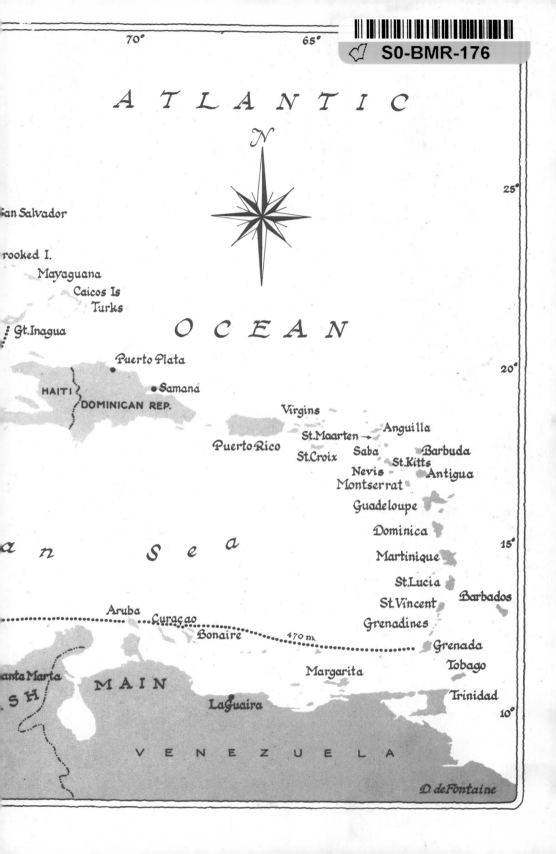

ATLANTIC

N

San Salvador

Crooked I.

Mayaguana

Caicos Is

Turks

Gt.Inagua

OCEAN

70°   65°   25°   20°   15°   10°

Puerto Plata

Samaná

HAITI

DOMINICAN REP.

Virgins

St.Maarten →   *Anguilla*

Puerto Rico   *Saba*   *Barbuda*

St.Croix   *St.Kitts*

Nevis   *Antigua*

Montserrat

Guadeloupe

Dominica

a n   S e a

Martinique

St.Lucia

St.Vincent   *Barbados*

Aruba   *Curaçao*   *Grenadines*

Bonaire   470 m.   *Grenada*

Margarita   *Tobago*

Santa Marta   MAIN   *Trinidad*

La Guaira

V E N E Z U E L A

D. de Fontaine

A Cruising Guide to the CARIBBEAN

A Cruising Guide to the CARIBBEAN

Including the North Coast of South America, Central America, and Yucatán

William T. Stone
AND
Anne M. Hays

COLLABORATORS

Jerrems C. Hart · PLANS, PREPARATIONS, AND CRUISING CONDITIONS

Jolyon Byerley · THE WINDWARDS AND LEEWARDS

Alexander C. Forbes and Robert Tonks · THE VIRGIN ISLANDS

Kit S. Kapp · THE SPANISH MAIN

Rodman A. Oakes · THE PANAMA CANAL

1993 Revised Edition, with Corrections

SHERIDAN
HOUSE

SHERIDAN HOUSE INC.
145 Palisade Street
Dobbs Ferry, NY 10522

First published 1991 by G. P. Putnam's Sons
Reissued with corrections 1993 by Sheridan House Inc.

Library of Congress Cataloging-in-Publication Data

Stone, William T.
    A cruising guide to the Caribbean: including the
north coast of South America, Central America, and Yucatán/William
T. Stone and Anne M. Hays; collaborators, Jolyon Byerley...
(et al.). —Rev. ed.
    p. cm.
    Rev. ed. of: Cruising guide to the Caribbean and the Bahamas /
Jerrems C. Hart and William T. Stone. 1988, © 1982.
    Includes bibliographical references.
    1. Caribbean Area—Description and travel—1981- —Guide-books.
2. Yachts and yachting—Caribbean Area—Guide-books. I. Hays, Anne
M II. Hart, Jerrems C. Cruising guide to the Caribbean
and the Bahamas. III. Title.
F2165.S89 1991   89-48896 CIP
917.2904'52—dc20

ISBN 0–924486–57–0

Printed in the United States of America
        3   4   5   6   7   8   9   10

PICTURE
ACKNOWLEDGMENTS

Credits for photographs and route and sketch charts

J. E. Allen: *pages 79, 126, 129, 131, 132, 143, 145, 407, 409, 410, 411, 412, 415, 423, 425, 428, 441, 444, 450, 452, 455, 456, 459, 469, 470, 475, 476, 478, 479, 500, 509, 510*

Tom Closs: *page 437*

CSY Ltd.: *pages 288, 294*

Dorothy De Fontaine: *endpapers; pages 40, 65, 68, 504*

Fishergate Reproduction: *pages 74, 84, 312, 334, 354, 364, 384, 403*

Alexander C. Forbes: *pages 124, 153, 157, 158, 159, 165, 170, 172, 174, 176, 177, 180, 181, 184, 186, 189, 194, 196, 197, 199, 200, 203, 204, 205, 206, 207, 208, 210, 212, 214, 216, 217, 219, 256, 393, 394, 397, 438–439*

R. K. Franks: *page 41*

J. C. Hart: *pages 76, 169, 187, 192, 240, 244, 285, 303, 304, 309, 318, 477, 480, 485, 499, 506, 508*

Hart's Camera (Curaçao): *pages 348, 349*

Anne M. Hays: *pages 23, 51, 97, 100, 103, 107, 161, 190, 231, 235, 237, 238, 247, 253, 264, 266, 275, 277, 279, 282, 286, 305, 306*

Kit S. Kapp: *pages 330, 331, 335, 362, 365, 371*

Nelson McClary: *pages 417, 421, 433, 435, 440, 449, 461*

V. E. B. Nicholson & Sons: *pages 257, 260, 267*

National Oceanic and Atmospheric Administration: *page 486*

Sid Stapleton: *page 332*

Jay Stone: *page 195*

U. S. Sailing Directions: *pages 99, 111*

***Yachting Monthly* (Winston Megoran):** *page 21*

ERRATA

page 26 para 1 - Write to SSCA, 521 South Andrews Ave., Suite 8, Fort Lauderdale, FL 33301-2844 or call (305) 463-2431 or fax (305) 463-7183

page 46 first line - replace "by Harry Kline" by "edited by Meredith Fields"

page 519 Appendix B - the nautical charts are now out of print

page 522 replace "Kline, Harry" by "Fields, Meredith, editor"

CONTENTS

FOREWORD

Almost 15 years have passed since the first edition of this guide appeared, and a good many changes have come about in many parts of the Caribbean Sea.

With this in mind, when Jerrems Hart was unable to participate in the updating of this edition, Anne Hays, and her husband, Jim, undertook to cruise to areas frequently visited by yachtsmen, including the Bahamas, the Turks and Caicos, the Dominican Republic, Puerto Rico, and the eastern Caribbean from the Virgin Islands south to Grenada for the purpose of gathering information for the book. Further, Anne agreed to act as coordinator for information coming in from other collaborators and fellow yachtsmen, in our attempt to bring you the best and most recent information possible about this vast and wonderful cruising ground.

While we were writing the first edition of this guide back in 1974 and 1975, cruising in the Caribbean was relegated largely to certain pockets: eastern Puerto Rico, the Virgins, and, for the most part, the island chain from Antigua to Grenada. As for the Caribbean as a whole, yachts were just beginning to spread their sails over this region, which is some 1,700 miles wide and almost a thousand miles from north to south. The popularity of the Caribbean basin has, in the meantime, grown by leaps and bounds throughout the yachting fraternity. White sails have spread like gypsy moths all over the eastern Caribbean and have pushed on into Venezuelan waters and the offshore islands of that country and the Netherlands; charter-boat operators have branched out into Belize, and hardened sailors who have tired of the Long-Island-Sound-like pressures in the Virgins and the Windwards have jumped at the chance to hoist sail on the other side of the Caribbean. This migration has, in turn, influenced private owners to cruise farther from the previously established grounds. Nevertheless, there still are multitudes of deserted lagoons, river mouths, jungle-bordered coves, and sandy, palm-festooned cays to be discovered; we hope this guide will entice you to exotic spots like these, because such private discoveries are the very essence of cruising, even if it takes a guidebook to get you there!

During the years since our first edition was published, cruising guides have proliferated, zeroing in on segments of the vast areas we cover here. We list these guides in the Bibliography and suggest you use them in their specific areas, because you will benefit, when moving from place to place, by a different emphasis and viewpoint.

Meantime, we have been busy cruising ourselves and have otherwise gleaned fresh information from our collaborators and from friends and acquaintances all over the region.

Beyond a mere digest of ports and places in this part of the world, we have tried

9

to give you a comprehensive résumé of the elements that constitute a successful cruising plan for these waters. For instance, if you have never before sailed below latitude 25°N, it is difficult to adjust to the constancy of the trade winds. You are in a belt above the equator in which air is constantly flowing in from the north to fill space being vacated by heated, rising air masses while, at the same time, this flow of surface air is being deflected to the right as a result of the earth's rotation. This constancy of wind direction, which is around 80 percent NE or E for most of the region, means in turn that open bays and headlands, when properly oriented, provide shelter that wouldn't even be considered in the temperate parts of the globe. Besides their convenient directional constancy, the trades seldom blow over Force 5, and calms are infrequent. The rise and fall of the tide is less than 2 feet in most places, and fog is unknown. In fact, the conditions are so perfect we might say that though the sea may never be completely forgiving to the careless sailor, it is more relenting here.

It's not all peaches and cream, however, for you will often be far from civilization as we are accustomed to it; you will need to plan for every contingency, to try to make your boat a self-sustaining entity, to realize that you will from time to time be thrown upon your own resourcefulness. Then, too, you may be disturbed by unpleasant racial incidents or by thievery provoked by poverty and growing disrespect for law (which is by no means confined to the Caribbean).

The area is understandably too vast for minutely detailed, up-to-date coverage by a mere pair of authors. We don't pretend to have been everywhere, but we've found others who have. For the Virgin Islands we enlisted the aid of Alex Forbes, who once operated a charter-boat fleet there and wrote his own guidebook to this immensely popular cruising ground; in fact his book and sketch charts are the basis for Chapter Eight, updated for the 1982 edition by Bob Tonks of the yacht *Seguin* and thoroughly covered for the 1990 edition by Anne and Jim Hays, who traveled throughout the Virgin Islands on their yacht *Blue Moon*.

Jolyon Byerley, who has skippered charter boats out of Antigua ever since the Nicholsons initiated the chartering scheme in the West Indies, knows the Windwards and Leewards like the back of his hand, and wrote both entertainingly and authoritatively about them for the previous editions. The Hays followed in his wake for this one, updating wherever necessary but preserving his fine stories. We are honored to have Kit Kapp as a collaborator, and we are fortunate that he has updated his own information. Kit started out as a charter-boat skipper out of Saint Thomas and eventually concentrated his attentions on the Spanish Main from Venezuela to Panama and beyond. He has since led expeditions into the area under the aegis of the Explorers' Club of New York to study Indian cultures, seek out lost historic sites, and conduct hydrographic surveys. As we began to develop information on this part of the Caribbean, people kept saying, "You'd better get in touch with Kit Kapp, he knows this area better than anybody." In addition to his chapters on Venezuela, Colombia, and the San Blas, Kit has also contributed valuable piloting advice drawn from his cruising experience along the Costa

Rican and Nicaraguan coasts. We're happy to have him on our team, and you will be, too, when you see how he has covered his territory.

For this edition Rodman Oakes, a Panama Canal pilot, completely rewrote the directions for transiting the Panama Canal. And Tony Piazza, a charter-boat skipper, gave us updates on the Quintana Roo section of Mexico.

Beyond these diligent collaborators, we have picked the brains of scores of other people who have recently sailed in the Caribbean, some of whom have spent enough time in certain places to give us very authoritative information indeed. The following are among those who have entered into rather exhaustive correspondence or meetings with us, beginning with the first edition: Bob and Ginnie Higman, of *Tormentor II;* Bob Fletcher and Tom Robson of Jamaica; Dick Steele of *Bonhomme Richard;* Jacques Kappes of *Liberty Belle;* Jack Laird of *Miss Applejack;* Tony and Jose de Pablo of the Dominican Republic; Michael Ronan and Sr. Christian de Lemos of the Dominican Republic; Nelson and Jane McClary and Dave Kimball (crew) of *Josefine;* Dr. Carlos Nouel and Dr. Victor Montoya of Venezuela; Captain "Henk" Hendrikse of the Netherlands Antilles; Ross Lysinger; Frank Glindmeier of *Summer Wind.*

We are grateful to John Van Ost for permission to use material from Caribbean Sailing Yachts publications, including harbor charts prepared for CSY charterers. We are also indebted to several Commodores of the Seven Seas Cruising Association who have cheerfully answered our queries about some of the out-of-the-way areas they have visited.

Following are others, not mentioned in the text, who have helped us in special ways or enhanced our coverage of certain places—and even this list is incomplete:

Bob Sparkman and Otto Doll on the subject of insurance
Corky Roberts in Barbados
Dr. Paul Chevalier in Trinidad and Grenada
Bill Rood and Captain Alberto Arvele in Santo Domingo
Frank T. Bonnin in Ponce
Esther Burnham of *Eventide* and *Chickadee*
James L. Madden of *Gesture II*
Stanley Livingston, Jr., of *Manukai*
Morton Gibbons-Neff of *Prim*
The Nicholsons of English Harbour
Edgard du Prey of Martinique

Marguerite Britter in Grenada
George T. Eggleston in St. Lucia
John Miles
Dick Avery in St. Thomas
Charles and Jinny Cary in Tortola
Daniel Valin, Roger Le Breton, Yves-Michel Barbe, and Serge Lodeon, all of Martinique
The Alburys of Man o'War Cay
Ralph Christianson of San Juan
Jack Vincent and Nick Zinkowski of Culebra
James L. Radawski of Roatán
Jack Allen of *Belinda*
Pearce Coady of *Cleopatra's Barge*

Wells Morse of *Legend*
Walter C. ("Wiki") McNiel of *Tropic Bird*
Dud and Barbara Dewey of *Nimbus*
Carolyn Hutchinson of *Tané*
George Bevier of Rum Point, Belize
Fred Hecklinger of Annapolis
Ron Barr of *Cibola* and Newport
Ken and Penny Saylor of *Barefoot*
Captain Robert D. McWethy of Annapolis

Jim Currie of the Angelus Press, Belize
Charles L. Ill of *Ill Wind*
David Gegg of Belize
Bob and Carolyn Paige of *Reality*
Lou and Barbara Martel of *Daybreak*
Bob and Carolyn Sperry of *Duet*
Malcolm and Debbie McCullouch of *Muscade*
Bill and Helen Weigel of *Wings*
Guy Patenaude and Veronique Kerbrat of *El Derf*
C. H. Murphy of *Tibona*

We are indebted to several yachtsmen-writers who have permitted us to quote liberally from their books or published articles, especially to Eric Hiscock for his sage advice on successful ocean voyaging, to the late Samuel Eliot Morison for permission to quote from his extensive writings on Columbus, to Bill Robinson for use of his commentaries in *Yachting* on passage-making to the Caribbean, and to Sid Stapleton for information concerning new facilities in the Dutch A-B-C islands and along the coast of Venezuela. For this same area we have had further valuable input from Brig and Louise Pemberton on the motor yacht *Victoire*. We are grateful to Dorwin Teague for permission to quote from a published article on his cruise in Belize.

Still others have helped us with valuable criticism, editorial review, and special research. These include F. G. Walton Smith, President, and May Smith, Secretary, of The International Oceanographic Foundation; and Clinton F. Loyd, a former shipmate and member of CCA, who directed us to the logs of many interesting voyages in the Cruising Club of America archives at Mystic Seaport.

Readers will recognize Dorothy De Fontaine's familiar hand and style in the endpapers of this book, together with several route charts. Kit Kapp has embellished his chapters on the Spanish Main with handsome sketch charts of places that are not detailed in any published charts. In the Virgin Islands, we have reproduced Alex Forbes's clear and concise sketch charts, which originally appeared in his *Virgin Islands Cruising Guide*, published in 1970. The late Jack Allen's distinctive sketch charts are scattered liberally throughout this book, to guide you into places not clearly shown in the government charts. Jack, a lifelong cruising yachtsman himself, understood how to present the details other yachtsmen need to know. We are glad to have been able to draw upon these talents to help remove some of the uneasiness that goes with cruising in unfamiliar waters.

Institutions that have assisted us with research, in addition to those mentioned above, include: Mystic Seaport Museum, Mystic, Connecticut; the Cruising Club of America; The Cruising Information Center in the Peabody Museum, Salem, Massachusetts; the National Oceanic and Atmospheric Administration and the National Weather Service in Washington (for data on Gulf Stream variability); and Yachting Publishing Corporation (particularly for permission to republish selected photographs from their outstanding collection of slides and prints on the Caribbean).

To all who have helped us in large measure or small, we extend our sincere thanks. We hope to make new friends among our readers, for we need the continuing cooperation of those who sail these waters to add to our store of knowledge, to correct us where we've been wrong, to amplify where we've been too brief, and to add deserving places that we may have missed.

Try as we did to make this guide accurate and dependable, it is of course manifestly impossible to guarantee our directions, many of which are a synthesis of information beyond our own experience, nor do we claim that our personal observations and recommendations are either infallible or complete. There may be some, too, who will misinterpret our text despite our earnest attempts to be exact. Therefore those who follow this guide are warned to use it with all the caution that becomes a good seaman for, after all, this is a guide, not a bible. Sketch charts and excerpts from government charts are intended as aids to piloting by eye and are not necessarily accurate enough to be used with rules and protractors.

WILLIAM T. STONE
ANNE M. HAYS

Chapter One

PLANS, PREPARATIONS, AND CRUISING CONDITIONS

Objectives

Not counting the zigs and zags that are part of any thorough cruise, the circuit from southern Florida out through the Antilles to Grenada, back along the Spanish Main to the Panama Canal, thence through the western Caribbean and the Yucatán Channel to Key West, is almost 4,000 miles. Only a fortunate few will have the time for such an ambitious expedition. The rest will content themselves with various goals to the east and south, working their way out the hard way against the trades, then coasting home in comfort with wind and sea abaft the beam.

The successive objectives of such a plan are fairly well defined, because each is separated by a significant body of open water.

Once Around, Clockwise

First, the Gulf Stream, 50 miles wide and often rough, must be crossed to reach the turquoise waters of the Bahamas. Then, running in the shelter of the larger islands, there is smooth sailing as far as George Town in the Exumas. As you proceed farther east, to the Caicos group, the islands dwindle in size and become too scattered to provide a lee, and fueling and repair facilities almost disappear.

From South Caicos, itself only an outpost, the next major objective is Puerto Rico, along the aptly named "Thorny Path." It skirts the rugged north coast of the Dominican Republic with only two intermediate shelters, at Puerto Plata and Samaná Bay, then leads 65 miles across the Mona Passage, where winds and countercurrents are apt to produce nasty conditions resembling those in the Gulf Stream. After this, the partial lee of Puerto Rico seems especially welcome; at least, the land breezes off this big island tend to dull the force of the trade winds, so that only in the afternoon do they reach their maximum onshore strength. In the appropriate chapters that follow, we will have more to say about how to manage the winds off these big islands.

Most cruisers who have come this far are heading at least for the Virgin Islands, through relatively sheltered waters. The next hurdle is the 85-mile Anegada Passage to Saint Martin, after which you will have "turned the corner" of the prevailing winds and can expect easier sailing down the string of islands to Grenada, which has for years been the terminus of most Caribbean cruises. Barbados and Tobago are seldom visited, because they lie upwind of Grenada— but the more adventurous, seeking new lands to discover, have begun to extend their cruising west to Isla Margarita and the other islands off the Venezuelan coast, and they bring back tales of unspoiled beauty, plenty of comfortable anchorages, and pleasant people.

Those who continue along the Spanish Main, now with the wind and sea generally astern, are usually bound for the Panama Canal. The Dutch islands of Bonaire, Curaçao, and Aruba are dividends along the way, and the paradisiacal San Blas archipelago is to be explored just before reaching the Canal Zone.

Cruising the western Caribbean is usually confined to the island stepping-stones of San Andrés, Providencia, Swan, and Cozumel in the course of passaging north from the canal. Coasting along the shores of Costa Rica and Nicaragua, where the trades tend to be deflected so that they blow more on the nose than on the beam, is infrequently attempted. This whole side of the Caribbean is of course a lee shore and thus not to be trifled with. On the other hand, Roatán, in the Gulf of Honduras, is well worth including in a cruise plan, and a growing number of hardy souls are snaking their way through the maze of cays that make up the barrier reef skirting Belize (formerly British Honduras). The wind pattern allows this virgin cruising area also to be approached comfortably from Key West or in the course of a swing through the Bahamas to Haiti, Jamaica, and the Caymans.

Except for the Thorny Path, the only easting in this clockwise cruising plan is the return to Florida through the Yucatán Channel, but there the trades are occasionally foiled by weather fronts that move across the Gulf of Mexico. We have slipped through that channel in between the usual procession of winter northers, while the wind was southerly and before it had time to swing into the north and northeast with its full intensity. Also, the north-flowing current, which later turns east, is a substantial help.

If you are simply seeking the easiest way through the Caribbean to the Panama Canal, we recommend taking the Windward Passage rather than the seemingly more direct route by way of the Yucatán Channel. Because the winds in the Bahamas tend to be more variable than farther south, you should have little windward work down to Inagua, where you should expect steady reaching winds for the rest of the way. This track will take you to Jamaica, where you will find it convenient to stop at Port Antonio or Port Royal (Kingston) for provisions, water, and fuel. To break up the trip still more, you might want to detour slightly to anchorages among the cays of the Pedro, Serranilla, and Serrana banks.

This track is roughly equal in distance to a southbound passage through the Yucatán Channel (bucking a substantial current), with the usual stops at Swan Island, Providencia, and San Andrés—about 1,250 miles.

The Hard Way

Yachtsmen coming from the temperate zones, accustomed to winds and tidal currents from every point of the compass, find it hard to adjust to the regularity of the trade winds and the predominately one-way ocean currents in the Caribbean. But the sheer discomfort and futility of trying to beat your way against them cannot be overemphasized. Many have set a counterclockwise course from the Panama Canal to Grenada and have had horrendous tales to tell of head seas encountered, and some have aborted their plans and headed north to Jamaica.

One hardy sailor who did it tells us: "The coasts of Colombia and Venezuela at that time of the year [January] are almost impossible; three boats before us were dismasted."

Another yachtsman remarks:

> From Cartagena to Aruba was by far the worst part of our trip except for the tehuantepecer we hit. The current, the wind and, most of all, the choppy seas are dead against you. We made Aruba before dark one night, and it took us 12 hours to get the last 6 miles, with wind, current, and seas pounding us to death. Aruba offers no abatement of wind on the lee side, only a little less sea.

We can add no more explicit advice than that of Kit Kapp, who has made six eastbound passages, in all seasons, from Panama to the Leeward Islands. In fact, he recommends that the owner of a small yacht should seriously consider shipping her from the canal as deck cargo on a freighter to Trinidad, to save wear and tear on the gear—in spite of the costs of a cradle and the transportation itself.

For those who persist, Kapp offers this experienced counsel:

a. Plan to make your passage from April to December, but preferably in October and November.

b. Allow plenty of time.

c. Be sure your engine is in good condition, because you will have to power much of the way.

d. Carry all the fuel you can and top off tanks wherever possible.

e. Secure all hatches, ports, and deck gear for heavy sea conditions, and by no means tow your dinghy. Have an extra hook handy on deck.

f. Plan to live on sandwiches and other snacks when underway, because cooking may be physically impossible.

g. Plan to make short hops from shelter to shelter as the weather allows; and plan your departures to take advantage of the daily cycle of the winds in a particular area. This may mean an evening departure when the trades have abated; or leaving in the very early morning, when near mountainous terrain, to take advantage of the land breezes.

Here is the way Kit would establish the successive legs:

1. The Canal Zone to Holandes Cays in the San Blas Islands, taking refuge at Isla Grande if necessary.

2. San Blas directly to Isla Tesora light and Cartagena, but bearing off to shelter in the San Bernadino or Rosario Islands if the weather is too much.

3. Cartagena to Santa Marta, which could be one of the roughest legs.

4. Santa Marta to Cape La Vela, taking refuge in Bahía Cinto if necessary. Keep within 2 or 3 miles of shore for an easier sea and less current, especially beyond Ríohacha.

5. Cape La Vela to Aruba, taking refuge in Bahía Honda if necessary. Skirt the Guajira peninsula, about 2 or 3 miles off, to Punta Espada, then run southeasterly across the Gulf of Venezuela until you are well under the lee of the Paraguana Peninsula before turning northerly toward Punta Salina. Stay in the lee of the land, about 4 miles off, to Punta Macolla, thence take up a course for a point to the east of Oranjestad on Aruba.

6. Aruba to Bonaire, taking refuge in Curaçao if necessary.

7. Bonaire to Puerto La Cruz. Make a long tack to the southeast, using the La Guaira area for refuge in adverse weather. Otherwise, upon reaching the coast, tack to the northeast for shelter at Los Roques, or try for the west end of Isla La Tortuga. When the weather improves, carry on to Puerto La Cruz for a well-earned rest.

8. Puerto La Cruz to Bahía Guamache on Isla Margarita. Favor the coastline to the vicinity of Cumaná, then head north, using the lee of Isla Cubagua, thence to Bahía Guamache.

9. Isla Margarita to Grenada, taking refuge in Islas Los Testigos only if necessary. In heavy weather, the prudent course would be southeasterly to Carúpano (or perhaps Esmeralda Bay), then to Puerto Santo, Cabo Tres Puntas, and northeast to Grenada.

Weather Wisdom

To understand the weather picture better, and for details of conditions to be expected in different parts of the Caribbean, *Sailing Directions for the Bahamas, Bermuda and Caribbean—Eastern Part* (S.D. 147, cat. no. 11086) and *Sailing Directions for the Caribbean—Western Part* (S.D. 148, cat. no. 14447), published by the Defense Mapping Agency, should be studied. The British publication *Pilots,* vols. 70, 71, and 69A, gives similar information.

However, we think the most valuable tools for planning a cruise around the Caribbean are the Defense Mapping Agency Hydrographic Center's *Pilot Chart Atlas, Caribbean and Central America* (cat. no. 10378) and *Pilot Chart Atlas, South Atlantic* (cat. no. 10377). Therein, by means of easy-to-read wind roses, current arrows, and comments about average conditions, you can almost "see" the weather pattern on a month-to-month basis. Remember, however, that these are averages and do not show the effects of "extended northers" during the winter that may reach as far as the Panama Canal or the Windwards.

Also, one must consider the effects of occasional "easterly waves," which are troughs of low pressure traveling from east to west across the Caribbean and causing a northerly slant to the winds ahead of them and a southerly flow behind them. These easterly waves with their wind and rain are in fact the very conditions under which tropical storms and hurricanes develop.

Hurricanes

Since the West Indies and the ocean to the east are the spawning grounds of hurricanes, the incidence of these ultimate storms must be considered in your cruising timetable. On the other hand, lest the fear of being caught in a hurricane becomes too inhibiting, consider that there are only four or five in a normal year and that the area of Force 12 winds averages little more than 100 miles from the eye, or storm center, and only occasionally as much as 200 miles. Then realize that, although the season officially lasts from June through November, the percentage incidence by month is: September 36 percent, August 29 percent, October 19 percent, July 7 percent, June 5 percent, and November 3 percent. Note, too, that these statistics include *all* Atlantic hurricanes, many of which reach this designation in the Gulf of Mexico and would be classed only as tropical storms or perhaps just "disturbances" in the Caribbean Sea.

As we have seen, the most dangerous months are August, September, and October, and the greatest percentage of these "high season" storms reach their hurricane intensity in the western half of the Caribbean. Furthermore, they invariably trend to the northeast and north. Therefore, the farther south and east you are during the height of the season, the less likely you are to be clobbered.

With the advanced state of the art of finding and continuously plotting hurricanes, as practiced by the National Hurricane Center in Miami, no alert yachtsman should find himself at sea in the path of one of these killer storms. In such an unfortunate event, however, he will obviously want to do what he can to mitigate the consequences. In the tropics, these storms tend to move quite slowly, perhaps 300 miles a day, so there is a chance to move out of the most destructive path. Because a hurricane is spiraling counterclockwise with the winds drawing toward the vortex, the semicircle to the right of the storm's path (as might be seen from an observation plane) is the most dangerous, since the winds are stronger to the extent of the storm's forward movement.

To help you avoid a hurricane or to make the best of a bad situation, here are some helpful hints:

Precursory signs:
Two days before—long, heavy swells, 4–5 per minute instead of 12–15. Thunderstorm clouds.
Day before—bright skies, above normal temperature, little or no cumulus clouds seen, unusual wind direction, barometer drops below 29.53 inches.
Immediate signs:
High cirrus ("mares' tails") followed by cirrostratus clouds, halos around sun

BEAUFORT WIND SCALE

Beaufort Number (force)	Limits of Wind Speed in knots.	Descriptive Terms.	Sea Criterion.
0	Less than 1	Calm	Sea like a mirror
1	1–3	Light air	Ripples with the appearance of scales are formed but without foam crests.
2	4–6	Light breeze	Small wavelets, still short but more pronounced. Crests have a glassy appearance and do not break.
3	7–10	Gentle breeze	Large wavelets. Crests begin to break. Foam of glassy appearance. Perhaps scattered white horses.
4	11–16	Moderate breeze	Small waves, becoming longer; fairly frequent white horses.
5	17–21	Fresh breeze	Moderate waves, taking a more pronounced long form; many white horses are formed. (Chance of some spray.)
6	22–27	Strong breeze	Large waves begin to form; the white foam crests are more extensive everywhere. (Probably some spray.)
7	28–33	Near gale	Sea heaps up and white foam from breaking waves begins to be blown in streaks along the direction of the wind.
8	34–40	Gale	Moderately high waves of greater length; edges of crests begin to break into spindrift. The foam is blown in well-marked streaks along the direction of the wind.
9	41–47	Strong gale	High waves. Dense streaks of foam along the direction of the wind. Crests of waves begin to topple, tumble and roll over. Spray may affect visibility.
10	48–55	Storm	Very high waves with long overhanging crests. The resulting foam in great patches is blown in dense white streaks along the direction of the wind. On the whole the surface of the sea takes a white appearance. The tumbling of the sea becomes heavy and shocklike. Visibility affected.
11	56–63	Violent storm	Exceptionally high waves. (Small and medium-sized ships might be for a time lost to view behind the waves.) The sea is completely covered with long white patches of foam lying along the direction of the wind. Everywhere the edges of the wave crests are blown into froth. Visibility affected.
12	64+	Hurricane	The air is filled with foam and spray. Sea completely white with driving spray; visibility very seriously affected.

Force 2

Force 4

Force 5

Force 6

Force 8

and moon. Then altostratus turning to altocumulus, becoming cumulus conges-
tus, black, with rising wind.

Maneuvering:

1. Determine bearing of storm from swell and wind direction. Bearing is wind
direction plus 115°.

2. If wind hauls to right (clockwise), you are in the dangerous semicircle. Bring
wind on starboard bow (45° relative) and make best speed.

3. Use radar, if available.

4. If wind remains steady and barometer continues falling, you are in direct
path. Bring wind on starboard quarter (160° relative) and make best speed toward
the "safe" semicircle.

5. Never try to cross direct path of storm.

6. If in the "safe" semicircle, bring wind on starboard quarter (130° relative)
and make best possible speed.

The Boat

Without our making any attempt to detail *the* perfect boat for cruising the
Caribbean, there are some parameters into which such a craft should fit. In the
first place, winds of 30 knots and waves of 8 feet on top of huge ocean swells are
not uncommon. A seascape so awesome (or gruesome, whichever way you are
inclined to look at it) is not the usual fare by any means, but any extended
Caribbean cruise will include some passages of that sort. Under such head-on
conditions, a sailboat under 35 feet or a powerboat much under 40 feet would,
to say the least, be highly uncomfortable. Fastnet conditions may not be encountered, although we have experienced them in the western Caribbean, but one is
nevertheless reminded that during that tragic 1979 race many fast, light-displace-
ment boats simply couldn't stand the gaff—usually the result of poor lay-up of
the fiberglass, particularly at such points of stress as fore and aft stays and
spreader fittings, spade rudders (also vulnerable in coral waters), and deep fin
keels. Draft, too, has much to do with seaworthiness, whether sail or power, and
we have no hesitation in recommending 4½ feet or more. In the Caribbean, draft
is not really an important consideration, and deeper draft will give you a stiffer,
steadier boat.

Tank capacities should be sufficient for at least a week on water and 500 miles
on fuel (750 miles in the western Caribbean) if power is the only propulsion, and
this is where most boats designed for U.S. coastal cruising fall far short. Know
in advance what your limits are and plan to carry extra rubber or plastic tanks
on deck to make up the deficiencies. To some Spartan sailors, 20 gallons of water
might be enough, but such a ration would hardly last a day on a powerboat with
pressure taps all over the boat and sailors used to daily showers.

A powerboat with a range of 200 miles at cruising speed may well go two or
three times as far at some slower speed, a factor that can best be determined by

adding a flowmeter to the fuel system. An auxiliary, working out against the trades, will want to use power on many occasions, at least as far as the Virgins. In determining range, however, it must be remembered that speed is not the only factor. Head-sea and wind conditions will materially affect consumption, and a reserve of 20 percent should be allowed for such contingencies.

Bear in mind that little painted anchors with bits of vinyl-covered chain don't "go" in the West Indies. You may learn a lot about anchoring out there, but you need to be equipped with the right ground tackle before you leave. Without going into a long dissertation on this subject, which is well covered in seamanship books, we suggest you take two different types of patent anchors (a Danforth and a plow, for instance), each with a nylon rode and 10–12 feet of chain, plus a spare to replace one of the standard anchors in case of loss or breakage—we have seen Danforths come up off a coral bottom looking like a piece of spaghetti.

The more opening portlights, hatches, wind sails, and awnings you have, the better, for the tropical sun beating down mercilessly on an unshaded, poorly ventilated boat can take all the pleasure out of island cruising. Awnings should be not only the width of the boat but should extend well forward and aft, not just

An awning over the forward hatch lets in the breeze and keeps out the rain, which comes in short but frequent showers during the day.

over the cockpit, for it is surprising how much a shaded deck will lower the temperature below decks. Side curtains are another benefit. The most effective cowl ventilators have really big mouths, and Dorade boxes are best fitted with two exterior openings so that you can swap the ventilator for a deck plate to get straight-through ventilation when in port.

Insect screens are a distinct convenience but not an absolute necessity; the bugs are at their worst for only a couple of hours around sunset and can be held more or less at bay with liberal use of repellents. We have found that the smoldering-incense repellent made in the Orient is especially effective. The trouble with screens is that they seriously cut down the flow of air on quiet nights.

A life raft with survival rations, water, and flares should of course be a part of every equipment list.

Charts and Other Published Aids

Although all U.S. charts, domestic and foreign, are now under a uniform number-ing system, they are far from uniform in detail, accuracy, symbols, scale, and general appearance. Some have been prepared from aerial surveys; others are adaptations of charts, mostly British, that derive from surveys a hundred years old or older.

Islands that once were British (the whole Caribbean, for that matter) are well charted by the British Admiralty, as the French islands are by the French government. Charts referenced BA are British Admiralty charts.

Charts referenced with the prefix CK- and a number refer to pages in the folios published by Better Boating Association, Inc., Box 407, Needham, MA 02192. These 17" × 22" books are currently available for the Bahamas and the Virgin Islands and contain exact reproductions of all the government charts of those regions (in some cases reduced by 15 percent) together with striking aerial photos in color to give you a preview of what lies ahead. Though they may seem expensive, a *Chart-Kit* actually costs considerably less than the sum of the official charts if bought separately.

The charts referenced KSK (numbers 1–9) are large-scale charts of certain popular or convenient areas along the coasts of Venezuela, Colombia, and Pan-ama (also one of Port Royal on Roatán Island, Honduras). The key to these charts along the San Blas coast and the Gulf of Darien is the orientation chart in Chapter Fifteen. Complete information about these charts, including a list of places where you can get them, appears in Appendix B.

The charts referenced I- are Imray-Iolaire charts, available for Puerto Rico, the Virgin Islands, the Leeward and Windward Islands, Venezuela, and the A-B-C islands. These are published in a standard size of 25" × 36" and incorporate large-scale plans of the more important harbors and anchorages within the areas covered. They are generally available in marine outlets in most of the areas covered, and may be mail ordered in parts of the United States where they are not available from yacht chandlers. A good source for these, as well as other charts and government publications, is Bluewater Books and Charts, 1481 SE 17th St., Fort Lauderdale, FL 33316, 800-942-BLUE or 305-763-6533. Another is the Armchair Sailor, 126 Thames St., Newport, RI 02840, 401-847-4252 or 800-29-CHART.

For a few places, seldom visited, we have continued to list discontinued DMA charts that seemingly have no direct replacements. They may still be available.

By all means stock up on the charts you'll need before you leave the States, but if you change your route or are still missing a chart or two, the following sources will probably have U.S., BA, Imray-Iolaire, or French charts of their immediate cruising areas:

Bahamas: Yacht Haven in Nassau
Jamacia: R.S. Gamble and Son Ltd, Harbour St., in Kingston
Virgin Islands: Island Marine Supply in Charlotte Amalie
Belize: The Angelus Press
Antigua: Carib Marine, English Harbour
Guadaloupe: Marina Bas du Fort in Point-à-Pitre
Martinique: Ship Shop in Fort de France
St. Lucia: Rodney Bay Marina
Bequia: Bequia Bookstore
Grenada: Grenada Yacht Services in St. George's
Trinidad: R. Landry and Co. Ltd, Port-of-Spain
Panama: Islamorada in Panama City

Aside from their climatological data, the *Sailing Directions* offer only limited help to yachtsmen, and some of their scary admonitions should not be taken too seriously if you are to persevere in your Caribbean cruising. After all, these publications are written primarily for big ships, and before that for clumsy sailing vessels; the best places for small craft, where the water may be a couple of fathoms or less, are usually not mentioned. If they are, reference is made to the need for "local knowledge," that elusive ingredient that never seems to be around in extreme situations when you really need it.

The nearest thing to local knowledge in these waters comes in the several spiral-bound guidebooks that give detailed directions, supported by numerous sketch charts, for getting into most of the important harbors and anchorages from the Bahamas to Grenada and the Bay Islands. Current guides are listed in the Bibliography.

Tidal differences for Puerto Rico and the Virgins, a listing of radio beacons for the entire Caribbean, and a light list for the whole chain down to Grenada are included in *Reed's Nautical Almanac & Coast Pilot,* together with a wealth of miscellaneous data such as first-aid advice, radio usage and weather forecasts, seamanship, and ocean and coastal navigation tables and procedures.

The monthly *Bulletin* of the Seven Seas Cruising Association contains very valuable cruising information in the form of letters from members and associates. The coverage is worldwide, but almost every issue includes some advice useful to those cruising in the Caribbean. You may become an associate and receive a subscription to the *Bulletin* at $20 a year. Write to SSCA, P.O. Box 1256, Stuart, FL 34995, or call 407-287-5615.

Aids to Navigation

You will have little occasion to use buoyage in the course of your navigation. In the first place, buoys are few and far between. Second, they are usually found only in the entrances to commercial ports, where they mark depths and dangers that seldom concern small craft. And third, buoy tending in the West Indies is usually lackadaisical at best, and buoys may be missing, out of place, or unlit. Lighthouses may also be extinguished.

Since big ships depend on radar and other electronic positioning devices, the reliability of aids to navigation is nowhere nearly as important as it once was. So never be upset if you fail to see a light you had planned to use in your overnight sailing.

Navigation Equipment

In the clockwise circuit of the Caribbean we have just described, most of your navigation will be in the coastwise category, and since the offshore legs are generally less than 300 miles, a carefully maintained DR track should suffice to put you close to your target, especially if you are in a powerboat or sailing steadily off the wind. Upwind sailing, particularly with head or crosscurrents to contend with, is another matter, however, and we recommend that every sailboat carry a sextant, even if you are only able to cope with noon sights for latitude. After all, that was the only technique known to seamen until the perfection of the chronometer.

In the choice of electronic navigation equipment, every yacht cruising the Caribbean should have at least a depth finder. A radio direction finder is a good backup for electronic gear, which is always subject to failure.

Loran C is of little value in most of the Caribbean. While it can be of great assistance in negotiating the Yucatán Channel with its strong and confusing currents, ground-wave coverage to the southeast extends only as far as Great Inagua. Before you buy, check the coverage carefully against your cruising plans.

SatNav will pick up where Loran C ends. And perhaps you will have GPS by the time you make your voyage. Frequent good satellite fixes are indeed a comfort when navigating unfamiliar waters.

Since fog is virtually nonexistent in the Caribbean, radar may seem unnecessary, but we well recall standing on and off the reef-strewn coast of Hispaniola during 30 hours of heavy rain and zero visibility when that bright orange picture of our position would have been very welcome indeed. Even in perfect weather, radar is a distinct boon every time you make a landfall; in fact, a radar set with moderate range, say 24 miles, coupled with a carefully kept DR track, should (with a depth finder) be all the electronics you really need to find your way in Caribbean waters, especially among the high islands and along the mountainous coasts of the Spanish Main.

Radio Communications

Simply from a safety standpoint, we would not put to sea without radio; it's also nice to be aware of what's going on at home and fun to be able to keep in touch with friends you've made along the way. And there may be crew changes to be arranged and spare parts to be ordered and expedited.

You will of course have a VHF-FM set, which, because of its clarity, uncomplicated installation, and low power drain, is the major means of communication between yachts and shoreside facilities. Excellent reception, especially between sailing yachts with masthead antennas, is assured to 25 or 30 miles, while reception to 50–80 miles is not at all unusual if you are talking to a shore station with an antenna atop an island mountain peak.

You can keep in touch with the States through your SSB set and station WOM for ship-to-shore calls. Having WOM also enables you to receive the weather forecasts for the Caribbean and the Gulf of Mexico.

If you have HAM radio, you will have a good way of keeping track of fellow cruisers through the daily Caribbean Maritime Mobil Net (7.230 MHz). This net can sometimes help in an emergency situation through access to the San Juan Coast Guard, and also has convenient liaison with the Waterway Net (7.268 MHz). You will sometimes be able to make calls home via a telephone patch with the help of the International Net on 14.313 MHz. (Remember, however, that you will have to get a reciprocal radio operator's license in each country that you visit in order to transmit there, and some countries do not allow third-party traffic. You can sometimes get a reciprocal license immediately by a single visit to the proper official and payment of a small fee; but it may require a wait of up to three months and a larger fee than seems practical if your visit is to be short.)

Insurance

This subject is very much in the hot-potato category, since there are no specific guidelines under which yacht underwriters operate, and they are all very individualistic in their thinking.

When they come to assessing their risk, your own experience and competence is extremely important to them, since you will be voyaging long distances in open ocean and in relatively primitive areas far removed from repair facilities. If you have proved yourself experienced and resourceful through your previous record as a policyholder, your first step toward widening the cruising limits of your policy should be to present to your broker a detailed plan of your cruising intentions, including the countries and ports you will visit and when, and where your boat will be during the hurricane season.

Depending on political conditions at the time, underwriters may look with disfavor on certain countries, even to the point of suspending insurance if you enter one that happens to be on their current blacklist. In the recent past, Jamaica, the Dominican Republic, and Grenada have been in this category. All policies exclude Cuba and Haiti, and you would be lucky to find coverage for cruising the north coast of South America.

The more complete your plan and the more knowledge of the Caribbean and its pitfalls you can display, the more reasonable your premium is apt to be. If, for instance, you have recognized certain problems and show that you have added certain gear and equipment or taken other logical steps to counter them, your plan will find favor.

If this sounds as if you must plead your case before an underwriter, that's exactly what happens! Yet you will or should have thought out all such details anyway, so it is just a matter of pulling it all together for a condensed presentation. As one broker said to us, "Any indication of knowledge is good!" Remember that the underwriter wants your premium as much as you want his insurance, but he wants his commitment to be safe. After all, there are not so many far-ranging cruising people that his business will be seriously affected if he turns down a few applications or occasionally makes himself uncompetitive.

Ship's Paperwork

You will, of course, be sure that your numbering certificate, or license-of-vessel if it is documented, is up to date. You should also review the renewal procedure if renewal will come up in the course of your cruise.

The crew list should contain names and middle initials, where and when born, citizenship, passport number (if any), and rating aboard the yacht—i.e., mate, cook, stewardess, and so on. Never list any of the ship's company as passengers; this implies commercialism and may complicate the procedures and cause extra charges.

To some foreign officials, the next most important paper (called *zarpe* in Spanish) is your clearance document from your last port. This is why it is so important to "clear" as well as "enter" in each country. You will have to do this over thirty times if you run the whole circle of the Bahamas and the Caribbean, and you'll also have to check in with officials in each and every major port in some of the fussy countries. All of this becomes tiresome, annoying, and occasionally costly; sometimes it involves detouring or backtracking if the official port of entry happens to lie beyond the harbor where you want to put in for the night. Unfortunately, this routine is just one of the facts of the cruising life.

To be correct, you must enter at a port of entry (which we indicate in the appropriate sections of this guide), drop anchor, hoist your Q flag and courtesy flag, and await developments. Incidentally, do maintain a complete inventory of courtesy ensigns, because some officials take real offense when they see a yacht without one. In fact, we have even heard of fines being levied for this oversight. Furthermore, these flags are likely to be very costly when bought under duress. If the whole town knows you are there and why, and nothing happens after a reasonable time, the master will probably be safe in going ashore with his papers to seek out the officials. However, he should instruct his crew to stay on board. Where we or others have observed the routines in various ports, we have reported them in the appropriate sections, but even so, you may run afoul of the law, depending on the individual who happens to be in charge at the time.

Defensive Weapons

So much has been said in the yachting press about the pros and cons of carrying guns aboard that we shall not dwell on the subject here, except to say that you might be molested a hundred miles from any possible help. Whether you believe that defense of your person(s) is practical or even righteous is for you to decide. Suffice to say, too, that punishment these days is so gentle as to be ineffective, which means that all who cruise alone must take into consideration the consequent breakdown of law and order everywhere.

Since they are so subject to change, it would be folly to try to pinpoint the danger areas—most of which have to do with drug smuggling. In any case, very little secrecy is involved anymore and, as you cruise from place to place, you'll soon find out where the action is. Outright piracy is a by-product of drug running, practiced as a sideline by those who have discovered how easy it is to break laws and get away with it.

In almost all countries firearms must be declared upon entering and in many places will be impounded during your stay in that port.

In suspicious regions it would be well to cruise in company with another yacht and in any case to keep in radio touch with friends you meet along the way. Be wary of calls for assistance in apparent distress situations and report the circumstances and your intended action by radio before being lured into a possible trap. Lastly, keep some trusted person aware of your itinerary and your crew complement.

Personal Documents

Although passports are not specifically required by some of the countries you are likely to visit, we strongly urge that you and each of your crew carry one, for then there can be no question of your identity. Otherwise, you will have to carry positive proof of citizenship—in the case of a U.S.-born person, a birth or baptismal certificate or an expired passport. A naturalized citizen should carry his certificate of naturalization; a person born outside the U.S. should have a State Department Certificate of Birth. For extended cruising, we think a passport is easier in the end, especially during the current instability in the islands and in Central America.

For long stays in any country, different regulations usually apply. Check the embassy or a consulate of the country involved.

Except in rare cases when you are acting on respected current advice, we do not recommend that you go to the trouble of obtaining papers to enter a certain country by going to one of their consulates in the U.S. or elsewhere. The procedure is time-consuming and frequently costly—and the papers are not likely to carry much weight at the other end.

Since you may want to rent a car, bring your driver's license. Licenses are valid wherever we have been, although in some places (such as Barbados and Antigua) a local operator's license will be issued and a fee charged, presumably in deference to the local taxi organization.

To stay out of trouble, do not sign on any seagoing hitchhikers. If you do, be sure of their background and carefully examine their personal documents. Remember that as master you are responsible for a member of your crew with inadequate or false papers; remember too that most countries do not allow you to discharge a crew member who does not carry an onward or return air ticket.

When you have changes in your crew list (friends arriving to replace others, for instance), make this situation clear to the immigration officials at the port where the changes will take place. Also, be sure your incoming friends have round-trip tickets, subject of course to refund later. Otherwise they may not be able to talk their way past the immigration desk at the airport.

Dogs and Cats

Animals from home or picked up en route have become members of many a yacht's company. Some cruising people think they're a nuisance, which they can be; others appreciate their trusting and usually quiet companionship in all sorts of places and all sorts of weather. To bring a pet along is a choice for some; for others there's really no choice at all, and their cruising plans will have to be adjusted to suit.

Unfortunately, island people develop insular attitudes, one of them being a lurking fear of animal diseases, such as rabies, which might come to their island by way of some pestilential animal from a disease-ridden mainland. Thus, on some islands pets are definitely banned or slapped into quarantine, which is the same thing. A few easy-going places have no restrictions at all; others have prohibitions that are not necessarily enforced; still others admit pets under certain stipulations that may or may not be enforced, depending on where you enter and who's in charge at the time. From country to country, we have found these regulations much harder to nail down than the entry requirements relating to the human species.

For up-to-date information on taking your pet to any foreign country, get a pamphlet entitled "Traveling with Your Pet." You can obtain a copy by sending $5 to the ASPCA, 441 E. Ninety-second St., New York, NY 10128.

Electricity

Heavy dependence on electricity is a mistake. Anchoring out will be the rule, and shore power, where it is available at all, is likely to be inadequate for the load imposed on the dock's wiring. Since bottled gas is available almost everywhere, cooking need not depend on electricity. Refrigeration, the biggest user of precious amps and so vital in warm climes, can best be handled by a heavy-duty compressor system, belt-driven by the main engine for a few hours a day, that stores cold by means of eutectic plates in a heavily insulated custom cabinet.

Down among the islands, variations in voltage and frequency are more the rule than the exception. To avoid damage to motors, large yachts that depend heavily on shore power would do well to install a separate transformer through which the incoming voltage can be adjusted to the normal 115 or 230 volts. It should be remembered that battery chargers, even though they may be rated for 50 to 60 cycles, do not operate at the same efficiency at the lower frequency. Some makes of charger are more sensitive than others in this respect; in fact, some will not function at all at the 50 cycles common in the formerly British islands.

Mooring

Outside of the Virgins and Venezuela, you'll seldom find marinas with finger piers and handy pilings. Nor will you be inclined to go alongside commercial docks, because of dirty walls and pilings or a heavy surge. This means you will have to get used to docking as it has been done in the Mediterranean for centuries: you set a bow anchor out and then back down so your stern is a couple of feet from the pier or quayside and your stern lines crossed.

Ordinarily this is a simple maneuver, except for judging the distance off for setting your anchor. You will do well to overestimate this rather than underestimate it. Calculate your scope using the HW depth multiplied by at least 5 with chain and 7 with rope. Actually, we like to drag the anchor under power for the last 10–15 feet to be sure it's securely set.

In a crosswind, this can be tricky, but here again you had best overallow for leeway, since you can always pause during the maneuver to let the wind straighten you out. Normally the bow will fall off more than the stern, in which case you snub your rode temporarily to straighten her up. This is an especially useful tactic with an auxiliary, which will seldom back straight anyway.

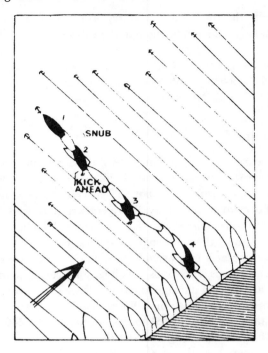

The Mediterranean moor

In the Mediterranean, stern gangplanks (usually collapsible) are standard equipment, with sturdy swivel fittings at the transom, rollers or wheels for the pier end, and an adjustable topping lift for raising the gangplank clear of the pier at night or under surge and wave conditions. For some reason, this very convenient apparatus is seldom seen in the Caribbean. If you think you can get by with some kind of jury rig like an old plank, a swimming ladder, or a network of stern lines, you will be following the crowd, but for convenience as well as safety we recommend fitting a substantial gangplank before you leave the States.

Medical Matters

The size of its cruising area should also be a measure of the size of a small ship's medicine chest—not only for the sake of the crew but for those you find along the way, from a Panamanian native on a faraway islet with a badly slashed foot to a professional skipper with a debilitating case of Montezuma's Revenge.

A comprehensive first-aid manual should of course be a part of every yacht's library.

No matter how inviting they may seem, avoid washing or swimming in slow-moving freshwater streams or pools in Hispaniola, Puerto Rico, Martinique, Saint Lucia (except the hot sulfur springs at Soufrière), and Guadeloupe. Although the whole Caribbean area is considered suspect, these islands in particular are known to harbor a debilitating parasitic disease called bilharziasis; its scientific name is *Schistosomiasis mansoni.* It derives from human or animal feces and requires hosting by snails that collect in slow-moving water. The larvae of such infected snails can penetrate the human skin to spread the disease through the blood stream; it eventually affects the liver in particular.

Everybody knows enough not to eat the fruit of the manchineel tree, but not that it drips its poison, too. Don't stand under one in the rain!

White sea urchins can be eaten, but the black ones are dangerous to touch and, unfortunately, all too prevalent in some of the most inviting swimming areas. If you tangle with one of these seagoing porcupines, you won't have to rush for the medicine chest, because the antidote is handy wherever you are. A quick application of urine will do wonders; its acid will neutralize the nitrogen in the urchin's poison.

Ciguatera was the term given to fish poisoning back in the days of Columbus, and it has ever since been a recognized health problem all over the eastern Caribbean. The greatest number of cases from the greatest variety of fish are reported in the Virgins and the other islands north of Antigua. The disease is not well understood, but is thought to be caused by toxin present in algae ingested by the fish—any species of fish. However, barracuda and amberjack are most often blamed, owing to their heavy diet of smaller, possibly toxin-carrying fish. The principal symptoms of fish poisoning are vomiting, cramps and diarrhea, a tingling sensation in the face and extremities, and pain and weakness in the joints. The best treatment is to induce vomiting. Atropine, calcium salts, or vitamin B may help. If you are unsure of your fish, taste a small quantity several hours before making a full meal of it.

Spares

Before you leave the mainland of abundance for the islands of scarcity, make sure you are adequately equipped with the things that no amount of ingenuity or talent with tools can replace. Make a careful study of the systems aboard your boat and, in a purposefully pessimistic frame of mind, consider the possible failures, item by item, that could delay your cruise and bring expensive consequences. Never mind if it seems to be a part or assembly beyond your capability to fix; you may very well find someone with sufficient experience to do the job, but he will be helpless if he doesn't have the parts.

Remember that customs duties are the primary source of tax income for many of the islands, so that importations are a costly business. The nature of the rates are such that some cajoling and perhaps a little bribery may be needed to obtain the most favorable one for your particular case. Then, when you add in radiotelephone charges, air-freight cost, agency fees, and impatience and anxiety, you will probably conclude that a generous stock of spare parts is good insurance for your peace of mind as well as your pocketbook.

Part I

ROUTES
TO THE
CARIBBEAN

Chapter Two

PASSAGING FROM THE U.S. EAST COAST

The Choice of Route

Whatever the points of departure or destination of an offshore passage, certain basics must be kept foremost in mind in choosing the route. Eric Hiscock sums them up in his book *Cruising Under Sail:* "The essentials when planning a voyage are to make the greatest use of fair winds and avoid dangerously bad weather by choosing a suitable course and being in the right place at the right time."

Making maximum use of fair winds is a relatively simple matter once you reach the Caribbean, where the NE trades blow with predictable regularity much of the year. But it's not so simple to select the right route at the right time for a small-boat passage to the Caribbean in the often unpredictable North Atlantic. Particularly careful planning is required for a successful passage from the East Coast, where weather conditions in the Bermuda-Hatteras region are controlling factors much of the year. Those who embark casually with dreams of sailing off into the sunrise are due for a rude awakening unless they have diligently studied their pilot charts and alternative routes.

Every seasoned mariner benefits from the experiences of other sailors. Sir Francis Chichester prepared himself for his epic single-handed circumnavigation by reading every log and printed account of sailing over the clipper-ship routes that he could lay his hands on. Skippers who are serious about taking the sea lanes to the Caribbean will do well to follow his example. Too often, bad advice is picked up along the waterfront at the last minute before departure, leading to mistakes that cannot be corrected once you are on your own offshore. On the other hand, with careful advance planning, there is no reason why a well-found boat, starting at the right time of the year on a suitable route with a competent crew, cannot make a successful passage to the islands.

In the following pages, we have made extensive use of logs and published records of many yachts that made successful voyages as a result of sound planning and seamanlike execution.

In planning a departure from the northeast coast of the United States or Canada, your first decision must be whether to make a direct offshore passage to your chosen destination in the Caribbean, or whether to begin your voyage with a coastwise or Intracoastal Waterway passage to more southerly departure points.

Several basic factors will determine the initial choice, the most important being: (1) suitability and readiness of your boat and crew for an offshore passage, (2) how much time you can afford to spend getting to your destination, and (3) whether you can get away at the time of year best suited for the course of your choice. Once these decisions have been made, you will be ready to consider alternative departure points and destinations, and to look more closely into the route options that are best for different times of the year. For those who have time for extended cruising, the options may be more numerous than one would suspect; they include several offshore routes, either direct or by way of Bermuda, and a number of alternative island-hopping routes for the cruising skipper who can afford to plan a more leisurely schedule through the Bahamas and along the coasts of Hispaniola.

If one is planning an offshore passage from anywhere north of Cape Hatteras, weather conditions, timing, and good judgment are the primary ingredients of a successful voyage. Unfortunately, it's not always convenient to leave at the time most suitable for an easy passage south—spring and early summer, when cruising happens to be at its best in northern coastal waters. Conversely, late autumn, when most cruising skippers feel the strongest urge to head south, is apt to be just the wrong time. And those who postpone their departure to winter months are asking for trouble, if not inviting disaster.

Bill Robinson, writing in *Yachting,* rightly warned that departure for southern waters via the offshore route can be hazardous in the late fall and early winter. Reviewing seasonal weather patterns, he states:

> The only really good season for passage in a small yacht . . . is late spring and early summer, and even here there can be freak storms or out-of-character weather, such as the hurricane that delayed the start of the 1968 Bermuda race by one day. From midsummer on, hurricanes have to be considered. Many a lucky voyager has skipped between them, but their usual track out of the Caribbean is to parallel the North American continent between the mainland and Bermuda. True, modern reporting methods give many days' warning in most cases, but sometimes things develop too rapidly and the storm starts moving too fast for a small boat to clear the danger area.

The hurricane season begins to taper off in late October, and by November the percentage incidence of tropical storms has dropped to 3 percent, as noted on page 19, but before the end of November, autumn gales take over quickly, followed by winter conditions that are highly unfavorable, if not dangerous, for an offshore passage in the North Atlantic. Winter passages from New York or New England ports should be ruled out as too hazardous for most small yachts from December through March, when the chances of escaping a combination of gale-force winds and freezing cold somewhere north of Bermuda and east of Hatteras are slim indeed.

Coast Guard search and rescue files contain the records of many yachts lost during winter gales on the North Atlantic track to the West Indies. Scarcely a year passes without the loss or disappearance of one or more vessels, and there need be no mystery about the so-called Bermuda Triangle, where weather-breeding conditions alone are sufficient to explain most of such losses.

These seasonal weather patterns leave two periods in which conditions are likely to be especially favorable for offshore passage-making: the spring and early summer months mentioned by Bill Robinson, and a brief period in the fall between the end of the hurricane season and the onset of winter gales. Both periods offer a variety of route options.

OFFSHORE COURSES AND DISTANCES

Distances are considerably less important than winds, currents, and regional weather conditions in planning your course, whatever the time of year. In spring and early summer, yachts starting from New York or New England may find it to their advantage to detour by way of Bermuda, breaking the long, direct passage with a stopover for provisions and perhaps a change of crew. The extra distance is slight, and a favorable wind slant at the outset may get you across the Gulf Stream sooner and give you the easting you'll need to pick up the NE trades south of Bermuda. The basic objective is to reach the vicinity of 65°W and 25°N as expeditiously as possible, taking advantage of the westerlies at the outset and hopefully avoiding calms and head winds in the variable belt before the trades set in.

The direct distance between New York and Saint Thomas is about 1,400 nautical miles, and there's very little difference whether you start from New London, Newport, or any departure point west of Cape Cod. Bermuda is only about 160 miles east of the rhumb line for Saint Thomas, and if you are lucky enough to pick up northerly or westerly winds, the longer route might prove to be faster.

The traditional course for the Bermuda race is 635 miles from Brenton Reef Light to Saint David's Head, with the larger classes usually finishing in three and a half to four days, the smaller yachts in four to five and a half days, and a few stragglers requiring up to six days. Not everyone races to Bermuda, however, and the average cruising auxiliary is almost sure to take longer, even with the use of power in periods of calm that may be encountered in spring and summer. Six to eight days is not unusual, even for a well-sailed 30-to-40-foot auxiliary that encounters several days of calm or squalls and head winds in the Gulf Stream.

Even the racing fleet often has a rough time crossing the Gulf Stream. The Bermuda-Azores high, with its clockwise circulation of air, gives no assurance of constant winds once you reach the Stream, the northern edge of which lies about 170 to 180 miles southeasterly of Newport. Frequent squalls and sudden windshifts are more often the rule than the exception where the warm waters of the stream meet the cold waters of the North Atlantic, and low-pressure disturbances

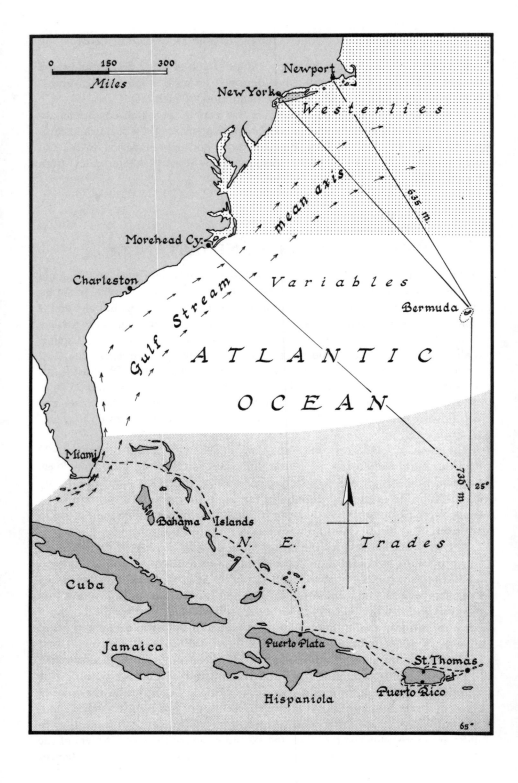

have given the ocean racers trouble more than once in recent years. Under such conditions, small cruising auxiliaries, often sailing with a family crew, may have problems in the Stream and even have some difficulty locating Bermuda or making a successful landfall when visibility is poor.

Most cruising boats plan to make their landfall off Saint David's Head, as the ocean racers do. However, this can be dangerous in stormy weather, as the racing fleet itself discovered in the 1972 race; three boats were dismasted in high winds and mountainous seas close to the reefs that rise steeply from the 100-fathom curve. A dozen other boats withdrew or failed to finish that race, and under similar conditions, most cruising boats would be well advised to stand clear of the islands and their dangerous reefs until conditions have improved. When visibility is good, it is not too difficult to sight Bermuda's two powerful lights at night, or to establish a radio fix from the RDF signals at Gibb's Hill and Saint David's Head before sighting land. Cruising skippers visiting Bermuda for the first time should study their *Sailing Directions* carefully before entering Saint George's or Hamilton Harbour, both of which may be reached through connecting channels leading from the Narrows at the northeast end of the island group.

BERMUDA

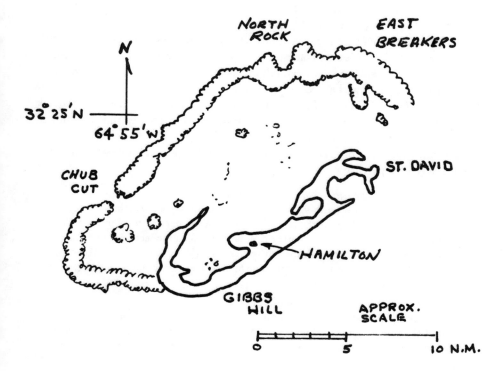

The course from Bermuda to Saint Thomas is almost due S, about 750 miles on the rhumb line, with variable winds for almost half the way until you pick up the NE trades between 25° and 22°N latitude. With a little luck and the use of power in periods of calm, cruising boats usually manage to reach Virgin Island Passage between Culebra and Saint Thomas in six or seven days under favorable conditions in spring and early summer. When you reach the trades, it can be a glorious reach in May or June, and often into July if long-range weather predictions indicate no hurricanes in the Caribbean. But don't attempt such a passage in August or September, when tropical storms are always a threat and may come up without sufficient warning for you to take evasive action.

Long-range weather predictions cannot always be trusted for offshore passages; freak storms may develop quickly at any time, especially during the fall and winter months. In late October and November, many amateur skippers and professional yacht-delivery captains prefer to make short coastwise passages from New York or New England to Norfolk, and then run down the Intracoastal Waterway to Morehead City or Beaufort, N.C., or Charleston, S.C., before jumping off for Saint Thomas or other destinations in the eastern Caribbean. Of course, under the right conditions, it is also possible to make successful voyages starting from Chesapeake Bay, although on that course you have Cape Hatteras and its outlying shoals under your lee, which can be dangerous in a northeast blow.

Looking over the logs of vessels we have known or sailed aboard leads us to the conclusion that there is really no such thing as a "normal" passage at any time of the year. There are records of fast passages and slow passages, of uneventful voyages and hazardous voyages, during the same periods year after year.

Delivery skippers, who have been taking yachts to the islands at all seasons for a number of years now, have developed much practical information from their experiences. One of them is Bruce Cameron, who began deliveries for Patrick Ellam, Inc., in 1970, making a number of noteworthy passages that led him to reevaluate various routes and departure dates.

The following excerpts are from Cameron's notes on five passages, all made from different departure points:

New York—Morehead City—Tortola (Feb.–Mar.)
This winter passage in a Carib-41 was made in unusually good weather—2 days to Norfolk in a bone-chilling northwester, 3 days on the Waterway to Morehead City, and several days' wait there for another NW breeze. Sailed the second leg to Tortola in 7 days, near record time, with the nor'wester carrying us to the Gulf Stream; but the remainder of the trip was a wet, gruelling fight to keep above the rhumb line, with winds from the east (Force 5).

New York—Bermuda—Tortola (June–July)
This summer trip, also made in a Carib-41, took 4 days to Bermuda under power much of the time in glassy calms, with fresh SW breeze on final day. The passage from Bermuda to Tortola was made in 7 days, starting with southerlies that carried

us 150 miles E of the rhumb line on starboard tack; then picked up easterly trades sooner than usual and by 25°N we were reaching along in warm breezes normally found farther south.

Morehead City—St. Thomas (November)
This fall passage was made in *Djinn,* a superb 63-foot S & S sloop, in 7 days after waiting 18 hours in Morehead to check weather with Coast Guard. Boats that had left a few days earlier had experienced moderate gales, and a menacing low system was coming in from the west. With locally west winds, we decided to leave before the low arrived, reasoning that the westerly would carry us out to the Stream and *Djinn* being a fast passage-maker would be far offshore before the low system reached the Carolinas. The predictions held true. We carried the westerly beyond the Stream, when it increased to Force 6 and we reefed down for a night. We stayed E of the rhumb line and picked up the trades about 22.5°N.

Charleston—San Juan (Dec.–Jan.)
This winter delivery of a new Columbia 43 began farther south than usual because of a weather pattern similar to that encountered with *Djinn.* Our wait in Charleston was 6 days, as unsettled conditions continued with a series of lows moving in from the west (one producing 60–70-knot winds). The National Weather Service office in Charleston was most helpful, making some sage predictions on our particular problem, with a real feeling for a sailor's concerns. They advised us to wait out the unsettled period when local conditions looked quite innocent. . . . When we finally took off the trip was slow: 30 hours of westerly winds which gradually decreased to motoring weather, eventually followed by SE winds, shifting more easterly about 21° and never exceeding Force 4. The trip took nearly 11 days.

In drawing conclusions, Bruce Cameron did not suggest any ideal route or schedule, but offered several basic recommendations:

A late spring or early summer departure makes for an easy and fast trip via Bermuda. School vacations ease the crew problem in this period.

Winter and indeed fall trips can be very hard. The trades are sometimes south of east and about 24°N. Get a lot of early easting. However, in the fall early southing is advisable to get out of the more gale-ridden middle Atlantic.

Care in getting a weather forecast before leaving is mandatory particularly in the "off" seasons. A look at a current map is invaluable. The National Weather Service is excellent for this information whereas the TV and newspaper maps may be outdated. Leaving when conditions are right, not on a schedule, requires more time. Thus the "off" season time for the trip is longer.

A radio contact with other yachts is useful. In the fall this is easy to establish with the many yachts leaving.

Have extra food and drink for at least 20 days total. Running out is not fun.

Carry as much fuel as possible and at least enough to get adequate sea room when leaving the Carolinas (two days' worth).

Enjoy it! It is a great passage if you do it right.

From the viewpoint of the cruising skipper, a few additional comments on route selection may be in order. The professional captain and the amateur skipper have an identity of purpose only when each is expected to get from Point A to Point B as quickly as possible. The professional delivery captain usually is. But there are many situations in which the owner-skipper has choices not open to the delivery captain. For one, he can afford to wait longer for settled weather. He can change his plans more easily and choose another port of departure with greater freedom. If the outlook is poor for an offshore passage from Charleston, he can continue down the Intracoastal to Florida and still have a chance to make his easting from the Bahamas. Finally, if time is not a controlling factor, he can consider an altogether different route by cruising southeast into the Caribbean through the Bahamas.

ROUTES VIA THE BAHAMAS

A number of alternative routes are available to the cruising skipper who is not pressed for time and can afford the luxury of leisurely island-hopping through the 600-mile chain of the Bahamas to the Caicos Islands, Grand Turk, or Great Inagua at the southern end of the chain, where he is only an overnight passage away from the north coast of Hispaniola. For those who cannot afford to tarry in the Bahamas, other options are open. Deep-water sailors may prefer a direct passage to San Juan or Saint Thomas from departure points several hundred miles southeast of Florida.

The direct distance from Palm Beach or Miami to Saint Thomas is approximately 1,000 miles, although the actual sailing track is substantially longer when you zigzag through the islands or encounter head winds much of the way on the offshore passages. Most yacht-delivery skippers avoid these routes because they are too time-consuming and are likely to prove a hard upwind battle. Yet there are often advantages for cruising boats that can wait for the right weather to start from a preferred departure point, and there are special rewards for those who can linger long enough in the Bahamas to savor the distinctive combination of bank and deep-water cruising in those lovely islands.

In this chapter, we are concerned with routes to the Caribbean rather than with descriptions of the individual islands. They are discussed in separate chapters of Part II covering the Caicos Islands and Grand Turk, and Hispaniola on the Thorny Path to the Lesser Antilles. We have traveled the island-hopping routes under both sail and power, making the passage between Florida and the Virgin Islands in both directions and at different times of the year, under both sail and power. We have made the eastbound passage in November and early December and encountered northeast winds that made it a close reach most of the way to the Caicos Islands and Hispaniola, but not the hard beat to windward one is likely to experience in late December or January. Furthermore, we have studied the logs of other vessels that followed much the same routes, and of some that made direct offshore passages from various departure points. The following is a synthesis of those experiences.

Florida to the Bahamas

From the East Coast of the United States, a Florida port is the most usual embarkation point for the northern and central Bahamas. The 55-mile Gulf Stream crossing between Palm Beach and West End, Grand Bahama, is one of the easiest routes to the islands, longer by a few miles than the Miami-Bimini or Gun and Cat cays route, but with a better landfall channel for entering at West End. Crossing the Little Bahama Bank to the Abaco Cays is generally easier—at least for sailboats—than making the long run from Bimini across the 90-mile stretch of the Great Bahama Bank to the Berry Islands and beyond to the central Bahamas.

Approaching the Abacos from West End, most cruising powerboats allow two days for the 125-mile run across the bank to the Marsh Harbour–Hope Town area, while small sailing auxiliaries often take three days, with overnight stops at Great Sale and Green Turtle cays. The bank waters on this route range from 1 ½ to 3 ½ fathoms over clear sandy bottom with virtually no hidden dangers.

The shortest distance (45 miles) across the Gulf Stream is from Miami to Bimini or Gun and Cat cays, with a powerful beam current all the way. But in terms of time, it is almost the same to start off from, say, Key Largo, since you will get a lift from the current and often a better slant of wind. In the winter season, the northers seem to come through with exasperating regularity, so you may have to figure on waiting several days for the right conditions to make the crossing—and we can assure you that the Stream is no place to be during strong northerly winds, when conditions in the "hump," where the current is running at its maximum pace against the wind, must be seen to be believed. Rather than cross from Miami, we often use the waiting time to wend farther south.

To come in off the deep dark blue of the Gulf Stream to the unbelievably clear water of Bimini or Gun and Cat cays, with its vivid hues of blue and green and almost white, to feel a softer wind in one's face and to see the restless surge chomping at the undercut coral edges of the cays, is an experience to be savored again and again, no matter how many times one makes the crossing from Florida.

If you are headed for Nassau on New Providence Island and for the Exumas and the islands beyond, the various routes across the banks converge on Northwest Channel Beacon with the excellent shelter of Chub Cay just beyond, thence across another stretch of deep water where the conflicting ocean currents tend to set up a confused sea under windy conditions.

Several texts exist that contain detailed information about cruising in the

Bahamas. Among these are *Yachtsman's Guide to the Bahamas,* by Harry Kline, and *Cruising Guide to the Abacos and the Northern Bahamas,* by Julius Wilensky. (See Bibliography.)

Northern and Central Bahamas to the Virgin Islands

Many cruising boats have made successful passages from the northern and central Bahamas direct to the Virgins by waiting for a moderate norther to give them their necessary easting early in the voyage, making it possible to carry the NE trades all the way to their destination. Northers occur regularly from December through March. Some of them are too boisterous for comfort or safety in a small cruising boat; others, lighter at the start, may peter out before you are far enough east to pick up the trades. You can run offshore from any point in the Bahamas; the farther south you depart the more likely you are to start with a light northerly that dies out entirely before the trades come in.

Abaco to the Virgin Islands

One example of a yacht making good use of a norther is the mid-January voyage of Stanley Livingston's 50-foot yawl *Manukai* from Man-o-War Cay in the Abacos. The breeze was relatively light at the outset but freshened as it moved around from N to NE, giving the crew boisterous winds and seas along the way. The unusual feature of the voyage was that *Manukai* was on port tack for the whole passage, with the exception of about three hours before making its landfall on Jost Van Dyke. The passage was made without incident in seven days and one hour. On a later voyage, *Manukai* followed much the same course, but took nine days, in lighter airs.

Newer and larger racing yachts report some faster passage times, but very few take less than six days to reach the Virgins by this route.

The track for commercial vessels from Florida ports and Nassau to the eastern Caribbean is by way of the Northeast Providence Channel and is favored by some sailing auxiliaries and long-range cruising power yachts. The direct distance from Hole-in-the-Wall Light at the NE end of Providence Channel is about 660 miles to San Juan, or 710 miles to Saint Thomas, but the ESE course makes it a close beat for sailing vessels after a northerly swings into the east. During the winter months, this is likely to be a rough trip even for true seagoing powerboats. In spring and early fall, when the prevailing winds are E to SE, this route often involves tedious hours of tacking upwind into the long Atlantic seas, or exasperating periods of calm in the oily swells. We know of an Alberg-35 with a husband and wife crew that alternated between light head winds, variables, and flat calms for 11 days until the engine failed within sight of Puerto Rico. At that point, without a zephyr of breeze, and without power, an onshore current carried them across a fringing reef and deposited the boat on a beach north of San Juan. After several months of arduous repair work on the damaged hull and engine, this doughty retired couple continued their cruise to the Virgin Islands, where they spent a pleasant winter.

Southern Bahamas to the East

After island-cruising through the Bahamas as far southward as George Town, Great Exuma, there are several other departure points from which cruising boats have made direct ocean voyages to Puerto Rico or the Virgin Islands. These are from Cape Santa Maria at the northern end of Long Island; out through Crooked Island Passage; or, farther down, through Mayaguana Passage, Caicos Passage, or Turks Island Passage, each of which provides a deep-sea track frequented by eastbound and westbound commercial traffic. For sailing vessels, a departure eastward from any of these passages is sure to involve a long, hard beat to windward, even when you start with a norther (and as we've noted, they are more likely to be short-lived the farther south you start).

If you start offshore from Caicos or Grand Turk, at the southern end of the island chain, you encounter another hazard: the treacherous shallows of the Mouchoir and Silver banks, which extend more than 150 miles southeast of Grand Turk and have been the graveyard of many good ships since the days of Spanish galleons. The few successful eastbound voyages that we know about through these passages have been made when N to NNE winds continued long enough to carry vessels almost all the way to Puerto Rico. Such conditions are unusual, and more often than not cruising boats have abandoned the ocean voyage entirely or returned to the Bahamas in search of an easier route to the east.

Under settled conditions, the island-hopping route from the southern Exumas to the Caicos Bank, a direct distance of about 250 miles, can be made in a series of daylight runs with overnight anchorages at each of the major islands along the way. When you have reached South Caicos, you are only about 110 miles NW of Puerto Plata, a port of entry on the north coast of the Dominican Republic, within two or three days' sailing distance of Puerto Rico. (The other port of entry on the north coast of the Dominican Republic is Pepillo Salcedo in Manzanilla Bay, farther west, near the Haitian border.)

The best seasons for taking this route are spring and fall, when conditions are generally favorable for fast runs across the three deep ocean passages, with good visibility for landfalls on the larger islands. We have made the eastbound trip from Long Island to the Caicos Bank in three or four days under sail in late November, with NE winds giving us a fair breeze during daylight and only a few hours of windward work approaching West Caicos. Other cruising boats have encountered frustrating head winds and steep seas that made it an uphill battle, taking a week or more to reach Caicos. Still others have tired of the windward beating, and given up the battle or headed for Great Inagua, southwest of the Caicos Islands and Grand Turk.

Powerboats can plan their daily runs with considerable precision, making landfalls earlier in the day and finding a good anchorage for the night in protected harbors on most of the islands. But those who follow this course, whether by sail or power, should realize that conditions in the open passages may be quite different from those in the sheltered sounds of the central Bahamas, and that finding a safe harbor may be difficult or impossible in gale-force winds and heavy rain.

On the other hand, sailing the windward side of these outer out-islands is an exhilarating experience in a fair breeze. The 1,000-fathom line is only a few miles offshore, and the barrier reefs are close enough that you can see the surf breaking and piling up on the sandy beaches beyond. Harbors and anchorages on each of these islands are described in Part II, and the approaches should be studied carefully on the largest-scale government charts, harbor plans, and sketch charts before entering. Here we list only the principal harbors and approximate distances between them, for planning daily runs.

Clarence Harbour, Long Island (26253, 26240, CK-55),

is about 40 miles SE of Cape Santa Maria, which is the northern tip of Long Island, and can usually be reached in one day from George Town, Exuma. It is exposed to the north but offers protection in prevailing trades. Water and fuel available.

Portland Harbour, Crooked Island (26240, CK-14/54),

is another 40 miles ESE across Crooked Island Passage, with Bird Rock Lighthouse often visible many miles out at sea. Columbus anchored here on October 19, 1492, but there are better anchorages nearby.

Major's Cay Harbour (26240, CK-14/54)

lies 14 miles ESE of Bird Rock Light on the north coast of Crooked Island, and is entered through a narrow break in the reef that should not be attempted in stormy weather.

Atwood Harbour, Acklin's (26240, CK-13A/14),

is 12 miles E of Major's, marked by a light at the harbor entrance. It's a tiny harbor exposed to the northeast, but a good jumping-off place for Mayaguana.

Abraham Bay, Mayaguana (25263, CK-60/61)

lies approximately 50 miles across Mayaguana Passage. This may be a long windward leg if the trades are from E to ESE. Several anchorages are described in Part II. On an eastbound passage in *Brer Fox*, we sailed north of Mayaguana on a 30-hour overnight run direct from Crooked Island to Providenciales on Caicos Bank with NNE to NE winds all the way. A lucky break!

Providenciales and West Caicos (26260)

lie approximately 45 miles SE of Abraham Bay across Caicos Passage, where a night run in good weather may be preferable to a daytime crossing. Even under the best conditions, it's not easy to identify the entrance to the west side of Caicos Bank; the entrance is completely surrounded by reefs correctly described in the

Sailing Directions as "extremely dangerous." A landfall in midmorning after a night run is easier and safer than a late-afternoon arrival, when a low sun makes it difficult or impossible to read water depths. At night, we would dare to enter only through the reef at Fort George Cut on the northwest coast of Providenciales, described in Chapter 5. Directions for entering and crossing the 50-mile-wide Caicos Bank at various points are also discussed in that chapter.

Cockburn Harbour, South Caicos (26261),

is the best jumping-off point for Hispaniola and Puerto Rico. The protected anchorage here is preferable to the open roadstead at Grand Turk, 20 miles across Turks Island Passage.

Great Inagua (26240, CK-15).

For yachts making the Windward Passage route to Jamaica, Panama, or the western Caribbean, Great Inagua is the last stepping-stone in the Bahamas chain. Although it is one of the largest islands, Great Inagua provides the poorest anchorages in the entire chain.

Mathew Town (26267, CK-63)

is an open roadstead that provides a rolly anchorage under the best conditions and becomes completely untenable in a norther. There is a small man-made basin 200' × 200' about a mile NE of the town that carries 5 feet in the dredged entrance channel at low water and 8 to 10 feet along the cement bulkhead, but no yacht facilities are available. Fuel can be delivered alongside by truck and carried aboard by jerry cans. Mathew Town is a port of entry for the Bahamas.

The chart does not show the dredged basin. On our last southbound passage in *Brer Fox* we were confused about midnight by sighting the bright lights of what seemed to be a sizable town when we were still 30 miles from Mathew Town. The bearing of these very bright lights, moreover, was at least 20°E of the charted position of Mathew Town. Had we altered our course and steered for the lights we would have arrived at the new Morton Salt Company plant and ship pier 10 miles from Mathew Town, in Man of War Bay!

The Thorny Path, via Hispaniola (25720)

In recent years, an increasing number of eastbound cruising yachts have followed the old sailing route by way of the Dominican Republic, which was "out of bounds" during the troubled years of the Trujillo dictatorship in the Dominican Republic. Many have found the route a thorny path indeed, beating much of the way into the teeth of boisterous winter trades, with few protected harbors along the way; others have experienced relatively easy overnight runs to Puerto Plata and interesting coastwise cruising to Samaná Bay and across the Mona Passage to Puerto Rico.

Cruising conditions in Hispaniola are fully described in Chapter Six, including approaches and entry procedures for all major harbors in both Haiti and the Dominican Republic. (Information previously gathered about Haiti has been included, but edited to reflect the current restrictions to cruising there. These restrictions are discussed in Chapter Six—Hispaniola.)

Here we will make only general observations about routes and offshore weather conditions in the open passages, drawn from our own experiences and those of others.

Once you are clear of the island-hopping to the Caicos Islands and are approaching the large, high land mass of Hispaniola, a powerboat skipper's tactics will differ from a sailor's. The object is to avoid the prevailing wind as much as possible. Yet both sailboats and powerboats can take advantage of special wind conditions that prevail around all the large mountainous islands, and learn to avoid some of the strongest head winds. More often than not, we have found the winds to be more moderate at night along the coasts of Hispaniola and Puerto Rico, when the cooled air is flowing down off the hills and out to sea. Sometimes this offshore flow is enough to counter the trade winds completely, providing a welcome spell of coastwise running in calm conditions under a starry sky with the brooding mountains close by and only the ever-present swell to disturb one's balance. Having carefully noted the courses and distances while making the daylight approach to an overnight anchorage, we often got under way at 0200 or 0300 in the morning and tried to time our arrival at the next stop before the trades really piped up in the early afternoon. With a fast powerboat, there is considerable flexibility in such tactics. Sailboat tactics naturally will differ on the longer passages, but we've also taken advantage of the offshore winds at night by getting an early start or, when conditions are favorable, continuing alongshore in the evening breeze.

The open water passage from the Caicos Islands to Puerto Plata in the Dominican Republic is approximately 110 miles SSE, usually made in an overnight run by sailboat or trawler-type yacht, and often in a daylight run by a fast seagoing powerboat. In winter months, it is generally a rough passage, with 10-to-12-foot seas when the trades are blowing hard. Long-range weather forecasts are hard to come by, unless you have a single sideband radio.

Conditions may also change suddenly, as we discovered on a passage in December 1971. Although we had been unable to get any regional weather forecast before leaving the Caicos Islands, a moderate northeast breeze promised a fast overnight passage on a comfortable reach. But that hopeful promise failed to materialize. A low-pressure system was soon upon us, with severe squalls and heavy rain that reduced visibility to near zero. We furled the main before dark and ran off comfortably enough under our low-cut No. 3 ("mule") genoa and mizzen, logging 7 knots until midnight, when the squalls became almost constant, with sudden shifts in wind direction and velocity. Backwinded by one such shift, the boat fell off into a trough, momentarily losing steerageway and fouling the taffrail log line around the rudder. It took us several hours to clear that fouled line and reset the log, during which time we could only guess our speed and distance run.

By daybreak of December 7, the storm was generating Force 8 winds and building up 15-foot seas with breaking tops. There was no letup in the torrential rain, which obscured everything outside the boat. By that time, we estimated we should be approaching Cape Isabela at the northern tip of Hispaniola, some 20 miles NW of Puerto Plata.

The coast of Hispaniola is mountainous here, rising steeply from the sea to bold headlands visible for more than 30 miles in good weather. The 100-fathom curve lies less than 1½ miles off Cape Isabela and trends irregularly southeastward, following the steep, reef-fringed coastline toward Puerto Plata, the only real port on the north coast of the Dominican Republic.

With less than a half-mile visibility between rain squalls and no accessible radio or other navigational aids to guide us, our only safe course was to stand offshore before getting too close to the breaking reefs. So we tacked on and off soundings for almost seven hours, waiting for a break in the storm. When there was no change by early afternoon, we feared we'd have to put through another night under these conditions, beating off a dangerous lee shore. Then, through a sudden break in the rain-laden storm clouds, we caught a fleeting glimpse of Mount

Puerto Plata is not the best place to take your boat when the wind is in the north. But later in the spring, when the trades blow, this government dock is a popular place to spend a few days.

Isabela de Torres rising from the sea some 15 miles to the southwest. This was the 2,600-foot mountain that guided Columbus to Puerto Plata in 1493, and it gave us an unmistakable landmark from which to set our course. Although the squalls continued intermittently, we ran our distance with assurance and three hours later were at anchor behind the sheltering reefs of Puerto Plata's harbor.

Almost a decade later Bill Robinson sailed much the same course between the Caicos Islands and Puerto Plata. This was a springtime cruise, with Bill taking his CSY-37 *Brunelle* along the Thorny Path in bright sunshine with light and variable winds that made the rugged north coast of Hispaniola a "not so thorny path." Listen to Bill's report on the approach to Puerto Plata:

> I had visualized a hard, dusty thrash into a southeast trade. It was almost like waiting for a firecracker to pop and then have it fizzle when we encountered 24 hours of motorsailing in light zephyrs. There was a big swell over which we heaved and bobbled, but no surface waves. Dolpins played around us for a while, but otherwise it was an empty, quiet ocean until the great bulk of Hispaniola loomed out of the morning haze at dawn.

Puerto Plata to Puerto Rico

Although the direct distance from Puerto Plata across Mona Passage to the west end of Puerto Rico is only about 220 miles, the time required to make good that distance in a cruising auxiliary may range anywhere from 35 to 40 hours under favorable conditions, and up to twice as long when the trades are right on the nose, as they are likely to be much of the year. We were fortunate to pick up moderate NNE winds after a welcome two-day layover at Puerto Plata. This gave us a favorable slant to clear Cape Cabron at the northeast tip of Hispaniola with only two short offshore tacks around the headlands of Cape Macorís and Cape Francés Viejo. There are no good harbors on this section of the coast, but one can find shelter at Santa Barbara inside Samaná Bay. Most sailboats prefer to continue southeastward across Mona Passage to the west end of Puerto Rico, where wind and sea conditions should determine whether you ought to take the north or the south coast around that large island. Our eastbound passage in December 1971 was favored by NE winds that made it possible to continue up the north coast to San Juan, doing the last eight hours under power and sail. From Puerto Plata to San Juan our taffrail log showed we had sailed 310 miles over the bottom, mostly hard on the wind, in 58 hours, about four hours better than our return over a somewhat shorter route in light SE winds with periods of calm in April.

In recent years the island-hopping route has been attracting more and more cruising yachts on both the eastbound and westbound passages. In winter months it is still the Thorny Path, beating to windward along the north coast of Hispaniola; but in fall and spring months you may be as lucky as Bill Robinson and find it "not so thorny a path" after all.

SUMMARY

How much time should one allow for the entire island-hopping route from Florida to Puerto Rico? The answer, of course, depends on what kind of boat you have and how much time you can spare for overnight stops and gunkholing along the way. Our logged distance under sail was just over 1,000 miles; we made it in three weeks, anchoring almost every night in the Bahamas, with two-day layovers at George Town, the Caicos Islands, and Puerto Plata. A larger cruising auxiliary could do the same eastbound route, with fewer stopovers, in two weeks or less with favorable NNE to NE winds, but if the trades are E to SE, as they frequently are in the spring and early summer, this passage might take a month or more for the average small sailing vessel.

Cruising powerboats make the same voyage in considerably less time, of course. A recap of *Out Islander*'s log on an eastbound passage cruising at 15 knots from Miami to Ponce, Puerto Rico, from March 21 to April 1, gives the following daily runs:

	Winds	*Nautical Miles*
Miami to Chub Cay	ESE 4, diminishing through the day	129
Chub to Compass Cay	Variable light breezes, smooth	105
Compass to Clarence Town, Long Island	N 2 to 3, smooth sea	125
Clarence Town to Abraham Bay, Mayaguana	NE 3, little swell	122
Mayaguana to Cockburn Harbour, S. Caicos	ENE 4 in the afternoon	113
S. Caicos to Puerto Plata	E 4, 4–5' seas. Dep. 0537, arr. 1243	115
Puerto Plata to Samaná	SE 3–4, confused swells. Dep. 0400, arr. 1135	118
Samaná to Puerto Real via Mayagüez	Heavy rain squalls at first, then E 3–4 but 6' to 7' seas in western half of Mona Passage	146
Puerto Real to Ponce	SE 4 along S coast of Puerto Rico	46
	Total miles	1,019

To our way of thinking, the island-hopping route offers something more than just one way to get your boat to the Caribbean. It is a unique cruising experience in itself, providing opportunities for those who are making the trip for the first time to test their navigational skills in relatively short interisland passages, and offering more experienced skippers a wide variety of offshore and coastwise cruising in areas that are off the beaten track. Despite the increasing number of cruising yachts following the Thorny Path, you'll find many long stretches of Hispaniola's barren coastline that are still well off the beaten track.

Chapter Three

PASSAGING FROM THE U.S. WEST COAST AND THROUGH THE PANAMA CANAL

More than 3,000 miles lie between San Diego and the Panama Canal. You'll hug the coast for most of it: miles upon miles of uninhabited coastline along the desolate and treeless peninsula of Baja California, then a 290-mile open-water hop across the Sea of Cortez to lively and splashy Puerto Vallarta (or a slight detour via Mazatlán); then along a stretch of coast marked by low cliffs, with a backdrop of magnificent mountains—and then to pleasure-crazy Acapulco. Beyond that resort of resorts lie a thousand miles of seemingly endless beaches, lagoons, and occasional volcanos until you reach the mud, silt, and breathless heat of the Costa Rican port of Puntarenas.

Next comes the crenated coast of Panama, pocked with islands, splashed with verdant jungle growth, and almost uninhabited, to the most southerly point of the passage—just over 7°N—at Cape Mala, a name that needs no interpretation. Here the trade winds, now released to flow unhindered across the low isthmus, rush to meet you in one violent blast, as though to prove that the Pacific isn't always pacific. And here, having trended east as much as south along the entire coast of Central America, you will turn your course north to Balboa, the western end of the Panama Canal.

Just to show how distorted the geography of this passage can be in the mind's eye of most people, ask anyone what major U.S. city lies due north of the canal. The usual answers will be New Orleans or even Houston. It's hard to realize that Miami is actually a little *west* of the meridian of Cristóbal and that it's only 1,226 more miles to Key West by the shortest route.

Between San Diego and the canal, the usual stops for provisioning, fueling, rest, and relaxation are:

San Diego	0	miles
Turtle Bay	365	"
Cabo San Lucas	395	"
Puerto Vallarta	291	"

Acapulco	452	"
Puerto Madero	502	"
Puntarenas (Costa Rica)	588	"
Balboa	469	"
	3,062	

Mexican tourist cards for each of the crew members should be obtained at a Mexican tourist or consular office before you leave California. Whether or not you really like fishing, fish are so plentiful in Mexican waters that you definitely should pick up a fishing permit along with your tourist card. As a matter of fact the simple possession of fishing tackle on board requires that you have a license. A sierra mackerel on your dinner table, less than an hour out of the water, is a delicious treat. We have provided our dinner after only 50 yards of trolling with the dinghy!

The months during which this coast can be most safely run are limited by the hurricane season, which begins in late June or in July and carries through October. Standard practice among cruising people who know this area well is to leave San Diego around November 1 and be back in June. Winds are northwest most of the time down as far as Cape Corrientes or maybe a little farther, but after that you are in the lee of the mountainous backbone of Central America and will feel only the light sea and land breezes blowing on and off the coast as the land mass alternately heats and cools the air above it.

There's a chance of strong winds down the Pacific side of Baja, and there are three other places where you may take a drubbing: the dreaded Gulf of Tehuantepec, the somewhat less feared Gulf of Papagayo—in both gulfs the winds come in hard and suddenly from the northeast, amplified by the topography of the coast—and the bash to the canal after you leave the shelter of Cape Mala.

The tehuantepecer in particular must be treated with utmost respect. It is extremely local and difficult to forecast, and its wind velocity may go from Force 2 to 8 within a matter of minutes. The firmly accepted strategy of all who pass that way is "to keep a foot on the beach," in order to avoid the vicious sea that builds up only a mile or so offshore. We saw a yacht that had been literally sandblasted by following the beach so closely, and were told the crew had had to don snorkel masks to protect their eyes. Nevertheless, this is the tactic to follow.

Another bane of this coast that needs mentioning is the incessant Pacific swell. West Coast sailors take it in stride, sometimes with boomed-out stabilizing devices, but it remains a novel discomfort to sailors from the Atlantic coast. Sometimes the judicious setting of a stern anchor may turn the roll into a pitch, but the flukey night breezes tend to foil that tactic. In any case, most anchorages that are not completely enclosed will subject you to swell, and you'll frequently find it a good reason to keep going through 24 hours rather than roll all night at anchor in an open bight.

Water quality and availability down this coast present a problem. If you have the space and the wherewithal you will do well to install a water maker before leaving the States.

THE PANAMA CANAL
BY RODMAN A. OAKES

After 75 years of operation, the Panama Canal continues to be one of the great engineering feats of all time. The massive locks, their gates, the huge culverts and valves that fill and empty the chambers, and the one-and-a-half-mile-long Gatun Dam that holds back the waters of the Chagres River all continue to function as they did when first put into service in 1914.

There have, however, been many changes in Panama and in the operation of the 50-mile canal since it opened. The most notable change for canal users occurred in 1979, when the Panama Canal Treaties of 1977 went into effect. The former 10-mile-wide U.S. Canal Zone became part of the Republic of Panama, and the binational Panama Canal Commission took over the administration and operation of the canal for the 20-year term of the treaties.

For yachts transiting the canal there has been a more recent and more important change in procedure: consolidating small-vessel transits on Tuesdays and Thursdays. On these two days, yachts are locked up en masse as the last lockage of the morning run without a large ship in the lock chambers. This eliminates one of the hazards of a canal transit—the propeller wash from an upbound ship ahead in the chamber. The trade-off with this system is that transits usually take a second day to complete, since most yachts arrive up at Gatun Lake level too late to make a down-lockage the same day. Yachts are usually anchored at the Gatun Yacht Club northbound (at the Gamboa mooring area southbound) to await the first available down-lockage the following day. Exceptions are made for larger vessels that can safely lock up with a ship and faster vessels that can cross the lake in time to make a down-lockage the same day.

Otherwise, the procedures, problems, and pleasures of going through "the ditch" are pretty much as they have been since the Panama Canal Commission took over in 1979. The commission's first obligation is to operate the canal for commercial interests, and if some of the rules and regulations seem arbitrary or overly restrictive for yachts, remember the canal was designed and built at a time when few yachts were sailing around the world.

Arrival at the Canal (21603)

Upon arrival at the sea buoy, call Flamenco Island Signal at the Pacific entrance (Cristobal Signal at the Atlantic entrance) on VHF Channel 12 or 16. You will be directed to proceed to the anchorage of the Balboa Yacht Club (Panama Canal Yacht Club, Cristobal), since officials no longer board yachts upon arrival. This will be no problem in clear weather, when the IALA District B aids to navigation are easily identified; but if it is raining or if you are in doubt, stand off until the visibility improves. The shoals alongside the Pacific entrance channel and coral reefs at the ends of the Atlantic breakwater stand ready to welcome unwary vessels. Keep a constant fix on your position as you enter the channel. There are excellent high-visibility green range lights on the centerline of both Atlantic and Pacific entrance channels. Use them to confirm the often strong current set— usually to the west—at the entrance to the Pacific channel, but don't stay on the ranges when large ships are in the channel. Run the buoy lines instead! Do not anchor off any of the islands at the seaward end of the 1-mile-long Pacific causeway. These islands are Panama Defense Forces controlled.

Balboa Yacht Club (21603)

The club is located on the east bank of the channel opposite Buoy No. 16. Due to the up to 20-foot tidal range on the Pacific side, there are no slips at the Balboa Yacht Club. There is 24-hour launch service, such as it is, and the launch operator should be able to direct you to a vacant mooring. Use great care maneuvering in the mooring area off the club, as there is an almost constant strong ebb current due to the spilling of water from Miraflores Locks. Moorings have been known to drag!

In a worldwide survey of yacht clubs, Panama's ranked at the top of the list of the worst. Available facilities at the clubs are, of course, primarily for members' use. Don't expect much service, if any, though club members can be very helpful with local knowledge and assistance with problems. At Balboa Yacht Club dockage at the club float for fuel and water can be difficult. The float is reserved for members only on Friday, Saturday, and Sunday. There are showers but no washers or dryers at the club.

Transit Clearance

As soon as convenient after arriving at the yacht club, take passports and related documents to the Panama immigration personnel at the small office manned around the clock at the head of the dock. If you approach the personnel in a positive, friendly manner, this should be your first pleasant experience dealing with Panamanians. Wear proper dress on all official business. Tank tops, shorts, and flip-flops are not worn on the streets of downtown Panama.

The next official stops are made during business hours (0700–1500) at the offices of the Panama Canal Commission's Admeasurers and Canal Operations. Take all appropriate vessel documents, including your PCC admeasurement certificate if your vessel has transited before. If you do not have a PCC admeasurement certificate, you will find out how to obtain one. It is possible to arrange for measuring before visiting the PCC offices. Call the admeasurers at 52-4570 (Cristobal 46-7293).

If required, the measuring of your yacht can be accomplished the same day if you contact the admeasurers' office before noon. After that time, measuring will probably take place the next day. The minimum fee for admeasuring is $50 for up to 50 tons and $1 more per additional ton thereafter, up to 100 tons. There is a sliding diminishing fee per ton over 100 tons. The transit fee is based on your Panama Canal net tonnage (the vessel's interior volume in cubic feet divided by 100) multiplied by $1.60. For example, a 47-foot auxiliary sailboat with a net tonnage of 30 would pay a toll of $48—a bargain compared to the $100,000+ fee paid by the *Queen Elizabeth 2* for a one-way transit. Your transit date will be scheduled when the commission's paperwork is completed, and *cash payment is made in U.S. dollars.* A 30 percent contingency fee will be included, and a fine of $295 will be levied if you fail to make a timely cancellation of your transit date. You will also be required to sign a waiver that relieves the PCC from responsibility for damage to your vessel during transit. The Canal Operations office telephone is 52-4211 (Cristobal 46-7637).

Taboga Island (21603)

If you have more than a day or so to wait for transit, consider moving over to this tropical island, just 8 miles off commercial Balboa Harbor. Anchor off the small attractive community, where the water is usually clean and quiet, a peaceful world away from the almost constant rolling at the yacht club due to canal traffic, the strong current, the potential for bunker spills at the ship piers, and the roar of traffic from the Bridge of the Americas. Proceed well into the anchorage off the hotel as far as your draft will allow with consideration for the tidal range, which uncovers the sand spit between the hotel and the small island (Morra de Taboga) to the east during low water. At Taboga there is good swimming, fishing, exploring, and an excellent inexpensive restaurant all just a one-hour ferry trip from Balboa Harbor. The ferry docks in Balboa basin alongside the duty-free store, and taxis are usually available just outside the large-ship-pier gate. On weekends, be prepared for a small invasion on Taboga of Panamanians getting away from it all.

The Canal Transit

Vessels less than 125 feet in length are known as handliners, since their mooring lines are tended on the lock walls by line handlers rather than being secured by wires to electric locomotives, as larger ships are. One of the official transit requirements is to have four good 100-foot dock lines and crew to handle them—a minimum of five adults, including the skipper. Dock lines can be married together, but it is not recommended. Shorthanded yachts may assist each other with extra crew, taking the train or bus back across the isthmus after the transit. The ride through the jungle and around Gatun Lake on the world's first transcontinental railroad should not be missed! It costs only $1.25 each way, but service has been reduced to commuting hours only. It is also a worthwhile experience to make a canal transit on board another boat before you take your own vessel across the isthmus.

There are three possibilities for securing handline vessels in the locks chambers:

1. A center chamber lockage uses two bow lines and two stern lines secured to bollards on the lock walls to position the vessel in midchamber. This is the safest system for the turbulent up-lockage when 26 million gallons of fresh water fill the chamber in about 10 minutes.

2. If a PCC tug happens to be locking up at the same time, you may be lucky enough to secure alongside and get a free ride up while the tug crew does the line handling.

3. The third possibility for handliners is a sidewall lockage with one bow line and one stern line—not recommended for upbound lockages unless your vessel is built like a tug with stout fenders. It is possible to safely lock down sidewall as the chambers empty like a bathtub, with little turbulence.

Depending on the number of vessels in the lockage, two or three may be rafted—the term is "nested" at the canal—together and moved as a twin- or triple-screw vessel from chamber to chamber. Whichever lockage method is used, beg, borrow, or steal all of the fenders that you can lay your hands on, and then rig fender boards to save your fenders from the rough concrete, algae, and grease of the chamber walls. Tires rigged over the fender boards will provide maximum protection. Avoid coming alongside the lock walls at the entrance to the chambers where the locomotives drag their wires, depositing grease that is difficult to remove from fenders and topsides. Look out for the monkey's fist on the heaving lines thrown by the PCC linemen from the lock walls to pull your mooring lines up to the bollards. Crew members have been hit and ports and windows broken by these potentially lethal missiles.

Depending on the size of your vessel, you will have a pilot or a transit adviser. Less than 65' LOA, a PCC tugboat mate with a motorboat operator's license will be assigned as transit adviser. Over 65' LOA, you will have a genuine Panama Canal pilot, although he'll probably be a "shorthorn" of limited experience. In either case, he is unlikely to be a small-boat sailor, and the transit may be a learning experience for both of you.

You must be able to safely handle your vessel in the often turbulent conditions while approaching and in the locks, with your pilot/adviser telling you only where and when to proceed. Your crew must be able to quickly and safely handle your mooring lines to prevent damage in the chambers. Chocks, bitts, and cleats must be securely through-bolted to take the heavy strains. If you do not have closed chocks, rig snatch blocks to prevent tearing out lifelines due to the high leads to the lock walls, which are over 30 feet above water level in a spilled chamber.

On your assigned day, have your vessel ready in all respects for transit at the scheduled time. Have sufficient food and drink for your crew and pilot/adviser for what may be a long, hot day or two. An awning for sun and/or rain can make the transit more pleasant; but discuss with your pilot/adviser before rigging, as it may interfere with line handling in the chambers. Be prepared to anchor for the overnight layover if you are not able to lock down the same day, and be ready for an early departure the next morning when your pilot/adviser returns.

The three steps up 85 feet from sea level to Gatun Lake are divided into two sets of locks on the Pacific side. The first, Miraflores Locks, has two chambers, which lift vessels 54 feet up to 1-mile-long Miraflores Lake, where the Pedro Miguel Yacht Club is located. There is a single chamber at Pedro Miguel Locks for the final step, up to Gaillard Cut, which winds 7 miles through the mountains of the Continental Divide. Thousands of workers died here in the landslides during construction days. The cut is all the more awe-inspiring when you realize that there is a minimum water depth of 50 feet in the 500-foot-wide channel.

The 20-mile trip across Gatun Lake begins after leaving the cut at Gamboa, where the Chagres River flows into the lake. Here the channel follows the straightened course of the river to Gatun Anchorage, where the Gatun Yacht Club is located. The trip across what was the world's largest man-made lake when completed is a beautiful experience, especially if your pilot/adviser takes you through the Banana Channel. This shortcut over the route of the original Panama Canal Railroad takes 1 mile off the crossing and provides a close-up look at the jungle on either side.

The three steps back to sea level are accomplished in three continuous chambers at Gatun Locks, where there was sufficient rock base to build all three chambers together. The down-lockage is tranquil compared to the turbulence of the up-lockage. Leaving the last chamber, be ready for the strong outbound current generated by the intermixing of the fresh water in the chamber with the salt water in the sea-level channel. A 5-mile run to the Panama Canal Yacht Club is the usual completion of a northbound transit. Here your pilot/adviser will leave your vessel.

The Panama Canal Yacht Club (26068)

At Cristobal, if slip space is not available at the PCYC, anchoring on "the flats" in Cristobal Harbor can be a real chore, particularly during the trade-wind season—usually mid-December through April. The holding ground is poor, so make certain your anchor is well set. A local motorboat operator's license is required to use an outboard-powered dinghy, and there is no launch service at the club. Fuel is now available at the yacht club, as is water. A restaurant, bar, showers, washers, and dryers are located at the club.

For long-term layovers, a berth at Pedro Miguel Yacht Club in freshwater Miraflores Lake is ideal for avoiding the problems of the other clubs. Contact the club at 32-4985/4509 to determine if space is available.

Ashore in Panama.

Every vessel arrives in port with its own unique problems. Dealing with them in Panama is no more difficult than in most countries and perhaps easier than in many. Panamanians are generally very friendly and maintain close ties to the United States. Despite the efforts of the two governments to destroy this good relationship, there is little "Yankee Go Home" sentiment (even though you may see carefully painted signs to the contrary). Since the political climate often changes rapidly in Latin American countries, try to obtain information prior to arrival in Panamanian waters on the current state of affairs, requirements for visas, cruising permits, and islands or coasts to be avoided. Yachts outbound from Panama are probably the best source of up-to-date reports on conditions.

Due to the current U.S. economic sanctions against Panama, banking transactions may be difficult or impossible. If required, they should be prearranged. The official Panamanian currency is the U.S. dollar, although prices are expressed in balboas—one balboa to the dollar. Panamanian coinage up to one balboa (featuring a likeness of the explorer Balboa) is used interchangeably with U.S. small change. You can buy traveler's checks in Panama, but cashing them is difficult if not impossible in most places. Cash is in very short supply and is preferred to credit cards.

Shopping for provisions should present no problem other than the high duty on U.S. items. Local, European, and Asian products are sold at or below Stateside prices. Produce in the markets is excellent and reasonably priced, as are seafood and local meat. Liquor can be a bargain at the duty-free shops within the ports. Taxis are reasonable and usually reliable, but settle all fare arrangements in advance. Taxi fares range from $1 to $3 for most short trips. You will want to get local advice on neighborhoods to avoid. Most areas of Panama City are usually safe day and night, but downtown Colón should be completely avoided.

Marine supplies for small vessels are difficult to find and generally expensive. Panama does have some excellent general hardware stores, particularly on the Pacific side. Marine electronics firms serve ships around the clock on both sides. Free-lance craftsmen and mechanics found at the yacht clubs can be very good, but you should get local recommendations. Getting parts in or into Panama can be difficult and costly, particularly via normal mail service, since duty will probably be charged. Consider using the international courier services. If you do use a yacht club as a local mailing address, be sure to include its post office box number.

The following information will be useful to the skippers of all boats making a Panama Canal transit:

Panama Canal Commission
Mailing: APO Miami, FL 34011
Cristobal Port Captains 46-7637
Balboa Port Captains 52-4214

Cristobal Admeasurers 46-7293

Balboa Admeasurers 52-4570

Transit Scheduler 52-4202

Panama Canal Yacht Club

Cristobal, Panama (507) 41-5882/5883

Mailing: Apartado 5041, Colón, Republic of Panama

Office open: 0900–1700, Monday through Saturday

Slips: $.30/ft/day Stern to: $.25/ft/day

Diesel: $1.30/gallon—No gasoline at club

Coin-operated washers and dryers; showers available

Marine railway up to 70 ft/35 tons

Balboa Yacht Club

Fort Amador, Panama (507) 28-5794/5196, Pier 28-2313

Mailing: Apartado 552, Republic of Panama

Moorings: $.35/ft/day; Free 24-hour launch service

Diesel: $1.60/gallon; Gasoline $2.46/gallon—not available Friday through
   Sunday

   No washers and dryers; showers available

   Marine railway up to 50 ft/25 tons

Pedro Miguel Yacht Club

Miraflores Lake (507) 32-4985/4509

Mailing: Apartado 2613, Balboa, Republic of Panama

Long-term storage in fresh water; $6 ft/month

Panama "Yellow Pages"

Let your fingers do the walking—check the excellent Intel Yellow Pages for
   goods and services. Consult yacht club members for recommendations.

Chapter Four

PASSAGING FROM EUROPE BY THE TRADE-WIND ROUTE

For nearly 500 years, sailing vessels have been navigating along a well-established Atlantic track from the Madeira or Canary Islands to the isles of the Caribees and the Spanish Main—the trade-wind route. Columbus found and established it on his four voyages, and it has been followed ever since by all manner of ancient and modern mariners. Probably no other sailing route in the world, not even the clipper-ship routes, has had more consistent use or been traveled by a greater variety of wind ships.

The recommended route for the trade-wind passage, as Eric Hiscock states it in *Cruising Under Sail,* is "to make 25°N in 25°–30°W, then to 18°N in 40°W, and thence to destination; but the season of the year must be taken into consideration when judging how far south it will be necessary to go to ensure holding the trades."

Jimmy Cornell, yachting writer and organizer of the ARC (Atlantic Rally for Cruising Yachts, an annual event since 1986 that has been a popular way for cruisers to make the passage in company with other cruising boats), interviewed 50 skippers who had made the crossing in 1985. He found that most sailed south to about 20°N and 30°W, where they found the trades, and then sailed southwest to about 15°N and 40°W, thereafter altering course for their destination, with the best crossings made by those who left in late November.

Columbus found that the trades become steady and strong out of the northeast at about 20°N—about 500 miles, say, southwest of the Canaries. But many voyagers, including the admiral himself, have found that neither the direction nor the strength of the trades is always to be relied on. You can sail from the Canaries to the Caribbean in 21 days, as Columbus himself did. You can also take a month and a half or more to make the same passage.

Getting to the Madeiras or the Canaries is, of course, your first step.

To the Madeiras and the Canary Islands

The Madeiras lie about 1,250 miles southeast of Falmouth; the Canaries are about 250 miles farther south. The passage requires from 10 to 25 days, largely depending on the kind of weather you encounter in the Bay of Biscay. As Hiscock points out in *Cruising Under Sail,* the north-to-northeast winds known as the Portuguese trades predominate during the summer from Cape Finisterre southward, but tend to become variable in September and October, with an increasing proportion of southwest winds and a higher percentage of gales during the fall months. Therefore, Hiscock suggests that if time permits, it may be better to leave from the English Channel earlier and spend more time in the Madeiras or Canaries before making a late-fall or early-winter departure on the trade-wind route to the Caribbean.

Over the years, many cruising yachts have preferred to sail first to Spain or Portugal, or Gibraltar, stopping off for final preparations on the Continent before leaving for the islands. Gibraltar is about 1,100 miles from Falmouth, a passage of 10–14 days; it's 760 miles farther to the Canaries. Older cruising boats took anywhere from 10 days to two weeks to get from the Channel to Gibraltar, and another week or 10 days to get to the Canaries. With favorable winds, modern yachts may take five or six days for the relatively short offshore passage to the Canaries, although light airs and head winds may be encountered at any time.

In considering the passage from Madeira or the Canaries, it is important to bear in mind that these island groups are about 250 miles apart, and that the major islands of the Canaries extend east and west for approximately that distance, and north and south about 60 to 75 miles. Thus a passage departing from Lanzarote at the northwest end of the island group may be a couple of hundred miles longer than a passage starting from the easternmost islands. Tenerife and Grand Canary lie approximately in the center of the archipelago, between 27°30′ and 28°30′N and between 16° and 17°W, some distance above the northern limits of the northeast trades.

The small boat harbor at Las Palmas on Grand Canary has been improved since 1986, when the boats participating in the first ARC gathered there, and is now a good port for all cruisers to use as a departure point.

Fewer yachts depart from the Madeiras; from them, it usually takes several days longer to reach the steady trade-wind belt. The port of Funchal on the main island of Madeira offers a convenient stopping point with good provisioning. Recent visitors report that cruising yachts are made very welcome.

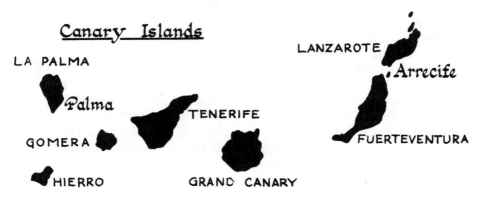

Observations on the Voyages of Columbus

There has been no dearth of information about the trade winds and their vagaries since the days of Prince Henry the Navigator, when Portuguese mariners found their way southward along the west coast of Africa and westward to the Madeiras and Azores long before Columbus. As Samuel Eliot Morison notes in *The Southern Voyages* (the second volume of *The European Discovery of America*), considerable data gathering had been going on since about 1430, when Prince Henry "set up a sort of information service where shipmasters might consult the latest charts and pick up useful data about winds and currents."

Columbus studied many of these early maps and charts and picked up much practical information on his own previous voyages along the African coast and into the North Atlantic. He learned a lot about prevailing winds and also much about ships and their sailing characteristics from the Portuguese, who had already developed the lateen-rigged caravel, which could sail closer to windward than the old square-riggers. Columbus had learned from his Portuguese tutors, in Morison's words, "how to handle a caravel in head wind and sea, how to claw off a lee shore, and what kind of sea stores to take on a long voyage." So his discovery of the trade-wind route to the West Indies was grounded in his earlier experience, though it took him four voyages over a period of 12 years (1492–1504) to learn how to use the trades to best advantage.

Several particulars about the four voyages of Columbus are worth recalling. Apart from the primitive state of celestial navigation in the fifteenth century, Columbus and other early navigators lacked any accurate knowledge of seasonal weather patterns in the tropics. That made it impossible for them to determine the best times of the year to plan their departure in order to avoid tropical storms. Yet even on his first voyage, the admiral had a seamanlike plan for avoiding head winds in the northern latitudes and taking advantage of the prevailing northeast trades on the westward passage. By the time of his final voyage, he had encountered enough hurricanes to predict the probable months of their occurrence and to plot the general pattern of these revolving tropical storms. As a result of his intuitive sea sense and his increasing knowledge of the behavior of the trades, his fastest passages followed a course very close to the preferred route of present-day deep-water skippers.

In comparing the passage times of ancient and modern sailing vessels, there is another factor that present-day navigators are likely to overlook: on all his voyages, Columbus sailed in company with other ships of various types and sizes, keeping in touch night and day as far as possible. On the first voyage, contrary to later experience, Columbus left the Canaries with a fresh easterly wind that carried the little fleet *(Santa Maria, Niña,* and *Pinta)* a distance of approximately 1,163 nautical miles in the first 10 days—not bad going, when you consider that the fleet kept in sight every day, the fastest vessel rounding up to allow the slower ones to come within hailing distance toward sundown. The best day's run on that voyage was 182 miles, according to Morison, and for five consecutive days the fleet averaged 141 miles a day.

On his second voyage, from the Canaries to Dominica, Columbus followed the same procedure, with a large fleet of 17 vessels. He made a remarkably fast passage—21 days—considering that the entire fleet kept their stern lights in sight of one another throughout the hours of darkness. On his fourth voyage, Columbus made an even faster passage—21 days from Grand Canary to Martinique, a route about 100 miles longer than that of the second voyage. That 21-day passage established a mid-Atlantic crossing record that was unsurpassed for more than a century.

On both of these very fast voyages, Columbus set a course from the Canaries of W by S until he picked up the steady trades after leaving the frequent calms and variables encountered near the Canaries. He had learned that the trades became steady and strong when he reached about 20°N, where he set his course westward to the islands. The exhilaration which must have been experienced by the early explorers, as well as by those who followed into this fair-wind belt, is vividly described by Morison in his *Southern Voyages:*

> Sailing before the trades in a square-rigger is a sailor's dream of the good life at sea. You settle down to the pleasant ritual, undisturbed by shifts of wind and changes of weather; and the ocean crossing seems to have been pure joy for everyone who loved the sea. There is the constant play of light and color on the bellying square sails (gold at sunset, silver in the moonlight, black in starlight, white as the clouds themselves at noon). The sea, flecked with whitecaps, is of a gorgeous deep blue, the schools of flying fish spring like a flash of silver from the bow wave.

But Columbus, like other mariners who followed him, discovered that the trade-wind belts are neither easily predictable nor precisely defined. The first and third voyages of Columbus were slow passages, caused by long periods of light airs, calms, or head winds, usually encountered at the northern or southern limits of the northeast trades. On his first voyage, the fleet ran into light variable winds and rain, lasting several days, during which they averaged about 46 miles a day; they made only 234 miles in five days. This was at the northern limits of the trades, since the fleet had been steering a magnetic course W from the Canaries, which was about W by S true, owing to the variation that Columbus had no way of suspecting when he set out from the Canaries, but noted and compensated for during the course of the voyage, much to the consternation of his crew. Columbus is said to be the first navigator to have recognized and dealt with westerly variation.

On his third voyage, in the summer of 1498, Columbus encountered eight days of calms after his little fleet of three vessels left the Cape Verde Islands, where they had stopped briefly seeking fresh meat and cattle. This time they sailed a SW magnetic course, which carried them to about 9°30'N in 29°W near the southern limits of the trades, where the equatorial current put them into the doldrums.

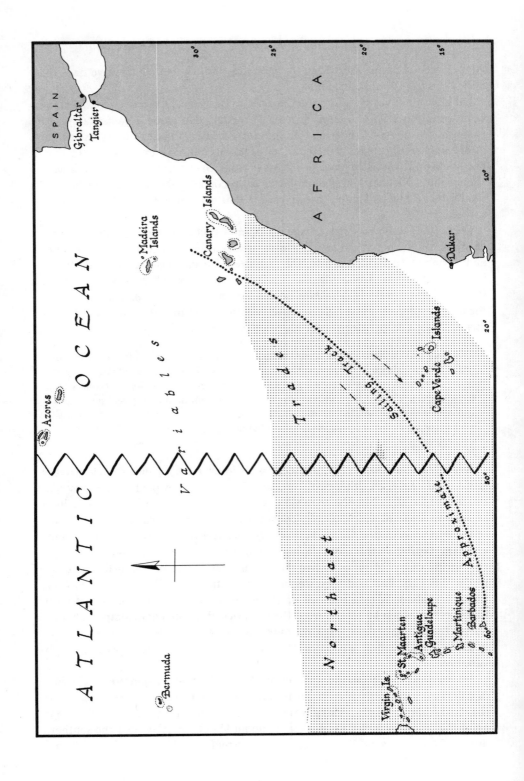

Modern Trade-Wind Passages

Modern sailing vessels have encountered conditions very similar to those experienced by Columbus, making both faster and slower passages over much the same routes.

The slowest passage recorded by Hiscock was the 44-day crossing made by the 30-foot, gaff-rigged cutter *Diotema,* sailed by Vice-Admiral Sir Lennon Goldsmith in 1949. This Hanna-designed vessel ran into seven days of calm and four days of head winds along the usually reliable trade-wind route.

In 1985, when Jimmy Cornell interviewed 50 skippers who made the trade-wind crossing that year, the average time was 22 days, and most of the boats were production cruising boats or boats built by their owners. The fastest passage among the skippers Cornell contacted that year was 17.5 days, made by the German sailors Robert and Waltraud Bittner in *Lorebella* as part of their circumnavigation.

That time was soundly beaten by the Swan 57 *Tenareze,* the first boat over the finish line in the 1988 ARC, with a time of 15.5 days. Ninety-five percent of the approximately 150 boats, ranging in size from 24' to 80', sailed the 2,700-mile course in the 1988 ARC in under 24 days.

The Cruising Club of America has been awarding its Blue Water Medal since 1923 in recognition of noteworthy voyages made in small boats by amateur sailors of all nationalities. Many winners of this coveted award have made passages to the West Indies by the trade-wind route as part of more extended voyages or circumnavigations. In 1947 Ernesto Uriburu of Argentina won the award in his 50-foot ketch *Gaucho,* after sailing from Buenos Aires to the Mediterranean and then returning across the Atlantic, following the route of Columbus from Palos, Spain, to San Salvador, and then to New York. Sten and Brita Holmdahl of Sweden won the award in 1954 for their circumnavigation in *Viking,* with a trade-wind passage to the islands included. Eric and Susan Hiscock were similarly honored the following year for their circumnavigation in *Wanderer III;* part of their voyage was the Atlantic crossing by the southern route.

Special mention, apart from his other awards, must be made of the 10 Atlantic crossings made by James W. Crawford, Jr., seven of which were made in his 61-foot steel cutter *Angantyr.* One extraordinary passage of his, in *Angantyr* in 1970, was single-handed; he did it alone in 19 days, from the Canaries to Antigua.

Many other fast passages by the trade-wind route have been made by cruising couples, with or without extra crew, participating in the ARC or alone, many flying the burgee of the Seven Seas Cruising Association.

Part II

THE CLOCKWISE CIRCUIT

Chapter Five

THE TURKS AND CAICOS ISLANDS

Island-hopping through the Bahamas (see Chapter Two, "Passaging from the U.S. East Coast") will bring you to a port in the Turks and Caicos.

These islands are actually the southeasternmost islands in the Bahamian chain in the geographic sense, but they hold the distinction, and in some ways the advantage, of being one of the few Crown Colonies remaining in the formerly all-powerful British Empire. Appearing as "Yucayo" on a map of the West Indies dated 1500, this remote and sparsely settled group of islands has, throughout its history, been both orphaned and fought over.

Originally settled in the 1670s by Bermudian salt rakers, the group was occupied briefly by the Spanish and by the French, reluctantly joined the Bahama Colony between 1799 and 1848, later became a dependency of Jamaica until that island gained its own independence, and finally ended up as a Crown Colony of some 6,000 people presided over by a governor appointed by the queen.

Until about 1963, the production of salt was the mainstay of these islands, but inefficient methods have taken their toll. The salinas of South Caicos, Grand Turk, and Salt Cay are now only tourist attractions, although some minor production continues on Salt Cay as a subsidized make-work project. How different from the days when Yankee trading schooners used to fill their holds with this commodity for the homeward voyage! But those were the days before refrigeration, when salt was the primary means of food preservation.

It is of course necessary to go through the usual entry and clearance procedures when passing through this archipelago. U.S. citizens do not need passports, although some proof of citizenship may be required: even a driver's license or Social Security card may suffice. Providenciales, Cockburn Harbour (pronounced "Co-burn") on South Caicos, and Cockburn Town on Grand Turk are ports of entry.

Caicos Bank (26260, 25720)
is apparently shoaling gradually, judging from depths shown on early charts, but is regularly being crossed by yachts of up to 7-foot draft.

Even under ideal conditions, it is not easy to identify the Sand Bore Channel leading on to the W side of the bank until you are quite close to the reef and can see the breakers on Shoe Reef on the northern side of the channel. Approaching

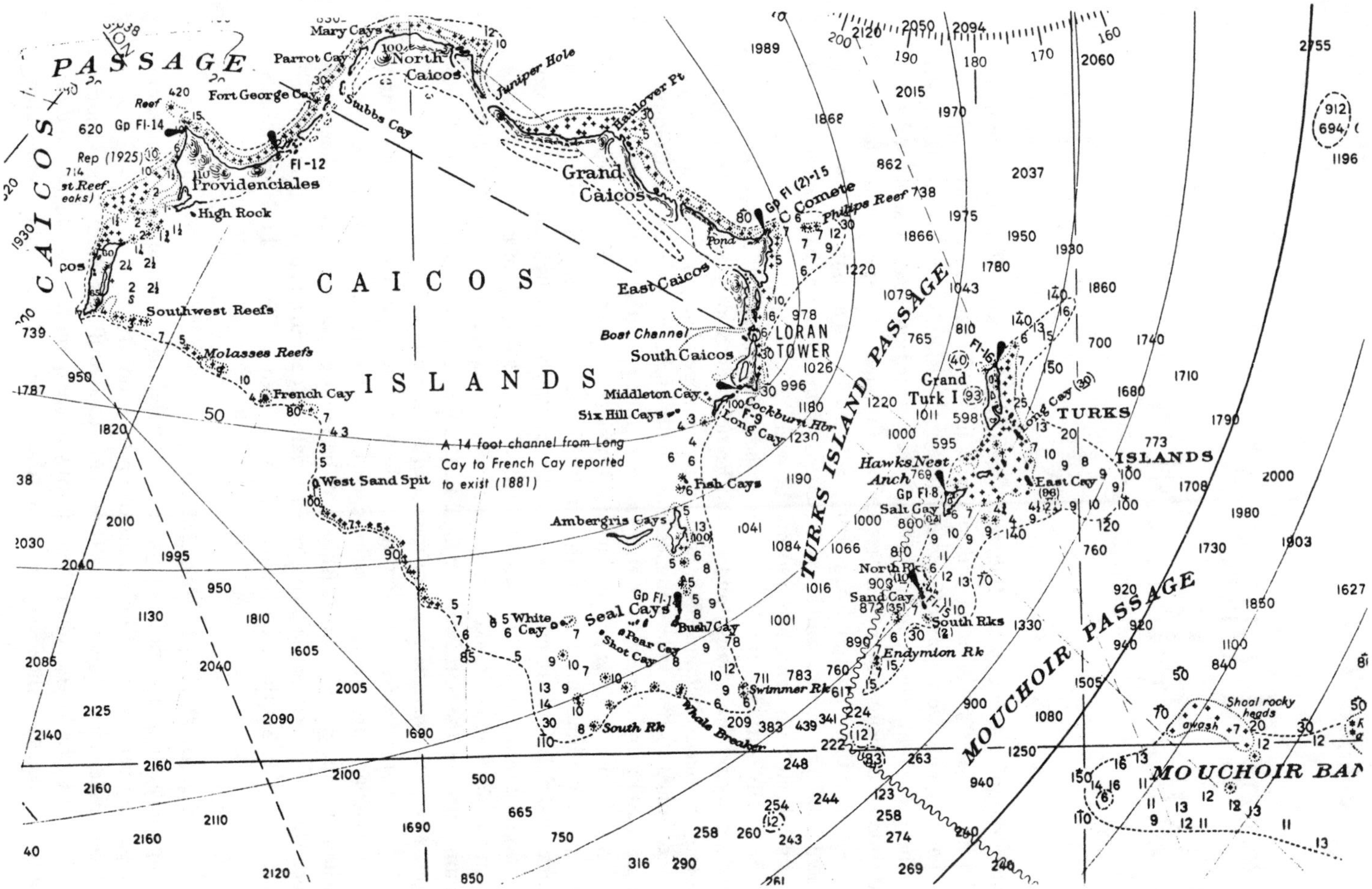

CAICOS PASSAGE

PASSAGE

TURKS ISLAND PASSAGE

MOUCHOIR PASSAGE

MOUCHOIR BANK

CAICOS ISLANDS

TURKS ISLANDS

Mary Cays
Parrot Cay
Fort George Cay
Providenciales
High Rock
Southwest Reefs
Molasses Reefs
French Cay
West Sand Spit
Sandy Pt
Jupiter Hole
North
Caicos
Sabba Cay
Grand
Caicos
East Caicos
South Caicos
Boat Channel
Middleton Cay
Six Hill Cays
Cockburn Hbr.
Long Cay
Fish Cays
Ambergris Cays
White Cays
Seal Cays
Bush Cay
Bear Cay
Shot Cay
South Rk
Whale Breaks
Swimmer Rk
Endymion Rk
South Rks
Sand Cay
Salt Cay
North Pt
Hawks Nest Anch
Grand Turk I
East Cay
Cotton Cay
Pelican Reef

LORAN TOWER

Gp Fl (2) 15
Gp Fl 18
Fl 12
Gp Fl 14
Fl 9
Fl 16

A 14-foot channel from Long
Cay to French Cay reported
to exist (1881)

Shoal rocky

Turks and Caicos group

from the W, you will sight the Blue Hills of Providenciales at the N end of the island long before you pick up West Harbour Bluff at the S end, or the low profile of West Caicos Island further S.

We made our landfall N of the Shoe Reef and had to run back almost 6 miles outside the breaking coral heads before finding the opening. Once in the channel, however, we found 12–20-foot depths on an easterly heading to the rocky bluff at West Harbour, becoming 6–9 feet as we proceeded to an anchorage off a sandy beach W of Gussie Point, the next point E of West Harbour Bluff.

Alternatively, you can round the southern tip of West Caicos, where a channel over clear sand leads N to West Harbour and Gussie Point. In failing light you can anchor in reasonable comfort in this channel, which is protected by the Molasses Reef.

In our experience, the best track across the bank is 110°T from West Harbour Bluff for about 44 miles to a position just N of Six Hills Cays, where you will eyeball through the heads until you gain the deep water off the S end of Long Cay. Do not stand in too close to the tip of Long Cay, because it is necessary to round Middle Reef, which makes out SW from Long Cay. We followed this track in *Brer Fox* in 1971, only to find ourselves in very shallow water about halfway across, with no landmarks visible anywhere on the horizon. We assumed we were on Foot Shoal, which appears on both the U.S. and British charts, but soon discovered our error when we ran into even shoaler water to the N, and finally grounded gently on a soft grassy bottom inside the 1-fathom line shown on the charts. The northeasterly set of the flood current had carried us at least 4 miles N of the track in about three and a half hours of running time.

Unfortunately the currents have never been studied for this or any of the Bahama banks, so you have to be alert to the possibility of being set probably, but not necessarily, to the N of this track.

Bob Wilke, who crossed with his deep-draft shrimper *Lady Jane* in 1974, advises running from Gussie Point on 135°T for 6 miles before taking up a course for the Six Hills Cays. He reports 8 feet or more all the way.

For a crash course in eyeball piloting (no pun intended), you might prefer to run SE from West Caicos along the outside of the reef (which is not continuous) to French Cay, a low scrubby island, where overnight anchorage may be taken along the western shore. From the S end of this cay, take up a course due E to the eastern edge of the bank S of Six Hills Cays. In all our Bahamas cruising we have never experienced a run so infested with ugly, black, and sprawling coral heads. In fact, it makes the Yellow Bank on the Nassau-Exumas run seem like a dredged channel. Of course, in the sunlit water the heads stand out sharply against the clear white sand, but in poor light this route would be impossible. We do not recommend this track westbound, because the sun would be in your eyes during an afternoon approach to French Cay, where the heads are the thickest— and French Cay is not conspicuous, although it is the key to getting off the bank at the W end of the run.

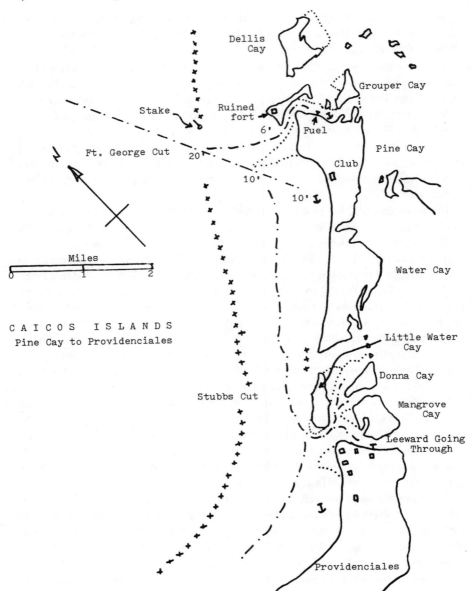

Dellis
Cay

Grouper Cay

Stake

Ruined
fort

6'

Fuel

Pine Cay

Ft. George Cut

20

10'

Club

10'

N

Water Cay

Miles

0   1   2

CAICOS ISLANDS
Pine Cay to Providenciales

Little Water
Cay

Donna Cay

Mangrove
Cay

Stubbs Cut

Leeward Going
Through

Providenciales

Only on the Caicos Bank have we chanced to see the phenomenon known as "bank blink." Like a mirage on the desert, it seems to reflect the white water of the shoals and sandbars into the atmosphere immediately above them. On a shallow, shimmering sea over a bottom of gleaming sand, the effect is eerie, foreboding, and somewhat claustrophobic—especially when seen over the bow!

Providenciales and Pine Cay (26260)

are developing at a fast pace as a residential resort area, no doubt because they enjoy the greater political security and stability of a Crown Colony. Club Med, the Ramada Inn, and other hotels, large and small, have been built, and more tourist facilities are under construction. Regular air service was bringing 42,000 visitors a year directly from Miami to the island in 1988, with 60,000 projected for 1990. Despite the fact that these islands lie 200 miles dead to windward of Cape Santa Maria, cruising yachtsmen too are steadily becoming attracted to them and liking what they find in the area.

After the long passage from Mayaguana or Great Inagua, the easiest entrance through the barrier reef is via Fort George Cut, which is about a mile wide and perfectly straightforward and safe even in poor light conditions. Inside you'll find a restful anchorage along the beautiful beach at Pine Cay. A more secure anchorage is up in the cut just beyond the Meridian Club's fuel dock, where the shallowest section, between Fort George and Pine Cays, will carry about 7 feet at half tide. From the Meridian Club beach for about one half mile beyond Leeward Going Through, you will have easy sailing inside the reef, for 7-foot draft and under, but from that point to the channel into Sellar's Pond there are numerous heads.

Stubbs Cut requires good light and a smooth sea, and considering the safety and convenience of Fort George Cut, we see no reason to use it until you are more familiar with the area.

It is no longer possible to continue on through the Leeward Going Through, but Leeward Marina, accessible to yachts of no more than 7-foot draft, has a variety of facilities. Nearby, the Caicos Conch Farm, where millions of conch are hatched in the geodesic dome, raised to the larval stage, and finally put out to grow to maturity in large undersea pastures, makes an interesting side trip. The farm is open seven days a week, from 8:00 A.M. to 4:30 P.M., and offers tours, slide shows, and a gift shop.

Turtle Cove Marina may be approached via Sellar's Cut or, with due caution, via the passage inside the protecting reef from Leeward Going Through. Immediately beyond Sellar's Cut, a secondary reef (approximately N-S) makes out from the shore to the outer reef. Through this secondary reef a very narrow channel has been blasted and marked with white PVC pipe stakes, maintained by the Turtle Cove Marina. There is barely 5 ½ feet LW in this blasted channel, but most yachts can use the tide to reach the perfectly landlocked pond, where there is ample room for docking or anchoring. Carefully follow the markers that lead from the blasted channel through a forest of heads and sandbars. Even with the markers (which may not be there), you will need to resort to some eyeballing to get in here; if the light is poor or you are unsure of your ability to read the water, you should call Turtle Cove Marina on VHF-16 and wait for a boat to lead you in. (A fee will be charged for this service, as well as for either a slip or for anchoring in the pond.)

Although we have circled Providenciales via Wheeland Cut and a break in the reef about one half mile off Northwest Point, thence across Malcolm Roads and through the reef again at Wylie Cut, the lack of reference marks makes it very difficult to describe. Suffice to say that it can be done under ideal light and sea conditions.

Cockburn Harbour (26261)

on South Caicos gives far more protection than might appear from the chart. In fact, it is the only really secure anchorage on the E side of the Caicos Bank. The shallows to the S and W break up any sea from those directions, the island itself

Cockburn Harbour at South Caicos held only one other boat when *Blue Moon* anchored there. A new casino on a beautiful beach north of the harbor may bring more traffic.

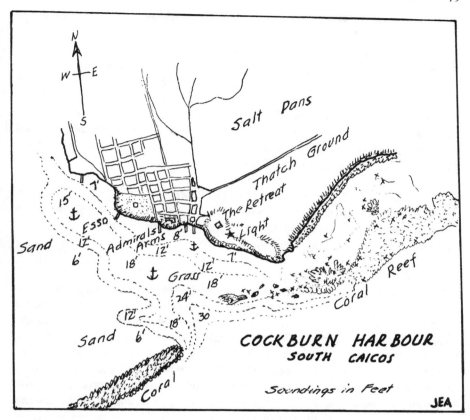

Soundings in Feet

COCKBURN HARBOUR
SOUTH CAICOS

provides a lee from northers, and in the event of a real blow from the SE, one can move across the harbor to a lee under Long Cay.

In order to be close to town, anchor under the cliffs where the Admiral's Arms Inn is—or was—situated. This establishment had been sold and was awaiting refurbishing in 1989, and may possibly have a new name by the time you anchor here. Next door, the Harbour View Hotel was also being renovated, to house the employees of the large casino-hotel complex Club Carib Casino Resorts, being built on the beautiful beach east of town. In conjunction with the resort, there are plans for two flights a day in and out of South Caicos's International Airport (built by the U.S. Army Engineers during World War II), originating in the Dominican Republic and in Miami. A marina may be built in the future as well. In the meantime, check your anchor to be sure it is in well. The bottom is a mixture of sand, rock, and grass.

In days gone by, South Caicos was an active producer and exporter of salt. The old salt pans can still be seen, as well as rusty machinery that was used for its loading, and old warehouses and docks along the waterfront. With the exception of some fishing, there is little evidence of any money-making activity going on here now.

No more than basic supplies are available in South Caicos. With only 16 inches of rain a year, few things can be grown. There are several small grocery stores.

The customshouse is at the east end of town. If there is no surge, you can tie your dinghy carefully to one of the old docks and be only a few steps away from it. A better place to leave your dinghy is on the ramp beyond the two piers on the west side of town, next to the police station. The customs officer can be called on VHF-16. He is available to clear you in or out at just about any time of the day, including Saturdays and Sundays.

Big and Little Ambergris cays (26261),

approximately 13 miles south of South Caicos, are a popular stop for boats crossing the banks. There are no facilities of any kind there. Anchor between the two islands, wherever your draft allows.

Grand Turk (26261, 26262)

is the administrative center of this island group. Cockburn Town, on the west side of Grand Turk about midway between the north and south tips, is an attractive town to visit, with only a few modern buildings among many old West Indian–style structures. It is a port of entry. Its harbor, however, is an open roadstead, sheltered from the prevailing easterlies but wide open to winds from SW to N.

The entrance to the anchorage is through a narrow opening in the reef, W of the two small piers in the center of the town. In making the approach, you will first sight the radio tower S of the town and the large buildings of the inactive missile base at the southern end of the island. The reef is only about 600 yards off the shore. You will usually find a few boats anchored in 6 to 20 feet about 100 yards off the beach near the government pier. When we arrived there in 1989, we encountered a mild west wind that produced a violent surge in the harbor. After checking in, we exited the reef and sailed past the south end of the island until we could turn due E toward a white ball marking the cut into the Hawks Nest anchorage, on the SW corner of the island, where we passed a quiet night in reef-protected water.

Had we had a shallow-draft boat and a rising tide, we might have tried the passage into North Creek, at the north end of the island. The entrance has been dredged to accommodate boats of up to 6-foot draft. Inside there is 10 to 12 feet of water. There are plans for some facilities to be built on the creek. You should check in with the officials at Cockburn Town before proceeding to this or to the Hawks Nest anchorage.

Salt Cay (26261)

is low, flat, and ideally suited to the production of salt, which in times past made it a prosperous place, as the remains of some grand old homes will attest. As a relic it is interesting; as an anchorage it is comfortable off the settlement only in moderate easterly weather. Tourist hotels are planned for Salt Cay, but were not yet in evidence in 1989.

Sand Cay (26261)

is little more than a sand pile about 35 feet high, with a light on a frame tower. Lying about 25 miles SE of Cockburn Harbour, it makes an ideal stopover for the night when on passage to or from the Dominican Republic. Anchorage may be taken quite close up to the shelving beach.

Chapter Six

HISPANIOLA

Almost 500 years after its discovery in 1492, Hispaniola is beginning to be rediscovered by cruising yachtsmen, who are finding its exotic tropical seascape just as alluring as Columbus found it on his first voyage. The admiral called it his favorite isle in the Caribees—"the fairest land human eyes have ever seen"—and though cruising skippers who sail along the same track today may have their own favorite isles elsewhere in the Caribbean, they are not likely to quarrel too much with his descriptive eloquence.

The second-largest island of the Greater Antilles (only Cuba is larger), Hispaniola has had a more turbulent history than most of its Caribbean neighbors. Fought over and divided by France and Spain in the colonial era, raided by pirates and freebooters in the seventeenth and eighteenth centuries, ruled by native tyrants and military dictators since the nineteenth century, and plagued by civil strife, poverty, and political unrest, the island has nonetheless managed to continue its tortured life into the twentieth century. Today, the eastern two thirds of this 28,000-square-mile island are occupied by the Spanish-speaking Dominican Republic; French-speaking Haiti occupies the western third.

While Rafael Trujillo and "Papa Doc" Duvalier ruled the Dominican Republic and Haiti, respectively, yachts were not encouraged to visit any part of Hispaniola. But Trujillo died in 1961 and Papa Doc in 1971.

Papa Doc was succeeded by his son Baby Doc, but Baby Doc's regime came to an end in 1986 by way of an uprising followed quickly by a military coup. At that time the United States government issued a travel advisory cautioning U.S. citizens to undertake only necessary travel to Haiti. This advisory may still be in effect at the time you wish to cruise. U.S. citizens should check with the State Department.

From Haiti's end, travel restrictions for private vessels in 1989 were as follows:

Cap-Haïtien and Port-au-Prince are the only official ports of entry.

Private vessels should notify in advance by registered air mail, or preferably cable, the Director of Port Administration, Port-au-Prince, Haiti.

A copy of the notification must be sent to the Director General, National Office of Tourism, Port-au-Prince, Haiti.

Notification must contain the following information:

1. Name and specifications of vessel.
2. Port of registration.

3. Names and nationalities of all passengers and crew.
4. Estimated date and time of arrival, and desired port of call.

Passengers aboard private vessels who are not citizens of Canada, France, Great Britain, the United States, or West Germany should possess valid passports. U.S. citizens must possess proof of citizenship (passport, birth certificate, or naturalization papers).

Information in this chapter on Haiti has few updates and has been retained from the 1982 edition as if it were possible to visit Haitian ports on all parts of the coast.

During the early 1970s numerous reports came to us of boardings at sea by Dominican gunboats and one case of a boarding by armed bandits, but conditions along the north coast of Hispaniola now seem to be much improved, perhaps because yachts have become more commonplace in these waters and less subject to suspicion. At any rate, when we cruised this coast in 1979 aboard *Quo Vadis* skippered by Jim Fox, then Commodore of the Sailing Club of the Chesapeake, we stopped at several small places that were not ports of entry and had no difficulty whatsoever. Veteran cruising man Bill Robinson, on a more recent eastbound passage, found a friendly welcome at every port he put into.

In 1989, however, foreign vessels were being allowed only to clear in and out of the Dominican Republic at a few designated ports, and were not being given cruising permits to visit other anchorages. Yachts stopping at unauthorized ports to make necessary repairs or to gain temporary shelter from bad weather were visited by local officials and told not to leave the boat and to proceed as soon as possible. Ports of entry included Manzanillo Bay and Puerto Plata on the north coast, Santa Barbara de Samaná on the east coast, and Boca Chica and Santo Domingo on the south coast. One more, Puerto Blanco at the village of Luperon on the north coast, may be added to this list sometime soon.

Our earlier suggestions for planning a Caribbean cruise apply particularly to the Dominican Republic. It is essential to have clearance papers from your last foreign port, designating your intended port of entry. Make your first entry at a major port. You should have a valid identification document for every member of your crew, with evidence of citizenship. Passports, though not required for short-term tourists with return tickets, should be carried by the owner and crew members of yachts intending to cruise the area.

Don't neglect to check your chart inventory before departing for Hispaniola. There are 26 U.S. coastal and harbor charts covering the island as a whole—13 for Haiti, 13 for the Dominican Republic, including large-scale plans, which are essential for entering ports and bays. You may not need them all, but the coastal reefs of Hispaniola are not a place to practice eyeball navigation without the aid of the best large-scale charts obtainable, which in this instance are considerably better than those available for the Bahamas.

In the following sections, we take a close look at coastal features, harbor entrances, and port facilities, starting with the north coast of Haiti from west to

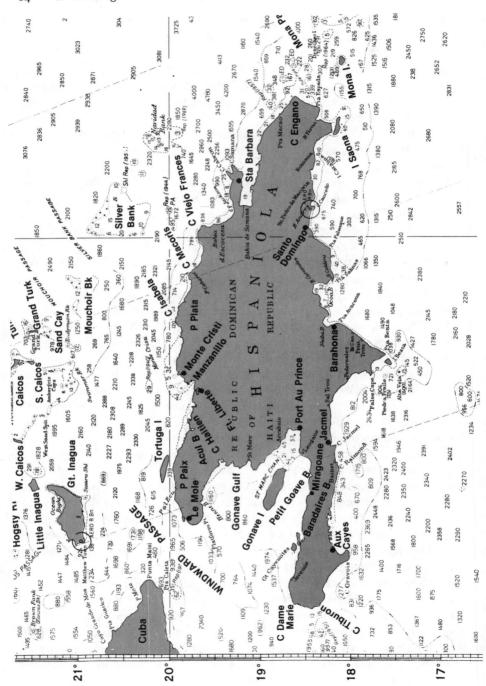

east, continuing along the north coast of the Dominican Republic to Samaná Bay and Mona Passage, as one would in making an eastbound passage to Puerto Rico and the Virgin Islands. Then we return to the west coast of Haiti, look at interesting harbors in the Gulf of Gonâve, port facilities at Port-au-Prince, and continue counterclockwise around the south coasts of both Haiti and the Dominican Republic to the eastern end of the island.

THE NORTH COAST OF HAITI (26260)

The veil of mystery that enshrouds Haiti may apply even to your landfall if you are approaching from the north, for though the hills of Tortuga Island rise to 1,200 feet and the mountainous mainland reaches heights of 3,000 feet a few miles inland, the land itself may often be hidden in haze until you are quite close inshore. This condition is more than symbolic and can be confusing to navigators approaching for the first time, expecting to sight distant mountains from 30 or more miles at sea. Haze, caused by hundreds of burning charcoal fires in the hills, often shrouds much of the north coast of Hispaniola, making it difficult for those who have not experienced it before to judge distances accurately in making their approach to the coast and its fringing reefs.

Winds and currents are the major elements with which navigators must contend in approaching from the north. Yachts making the 70-mile passage between Inagua and Haiti must make allowance for the usual strong ocean current that has set more than one small vessel westward into the Windward Passage to an unexpected landfall on Cuba. While the pilot charts show an average westerly set of less than 1 knot most of the year, this may increase rapidly in winter months when the northeast trades are blowing their strongest.

On the other hand, our last passage to Haiti in *Brer Fox* taught us an important lesson concerning surface currents under unusual storm conditions. We had left Mathew Town, Great Inagua, shortly after sunset in early December, expecting to make the 70-mile passage to Cap du Môle at the western tip of Haiti in about 12 hours with a strong NW wind that began to pipe up to 40 knots before midnight. Running downwind under small jib and mizzen, we logged 6K on a course of 162° that allowed for the 0.7K current which normally sets west along the north coast of Hispaniola. We came on watch at 0400, and the log showed we had made 48 miles, which should have put us about 20 miles north of the Haitian coast but, much to our surprise, the high coastal mountains loomed up directly ahead and breakers were visible in the moonlight.

How could this discrepancy be explained? Though it was difficult to judge our distance offshore, the coast seemed no more than 6 or 8 miles away, while the log implied we still had over 20 miles to go. Moreover, there was no sign of a light at Cap du Môle nor any break in the coastline where we should have been able to see the open water of the Windward Passage in the moonlight. Not until we had hardened on the wind and run back more than 6 miles to the west, were we able to discern the bold headland of the cape (we never did see the light). It was obvious by then that we not only had allowed too much for the current but had made considerably more distance over the bottom than our log had recorded through the water. This could only mean that the normal westerly current had been stopped in its tracks by the norther and deflected to the south in the direction of the wind.

Later, as this combination of strong northerly winds and wind-induced current swept us around Cap du Môle and into the Windward Passage, we were able to check speed and distance run against coastal landmarks on the run to Cap Dame-Marie at the southwest tip of Haiti. Once again we were about three hours ahead of our ETA and 20 miles ahead of our log. Therefore, within 24 hours after a strong norther takes over from the easterly trades in this area, one should figure on a surface current of 1 to 1½K setting with the wind, regardless of what the pilot charts may indicate.

Cap du Môle to Cap-Haïten (26260, 26141)

Yachts approaching Cap-Haïtien from the western end of Tortuga or from Cap du Môle, the westernmost point in northern Haiti, are likely to find this 70-mile stretch of mountainous coastline rather forbidding when the winter trades are blowing boisterously. Most of the coast is bold and steep-to, with only a few bays where one might hope to find shelter. In the western half of this section, the 100-fathom line follows the rugged coast a mile or less offshore from Cap du Môle to Port-de-Paix about 35 miles ENE, or directly upwind for eastbound vessels. Tortuga Island, also high with a bold shoreline, fronts the mainland coast about 4 to 5 miles offshore in the vicinity of Port-de-Paix.

Unless you are already familiar with Haiti's inshore waters, we don't recommend entering any of the small bays in this 35-mile coastal sector. However, there are several bights and indentations with anchorages used by small coastal vessels. These are described briefly below for those with previous experience in Haitian coastal waters, or for anyone cruising this area in settled weather conditions.

Juan Rabel Anchorage (26260)

is an open roadstead off the village of Magasins, about 2 miles SW of Point Juan Rabel, some 15 miles eastward from Cap du Môle. A white cliff and a long sandy beach are skirted by a reef that lies about 200 yards N of the village. Coastal vessels anchor in 10 fathoms off a shallow, foul-bottomed shorebank that extends about one quarter mile offshore. It's not a good anchorage for yachts.

Baie du Port à l'Écu (26260)

is a small sheltered cove less than one half-mile wide about 7½ miles eastward of Point Juan Rabel, with a deep-water approach to a high brown bluff marking the eastern entrance. There is a small fishing village on the SW shore and good holding ground over a sand and mud bottom S of the eastern entrance. In the prevailing trades, this is a comfortable overnight anchorage.

Baie des Moustiques (26146, Plan F)

is a deep indentation about 4 miles E of Port à l'Écu, which was visited by Columbus on his first voyage. The anchorage is exposed to the N, and the bottom is rocky and should be sounded before you drop the hook. The village of Cabaret is about one half mile inland, where you will see outdoor cooking by charcoal.

Port-de-Paix (26141)

is the second-largest town on the north coast of Haiti and a port of entry about halfway between Cap du Môle and Cap-Haïtien. The "port" is a roadstead in the center of a small bight that recedes less than 500 yards between two entrance points about one half mile apart, each marked by the ruins of an old fort. The anchorage off town is wide open to northerly winds but affords limited shelter in the prevailing easterlies. There is always a surge. The mud-and-sand bottom is foul in places, and holding ground is poor in a blow. There is a small pier used by local boats and lighters for unloading cargo from vessels anchored in the bight. The customshouse is close by on the waterfront, and it does handle occasional foreign yachts, though we favor proceeding directly to Cap-Haïtien if possible. The Bon Accueil Hotel in town has the reputation of serving fine charcoal-broiled fish dinners. Fuel and water are available, with limited provisions in the markets.

Tortuga Island (26141)

This high, wooded island is about 20 miles long and, 3 to 4 miles wide, with a bold steep-to coastline fronting Tortuga Channel on its south side. The only anchorage is at Basse Terre, about 5 miles westward from the SE point, where a break in the fringing reefs provides some protection from the seas but not from easterly winds. You can identify the village by boats at anchor and under construction ashore, houses on the hillside, a bluff to the west, and a sandy beach to the east. If you are coming from the east, we suggest you hold about 100 yards off the line of reefs, knowing that you will have to "eyeball" your way through the opening off the village. Once inside, anchor as close to the beach as your draft permits; the holding seemed good when we were there. Bring your ship's papers ashore as soon as you have anchored; there should be no fee involved, although the official may make overtures in that direction. The people are friendly but shy. Basse Terre, it seems, has the reputation of being one of the best boat-building centers on the north side of Haiti, although the methods are anything but modern, including using natural knees and caulking with pitch.

Tortuga provided a stronghold out of which operated some of the earliest buccaneer bands in the Caribbean. It is interesting to recall their history and the origin of the word, which came into common use during the 1600s when the "Brethren of the Coast" established the first settlements on Tortuga. "Buccaneer" was the English version of the French word *boucanier,* one who cures meat over an open fire by the *boucan* process. The first bands to reach Tortuga arrived from Saint Kitts after being driven out by a Spanish raid in the 1630s. Alec Waugh tells their story in his classic history of the West Indies, *A Family of Islands.* At the beginning, their life was relatively peaceful. They had plenty to eat. They enjoyed hunting and led a free and easy existence. Pork was the staple of their diet, and they cut the meat in long strips that they laid over open fires *(boucans)* on gratings made of green sticks, a kind of barbecue.

The buccaneers might have been content to lead their life in the bush if they had been left alone. But the Spanish attacked Tortuga in force in 1638, driving out all the inhabitants in a violent raid. The buccaneers came back a few months later "in far from a pacific mood, ready for revenge." They were joined during the next few decades by freebooters from Jamaica and by traders whose ships had been intercepted by the Spanish. They too were ready for revenge and plunder. They were, in Waugh's words, "a motley crew, from many stocks, from many ways of life." In a short time they attracted still others, "the riffraff of seven nations and the seven seas; they were homeless, rootless, with families long since forgotten. They were mutineers, escaped prisoners, shipwrecked pirates; they had no country, they owed no allegiance to anyone except themselves."

Half a century later, Henry Morgan gave a different connotation to the word "buccaneer" when he led his well-organized raids on Spanish commerce in British ships and assembled the armadas that sacked the rich colonial cities of the Spanish Main with the backing of the British Crown. But some of Tortuga's Brethren of the Coast may well have served with Morgan in the sack of Porto Bello and the raid on Panama in 1671.

Today one hears occasional tales of cruising yachts boarded by bands of native ruffians along the rugged shores of Tortuga. We have not been able to verify any recent cases of such boardings; in fact, our own experience has been entirely favorable.

Port-de-Paix to Cap-Haïtien (26141)

This 36-mile section of the coast is indented by a series of small bights and one large bay in which a number of good anchorages may be found. Here the coastal mountains recede inland but become higher, rising to peaks of nearly 4,000 feet a few miles from the coast. The 100-fathom curve continues close offshore except at the eastern end near Cap-Haïtien, where reefs extend 3 to 5 miles north of the coast. There are several temporary anchorages south of Marigot Head, a prominent 500-foot-high island with four small islets around it about one half mile offshore and 2 miles west of Limbé Point. Caution should be exercised in navigating around the islands and in Marigot Bay, as there are few charted soundings in the area. The outlying reefs and shoals begin east of Limbé Point and continue northeasterly for about 8 miles, all the way to Cap Haïtien, with channels leading into deep Acul Bay to the south and Port Francis to the east. Both of these places are definitely worth exploring.

Acul Bay (26148)

is the second-largest harbor on the north coast of Haiti, penetrating almost 4 miles into the surrounding hills, which provide complete protection in all weather. Large coastal vessels enter through one of the deep-water channels leading across the outer reefs (the Limbé Channel west of the reefs is the safest approach for yachts), then continue into the narrow harbor channel between a 400-foot hill behind Morro Roxo on the eastern shore and a sand spit extending off the low western shore. Cruising boats will find quiet anchorages in Lombarde Cove, just S of Morro Roxo, or farther S, near the head of the bay.

Port Francis (26148),

known locally as "Labadie," is a lovely little bay on the western side, or "back-side," of Cap-Haïtien, protected by the surrounding mountains to the E and the reefs in the NW. It's a favorite anchorage for yachtsmen from "Le Cap," who find its peace and quiet a pleasant contrast to the noise and bustle of the city. The small village has good water, clean beaches, and friendly people who will char-coal-broil you a fish dinner in the native style.

On our last visit in 1980 we found that one cannot simply drop the hook off the lovely clean beach; it is necessary to check in with the dock officials upon arrival. At that time the anchorage had been placed out-of-bounds temporarily as a result of the irresponsible behavior of the crew of an American yacht a few years previous.

Approaches to Cap-Haïtien (26147)

Inbound sailing vessels that have successfully cleared the eastern point of Tortuga will have a straightforward approach to Cap-Haïtien, although they'll probably have to beat part of the way unless they are lucky enough to pick up N to NE winds. In order to allow for the westerly set of the current, you may have to hold a course of 110° to keep clear of the reefs and shoals that extend northward of the cape. Power cruisers approaching from the west through Tortuga Channel or coming from Acul Bay will also have to contend with winds and currents in rounding the cape.

The final approach to the port of Cap Haïtien should always be made in daylight, as the lighthouse on Pointe Picolet is no more reliable than most other such aids to navigation in Haiti, where unreliability is more the rule than the exception. In any case, if your approach is from the NW, take note that this lighthouse is not visible from W of a line bearing 140°, as shown on Chart 26141.

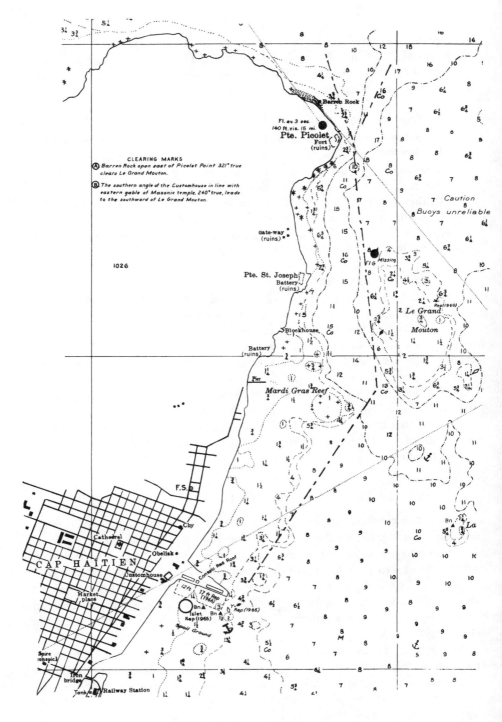

Approaches to Cap-Haïtien

Three mountain peaks behind Haut-du-Cap are conspicuous from offshore, however, and the ruins of the old fort become visible as you approach the light.

When abeam of the light, take the western channel, leaving Grand Mouton Reef to port, the first two buoys to port, and the next buoy to starboard. Before you will have sighted the channel buoys, beware of what looks like a navigational aid to port: it turns out to be the mast of a sunken ship on the reef. Columbus lost his flagship, *Santa Maria,* on one of these harbor reefs on Christmas Eve, 1492; don't follow his example. As we've noted elsewhere, you can forget the "red, right, returning" jingle when entering most Caribbean ports, but here at Le Cap recent arrivals report that all the buoys appear to be red—from red rust, that is.

George and Jacques Kappes, reporting on a 1973 visit to Cap-Haïtien in the ketch-rigged motor sailer *Liberty Belle,* provided helpful information about entry procedures and shoreside facilities. We summarize them as follows, because they may still be applicable.

The customshouse is located just across the street from the commercial concrete dock, where visiting yachts may lie alongside if there's room. Native boats tie close to the foot of the dock, new arrivals in the middle, and large cruise ships and freighters at the outer end. There is usually some surge, so be prepared for liberal fendering. Customs and immigration officials are polite and helpful. They come aboard carrying guns, but don't be disturbed by that, as it's all part of the scene. With passports, health certificates, documentation papers, crew lists, and a letter from the Haitian consul in Nassau, *Liberty Belle* had no trouble clearing. But the Kappeses had firearms aboard, which they declared and which were promptly taken by the authorities to be held until the yacht's departure some four months later.

If you are planning to visit other ports in Haiti, or merely do some gunkholing nearby, clearance must be obtained from the port captain, and you will need final clearance papers before leaving the country.

After clearing customs, most cruising boats prefer to lie out in the harbor, where anchorages may be found in 2 to 4 fathoms not far from the dock. The surge is more or less constant, but it's not too uncomfortable except in storms or severe N to NE winds. Safely anchored out, you can avoid the inquisitive stares of the scores of townsfolk, young and old, who cluster on the dock to watch every move you make.

The reactions of cruising people naturally differ, but most of the people we've seen or heard from recently have been favorably impressed by the friendliness of the Haitians, though somewhat baffled by the country itself. Bob and Ginnie Higman, cruising the coastal waters of Haiti in 1971 in *Tormentor III,* found the country "baffling, beautiful, and exasperating." They were impressed by the stark contrasts: "A country of friendliness and fear; generosity and beggary; barren mountainsides and lush tropical valleys; so much loveliness and so much poverty, too." Ginnie acknowledged that she and her skipper husband, Bob, had two completely different sentiments about the country. "Bob hated the hassle he had to go through at every anchorage; he hated the lack of privacy, the beggary, the lack of communication, which to me were only minor inconveniences . . . it was going ashore and getting acquainted with the people that attracted me most."

For those lingering at Cap-Haïtien for more than a few days, the skipper and mate of *Liberty Belle* had a number of practical suggestions. In such an environment, there are street urchins everywhere, so if you want to help the economy as well as make life ashore easier for yourself, it is best to select your own boy. He will go to market with you, carry your tote bag, and fetch ice for you from the Veau d'Or market (where it's clean). Of course, he will expect a tip, which will vary according to the size of your bag and the quality of his services.

When we were in Cap-Haïtien in 1979 we made the mistake of ignoring this advice and ended up, like the Pied Piper of Hamelin, with a whole horde of little urchins trailing us around town and competing for the job of serving us. Obviously one can do best by picking the first bright-faced lad that applies for the job and settling quickly with him at a price that, once established, is not disturbed.

A good friend of yachtsmen at Le Cap is Walter Bussenius, owner-manager of the Mont Joli Hotel just off the main street on a steep rise about a mile from the dock. The view of the harbor and the swimming pool surrounded by a terraced garden is superb. Also the German consul, Carl Otto Schuet, is always helpful if you have a problem. Having lived at Cap-Haïtien for over 30 years, he knows everyone and can tell you how and where to get things done. Either of these good people can advise you about water, fuel, engine repairs, or refrigerator problems.

A visit to the public market at Le Cap is an experience not to be missed. The market covers two city blocks and is roofed over, with stalls spilling out into adjacent streets. The activity is usually frenzied, with bargaining expected for every purchase.

Food is a delight, thanks to Haiti's French heritage, and there are several good eating places around town. The Brise de Mer is a pension near the Careenage where the proprietor will prepare an excellent meal of soup, crêpes, salad, main course, and dessert if you call ahead. The restaurant at the Mont Joli is also good, if somewhat more expensive. Be careful of what you eat and drink, however, as dysentery ("Christophe's Revenge," as it's called locally) is not unknown. Best avoid clams, lettuce, watercress, and things grown in water. Malaria, too, is still extant, so pills such as Campoprima would not be amiss.

No one visiting Cap-Haïtien should forego the pilgrimage to the Citadel, the huge fortress perched atop a mountain above the town of Milot, built by Henri Christophe, the black ruler who proclaimed himself emperor of Haiti in 1806. La Citadelle took 13 years to build, and 20,000 lives were lost in the process, so it's said. All the stone, timber, cannon, and shot had to be carried up the steep mountainside by sweating, toiling humans. By one account it took 100 men two weeks to drag each of the 375 cannon to the parapets at the top. Christophe's great Citadel, which never fired a shot in anger, still stands in remarkable condition today, well worth the time and effort required to follow the narrow, winding trail to the summit, where you will be rewarded by a magnificent view of the valleys below. When we were there last, we heard the echoes of distant drums coming from different points in the valleys, intensifying the mysterious spell that seems to hang over the place.

At the base of the trail to the Citadel are the gutted remains of Christophe's palace, Sans Souci, now only a vague monument to this vain man's grandiose reconstruction of the elegance he had seen in his visits to France.

In negotiating with a taxi driver for the 15-mile trip to the Citadel, make sure whether he is quoting to take you to the "first parking," where the horses and guides are, or to the "second parking," just under the summit. In our case the four of us settled on three horses and a mule at the "first parking," although none of us had been on a horse for years and we were all somewhat advanced in age. The trip up the mountain was steep indeed and, after an hour, with each horse led by a lead boy who guided him safely past the numerous rocks and ruts along the route, we paused at a welcome lunch stop near the halfway point. Here little native Indian girls came out from the bank of a fresh flowing pool to offer us soft drinks and even beer cooled in the mountain stream. After refreshing ourselves, we resumed the upward path with our nags stumbling along over the rough terrain. Our own condition began to deteriorate rather markedly as the grade became steeper and we progressed toward the summit, which was now visible through the tropical foliage. The last few hundred yards, which seemed to rise almost vertically from the terminus of the Jeep track, was made on foot, but when we reached the top we were rewarded by a splendorous view of the surrounding hills and valleys, which descended from the fortress in successive waves much like the waves of the sea.

Cap-Haïtien to Manzanillo Bay, D.R. (26260, 26142)

This section of the coast trends WSW for about 25 miles to the boundary between Haiti and the Dominican Republic, which is marked—appropriately, perhaps— by the muddy waters of the Massacre River. The coastline here is low and fringed by a barrier reef that rises steeply from the deep seabed with openings leading into two large bays.

Caracol Bay (26260)
is a shallow estuary entered through a narrow channel that meanders southward into numerous uncharted shoals. Unless you enjoy sounding the flats by dinghy (which could be rewarding), we would suggest continuing eastward for another 8 miles to Fort Liberté Bay, where you will find a number of fine anchorages in the largest all-weather bay on the entire north coast of Hispaniola.

Fort Liberté Bay (26145)
is entered through a deep, narrow channel between West Point and Saint-Louis Redoute, a promontory on the eastern shore. The ruins of an old fort are visible as you approach the entrance, and when they are directly abeam, you may safely follow midchannel until it widens into the landlocked harbor of Fort Liberté on

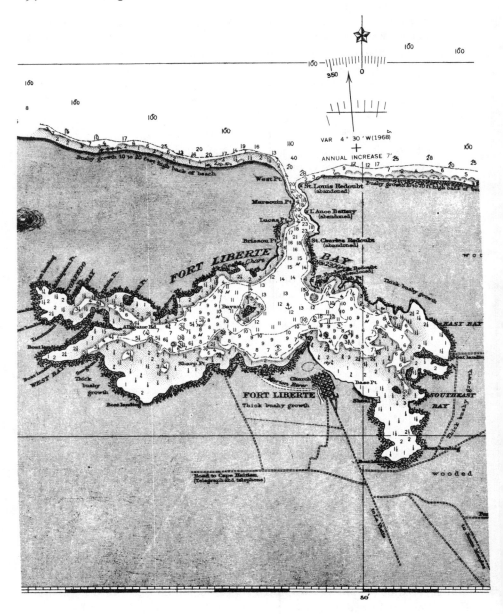

Fort Liberté Bay, north coast of Haiti

Milot and ruins of the Sans Souci palace

Cristophe's fortress, La Citadelle, above Milot

the SE side. Or you may swing westward past a small island into another arm of the bay. The island may be passed on either side, but keep a safe distance off to avoid shoals that extend 200 yards off its NE side.

On entering the bay, it is advisable to proceed first to the town of Fort Liberté, where you must clear customs even though you may be making only a day trip from Cap-Haïtien. The best time to enter is in the morning before the sea breeze starts to pipe up, as the outlying reefs and shoals show up better in calm water. Vessels are not permitted to enter at night. Depths in the bay range from 1 to 11 fathoms, but there are a number of shoal spots around the shores and off the points. There is a pier about 360 feet long on the western side of the entrance channel and a boat landing near a flagstaff at the NE end of the town. Cargo vessels are loaded and unloaded by lighter. Limited provisions are available in the town, but fuel and good drinking water may be hard to find. A banana plantation at the N end of town is reported to have a machine shop with facilities for engine repairs.

In the spring of 1979 we made Fort Liberté our initial port of entry into Haiti. If the pier is not crowded, your best bet is to tie alongside in about 5½ to 6 feet MLW. Just a few steps from the pier is the red-roofed customshouse, where our papers were promptly taken by an elderly clerk who solemnly assured us they would be processed within the hour.

This gave us a welcome chance to stroll through the ancient town, now falling into ruins, but nonetheless interesting for exploration. The old churchyard has graves dating back at least two centuries, and a handsome plaza and facade face the dusty square in front of the cathedral. At noon hordes of schoolchildren poured into the streets, kicking up the dust and dribbling a soccer ball down to the church square in their enthusiasm at being free of academic bondage. At 1430 we were ready to depart, saying farewell to the customs officials and heading north toward the narrow harbor entrance. On the way we passed a tiny fishing boat sailing in with the freshening breeze and carrying a freshly cut pine tree as its mast and sail. It was quite surprising what speed these well-crafted log canoes can make with this primitive rig. We were told that the local fishermen head out early each morning with the offshore breeze, fish all day, and return at dusk with the easterly trade wind "filling" their rig of pine needles.

The frontier between Haiti and the Dominican Republic is only 5 miles E of the entrance to Fort Liberté Bay, where forts on both sides of the Massacre River are a reminder of bloody battles in years past.

THE NORTH COAST OF THE DOMINICAN REPUBLIC

Judging from the charts alone, one might conclude that the rugged north coast of the Dominican Republic is even more formidable than the Haitian coast. Starting at the Dominican border, the mountainous coastline trends ESE for 235 miles—more than twice the length of Haiti's north coast—with only a few indentations where a cruising yacht might expect shelter from the strong winter trade winds. In all, there are no more than four or five anchorages offering all-weather protection, and cruising yachts were being officially welcomed at only two of these, Puerto Manzanillo and Puerto Plata.

Yet, despite its lack of good harbors, this coast is not quite as formidable as it appears on the charts, and need not be out of bounds for well-equipped sailing vessels or power yachts capable of making the long coastwise runs. Navigation is relatively straightforward, as the 100-fathom curve follows the coastline only a few miles offshore and is free of outlying dangers. Although there are virtually no aids to navigation and few of the lights are dependable, the coastal mountains provide good landmarks that are not hard to identify from the charts. For those who have time for leisurely cruising, this area has its special attractions, as we shall see.

Manzanillo Bay to Puerto Plata (25720)

Four of the five "ports" or anchorages on the north coast are situated in the NW corner of the Dominican Republic in the 75-mile stretch between Manzanillo Bay and the principal port of entry at Puerto Plata. This historic district is closely

The customshouse in Puerto Plata

associated with Columbus and his second-in-command, Martin Alonso Pinzon, who rendezvoused here on the first voyage and named most of the harbors and principal landmarks. Columbus returned on his second voyage to establish the first Spanish colony in the New World, which he named Isabela. The four ports, proceeding eastward, are as follows:

Puerto Manzanillo (26142, 26145)

is an open roadstead and deep-water port on the south shore of Manzanillo Bay, with a straightforward approach. The 100-fathom curve is less than a mile off-shore. The harbor and town are in the process of transformation from a banana-loading port and Dominican naval station to a projected seaside resort area with the inevitable condominiums, tourist hotels, swimming beaches, and golf courses. In 1989, the project was still on paper and the commercial pier was being used by only one naval vessel and some small trading boats. The customshouse and port captain's office are near the end of this pier. Visiting yachts should anchor to the west of the commercial pier, and the skipper should dinghy ashore to arrange clearance with the *commandante,* whether or not the vessel has previously cleared into the Dominican Republic.

After clearing, most boats move away from the open harbor, where there is usually an uncomfortable surge, into Estero Balza, east of the pier and town. A local dive shop has marked the entrance, so yachts do not need to run aground on the shoal at the mouth. As the water shoals, the channel entrance is marked with a flag on a wreck to port and a pole to starboard. Straight ahead the way is marked with a range on shore. Best to make this approach on a rising tide. This anchorage will easily accommodate boats of up to 7-foot draft. The limiting depth is at the entrance.

The town of Pepillo Calcedo is small, and this is not a place to do major provisioning. But the growing number of cruisers who stop here find a ready welcome and a safe haven.

Monte Cristi Bay (26143)

enticed Columbus to lay over for three days in January 1493, while he took on wood and water. He named the place Monte Cristo, and it was here that he discovered the first gold in the New World, brought to him by Indians who were panning nuggets in the nearby river now called Yaque del Norte.

Present-day mariners can follow Columbus's track across the extensive bank that fronts the coast between Manzanillo and the conspicuous promontory of El Morro, 2 miles N of the town of Monte Cristi. From the SW, the best approach is through Bradford Channel, past a group of small islands known as the Seven Brothers, to an anchorage a mile off the pier, where the port offices are located.

Two other approaches, from the W and N, are described in the *Sailing Directions,* which gives courses and bearings based on the 825-foot summit of El Morro and a conspicuous clock tower in the town of Monte Cristi. George and Jacques

El Morro from northward

Kappes, who cruised these waters in *Liberty Belle,* reported no problems in making the approach through Bradford Channel, but found shallower water inshore than indicated on the chart. They advised lying not less than a mile off, outside the shorebank.

Monte Cristi is not a port of entry, but in an emergency officials will travel the 30 miles from Pepillo Calcedo to check you in. You should expect to show your appreciation for this in some fashion.

Cape Isabela and Puerto Blanco (25720)

Monte Cristi Bank extends eastward for more than 30 miles between El Morro and Cape Isabela, with a barrier reef fronting the coast about 1 to 2½ miles offshore for most of that distance. Much of this section of the coast is backed by a mountain range rising to more than 2,600 feet a few miles inland. Skippers unfamiliar with these waters are advised to stand at least 3 miles offshore until clear of the shoals north of Isabela Bay, the bight on the western side of the cape.

It was here that Columbus attempted to establish a city, which he called Isabela, but it was a poor site, without a good harbor, and was abandoned in less than two years. It is still a poor anchorage today, and there is no trace of the old town.

Continuing E for another 10 miles around the bold headland of Cape Isabela, present-day cruising skippers will find perhaps the snuggest all-weather small-boat harbor on the north coast, called Puerto Blanco, about 15 miles W of Puerto Plata. (Consult local authorities to ascertain if Puerto Blanco has been made an official port of entry where foreign yachts are welcome at the time of your planned visit.)

We found this delightful little harbor on a westbound passage between Puerto Rico and the Caicos Islands, when an unexpected norther caught us off Cape Isabela and led us to seek overnight shelter. As we approached on a course of 180°, a channel opened up about midway between the two shores, leading into a tight little Y-shaped harbor with one branch to port and another to starboard. We found the best anchorage to starboard in the SW branch about 200 yards off a small boat dock at the western end. The village of Luperon is hidden behind a lush hillside plantation on the SW shore, with coconut palms and banana plants on its slopes.

The eastern branch shoals rapidly beyond the entrance, and there are unmarked shoal spots in the western branch, so yachts entering for the first time should proceed cautiously with depthfinder or leadline. You will find any number of good places to drop your hook in 8 to 12 feet over good-holding mud or sand bottom.

Puerto Plata (25803)

was founded by Nicolas de Ovando in 1502 and today is the largest town on the Dominican north coast, with a population of 20,000 and a small harbor that is the only port of entry on this section of the coast. Limited yacht facilities are available in the harbor, which is being developed as a commercial port for cruise ships, tankers, and general cargo vessels.

The approach from seaward presents no difficulties in good weather, with Mount Isabela de Torres rising to a height of 2,600 feet behind the town and the 100-fathom curve only about 2 miles off the entrance channel. (Don't count on fair weather at all times, however, because occasional storms can reduce visibility

This unique building houses the market in Puerto Plata.

to zero, as we discovered on our first visit.) The entrance channel, about 300 yards wide, leads between two reefs that break heavily in rough weather. The channel is marked on its western side by two buoys, which should be left to starboard. We found it difficult to identify the entrance range (described in the *Sailing Directions* as two light beacons in range at 218°) until after we had sighted Owen Rock on the outer edge of the shoal bank half a mile northwest of the entrance markers. When Owen Rock bears about 309°T, you can alter course to 218° and eventually distinguish the range just before entering the marked channel. The white obelisk on Point Fortaleza, at the east side of the entrance, is visible from several miles offshore, with a tall chimney about one fourth mile south.

The inner harbor is small and exposed to the trade winds, which create a constant and uneasy surge throughout the anchorage. Both the British *Pilot* and U.S. *Sailing Directions* carry a cautionary note that swells from 4 to 18 feet are not uncommon between October and May. We have not encountered more than 2-to-3-foot swells on the few occasions we've been there, but each time we have found it necessary to lay two anchors to hold our bow in the general direction of the swells, but still the boat will roll.

On entering, yachts should proceed to the western side of the old commercial pier at the SE end of the harbor, where they will receive directions for anchoring or tying up. The Med-moor is customary here. There is no charge for tying up, water is available for a one-time charge of $5, and electricity is available as well. Special arrangements need to be made to obtain fuel.

The customs office is at the head of the old pier, and the commandant's headquarters are just outside the gate surrounding the commercial dock area.

Because of the ever-present surge, the unattractive waterfront, and the remnants of a large oil spill that rise to the surface and coat your topsides whenever the harbor is stirred up by a cruise ship, the harbor of Puerto Plata is avoided by many cruising yachtsmen.

The city of Puerto Plata, however, is well worth a visit if the weather is such that the conditions in the harbor are tolerable. Gothic revival buildings line the narrow streets, housing small businesses and restaurants. The ancient fort at the harbor entrance, San Felipe, dates back to 1540 and is being restored, along with other historic landmarks.

There are several good native restaurants in the town. A short walk of only a few blocks will take you to the modern city market, where fresh food supplies are available; it's situated atop a rise commanding a fine view of the port. If you have time to lay over for a few days, take a trip by car or bus through the surrounding countryside to nearby beaches or take the cable car up the wooded slopes of Mount Isabela de Torres with its lighted statue of Christ at the summit. Go early in the morning, because clouds usually wreath the summit after noon.

Hertz and Avis rental cars are available through local travel agencies, one of which is directed by a young American, Mike Ronan, who is especially helpful to yachtsmen, being a sailor himself. Mike first came to Puerto Plata as a Peace

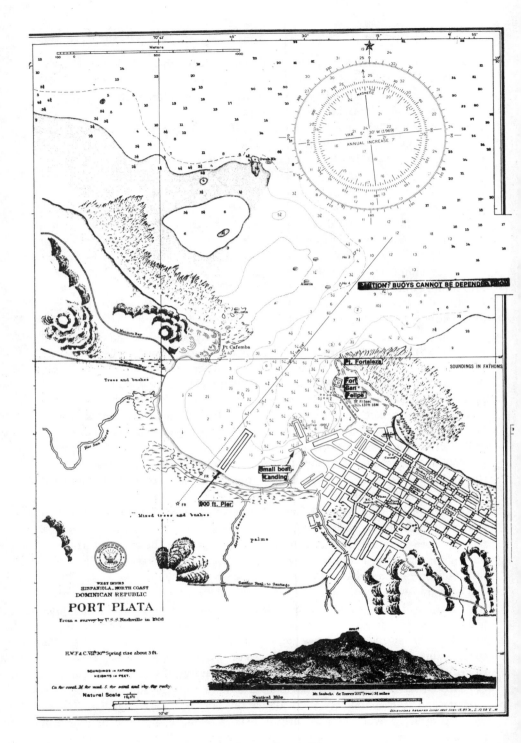

Approaches to Puerto Plata

These fishermen's boats found their way through the reef, where the water can be
seen breaking in the distance.

Corps volunteer and remained to establish his own travel firm, Agencia de Viajes
Cafembas. Mike is very busy these days showing cruise ship tourists around the
countryside, but sometimes he can find time to advise cruising skippers how to
get things done or where to find a good mechanic or electrician. Look him up
in any event.

Puerto Plata to Samaná Bay (25801)

Eastward of Puerto Plata, you will find no harbor providing all-weather protection for more than 100 miles, until you reach Samaná Bay and the port of Santa
Barbara. For the most part, this section of the coast is steep-to, fringed by inshore
reefs and backed by mountains that present some of the most spectacular coastal
scenery in the Caribbean. Several anchorages along the way afford temporary
shelter from easterlies, but are exposed to the N and NE. And, unless things have
changed and foreign vessels are welcome in harbors other than those previously
mentioned as ports of entry, you may enter these only when you can plead some
sort of an emergency.

Sosúa (25720)

lies about 10 miles SE of Puerto Plata in a tiny cove under the lee of Cape
Macorís, where anchorage may be found. This is an interesting place to visit in
settled weather, with a lovely sandy beach and a remarkable refugee community

close by. The best anchorage is in the NE corner of the bight, just N of a coral reef, in 1 to 3 fathoms over a hard sandy bottom. The approach from the 100-fathom line less than a mile offshore is straightforward, with no dangers N of the unmarked but clearly visible reef. Northerly winds make the anchorage untenable, and there is a constant swell even in the prevailing breeze.

The refugee community at Sosúa was founded during World War II, when Rafael Trujillo made a grant of land to refugees from Nazi Germany. More than 1,000 exiles from Hitler's Third Reich settled on the land and, without previous agricultural experience, established a successful farm cooperative that has survived to this day, producing meat and dairy products for the Dominican market and for export to other parts of the Caribbean. Some of the second-generation families have migrated to the United States or returned to Europe, reducing the size of the community, but the remaining group is a vital force in the area today. There are two other communities at Sosúa, a native settlement and a residential resort community that has become popular with affluent Santo Domingans, Americans and Europeans.

San Juan River (25720)

is a small estuary situated just S and W of the bold headland of Cape Francés Viejo with a daytime anchorage that is worth exploring. It can also be an overnight stop on this long, unbroken stretch of coast if the trades are south of east, in which case the mountainous terrain behind the cape provides adequate shelter. This anchorage is not easy to spot, because the shoreline is undistinguished at this point; but if you are proceeding eastward and closing on the first rocky promontories of the cape, look close inshore for a high barren tree with a prominent rock situated some 100 yards southwest of the river entrance. The San Juan River is little more than a shallow stream winding inland through a tangle of the largest mangrove trees we have ever seen. At the time of our visit in the spring of 1979 aboard *Quo Vadis,* soundings in the approach indicated we would not get far with her 6-foot draft, so we dropped our hook just N of the prominent rock and close by the tall tree on shore.

We had not been anchored more than 10 minutes when, somewhat to our surprise, a gaily painted green-and-black boat came chugging out from the river mouth, heading in our direction and coming smartly alongside with four officials aboard—the port captain and his assistants from the little fishing village of San Juan. After leafing through our papers briefly and finding them in order, they asked if we would like to return with them for a visit to the town. Three of our crew, with Jim Fox remaining on board, accepted with pleasure, and to our astonishment we discovered one of the most intriguing villages in the entire country.

The river depths are only 2 or 3 feet at most, but the outboard-powered dugout craft took us through a winding stream beset with mangroves for perhaps half a mile to a circular basin surrounded with 25 or 30 brightly painted rowboats ready to take native parties for a day of fishing at sea. Walking through town we were followed by a stream of little ragamuffins pulling from time to time at our hands to ask for a nickel or a dime to buy cookies or sweets along the way. Poor Jim Fox back on the boat missed this grand adventure, but later in the evening Hal Watson, our ebullient cruising companion, took Jim in our own dinghy for a private tour.

Port Jackson (25710)

is said to provide temporary anchorage in the lee of a small cay at the head of a very large bight about 50 miles SE of Sosúa and halfway between Cape Francés Viejo and Cape Cabrón. Although it is called Port Jackson, there is no port, no harbor, no town, and very little protection except that provided by the tiny cay and the breaking reef on which it stands. It is out of the way for vessels making a coastwise passage and has nothing whatever to recommend it as an anchorage for yachts.

Port Escondido (25723)

is a small bay situated at the head of a deep indentation in the coast about 6 miles W of Cape Cabrón. This bay is exposed to the N and W but may offer some protection when the trades are easterly. The anchorage is in a most attractive setting just off a white, palm-fringed beach backed by green hills that surround the harbor on three sides.

When we were there in 1979, we spent a memorable night anchored in the brilliant light of the moon, which left its shimmering reflection on the quiet waters of the Bay of Escondido. Since it was one of those ever-frequent religious holidays, not a soul came down to the shore to wave at us.

Proceeding eastward around Cape Cabrón you will pass one of the most spectacular coastal areas in the eastern Caribbean. White rocky cliffs rise perpendicularly from the sea to heights of more than 800 feet. Deep water carries right up to the base of the cliffs, where the ocean swells break thunderously, throwing spray and spume high in the air and echoing in huge caves and recesses in the rock. Cape Cabrón is the departure point for vessels bound for Puerto Rico and the Virgin Islands, but if you need fuel or provisions before crossing the often turbulent Mona Passage, your last port of call will be in Samaná Bay a few miles to the southeast across the deep bight of Rincón. Cape Samaná with its lighthouse perched atop a 500-foot cliff is almost as spectacular as Cabrón, and marks the northern entrance into the huge Bay of Samaná.

Santa Barbara de Samaná (25723, 25724)

lies about 15 miles SW of Cape Samaná, protected by a mass of coral reefs extending most of the way across the mouth of the bay, reefs so numerous and interconnected that the chart simply calls them "foul ground." However, the approach is actually less formidable than it appears on the chart, with 5 to 6 fathoms of water across Canandaiqua Bank about a mile off the light on Balandra Head, leading into a deeper channel along the shore inside Leventado Cay

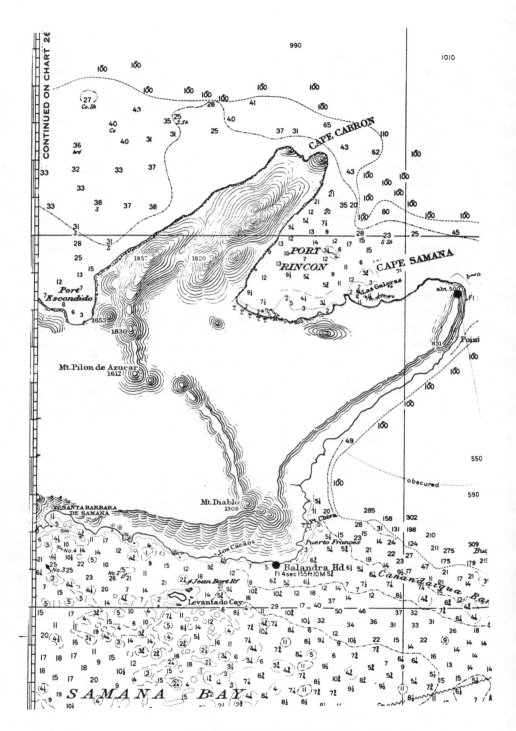

The approach to Samaná Bay

A small but very pleasant French hotel looks out over this beautiful beach on the
northeast corner of the Dominican Republic.

and Jean Bart Reef. This passage is wide and easy of access under normal weather
conditions and, with due caution, could be used at night. Only when heavy ocean
swells or gale-force winds create a "rage" on Canandaiqua Bank does this passage
become dangerous. At such times cruising yachts should not have left the last
port.

This is another beautiful coastal area, well worth a visit in its own right, as well
as for the excellent shelter it provides in the harbor of Santa Barbara, or simply
Samaná, as it is now called. Past Balandra Head, steep hills covered with coconut
and banana trees lead down to the water, with brown slashes of road attesting
to their cultivation, as do the clusters of thatched roofs of the plantation workers'
huts. Several small bays open up before you enter the harbor between Gorda Point
and two small cays to the S.

The head of the harbor is shallow, but good anchorage will be found off the
town wharf or anywhere in the center of the harbor. But first, if there is space,
Med-moor to the dock and wait for the port commander, accompanied by customs and immigration officials, to arrive. Young men waiting on the dock, who
make a business of assisting visiting yachtsmen, will help you moor and will

summon the proper officials. If local boats, a small Naval vessel and the ferry to Sabana de la Mar across Bahía Samaná have preempted all the dockage, anchor nearby until there is room or until the skipper goes ashore to make arrangments with the officials, who are not keen about going out to process boats in inflatable dinghies.

The main wharf area has been dredged to 15 feet. Good drinking water, gasoline, and diesel fuel *(gasoil)* are available at the wharf.

The picturesque old town that we visited before the 1970s has been leveled to make way for a tourist development project embracing the entire harborfront and adjacent cays. Gone are the narrow, dusty streets and alleys with their clapboard houses and shanties. A broad boulevard has been built along the waterfront, and a hotel overlooks the town.

Nearby, however, you will find unspoiled countryside, sheltered beaches and coves, and a historic site at the Bay of Arrows, where Columbus battled briefly with the first hostile Indians he had seen in the New World. They were Arawaks, normally peaceful, but they had acquired warlike ways in defending their lands against the invariably hostile Caribs. If you have the time, hire a taxi or dirt bikes for a drive to the northeast end of the island to visit the several lovely beaches and waterfalls in the great bight between Capes Cabrón and Samaná. It's a rewarding side trip.

THE WEST AND SOUTH COASTS OF HAITI

When winter trade winds make the rugged north coast of Hispaniola a Thorny Path, an alternative route around the western end of this large, mountainous island may have certain attractions for eastbound cruising yachts. Although this route is longer by almost 200 miles (300 miles if you detour to include Port-au-Prince), it has the advantage of providing better protection in a number of small bays, harbors, and sheltered anchorages in the Gulf of Gonâve and along the south coasts of Haiti and the Dominican Republic.

The huge Gulf of Gonâve lies eastward of the Windward Passage and is out of the way for vessels bound for Jamaica or the south coast of Hispaniola. But it is a starkly dramatic land and water area well worth visiting. Its bold headlands rise steeply from the sea, backed by arid mountains that reach heights of more than 5,000 feet a few miles inland, and depths plunge to 1,000 fathoms only a few miles offshore. Port-au-Prince, the populous capital of Haiti, lies at the head of the gulf, about 100 miles east of the Windward Passage, and the mountainous Île de la Gonâve, some 30 miles long, occupies the center of the gulf, between the northern and southern approaches to the Baie de Port-au-Prince.

Winter winds are less boisterous in the gulf, though an occasional norther may sweep down to interrupt the prevailing pattern. In the Bay of Port-au-Prince, an offshore land breeze sets in at night, continuing through the morning hours until almost noon, when it is followed by a gentle sea breeze coming in from the W and lasting until evening. This pattern extends over most of the Gulf of Gonâve and is used to advantage by native fishermen, who sail westward on the morning land breeze to their fishing grounds in the gulf, returning in the afternoon with their tattered sails billowing from the sea breeze behind them. Although offshore winds are common at night in all of the larger mountainous islands, nowhere else in the Caribbean have we encountered a similar daytime pattern over so large a water area as the Gulf of Gonâve. During the summer months winds are somewhat more variable, with more westerlies, squalls, and periods of calm extending as far west as the Windward Passage. Although Hispaniola lies in the hurricane belt, there are enough protected harbors in the gulf for cruising boats to find a safe hideout when a tropical storm comes their way.

Currents vary in different parts of the gulf, and one should always be aware of the strong set close to the shores in cruising these reef-fringed bays. In the Windward Passage, the prevailing current sets westward toward Cuba, but close to the Haitian coast it sets northward in the vicinity of Cap du Môle. In the approaches to Port-au-Prince Bay, the current is said to set NW in the Saint Marc channel and E in the channel south of the island of Gonâve.

Ports of Entry in Western Haiti

If you intend to cruise for any length of time in the territorial waters of Haiti, it is essential to have an official cruising permit, or *Permis de Navigation,* authorizing you to visit other ports without restriction. This unlimited permit may be obtained only at Port-au-Prince and Cap-Haïtien, although there are several other ports of entry in the gulf (Gonaïves and Saint Marc on the northern peninsula) and on the south coast (Jérémie, Jacmel, and Aux Cayes) where you may enter if necessary. Cruising skippers find out sooner or later that it's worth the extra time and mileage to make their first entry at Port-au-Prince, where customs and immigration officials are used to dealing with foreign vessels. Bob and Ginnie Higman had this advice to offer others after their three-month cruise around Haiti in *Tormentor III:*

> Cruising was made much easier for us after we reached the capital and obtained papers for the rest of our voyage. M. Cadet, the Chef de Service (in 1971) typed out the one-page *Permis de Navigation* authorizing us to cruise all the territorial waters around the southern peninsula to Aux Cayes on the south coast. Up until then we'd had to obtain a new cruising paper at each town large enough to have a customs office, restricting us to anchorages only in the next governmental district . . . and woe be to the yacht that does not rigidly observe the rule of obtaining a cruising permit for every anchorage.

Cap du Môle to Port-au-Prince (26260, 26181)

Several small bays indent the 100 miles of coast between the northwest tip of Haiti and Port-au-Prince at the head of the gulf, providing safe anchorages for vessels making a coastwise passage with short daylight runs. Most vessels approaching from the north plan to make their landfall on Cap du Môle, but their first sight of land from seaward is more likely to be the high mountains a few miles inland behind the deep bay where Columbus first set foot on Hispaniola on December 5, 1492.

Cap Saint Nicolas Môle (26260)

is undoubtedly one of the most interesting bays on the northern peninsula but is seldom visited by cruising yachts, and we don't recommend anchoring overnight unless you have already obtained a cruising permit. It's not a port of entry, and the small village has no boat facilities. Furthermore, you could be detained by a boarding party with soldiers from the local army post. Jack Laird, an American yachtsman who entered Cap Saint Nicolas Môle in his 57-foot power cruiser *Miss Apple Jack* after a 1969 passage from the Bahamas, was struck with its beauty and gave this interesting description of the bay and his reception:

> The Baie du Môle contains 17 old forts in various stages of deterioration. It used to be an important strategic position, as whoever controlled Le Môle controlled the Windward Passage. . . . We had rather expected to be met by some type of Coast Guard vessel, but none was there, so we went straight up to the village and anchored in 10 feet of water about 50 yards offshore. This is where Columbus was supposed to have landed centuries before. A small sailboat and two rowboats were on the beach and some of the crude houses of sticks, with palm-leaf roofs, were visible but no one was in sight.
>
> Apparently we were taken as invaders from Cuba or Mars and were expected to start blasting away with guns. . . . Eventually with a little coaxing the town folk began to appear from behind trees, bushes, huts and houses, and soon there were several hundred men, women and children on the beach just staring. Shortly one of the rowboats set out from the shore with one man rowing and another with a rifle, who turned out to be a sergeant in the army. . . . He had his instructions, as I was rowed in to the beach and walked through the silent crowd of non-smiling faces and was taken into what I took to be the Town Hall. It was about 30 feet in diameter with sides made of small sticks placed vertically in the ground, and a roof. There was a small table and seven unpainted chairs. That was all.
>
> With voodoo-like magic, six men came out of the woodwork. One was a good-looking army lieutenant in full uniform who spoke a "little bit" of English. One man took our passports and papers into the corner for study. As we waited the conversation was strained and difficult, but finally after about an hour I was offered *café* and I knew we were accepted as tourists.

Other cruising boats have had similar experiences here and at other small towns around Haiti and the Dominican Republic where yachts are seldom seen. In encounters with local authorities, the inability of the visiting boat owner to communicate effectively often results in strained relations and misunderstandings that could be avoided if either side spoke the language of the other. Water and fuel are problems at all of the small ports and some of the larger towns as well.

At Le Môle water was carried down from the mountains in buckets; there was no fuel and no dock.

Continuing southward around Cap à Foux, cruising boats may run alongshore past a succession of bold headlands and rocky promontories backed by high hills and mountains. The 100-fathom curve lies less than a mile offshore for much of the 50-mile section between Cap à Foux and the entrance to Gonaïves, the first port of entry on the northeast side of the gulf. There are several conspicuous landmarks and a few anchorages on this coast.

Pointe la Plateforme

is a white rocky bluff rising steeply to a flat tabletop summit about 10 miles SE of Cap à Foux. It is easy to recognize from almost any point at sea. On a southbound passage we sailed by la Plateforme in a howling norther, with the mountain giving us welcome protection.

Baie de Henne (26181)

is a deep indentation in the coast about 9 miles eastward of la Plateforme, where anchorage may be found on the E side of the bay behind the encircling hills. It is exposed to winds from the S but affords protection in the NE trades. There's a small village at the head of the bay.

Port-à-Piment (26181)

is a tiny harbor about 12 miles eastward of Baie de Henne, with an anchorage used by local fishing boats but exposed to the S like others on this coast. When passing close offshore, you can identify the entrance by a conspicuous mound that rises from the flat savanna behind the cove. The nearest village is Anse Rouge, on the coast about 3½ miles to the W.

Pointe la Pierre

is a bold rocky headland about 16 miles SE of Port-à-Piment. It marks the northern approach to the Bay of Gonaïves. The light on the point is usually out, but the cliffs, which rise steeply from the shorebank, are easy to identify in daylight. The bank extends only about 350 yards off the cliffs.

Pointe la Plateforme, NW end of Haiti, southwestward

The Platform (bearing 315°)

Baie de Gonaïves (26181)

This large bay opens up into two smaller bays that provide a number of safe anchorages. The town of Gonaïves, with a population of more than 20,000, is a port of entry used by Caribbean trading vessels and local fishing craft. The commercial harbor is exposed to the W, but vessels anchor in 6 or 7 fathoms off the town or tie up along the pier with depths of 12 feet alongside. The customs-house is near the foot of the pier. Better anchorages for cruising boats may be found in Baie Carénage to the N or Baie de l'Hôpital to the S.

Yachts are not exactly a familiar sight in Gonaïves, as Jack Laird discovered when he spent six hours attempting to get clearance papers for *Miss Apple Jack.*

> Since we were apparently the first pleasure boat to enter this port, no one knew exactly what to do with us and whether to allow us to come ashore. A seemingly endless parade of officials descended on *Miss Apple Jack,* starting at the lowest echelon and working up to the heads of the state. . . . The parade of officials finally ended with the arrival of the colonel in charge of the army, a special representative of the President, and a decision to pass the buck to Port-au-Prince. . . . This is not to suggest that these six hours were strained or fearful. On the contrary, it was one massive party. Our bar was open. Since it was Sunday most officials had minimal duties and therefore went home to fetch their families. All were extremely pleasant and courteous. Through all of this (as we were tied to the pier) hundreds of town folk pushed their way forward for a look-see. The cops couldn't hold them back, nor was there any need, as all they wanted was to look into the goldfish bowl at us—the goldfish.

Gonaïves to Cap Saint Marc

In contrast to the mountainous terrain north of Gonaïves and south of Saint Marc, this 20-mile section of the coast is relatively low, with a succession of shallow bays, some of which provide anchorages for native boats.

Baie de la Tortue (26181)

is encumbered with shoals and is not recommended, although local fishing craft anchor SE of Frigate Isle or at Mangrove Island off the northern entrance, about 3 miles SW of Gonaïves.

Baie de Grande Pierre (26181)

is a large open bay just S of Tortue Bay, with a wide and deep entrance channel leading into an anchorage with depths of 10 to 30 feet over a mud bottom. The shoreline is covered with mangroves, and there is a small village on the southeastern shore. Pointe Dessalines marks the southern entrance to the bay.

Baie de Saint Marc (26188)

lies between two conspicuous points—Table au Diable on the N and Cap Saint Marc about 10 miles to the S—and leads to the harbor of Saint Marc 6½ miles eastward at the head of the bay. The harbor is an open roadstead exposed to westerly winds; the town is a busy coastal community of some 12,000 persons. It's said to be one of the most healthful spots in Haiti, with sea breezes from the W and encircling mountains in the E and S. Deep water can be carried right up to the harbor, with the 100-fathom curve nowhere more than three fourths mile offshore all around the bay. As you approach the town, the twin spires of a cathedral and a flat-topped hill, Morne à Vigie, rising more than 1,000 feet, provide conspicuous landmarks. There are several small piers used by coastal vessels, but larger ships are usually moored off the town, facing westward with their stern lines anchored on the beach. This is an exposed anchorage and may be dangerous in strong westerly winds. Gas and water can be brought to the pier, but not diesel.

Approaches to Port-au-Prince (26181)

Vessels approaching the Baie de Port-au-Prince from the north will find no harbors or temporary shelter of any kind in passing through the deep ocean channel of Saint Marc between the mountainous mainland and the almost equally unbroken shoreline of the island of Gonâve. The 100-fathom curve is less than a mile offshore along the northern peninsula from Cap Saint Marc to Pointe Trou Forban, which marks the entrance to Port-au-Prince Bay, where the depths shoal rapidly to between 6 and 60 fathoms for the next 20 miles. As the mountains recede, the entire northeastern shoreline seems to disappear in the haze that often hangs over the low coastal plain.

Cruising yachts approaching the bay for the first time should plan to enter around midday, if possible, or at a time when visibility is good and the westerly sea breeze is behind them. We won't attempt to summarize the *Sailing Directions,* which are essential for making the final approach through the numerous reefs and shoals that protect the harbor of Port-au-Prince. No one should try to enter at night, for several obvious reasons, as noted by Jack Laird:

> As an example of navigating here, and why you shouldn't proceed at night, the light shown on the Arcadins Islets (three small islands off the northern peninsula) is out and has been for several years. . . . Also do not depend on the harbor buoys, as they are either not there or have been changed, an indication of the difficulties our Hydrographic Office has in keeping up with local changes in many foreign lands.

Port-au-Prince Harbor (26186)

is an open roadstead exposed to the W but sheltered to some extent by the fringing reefs and shoals. Pilotage is compulsory for commercial vessels, and a pilot boat is usually seen in the entrance channel or just off the quarantine anchorage adjacent to the 2,000-foot pier with a long warehouse at the outer end. The twin spires of the cathedral and two masts of the radio station provide conspicuous landmarks from the entrance channel. Once inside, most yachts will be directed to the anchorage or told where to tie up along the pier. If you don't see a pilot boat, anchor first off the south side of the pier until port officials come aboard. Advance notice of the date and expected time of your arrival helps expedite clearance procedures. The port pilots monitor channel 2738 kHz on a 24-hour basis and generally can be reached from 40 miles out, according to recent cruising visitors.

There is no really good anchorage in the commercial harbor, and the only place to tie up is the Casino Dock, whose number of small boat slips is limited. All of them were occupied when we were there in 1973. This facility is operated by Gaston Boussan, who also runs a glass-bottom snorkeling boat making daily visits to Sandy Cay and outlying reefs. M. Boussan keeps a register of visiting yachts; it includes the names of well-known transatlantic sailors like Eric Tabarly and *Pen Duick III* (on a 1972 passage), and a number of U.S. yachts from Florida and Pacific coast ports. His pier carries 6 feet alongside, with water, electricity, and fuel, and if he can't find you a slip he will be helpful in suggesting alternative anchorages. His address is P.O. Box 923, Port-au-Prince.

The American embassy and consulate are near the waterfront, only a few blocks from the commercial pier, and you are almost certain to find someone on the staff who is active in sailing and willing to share his knowledge of local waters and facilities. When we were there in 1973, a member of the embassy staff was one of a group of 50 boating enthusiasts who were then organizing the Port-au-Prince Yacht Club; they hoped it would soon have a small marina and yacht facility on the bay. A new marina was being developed on the N side of the bay, about 15 miles from the capital.

Cruise ships call regularly at Port-au-Prince, and you'll see more tourists ashore here than anywhere else in Haiti. There are usually one or two sailing vessels for charter in the harbor, but they are likely to be crewed by itinerant "yotties" trying to raise enough cash to clear for their next port; their credentials should, of course, be checked out carefully.

A good friend of visiting yachtsmen and a helpful source of information is the American owner of the local Coca-Cola plant, Mr. Richard Forgh…am, who is also commodore of an unofficial group called the Kaka Poul Yachting and Drinking Association. Bottled water, beer, and soft drinks may be bought at the Brasserie de Couronne, operated by Mr. Forgham.

A walk around the busy, dusty streets of Port-au-Prince is always interesting. Or you can negotiate with a "share-the-taxi" driver to take you to almost any destination around town. There are several fine old hotels in the downtown area, some of them (like Sans Souci and the Oloffson) occupying colonial mansions in a garden-like setting, excellent restaurants, and all manner of outdoor markets and stalls. Filet mignon and other meats can be bought at a smaller "supermarket" called The Food Store near the Presidential Palace. Everywhere you go you are caught up in the moving streams of pedestrian traffic—barefooted, ill-clad black folk crowding the narrow streets and sidewalks, packing into the tiny, dilapidated, but brightly colored buses with names such as "Mon Dieu," "Notre Dame," "Jesus Christ," and beggars and street urchins everywhere constantly reminding you of the appalling poverty of Haiti.

Port-au-Prince to Cap Dame-Marie (26181, 26147, 26184)

The south coast of the Gulf of Gonâve trends westward for approximately 120 miles to Cap Dame-Marie, closely backed by a coastal mountain range that extends to the western end of the southern peninsula. Once you have left Port-au-Prince Bay, deep water can be carried through the Gonâve (or south) channel westward to the Windward Passage, with several interesting overnight anchorages in protected coves and harbors on the peninsula, and at least one anchorage on the island of Gonâve.

Petit Goâve Bay (26181)

lies about 32 miles SW of Port-au-Prince; the town of Petit Goâve is situated on the western side of the bay, and a coffee mill and old fort on the southern side. The Lairds found this "a beautiful, well-kept town, slightly richer than most due to coffee growing. The officials here were most gracious and helpful and asked us to stop by on our return trip. This we did, and were utterly flabbergasted to have practically the entire town present us with a large primitive oil painting inscribed to Capt. Jack Laird and his wife 'in remembrance of their visit.' "

Miragoâne Bay (26188)

is another open bay, about 12 miles W of Petit Goâve, with a wide entrance that is easy to enter whether the lighted marker shown on the chart is operating or not, or is even there. There is a beautiful cathedral in the town on the S side of the harbor. Bauxite is shipped from this port, and the loading dock in the western part of the harbor fills the air with red dust. It should be avoided when it's operating. Better anchorage is found in the SE part of the bay.

Baradaires Bay (26181)

is the largest and most interesting bay on the southern peninsula. It lies about 25 miles E of Miragoâne and is almost 10 miles long and 2 to 3 miles wide, with several primitive fishing villages around its shores and a variety of sheltered anchorages. The entrance at the N end of the bay is unmarked and less than one half mile wide, but carries depths of over 100 feet between the reefs and shoals to the S and the small town of Gran Boucan on the northern peninsula. The water

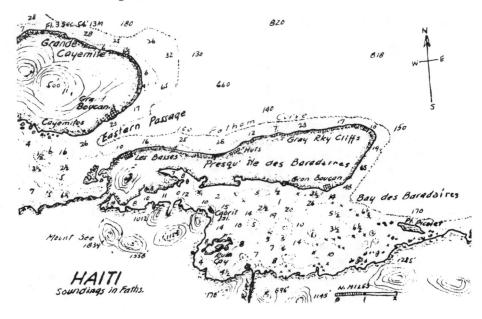

Baradaires Bay

shoals rapidly about 400 yards off the town and is less than 4 feet at the small pier. Better anchorages can be found behind several rocky cays and islets 4 to 6 miles inside the bay. The most accessible are Rum Cay, a hilly, wooded island with white cliffs and bluffs about 4 miles SW of Gran Boucan, and tiny Cabrit Islet 1 mile NW of Rum Cay. Deep water can be carried all the way to the western end of the bay, with mountains rising more than 1,100 feet along the S shore. There's a fjordlike entrance into a lagoon with depths of 78 feet, well worth exploring if you can clear the 6-foot bar at the narrow entrance. Local guides can take you in a native canoe (or your own dinghy) for a fascinating trip 2 miles up the narrow Baradaires River to the town of that name.

Park Bay, Gonâve Island (26181, 26184)

is the only semiprotected harbor on the N side of Gonâve channel, and it's hardly worth visiting unless you want a close look at the bare, eroding mountains of this 30-mile-long island. Situated in the SE corner of the island, Park Bay is exposed to the W but sheltered by the mountains from winds from NW to SSE.

Baie de Cayemites (26181)

lies a few miles NW of Baradaires Bay and provides the last chance for westbound vessels to find much shelter en route to the south coast of Haiti. Great Cayemite Island is a high, thickly wooded isle a few miles NW of Baradaires, with a light on its northern shore and a deep channel between its southern shore and the mainland, leading into a large bay with a number of small islets and cays. Much of this bay is encumbered with coral reefs, shoals, and unmarked rocky heads. There are two fishing villages on either side of the eastern passage—Cayemites on the island and Les Basses on the Bec du Marsouin peninsula—both of which are exposed to winds from the E and W. Anchorages may be found at the western end of Great Cayemite in the channel separating it from Little Cayemite Island, but the passage through the reefs to the N and W is not recommended without a local pilot. The village of Corail at the SW end of the bay looks interesting, but the approach is encumbered by reefs and unmarked shoals.

Jérémie Bay (26147)

lies about 12 miles southwestward of Cayemite Bay and is little more than an open roadstead exposed to the full force of the NE trades. The town of Jérémie, with a population of about 15,000, is a port of entry. It has a customshouse, a small stone pier with 6 feet at the outer end, a prominent cathedral with a clock tower, and the ruins of an old fort. Water and limited provisions are available, but the anchorage is not recommended except in settled weather. The harbor is filled with breakers in a strong breeze, and northers may come up without warning, often accompanied by heavy squalls during the summer months. Under such conditions the bay becomes unsafe. The *Sailing Directions,* while noting that the holding ground is good in the anchorage off the town, cautions vessels to "be prepared to get underway at a moment's notice." Some of our cruising friends are inclined to bypass Jérémie, although it's the last anchorage worth mentioning until after you have rounded Cap Dame-Marie at the NW end of the peninsula. However, it provides a convenient overnight stopping point for fuel and provisions if you are continuing on around the peninsula to the south coast of Haiti, where you won't find another real harbor short of Aux Cayes, about 86 miles away.

Cap Dame-Marie to Pointe de Tiburon (26191)

Several small bays indent the coast, which trends southward for 16 miles between Cap Dame-Marie and Pointe de Tiburon. Temporary anchorage may be found in any of these bays during periods of settled weather when the trades are blowing offshore, but they are completely exposed to the westward. A large triangular bank fronts this entire section of the coast, with its apex more than 12 miles offshore. Depths on the bank range between 5 and 20 fathoms, over sand and coral, in waters so clear that the bottom is plainly visible. You will find fish traps and buoys all over the bank. If you plan to anchor in any of the small bays, the large-scale chart plans are essential.

Baie de Dame-Marie (26210)

lies between the cape of that name and Pointe Rousselin, about 3½ miles southward, with the best anchorage off the village of Petite Rivière at the NE end of the bay. A strong current sweeps around the bay at times.

Baie de Nault (26210, 26147)

lies about 4 miles southward of Pointe Rousselin in a bight SE of Pointe à Bourry, a reddish-brown cliff that is difficult to identify from offshore. The approach from seaward is free from outlying shoals, and anchorage off the town of Anse d'Hainault affords good shelter from the trade winds during the winter months. Other bays in this section are not recommended; they are less than adequately charted, with few identifying landmarks.

Pointe de Tiburon to Cabo Beata (26210)

From the white cliffs of Tiburon to Cabo Beata in the Dominican Republic, the coast trends irregularly to the SE for about 185 miles, backed by mountains most of the way, with many small rivers and streams emptying into the sea. There are two ports of entry on the south coast of Haiti, Aux Cayes and Jacmel, and a number of good anchorages in sheltered bays within the large bight that forms the Baie des Cayes in the central section.

Yachts heading eastward from Tiburon can run along the 100-fathom curve about 2 miles offshore past a succession of high cliffs alternating with sandy beaches for almost 37 miles to Pointe-à-Gravois, where the coast recedes to Pointe l'Abacou and then opens up into the relatively protected waters of Baie de Cayes. Here eastbound vessels have a choice between standing on for a deep-water passage around Cabo Beata, about 140 miles ESE of Pointe l'Abacou, or turning N in search of an anchorage at Aux Cayes or one of the many finger bays in that area. Sailing vessels may find the offshore route rather strenuous at any time of year, as the trade winds tend to draw in along the coast, making it a long beat to windward into the steep Caribbean seas. This is particularly true in winter months, when the easterly trades blow fresh throughout the daylight hours, moderating only slightly at night if you are more than 16 miles offshore. In summer the winds are likely to be variable, with southerlies frequently interrupting the easterly flow.

The alternative inside course is made more attractive by the choice of sheltered anchorages and the kindly land breeze that comes in from the NW during the night and gradually veers around into the NE until about noon, when the sea breeze sets in from the SE and continues until evening. Strong easterly winds cause a heavy surf on the outlying islands and reefs and create a surge in the harbors, but most of the Baie des Cayes affords a welcome respite from the relentless ocean seas outside.

Baie des Cayes (26203)

This large bay is undoubtedly the most interesting cruising ground on the south coast of Haiti, and is well worth a visit. The western end of the bay is protected by Isle-à-Vache, a low, wooded island about 8 miles long and 2 to 3 miles wide, which lies about 6 miles offshore and approximately the same distance eastward of Pointe l'Abacou. There are two entrance channels, one to the SW of the island and the other to the NE, both of which are wide and deep. The south channel carries depths of 5 to 20 fathoms to a point about 1 mile S of the town of Les Cayes, where you must keep clear of the clearly visible reefs shown on the large-scale charts. In approaching through the eastern channel, yachts should keep well clear of the fringing reefs and small cays that extend 3 miles N of the island. There is a lovely protected anchorage on the N shore of the island. The following harbors and small bays all have reasonably good anchorages, and some offer complete protection, with lovely beaches.

Les Cayes (26203)

is a small commercial port in the NE corner of the bay with depths of 2 to 4 fathoms in the inner anchorage off the town. Larger ships anchor outside in 4 to 10 fathoms. There is a small pier with about 6 feet at the outer end. The best yacht anchorage is NE of the pier, where partial protection is provided by Tourterelle Battery point and its fringing reef. Provisions and water are available in the town, but visiting boats report that fuel can be obtained only "tediously from the lightered drums." The town has air service three times a week to Port-au-Prince and Jacmel, and there is a small inn offering rooms and meals to travelers.

NE of the anchorage there are five deep, fingerlike bays, each of which offer all-weather protection in deep water. Jack Laird visited most of them in *Miss Apple Jack* (in 1969), and the Higmans passed this way in *Tormentor III* (in 1971), both reporting good gunkholing.

Baie de Saint Louis (26203)

is the largest and easternmost of the five finger openings off Aux Cayes Bay, with deep water right up to the head of the bay. The Lairds anchored here "in quiet water off a lovely beach near the town of Saint Louis. Here we had full protection in Hispaniola's lee from the NE winds of winter. . . . The whole area is loaded with beaches, the fishing is fine, and the weather and seas seemed to prove my contention that the southern route to Puerto Rico in the winter is much preferable to the northern one with rough seas on that coast." This may depend upon how much time you have to cruise in these small bays. Those who stand offshore also encounter rough seas on the south coast.

Continuing eastward from Baie de Saint Louis, two more bays open up behind a long chain of protecting islands, cays, and reefs.

Baies Anglais and d'Aquin (26203, 26206)

extend for 10 miles E and W, with many pretty little coves backed by mountains rising to heights of 1,200 to 2,400 feet and sheltered from the sea winds by the outlying reefs and isles, through which there are several deep channels. The best anchorages in Baie Anglais are at the NE end in the two coves behind Trompeuse

Cay, and N of Grosse Cay, largest and highest of the outlying isles at the eastern end of the chain. Baie d'Aquin lies NE of Grosse Cay and offers good protection in the fingerlike arm leading to the town of Aquin at its head. The water shoals rapidly off the town, with depths of less than 6 feet over sand and mud flats. Cargo vessels anchor out in the bay in 4 fathoms and are loaded by small lighters.

Baie de Jacmel (26206)

lies about 50 miles eastward of Aquin Bay, with no shelter on the bold and steep-to coast W of Cap Jacmel. The 100-fathom curve follows this section of the coast from one half mile to 3 miles offshore, and if you start early enough in the morning you can usually carry the offshore land breeze at least part of the way. In approaching Jacmel from the westward, your only sure landmark is the end of a mountain range that drops off precipitously back of the town to form a shoulder that can be seen from a great distance at sea. Cap Jacmel is a broad headland with an isolated rock standing 25 feet high at its southern end. The bay opens just eastward of the cape and is very deep, with soundings of more than 100 fathoms to within one half mile of the town of Jacmel at its head. An easily recognized landmark in the town is the cathedral, which has two red-topped steeples. Much of the town is built on a hillside; French architecture and flowering shrubs give it a Mediterranean atmosphere. Vessels entering the port usually anchor off the 335-foot commercial pier in 3 to 4 fathoms, within sight of the customshouse, or in shoaler water on the shore bank.

This was once a rich coffee area, but several severe hurricanes have damaged the crop and reduced coffee exports from the port. The Lairds had trouble fueling and taking on water at the pier (with hundreds of sightseers looking on, as usual), but they reported the drinking water was good. They met a local coffee exporter, Mr. Masden, who was most helpful.

If you are continuing to the Dominican Republic, be sure to get your clearance papers before leaving. Jacmel is about 48 miles from the Haitian-Dominican border at Pedernales, and you should plan to enter the Dominican Republic officially at Barahona or Calderas Bay.

DOMINICAN REPUBLIC, SOUTH COAST (26210, 25800, 25842, 25849)

From Pedernales, which is not a yacht stop, you will find fair protection as far as Cabo Falso. Approaching Cabo Beata, you can expect big seas and a funnel of wind (as is the case with capes everywhere), and when you get around this obstacle you will feel the full brunt of the trades—and then some, due to the air flowing in to fill the trough caused by the air masses rising over the mountainous peninsula. Your course from Cabo Beata will be generally dictated by the winds you happen to encounter, more than likely E or ESE, and we recommend making for Calderas Bay if you can, rather than becoming further embayed by coasting down to Barahona, which is the first available shelter along that stretch of coast. Calderas Bay is only about 20 miles farther, if you can lay a comfortable course for it.

Thence you will do best to make for Boca Chica (bypassing Santo Domingo) and on to La Romana, which is an area definitely worth lingering in before the hop across the Mona Passage.

Bear in mind that this is a coastal area in which you can take advantage of the land breezes from W and WNW to help you with your easting.

Bahía Agujas (26210)
affords excellent anchorage at the foot of the high cliffs that make out to Cabo Falso, and is to be preferred over the bay at Cabo Rojo, where there is a bauxite-loading plant.

From Agujas we recommend an early-morning departure in order to pass through the channel between Isla Beata and the cape before the trades reach their afternoon strength, since the 12-foot depths generate a heavy swell and you will have the wind dead on the nose. There is no shelter along the E side of the peninsula, and the current will be heading you, until you reach Barahona.

Barahona (25842)
is a port of entry and an important sugar port with the usual commercial aspects. Water, fuel, and provisions are available, and the customshouse is at the end of the 675-foot government pier. A fully protected and safe harbor for a yacht is inside the Sugar Company's area in the northern extension of the harbor.

Puerto Viejo de Azua (25845)
is an attractive little bay about 15 miles NE of Barahona, with good protection behind a narrow sandy island with a 60-foot bluff and a light at its eastern end. The channel between the island and the two low-lying points leads through deep water to several good anchorages in the lagoon. A dredged channel leads to a commercial pier at the NE end.

Bahía de las Calderas (25845)
affords excellent shelter, and the approach is easy even if you do not have the large-scale chart. Round Punta Calderas and head W of S toward the little village of Las Salinas in order to avoid the rocky patch on your port hand; the patch may or may not be buoyed (black). Keep out of the E end of the bay, which is reserved to the naval and air station.

Puerto Palenque (25842)
is a small port offering limited protection behind a low point and fringing reef. You will find a small pier with 4–8 feet alongside and several moorings in the harbor, such as it is. Although exposed to the SW and subject to some swell, it is the only shelter on this section of coast until Puerto de Haina.

Puerto de Haina (25848),

another large sugar port, really offers nothing for a yacht except protection under arduous conditions.

Santo Domingo (25848 Plan)

is a clean, modern city built on the rubble left after a devastating hurricane in 1930. But for this catastrophe, Santo Domingo would be a far more interesting relic of the era when it was an important way station for Spanish explorers on their way to Central and South America during the great gold rush. Sir Francis Drake burned this gracious city in 1586, another catastrophe. The first cathedral in the New World was started here in 1514, and still stands in most of its colonial glory, and the castle of Columbus's son, Don Diego, has been painstakingly restored.

Unfortunately, the harbor of Santo Domingo is one of the Caribbean's most unattractive places for a yacht. It lies at the mouth of a river of orange-brown mud cluttered with debris both natural and unnatural.

Boca Chica (25849),

on the other hand, sports the Club Nautico de Santo Domingo in a lovely bight of crystal-clear green water and white sand, thoroughly protected by an off-lying island and an awash reef. No wonder this was once the site of a beach villa belonging to one of the Trujillo clan.

The modern clubhouse and its bar, restaurant, pool, and manicured beach lie within a walled compound that protects this smart place from the drab, dusty village outside, with its hogs and chickens roaming the streets.

Local sport fishing boats occupy most of the slips. The shower and toilet rooms are immaculate, the fuel dock will take 6-foot draft, and the club operates a 20-ton travel lift.

This attractive place is called Puerto de Andrés on the chart. You can pinpoint it from seaward by the stacks of a large sugar mill a couple of miles E of the airport. Proceed boldly past the commercial quay in the top right corner of the plan in 25849 and do not be concerned that the chart soundings end some 400 yards short of the yacht club dock; the channel will carry better than 15 feet, though you must avoid the obvious shallow bar on your port hand.

This is a fancy club, and it quite properly goes through the formality of issuing temporary memberships to members of other yacht clubs. If you are able to do so, make your arrangements in advance.

Boca Chica is about 18 miles from the capital, via a beautiful landscaped superhighway.

San Pedro de Macorís (25849)

is an active sugar port; we saw three large freighters loading thousands of bags of sugar while we were there. The town is rather dry and dusty, with an impressive church dominating a plaza, as one would expect in a little Spanish town. Donkey carts and even horse-drawn buggies clop through the streets. Along the boulevard fronting the water and just E of the E breakwater is an attractive hotel called the Macorix.

One might be tempted to avoid this commercial harbor, yet it is attractive in an Old World way, and spacious and easy to enter. Anchorage may be taken wherever the spirit wills, but we suggest the indent just N of Ellen Point or the area just beyond the second wharf and the customshouse. You may land a dinghy at either place; the farther in you go, the less chance of any swell.

Cumayasa River (25849)

is said to be navigable by yachts for at least one fourth mile from its mouth. The river is enclosed by rocky cliffs 10–15 feet high, but there are a couple of sandy beachlets for landing a dinghy. In the very heart of the sugarcane plains, this place is wild and pretty, and the water is very clear, for a river. You'll feel a surge, since the rocky walls set up a perpetual ricocheting effect.

Isla Catalina (25849),

just W of La Romana, offers a good lee on its NW side.

La Romana (25849)

is two worlds in one: the seat of a vast cane and cattle operation by Gulf & Western Americas Corporation, and a mini-Riviera growing up, under the aegis of G & W, along a shoreline of clean white sand and rustling palms.

Since the economy of most West Indian islands was, and in some cases still is, so dependent on the cultivation of sugarcane, perhaps a capsule history of sugar will be instructive here.

Sugar (sucrose) is a chemical found in all plant life, but is commercially derived only from sugarcane in tropical climates and from sugar beets in more temperate zones. (It was the discovery of the value of sugar beets that, for a time, ruined the cane industry in the Caribbean.) Sugarcane is said to have originated in the South Pacific 8,000 years ago, but there was no historical reference to it until 325 B.C., when one of Alexander the Great's officers in India described its qualities.

Sugar was unknown in Europe until the eleventh century. By the Middle Ages, it had become a luxury available only to the nobility. More than just a sweetener of food and drink, it was claimed to have miraculous curative powers. Cultivated by the Portuguese in Madeira and later in Brazil, it was eventually imported into the Caribbean, where the climate was ideal. Cane-cutting by hand, said still to be the most effective way to harvest, has since become the source of income for thousands upon thousands of native laborers. G & W at La Romana alone employs almost 14,000 workers in the cane fields.

As might be expected, the most conspicuous landmarks along this low coast are the stacks of the sugar mills spewing smoke by day and alight at night. La Romana is thus visible for 20 miles or more at sea.

LA ROMANA

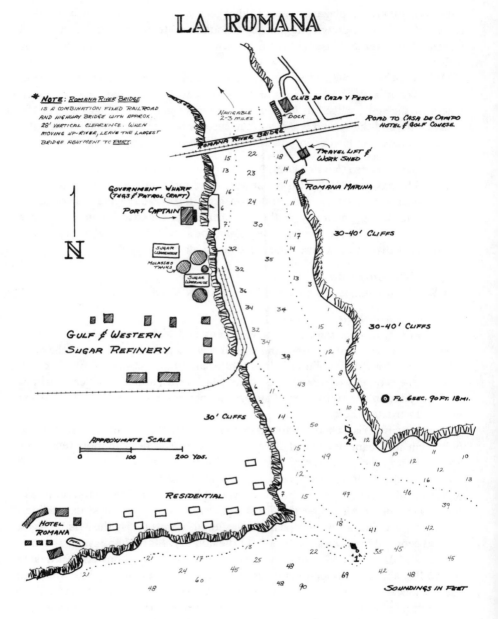

NOTE: ROMANA RIVER BRIDGE IS A COMBINATION FIXED RAILROAD AND HIGHWAY BRIDGE WITH APPROX. 28' VERTICAL CLEARANCE. WHEN MOVING UP-RIVER, LEAVE THE LARGEST BRIDGE ABUTMENT TO PORT.

NAVIGABLE 2-3 MILES

CLUB DE CAZA Y PESCA

DOCK

ROAD TO CASA DE CAMPO HOTEL & GOLF COURSE

ROMANA RIVER BRIDGE

TRAVEL LIFT & WORK SHED

GOVERNMENT WHARF (TUGS & PATROL CRAFT)

PORT CAPTAIN

ROMANA MARINA

SUGAR WAREHOUSE

MOLASSES TANKS

SUGAR WAREHOUSE

30-40' CLIFFS

N

GULF & WESTERN SUGAR REFINERY

30-40' CLIFFS

FL. 6 SEC. 90 FT. 18 MI.

30' CLIFFS

APPROXIMATE SCALE

0   100   200 YDS.

RESIDENTIAL

HOTEL ROMANA

POOL

SOUNDINGS IN FEET

The Río Romana, on which the mill and the town are situated, is only 150 yards wide, where its surprisingly clear waters spill into the sea between steep cliffs 30–40 feet high. Only 3 cables inside this fjordlike entrance, where the water runs deep to each shoreline, are the big ship wharf to port and the Romana Marina to starboard, just before the fixed bridge.

Yachts are moored Med fashion, with their own anchors in the good holding ground, to a narrow wooden walkway built out from the base of the cliff. This marina, which is part of G & W's hotel operation, is equipped with water and 110V–220V power, but there is no clubhouse. Adjacent is a slipway with a travel lift accommodating 50 feet and 30 tons.

After you pass under the combination railway-highway bridge (said to have 28 feet clearance, but don't be too sure), the river may be navigated 2–3 miles farther.

Immediately beyond the bridge, on the same side as the hotel marina, is the private Club de Caza y Pesca, where 6 or 8 sportfishing boats are usually moored stern-to. This club sponsors a tournament each year that draws fishing enthusiasts from Puerto Rico, Florida, Jamaica, and sometimes as far as Venezuela. The hunting *(caza)* aspect of the club refers to the shooting of pigeons, which are prolific in the wild country to the SE. When passing upriver under the bridge, leave the solid and most substantial bridge pier to port.

At either marina, if you are obliged to moor crosswise to the channel, as most boats are, you will have to live with some roll from the swell.

The prospect of mooring in a rather narrow river mouth near a town and a sugar factory may induce some negative thoughts about La Romana, but do not be misled. The town itself is cleaner than most, the residential area near the mill where the managerial people live is prim and pleasant, and all the smoke from the mill blows off to leeward. The Romana Hotel, which actually fronts on the high mill building, was formerly a hostelry for visiting technicians and other businessmen, but has now been turned into a tasteful resort hotel with all the amenities and a cliffside view of the sea.

The mini-Riviera we mentioned is developing along the coast W of the river. A posh hotel of weathered wood, elegant planting in and all around it, is called Casa de Campo and is well worth a visit, if only to see the exciting horticulture. Beyond are condominium clusters with a definitely Spanish Mediterranean look, while farther along the hillside are a small airstrip, a well-kept golf course, and a swimming beach.

Minitas Beach (25849),

less than 3 miles E of La Romana, is a resort beach maintained by G & W, where good shelter will be found in the lee of Punta Minas (as it is named on the chart) in 8 feet or more. Sweep wide around the point if entering from the SE to avoid some rather inconspicuous rocky ledges. As the sketch shows, there are lines of reefs just off the beach, so do not move in too close.

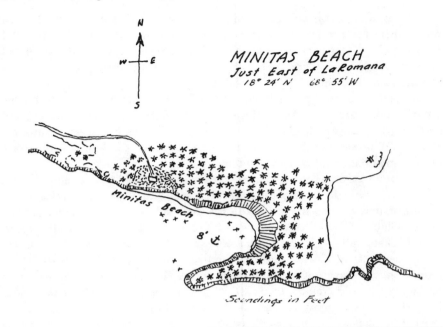

MINITAS BEACH
Just East of La Romana
18° 24' N   68° 55' W

Minitas Beach

8'

Soundings in Feet

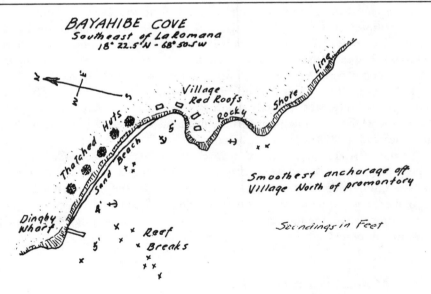

BAYAHIBE COVE
Southeast of La Romana
18° 22.5' N - 68° 50.5 W

Village
Red Roofs

Rocky   Shore   Line

Thatched Huts

5'

Sand Beach

4'

Smoothest anchorage off
Village North of promontory

Dingby
Wharf

5'

Reef
Breaks

Soundings in Feet

Bayahibe (25849)

is an idyllic spot. Its curving white beach and ubiquitous palms are proof positive that you don't have to cruise all the way to the South Seas to find such beauty. Constantly breaking, the few reef areas that encumber the bay are easily detected.

The calmest anchorage is off a tiny fishing village with red-roofed houses in the cove just N of the small, rocky promontory. Sound your way in over the gradually shoaling sandy bottom. At the NW end of the beach is the bathing area for Romana Hotel guests, who are ferried here in small launches and landed at the small pier at the farthest end of the bay.

Isla Saona and Bahía Catalinita (25800)

provide a welcome place to stop and relax before or after the strenuous run across the Mona Passage. Just N of Punta Cacón is a quiet anchorage off a white sand beach, where some brightly painted buildings stand in a grove of coconut palms. The bottom is clear sand and good holding. Landing is not allowed on government-owned Isla Saona unless you have first obtained permission from the authorities in La Romana.

Sportfishing boats, with their relatively shallow draft, regularly pass inside Isla Saona en route to and from Puerto Rico. They avoid the clearly visible reef that makes out N from Punta Catuáno and pass into the open sea fairly close N of Punta Balajú. This is strictly eyeball piloting for drafts up to 3½ feet under reasonably smooth conditions—that is, as early in the morning as the light will permit. Later in the day, the sea conditions make this passage dangerous.

Anchorage may be taken just N and W of Las Calderas, where the water has a Bahama-like clarity, but deep-draft vessels will have to stay well offshore, as the bottom shoals very gradually. Fishermen living in the huts along this shore may have lobsters for sale.

The 30-mile peninsula between Isla Saona and La Romana is devoid of roads or of any access except by boat; it is almost as wild as it was in the days of Columbus, decidedly scenic, and quite sheltered from the trades. We think you'll enjoy it, as we did.

Chapter Seven

PUERTO RICO AND VIEQUES SOUND

MONA PASSAGE AND THE SOUTH COAST

The prevailing winds flowing around Puerto Rico are northeast in the winter, becoming more nearly easterly during the summer, when the Bermuda High has shifted more to the north. This wind pattern *should* produce a lee under the south coast of the island, but unfortunately the daytime wind tends to "draw" in toward the coast. The result is that you have southeasterly winds all along this coast, usually of considerable strength in the afternoon. This condition reverses itself at night, and once again we wish to emphasize the strategy of making your easting during the night and into the forenoon, in order to take advantage of the nocturnal flow of cooled air off the land. The temperature of the land cools in relation to the sea; the air mass over the land drops; this in turn forces the night air out to sea. This reversing flow pattern is a daily performance along the coasts of the large islands.

The wind that has been split and deflected by the island mass must naturally unite again. So must the wave actions that have been generated during the split, and it is this confluence of sea and swell that makes the Mona Passage such a rough body of water. For example, our log of one eastbound passage says, "Sea running 6–7 feet, but only 12–15 knot breeze." The convergence of the currents flowing along each side of Puerto Rico may also have something to do with the turbulence, but a study of the various *Sailing Directions* and pilot charts will leave you completely baffled as to what the currents may be doing to you at any particular time. The pilot charts show a current set to the northwest from January through March, and southwest or indefinite during the rest of the year; the *Sailing Directions* speak of a general set to the northwest all year long. They further confound their observations by mention of tidal currents that flood SSW for nine hours and ebb NNE for three hours. However, all these variable currents are usually within the one-half-to-1-knot range and are not likely to seriously affect your reckoning.

On the other hand, there are strong local currents indicated across the bank that stands out about 22 miles from Cape Engaño. It is not by any means a shallow bank, but it does drop off sharply from 35 to over 150 fathoms, and this abrupt change in the sea bottom seems to rile the surface to the extent that, coming from the north coast of Hispaniola, you had best make a dogleg in your course toward Isla Desecheo.

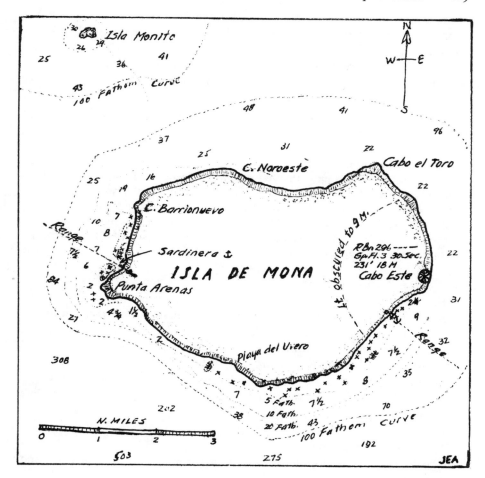

Mona Island

This island, incidentally, makes a beautiful mark for crossing the Mona Passage, since it rises to a 715-foot peak and can be seen for almost 30 miles. Desolate and steep-sided, it lacks any landing places or even a respectable lee, and is literally fit for the birds, whose habitat it is. As if to drive us off with their threat of droppings, some of the outriders from this forest reserve and bird sanctuary picked us up long before we reached their aerie and swooped and banked around our bridge long after we had passed.

Mona Island (25671)

Frequently visited by sportfishing boats running between Puerto Rico and Isla Saona, this wild island offers two reef anchorages for yachts of modest draft.

Mona is now operated as a commonwealth forest preserve; the only inhabitants besides the wild pigs and iguanas are a couple of wardens headquartered at Punta Arenas.

Fascinating caves riddle the island, once the dank and dripping lairs of pirates who used this strategic island as a base from which to waylay shipping that regularly used this important exit from the Caribbean. It has even been said that one could crawl the whole width of Mona underground! Of the largest of the caves near the western anchorage, Ginnie Higman of *Tormentor III* tells us:

> It's on the left-hand side of the road going up to the airstrip, about two blocks beyond the primitive camp at the west anchorage. There's a vaguely marked trail, and it's only about 200 feet from the road at the bottom of a climbable cliff and in a dense grove of coconuts. It was a legitimate cave with stalactites and stalagmites glistening in the glow of our flashlight. We quit when we were forced into the crawling stage. We found other caves, used by fair-sized iguanas for their homes, immediately above our anchorage.

Sardinero Anchorage

at the W end is the most secure place to lie in normal weather, but would be untenable in northerly blows. These are frequent from November through February and bring in huge, breaking swells right across the entrance. Come in on a rather inconspicuous range, which consists of a front marker on the pier head and a rear marker on the land just behind. The opening in the reef is not more than 10 yards wide and will carry about 8 feet with good-holding bottom inside.

There's good snorkeling, crayfishing, and spelunking here, but get away fast if a northerly swell develops.

Playa del Uvero

may be approached as close in as your draft permits, but this is an open and emergency anchorage useful only if you are overtaken by northerly winds.

East Anchorage

is entered through the reef on range markers about 1 mile SW of the lighthouse. The Higmans made it in here with their 6-foot-draft ketch, *Tormentor III*, bounced around all night, and advise that the holding is poor.

Mayagüez to Ponce (25671, I-A11)

Lying under the impressive Montañas de Uroyan, which rise to 2,000 feet and more, this end of Puerto Rico provides a perfect lee most of the time, with possible hurricane shelters at Puerto Real (shallow-draft boats) or the channel into the mangroves at Boquerón should the need arise. Here you are back in U.S. waters, where there are buoys to occupy your attention again.

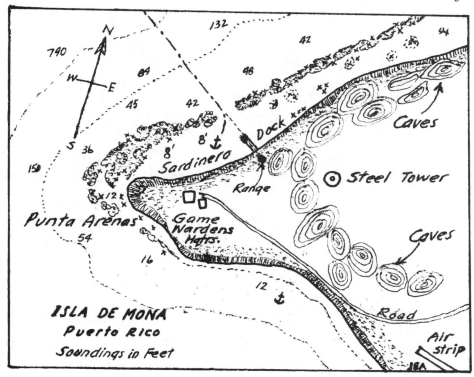

Sardinero anchorage

Mayagüez (25673, I-A11)

is really no place for a yacht to tarry, because of its commercial aspect, unattractive beachfront, and swell from the northwest during the winter months. However, it is one place you can stop for customs and immigration. San Juan, Ponce, and Fajardo are the others. If you are a U.S. boat coming directly from a U.S. port, you will not need to check in. Because of their free port status, you must check in if you are coming directly from the U.S. Virgin Islands. It is acceptable to continue on to Boquerón, where there is a good anchorage, and go to Mayagüez by *publico* should you wish to see customs and immigration; you may call the officials from Boquerón if you do not need to have paperwork processed. For example, you must go see the officials if you want exit papers to show officials in another country.

If the weather is good and you are not put off by the commercial aspects of the harbor and the difficulty of tying up at a large commercial dock, you can certainly do this at Mayagüez. The customs office is about a mile from the waterfront.

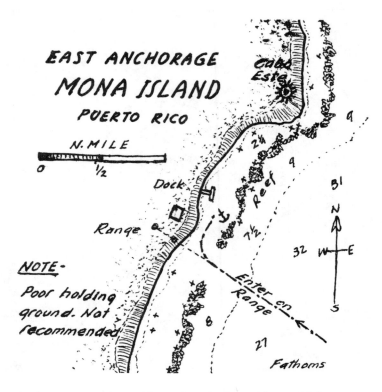

The trip from Boquerón to Mayagüez by the *publico,* which you must do in two hops, Boquerón to Cabo Rojo and Cabo Rojo to Mayagüez, will occupy about an hour and should cost less than $5.

The Mayagüez Yacht Club is located at 18° 09.9′ N, and a private marina called Club Deportivo Oeste at 18° 06.2′ N.

Puerto Real (25671 I-A11)

is only 11 miles S of Mayagüez, and here you will avoid the persistent lazy swell. If your draft is as much as 5 ½ feet, you will probably drag through the muddy bottom. A fisherman's cooperative there will haul yachtsmen's boats for a reasonable fee, and you can do your own work if you wish. The tidal range around Puerto Rico is only about 1 foot, so you won't get much help from the tide getting into this small bay.

Bahía de Boquerón (25675 I-A11)

is simple to enter on either side of the reef that extends partway across the mouth. The southern entrance is marked with a lighted buoy. The best anchorage is between the yacht club dock and the cottages on the beach. You can tie your dinghy at the town dock and also dispose of your trash there. The yacht club docks are crowded with power boats, mostly of the type used for fishing, and the club is generally closed during the week. Water and fuel are available if you can get to the dock (depth 6 feet maximum at high tide) at a time when there is someone to help you.

Boquerón is a resort town, and most items of general use that you might need can be found here. Should you wish to indulge in a splash of the U.S. you left behind, take the *publico* first to Cabo Rojo and then to the Mayagüez Mall. You'll find such stores as Sears Roebuck and Radio Shack and an incredible group of familiar fast-food franchises.

At the southeast corner of the bay, there is a dredged channel into the mangroves. Facilities of the University of Puerto Rico and of the Puerto Rican marine police are sheltered here. We measured the channel depth at 10 feet, and the water outside the channel at about 3 feet. Pick up the first marker on a pole close to the beach and follow the channel around to port. It would be a very secure place in a storm.

Cabo Rojo

is a promontory with strikingly red cliffs. Like strategic capes everywhere, Cabo Rojo is likely to give you a pounding. We advise planning to round it as early as possible in the morning, since the seas will be running 5–8 feet on a normal afternoon.

La Parguera (25671)

is well protected by the outlying reefs. These in turn make the entrance somewhat tricky, at least for the first time. This place is popular with local small craft, and the emphasis here is on fish. It is famous, too, for the flamelike phosphorescence of the water in the little cove immediately N of Isla Matei, which you will want to inspect by dinghy.

On the E side, a group of buildings, including a prominent pink hotel, stands at the end of the charted road, and will be seen from seaward over the small cays that front La Parguera. Approach via the Pasa del Medio, leaving the Media Luna Reef to port and Turrumote II to starboard, whence you may steer either way around Cayo Enrique. Anchorage can be found in its lee or in the lee of the string of cayos to the NE. From Cayo Enrique, a buoyed channel leads through the reef to the small town. Alternately, after negotiating the Pasa del Medio, turn to the E, keeping Arrecife Enmedio to starboard, and anchor off the beach below the pink hotel at Punta Montalva.

Guanica (25679, I-A11, A12),

with its high shores, makes an excellent storm shelter, but there are no yacht facilities, and the two commercial facilities, one on the E shore and the other on the W arm of the bay, do not enhance the surroundings. In fact, they "muddy" the waters, and you'll see the water turn from blue to brown as you enter. The water shoals off Playa de Guánica, so sound your way in to the anchorage depth you prefer. Or turn to the W and enter the small bay. You may see a classic ketch anchored there, owned by a downeaster named Peter. He rowed out to greet us and offered us the use of his telephone and the opportunity to fill our water tanks at his barn-red house on the shore. He told us the villagers call him El Gringo Loco, but can a Maine man who spends his winters in balmy Puerto Rico be crazy?

Guayanilla (25681)

is strictly a port for the oil refinery and no place for a yacht except as a storm refuge. The entrance is well marked and lighted.

Ponce (25683, I-A12)

is Puerto Rico's number-two city, but might well be classed number one with yachtsmen because of the cool and pleasant situation of its yacht club and the exceptional hospitality of its members.

Situated on Cayo Gato, outside the main harbor, where the water is unpolluted, the view of sea, city, and mountains from the second story of the clubhouse is spectacular. Ponce Yacht and Fishing Club has fueling facilities, a 40-ton travel lift—which is, however, available to nonmembers only in an emergency, and limited transient dock space.

If you anchor in the basin, the club offers the use of its facilities (dinghy dockage, telephones, showers, swimming pool, tennis courts, and restaurant) free for the first 24 hours and charges a modest per-person fee daily thereafter. There is security at the gate, and, if you choose to rent a car and leave your boat and dinghy unattended for a day or more, you can do it here without concern.

If you will be staying for a few days, you may also wish to rent a car to travel to and from the city, a trip taking about 15 minutes. There is no public transportation, but taxis are reasonable. A large grocery store is within walking distance.

In addition to the main channel approach, a course from the W may be laid between Isla de Cardon, recognizable by its 46-foot light, and Las Hajitas, leaving R4 to starboard and proceeding directly to the yacht club.

There are two drawbacks to Ponce, though neither is enough to make you pass Ponce by. One is the odor of the fish processing plant, which may descend at night when the wind normally swings to the NE, and the other is the noisy gathering of people of all ages in the evening near the ferry dock. After dark, small stands selling food and drink are set up, and each vendor tries to draw attention to his stand by turning up the volume on his boom box. On a Friday night, the last loudspeaker was turned off at 3:00 A.M. On the theory that if you can't beat them, join them, we strolled over on Saturday night and joined the fun, sleeping soundly in spite of the noise when we returned to the boat, with the gathering still in full swing.

Ponce to Punta Tuna (25677, 25650, 25685, 25687, 25689, 25659, I-A12, A13)

This 42-mile run along an exposed coast can be made a little more comfortable, at least for 12 of those miles, by ducking inside some of the reefs and mangrove cays that line this shore. A glance at 25687 will suggest a number of anchoring possibilities N of the cays along the channel leading to Central Aguirre. There is good protection in pleasant, inland lakelike surroundings in the small bay at Playa de Salinas, where the shore is ringed with small marinas, restaurants, and homes. Protection from wind and waves, but not from mosquitoes and no-see-ums, can be had in a mangrove-surrounded anchorage indented into the shore N of Cayos de Barca. Still more protected anchorages can be found in Bahía de Jobos, E of Central Aguirre, itself a commercial port and not a good place for yachts. The narrow entrance to Bahía de Jobos is buoyed, and the shoals are easily seen. Inside, on the south shore, is the small Jobos Yacht Club, and a pier and restaurant occupy the NE corner at Puerto Jobos. You can anchor almost anywhere in this small bay in from 8 to 19 feet of water.

Continuing along this partly sheltered route, you can run inside Cayo Berberia. Pass either N of Cayos Cabezazos, Cayos de Caracoles and Cayos de Alfenique or S of them, depending on whether you wish to negotiate the narrow and shoaling channel between Cayos Cabezazos and Punta Petrona. In either case, proceed to the channel inside the Ratones and Barca Cays, and out through the dreadful-sounding but easily identified Boca del Infierno.

From here there is little protection, except where the route passes inside the Guayama Reef off Punta Figuras, and very close under Punta Tuna, to take advantage of the shelter of Sargent Reef. Upon rounding Punta Tuna, you will have virtually "turned the corner" of the island and can look forward to the smoother waters of Vieques Sound.

Isla Caja de Muertos (25683 or 25685, I-A12)
provides a lee for anchoring off its beautiful beaches. Drop the hook just W of the light or just inside the SW tip of the larger island. The island is under the jurisdiction of the Department of Natural Resources. A caretaker lives ashore and maintains the beach and picnic shelters. A ferry runs to the island, bringing visitors from Ponce to enjoy the good swimming and snorkeling.

Puerto Patillas (25677, I-A12)
is a suitable overnight anchorage in depths of 1 to 1 ½ fathoms, but expect a swell. There are some small beach-type facilities ashore.

THE NORTH COAST OF PUERTO RICO

Except for the large commercial harbor of San Juan, the 90-mile-long north coast has no fully protected bays or anchorages comparable to those on the south coast, and its ocean beaches are more exposed to the relentless northeast trades in winter. If you are coming in from the Bahamas or Hispaniola for a landfall at the northwest end of Puerto Rico, however, you will be far enough north to avoid the confusing tidal currents of Mona Passage mentioned above. From there, eastbound yachts may continue along the coast for 60 miles to San Juan, although this may be a long day's passage in the strong head winds one encounters from December through March.

If your approach is from the vicinity of Isla Desecheo, about 12 miles W of Punta Higuero at the westernmost tip of Puerto Rico, it may pay you to stand into Aguadilla Bay, which offers some protection in the prevailing easterly winds. The port has little to attract yachts, however; it is an open roadstead used by commercial vessels. The anchorage is exposed to winds from north and west.

Punta Borinquen to San Juan (25671, 25668, I-A14)

West of San Juan along this rather inhospitable coast the only indentations worth mentioning are the following.

Punta Sardina (25671)

is a small promontory about 7 miles E of Punta Borinquen, with a semiprotected sandy cove and boat landing where you can enter in calm weather. The anchorage is obviously unsafe in a norther and uncomfortable in the surge created by the winter trades. But the setting is attractive, with green hills rising several hundred feet to the town of Isabela, identified by a radio tower one half mile to the SW of the settlement.

Puerto Arecibo (25668)

is the only harbor of any consequence on this coast; it is a small commercial port about 26 miles E of Punta Borinquen and 33 miles W of San Juan, providing a stopping place halfway for vessels in transit. The harbor occupies a bight protected by Punta Morillos on the E side of the promontory and by a 1,200-foot breakwater extending from it toward the SW. A well-marked, dredged channel leads from deep water to a bulkhead wharf on the S side of the breakwater, where fuel and water can usually be obtained. A pipeline on the wharf is used by barges to supply liquid chemicals to storage tanks. Fishing vessels and small craft anchor S of the wharf. Don't anchor off the town of Arecibo, on the SW side of the bight, where the water shoals and is muddy near the mouths of the Río Grande and La Vega rivers. The best anchorage is in the shelter of the breakwater off Punta Morillos. There is a small, crowded, powerboat marina tucked into the Río Grande de Arecibo.

Punta Palmas Altas (25668)

is a low peninsula with tall palm trees and a sandy beach about 7½ miles E of Punta Morillos. A rocky reef extends W of Punta Palmas Altas, affording limited protection in easterly winds, but the tiny anchorage is exposed to the N and shoals to less than 1 fathom in places.

Punta Puerto Nuevo (25668)

is a rocky promontory about 9 miles E of Palmas Altas and 15 miles W of San Juan, where boats can enter in calm weather inside the rocky islets that extend almost a mile W of the point.

The coastline from here to San Juan is irregular, fringed in parts by reefs that extend one half mile or more offshore. U.S. *Coast Pilot* 5 shows a danger zone. There are artillery and small-arms ranges extending up to 10 miles seaward in the vicinity of Puerto Nuevo. There is seldom any military activity in this zone, however, and coastwise vessels regularly hold a course parallel to the coast between the 20- and 100-fathom lines.

San Juan (25670, 1-A14),

whose bay and harbor form the largest commercial port in Puerto Rico, is one of the best all-weather harbors in the entire Caribbean. The approach from sea is direct and well marked, leading close in under the ancient battlements of Morro Castle on the east side of the entrance, which connects with the high city wall that continues along the channel side of the Old City to La Fortaleza, now used as the governor's residence. San Juan Light sits atop Morro Castle 181 feet above the entrance, and the white marble dome of the capitol building provides a conspicuous landmark overlooking the sea about a mile east of the light.

There are several clearly marked channels leading off the entrance (or Bar Channel) to commercial piers and anchorages around the large Bay of San Juan. Cruise ships, as well as pleasure craft, turn E into San Antonio channel between Isla San Juan and Isla Grande, leaving the governor's palace and the Old City to port and the container-ship terminals on Isla Grande to starboard. Most yachts continue to the head of the San Antonio channel, hoping to find a temporary slip available at Club Náutico or the public marina nearby. The club is very hospitable to visiting yachtsmen and extends guest privileges to members of accredited yacht clubs, though it may be unable to provide a slip at its own limited dock facilities. The clubhouse, with its showers, bar, and fine dining rooms, is located at the SE end of Isla San Juan, close to the center of everything in old and new San Juan. Gas, diesel, water, and a 20-ton lift are under the charge of the club's capable dockmaster, who will help you call customs if you are entering here. If you have come direct from the continental United States, you won't have to clear, as this is a U.S. port; but if you are entering from the Bahamas, the Dominican Republic, or any foreign country, you should notify customs and immigration authorities as soon as you have docked. It is easier to phone them than to go to the customs-house when they are busy with commercial vessels and cruise ships, and the officials usually prefer to clear yachts at the club or nearby marina in the harbor.

Should you be unable to get a slip at the club, try the marina just across the channel at the S end of the bridge, where a number of local boats and a few transient yachts are usually moored. Most marine supplies are available in San Juan, and several small shipyards can haul yachts and do major repair work. We found one of these yards at the SW end of Isla Grande, near the old navy airstrip, doing satisfactory maintenance and repair work on Coast Guard patrol boats and other small craft. The Coast Guard base is located on the N side of San Juan harbor at La Puntilla, near the customshouse, and its boating-safety personnel are well informed about conditions and marine facilities throughout Puerto Rican waters and eastward to the Virgin Islands. Many U.S. yachts bypass San Juan, but we have always found it a useful stopover for supplies, and the local yachtsmen could not be more friendly and helpful.

On an islet, separated from the city proper, is Old San Juan, now protected against the depredations of modern architecture and gradually being restored to its sixteenth-century Spanish glory. This historic area is not far from the yacht club by bus or taxi and is well worth a visit if you are tarrying more than a day or so in the harbor. We particularly recommend a walk through the moss-covered old fortress, El Morro, and the marble palace that houses the capitol of Puerto Rico, facing westward across the blue Atlantic.

San Juan to the East End of Puerto Rico (25668, 25650, I-A14)

The 30 miles of coastline between San Juan harbor and the northeast end of Puerto Rico is fringed by a long line of reefs and rocky heads. They prevent easy access to a succession of small coves and sandy, palm-lined beaches that look inviting from seaward but should not be approached without local knowledge. There is no harbor on this section of the coast. The only facilities are a yacht club and marina, available only to small powerboats, located in a lagoon W of Punta Congrejos, near the San Juan International Airport, and entered only through a shallow inlet crossed by a bridge with 15-foot clearance—obviously no place for sailboats and larger cruisers.

Vessels making this 30-mile coastwise passage should keep well clear of the fringing reefs and rocks, as tidal currents set onshore; but you will clear all dangers by staying 2 miles or more off the coast. In periods of calm weather, this is an easy run for both sailing yachts and cruising powerboats, but during winter months, it can be a long, hard beat to windward, particularly when heavy Atlantic swells are rolling in from the northward to encounter fresh northeast trades in the shoaling waters of Puerto Rico's continental shelf. Under such conditions, it's wise to allow ample time for this long upwind passage, standing far enough offshore, if necessary, to avoid the steep confused seas that often build up off the fringing reefs. More often than not, you'll find it takes longer than you counted on to clear the rocky headland of Cabo San Juan at the northeast end of the island. Under sail, it is a good plan to leave San Juan harbor soon enough in the morning to reach Fajardo Roads by early afternoon, giving you time to explore a choice of harbors on the east coast or nearby in Vieques Sound.

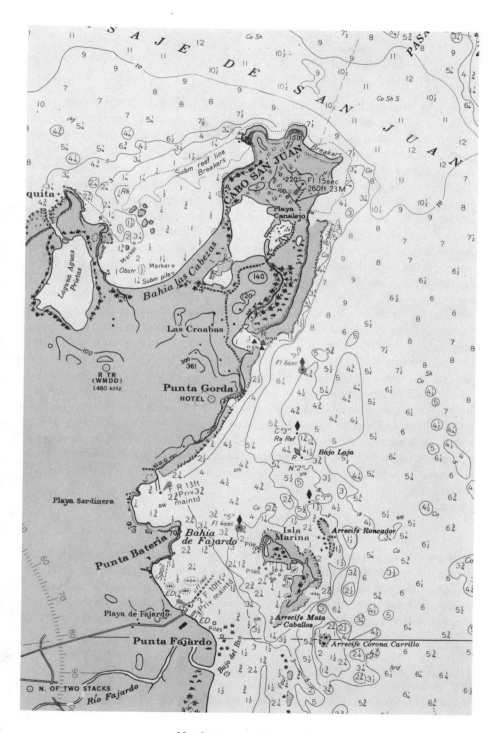

Northeast end of Puerto Rico

THE EAST COAST AND VIEQUES SOUND (25663, I-A14)

Except for cruising boats in transit between San Juan and Saint Thomas, relatively few visiting yachts know much about the east coast of Puerto Rico or the numerous coves and harbors in the chain of islands, rocks, and cays that extend eastward toward Culebra and the Virgin Islands. Yet this area offers a variety of sharply contrasting cruising grounds, ranging from the unspoiled beaches of Culebra and Vieques to the sophisticated resort hotels and condominiums that are rapidly transforming the eastern end of the Puerto Rican mainland.

The 10 miles of scenic coastline between Cabo San Juan and Punta Puerca, just north of the sprawling U.S. naval base at Roosevelt Roads, has been transformed from a remote rural farming and fishing area to a water-oriented residential and resort region, with housing developments, high-rise condominiums, and large resort hotels. Along with this economic growth, the east coast is becoming the leading yachting center of Puerto Rico; new marinas and boatyards provide literally hundreds of slips for the fast-growing fleets of yachts that now berth permanently at this end of the island. It includes all types of pleasure craft, from large power cruisers to sportfishermen, from big ocean-racing sailboats to tiny catamarans that stage their own annual offshore race to Culebra. Although new boating facilities seem to be keeping pace with the increasing boat population, visiting yachts may find it difficult to locate a vacant slip. However, most of the harbors or marinas mentioned below make some provision for transient yachts.

The E coast of Puerto Rico was in the direct path of Hurricane Hugo, which struck in September 1989, shortly after we visited that area for the purpose of updating this guide. Although most major facilities will be rebuilt, it is impossible to predict how much of the damage will have been repaired at the time of your visit.

Las Croabas (25667, I-A14)
is an old fishing village about a mile SSW of the lighthouse atop Cabo San Juan. Its tiny harbor is very crowded with local boats. The government established a school at the marina there to teach the marine trades to young Puerto Ricans, and has handed it over to be used as a commercial facility. Boats with a maximum draft of 6 feet can be hauled, and you can do your own work if you prefer.

El Conquistador Marina (25667, I-A14)
is in a man-made yacht basin less than half a mile S of Las Croabas. It was operated for several years in connection with the resort hotel on the hilltop above. But when the hotel closed in 1981, the marina fell into disuse. It may be operating again when you reach the area.

Marina Puerto Chico (25667, I-A14)

is another relatively modern facility, at the N end of Playa Sardinera, with fuel, water, and electricity available. Most of the slips are occupied by local power-boats.

Villa Marina (25667, I-A14)

is a yacht harbor and residential development that opened in 1975 on reclaimed land toward the S end of Playa Sardinera. A dredged channel entrance leads directly from Fajardo Roads into a landlocked basin with 218 slips for yachts up to 60 feet overall and 8 feet draft. All docks are of concrete construction.

Isleta Marina (25667, I-A14),

with its high-rise apartment buildings, is the oldest yacht facility in this area and is still preferred by those who enjoy lying to a mooring or anchoring in the shelter of the small cay half a mile off Fajardo beach, looking back toward the towering peak of El Yunque, the impressive and dominant rain forest mountain rising 3,500 feet above the coastal plain. One of the best boatyards in Puerto Rico is here, and its marine railway and repair facilities are in demand by yachts through-out the area. Fuel, water, and electricity are available, but slips are seldom open for transient boats except by advance arrangement. There is a regular launch service between Fajardo and Isleta Marina.

From Isleta Marina there is a protected passage south behind Cayo Ahogado and Isla de Ramos to the Passaje Medio Mundo in the lee of Isla Pineros. The passage is wider and deeper (10 feet least depth) than it appears on the chart and allows you to sail in scenic and sheltered waters.

Gaviota Marina (25667)

is the most recent marina facility to be opened on Puerto Rico's east coast. Located below the Gaviota Estates development, it is similar to Villa Marina.

Playa de Fajardo (25667)

is a port of entry for Puerto Rico used by commercial vessels from the Virgin Islands and other Caribbean or continental ports, but it is not a yacht harbor and not the best place to find an overnight anchorage. If you need provisions from the town of Fajardo, 1½ miles inland, leave your boat at Isleta Marina and take the launch to the Playa dock, where you can take a taxi or *publico* to town. There is daily ferry service between Fajardo and the islands of Culebra and Vieques, much used by local residents for transporting passengers, freight, and livestock.

Even though you may be an American vessel entering directly from the U.S. Virgins, you are required to clear customs in Puerto Rico. Although you are officially expected to enter here, it is recognized that dockage for yachts is inconvenient as well as a nuisance for all concerned at Playa de Fajardo; therefore you will probably be able to arrange for an agent to come over to Isleta Marina to inspect and clear your vessel there.

Roosevelt Roads (25666),

the large U.S. naval station at the SE end of Puerto Rico, preempts Ensenada Harbor, which lies within a restricted area and may be closed to civilian navigation during periods of military activity. However, the navy has a small yacht club at the NE end of the harbor, where active duty or retired military personnel and sponsored visitors will be made welcome when they present identification. After passing the navy docks in Ensenada Honda, continue to Buoy 13, from which you can see private yachts off the club. Pass yellow Buoy C to starboard before heading toward the docks. Check with the harbormaster concerning availability of a slip or mooring, or lie to your own anchor. Fuel, water, and supplies are available.

Palmas del Mar (25650)

seems finally on its way to becoming an international resort community with the tastefully contrived Old World elegance of Port Grimaud on the French Riviera or Porto Cervo on Sardinia, replete with picturesque villas on the hillsides and town houses on the water, a championship golf course, 20 tennis courts, boutiques, stables, and seven restaurants to tempt your appetite, all spread over 2,700 acres of rolling countryside under a backdrop of verdant mountains. The marina segment of this vast development is called Cala de Palmas and is only one of the five different "villages" that make up the complex.

The entrance lies in 18–04.6N, immediately S of Punta Fraile, and is marked by a tilted, rectangular concrete block with a light on it.

Severely battered during hurricanes David and Frederick in 1979, the breakwater has been partially repaired. Keep at least a half mile offshore until you have identified the tilted block, then come in on it on a 300°M heading, taking care to avoid the reefs N of the entrance. You may anchor in the outer harbor or tie up at the restaurant dock to port after entering the inner harbor. Contact the harbormaster at his office or on VHF Channel 16 or 68 concerning use of a slip. Fuel and water are available, and repairs can be made at the boatyard, on the port side as you enter the inner harbor.

Culebra and Adjacent Islands (25650, I-A131)

Some of the finest cruising waters in the eastern Caribbean are found in the area between Puerto Rico and the Virgin Islands known as Vieques Sound. These are U.S. territorial waters belonging to Puerto Rico, bounded on the north by a chain of small islets and rocky cays leading eastward for 20 miles to the populated island of Culebra, thence southward about 10 miles to Vieques, largest of the group, 18 miles long and extending east and west to within 6 miles of the Puerto Rican mainland just S of Roosevelt Roads.

One reason why this attractive cruising ground remained almost unknown to cruising yachtsmen for so many years was that until July 1, 1975, much of the

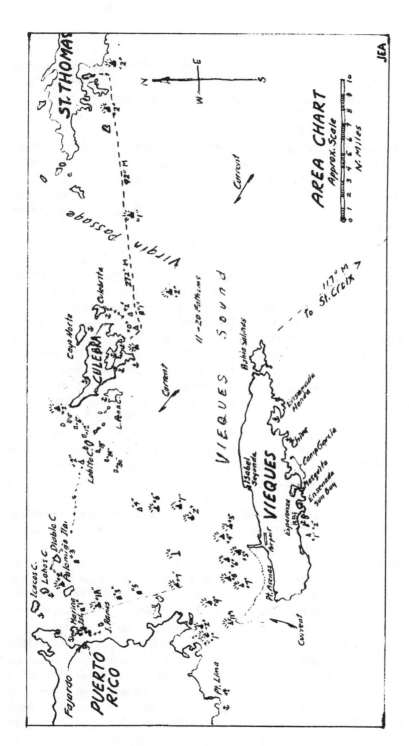

Vieques Sound

area had been designated a "danger zone," due to offshore gunnery, aircraft bombing practice, and unexploded ordnance around some of the islands. Your charts may still show an area northwest of Culebra as a danger zone.

Culebra Island (25655, 25653, 25654, I-A131)

is one of the most intriguing islands we have found anywhere in the Caribbean. It has a superb natural harbor, any number of fine anchorages, crescent beaches backed by palm groves and fronted by sheltering coral reefs. We based here for several months in *Brer Fox* and found the quiet anchorages a pleasant change from the overcrowded harbors in some parts of the Virgin Islands only 20 miles to the eastward.

The island is only about 7 miles long and 3 to 4 miles wide, but is surrounded by a score of smaller islets, cays, and rocks with their own fringing reefs and protected coves, which make the cruising area seem much larger. Now that the entire group of islands is safe from bombing and shelling, you could spend a week going from beach to beach for swimming, fishing, and snorkeling in unspoiled surroundings. The great harbor of Ensenada Honda is big enough and deep enough to moor a fleet of warships, which is undoubtedly why President Theodore Roosevelt chose it for a naval facility at the end of the Spanish-American War; but the station has been inactive for many years, and the shoreline of the bay is backed by peaceful hillsides where cattle graze on steep slopes that rise to the 650-foot summit of Monte Resaca, near the center of the island. The harbor is entered from the southern side of the island, on a NW heading through a narrow but well-marked channel that leads between two lines of exposed coral reefs, and then opens up into a mile-long bay, with depths of 30 to 40 feet almost to the town of Dewey at the NW end. Numerous smaller bays and coves lead off both sides of Ensenada Honda, providing snug anchorages under the protecting hills.

The town has a population of about 2,200 Spanish-speaking inhabitants and is a port of entry. The entire island is a municipality of Puerto Rico. The island people don't refer to the town as "Dewey"—the name shown on the charts—but call it Culebra; the mayor is not just mayor of the town but mayor of Culebra Island. His office is an imposing structure on the spur of a hill overlooking the two main harbors of Culebra. This building also houses the Department of Tourism. One of the harbors is located at the SW end of town, overlooking Bahía Sardinas, with a dock large enough to handle the Fajardo-Vieques ferries and interisland freight boats; the other is Ensenada Honda, on the eastern side of the closely built little town, and is connected with Bahía Sardinas by a small canal too shallow to allow passage for anything larger than an outboard. All yachts entering from the U.S. Virgin Islands are required to clear with customs, because the U.S. Virgin Islands are free ports. The customs office is a short walk from the town dock in Ensenada Honda, and the formalities here have been easier than at Fajardo or San Juan. Both harbors at Dewey have good holding ground,

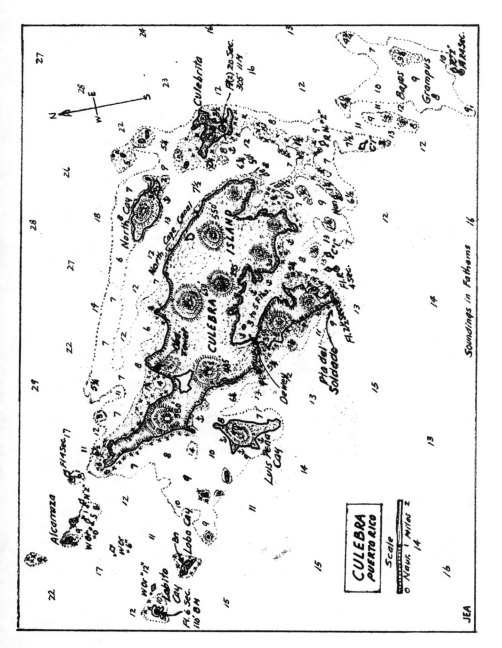

Culebra Island, between Puerto Rico and Saint Thomas

although there is sometimes a swell in Bahía Sardinas. If you are remaining at
Culebra for more than a day or so, you'll find a wide choice of all-weather
anchorages in the protected coves of Ensenada Honda and around the southeast
end of the island, where there is a lovely surge-free anchorage behind the reef
sheltering Puerto de Manglar. Other islands, islets, and reefs on the southern and
eastern sides of Culebra form a protected passage, with several sandy beaches and
sheltered daytime anchorages.

Culebra is not yet a resort island, and that has been one of its greatest charms—
you may enjoy cruising without elaborate shore facilities. When we were last
there, in 1989, there were no marinas, no supermarkets (but several small super-
ettes), and only one gas and diesel station, near the government dock on Bahía
Sardinas. The town boasts a number of small bars and guest houses. There is a
laundromat at Ricky's Garage at the ferry dock.

The canal connecting Bahía Sardinas and Ensenada Honda may have been
dredged to allow some development of marine facilities by the time you visit. A
well-stocked hardware store and a new marine supply store are already located
there. But a low bridge at one end and an overhead cable at the other end of the
canal will always limit the access to only low-profile vessels.

Culebra gets its water from a small desalination plant now, and water is in short
supply. Water will become available to visitors when the pipeline arrives from
Vieques, probably in 1989 or 1990.

Club Seabourne, on Fulladoso off Ensenada Honda, is a small resort that plans
to grow when the freshwater pipeline arrives. An expanded charter-boat operation is part of the future. Currently the inn's bar is a gathering place for thirsty
yachties at happy hour, and the restaurant has enjoyed a reputation as the best
on the island.

A small airport, walking distance from a dinghy landing, has both scheduled
and charter flights daily to San Juan, Vieques, Fajardo, and Saint Thomas.

Both harbors may be somewhat crowded with visiting yachts from the mainland of Puerto Rico on weekends or on gala occasions when Culebra is playing
host to the popular sportfishing tournaments or sailing regattas held in recent
years. Usually, however, the island and its harbors are quiet and peaceful spots.

Further information on anchorages in the islands around Culebra was available
in a regional cruising guide entitled *Westward from the Virgins,* by Raymond N.
Auger, which we list in the Bibliography, although it has been out of print for
some time.

Isla Culebrita (25653),

which lies half a mile E of Culebra, is a hilly, cone-shaped little island with a
lighthouse atop its 300-foot peak and a crescent beach fringed by reefs on its NW
peninsula. Once used as a navy bombing target, it is now a favorite weekend picnic
spot, with several good daytime anchorages but too exposed to the N for mooring
overnight.

Cayo Norte (25653),

off the NE coast of Culebra, is a privately owned island with steep cliffs rising from the sea, backed by wooded hills and fronted by a sandy beach on its S shore. There is a constant surge, and the anchorage off the SE end of the island is not recommended except in settled weather. It's best to have a local pilot on your first visit.

Cayo de Luis Peña (25655)

is the largest of a chain of islands and cays extending off the NW peninsula of Culebra and formerly was in the range of fire when gunnery exercises were in progress. There used to be a navy observation post at the top of the central peak, lighted at night. You'll find several daytime anchorages in semisheltered waters on the western side and in a sandy cove protected by coral reefs on the N coast. None of these anchorages is comfortable when swells are rolling in from the open Atlantic, and they become untenable in a norther.

Flamingo Beach, Culebra (25653),

has long been one of the favorite watering places of the Culebran islanders and their ancestors before them, and no description of the island could fail to mention the symbolic role it played in the long-lasting controversy between the navy and Puerto Rico over the issue of the live shelling that continued from the mid-1960s until 1975. The beach, called Flamenco in Spanish, is the most beautiful on the island and continued to be used by the islanders and Puerto Rican visitors when it was right on the edge of the target range. Now that bombing and gunnery practice has come to an end, visiting yachtsmen are discovering that the half-moon bay and its sparkling white-sand beach are among the finest in the Caribbean. It is only a little more than 1 ½ miles from town and a pleasant walk through the hillside pastures beyond the airstrip. Yachts may enter the bay from the N, but the approaches are lined by dangerous reefs, and there is usually a swell during the winter months, so it is no place to be caught in a norther. Best to visit it by land. An undeveloped national park is located adjacent to the beach, at Punta Molinas.

Isla Vieques (25650, 25664, I-A131)

Vieques is not only the largest of Puerto Rico's outlying islands but is actually larger than any of the U.S. or British Virgins except Saint Croix, which it resembles geographically. Vieques is 18 miles long and 3–4 miles wide, with rolling hills and pastures that have made it a principal cattle-producing area for Puerto Rico. The N coast is exposed to the NE trades and provides only one semiprotected harbor, at the port of Isabel Segunda, about 8 miles from the western end of the island and approximately 10 miles SW of Culebra across Vieques Sound. The S coast, on the other hand, is indented by a series of small bays and sheltered coves that offer a number of good anchorages in attractive rural surroundings. Much of the western end of the island and parts of the S coast have been restricted naval areas that may be closed to navigation during periods of navy and marine corps exercises, although access to some of the best harbors on the southern shore is generally available. Call the Navy Range on VHF Channel 16 when you are close enough to reach them to find out if firing is in progress and which areas are restricted. This information is also available in the local Notices to Mariners and may be posted at nearby facilities.

Isabel Segunda (25664)

is the largest town on the island, with regular ferry service to Fajardo and Culebra, and daily air service by two small airlines that also serve Culebra and Saint Thomas. Facilities for yachts are limited, and the anchorage off the town dock is exposed to more or less constant swells in winter. Fuel and water are available.

There are several restaurants within walking distance of the dock and the old town square, which dates back to Spanish colonial days.

Yachts rounding the western end of Vieques should keep well clear of the mile-long breakwater and munitions pier about halfway between Isabel Segunda and Punta Arenas at the westernmost end of the island, and don't cut corners too sharply in crossing the sand spit of Arenas Shoal, which extends more than 3 miles NW of the point. There are strong currents across this long shoal, with depths of less than 1 fathom in areas of shifting sand that are not shown on the charts. So use your sounder or lead line if you pass E of the flashing buoy at the W end of the spit.

Arenas Beach (25664)

is a public playground and beach right in the middle of the restricted naval area at the western end of the island. On weekends and holidays it's a popular spot for navy personnel from Roosevelt Roads and is used by islanders from Isabel Segunda and neighboring villages. The anchorage is exposed to a moderate swell but is safe enough for a daytime visit in settled weather.

Anchorages on the South Coast of Vieques (25650)

are seldom visited by cruising yachts, although there are any number of snug harbors and sheltered coves in the 10-mile coastal section between Esperanza at the west and Bahía Salina at the eastern end of the island. Here are a few that are worth a visit if you are cruising the area with time for gunkholing:

Puerto Real (25664)

is about 6 miles E of the western end of Vieques. A channel leads to the small resort town of Esperanza, identified from seaward by the radio tower, and from closer inshore by the pier used by local fishing boats. The pier is not a safe place for yachts, and the grassy bottom provides only fair holding ground. Use your depth finder when approaching the pier. Two small islands protect the anchorage from swells when the wind is in the SE.

Ensenada Sun Bay (25664)

with its crescent beach occupying most of the shoreline is truly beautiful, and you are likely to have the place to yourselves except on weekends. To the westward, at sunset, with waving palms on the low shore silhouetted against Monte Pirata, it seemed to us like a "Bali Hai" landscape.

We found 15 feet only 50 yards off the eastern shore, with enough surge to cause a slight roll following several days of light winds from south of east.

Puerto Mosquito (25664)

is a tight little hurricane hole about a mile east of Ensenada Sun Bay. It is justly famous for its phosphorescent waters, but its narrow entrance channel has a controlling depth of 3 feet that makes it inaccessible to most cruising yachts. It's worth exploring by dinghy from an anchorage just off the coral reef on the E side of the entrance.

Naval restrictions eastward from Puerto Mosquito hamper cruising or anchoring in other small bays until you reach the lighthouse at Punta Coneja, at the western entrance to another Ensenada Honda.

Puerto Ferro (25664)

can be identified from sea by the 56-foot light at the western side of the entrance. A narrow channel, deepest on the east side, leads into a snug, mangrove-surrounded bay.

Bahía de la Chiva (25650)

affords good anchorages off the beach on both the northeast corner of the bay and the northeast corner of Isla Chiva, which divides the bay. The easternmost anchorage, sheltered by an offshore shoal, is the quietest.

Ensenada Honda (25650)

is, as the name implies, the largest bay on Vieques, but it is exposed to SE winds and has several shoals and rocky reefs. There is a light on the western entrance on Punta Conejo, which is not readily seen from any distance. Bearings on the navy observation post on Cerro Matlas and on Punta Este helped us find the entrance. Favor the western side of the bay, and proceed slowly past Punta Carenero and the shoal southeast of it and you will be in deep water again. Enter while the light is still good, and you'll be able to eyeball your way in with no trouble. The water is not crystal clear, but there are lots of fish to see if you snorkel on the reef sheltering the bay to the south.

THE VIRGIN PASSAGE (25650)

Yachts bound eastward from Puerto Rico to the Virgin Islands can make the run through Vieques Sound in relatively protected waters under the lee of Culebra and its surrounding islets and reefs. Once they clear Culebrita, however, they encounter the north Atlantic swells, which tell them in no uncertain terms that they have reached the Virgin Island Passage. The distance between the eastern-most point of Culebrita and the western end of Saint Thomas at David Point is less than 12 nautical miles; another 6 miles takes you into the shelter of Saint Thomas Harbor. Depths in the Virgin Passage are not much greater than those in Vieques Sound, ranging generally from 15 to 25 fathoms, but wind and sea conditions may be totally different, when rollers from the open Atlantic pile up on the Virgin Bank to encounter steep cross-seas kicked up by the winter trades. So don't count on a fast upwind passage under sail, but plan your course to take advantage of the trades: pass close to Sail Rock if the winds are from the NE, or enter through Savana Passage when SE winds allow you to carry a northeast-erly course. It's usually a glorious 3-hour sleighride downwind from Saint Thomas to Culebra, but the eastbound passage may take 4 or 5 hours of wet slogging to windward.

Chapter Eight

THE VIRGIN ISLANDS

BY ALEXANDER C. FORBES

Updated by Robert Tonks

Between Puerto Rico and the Anegada Passage are the Virgin Islands, one of the world's most compact cruising areas. Lying in a 45-mile chain, the main islands are mostly mountainous, with a maze of passages between them, and indented every few miles by a tempting cove or bay. Only Saint Croix is separated from the chain—by a 40-mile stretch of truly open water. The Virgins are set in a region of constant summer. Their pattern of wind and weather is predictable. Yachtsmen find it hard to fault even the most extravagant descriptions of these islands. Swimming and snorkeling are superb, and the fishing matches the best in the world.

The Virgins are owned in part by the United States and in part by Great Britain. Under the American flag are Saint Thomas, Saint John, Saint Croix, and approximately 50 other intriguing islands and cays, many of which are uninhabited and ripe for exploring. The British Virgin Islands include Tortola, Virgin Gorda, Anegada, Jost Van Dyke, Peter Island, and about 23 smaller islands and cays. The demarcation line between the U.S. and British islands runs north to south: between Little Hans Lollik and Little Tobago, through The Narrows between Saint John and Great Thatch islands, around the eastern end of Saint John, and then through the Flanagan Passage between Flanagan and Pelican islands. All islands west of this boundary are U.S. possessions; all to the east are British.

In the U.S. Virgins, the major ports are Charlotte Amalie (rhymes with family) on Saint Thomas, and Christiansted on Saint Croix. Both do a booming tourist business, catering primarily to visitors from the continental United States. Both towns are amply endowed with mainland-style supermarkets and good restaurants and hotels. And they provide nearly all the usual yachtsmen's necessities.

Over the past 20 years, this business has overflowed into the British Virgins, resulting in expanded development and services there. The major British port is Roadtown, Tortola. Although she's not as sophisticated as her American sisters, Roadtown offers an ever-growing variety of rooms, restaurants, shops, pubs, and yacht-repair facilities. Marine supply inventories on the three main islands range from sparse to adequate.

Tides and currents are a problem in only a few places. The wind is usually constant, blowing from the east. During the winter, the trade winds usually come in slightly north of east and reach velocities of 18 to 22 knots, with gusts as high as 40. During the summer, they usually veer slightly south of east and decrease to 12 to 15 knots, occasionally gusting to 25 or 30.

The seas in Pillsbury Sound and Sir Francis Drake Channel seldom exceed 2 or 3 feet, except when affected by tidal streams. Away from the lee of the islands, however, the seas can build up to formidable size. The 40-mile southerly passage from the main group of the Virgins to isolated Saint Croix should be considered carefully; the passage can get quite uncomfortable when a fresh wind is blowing. So can the Virgin Passage and the Anegada Passage: none of these should be attempted in a blow by inexperienced sailors.

Customs and Immigration

In general, all vessels must clear and enter through U.S. Customs and Immigration when leaving and entering U.S. waters. This can be accomplished at Cruz Bay on Saint John, Charlotte Amalie on Saint Thomas, or Christiansted on Saint Croix, during normal working hours on weekdays and until noon on Saturdays. Although Coral Bay on Saint John is a port of entry, the part-time official may be hard to locate when needed. Clearing at any other times involves substantial overtime charges. American flag vessels need not clear customs when leaving U.S. waters provided there are no aliens or paying passengers aboard.

When entering and leaving British waters, all vessels are likewise required to clear, at West End or Roadtown on Tortola (the principal ports of entry), at Great Harbour on Jost Van Dyke, or at Spanish Town on Virgin Gorda at the airport. As of 1981 passports were required. If you are planning to spend only five days or less in the British Virgins, you may arrange to enter and clear simultaneously, at the discretion of the customs officer. This has become an accepted practice in recent years.

Radio

"Whiskey, Alpha, Hotel" (WAH), your friendly Saint Thomas marine operator with antennas and offices high atop Peter Mountain, offers more services on VHF than any Stateside station we have ever known. Now owned by Global Communications Corporation, they stand ready to handle messages between boats and the land in addition to the usual telephone link calls within the Virgins, or long distance calls anywhere.

WAH works Channels 25 and 28 from 0600 to 2200 daily and broadcasts traffic lists on even hours over Channel 28, odd hours over 25. In addition, weather forecasts are broadcast at 0800 and 2000, to which you are alerted on Channel 16. At 1700-feet elevation, WAH operators can of course hear many more sta-

THE VIRGIN ISLANDS

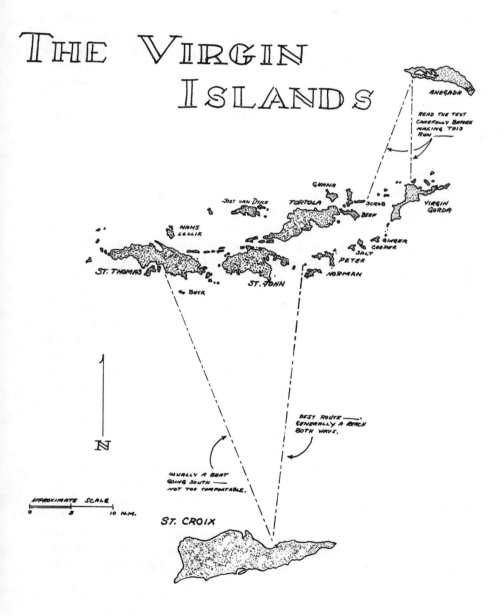

ANEGADA

READ THE TEXT
CAREFULLY BEFORE
MAKING THIS
RUN

GUANA

JOST VAN DYKE   TORTOLA

SCRUB

VIRGIN
GORDA

HANS
LOLLIK

REEF

GINGER
COOPER
SALT
PETER

ST. THOMAS   ST. JOHN   NORMAN

BUCK

N

BEST ROUTE —
GENERALLY A REACH
BOTH WAYS.

USUALLY A BEAT
GOING SOUTH —
NOT TOO COMFORTABLE.

APPROXIMATE SCALE
0   5   10 N.M.

ST. CROIX

tions than you can. If you have difficulty getting through on Channel 16, try 25 or 28, but listen well beforehand in order not to interfere with traffic that may be in progress.

For emergencies, the U.S. Coast Guard Auxiliary in Saint Croix stands by on Channel 16 from 0700 to 2200 and is very efficient and helpful, but they are not authorized to relay messages. You may also call U.S.C.G., San Juan, at any hour.

Tortola Radio, with its antenna likewise on the island's highest peak, monitors Channel 16 and handles traffic on Channel 27 at all hours of the day and night. The weather and their traffic list come on at 0900.

With this expansive VHF service available, you really have no need for SSB while in the Virgins.

Currents, Tides, Tidal Streams, and Rollers

The prevailing ocean current runs from east to west at one half to 1 knot throughout the islands. Its direction and velocity can be greatly affected by tidal streams and wind. The current usually increases slightly as the wind increases from the east, though only in isolated places does it ever exceed 1½ knots. Conversely, there are certain areas where the current is considerably lighter. For example, when sailing east along the southern coast of Saint Thomas, it helps to stay close to shore, since the current is considerably less and the seas easier there.

Tides in the Virgin Islands have been a source of confusion for years. The British *Pilot* states that the area experiences the standard two tides daily, while their charts mention a diurnal condition. The U.S. *Sailing Directions,* on the other hand, state that a diurnal condition prevails on the Caribbean side only and that a semidiurnal condition is found on the Atlantic side. Tide tables for the Virgins are based on San Juan, Puerto Rico, for the north side of the islands, and Galveston, Texas, for the south side. Needless to say, these tables are not too accurate. However, the standard rise and fall of the tide is only 10 to 16 inches, so there is not really much of a problem.

Tidal streams run in various directions throughout the islands, and they sometimes drastically affect both The strength and direction of the prevailing ocean current. The situation at The Narrows between Saint John and Tortola is a good example of this effect. When the tide is flooding (from north to south), a tidal stream funnels through Thatch Cut and runs directly across The Narrows. Turning eastward along the Saint John shoreline, this stream follows the contour of the island and finally flows into the Caribbean through the Flanagan Passage. During this period, a current in excess of 2 knots may be found close to the Saint John shore, while a light westerly current, or none at all, will be found along the Tortola shore. A yacht sailing eastward through The Narrows on a flood tide will certainly benefit by staying close to the Saint John shoreline, while one making a westbound passage would do well to hug the Tortola side.

Rollers are a formidable type of ground swell frequently experienced from

October to May. They may continue for three or four days at a time. These swells move in from the north after several days of light east to southeast winds. They may exceed 6 feet, and have been observed to break in 9 fathoms off the northern coast of Tortola. In some places near the western end of Anegada Island, where the bottom is composed of fine sand, the formation of banks is often changed by rollers. In winter, great care must be taken when anchoring in harbors exposed to the north. Several yachts have come to grief in recent years because their skippers either ignored this hazard or were unaware of it. We indicate in this chapter all anchorages that in our opinion could be subject to this danger.

Marine Supplies

The amazing growth of yachting in these islands has fostered the establishment of several marine supply stores. Shipyards and bareboat charter centers have also capitalized on the demand by opening small stores in conjunction with their maintenance and repair facilities. Ice and water are now generally available at all marinas and bareboat charter centers.

Fishing and Scuba Diving

The Virgin Islands offer some of the best game fishing in the world. Professional fishing guides and deep-sea fishing boats are available for charter in Saint Thomas, Saint Croix, and Tortola. The good fishing boats are booked well in advance of the season, so reservations need to be made early. Diving facilities in Red Hook, Christiansted, Roadtown, and Virgin Gorda offer instruction in scuba and snorkeling, and provide tours of wrecks and reefs in their respective areas.

CHARTS

In the heading for each port or anchorage we have listed the largest-scale U.S. chart available, issued by the Defense Mapping Agency and readily available at chandleries.

The prefix CK- refers to pertinent pages in *Chart-Kit,* a folio of all the U.S. charts of the Virgin Islands. *Chart-Kit** costs less than a set of government charts, from which it is derived, and is more convenient to use in a cockpit. In addition, it is replete with aerial photographs to give you an excellent preview of the places you are about to visit. In our opinion, you will be sufficiently equipped chartwise to have aboard the *Virgin Islands Chart-Kit* and DMA chart 25641, this last in

*Published by Better Boating Association, Inc., Box 407, Needham, MA 02194, 800-225-8317.

order to give you all the islands, except Anegada, on a single sheet. You might wish to supplement these with Imray-Iolaire Charts A23, A231, and A232.

Another helpful publication to supplement your charts is *Virgin Anchorages,* a book of aerial photos with, side by side, a black-and-white photo page marked to show recommended tracks and certain dangers that are not always apparent in the aerials. This useful book is published by The Moorings Ltd, of Road Harbour, Tortola, and is usually available wherever charts are dispensed.

Route Charts

These charts show the customary routes to and from favorite anchorages. All the anchorages shown are not necessarily safe for overnight. Check the text, as well as the larger-scale charts, for greater detail when choosing an anchorage.

Where there are two or three possible routes to a particular destination, the favored routes are those that lead through the most protected water. For instance, the preferred route from the main harbor in Saint Thomas to Roadtown, Tortola, under normal conditions would proceed along the coast of Saint Thomas, through Current Cut, then along the west coast of Saint John, leaving Johnson's Reef to port, through Fungi Passage (between Whistling Cay and Mary's Point, Saint John), then through The Narrows and up to Road Harbour. You may, if you wish, go up the south coast of Saint John when making this trip, but the going is likely to be more rugged because of the open water and the prevailing winds booming out of the east. If you want to cruise the south coast of Saint John in normal weather, you'll find it much more enjoyable to approach from the east on a broad reach or a run. If the wind happens to be blowing out of the north, as it sometimes does in winter, cruising along the south coast of Saint John will of course be quite comfortable in either direction.

The north coasts of Saint Thomas and Tortola offer very little protection and may become unsafe, or at least uncomfortable, during the winter whenever the winds are blowing from north or east, or when heavy rollers are coming in. However, both of these coasts offer pleasant cruising in periods of settled weather, especially during late spring and summer, when sea conditions are easier. A number of good daytime anchorages along these coasts are described in the following sections. Safe overnight anchorages are hard to find on the north side of either of the big islands, however, and Magen's Bay, on Saint Thomas, is the only harbor we can recommend for an overnight stopover. Even this harbor may become untenable in a northerly blow or when ground swells are running.

The most protected, and therefore the most popular, all-weather cruising areas are those in Pillsbury Sound and Sir Francis Drake Channel, where sheltered anchorages are seldom more than a few miles apart.

The U.S. Virgin Islands bore the brunt of Hurricane Hugo, which passed over the islands with winds in excess of 100 miles per hour in September of 1989.

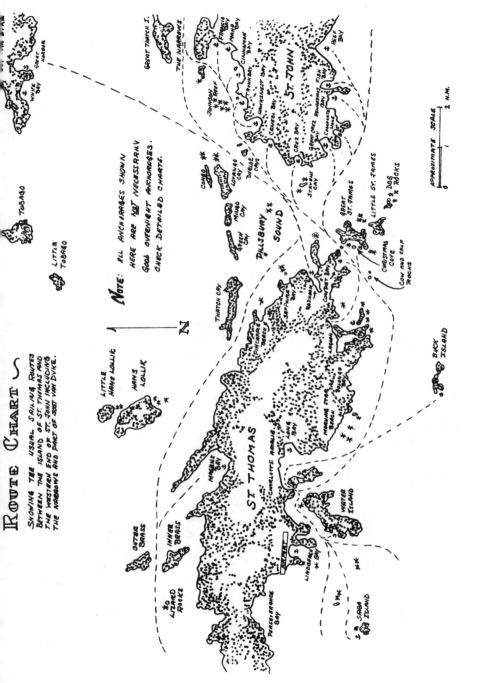

The western Virgins

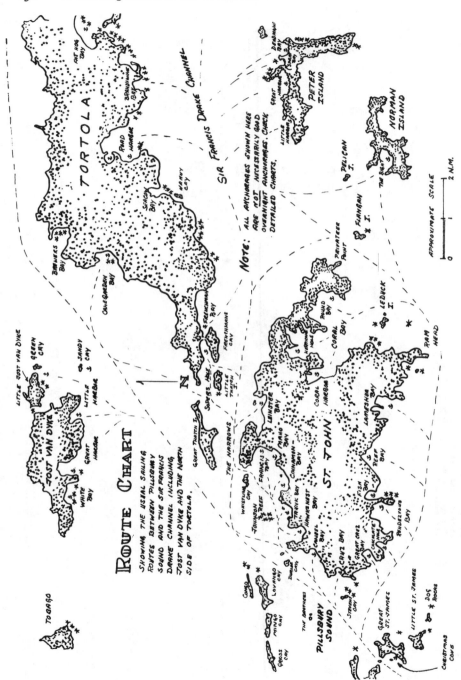

The central Virgins

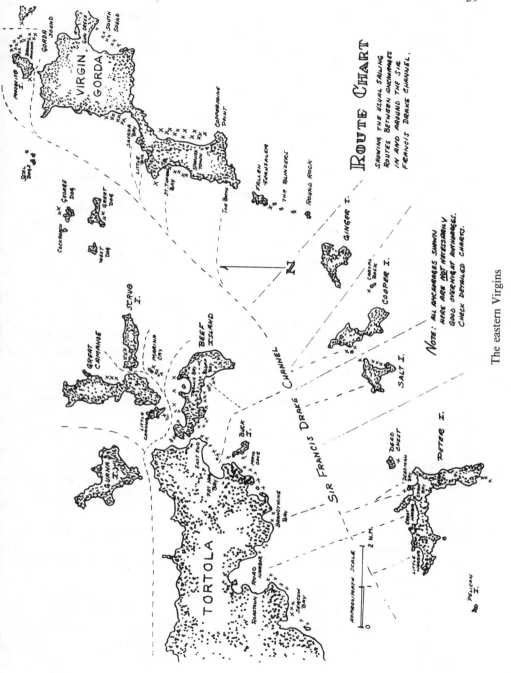

The eastern Virgins

Research for updating this text took place just prior to that storm, so be aware that facilities described here that were damaged by Hugo—or perhaps by subsequent violent weather systems—may or may not have been rebuilt at the time of your visit.

THE U.S. VIRGIN ISLANDS

St. Thomas

To sit contentedly on deck in Saint Thomas Harbor after a pleasant dinner ashore can be a beautiful experience, especially now that the harbor pollution has been somewhat cleaned up. The twinkling lights of Charlotte Amalie dot the steep surrounding hills, a cruise ship departs, the warm night breezes play on your face. The background of the Old World is omnipresent here, as it is everywhere in the Virgin Islands. Each European power that competed in the Caribbean has left its imprint in the islands' history, architecture, economy, and food. All are interwoven into the culture of the area.

Archaeological research has shown that Saint Thomas, as well as Saint John and Saint Croix, were inhabited by Arawak Indians for some centuries before Columbus. Although there is no mention of them in the earliest Danish records, pottery, arrowheads, stone implements, and weapons suggesting natives even earlier than the Arawaks have been found at Magen's Bay.

On his second voyage, in 1493, Columbus landed some men at the entrance to the Salt River on Saint Croix (which he named Santa Cruz), but they were unceremoniously driven off by hostile Indians who seemed not to recognize the historical importance of the event. Sailing north he promptly came upon a host of islands—so many that it seemed appropriate to name them after the legendary 11,000 Cornish virgins of Saint Ursula who died in Cologne while protecting their chastity from the evil Huns. For more than a century after Columbus this circle of islands was frequented by rapacious Spaniards and adventurous Englishmen. However, the Dutch seem to have established the first colony on Saint Thomas in 1657, but they soon gave up the effort and migrated to more fertile fields at New Amsterdam, now referred to as the Big Apple.

A Danish skipper, Erik Nielsen Schmidt, who had been trading with the Danes and other Europeans living on Saint Thomas, was granted permission by King Frederick III of Denmark to take control of the island as royal commandant and governor. Following the king's instructions, Schmidt brought with him a Lutheran minister, one Kjelt Jensen Slagelse. Together they sailed aboard the ship *Erik* and arrived at Saint Thomas around the first of January, 1666. Three months later, simply by hoisting the Danish flag and firing a salute, Governor Schmidt took possession of Saint Thomas. Thereupon, he selected a suitable hill, laid out house plots, and built a fortified tower, the site of which is now known as Bluebeard's Castle.

Interisland ferryboats like this one provide fast transportation between Saint Thomas and Saint John.

Another fort, built on a hill to the west, was known as Kjaer's Tower until the end of the seventeenth century, but is now known by a beard of another color, Blackbeard. Fort Christian was built in 1680 and had a luxurious room of gilded leather used by the governor. Other rooms were built for the use of the Lutheran and Dutch Reformed congregations. Fort Christian was rebuilt in 1870.

Governor Schmidt died just three months after the flag-raising ceremony, and Pastor Slagelse took over the conduct of the colony's affairs. The tiny settlement struggled to grow and increase its population, but the rigors of the life took a toll in European lives. Pastor Slagelse went back to Denmark and returned with settlers, soldiers, clerks, and 61 convicts in the *Fero* in 1671. This voyage took almost a year instead of the normal six months, and the pastor and 80 of the 128 people on board died and were buried at sea.

It was soon decided that the importation of Danish criminals was economically unsound, and the infamous slave trade began when the Danish West India Company settled in Saint Thomas. Slaves were brought to work the sugarcane fields as well as to be reshipped to other areas.

Under almost continuous Danish control until 1917, Saint Thomas prospered. Charlotte Amalie became a famous port, owing to liberal Danish trading laws. There is a long, but not too well documented, pirate history. Most of the buccaneers evidently preferred wealthier neighbors, such as those who lived in San Domingo, in Cuba, and along the Spanish Main. However, the pirates did use Saint Thomas's snug harbor to repair their vessels and sell their loot.

Beginning in 1865, the United States, which had felt the lack of a naval base in the Caribbean during the Civil War, made overtures to Denmark concerning purchase of the islands. Negotiations were carried on spasmodically over the years, but the fear that Germany might buy the islands finally brought action. The transfer, for $25 million, was completed in 1917, only two weeks after the U.S. entered World War I.

Saint Thomas Harbor (25649, CK-7, I-A231)

has two entrances. The main channel, deep enough for cruise ships, lies between Hassel Island and the eastern side of the harbor. The other, Haulover Cut, which is suitable for vessels drawing less than 10 feet, is a man-made passage between the NW end of Hassel Island and the westernmost corner of the harbor.

The approach to the main entrance is clear, although care must be taken to stay outside Triangle Reef, which lies SW of the entrance and is buoyed. Yachts may safely pass on either side of Rupert Rock, but not between the rock and the lighted buoy several hundred feet NW of it.

Of the two approaches to Haulover Cut, East Gregerie Channel, between Hassel and Water islands, is deep and free of hazards. West Gregerie Channel, between Water Island and the mainland, is also deep and unobstructed, except for a patch of coral heads extending from Sandy Point on the NW corner of Water Island to Sandy Point light buoy. These underwater heads are difficult to see. Pass W of Sandy Point, and stay in midchannel through Haulover Cut. At one time, a reef, with a marshy area behind it, connected Hassel Island to the mainland. In 1937, the government dredged the cut to promote a better circulation of water through the harbor.

Saint Thomas, the largest commercial harbor in the Virgin Islands, has several yacht anchorages. Long Bay has become the most congested anchorage in the Virgins, since most of the crewed charter fleet headquarters here, along with a colorful assortment of private yachts of every description. When anchoring here, give consideration to the numerous private moorings that infest the area; and stay well clear of the big-ship turning basin. The Ramada Yacht Haven and Marina is located at the head of this bay. With slips for 200 yachts, it offers all the usual marina facilities, including showers and a coin laundry.

The holding is good in midharbor, and you will have good protection under almost all conditions. Because of the high mountains, the wind can be changeable, so anchor carefully.

The bulkheaded area on the northern side of the harbor is known as "the waterfront." Commercial boats tie up here, and a few yachts moor stern-to. This is the least protected anchorage in the harbor, and if a heavy ground swell works in through the entrance, this place can become untenable. However, it's a convenient spot for taking on supplies in town, or for clearing through customs and immigration. The holding is good in mud.

Cay Bay, in the western corner of the harbor, adjacent to Haulover Cut, is the place where sailing ships used to dump their ballast before loading cargo. There's protection here for a limited number of yachts. Be sure to anchor clear of the channel, which is used by commercial traffic moving through the cut. Dick Avery's Boathouse, on the Frenchtown side, has facilities for visiting yachts. Holding is good in mud and the bay is generally smooth, except for the wash of passing commercial traffic.

The site of the old Prince Rupert Dockyard, on the eastern side of Hassel Island, has a limited anchoring basin. Holding is good in mud and conditions are calm unless a ground swell works through the main harbor entrance.

Two other facilities, within reach of Charlotte Amalie, are Shoreline Marine, where a few boats can Med-moor in water protected by a small rock jetty just west of Haulover Cut, and the Leeward Islands Sailing Center, on the NW side of Water Island.

Swimming is not recommended here or elsewhere in Saint Thomas Harbor, although the earlier sewage-pollution problem has been largely corrected.

Water Island, Western Side (25649, CK-7, I-A231)
provides protected anchorages in Ruyter and Elephant bays.

Honeymoon, or Druif, Bay is a lovely little anchorage, well away from the main harbor. The sandy beach at the head of the bay is used by residents of the island and guests at the Seacliff Hotel on the southern bluff. The usual anchorage is about 50 yards off this beach or off the swim buoys in 15 to 20 feet. Although a slight ground swell is sometimes experienced, the sea is usually calm and the protection good when the wind is out of the E. There is a small restaurant on the beach, and you can dinghy ashore to it for refreshments.

For snorkelers and divers, the wreck of an old iron steamship lies in about 10 feet of water just off the southern point of this bay.

Finally along this shore is Flamingo Bay, which has become quite popular of late. A dredged channel leads into the lagoon, where there is a small marina facility, part of the hotel. This channel has filled in to some extent, and in any case the lagoon is strictly for shallow-draft boats.

Lindbergh Bay (25649, CK-7, I-A231)
is a fairly satisfactory overnight anchorage and puts you in easy walking distance of the airport in case you are meeting someone.

Brewers Bay (BA2452, CK-1, I-A231)
is a popular weekend anchorage because of its fine beach. If you can tolerate the noise of aircraft coming in for a landing, anchor in 12 to 15 feet below the three-sectional building of the College of the Virgin Islands, staying well away from the end of the runway.

Cowpet Bay (25647, CK-8, I-A231)

is located on the eastern end of Saint Thomas, just S of Current Cut. You will recognize it by the private homes that spread across Deck Point and the garish condominium development at the head of the bay.

The Yacht Club of Saint Thomas is located here, and on weekends the area teems with boats. Three lines of moorings are rented to club members. Visiting yachtsmen from other recognized clubs can usually arrange to use the moorings by contacting the chairman of the house committee.

There are two beaches, one in front of the Yacht Club and the other just to the N. The swimming is good, though the water is not always clear, due to the influence of the current that runs through the cut. This current is primarily responsible for the rather uncomfortable ground swell that prevails most of the year. Otherwise, this is a safe overnight anchorage with good holding in deep sand.

When the wind is blowing decidedly N of E, a comfortable anchorage will be found in either of the two indentations along the northern side of the bay.

Christmas Cove, Great Saint James (25647, CK-8, I-A231),

is immediately S of Current Cut and opposite Cowpet Bay. Anchor either N or S of Fish Cay, keeping in mind that the lay of the boat is sometimes influenced by the wind blowing through the cut in the island. The approach to either anchorage is clear of dangers, but be careful of the reef area, which extends E and slightly N of Fish Cay. The protection is good in easterly winds and the holding excellent in sand. Swimming and snorkeling are superb.

Although the shoreline of the reef area appears desolate and rocky at low tide, closer observation will unfold a teeming intertidal community of marine life.

This anchorage is popular with charter boats based in Saint Thomas because it is the first or last stop when running to or from Saint Thomas.

Current Cut (25647, CK-8, I-A231)

derives its name from the strong tidal current in the passage between Saint Thomas and Great Saint James islands. As you approach the cut, determine the direction of the current by looking for the rip that is almost always present. The smooth-water side of the cut is the side from which the current is coming. The rip is formed *after* the current has passed through the cut. If you see no rip, you can assume the current is slack.

Of the two passages through the cut, the eastern passage (leaving Current Rock to the W) is favored by most commercial boats. There's a minimum of 23 feet through here, with ample room for two boats to pass. If you plan to sail through when the wind is E, or S of E, expect to be blanketed by Great Saint James just as you reach the narrowest part of the passage.

The western passage is neither as wide nor as deep as the other. At its shallow-

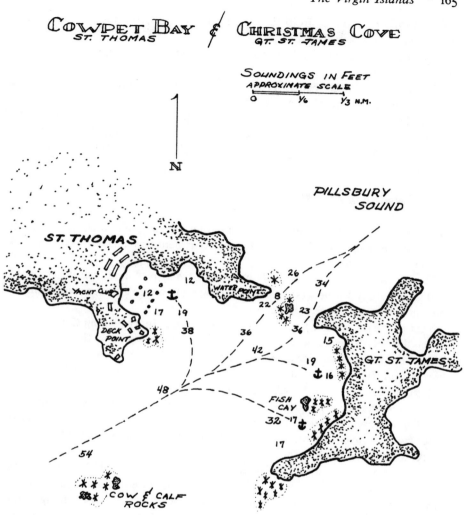

COWPET BAY & CHRISTMAS COVE
ST. THOMAS   GT. ST. JAMES

SOUNDINGS IN FEET
APPROXIMATE SCALE
0   ⅙   ⅓ N.M.

N

PILLSBURY SOUND

ST. THOMAS

est point, this channel has 8 feet, but stay in midchannel, because there are rocks and reefs on both sides. The current is less on the W side of Current Rock, and there is little or no blanketing effect from Great Saint James.

Pillsbury Sound (25647, CK-8, I-A231)
is generally clear of dangers, with only a few exceptions.

In the vicinity of Cabrita Point—the headland between Great Bay and Red-hook—stand well clear of the underwater rocks that extend from the point. It's wise to hold at least 100 yards off the point, for these rocks are just under the surface and practically impossible to see until you are on top of them. Then they seem to "jump" right up from the bottom. No wonder that the outermost rock is known as Jumping Rock.

Crossing the sound toward Cruz Bay, the recommended route is north around Steven Cay.

Pass inside of Shark Island off the NE coast of Saint Thomas if you wish. The Brothers are clearly marked and can be left close at hand. There are no hazards around Durloe Cays except for the obvious sandbanks extending from the shore, and the water is so clear that any rocks are easily seen. Between Durloe Cays and Saint John, the tide runs quite a bit stronger than between Durloe Cays and Lovango Cay.

Redhook (25647, CK-8, I-A231)

is located at the eastern end of Saint Thomas, just N of Cabrita Point. Ferries running between Saint Thomas and Saint John use the government dock, while the Caneel Bay ferry boats and the Park Department boats have their own dock on the S side of this bay.

To visit the park (which is really just a narrow strip of land fronting the bay), land your dinghy on the west side of the park dock, where a sunken wreck makes the water too shallow for the ferries.

Next to the government dock is the Saint Thomas Sport Fishing Center, know also as Piccola Marina, because there is a café of that name at the head of the dock. This is a full-service operation and an excellent source for sportfishing information. Just to the west are the five docks of American Yacht Harbor. The bottom shallows to 3 or 4 feet at the head of the bay.

Redhook has become a center for charterers and yacht services. It is possible to get most repairs made. Convenience-type groceries, drug-store items, hardware, videos, travel service, and ice cream are available at a small plaza across the road from the docks. There is no local laundromat or laundry service, but laundry can be picked up and delivered if you will be in Redhook a couple of days.

Although the protection is fair to good, a ground swell usually runs into the harbor, which can make living aboard rather uncomfortable. Swimming is not recommended because of the generally murky water. This is a convenient anchorage if you want to pick up passengers without going all the way back to Saint Thomas Harbor. Taxis can usually be found (at least during the day) for trips to town (about 30 minutes) or to the small shopping center and supermarket at Fort Milner (about 10 minutes).

Magen's Bay (25641, CK-1, I-A231)

on the N side of Saint Thomas has one of the island's loveliest beaches.

Approaching from the east, care must be taken to avoid Ornen Rock, lying one half mile NW of Picara Point, and also the rocks lying 30 yards NE of that point. Clear Picara Point by 100–150 yards and you will be clear of trouble. Then favor the northern side of the bay as you enter, but not too close because several reefs make out 50 to 100 yards from shore. The southern side of the bay is shoal. The best anchorage is about 100 yards from the beach in the eastern corner, where the holding is good in sand. A slight ground swell is usually present; otherwise, protection is good under most conditions, except in the winter, when rollers may make the anchorage untenable. It is not recommended as an overnight anchorage from October through May.

A restaurant of sorts dispenses hamburgers and beer during the day.

Saint John

Practically uninhabited until 1717, although under Danish sovereignty, Saint John suddenly felt the effect of the boom in sugar, and within 10 years most of the island was taken up with prosperous plantations—109 of them, to be exact. The population had risen to about 200 whites and over 1,000 slaves. A dry summer in 1733 reduced the food supply and caused much discontent, which, along with other harsh conditions, resulted in a bloody slave revolt that left most of the whites on the island dead, except those who were able to find refuge at the plantation at Caneel Bay.

The slaves roamed the island for five months. Then a force of 200 Frenchmen from Martinique arrived to help restore order on the island, but it never seemed the same after the massacre.

The abolition of slavery in 1848 brought a definite end to what little was left of the sugar economy of Saint John, and the island remained very sparsely populated and poverty stricken until Laurance S. Rockefeller began to buy up property.

Mr. Rockefeller has long been interested in the Virgin Islands, and his commercial operations (Rockresorts) there include Caneel Bay Plantation, on Saint John, and Little Dix Bay Hotel, with its associated yacht harbor, on Virgin Gorda. In 1956 Mr. Rockefeller gave over half of Saint John to the U.S. for use as a national park. The park area has been gradually expanded, and now more than two thirds of this heavily wooded island, with its mountain trails, sandy beaches, and wonderland of submerged reefs, is under the management of the Park Service and open for all to enjoy. The southwest corner of the island and some waterfront property on the west side of Coral Bay are privately owned and may be headed for aggressive development.

While you are in park waters, there are a number of regulations that must be observed; breaking these rules may bring heavy fines. National Park Rangers may at any time board any vessel to examine documents and licenses or simply to inspect the vessel.

Here are some of these regulations:

1. No damaging, breaking off, or removing any underwater growth or formation (coral, sea fans) or in any other way impairing the natural beauty of the underwater scene.

2. Anchors must not cause damage to underwater features.
3. No tampering with wrecks without a written permit from the Park Department.
4. No boat may anchor or maneuver within waters containing marked underwater trails.
5. No water skiing.
6. No rubbish or other refuse may be discarded.
7. Cats or dogs are not allowed ashore at Hawksnest, Trunk Bay, and Cinnamon Bay. Elsewhere, pets must be on a leash at all times.
8. Do not moor boats to trees or other vegetation ashore.
9. Keep beaches clean. No beach fires permitted.

For additional information contact the Ranger Stations at Redhook, Cruz Bay, or Lameshur Bay; or the Superintendent, Virgin Islands National Park, Box 1707, Charlotte Amalie, Saint Thomas, V.I. 00801.

Cruz Bay (25647, CK-9, I-A231),
on the western side of Saint John, is the major harbor and the largest town on the island. It boasts a telephone service, a small hospital, a bank, a department store, a grocery store, and the Park Service Headquarters, where you can get charts and park literature. A short walk north will bring you to Mongoose Junction, where you will find a bakery, a luncheonette, and a few other shops. The administrator's home and office are located on the headland in the center of the harbor, and the U.S. Customs and Immigration offices are across the street from the town jetty.

The town is usually quiet, except on Friday and Saturday nights. Taxis are available at the head of the jetty for tours around this lovely island.

The approach to Cruz Bay is partly obstructed by a reef that extends N from Galge Point, but a lighted marker marks the northernmost edge of this reef.

As shown in the sketch chart, there are two buoyed channels, one leading to the Park Service dock, the other to the ferry pier. You may anchor out of the channel in the general area of the seaplane ramp (Cruz Bay is no longer a regular stop), within the triangle delineated in the sketch chart, or S of a line from the light structure to just S of the ferry pier. The holding in sand is good. Be wary of the southern portion of the bay, because the bottom shoals rapidly.

The jetty is used by the ferries from Saint Thomas, as well as by all the rest of the commercial traffic, and cannot be recommended for a yacht. The protection is good, and except for the wash created by the commercial traffic, the anchorage is calm. However, the harbor is apt to be extremely crowded. After we have accomplished our business, we usually go elsewhere for the night.

Caneel Bay (25647, CK-9, I-A231),
less than a mile NE of Cruz Bay, is the site of the well-known Caneel Bay Plantation, one of the loveliest and best-run hotels in the Virgins. This elegant

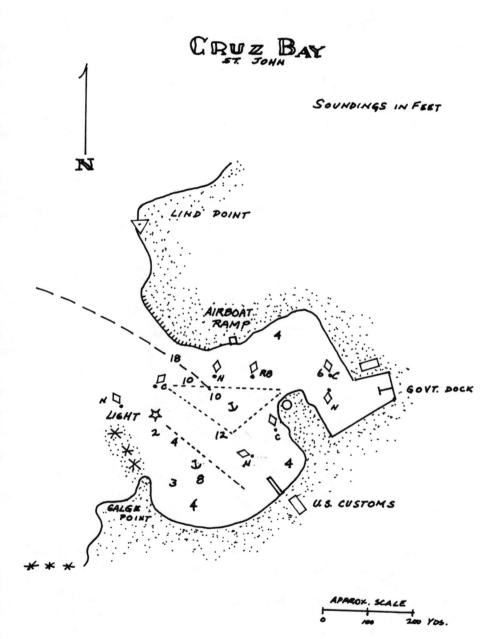

CRUZ BAY
ST. JOHN

SOUNDINGS IN FEET

LIND POINT

AIRBOAT RAMP

18

10

10

12

2   4

LIGHT

3   8

GALGE POINT

4

4

RB

GOVT. DOCK

U.S. CUSTOMS

APPROX. SCALE

0   100   200 YDS.

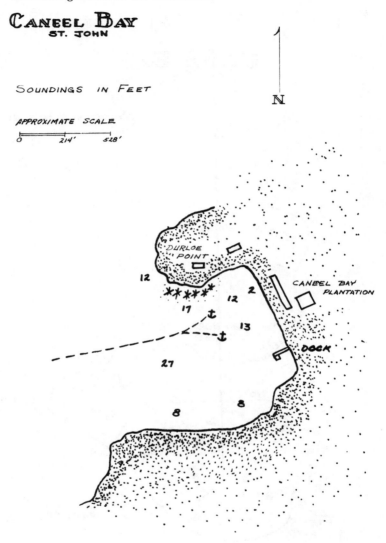

CANEEL BAY
ST. JOHN

SOUNDINGS IN FEET

APPROXIMATE SCALE

establishment was conceived by Laurance Rockefeller and tastefully designed and built about the time the Virgin Islands National Park came into being. Advance reservations are necessary to dine in this splendorous setting overlooking a fleet of anchored yachts and, in the distance, the line of islands that encloses Pillsbury Sound.

On the rise of land behind the main hotel, you can walk among the ruins of the sugar mill and the Greathouse of what was originally the Durloe Plantation. Durloe must have had a premonition of impending trouble, because he built his home in the manner of a fort, maintained a small arsenal, and even mounted a small cannon on the roof. This house was the one place on Saint John where the whites were able to hold out against the maddened slaves during the 1733 revolt.

The approach is open from all directions. The best anchorage is in the NE side of the bay, over a sandy bottom, and outside of the swimming buoys. You may find it crowded, though. The swimming is excellent everywhere, and the little reef on the N side of the bay will interest the snorkelers.

Although this anchorage offers excellent protection in easterly winds, it can become quite uncomfortable, even untenable, if the wind moves W of N, or if ground swells come in.

Hawksnest, or Hogsnest Bay (25647, CK-9, I-A231),

located just around the point from Caneel Bay, boasts three separate, lovely beaches. Unfortunately, this bay is so open to the N that we cannot recommend it as an overnight anchorage during the winter, but it makes a fine lunch or afternoon stop under the right conditions. The center beach is equipped with barbecue pits and tables. The best anchorage seems to be in the SE corner, 50 to 100 yards off the beach. Stay clear of the reef in the southern part of the bay.

The holding is good in sand, and the swimming excellent. Be prepared for a constant ground swell, caused primarily by the strong tidal stream running across the entrance.

Trunk Bay (25647, CK-9, I-A231),

just E of Hawksnest Bay, is the most popular swimming and snorkeling spot E of Saint Thomas—and with the crowds have come the regulations. An underwater trail, supervised by the Park Service and complete with signs and labels, may appeal to the beginning snorkeler. Ashore is a lunch counter and a bathhouse with showers—nothing primitive here.

You are expected to anchor (without breaking any coral) seaward of the buoys marking the swimming area, and you must land your dinghy (propelled by oars alone) at the western end of the beach.

A slight ground swell is almost always present, and because of the possibility of rollers, this is yet another anchorage that cannot be recommended for an overnight stay during the winter.

Johnson Reef (25647, CK-9, I-A231),

lying immediately N of Trunk Bay, is now flanked by buoys; it is not the navigational hazard it once was. The western side is steep-to, but the eastern side shoals rather slowly in spots, with isolated outcroppings, and should be approached with caution. A nun buoy marks the southern extremity of this reef, and a black, lighted buoy defines the northern limit.

The reef breaks in all but the calmest conditions, and when the rollers are on the move, seas have been known to break all the way from the reef to the headland of Saint John.

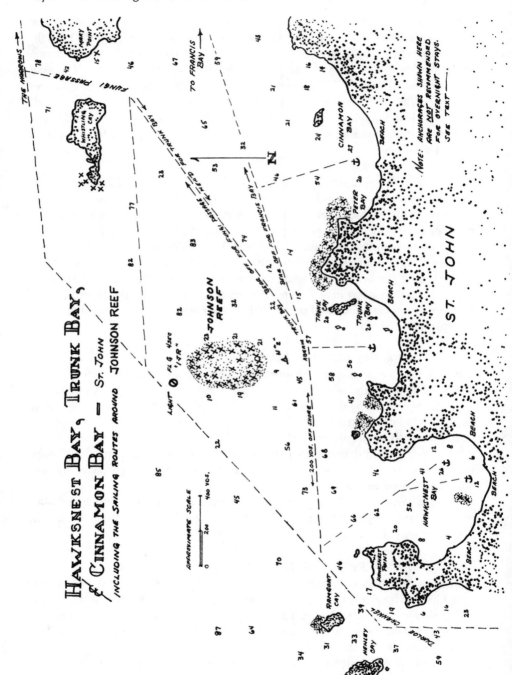

HAWKSNEST BAY, TRUNK BAY, & CINNAMON BAY — ST. JOHN

INCLUDING THE SAILING ROUTES AROUND JOHNSON REEF

The underwater scenery will appeal to the skin diver or snorkeler when the sea is calm. Park Service regulations apply to this reef, so be guided accordingly.

Cinnamon Bay (25647, CK-9, I-A231)

has a lovely beach under Park Service supervision. Along this strand are complete camping facilities, barbecues, a store, and a cafeteria—for those who like the rough life. Cabins and tent sites are so popular that reservations have to be made far in advance.

The anchorage is comfortable enough under standard conditions, with just a hint of a ground swell. Being exposed to the N, it's not recommended as an overnight anchorage in winter.

Maho Bay (25647, CK-9, I-A231),

the small area in the S corner of larger Francis Bay, is a lovely overnight anchorage during the summer, but in winter you may find an uncomfortable ground swell. The approach is straightforward, and a good anchorage, in sand and grass, will be found 50 to 100 yards off the beach. Watch your depth finder as you move in.

The house on the bluff above the bay was built by six donkeys, a couple of natives, and Mrs. Ethel McCully. She wrote an amusing book about it, which she originally entitled *I Did It with Donkeys*. When the publisher said no to this title, she changed it to *Grandma Raises the Roof.*

Francis Bay (25647, CK-9, I-A231)

offers a comfortable anchorage under almost all conditions. Drop the hook 50 to 100 yards off the beach, where there is a picnic area just N of a post marking the boundary of the National Park. Holding is good in the sand-mud or grass bottom.

From the picnic place, a hiking trail leads to an abandoned plantation house in the col above, whence a new black-topped road runs along the shore of Leinster Bay to the Annaberg sugar mill—but it's a long walk.

At night, in this crystal-clear bay, the beam of a flashlight directed into the water looks like a yellow-white column straight to the bottom. Held still, this column of light will attract a variety of fish. Some will attack it, others come for a look; all are interesting to watch. If you look closely, you may see a small, white sand shark circling quietly just outside the shaft of light.

Fungi Passage (25647, CK-9, I-A231)

is a deep passage between Whistling Cay and Mary Point, with very little current. A shoal extends a short way S from the SE tip of Whistling Cay.

As you pass through the cut, you will see the ruins of a customshouse or signal post that may have been used to communicate with a similar post on Little Thatch or Frenchman's Cay on the north side of the Narrows. Another conjecture is that the building was manned by armed lookouts stationed there by the Danish

Francis Bay & Maho Bay
St. / John

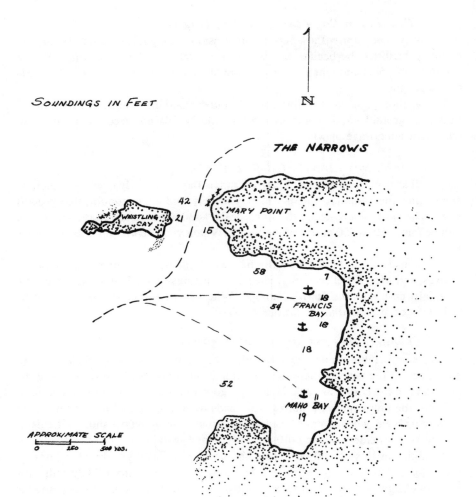

Soundings in Feet

N

THE NARROWS

WHISTLING CAY

MARY POINT

42
21
15

58   7
            18
54   FRANCIS
      BAY
            18

18

52

11
MAHO BAY
19

APPROXIMATE SCALE
0   150   300 YDS.

planters to intercept slaves attempting to run away to Tortola, where they hoped to find asylum at the British settlement at West End.

Mary Point, on the north side of this passage, is the spot where hundreds of slaves are said to have jumped to their death rather than submit to capture after the great slave uprising of 1733.

The Narrows (CK-2, I-A231)
creates a funnel of wind and current, but the seas seldom exceed 2 or 3 feet. There are no hazards, and yachts may sail to within 50 yards of either shore. To "play"

the current most effectively, hold to the Saint John side of the passage when eastbound, and to the Tortola side going west.

Leinster Bay (CK-2, I-A231)

gives you a choice of three anchorages, all of them safe in any but the most unusual conditions. The normal approach is W of Water Lemon (or Watermelon) Cay, but you may pass cautiously on the other side of this cay through a 12-foot-deep channel.

The two most popular anchorages are on the eastern side. One just S of Water Lemon Cay offers little protection from the trade winds (which is a happy choice when it's buggy), but the sea is always calm behind the cay. The holding is excellent in sand, but space is limited, since the bottom drops off rapidly. The cay was serving as a landing pad for a large group of pelicans the last time we were there.

The other anchorage in the eastern part of the bay is in Water Lemon Bay (sometimes called Limejuice Bay, sometimes Watermelon Bay). In any case, this anchorage is in the SE corner of Leinster Bay. Depths hold at 20 to 25 feet within 50 or 100 feet of this entire shoreline, until you approach the very head of the bay, where it shoals slightly. The holding is good, in sand and grass.

The ruins of Limetree Plantation standing at the head of the bay will interest the explorers in your crew. So will the ruins of a school at the top of the hill on the NE point of Leinster Bay. This building was originally a Masonic Lodge, the first one built in the Western Hemisphere. The view is spectacular and well worth the rugged climb. Take your camera.

The third and least used anchorage is Mary Creek, in the western part of the bay. The sandbank that straddles the entrance to this anchorage limits draft to 4 feet or less, but once you are over the bar, the creek becomes wider and deepens to about 6 feet. Holding is excellent in sand, and conditions are always calm, despite the exposure to the wind. In fact, this windward situation makes this anchorage relatively bug free during the damp seasons. Two or three yachts can anchor here comfortably.

On sailing into Leinster Bay, you will notice some ruins on the southern slope overlooking the bay. These are all that remain of the Annaberg Plantation, once one of the largest sugar plantations on Saint John. Along the path leading to the mill, you will find a small stand that usually contains pamphlets describing the ruins, which are supervised by the Park Service. There is a dinghy landing W of the ruins, or you can walk along the road from Limetree Plantation.

From Leinster Bay and the Narrows you look across to Great and Little Thatch islands and to Soper's Hole, which is the first port of entry for the British Virgins after leaving Saint John.

Haulover Bay (CK-2, I-A231),

just 2½ miles E of Leinster Bay, is the only other anchorage on the north coast of Saint John that holds much interest for visiting yachtsmen. In times gone by,

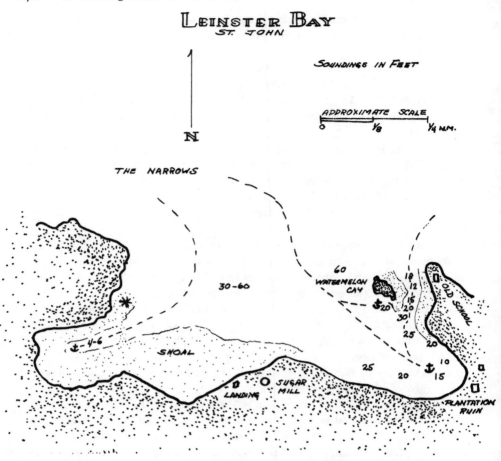

fishermen hauled their boats over this low land into Coral Bay in preference to sailing or rowing around the point.

Shoals encroach slightly from both sides of the entrance, so keep to the center as you come in. The best anchorage is in the SE corner near a small beach. Depths range from 60 to 20 feet, until you come within 10 yards of the beach, where it shoals to 10 feet or less. This is a very constricted anchorage; it would be crowded with two boats, but the protection is good under almost all conditions.

Coral Bay (CK-2, I-A231),

the largest bay on Saint John, will be considered in three sections.

The easternmost, little frequented and undoubtedly the most beautiful, is Round Bay. Stay well clear of the reef off Moor Point as you enter, and pick an anchorage off any of the beaches on the eastern side. Holding is excellent in sand, and the protection is good under almost all conditions, though there is always a slight ground swell. The two little beaches on the N side of Round Bay are rocky,

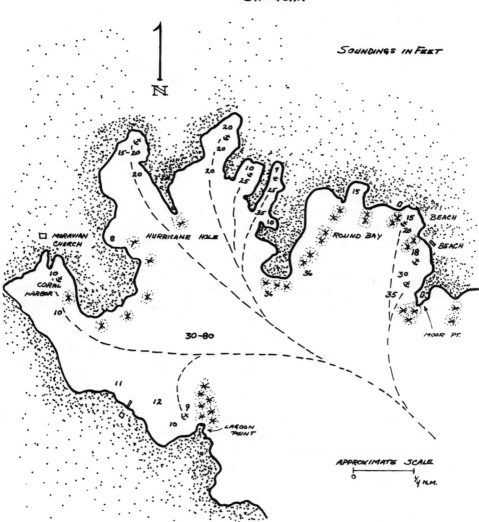

and anchoring off of them is less comfortable. The western side of the bay should be avoided. A rather nasty reef, always awash and breaking, extends its full length.

If the ground swells become uncomfortable in Round Bay, you can move into one of the four small bays in Hurricane Hole. There is nothing much here but solitude, and the bugs are usually fierce during the rainy season. However, this midsection of Coral Bay is a major haven for yachtsmen during the hurricane season. All four bays are deep and free of hidden dangers, although they shoal rather rapidly close to shore. Actually, there are only two completely landlocked spots, one a cove off the easternmost hole, the other behind the hook of land in the westernmost. Shoals extend from all the points that form these holes.

Coral Harbor is not as deep as the rest of Coral Bay, and yachts drawing over 6 feet should stay in midchannel and proceed cautiously. There are no dangers in the approach, except shallow water and a rock here and there off the northeastern shore. Nevertheless, deep-draft yachts should favor that shore slightly when entering. The anchorage is well protected and calm under most conditions, and the holding is good in sand and mud.

A small native community is clustered around the head of the harbor. Practically nothing can be obtained there except smiles and conversation. In a move to modernize the place, a telephone has been installed next to the school. The Moravian Church has an interesting history, if you can persuade one of the local residents to tell you the story. It may seem hard to believe now, but in Saint John's sugar-producing days, Coral Harbor was as busy as the harbor at Saint Thomas.

There's another anchorage in Coral Bay, just off the southern shore of Lagoon Point, and well protected by a reef that extends N from that point. When approaching from the E, be sure to stand well clear of the reef. The swimming is excellent here, and the reef affords good snorkeling on calm days.

When you are approaching Coral Bay from the S, extreme care should be taken to stay clear of the Eagle Shoal one half mile E of Ram Head. If passing inside this shoal, keep the shore close at hand and continue northward between Sabbat Point and Leduck Island. Once past the island, you will be clear of dangers. When passing outside of Eagle Shoal, keep S of a line between Ram Head and the southern shore of Norman's Island. When Leduck Island bears 359°T, you will be clear of the shoal.

Salt Pond Bay (CK-2, I-A231),

the first cove around the corner of Ram Head, is an excellent anchorage. The big reef in the middle of the entrance has deep water on both sides and well up toward the beach. Anchor in the NE corner on a sandy bottom. The Park Service maintains a picnic area on the beach and some pleasant hiking trails.

Great Lameshur Bay (CK-2, I-A231)

is a well-sheltered overnight anchorage. In 1970 this was the site of the Tektite Project in long-term undersea living. All that remains of this important undertaking is the stone dock and the headquarters building on the cliff.

Little Lameshur Bay (CK-2, I-A231)

is as well sheltered as its bigger brother. Favor the western shore.

Reef Bay (25647, CK-9, I-A231)

is an interesting lunch stop or afternoon anchorage, but is not recommended for overnight unless the wind is well to the N and expected to stay there. Since the bay is wide open to the S, a ground swell is usually present. This bay is "Genti Bay" on Chart 25647.

When approaching, stay clear of the reefs, which are awash or breaking along both sides. The center of the bay is deep and clear. As you approach the anchorage ahead, you'll notice the reefs on both sides dwindle to nothing. Continue slowly past the reefs and into the head of the bay. Anchor in 7-to-10 feet about 200 feet from shore, just W of the old sugar mill (the stack is visible above the treetops). In the afternoon it is difficult to spot the reef on the western side.

The area abounds with lime trees. A path leads to a waterfall (it performs during the rainy season) and some ancient Indian petroglyphs.

Fish Bay (25647, CK-9, I-A231),

immediately W of Reef Bay, is a good anchorage under normal conditions, although a slight ground swell is almost always experienced.

Stay in midchannel; reefs extend a short way from both sides. Proceed cautiously into the bay, as the bottom shoals rather rapidly. Yachts drawing 8 to 10 feet should anchor just outside the mouth of the bay; those of lesser draft may continue well in, where it is generally calm. The holding is good in sand and mud.

A little beach on the eastern side of the entrance is surrounded by reefs but fun to explore. Farther E, just outside the entrance and behind Cocolobo Cay, is a larger beach that can be approached by dinghy through the coral heads, when sea conditions allow.

Fishermen will appreciate the bonefish flats at the head of the bay.

Rendezvous Bay (25647, CK-9, I-A231)

offers little protection for overnight unless the wind is well N of E. However, one anchorage within this rather open bay is adequate under normal conditions—at least as a lunch or afternoon stop. It's just off the small beach in Ditleff Bay. Holding is good in sand and grass. Expect a slight ground swell at any time of the year.

Chocolate Hole (25647, CK-9, I-A231),

just W of Rendezvous Bay, is pleasant, quiet, and well sheltered. The approach is straightforward, though you should favor the western side, as a small reef makes out about 15 to 20 yards from Sam Point. Yachts drawing 6 feet or less may approach to within 20 yards of the first line of moorings. From this point to the head of the bay, the bottom shoals rapidly to 4 feet and less. Holding is good in sand and grass.

The little reef on the E side of the entrance will interest snorkelers.

Great Cruz Bay (25647, CK-9, I-A231),

on the SW corner of Saint John, is not particularly scenic but does afford good protection in most conditions. The sea is generally calm, but with a slight ground swell, and holding is good in sand and grass.

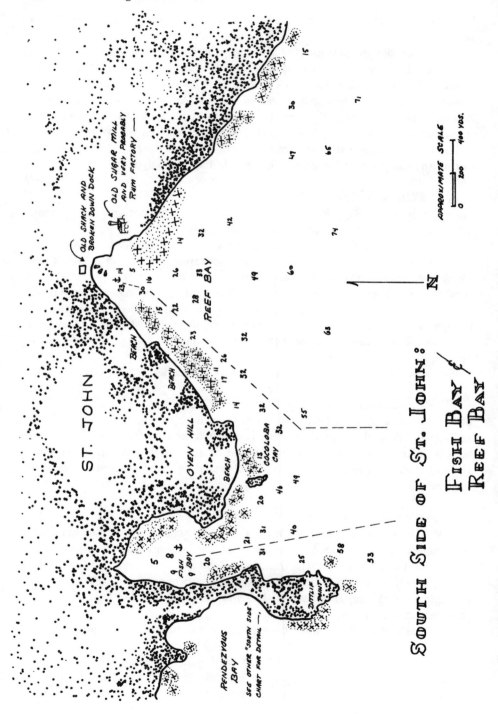

SOUTH SIDE OF ST. JOHN:
FISH BAY & REEF BAY

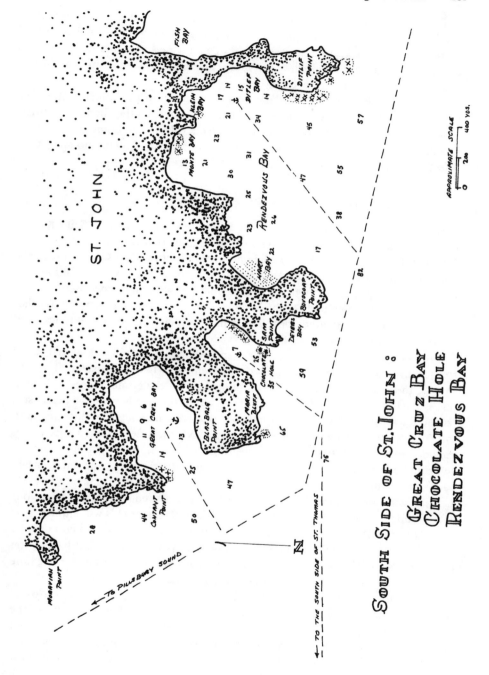

ST. JOHN

MORAVIAN POINT

TO PILLSBURY SOUND

GREAT CRUZ BAY

CONTANT POINT

ISLAS BRAS POINT

MARIA BLUFF

CHOCOLATE HOLE

SAFIR POINT

DEVERS BAY

BOVOCOAP POINT

HART BAY

RENDEZVOUS BAY

MONTE BAY

KLEIN BAY

FISH BAY

DITLEF BAY

DITLEF POINT

TO THE SOUTH SIDE OF ST. THOMAS

N

SOUTH SIDE OF ST. JOHN :

GREAT CRUZ BAY
CHOCOLATE HOLE
RENDEZVOUS BAY

APPROXIMATE SCALE
0   200   400 YDS.

The entrance is wide and unobstructed, except for a small reef extending from the N side. The best anchorage is about halfway to the head of the bay and 50 yards or so off the southeastern shore, but you'll find the area crowded, and private moorings take up much of the space. The bay is shoal near its head, where you'll see the elegant Virgin Grand Resort.

If you are proceeding to Cruz Bay, it is customary to pass outside of Steven Cay in spite of the considerable detour involved. On the other hand, the outermost part of the reef, which extends SW from Moravian Point, is awash or breaking in all weather so that, with due caution, yachts drawing no more than 9 feet may pass around this reef and inside of Steven Cay.

Saint Croix (25641, CK-5, I-A23)

Although the largest of the U.S. Virgins, Saint Croix (pronounced "Saint Kroy") is not a cruising ground to compare with the islands that ring Sir Francis Drake Channel. In fact, Christiansted is the only real harbor in Saint Croix, and Christiansted depends upon a protecting reef to the north to earn its definition as a harbor. Lacking are the high hills that encircle so many other harbors and anchorages in the main body of the Virgins. But Saint Croix has attractions other than the usual cruising amenities. Its Danish heritage is more evident here, and a stronger sense of history seems to pervade the place.

Sugar was always king on Saint Croix, and because its terrain was so well suited to the cultivation of cane, the industry died very slowly on this island. The mill towers, the brick stacks, and the crumbling walls of the estate houses still stand out against the shoreline. To see such sights out of the past is the most persuasive reason for sailing to Saint Croix—but isn't that reason enough? Sightseeing is so much of what cruising is all about, anyway. All too often, Saint Croix is not included in the brief itinerary of the visiting yachtsman, but if you have time to spare and can afford to choose your days to make the crossings, the sail over and back can be an exhilarating experience in ocean sailing.

If the wind is from the east or southeast, which is usually the case, start your southbound crossing from Flanagan or Salt Island Passage. This will allow a close reach, or at least the cracking of sheets, on the way across, and will certainly be more comfortable and faster than the wet beat to weather that you'll have if you leave from Saint Thomas Harbor. Plan to leave by 0900, so you'll have ample time to make your anchorage in Christiansted before dark.

During much of the year, the northbound trip is usually the easier crossing, with a comfortable reach or run all the way. But the wind often blows out of the north during the winter, which makes the trip a dead beat to weather. At such times, it's nice to have a few days in hand so that you can afford to wait for more favorable conditions. This north wind, though, has been known to continue for weeks at a time.

Remember that the current sets west between Saint Thomas and Saint Croix;

the velocity depends on the strength of the trade winds. Generally, you are safe in figuring on an average drift of 1½ knots for the entire passage.

Christiansted (25645, CK-6, I-A23)

is the major harbor and town, located almost in the middle of the north coast of Saint Croix. The circuitous entrance to Christiansted Harbor, though well marked, can prove confusing to strangers. While you are still well offshore, it is possible to identify the red-and-white-striped radio tower at Fort Louise Augusta. A course of 174°M on this tower will keep you clear of the Scotch Bank and bring you to the lighted sea buoy #1. At #4 buoy the well-marked deep-water channel bears off to starboard and passes north of Round Reef, a treacherous obstacle that has claimed more than its share of wrecks.

An alternative route, Schooner Passage with a least depth of 9 feet, continues from the sea buoy straight for the radio tower until about 100 yards off the point and takes red beacon #2 to starboard as the sketch chart shows.

Do not try to cross from one channel to the other. Also, try to avoid entering at night. Identifying the channel is very difficult because of the many lights in the harbor.

The anchorage off Protestant Cay is usually crowded, and considering all the private moorings with their short scope, and the easterly current which runs through here, you will have to use some rather delicate judgment in placing your anchor. Don't head for the wide open water W of the anchored fleet; that is the landing area for the seaplanes that shuttle back and forth between Christiansted and Saint Thomas, making 22 trips per day!

Saint Croix Marine and Development lies E of the channel, before you make the swing toward the town docks. The breakwater project charted N of the yard has been abandoned. This is a full-service marina and a competent shipyard, capable of hauling large yachts by railway and by travellift. A laundry is located here, which gives one- or two-day service. To avoid the congestion in the lee of Protestant Cay, you may well prefer to anchor off here.

For security reasons, do not leave dinghies in isolated spots, especially those with outboards. If anchored back of Protestant Cay, dinghies are best left at the end of the wharf adjacent to the King's Alley Hotel. If anchored on Welcome Bank, leave them at Saint Croix Marine.

Enough of the early buildings of Christiansted remain, in spite of fires, an earthquake and tidal wave, two hurricanes, and labor riots, to remind you of its opulence in the late eighteenth and early nineteenth centuries—landmarks such as Government House with its ballroom; the Steeple Building, once a church and now a museum; the fascinating Fort Christiansvaern; and the old Scale House near the waterfront, which now serves as the tourist information bureau.

Many shops carry a variety of tourist-oriented merchandise, and there are a number of good restaurants. Unfortunately you need a car or taxi to get to the several supermarkets.

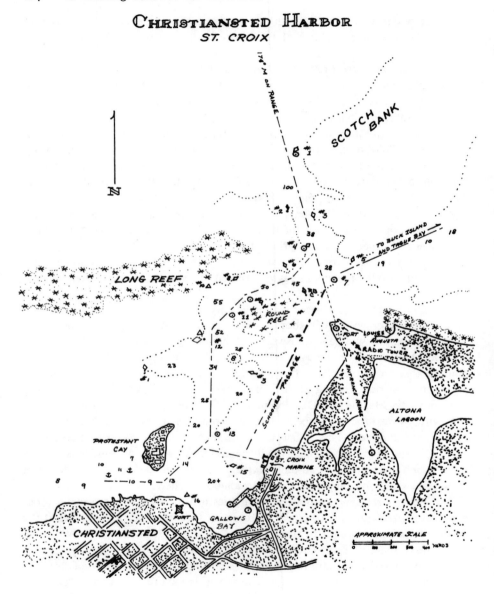

CHRISTIANSTED HARBOR
ST. CROIX

Green Cay Marina,

just south of Green Cay, is part of a development that includes a hotel, restaurant, ship store, yacht broker, dive shop, and more. The entrance is through a cut protected by stone jetties. Slips are usually filled by local boats, and there is no room to anchor. Call on VHF Channel 16 or 68 to check on availability of space for your boat at a dock.

Buck Island (25641, CK-5)

is a lovely spot for a day's outing from Christiansted, or even an overnight stay. It has the status of a U.S. National Monument.

Follow the main channel out of Christiansted Harbor to Green Flasher 7 and set a course directly for the anchorage on the western end of Buck Island, leaving Can 5 to port and Green Cay at least 50 yards to starboard. Often you'll find the wind directly on the nose, so keep a careful eye on Scotch Bank when short-tacking along this course. This bank is hard to detect under some light conditions.

The best anchorage at Buck Island is just off the lovely sand beach at the western tip of the island. The approach from the SW is clear of hazards, and you should anchor very close to the beach because the bottom is scoured to a hard finish only 50 feet out. Alternatively, if you are staying the night, you may find a spot of softer sand farther offshore. Incidentally, no one is allowed to spend the night ashore here. Picnic tables and pit toilets are provided for daytime use at the SW beach.

On the SE side of the island is a marked opening through the outer reef. Yachts entering here can make their way to an underwater trail, which is defined by the National Park Service by means of submerged signs here and there to describe the sea life and keep you on the trail.

Entering the lagoon between the red and black buoys, give the park sign a reasonable berth and hold directly for one of the 11 Park Service moorings, located in at least 8 feet of water. Proceed cautiously because of the scattered coral heads hereabouts. Do *not* anchor. To do so would risk damaging the coral.

If the prospect of eyeballing your way into the lagoon bothers you, go on one of the excursion boats that leave from Christiansted every day, taking eager snorkelers to the reef.

Tague (Teague) Bay (25641, CK-5, I-A23)

is protected by the reef that stretches along the entire northeastern end of Saint Croix. It is the home of the Saint Croix Yacht Club, which welcomes visiting yachtsmen by extending guest privileges for three days and temporary guest memberships after that at a very reasonable rate by the week, for a maximum of four weeks in any calendar year.

Approaching from the W, take up an easterly heading after passing Green Cay, until the old mill tower on the beach at Coakley Bay bears S. Alter course directly toward the tower, and pass through the reef opening, leaving the sand spit to starboard and the breaking reef, marked by FG #1, to port. The pass is approximately 150 yards wide and 12 feet deep. Continue toward the sugar mill until you are more than halfway across the bay before turning east, then hold down the middle of the bay. If you deviate at all, favor the shore side. If you draw 6 feet or more, anchor when you come abeam the yacht club, about halfway between it and the outer reef. From this position, yachts drawing less than 6 feet can turn in for the yacht club pier but must watch for a shoal close to starboard.

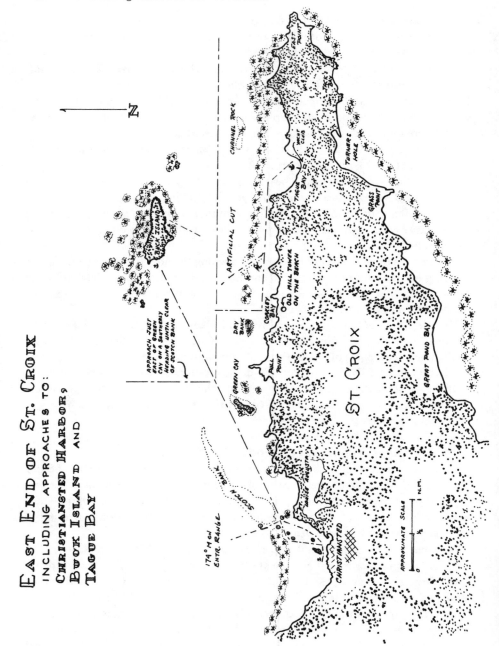

EAST END OF ST. CROIX

INCLUDING APPROACHES TO:

CHRISTIANSTED HARBOR,
BUCK ISLAND AND
TAGUE BAY

Once you are inside Tague Bay, the bottom shoals rapidly; the southwestern section is especially shallow and should be avoided. Holding is good in sand and grass, and sea conditions are always calm. Swimming is excellent.

Shown in the sketch chart is an alternative access into Coakley Bay—an artificial cut marked by a red-and-black buoy that has been blasted through the reef in a southeasterly direction. We suggest it be used only in conditions of good light and smooth seas.

Around We Go

Too many Saint Croix cruises take in Christiansted, Buck Island, and maybe Tague Bay, then back to the main islands, whereas an interesting clockwise circumnavigation of the island can be accomplished in three or four days, with only a bit of powering involved.

Great Pond Bay (25641, CK-5, I-A23)

provides the necessary overnight anchorage on the south shore for a cruise around the island. When it comes to a "countdown" of coral patches on the way in, the route may seem a bit perilous, but in fact it's more easily done than said. You must have good light, though, and this should work out conveniently, since you can expect to have the afternoon sun over your shoulder on the way in, and the converse for a morning departure.

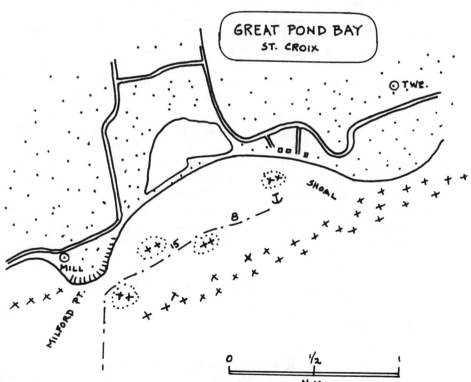

Come in on 010°M on the E end of the cliff at Milford Point and look for a distinct patch of coral about 0.1 mile beyond the tip of the outer reef. Leave this patch to starboard and turn up the middle of the bay for about 0.3 mile, when you will observe another clump of coral, which you will leave to port. Up to this point you will have been in no less than 15 feet of water. Continue another 0.3 mile, now in 8 feet, to a third patch of coral, which will be left to starboard. Carry on for 0.6 mile, still in 8 feet, till you see coral to port in the vicinity of several houses on the shore. Drop anchor outside this patch.

Frederiksted (25644, CK-5, I-A23),

on the western end of Saint Croix, is the second-largest town on the island. Bars, restaurants, and shops do a lively business, catering to passengers from the cruise ships, which use the large commercial wharf.

This anchorage is an open roadstead and cannot offer positive protection except in a period of normal trade winds. Most boats anchor or moor in the vicinity of the wharf. The holding is good in sand, and the sea is generally calm.

Because of its remoteness and wide-open aspect, this anchorage is not very popular. Nevertheless, it is a rather lovely spot, and the town, with its old buildings, has a certain quiet charm.

Salt River (25641, CK-5, I-A23),

about 4 miles W of Christiansted and the home of Salt River Marina, is a small, mangrove-surrounded haven sheltered at the mouth by a reef. Eyeball your way in if your vessel requires no more than 6 ½ feet at high water in the channel.

This is a scene of early Indian settlements. A little digging may unearth bits of pottery and primitive tools and weapons. Columbus stopped here, seeking to refill his water casks, on November 14, 1493. He skirmished briefly with some Indians in a canoe, then sailed away to Haiti.

Salt River is the scene of Hydrolab, an underwater chamber where researchers may live for lengthy periods. This facility is a part of West Indies Laboratory, which in turn is a part of Fairleigh Dickinson University. The laboratory itself is situated across the street from the Saint Croix Yacht Club in Tague Bay. In preparation for the hurricanes David and Frederick in 1979, the Hydrolab personnel temporarily buoyed the channel so that a veritable fleet of boats was able to seek shelter in Salt River. Many sought shelter there during Hugo in 1989 as well, but the damage was high, even in this protected spot.

THE BRITISH VIRGIN ISLANDS

Tortola and Adjacent Islands

During the eighteenth century, the residents of Tortola were quite openly engaged in the business of piracy. Businessmen, planters, doctors, and other respected members of the community apparently owned privateer sloops and cobles, which

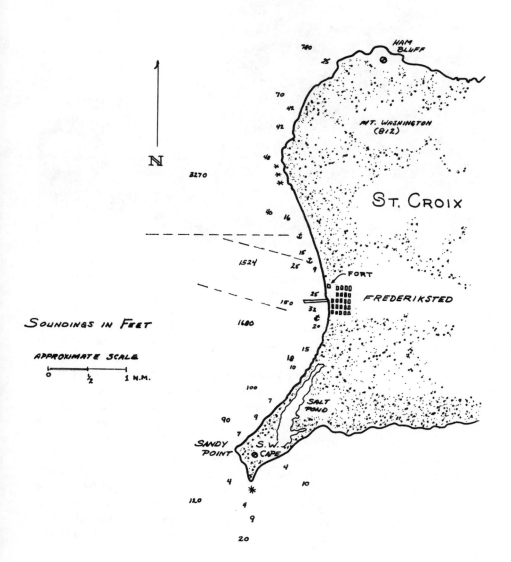

FREDERIKSTED
ST. CROIX

N

SOUNDINGS IN FEET

APPROXIMATE SCALE

0   ½   1 N.M.

Trees like this illustrate the direction, velocity, and consistency of the trade winds in the British Virgin Islands.

preyed on shipping throughout the islands. Goods, slaves, and produce were hijacked by these "Tortola Pirates" and either ransomed back to the owners or sold elsewhere.

During a period of overlapping states of war, declared or not, between the major European powers, and lacking any intervention by the local government, such as it was, this grim business flourished for many years. Some historians surmise that the customshouse on Whistling Cay was used as a signaling station to alert the privateers of approaching ships.

Tortola has had periods of wealth and fame, poverty, and hurricanes; it has had slave uprisings, warfare, and religious dissension among Quakers, Anglicans, and Methodists. Tortola today is the most populated of the British Virgin Islands and has recently experienced something of a building boom brought on by the burgeoning tourist trade. Roads have been improved, and large hotels and condominiums are going up. New marinas and yacht-chartering enterprises are being established as well.

West End (25641, CK-2, I-A231)

is a small community with meager supplies, located in Soper's Hole at the western end of Tortola. The ferry from Saint Thomas stops here, and taxis are available for trips into Roadtown or tours of the island. Decide on the price, however, before you hop in.

Customs and immigration officials are usually on the dock or in the immediate vicinity during normal hours. West End is a convenient port of entry if you are coming from the U.S. islands.

Enter from the Narrows around either side of Little Thatch Island, or from the N through Thatch Island Cut. The best anchorage is in the NE corner in 20 feet of water just 50 yards offshore, with good holding and excellent protection. Another anchorage, but with less protection, is just off the shoal ledge that runs out from Frenchman's Cay.

Little Thatch Island (25641, CK-2, I-A231)

has a lovely anchorage off a beautiful little beach on its northwestern corner.

Uncomfortable sea conditions caused by the tidal stream that sweeps through Thatch Cut make this a poor overnight anchorage, even during the summer.

Frenchman's Cay (25641, CK-2, I-A231)

across the harbor from the customshouse is the headquarters for the Stevens charter operations, with moorings, provisions, ice, fuel, and a restaurant open to visitors.

West End Slipway, next to Stevens, operates a railway capable of handling 150 tons, 100 feet length, 40 feet beam, and 15 feet draft.

Passing along the south shore of Tortola between Frenchman's Cay and Road-town, stand well offshore to avoid the charted reef about midway between Fort Recovery and Sea Cow Bay.

Nanny Cay (25641, CK-10, I-A231)

has a dredged harbor and an apartment/hotel complex on 25 acres of reclaimed land. The aerial photo on page 18 of *Chart-Kit* will give you a good preview of this harbor. The channel is buoyed, and the controlling depth is 10 feet. The modern facilities include a 30-T crane and a 50-T travel lift that can handle vessels 70 feet in length by 18 feet beam. Fuel, water, ice, provisions, and a chandlery are all here. A large fleet of charter yachts is berthed in the harbor.

Sea Cow Bay (25641, CK-10, I-A231)

can be entered by way of a dredged channel for shallow draft only. Eyeball your way in and do not approach the shore too closely.

Prospect Reef (25641, CK-10, I-A231)

is about a mile beyond Sea Cow Bay and around Slaney Point, but before you come to Road Harbour. This is a new marine-oriented residential complex with town houses, hotel, two swimming pools, other luxury trappings, and a small but modern marina, but limited to 5½-foot draft. In a strong easterly swell the entrance could be difficult if not impossible.

Road Harbour (25641, CK-10, I-A231, A232)

is the center of all commerce in the British Virgins. From a sleepy settlement 10 to 15 years ago, it has become a boom town, and, with its more central location among the islands, it may someday surpass Saint Thomas as the center of yachting activity. Already it boasts a liberal assortment of hotels and appealing restaurants with lovely views of the harbor and the Sir Francis Drake Channel, plus specialty food shops and supermarkets, a modern ice plant, grog shops, and English-style pubs.

The relatively sheltered southern corner of the harbor is still the popular anchorage area that it always was, and the Fort Burt Marina (below the round-roofed hotel of the same name) provides all the usual facilities, in addition to a chandlery and limited food supplies. Draft is limited to 6½ feet at the outer slips. Continue past the marina into Careening Cove, dredged to accommodate at least 7-foot draft at the Reef Rock Marina, a charter operation.

In making your approach, keep well clear of the rather indistinct shoals about 150 yards NW of Burt Point. We recommend heading toward the town docks on 290°T until you have Fort Burt Hotel abaft your beam; then round up slowly to

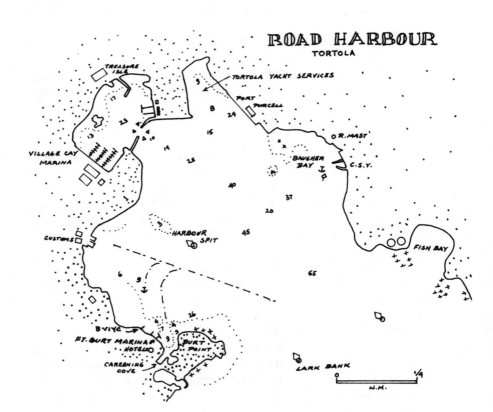

ROAD HARBOUR
TORTOLA

port and drop your hook, or continue to the Fort Burt Marina docks. Note in the sketch the 4-foot patch of shoal water projecting into this anchorage area. In the cloudy water, it is difficult to discern. The holding here is excellent in sand.

Docking at the town wharf is definitely not recommended because of the commercial traffic and general activity. It may seem convenient to go in there for entering or clearing; the customs and immigration offices are located just across the street, but don't be tempted. Anchor off and come in by dinghy.

A major face-lifting has taken place at the north end of Road Harbour—to wit, the development of port facilities for large ships at Port Purcell and a well-conceived yachting complex in the Wickham's Cay area. The artificial basin that has been created between the two landfill areas contains the elaborate Village Cay Marina and, across the way, the charter-boat base of The Moorings, with full-service facilities for visitors and additional docking space along the jetty that makes out from the Treasure Isle Hotel.

Across from The Moorings and facing Port Purcell are the shipyard and huge dry storage area of Albie Stewart's well-respected Tortola Yacht Services, with its 37-T travel lift and 80-T railway. In addition to hauling and painting, almost any kind of repair work can be handled, including hull, electrical, engine, and electronic jobs. On the premises are a sail loft, machine shop, and a refrigeration specialist. Fuel is available here for those who cook with gas.

When crossing the harbor between the Fort Burt anchorage and Wickham Cay, do not stray very far inside the Harbour Spit buoy E of the town docks.

At times, especially when the wind is N of E, you will find relatively calm conditions for anchoring in Baugher's Bay, although a slight ground swell is always present. The best anchorage is just inside the large mooring buoy, where holding is excellent in sand and the effect of commercial traffic is not bothersome. Caribbean Sailing Yachts (CSY) now base their large fleet of bareboat charter yachts here, having moved from Maya Cove in 1975. Transients may rent a mooring from CSY in the area just off the CSY docks where there used to be room to anchor.

Brandywine Bay (25641, CK-10, I-A231)
is likely to become far more crowded than it has been, considering its proximity to Road Harbour. The aerial on page 19 of *Chart-Kit* will give you a good picture of the shoal areas. Enter in plenty of water about midway between the points and anchor in the center or toward the eastern shore, as your draft permits.

Maya Cove (25609, CK-3, I-A231)
is home base for Tropic Isle Yacht Management, which operates a large fleet of bareboats. Visitors are welcome, and fuel, ice, water, and dinners ashore are available. A reef extends nearly across the mouth of the cove, giving protection from the surge but allowing the wind to deter the bugs. At the NE end of this reef is a pair of entrance buoys. The channel beyond will carry 8 feet and is

marked. Anchor in 10 feet, mud, but stay W of a line between a square brown mooring buoy and the entrance. This mooring is for *Charmaine IV,* a freighter that frequents this harbor and demands clear passage from its mooring to the entrance—and never mind damage to any pleasure craft in her way!

Fat Hog and East End Bays (25609, CK-3, I-A231),

on the southeastern end of Tortola, offer lovely, quiet overnight anchorages. Holding is good in sand and grass, and the sea conditions are usually calm. After passing S of the rocks at the entrance, simply bear off to starboard and drop your hook about 100 yards farther in. Stay well out from the head of the bay, as the bottom shoals rapidly 200–300 yards off the shore. The town of East End is located here. Some supplies and facilities, such as a laundromat, small grocery, and restaurant, are available. Go Vacations, a Canadian charter company, is headquartered here. The frequent landings and take offs at the Beef Island Airport are a detraction.

Bluff Bay (25609, CK-3, I-A231),

on the S side of Beef Island, is a quiet and little-used anchorage, undoubtedly because the entrance is narrow with dangerous heads and reefs on both sides. Do not attempt this entrance unless you have the afternoon sun at your back and good visibility.

As you make your approach, identify the beach with boulders (similar to those

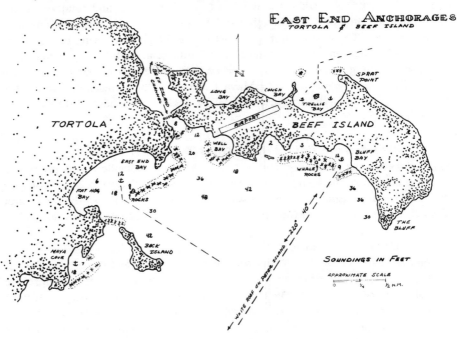

EAST END ANCHORAGES
TORTOLA & BEEF ISLAND

SOUNDINGS IN FEET

APPROXIMATE SCALE

Bluff Bay, Beef Island

at the Baths on Virgin Gorda) on its NW end. The aerial photo on page 20 of *Chart-Kit* is of some help here. The pass is E of the boulders on shore and E of some guano-covered rocks. Proceed in toward the beach, favoring the visible reef to starboard, until deep water opens up to the west. Give the guano-covered rock that lies just offshore a berth of 50 feet to starboard in order to avoid a submerged boulder, then stay in the middle while paralleling the shore and watching your depth finder to a suitable anchorage. The entrance channel, which runs approximately NE, will carry 7 feet at least. Inside it deepens to about 15 feet.

Trellis Bay (25609, CK-3, I-A231)
is the largest and best-known anchorage on Beef Island. Though open to the N, it offers excellent protection and calm water under most conditions. Restaurants are located on Bellamy Cay and on Conch Shell Point. Anchor on either side of Bellamy Cay, or S of it. Holding is good in sand, mud, and grass.

Approaching from the E, keep clear of the rock just above water off the eastern point of the bay. Approaching from the N or W, be careful of the foul ground that extends out from Conch Shell Point. Approximately 200 yards N and slightly E of Conch Shell Point, there is a nasty little reef lying about 3 feet below the surface. You may pass between this reef and the point, if you have positively spotted this outlying reef.

Yachts drawing 9 feet can circumnavigate Bellamy Cay, but note that a shoal extends from the E side of the cay and another from the opposite shore.

Marina Cay (25609, CK-3, I-A231)
is a small island just S of Scrub Island and E of Great Camanoe. Sheltered by these larger islands and by Marina Cay reef itself, the anchorage off the south-

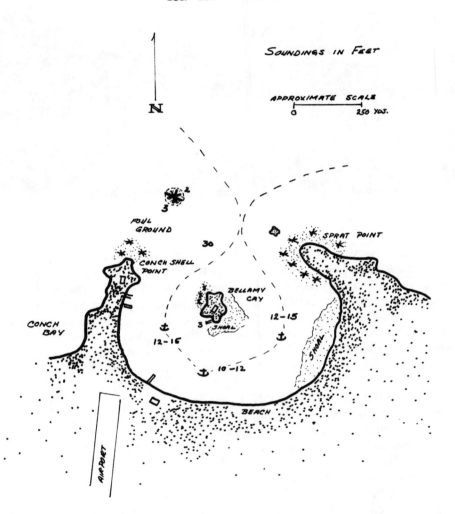

western shore is always smooth. The approach from N and NE is clear of dangers, except for the reef extending E from the NE corner of the cay. The channel between Great Camanoe and Scrub Islands is clear of hazards if you stay in the center.

From the S or SE, take care to identify and pass well clear of the protecting reef that extends about 500 yards SSW from Marina Cay. There is a red daymark at its extremity. Your anchor will hold well in the sandy bottom here.

Moorings are available, and the hotel dining room and the beach bar restaurant are open to visiting yachtsmen. Dinner reservations are necessary and may be made before 1700 through Tortola Radio or VHF Channel 12.

Long before the British Virgins were "discovered" by tourists and bareboat charterers, young Robb White and his wife came to Marina Cay to seek the idyllic, away-from-it all existence. He wrote an engrossing book called *Our Virgin Island* (now out of print) about their trials and tribulations in trying to make ends meet. It later became a movie.

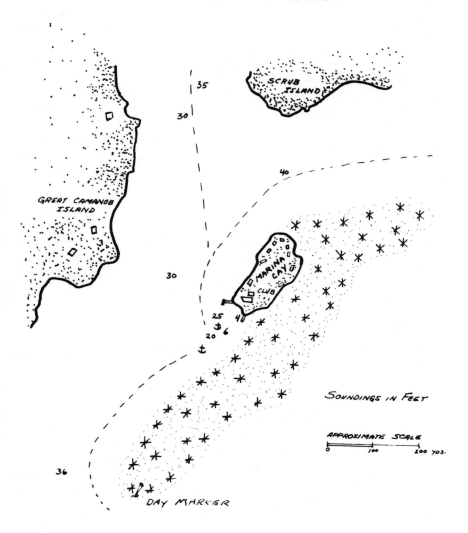

MARINA CAY

The North Shore of Tortola,

on a nice day, when no ground swell is running, can be the backdrop for a very pleasant sail. Although there are numerous coves and sandy beaches along here, none can be recommended for overnight anchoring during the winter months. In fact, many of these spots are relatively uncomfortable even in the summer, due to the unsettled conditions caused by current and tides.

The route is generally clear of dangers except for the passage between Beef Island and Little Camanoe. Just N of Conch Bay, Beef Island, there is a reef right in the middle of the passage. It is best to pass N of this one, as another reef extends N from the headland as you pass between Conch and Long bays.

To wend your way through these obstacles, leave the southernmost points of both Great and Little Camanoe close on your starboard hand, about 20 to 30 yards off. As you come abeam of the tip of Little Camanoe on your westerly heading, adjust your heading toward the nearest high mountaintop on Tortola, the 878-foot Lloyds. Hold this heading until you are well past Little Camanoe and the sand bar that extends S from it.

Once you are clear of this tricky spot, the remainder of the route down Tortola's north coast is uncomplicated. It is usually wise to stay rather well offshore in order to get a clear wind.

Alternatively you can run between Great and Little Camanoe, staying close to the former to avoid the reef on the NE corner of Little Camanoe. This channel, narrow and exposed to the N, should be used only in settled weather and under power.

Lee Bay (25609, CK-3, I-A231)

on Great Camanoe is a suitable anchorage provided there is no ground swell running. Come in on the beach to about 20-foot depth, drop a stern anchor, and proceed as far as your draft allows. Take your bow line ashore, tie to a tree, and you will seem to have pulled the land in all around you.

White Bay (25609, CK-3, I-A231)

on Guana Island is suitable as a daytime anchorage under quiet conditions. The island is privately owned, and it would be inappropriate to trespass beyond the beach itself.

Cane Garden Bay (25609, CK-2, I-A231)

is one of the most beautiful bays in the entire Virgin Islands, but unfortunately it's not a safe overnight anchorage during the winter, because the Atlantic swells can make it dangerous and even untenable within a few short hours. During the late spring and summer, it's an excellent overnight anchorage, and in calm weather it provides a safe lunch anchorage behind the reef, even in winter months.

When approaching from the W, favor the northern side of the bay; a reef extends from the southern side almost three quarters of the way across it. There is also a small reef off the northern point of the bay. The pass between these reefs has 15 to 20 feet of water. In the afternoon sun the southern reef is difficult to see; at such times favor the reef on the northern side of the pass.

Once you are inside the reef, the best anchorage is in the southern part of the bay, where the holding is excellent in sand. A lovely crescent beach with a pleasant community, palm trees, an old rum distillery where a local product can be purchased, and lots of friendly children will make your visit one to remember.

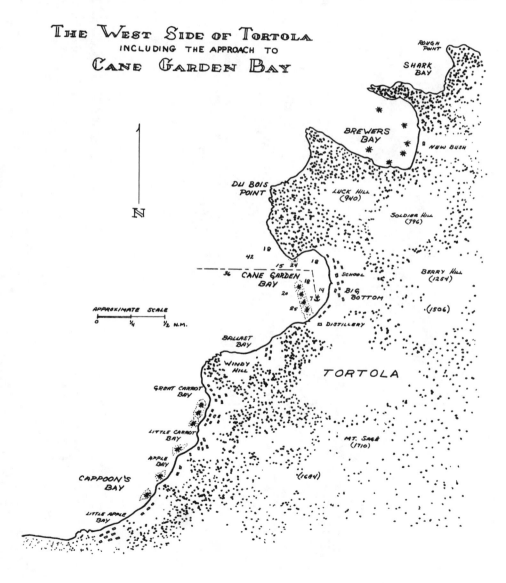

THE WEST SIDE OF TORTOLA
INCLUDING THE APPROACH TO
CANE GARDEN BAY

ROUGH POINT

SHARK BAY

BREWERS BAY

NEW BUSH

DU BOIS POINT

LUCK HILL (940)

SOLDIER HILL (796)

CANE GARDEN BAY

SCHOOL

BERRY HILL (1254)

BIG BOTTOM

(1506)

APPROXIMATE SCALE
0   ¼   ½ N.M.

DISTILLERY

BALLAST BAY

WINDY HILL

TORTOLA

GREAT CARROT BAY

LITTLE CARROT BAY

APPLE BAY

MT. SAGE (1710)

CAPPOON'S BAY

(1684)

LITTLE APPLE BAY

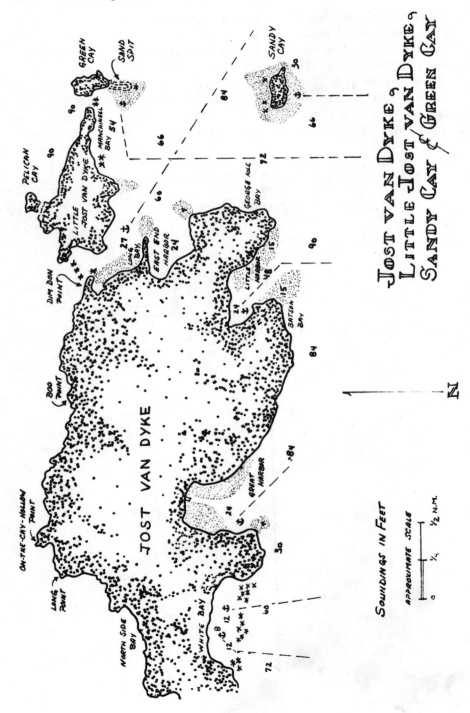

JOST VAN DYKE,
LITTLE JOST VAN DYKE,
SANDY CAY & GREEN CAY

SOUNDINGS IN FEET

APPROXIMATE SCALE

0   ¼   ½ N.M.

N

Jost Van Dyke and Nearby Islands

Great Harbour (25609, CK-2, I-A231),

whose exposure is to the south, is normally well protected. It is also by far the most pleasant spot in the British Virgins to go through the customs and immigration formalities. The official is usually around during regular working hours, but if you can't find him, ask anyone. There is a small extra charge after regular hours, which are 8:30 A.M. to 3:30 P.M.

The best anchorage is in the SW part of the bay just inside Dog Hole Point. The bay shoals rapidly to 3 or 4 feet, with a narrow channel running through the

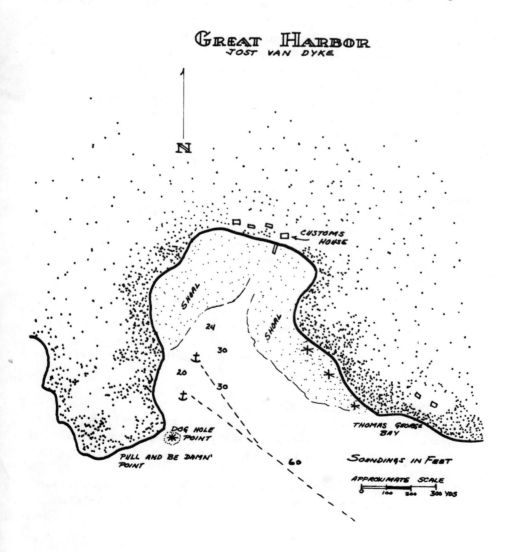

GREAT HARBOR
JOST VAN DYKE

shallows to the dock. You may go up to the shoal area, but don't drop your hook in the channel; local fishing and freight boats use it day and night. The bottom is sandy mud and grass, giving good holding.

There are several restaurants, bars, a bakery, a superette, and a guest house here. Fresh fish can sometimes be purchased at the superette in the afternoon, after the fishermen come in. When you go ashore, you'll quickly know where the action is.

White Bay (25609, CK-2, I-A231)

is located just W of Great Harbour and has a lovely sandy beach that extends the entire length of the bay. There are two approaches through the reefs. The passage on the western side is about 50 yards off the SW corner of the bay. As an alternative, a pair of small red and green marks will bring you in through a 15-foot channel between the two large reefs in the center of the bay. Once inside, anchor in 8 feet over sand. There's dinner ashore at the Sandcastle (make reservations) if you wish, and the swimming is perfect.

A swell sometimes makes this an uncomfortable overnight anchorage. Should you wish to have dinner here, you'd do better to anchor for the night in Great Harbour and dinghy around.

Little Harbour (25609, CK-2, I-A231)

is usually a quiet anchorage and not frequently visited by yachts. There is a tiny settlement here and restaurants on each side of the harbor.

When entering, stay in midchannel, as there are sandbanks on each side of the entrance. Continue to the head of the bay, where you will see on your port hand a tiny beach tucked into the corner. It is called Careening Hole and has 12 feet of water right up to the beach. It's a good idea to set a stern anchor here, because there is little swinging room.

Green Cay (25609, CK-2, I-A231),

lying just E of Little Jost Van Dyke, is well worth scrambling over, if only to visit the miniature crater on the eastern side. The best anchorage is on the edge of the sandbank that extends westward from the sand spit off the southern tip of the cay. This is not an overnight anchorage.

Sandy Cay (25609, CK-2, I-A231)

is a lovely "desert island" type of place for lunch or a swim. It is owned by Laurance Rockefeller, who has endeavored to keep it unspoiled and has planted almost every type of vegetation that will grow in the sandy soil. A delightful path runs around the island.

The best anchorage is on the sandbank to the SSW of the cay, about 50 yards from shore. Because it is exposed to the ground swells, it is not a good overnight anchorage.

LITTLE HARBOR
JOST VAN DYKE
ALSO KNOWN AS
GARDNER BAY

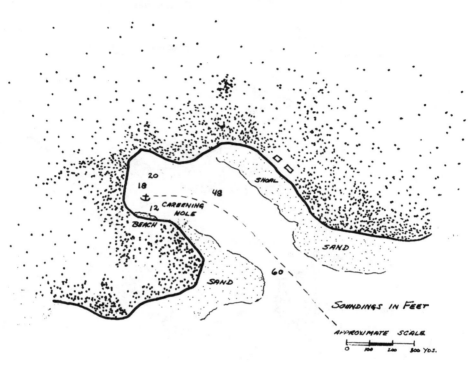

SOUNDINGS IN FEET

APPROXIMATE SCALE

Norman, Peter, Salt, Cooper, and Ginger Islands

The Bight on Norman Island (25609, CK-3, I-A231)

is a large and very popular bay offering good protection under almost all conditions. A fleet of 90 boats anchored here would not be unusual. The approach is clear except for a reef that projects N for about 200 yards from Treasure Point. You may anchor almost anywhere in the bay, though we prefer a spot about 50 yards off the beach at the very head of the bay.

Just S of Treasure Point, on the W side of Norman Island, are the three so-called Treasure Caves. Rumor has it that, not too many years ago, quite a fortune was found on a ledge in one of them. Norman Island has long been associated with pirates and their treasure, but the substance of this association is elusive. The island is reputed to be the famous *Treasure Island* immortalized

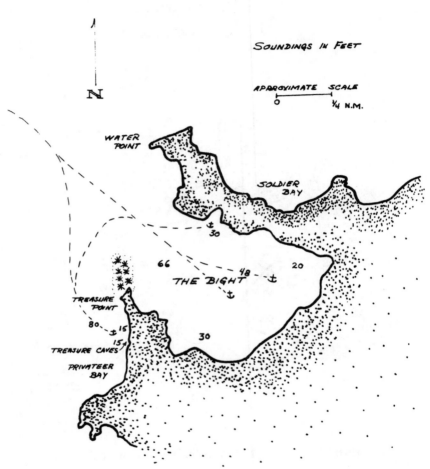

THE BIGHT
NORMAN ISLAND

N

SOUNDINGS IN FEET

APPROXIMATE SCALE

0   ¼ N.M.

WATER POINT

SOLDIER BAY

30

66   48   20

THE BIGHT

TREASURE POINT

80   15

15

TREASURE CAVES

PRIVATEER BAY

30

in Robert Louis Stevenson's novel. Other islands in other parts of the world have claimed this distinction, but Norman Island probably fits the story as well as any. In fact, Stevenson is said to have written part of the book while living in a camp on the beach at the head of the Bight.

Yachts may anchor on the narrow shelf that runs along this shore, and all three caves can be entered by dinghy under normal conditions. This is a lovely lunch or afternoon stop, but is not recommended for overnight. The swimming is good, though you're likely to see a lot of barracuda about.

Little Harbour on Peter Island (25609, CK-3, I-A231)

is the westernmost and most popular anchorage on this relatively large island. This anchorage is deep and affords good protection. Because of the topography of the surrounding land, the wind tends to swirl at night, causing yachts to swing and foul their anchors. A stern anchor is advisable.

All the land around Little Harbour is owned by Percy Chubb, of marine-insurance fame. His home overlooks the anchorage from the northeastern bluff. Permission should be requested before going ashore here.

Great Harbour (25609, CK-3, I-A231),

the largest bay on Peter Island's north coast, offers good protection, but the problem is to get your anchor on the bottom—the water is extremely deep. If you

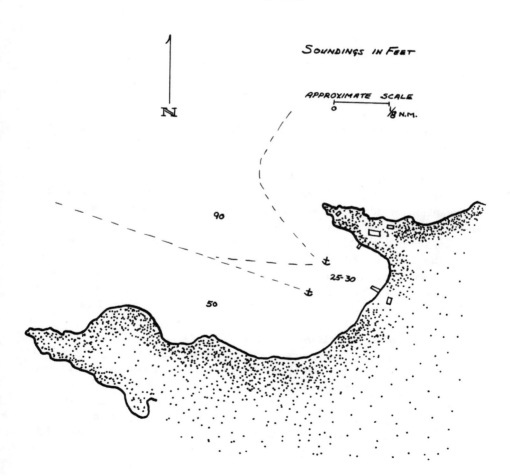

LITTLE HARBOR

PETER ISLAND

SOUNDINGS IN FEET

APPROXIMATE SCALE

⅛ N.M.

N

90

25-30

50

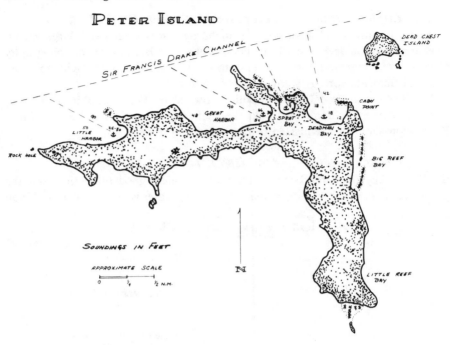

have plenty of chain or line, anchor in the SE corner, where the holding is good in sand.

Sprat Bay (25609, CK-3, I-A231)

is the site of the popular Peter Island Yacht Club, an elegant facility, with a 40-room hotel standing on a bulkheaded area over the reef. If it's not too crowded, this is a comfortable overnight anchorage amid luxurious surroundings.

Favor the E side of the opening as you enter, since there are rocks and reefs along the western shore. Allow plenty of swinging room for the fluky wind conditions or use a stern anchor. Anchor S and W of the dock, or moor stern-to on the inside of the bulkhead. A ferry runs between Sprat Bay and the Moorings at Road Harbour, for the convenience of yachtsmen as well as the hotel guests.

Deadman Bay (25609, CK-3, I-A231),

on Peter Island's northeastern end, is generally regarded as one of the most beautiful bays in the Virgin Islands. With its crystal-clear water and lovely beach backed by a grove of palms, it looks like a picture out of a travel brochure. Unfortunately, it is not suitable as an overnight anchorage in winter; it is too vulnerable to large swells that can come in without warning. In fact, a slight ground swell is almost always present here. Furthermore, you can expect difficulty setting your anchor in the extremely hard bottom.

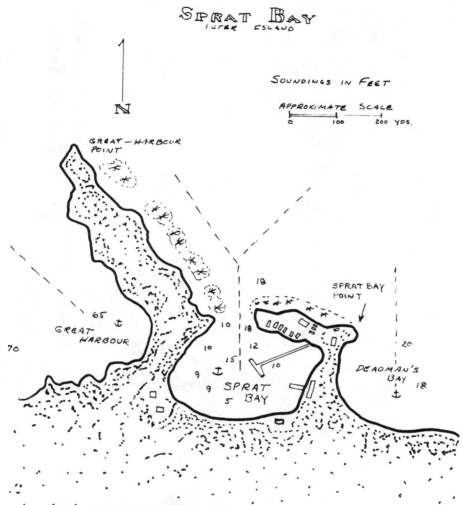

SPRAT BAY
INNER ISLAND

SOUNDINGS IN FEET

APPROXIMATE SCALE

0   100   200 YDS.

N

GREAT—HARBOUR
POINT

SPRAT BAY
POINT

18

65

GREAT
HARBOUR

70

10   18

10   12

15   10

9

9 SPRAT
5   BAY

DEADMAN'S
BAY   18

20

A path takes you over to Big Reef Bay, where you can enjoy fine swimming and snorkeling in the shallow water behind the reef.

Salt Island (25609, CK-3, I-A231)

has a small settlement in a shallow bight on the island's north side. At a distance, it appears to have an attractive beach, but on closer examination, both the beach and the village lose their allure.

Off the SW corner of the island, in 30 to 80 feet of water, lies the wreck of the *Rhone.* When she sank in 1867 during an October hurricane, with great loss of life, she was one of the newest ships of the Royal Mail Steam Packet Company— steam powered but fully rigged (just in case). Today she is a major scuba attraction.

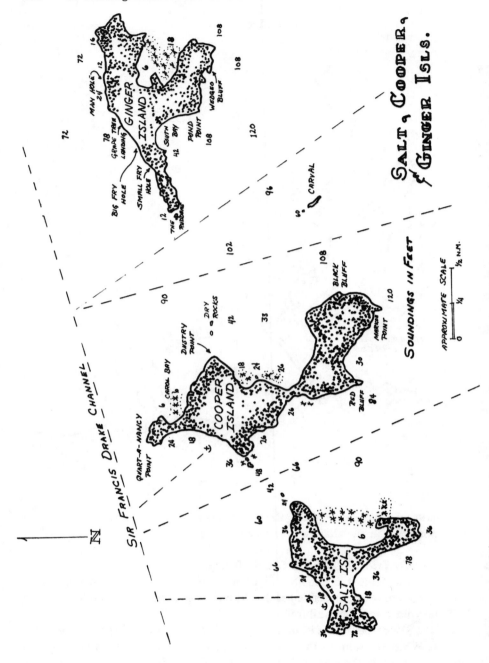

SALT, COOPER, & GINGER ISLS.

SOUNDINGS IN FEET

APPROXIMATE SCALE

A slight ground swell is incessant. This is strictly a daytime stop.

The passage between Salt and Cooper islands has rocks and reefs on either hand in the narrowest part of the channel. Favor the eastern side, leaving the exposed rocks on the Cooper Island side about 20 to 30 yards off.

Cooper Island (25609, CK-3, I-A231)

has several vacation homes on its slopes and seems crowded when compared with the adjacent islands. In the lee of Quart-a-Nancy Point, on the island's NW side, is an anchorage of sorts, but it is not recommended for overnight during the winter because of its exposure to the N. The best spot is in the lower part of this bay. The holding is good, though a slight ground swell is always to be expected, and the fluky wind conditions suggest setting a stern anchor if other boats have done the same. If you dine ashore, you may use one of the restaurant's moorings.

There are no hidden dangers in the passage between Cooper and Ginger islands.

Ginger Island (25609, CK-3, I-A231)

is currently uninhabited and offers no safe, all-weather anchorage. There is a bay on the E side of the island, with a 6-foot entrance through the reef, which sometimes offers protection. However, when the wind blows strongly out of the ESE, the entrance becomes dangerous and quite impossible to use.

Virgin Gorda

The Fat Virgin is the second largest of the British Virgins and, to some, the most beautiful. From the grotesque boulders strewn around the southern end to the flat middle area, and on to the high, lovely mountains of the northern section, it is certainly an island of contrasts. Beautiful beaches, some fine anchorages, and ideal snorkeling reefs are to be found around its shores. No wonder it is beginning to feel the hand of the resort developer.

The Baths (25609, CK-3, I-A232),

a phenomenal pile of huge boulders located on a lovely beach in a small bay on the western side of the island, derives its name from the pools of crystal-clear water formed in the sand at the base of the pile. Inside this jumble of monstrous slabs and boulders is a network of caves, archways, paths, and mysterious pools, some in complete blackness, others lit by bright shafts of sunlight bursting through the cracks in this edifice of nature. It is truly one of the wonders of the tight little world of the Virgin Islands.

The bay is easy to spot from seaward. Simply set a course for the southern tip of Virgin Gorda. When you are within 2 miles of the western shoreline, a string of pretty beaches will be clearly seen, stretching northward. The second beach to the N is your destination, and the pile of boulders in the southern corner of this

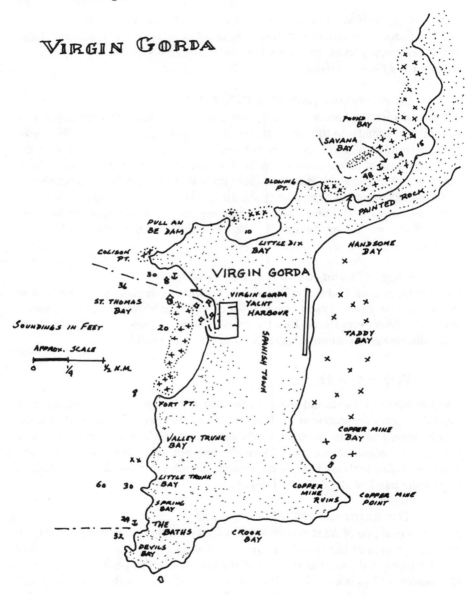

VIRGIN GORDA

beach is the Baths. Anchor 75 to 100 yards off the beach in 25 to 35 feet of water. Then check your anchor with mask and flippers, as there are numerous coral heads hereabouts that could foul your anchor or sever a nylon line. A ground swell is almost always felt here, sometimes of uncomfortable proportions.

If you run into poor conditions, better postpone your visit until another time, or tie up at Virgin Gorda Yacht Harbour and hire a Jeep for a visit by land. But do make the effort.

Virgin Gorda Yacht Harbour (25609, CK-3, I-A232),

marked by lighted buoys for entering just S of Colison Point, is in all respects a full-service marina. It has floating slips for over a hundred yachts, along with such welcome amenities as a food commissary, ship's chandlery, restaurant, bar, showers, coin laundry, and an ice-making machine. If this is not enough, a shopping center is nearby. You can also clear customs and immigration here. Rockresorts runs this highly civilized place, and also the nearby Little Dix Bay Hotel and Caneel Bay Plantation back on Saint John.

One may anchor overnight comfortably outside the marina, S of Colison Point and clear of the traffic.

Immediately SW of the yacht harbor is a 4-acre yacht yard with a 60T lift and ample storage space. The facility is a part of the Virgin Gorda Yacht Harbour complex.

Spanish Town is a small and rather sleepy settlement that was the capital of the British Virgins back in the eighteenth century. A goodly percentage of the native population works for Rockresorts.

Across the island from Spanish Town are the ruins of a copper mine and smelter originally worked by British and Welsh miners. A native boy will lead you there, or you can find your own way by crossing to the eastern shore and turning S. After rounding a few boulders, you will spot the stack of the copper works. This is a long hike on foot, but the mine can be reached by rental Jeep or mini-moke, available at the Yacht Harbour.

Savana and Pound Bays (25609, CK-3, I-A232)

provide good holding in sand. While sea conditions are generally calm, this anchorage is not recommended for overnight during the winter season.

In order for you to see the bottom, Savana Bay should be entered only in the middle of the day when the sun is high. Steer initially for a rock painted with white diagonal stripes, leaving it about 200 yards off, then head for a house to the E while keeping a sharp eye for coral heads.

Yachts are discouraged from entering Little Dix Bay, which is particularly subject to a ground swell anyway.

GORDA SOUND (25610, CK-11, I-A232)

Here is probably the most magnificent piece of protected water in the entire Virgin Islands. Once you have reached this outpost area, treat yourself to several days of exploring, swimming, snorkeling, fishing, and visiting the guest houses and resorts that have cropped up here.

The northern entrance into the sound is the safest entrance, being 20 feet or more deep and passable in heavy seas. It lies between the NW tip of Prickly Pear Island and Colquhoun Reef. When approaching from the W, keep the reef 30 to 50 yards on your beam until the entrance opens up, at which time you'll see one

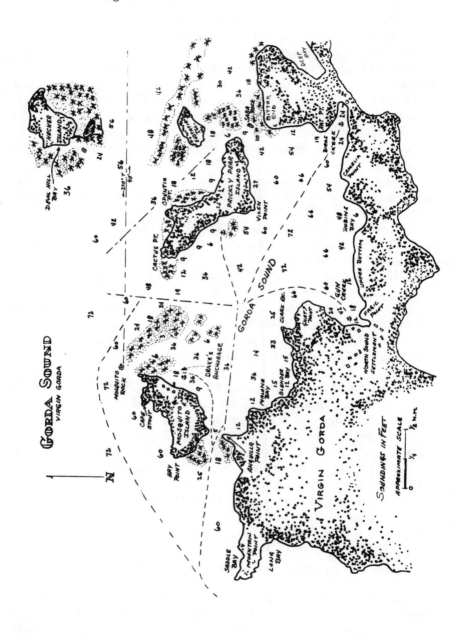

GORDA SOUND
VIRGIN GORDA

N

SOUNDINGS IN FEET
APPROXIMATE SCALE
0   ¼   ½ N.M.

pair of red and green buoys marking the channel. The reef is always breaking or awash. Turn into the entrance on 180°T, favoring the western side of the channel, to stay clear of the small reef extending from Cactus Point. Once you are inside the reef, Gorda Sound is relatively clear of hazards to the S and E. While it hardly seems necessary to warn against trying to use this entrance at night, a number of boats have piled up here trying to do just that. One bareboat charterer, mindful of the usual instruction "Don't sail at night," figured it would be OK to run the passage under power and ended up on Colquhoun Reef!

If you are planning to anchor off Mosquito Island, note the three small reefs that extend southward from Colquhoun Reef. (The southernmost is marked with a white buoy.) To avoid these reefs, maintain your course of 180°T (and directly toward Gnat Point) until Anguilla Point bears due W, or until Seal Dog Rocks (outside the sound) drop behind the point. Then turn westerly until Drake's Anchorage is approximately N, then continue to the anchorage.

The western entrance, a narrow passage between Mosquito Island and Anguilla Point, can be used by yachts drawing 7 feet. However, heavy ground swells may break across the entire entrance, making it unusable.

The reef extending S from Mosquito Island is always awash and sometimes breaking. Leave this reef approximately 30 yards off the port beam as you approach on a course of 090°T. Stay in midchannel until just inside Anguilla Point, then head southeasterly for the middle of the Leverick Bay Estates, a group of mostly circular buildings. Crossing the sand bar in this vicinity we have found no less than 7 feet. Beyond this shallow spot, the sound deepens to 20 feet or more. This southeasterly detour around the shallow spot is the most reliable, because the commercial boats going into Gun Creek tend to keep it open. It can also be easily seen when the sea is calm.

If continuing eastward from this entrance, be careful to stand S of the three reef patches that project S from Colquhoun Reef.

Drake's Anchorage (25610, CK-11, I-A232)
offers a small guest house, restaurant, and marina facility on the eastern shore of Mosquito Island. The anchorage itself is pleasant and usually quiet, being well protected by Colquhoun Reef. The holding is good in sand. Yachts of any draft can anchor within 50 yards of shore in the vicinity of the dock.

The flagpole here is the mast of Huey Long's first *Ondine,* which went on the reefs of Anegada some years ago. If this can happen to a modern sailing machine, well equipped with electronic gear, imagine what a hazard the Anegada Reefs were to the lumbering sailing craft of earlier days. The number of wrecks on Anegada is phenomenal, and they make for interesting diving. Records show that the reef claimed 90 vessels between 1653 and 1843.

Gun Creek (25610, CK-11, I-A232)
is the only native settlement in Gorda Sound. Supplies of any kind are very limited. The approach is straightforward. Anchor 30 to 50 yards from the head

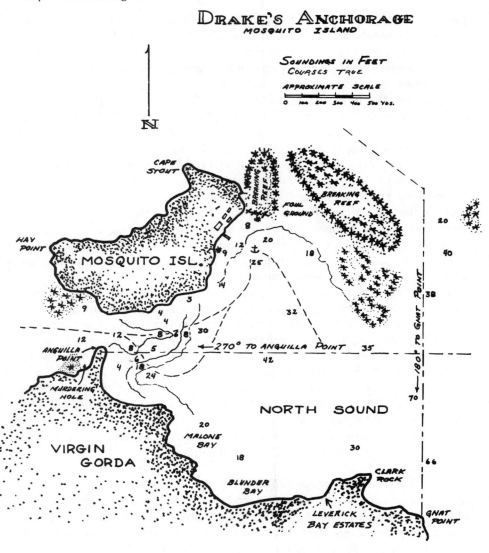

DRAKE'S ANCHORAGE
MOSQUITO ISLAND

SOUNDINGS IN FEET
COURSES TRUE

APPROXIMATE SCALE

0   100   200   300   400   500 YDS.

N

CAPE STOUT

BREAKING REEF

FOUL GROUND

BREAKING REEF

20

40

HAY POINT

MOSQUITO ISL.

8

12   20

9   18

25

4

3

4

9

32

30

38

180 TO GNAT POINT

12   12   8   8   8

ANGUILLA POINT

8   5

6

4   18

24

← 270° TO ANGUILLA POINT   35

42

35

70

MURDERING HOLE

NORTH SOUND

20
MALONE BAY

VIRGIN GORDA

18

30

66

CLARK ROCK

BLUNDER BAY

LEVERICK BAY ESTATES

GNAT POINT

of the bay, where it is generally calm and the holding is good in sandy mud. The swimming is fair, but there are more attractive places close by.

A climb to the top of the hill will reward you with views of the lovely South Sound, the nearby islands, and Anegada to the N.

Biras Creek (25610, CK-11, I-A232),

in the bottom corner of the sound, affords excellent protection under almost all conditions. The new resort there consists of cottages, pools, and a hotel offering fine meals with a beautiful view in lovely surroundings. The floating docks are for the hotel's small fleet of boats. You may anchor, or pick up one of the moorings after checking with the dockmaster. Water, fuel, and ice are available.

When approaching Biras Creek from the W, keep a sharp eye open for Oyster Rock, about 200 yards offshore, just N of Camelia Point. This menace is just below the surface and cannot always be seen. Otherwise the approach is clear.

Saba Rock (25610, CK-11, I-A232),

which divides the channel between Prickly Pear Island and Virgin Gorda, presents a lovely anchorage off its western side. But be sure to allow ample swinging room, or put out a stern anchor. As the tidal stream changes, it has been known to set the unwary skipper right against the rock. The approach from the W is clear of dangers.

It is usually calm here, and the holding is good in sand. Swimming is excellent, and the place is generally bug free even under the dampest conditions. Saba Rock is private property, so do not go ashore.

Just S of Saba Rock, you may anchor or pick up a mooring off the attractive Bitter End Yacht Club, or use their new marina facilities, which include showers and ice.

Prickly Pear Island (25610, CK-11, I-A232)

offers a pleasant anchorage on a sandy shelf 200–300 feet wide about halfway down its western side. The approach is clear except for one or two coral heads about 400 yards N of Vixen Point and about 150 yards from shore. It is usually calm here, and the holding is good in sand. Leverick Bay is the home of a Canadian charter organization. The moorings and dock accommodate both private and charter boats.

Eustatia Sound

The main body of this sound is well protected by an outer reef and provides good swimming and excellent snorkeling right from your boat. The approach should be made only under ideal conditions—that is, a calm sea, unriled water, and the sun overhead and slightly behind you. In such circumstances, all the rocks and reefs along the route can be spotted well ahead of time. Con your way from the rigging if you can. Enter the sound on the S side of Saba Rock on a heading of 060°T until you reach the deeper water. When entering from Virgin Sound, stay midway between Prickly Pear and Eustatia islands and be aware of the reef NW of Eustatia.

Start your return trip to Gorda Sound in good afternoon light or you will have a problem picking your way around the hazards while heading into the sun.

Deep Bay (25610, CK-11, I-A232),

in the southwestern corner of Eustatia Sound, has a clear approach except for some small reefs and rocks close to shore. For a good overnight anchorage, move well up into the bay and drop the hook in 10 feet. Holding is good in sand.

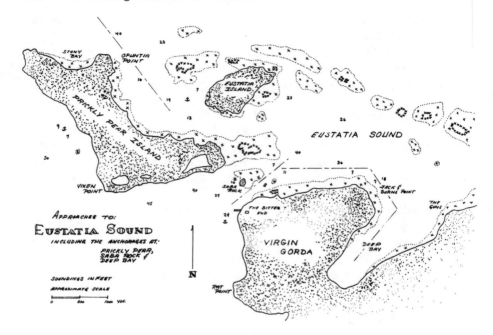

Virgin Sound

Lying between Eustatia and Necker islands, this small sound is open to the N and E; it is not a really pleasant cruising area except under light sea and wind conditions. The reefs S of Necker Island are quite obvious, but those N of Eustatia Island are not so easily seen, even under ideal conditions. For a safe, midchannel passage through this sound, hold a course or a back bearing 270°T on Mosquito Rock.

Eustatia Island (25610, CK-11, I-A232)

may be easily and safely approached from the NW. Simply pass Opuntia Point (on Prickly Pear Island) about 50 yards off on a heading of 150°T and sail right on in. Anchor off the beach on Prickly Pear or in the lee of Eustatia. You are requested not to go ashore on Eustatia.

On a nice day, under the right conditions, this is a truly delightful spot, but it cannot be recommended as an overnight anchorage in winter because of its exposure to the N.

Necker Island (25610, CK-11, I-A232)

is a lovely spot with beautiful beaches and excellent snorkeling. A resort on the hill commands a spectacular view. The approach from Virgin Sound is straightforward. Look for the small rise of land on the island's SW corner; the rise flattens out to the eastward. Approach this rise, which is called Devil Hill, on a northerly

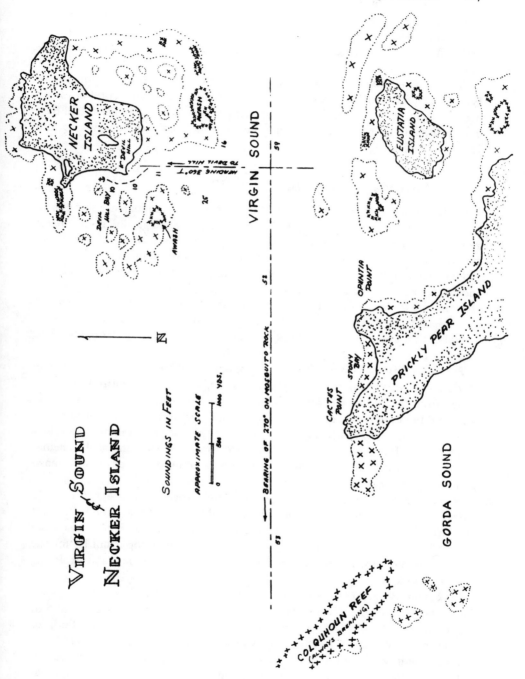

VIRGIN SOUND & NECKER ISLAND

NECKER ISLAND

VIRGIN SOUND

EUSTATIA ISLAND

PRICKLY PEAR ISLAND

OPUNTIA POINT

STONY BAY

CACTUS POINT

GORDA SOUND

COLQUHOUN REEF
(ALWAYS BREAKING)

SOUNDINGS IN FEET

APPROXIMATE SCALE

0   500   1000 YDS.

BEARING OF 270° ON MOSQUITO ROCK

HEADING 350°T — TO DEVIL HILL

DEVIL HILL

DEVIL BAY

AWASH

N

heading, with a watchful eye for a small, isolated reef on your port hand. In fact you will do best to favor the eastern side of the channel, since the reef on this side is more visible and continuous, whereas the coral patches to port are scattered.

Anchor about 100 yards off the rocky shore directly below this small rise, or bear off around the point, picking your way through the isolated coral heads, to a good anchorage not more than halfway along the lovely beach in Devil Hill Bay. This is a daytime stop, to be used only under ideal conditions for entering and leaving.

Anegada (25609, CK-4, I-A232)

Loosely translated from the Spanish, Anegada means "inundated"; and that it practically is! Contrasting sharply with the rest of this island group, this northernmost Virgin Island is nowhere more than 30 feet high. It is unapproachable except by eyeballing through a barrier reef that completely surrounds this seagirt patch of land. This combination of low-profile and dangerous fringing reef demands the most exacting dead reckoning, coupled with a healthy respect for the vagaries of the currents in this vicinity. Perhaps it is this last factor that has driven so many fine vessels to their death; perhaps it is the very immensity of the hazard, which stretches in a crescent of 23 unbroken miles, if you include the Horseshoe and Herman reefs to the south of the island itself.

For years this windswept island had been populated by 300 or so natives, who made their living primarily from the sea. Then, in 1968, the entire island was leased from the British Crown to an English land developer, who industriously set about building roads, docks, and airport, a hotel, and a smattering of model homes—in the hopes of generating more interest in Anegada, and more development money. But this bold project ran out of steam, as so many such schemes do, and Anegada is now back to its original population of 300 or so, who make their living primarily from the sea.

No one would dispute the island's potential for resort development. Almost 22 miles of unbroken beach, on an island in the middle of the trade-wind belt, is not an asset to be overlooked. But in the meantime, in a setting about as far from civilization as you can get nowadays, there are unlimited opportunities for the yachtsman (and others who can get there) for snorkeling, diving, and exploring reefs and wrecks.

Make your departure for a position about 2 miles 180°M from Anegada's West End. You are unlikely to sight the "inundated island" until you are within 5 or 6 miles of it, so be sure you are not set to the east of this line on West End, for obvious reasons! As you close the land, you will be able to identify Pomato Point and the buildings along the beach near Setting Point. The pass through the reef to the anchorage is marked by two widely separated posts sitting on the reef, as shown in the sketch chart. Line yourself up with the white hotel building

ANEGADA

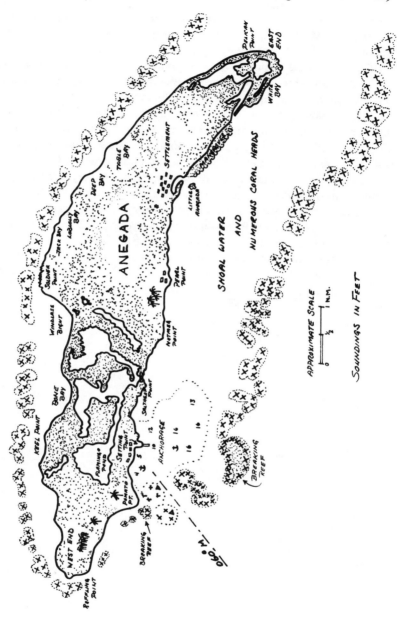

APPROXIMATE SCALE

SOUNDINGS IN FEET

N

SHOAL WATER AND NUMEROUS CORAL HEADS

ANEGADA

PELICAN POINT

EAST END

WHITE BAY

SETTLEMENT

TABLE BAY

DEEP BAY

BONES BAY

JACK BAY

SOLDIER POINT

WINDLASS POINT

KEEL POINT

BONE BAY

SETTING POINT

FLAMINGO POND

WEST END

BREAKING REEF

PABLINE POINT

SALTHEAP POINT

NUTMEG POINT

PEBBLE POINT

LITTLE FLAMINGO

ANCHORAGE

BREAKING REEF

(Anegada Reefs Hotel) on your bow and Jost Van Dyke dead astern while steering 060°M. If you are on a proper course, you will leave the first post marker about 250 yards off and the second one 150 yards off, both of course to port.

If you are at all unsure of your approach, establish VHF radio contact with Anegada Reefs Hotel or Neptune's Treasure Hotel. Someone from either facility will be able to guide you in simply by observation—just follow their directions.

Yachts drawing 5 feet or less may anchor well in the lee of Setting Point. Deeper-draft vessels may anchor S from Setting Point dock or farther E, where the water deepens to 16 feet. This anchorage is almost a mile wide and a mile and a half long and provides excellent protection under practically all conditions. The sea is generally calm in the lee of Setting Point. A very light chop sometimes develops in the more open anchorage. Holding is good in sandy mud and grass.

The Ministry of Natural Resources has proposed designating a 10-mile strip of Anegada's Horse Shoe Reef as a Fisheries Protected Zone. Both anchoring and fishing would thereby be forbidden in that strip, where 185 different species of fish and 30 separate species of coral have been identified.

Chapter Nine

THE WINDWARDS AND LEEWARDS

By Jolyon Byerley

When the Caribbean islands burst through into the sunlight, the gods in charge of the area must have had a pretty keen sailor on the board of directors. Admittedly, someone blundered a little in the vicinity of the Anegada Passage, but on the whole, the islands stretch away to the south an amazingly regular 20 miles apart and at a handy right angle to the bustling trade winds. The lee coasts have an abundance of perfect harbors, usually strategically placed at either end of the islands, and most of the loose bits of rock, which in the beginning must have splattered around, fell into deep enough water not to be a nuisance.

The original inhabitants were the Arawaks, a band of cheerful, peace-loving layabouts whose main occupation must have been breaking their cooking pots into a million pieces with a view to occupying the time of present-day archaeologists. Nobody is too sure exactly what sort of vessels the Arawaks used for their early exploring of the sometimes rather rough passages. We do know that the Caribs, a group of ferocious gentlemen with prodigious appetites, made long, light canoes from logs of the *gommier* tree: keeping their cooking pots whole, they ate their way northward from Venezuela as far as Haiti and possibly Cuba, much to the consternation of the Arawaks.

Much later, when the British, French, Spanish, and Dutch were squabbling mightily over the islands and blowing each other's heads off with cannonballs the weight and consistency of my Aunt Mabel's Christmas pudding, the Caribs in their almost unsinkable canoes very nearly overcame the might of the European navies pitted against them. Brave and skillful seamen, they easily outstripped the lumbering naval ships, pulling off incredible feats of daring into the bargain.

On one occasion, a war party from Dominica paddled to Antigua and landed just east of English Harbour in a tiny hidden inlet known as Indian Creek. Knocking off a few dozen Redcoats, they kidnapped the governor's good lady and a dozen bottles of his favorite port, had dinner, and paddled back to Dominica. They obviously had other attributes, for when Her Ladyship was rescued by all the king's men, she was most reluctant to return, preferring the wild mountain stronghold to the bright lights of Antigua.

Carib canoes are still built in the islands of Dominica, Martinique, and Saint Lucia, and are just as popular amongst the fishermen as more conventional modern boats. Now, mostly propelled by massive government-financed outboards

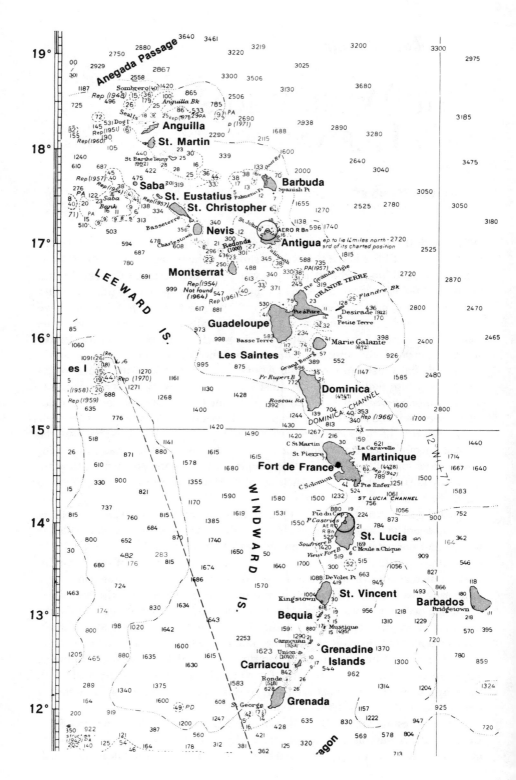

The Windwards and Leewards

instead of patchwork sails, they are a fabulous sight, screaming in rainbows of spray through the tumbling trade-wind seas or lying perilously ahull in midchannel while their occupants calmly tend their lines.

After the demise of the Caribs, the islands became a focal point in the European struggle for power. Most large vessels of the day, unable to do much more than lumber downwind like runaway haystacks, preferred to take the trade-wind route to the New World. These islands lay like a giant tollgate across their path. Therefore, whoever controlled these little outposts controlled the Americas. With a strange mixture of sadness, awe, and excitement, one can now wander through these old battlefields. Relative to the size of the area, more British and French troops died in combat on the slopes of Saint Lucia's Morne Fortune than anywhere else except the trenches of Flanders. Two thousand fathoms down, between the shrouded peaks of Guadeloupe and Dominica and under the hurrying, forgetful waves, lies almost the whole of Admiral de Grasse's battle fleet, outsailed and outmaneuvered by the vengeful tars of Admiral Rodney's West Indian Squadron.

The charm of cruising the islands these days is that, outside of the major cities, things have changed very little through the centuries. Even the most sluggish imagination can leap into the past: anchored in a moon-drenched bay, the watcher, already awed by the enormous tropical night, sees close inshore under the shadowy slumbering palms the indistinct image of a six-man Carib canoe slipping stealthily into the darkness. How many times on a similar night had the young Horatio Nelson looked into the depth of the jungle and pondered its secrets?

Yachtsmen were quick to discover the islands: Captain Slocum, Fritz Fenger, and Eric Hiscock were among those who wrote admiringly of what they saw. Only recently, though, has it become commonplace to sight another yacht crossing the passages, and even now, despite a fairly high density of yachts in English Harbour, Fort-de-France, Castries, Kingstown, and Saint George's, one cannot complain of overcrowding. The main reason this yachtsman's paradise is so free of traffic is undoubtedly that few Stateside yachtsmen relish the 1,800 miles or so of slogging to windward. And make no mistake—slog, slog, slog it nearly always is.

In jotting down these notes, I am making no attempt to give sailing directions in intricate detail. The intention is to make life a little easier for the cruising yachtsman. Having found his way to the islands in the first place, he can presumably manage another 400 miles without too much hassle. Finding a reliable taxi driver is generally more of a problem than finding the channel into the next harbor.

Wind, Seas, and Strategy

Weather conditions throughout the islands are fairly predictable. December through April, the trade wind blows at its hardest. I would put the mean at something between 18 and 23 knots from the east. However, I have known weeks at a time when the trades have seldom dropped below 30–35 knots, gusting to 45 at times, and persisting in the ENE or ESE. Conversely, I remember one February so calm that *Lord Jim*'s 2,000-square-foot golleywobbler was constantly in use, more to shade our gently broiling charterers than to catch the fitful puffs. But, luckily, the winter season is almost always a time of superb sailing conditions, when the accent is slightly more on the boisterous than the balmy. The rest of the year generally produces a wind that averages 12–15 knots and widens its angle to between NE and SE. In August, September, and October, it can get pretty warm ashore at times, although at sea the temperature would compare favorably to that of a summer day off the Chesapeake.

These months are also when most hurricanes pass through the Caribbean. Although the Windwards and Leewards are frequently bypassed, Hurricane Hugo crossed right over Guadeloupe in September of 1989, causing extensive damage there and, to a lesser degree, in Antigua. That storm followed on the heels of our trip made to update this text. You may observe considerable destruction resulting from that storm that will not be noted in these pages.

For 3,000 miles, the Atlantic has rolled itself along at a fair clip, with the constant trades using plenty of spur to good effect. No wonder, then, that by the time a much-traveled wave is bottlenecked between the islands, it has grown into a rare broth of a boy and eager to make itself felt. On a reach-through, the well-found yacht will find such a sea only exhilarating. To windward it's another matter. Squalls and the higher islands affect local conditions considerably. A West Indian squall, very common in slightly unstable weather, normally increases the wind strength by 10–15 knots.

After many years of shortening sail in such weather, I've eventually settled instead on running off, sheeting everything in hard to keep the speed down, and waiting it out. Five minutes usually does it. There is no hard and fast rule, but if the squall moves fast and you can't see through it, be prepared for a bit of a bashing. As a yacht leaves a high island, she will generally find that the wind will head for 15–20 minutes and blow a good deal harder than in midchannel. Likewise, the wind will both step up and free as the yacht runs under the lee of the next island. If it is a marginal reefing day as you poke your nose from under an island such as Dominica or Saint Vincent, hang on for 10 minutes or so, and the chances are you can then have a good full-sail breeze. In the lee, the wind will funnel down the bigger valleys, blow like Stan Kenton's old brass section, and then fan out to the N and S. Under the hills, it will die or even come in from the W. You'll probably do best to stay about one half mile offshore and play the puffs. At least the seas are flat and the scenery is great.

The traditional point of departure from the British Virgin Islands to the Leewards* is Round Rock Passage, just SE of Virgin Gorda. Many crews, having made it to the Caribbean, become a trifle blasé about the whole thing and are apt to swagger off southward, fully intending "to let the balmy trades waft them

*See Appendix A, The Leeward and Windward Islands and Vice Versa.

gently through the satin-smooth seas of the Indies." That's what it says on the travel posters, anyway, but the first of the slab-sided seas of the Anegada Passage is rather inclined to dampen their enthusiasm.

Between Round Rock and Philipsburg, Saint Martin, is 81 miles. The NE trades, which for most of the year can be relied upon to be easterly or even S of E, seldom allow even the most close-winded of vessels to lay Saint Martin. From Round Rock it's 82 miles to Saba, a magical, storybook island hardly ever visited before 1973, because it had no safe anchorage whatsoever. Many times we have stood forlornly off, watching the spray hurl itself up the rocks at both of the island's so-called landing places. Now, however, a substantial stone mole has been constructed by the Dutch government, and provided the wind is not in the N and the limited space not taken up by local trading schooners, a safe night can be spent alongside. Generally, though, a yacht heading S should not rely on finding favorable conditions at Saba, and may find it best to bash on to Saint Martin or the nearby islands of Anguilla or Saint Barts, where good, comfortable harbors abound.

A word about the Anegada Passage might be in order hereabouts. If you're going south, do not take the passage lightly. Your vessel should be prepared for steep, confused seas that sometimes bear little relation to the strength or direction of the wind. In February 1972, the experienced captain of a 130-foot motor yacht reported to English Harbour Radio, Antigua, that he was tangling with conditions as unpleasant as any he had met in 35 years of ocean cruising. Obviously the angle of attack has a lot to do with it, and certain Caribbean yachtsmen advise paying off a fraction, making a proper passage of it, and heading for the first island that can comfortably be reached—Montserrat, Guadeloupe, or Dominica, for example. Only conditions at the time can decide this, but should the wind have a slight northerly slant, jump at the chance to cross this aggravating bit of water.

A very large area of relatively shallow water lies SSW of Saba, with a least depth of 4½ fathoms on its NE corner. In blowy conditions, the local schooner men keep well clear, calling it "a damn vexin' piece of troublesome water."

The current in the Anegada Passage normally sets to the NW or W, but in places seems to have a mind of its own. On one occasion, after a quiet night crossing from the Virgins, we found ourselves so far to the east of our course that the low-lying island of Anguilla came up on the starboard beam instead of the port bow. But if the Anegada is unpredictable and aggravating, remember that, once he has crossed it, the sailing man is then in the most perfect sailing conditions in the world.

Radio Communications

Communication over the airways has changed considerably in recent years, and I have yet to be convinced that it is entirely for the good. In the past, everyone used AM (double sideband) on 2527 kHz, and it was nearly always possible to make contact throughout the island chain. Now, with the advent of VHF and

SSB, yachtsmen either jam the airways on VHF (even when within a stone's throw of each other) or go stark staring mad attempting to unscramble the weird Disney World sounds which emanate from SSB. Neither system appears to bridge the gap left by the demise of the "Children's Hour." Every island has vast quantities of VHF sets and a call on Channel 16 is sure to find some helpful soul. Channels 16 and 06 are the most commonly used chat frequencies.

The northern islands of the chain are best served by Saba Radio, with its 7-day, 24-hour listening watch on VHF-16. With its antenna located some 2,000 feet high, range and reception are excellent. Worldwide telephone calls can be made provided you can supply current registration details. In Antigua, English Harbour Radio monitors VHF-16 and SSB 4125.0 kHz, using 8291.1 kHz and 16587.1 kHz as alternatives after contact has been made. Phone patch facilities are not available. Listening hours are from 0830 to 1630 every day but Sunday. Destrellan Radio in Guadeloupe monitors VHF-16 and 2182 kHz, as do Fort-de-France Radio in Martinique and Barbados Radio. Phone calls can be made on all three. Stevens Yachts in Saint Lucia listens on VHF-16 and SSB 2527 kHz except for periods from 1130 to 1200 and 1530 to 1600, when they stand by on 4139.5 kHz. Most of the older resorts in the Grenadines monitor either VHF-16 or DSB 2527 kHz. Perhaps the best weather forecast is supplied by Radio Antilles in Montserrat on 930 kHz medium-wave band at 0805 and 1830 local time.

The Nicholson family of Antigua pioneered radio communications in the early 1950s, when they realized that their charter clients sometimes found it necessary to keep in touch with their homes and businesses. Commander V.E.B. Nicholson bought the second-oldest transmitter in the world, set up schedules at 0900 and 1600 hours, and kept in close contact with his little fleet, a happening that was soon to become a tradition enjoyed by charter crews and guests alike.

"Hello, *Carrina.* Ah, John, old boy," he would boom, "those head parts haven't arrived yet. I can send you down an old bowler hat of mine, or one of Emmie's flowerpots. Anyway, old boy, tell Mr. Smith [the charterer] that I hope everything's taking an equal strain. English Harbour clear with *Carrina,* and hello *Freelance.* Bruno, old boy. Good morning, afternoon, and evening to you."

The number of boats and the corresponding traffic density now preclude sheer entertainment, but it can still be amusing. For instance:

"Hello, such-and-such, this is PSV. We have a bikini top and a man's brown headpiece found under the bar after last night's jump-up."

On more than one occasion, these "yachty" radio stations have organized search and rescue operations. Several lives have definitely been saved as a result. There are no organized coast guard services south of Saint Martin and north of Trinidad; yachtsmen are rather on their own.

Lifesaving Equipment

Most of the islands are steep-to, and even Auntie Mabel, whose watery eyes once mistook a mustachioed Buckingham Palace Guardsman for a red postbox, would become dimly aware of such a land mass before it was too late. The exceptions, such as Antigua, Barbuda, Anguilla, and the Grenadines, have most of their reefs on the windward side, so that a mariner in real trouble, apart from getting scratched up a bit on the way in, would soon drift ashore, perhaps in the middle of the local hostelry's lobster barbecue. More of a problem would be the yacht that foundered because of fire, explosion, or tired caulking and happened to be in the middle of an island passage at the time.

An inflatable life raft, especially the type with a canopy, takes off to leeward at the very dickens of a rate in the usual trade-wind conditions, so the important thing (if it is impossible to work north or south across the trades to the nearest island) is to endeavor not to drift too fast to the west. Once through the island chain, it's a long haul to Central America; therefore, a larger-than-usual sea anchor should be carried, along with a good set of rockets for nighttime and a mirror and smoke for daylight.

Personally, my choice would every time be a good, nonsinkable sailing dinghy. Even a small one would stand a chance of towing a medium-sized life raft on a reach and into the lee of the nearest island. In recent years several yachtsmen have, in fact, been forced to put this theory to the test and all are alive to tell the tale.

Firearms

In recent years much hysterical publicity has been given to so-called acts of piracy in the Caribbean, and even the U.S. Coast Guard has suggested that firearms should be carried on board. In my 24 years in the Windwards and Leewards, I cannot recall one incident where a yacht has been boarded while at sea. On the other hand, there have been a few instances of a most unpleasant nature that have involved yachts at anchor. All island authorities require firearms to be declared on arrival and, in many places, police will hold the guns until the yacht's departure, which of course defeats the purpose of carrying them in the first place. If a sufficiently secure lock-up can be provided on board, small-caliber handguns and sporting guns can usually remain on the ship. The concern of the authorities is, of course, that weapons may be stolen while the yacht is in the harbor. Do not, however, expect to breeze through customs with a couple of M-16s and a bazooka; most small islands cannot boast of such an armory themselves. Truthfully, though, I would have no qualms about seeing my Auntie Mabel sail up and down the islands forever without even her dreaded hatpin.

Sunburn

For as long as I remember, I've had a horror of pajamas. At a very early age, I was given a pair by Auntie Mabel. They were bedecked with a ghastly maroon-and-blue stripe and had a weight and bristliness similar to the coat of an old Highland bull. I distinctly remember that you could stand them alone on the floor and crawl through their hairy interior; it was like entering an empty suit of armor. Regulation boarding-school and army pajamas did little to change my attitude. Anyway, I haven't owned a pair for 22 years. This fact, I am told, should stop me from ever emerging into the West Indian sunlight. Pajamas are the only way to avoid being frizzled to death, say the experts, and bound by this advice, there seems to be a never-ending parade of the nasty, floppy things.

The great pajama game has been going on for all my time in the islands, but unless you are one of those unfortunates who immediately becomes burnt to a crisp and never tans, common-sense exposure—with the help of one of the excellent, nongreasy liquid sun creams—will suffice. Make no mistake, however: the sun can be wickedly hot and damaging to an unbronzed northern skin; therefore I suggest you give serious thought to equipping your boat with a small sailing awning or a collapsible Bimini top.

A strong trade wind blowing against a salt-encrusted face can do just as much damage as the sun, so it's not a bad idea to rinse off with fresh water every so often, then apply a fresh load of gunk. A barrier cream such as "Shade," applied between 1100 and 1400, is very good protection.

In harbor, an awning is a must. It should be easy to rig, preferably of dark-colored material like blue Vivetex, and fitted with roll-down side curtains as a protection against driving rain and the late-afternoon sun. A roll-down curtain on the rear of the awning is a good thing if, as on most medium-sized yachts, the relaxing place is in the cockpit. One always lies at anchor facing east or thereabouts, and from 1600 until dusk the only shade is up at the pointed end! Whatever you do, make your awning simple and taut. The pretty, scalloped affair so carefully arranged with battens and myriad pieces of string may have looked shipshape in Force 0 up a quiet Florida creek, but during a squall in the Tobago Cays it will become a passable imitation of Aunt Mabel's washing in a wind tunnel.

The Northern Leewards—Saint Martin (25613, I-A24)

Anguilla, Saint Martin, and Saint Barts offer as much variety as one can expect to find in the West Indies. The only feature lacking on these three islands is the dense mountain foliage found on the higher, more tropical islands to the south. Saint Martin, very small, half French and half Dutch (the Dutch call their half Sint Maarten), is both bustling with commercial enterprise and lazing in the warm peace of the tropics. It is ringed with bays and beaches, and a yacht of moderate draft, say up to 8 feet, can find many anchorages around the coast. But with charter fleets now operating in the area, many anchorages are no longer empty.

Philipsburg (25613, I-A24)

is the capital of the Dutch section. By comparison, it makes the French capital of Marigot seem quaint. However, after one has sampled the pleasure of free-port

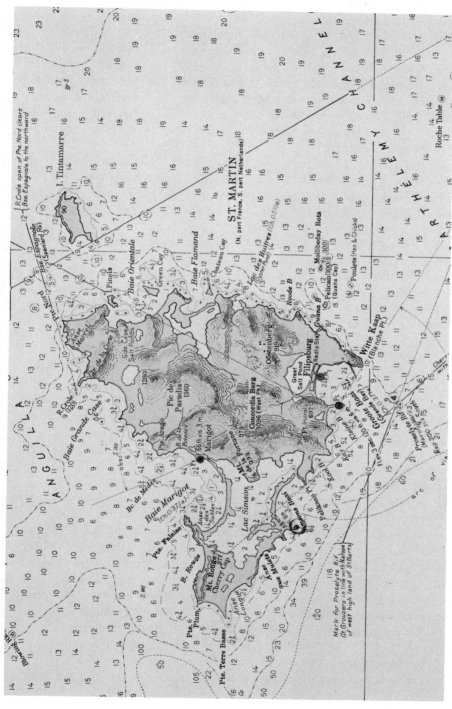

Sint Maarten/Saint Martin

shopping in Philipsburg (cameras, watches, tape recorders, binoculars, jewelry, and booze), I personally prefer the rural French side.

On entering Philipsburg, fly the yellow flag and, as a courtesy, the Dutch national flag (if you have forgotten to get one, then fly the French flag with the stripes horizontal, but don't say I suggested it). You will find that nobody is much interested in you, so the skipper should proceed ashore to the police station, just behind the church at the back of the main square. The officials will give you a form to fill out. Neither customs nor immigration worry as much on this island as they do on some others.

Favor the western end of the bay for the approach. Philipsburg, like most of the bays on the S and W coasts, occasionally suffers from a heavy swell, but the most comfortable and untroubled part of the bay is the NE corner, as close to Bobbie's Landing as draft allows. Bobbie's offers a wide variety of services, including hauling, and sells fuel and water.

Slightly to the W of Bobbie's is Great Bay Marina, a new enterprise with draft limited to around 7 feet. Chesterfield's Bar and Restaurant is a good spot both to leave one's dinghy and to cool off, and Great Bay Marina now has a jetty, with 9 feet alongside, where fuel, water, and ice are available. The bay shallows quickly about one half- to three fourths-mile from shore, and 7–8 foot draft is just about maximum to get close up to the beach.

Simson Lake (25608, I-A24)

is a large and mostly rather shallow lagoon that offers complete protection from the sea but little from the wind. To gain entrance, a swing bridge must be opened. At present, the bridge from Marigot opens at 0900 and 1700 daily. Yachts with draft up to 9 feet may enter and anchor or move around in a small area that is nicely developed with some places to Med-moor, cafés, restaurants, and shops. We saw a fleet of 20 or 30 miniature 12-meter boats tied up there, and were only sorry not to see them out racing.

Shallow water, 4 feet or less, precludes moving from the French to the Dutch side of Simson Lake unless a talked-about dredging project has taken place.

The bridge from the Dutch side at Simson Bay opens at 0630 and 1700 only. Just inside, several boats have anchors out, with bows tied to the beach. Depths in the channel and into the lagoon are over 20 feet for a considerable distance, probably dredged for fill to build the airport, which borders the lagoon. (Flights begin about 0900 and cease about 2130, and fly directly overhead.) Depths where most of the boats are anchored are 10 feet or less. Many of the boats anchored here have no one aboard for one reason or another, and it's a bit lonesome if you are looking for sociability. However, the absence of ground swell can be very welcome. It is an excellent hurricane hole, and services (a marina for shoal-draft boats, sailmaker, riggers, and electronic help) are available.

The holding is good, but the milky water and a number of shallows can make life a bit tricky. The place is certainly a godsend in the hurricane season though.

The Simson Lake Bridge, Sint Maarten, opens twice a day to allow yachts in and out.

Marigot (25608, I-A24),

on the French side, has recently been dredged and is a reasonable anchorage provided a northerly swell doesn't build up. If it is uncomfortable in Marigot, it's usually good in Philipsburg, and vice versa.

When I asked what the dredged depth was supposed to be, there was a great deal of shoulder-shrugging, but we found 9 feet in the vicinity of the moored boats close under the town.

Look for customs at the port (portside as you enter) where ferries and commercial boats are loaded and unloaded. The French official who checked us in made no charge, and took information about our boat on a blank sheet of paper after apologizing for running out of forms. We could have checked out if we wished, but it wasn't necessary. The process was very informal.

Don't rely on buying a lot of provisions in Marigot; you'll do better on the Dutch side. However, if you appreciate good food, toddle down to Le Mini Club, a waterside restaurant run by ex-yachtsman Pierre Plessis and his wife, Claude. Both speak English as it was spoken by Marurice Chevalier and are delightful hosts—and their food is the best on the island.

In their chartering days, Pierre and Claude had on their yacht a tame ocelot named Pompidou. It slept on Claude's bed in the master cabin, a situation obviously not possible when the cabin was given over to guests or on charter. At such times, Pompidou was banished to the fo'c'sle and exercised ashore in the dead of night—the charterers, of course, had no idea he was aboard. One night, by means of an open cupboard, the big cat found his way into the bilge and was able to creep aft and into the master cabin. The charterers were a hard-drinking elderly couple from Rhode Island. Pompidou padded onto his accustomed bed, put his paws on the good lady's shoulders, and with his big whiskery face inches from hers, began purring in loud contentment. The resulting scene hardly needs enlarging upon.

Marcel Cove (25613, I-A24),

on the northwest corner of the island, would make a good stop if you are looking for a marina in luxurious surroundings and excellent protection from any weather. The marina is part of L'Habitation de Lonvilliers Beach Hotel and Resort, which also includes shops, restaurants, and sports facilities.

Orient Bay (25613, I-A24),

on the E coast of the island, should be entered in good light. Enter midway between Caya Verte and Ile Pinels in 8 fathoms, while waves break on either side of you when the trade winds are blowing. When well in, turn right to anchor in the lee of Ile Pinel. Yachts with less than 6-foot draft can continue in behind Pit Petite Clef. A second good anchorage is at the opposite end of Orient Bay, in the shelter of Caya Verte. Both anchorages are reasonably free of ground swell. There is a naturist resort nearby, and quite a few naturists on the beaches.

Oyster Pond (25613, I-A24)

is a great place for the adventurous when a strong trade is blowing. There is a narrow entrance between the reefs, and since this anchorage is on the exposed eastern side of the island, a large, breaking sea can really enliven the proceedings.

I've entered Oyster Pond many times without incident, but once I nearly put *Mirage,* a single-screw, deep-draft trawler, halfway up a cactus bush on the nearest hill. Caught by a breaker, we were suddenly going sideways at an angle of 45° and at about 15 knots, with white water foaming angrily around the deckhouse. After the breaker had gone through, we clawed around again (thanks to a big rudder) and slipped inside before the next one grabbed us.

The channel, which is privately marked, has a red-and-white vertically striped stake at its entrance. Small red cans mark the starboard side of the channel, which should be favored. Do not rely on finding these buoys in place. Once around the dogleg to starboard, halfway along the channel, your problems are over.

Fuel, water, and electricity can be obtained inside the lagoon, where 10-foot draft is maximum. The hotel is delightful, and the staff is very anxious to please.

On another occasion we were in Oyster Pond during a period when the trades had been blowing at 30 knots for nearly three weeks. We had gone in with *Étoile de Mer* just as it started to blow, and getting out over the bar a week later was a hair-raising experience we won't soon forget. Mike Beal, the very experienced skipper of the Bill Tripp–designed *Katrinka,* watched us negotiate the channel from a vantage point about 12 feet above sea level and told us later that our 73-foot, heavy-displacement trawler completely disappeared in the troughs and looked like an exploding soufflé among the breaking crests. Obviously some of these waves must have been over 14 feet high.

I mention this as a reminder that the E side of any of the islands is no place to be during blustery winter weather. Save your exploring of the exposed coasts for another season.

Tintamarre Island (25613, I-A24),
once a secret airfield, was much used by a former mayor of Saint Barts. He assembled a veritable squadron of antiquated aircraft on the tiny strip. Quite what he did with them no one knows, but the remains are still there, littered over the tiny island. Anchor off the western tip in 3 fathoms.

Spaniard Rock,
a real hazard situated bang in the middle of the channel between Tintamarre and Saint Martin, is accurately charted and breaks in most weathers.

Anguilla (25613, I-A24)

You'll probably remember this little island's sudden climb to fame a few years ago. It went through a series of real-life events that would outdo a better-than-usual Hollywood farce. The scenario was written by Her Majesty's Britannic Government and was well up to its usual standard. The only snag was that someone forgot to invite the cameraman, which was indeed a great pity. Anyway, sandy little Anguilla used to be part of a group that also included Saint Kitts and Nevis, both relatively large and prosperous islands. The good people of Anguilla developed a "thing" about being poor relations, and one sultry day, in the best Gilbert and Sullivan tradition, armed with sticks and stones and the odd coconut, they packed their half-dozen Kittian policemen into a local schooner and sent them back to Saint Kitts with strict instructions for that island's leader. According to well-informed sources, the instructions had something to do with the bristly end of a pineapple.

Here the plot thickens. The government of Saint Kitts became convinced that nasty Sicilian-type gentlemen in wide-brimmed hats and sinister dark suits were behind it all and were planning to take over the island to build a private kingdom of naughtiness. Saint Kitts sent an impassioned appeal for assistance against the forces of evil to Her Majesty's Government, which lacking a gunboat but dying to do something exciting for a change, promptly dispatched a relief force of two

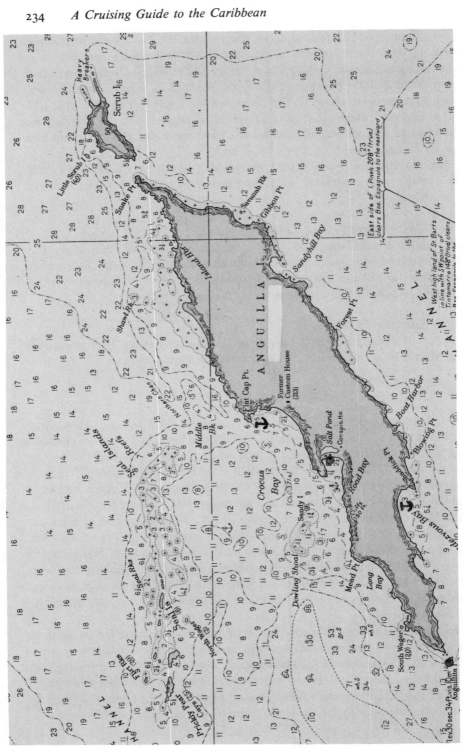

Anguilla

battalions of paratroopers, a squadron of helicopters, an antisubmarine frigate, six turboprop aircraft, and half the City of London police force, complete with blue serge jackets and pointed helmets.

Meanwhile, back at Anguilla, the citizens were employed in revolutionary activities like lobstering, boatbuilding, and lying in the sun. It obviously had to stop. At dawn one morning, the paratroopers, the helicopters, the antisubmarine frigate, and the London police force, backed by the six aircraft, stormed the beaches!

The opposing force—two small boys, one old lady, and six nanny goats—were soon in full flight back to the village, where the inhabitants were beginning another revolutionary day. Told of the landing, they rushed to the beaches. Soon the London police force was heavily engaged in solving two cases of poultry theft and a drunk-and-disorderly charge. The paratroopers, finding very few roads for their vehicles, proceeded to build some, plus a couple of schools, a clinic, and improvements to the airstrip. Never have an invading force and a crushed nation been so happy with each other. The actors having long since departed, the people

Outboards have replaced sails as the favorite means of propulsion for fishing boats in Anquilla and elsewhere in the Windwards and Leewards.

of Anguilla petitioned the British government in 1980 to allow them to remain a Crown Colony, to which a somewhat surprised cabinet duly agreed. So now sandy little Anguilla and its 6,000-odd people remain under the Union Jack—if there is a moral to this story, perhaps someone would be good enough to tell me what it is.

In any case, the cruising yachtsman will find it delightful. The people are very courteous and well-disposed toward visitors. For years they have held the position of being among the best seamen and shipbuilders in the West Indies. Now that the schooners are being superceded by small modern coasters, the shipwrights will be hard put to keep going.

Good ice can be obtained in this driest of dry islands by nipping over to the Valley, a 10-minute taxi ride from Sandy Ground.

A fee for a cruising permit was instigated in 1980. Both locally registered and visiting yachts are assessed. The regulation reads as if it applies only to charter boats, but was interpreted when we visited Road Bay to apply to all boats that wished to visit the outlying islands of the Prickly Pear Cays, etc. No fee at all was collected if your vessel would visit only the bays on the "mainland." A one-day cruising permit cost about U.S. $10. Though it was not clear how this tax was to be used, if one looks at it as a fee for a fishing license, it is high—but not exorbitant.

The customs official who met us as we beached our dinghy in Road Bay and directed us to his office in a building at the commercial pier was very courteous, and checking in took only a few minutes.

Sandy Ground, or Road Bay (25613, I-A24),

as the principal settlement is called, looks like a good, sheltered anchorage on the chart, but for much of the year it is plagued by an unpleasant swell. Several bar/restaurants front the bay, along with a boatbuilding shed and fishermen's homes and boats.

Rendezvous Bay (25613, I-A24)

is one of several around on the S coast opposite Marigot. At their extreme eastern ends, they usually give good shelter. The local sloops and schooners use 2 or 3 reef-fringed anchorages that are shallow and difficult to approach in a keel boat.

The island's beaches are the color and consistency of freshly fallen snow, and swimming off them is a sheer delight. Snorkeling is excellent all around the island.

Prickly Pear Cays (25613, I-A24)

will appeal particularly to the snorkeling enthusiast. Sneak just to windward of the easternmost island, between the reef and the little beach. Maximum draft is about 8 feet, but the fine sand bottom is subject to shoaling after heavy swells from the N.

All the reefs to the N of Anguilla offer some of the best diving in the Caribbean.

Native sloops and modern yachts anchor side by side in Road Bay, Anquilla. A steel band played on the afterdeck of this yacht during the cocktail hour, for the pleasure of all of us anchored nearby.

Dog Island (25613, I-A24)

is uninhabited, and is intriguing because of an unexplained, unused airstrip, but to find a good anchorage here is difficult indeed. Slip in through the coral heads on the western tip in good, calm weather only.

Sandy Island (25613, I-A24)

qualifies as a daytime anchorage and gives the crew a chance to explore everyone's dream island. Watch out for Long John Silver, though.

I would rather keep this last place a secret; as a compromise, it shall remain nameless.

A little way to the NE of Crocus Bay there is a long rocky point with a tiny sand beach at the eastern end. Anchor stern to the beach and make fast to a boulder. Jagged white cliffs fall into crystal-clear water, long-tailed bosun birds swoop through the masthead, and not a soul will you see. Absolutely idyllic.

Saint Barthélemy (Saint Barts) (25613, I-A24)

I suppose that Saint Barts is pretty close to being my favorite island, yet it's hard to say exactly why. It's a French island. Ever since I tacked the old schooner *Mollihawk* into Gustavia, way back in 1958, this tiny little fragment of Brittany has captivated me. The Swedes at one time owned the island, and maybe a little of their neatness has rubbed off on the more happy-go-lucky Breton fishermen who have lived here since the late 1800s.

Gustavia (25608, I-A24),

the island's minute capital, rings the harbor. Until a short time ago it was the base of smuggling operations for the entire Caribbean. Even now, battered old sloops from as far away as Trinidad and Venezuela can be seen alongside the dock loading up to the point of absurdity with case after case of Scotch whisky. Prior to 1973, only a quarter of the harbor was deep enough for anything but a short-legged seagull. Now just about all the space can be used, but so much mud and sand was removed from the bottom that some of the houses close to the water

Large yachts Med-moor around the seawall of Gustavia Harbor.

are leaning inward a little more than usual. Ten feet can go nearly anywhere, and it's quite normal to pick a spot and tie stern to the old walls.

Although customs and immigration formalities are minimal, the gendarmes sometimes feel a little neglected, and it's a good plan to nip along to their office (three minutes from the dock) and ask if they require anything. They will usually hand you a printed leaflet, which, among other things, tells you how to get to the *abattoir* and that riding a bicycle in the nude is prohibited. This apparently does not apply to motor scooters; recently, by the Eden Roc Hotel, two tanned and topless young things put the law regularly to the test.

Very good marine supplies are available from Loulou's Marine right on the town dock. Loulou, a cross between Ché Guevara and Harpo Marx, is one of the most helpful people to be found anywhere. A few years ago he started the now very popular Saint Bart's Regatta, one of the few sailing events where the actual results don't really matter—to be there is what counts!

Gustavia's good restaurants are so numerous it would be impossible to mention them all; but definitely give the cook a break and enjoy this little gastronomic heaven. Nearly everyone speaks fluent English here.

Baie de Colombier (25613, I-A24),

on the island's NW corner, is quite free of dangers right up to the beach.

Baie Saint Jean (25613, I-A24),

good in calm weather, is adjacent to the small and delightful Eden Roc Hotel. The wealthy young French jet-setters congregate here, and there is a little of the sparkle of Saint Tropez about the place. Nip along by taxi and have a look at the entrance before going in. On the way, if you are a light-plane enthusiast, pause for a few moments of thoughtful study of the airstrip.

High in the mountains overlooking this bay is a tastefully built and delightfully decorated hotel called Les Castelets. Managed by the delectable Madame Geneviève Jouney, this little place is a real surprise and as different from the average Caribbean hotel as you could imagine. The rooms are palatial, the view superb, and the restaurant excellent. Try to make it before sunset.

Isle de Fourche (25613, I-A24)

is a tiny but spectacular spot just to the NW of Saint Barts. Completely barren and deserted, except for a herd of about 50 very agile goats, and boasting an imposing skyline of humps and pinnacles, it offers a fairly good but blowy anchorage. Keep a good lookout on entering the bay; the odd rock is littered about.

For some reason, people always take their clothes off here. Maybe it's the solitude, but the dear old inhibited and morally constipated human being can be seen gamboling about, doing what he's always wanted to do, white rumps flashing like those of a herd of startled deer.

Saba (25607, I-A25)

This spectacular Dutch island, and nearby Statia (Saint Eustatius), are drifting along about 20 years behind the times. Particularly in Saba's case, that makes a stop quite delightful. The problem is finding a secure spot. On rare occasions, it is possible to anchor off or make fast to the large steel buoy off the customshouse landing. Before the stone mole was built in 1973, a surf boat would come out to ferry one ashore, and yachts would most likely stand off while shore parties explored this mountainous paradise. Now, with luck, you may be able to make fast alongside for a night, but keep in mind that commercial vessels have preference at all times.

The wind howls and moans fitfully around the great gray cliffs, and the sea does its best to reach over the stonework of the new wall. One becomes more aware than ever how fragile a creation a yacht really is. In spring, summer, and fall, long periods of really calm weather would make Saba a really attractive proposition, for with your yacht safely alongside, you could spend days ashore absorbing the marvelous beauty of this unique island.

The main town, Bottom, is about a quarter of the way up the steep-sided island,

The road from Bottom to Windwardside, Saba

snugly nestled in a bowl (*botte* in Dutch) among the hills. After an awe-inspiring ride up the unbelievable switchbacked road, the little town pops into view like something from a Hans Christian Andersen fairytale: neatly painted dollhouses are surrounded by a riotous explosion of flowers. Much higher still are the villages of Windwardside and Hell's Gate, where the little white houses cling to the cloud-shrouded side of the great green mountain.

Nearly two out of three Sabans are of pure white origin. The rest are of varying hues—and everyone is either very young or very old. The men and women of working age are all earning a living in Saint Martin, Curaçao, or Aruba. Considered to be among the best blue-water seamen in the world, Sabans will be found as deck officers and crew aboard freighters, coasters, and supertankers. But somehow, when you meet them in a far-off port, you get the impression that they are only waiting for the moment when they can step back into yesterday and sit with their blue-eyed, stubbly-chinned old uncles, high in their windy eyries, watching the sea below, which from 2,000 feet up looks almost benign.

English is spoken as much as Dutch, and dollars seem to outnumber the official guilders.

Tourists are beginning to find their way to Saba, so go quickly while the magic remains. If necessary, leave your yacht in Saint Martin and fly across (which is an experience in itself). Or make a round trip, which takes about an hour each way, on the speed boat that runs daily from Saint Martin.

Saint Eustatius (25607, I-A25)

Statia, as it's called locally, is also living in the past. Unlike Saba, though, the island has a slightly sad atmosphere; it has probably never recovered from the sacking administered in 1780 by Admiral Rodney because the Dutch were supplying provisions to American warships. The ruins of the demolished town of Oranjestad are still partially visible, but one finds it hard to believe that this tiny forgotten island was once the principal trading port in the West Indies.

The anchorage at Oranjestad shown on the chart is inclined to roll badly, but if you have a taste for out-of-the-way places, it's certainly worth it.

A large jetty has recently been built in Interloper's Bay that can accommodate the sizable vessels that bring oil into the tank farm on the shore.

But whatever you do, never leave your dinghy alongside for a long period. A good friend took his crew ashore for dinner at the lovely old inn at Gallows Bay. It was then a quiet night and hardly a ripple stirred the sea. Returning a couple of hours later, they saw the yacht rolling and plunging to her anchor and found the dinghy halfway up the beach, upside down and smashed. Don't be put off, though; just be careful.

The people of Statia are very pleasant, and I have the impression that this island will not remain "undiscovered" much longer.

Saint Christopher (Saint Kitts) and Nevis (25601, I-A25)

From Statia, the great bulk of Mount Misery on the northern end of Saint Kitts dominates the southeastern horizon. Along with its little sister Nevis, Saint Kitts was, in the early days of colonization, the most important island in the British West Indies. For some reason, the two islands lacked the density of mosquitos that, unbeknown to the settlers, were the principal carriers of the killing diseases on islands such as Antigua, Saint Lucia, and Martinique. Initially, the purity of the drinking water was thought to be responsible for this healthy situation, and Nelson, then a young captain, watered his squadron regularly at Saint Kitts.

Today, owing to a lack of good anchorages, these islands are not too popular with yachtsmen. However, with a little care, a comfortable night can be spent in one or the other of the islands without Auntie Mabel ending up with her head in the vegetable locker.

Neither island has any facilities for yachtsmen, but they are handy stopovers on the way north or south.

Basseterre (25601, I-A25)

is a tolerable roadstead when the wind and swell have a northerly slant to them, a quiet spot being as far to the NW as depth allows. A tripline on the anchor is a good idea here, since there is a maze of old moorings and odd bits and pieces on the bottom.

Another anchorage would be close in the lee of the cruise-ship dock on the east side of the bay. Customs is nearby. It is closed on weekends.

In a strong easterly, it is pleasant enough in one of the little bays on the hook of land known as Salt Pond, about 4 miles SE of Basseterre. With the wind further in the S, Nevis offers fairly good shelter, either off the beautiful beach that faces the Narrows or tucked up as close as possible to Charlestown.

Since Saint Kitts and Nevis are under the same jurisdiction, you may enter at either Basseterre or Charlestown.

Brimstone Hill on Saint Kitts, dubbed the Gibraltar of the West Indies, is truly worth a visit, especially for the view up and down the island chain from the old ramparts.

Saint Kitts remains one of the few large islands virtually untouched by the tourist trade. Thousands of acres of gently ascending sugarcane fields give the island a cool, green garden look.

The Narrows (25601, I-A25)

is the 2-mile-wide channel between Saint Kitts and Nevis. There are several rather dangerous shoals in the E and NE section of this passage, and it is no place to be fooling about with a deep-drafted, unhandy sailing vessel in failing light. With

The waterfront, Basseterre, St. Kitts

a clear sky and midday sun, however, there is no problem. Keep within three fourths of a mile of the Saint Kitts shore and all will be well. If the weather is fairly settled, by all means pop into Majors Bay or Cockleshell Bay, which adjoin each other at the SE end of the island. Both bays offer more protection than would appear from the chart, and the view of towering Nevis across the Narrows is quite beautiful.

On approaching a place such as the Narrows from, say, the NE, there are several complicated ranges published to lead you through the dangers, but in my view it is just too easy to make a mistake unless you have done it first under ideal conditions. "Is it a church or a windmill we want?" croaks Dad as his knuckles gleam white on the tiller and the wind blows the pages from Mother's nervous fingers. Remember, there is always a hefty sea running in exposed parts of the Caribbean, and you just don't go aground, you explode like a kamikaze bomber!

Statia and Saba (far distance) seen from the fort on Brimstone Hill, Saint Kitts

Charlestown (25601, I-A25)

is the port for Nevis, a quiet and beautiful island, surprisingly full of historic interest. The town itself is attractive and has plenty of fresh fruit and local vegetables in the market.

The shoal off Fort Charles should be given a wide berth—at least three fourths of a mile.

Not too long ago, all the traffic between Saint Kitts and Nevis was conducted by sailing lighters—huge, high-sided, straight-stemmed antiquities with booms extending 15 feet or more over their transoms. On the rare windless days, their two-man crews would labor at 30-feet sweeps propelling their 25 tons of cargo at a pace similar to Uncle Albert's on his way to the dentist.

On your leaving Nevis for Antigua or Montserrat, a rather uncomfortable sea may be encountered for 5–10 miles offshore.

Montserrat (25601, I-A25)

Although it's very beautiful ashore, Montserrat, the "saw-toothed" mountain, has little to offer the yachtsman other than an overnight shelter when on passage.

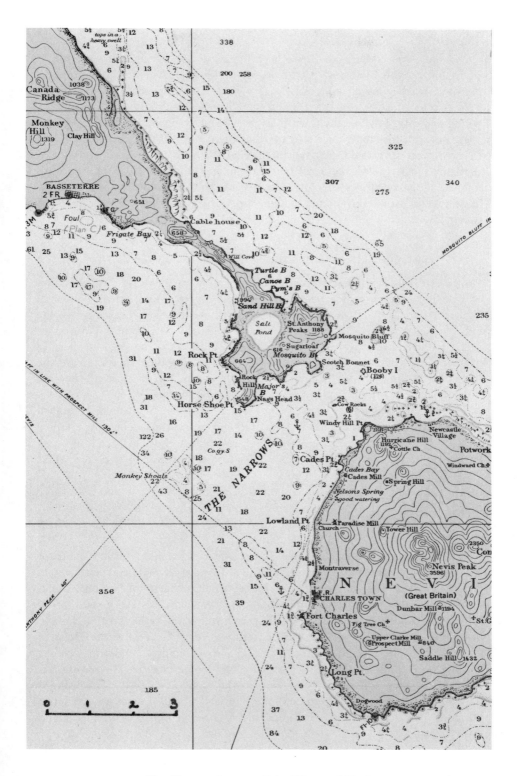

The Narrows between Saint Kitts and Nevis

Officially, one should go through the customs-and-immigration routine at Plymouth on the southwest corner. Here, under the usual conditions, even a half-mile-wide trimaran will usually turn itself into a passable imitation of a berserk windshield wiper. It's distinctly not Auntie Mabel's favorite anchorage, which is a pity, because the town is as pretty as any in the islands.

However, a little bird once told me that there is a roll-free cove right up on the northwest tip, called Carr's Bay on the charts. It's a beautiful spot, and a yacht that through stress of weather might find its way into the bay would be most unlucky if disturbed. Another alternative would be to clear at Plymouth and pop back to Old Road Bay about halfway up the coast. Most of the time it is reasonably quiet.

Antigua, the Yachtsman's Isle (25570, I-A27)

Southward from Antigua the voyage becomes a joyous sleigh ride. A succession of cracking reaches, which invariably leave all skippers in a delirious state of Walter Mittyism ("and with a last gallant effort, the little ketch eased across the line, just seconds ahead of the giant *Ondine*" is usually how it goes). No wonder then that after a few days in English Harbour, most crews, having had their fill of windward work, are eager to put to sea again, easing their sheets toward the hazy blue outline of Guadeloupe. It's actually a pity, for in so doing they are missing some of the most pleasant spots in the Caribbean.

There are four places to check in and out of customs: Saint John's, English Harbour, Crabb's Marina, and at the south end of Barbuda. You'll be charged a reasonable fee for a cruising permit and, at English Harbour, you'll also pay harbour dues for the boat and a landing fee for each member of the crew, since English Harbour is a national park.

Antigua's 60 miles of coastline abound in anchorages that match even those of the Grenadines and the Virgin Islands. And for the beachcomber or skin diver, the island of Barbuda (a dependency of Antigua), just 24 miles to the north, is probably without equal in the islands.

Nevertheless, to most yachtsmen Antigua means English Harbour, and for many years cruisers from both sides of the Atlantic have planned their voyages around a visit to this lovely old port. Indeed, the popularity of Nelson's Dock-yard—"the Dockyard," as it's universally known—increases every year.

Everyone knows that Horatio Nelson, then a young and rather acerbic captain, based his squadron here. And Prince William, later to become the Duke of Clarence and King William IV of England (he was known in Europe as "the Sailor King"), built Clarence House overlooking the harbor. It still stands today. Older yachtsmen will probably know that the pioneers of postwar cruising—Allcard, Hiscock, Pye, Johnson, and many others—regularly met up in English Harbour for Christmas and were, in those days, the only boats in that quiet and lovely place.

The megayacht charter fleet moors where once Admiral Lord Nelson's Squadron found shelter.

And of course everybody knows that English Harbour is the home of Commander V.E.B. Nicholson and his family.

English Harbour (25570, I-A27)

can hardly fail to impress one deeply, as, out of the tumble and jumble of the seas normally encountered at the foot of Shirley Heights, the yacht slips for the first time between the battlements of Fort Barclay on the port hand and Charlotte Reef to starboard. This description, written in 1800, tells us:

> The entrance to English Harbour is difficult and narrow, and resembles that of Malta. You give the ship good way through the water clue all up, and shoot her in to an anchorage; from which she is afterwards warped to that part of the Harbour she is destined for.*

Today, even with far more nimble craft, we prefer to give you more complete directions. The westernmost rocks of Charlotte Reef should be given a berth of

*From *The Romance of English Harbour,* obtainable at the dockyard.

about 50 yards. The old admiralty entrance range has become rather lost among the new hotel buildings, so stick to the middle of the channel all the way in, and the dockyard buildings will spring into sight, looking perhaps more like a film set than the real thing.

If you are under sail, a perfectly safe entrance can be made under easterly conditions, when at the worst the vessel may have to pinch a little as the wind heads in the narrowest part of the channel. Fifty yards farther on, it will usually free again, and the problem then becomes one of easing sheets in time for the 80° turn to port and the run down to the dockyard.

If the wind has a slight northerly slant, hug the eastern side, under the Pillars of Hercules (a striated, crenelated cliff to starboard of the entrance, eroded on the face to an appearance of vertical columns) keeping an eye on the quite rapidly shelving reef. The water is normally crystal clear here, and the reef very easily seen.

Under the Pillars, the wind will die, but the yacht will have enough way to shoot through the calm until fairly heavy puffs are met coming out of the NE. After paying off to meet this new wind, the yacht will be heading straight for Barclay Point, which has a rock with 4 feet of water over it, 12 feet off its eastern extremity.

Come about in good time, whereupon the wind will invariably head and follow you around. Sail half the distance back toward Charlotte Reef, tack again, and you should weather Barclay Point without trouble. If you keep in mind that 60 or 70 yachts used this same entrance for a starting line during Antigua's annual Race Week the last week in April, it will not seem so bad.

Immediately inside the entrance and slightly to starboard is Freeman's Bay, a beautiful calm-water anchorage five minutes away from the bustle of the dockyard. Anchor there.

The official procedure for checking into customs in English Harbour is as follows. After hoisting the Q flag and an Antiguan courtesy flag, wait for customs and immigration officials, who make regular tours of Freeman's Bay between 0800 and 1700. If they do not appear after a one-hour wait, the skipper alone may either go ashore to make contact or call on VHF-16 (call sign "Dockyard Immigration") for instructions. In practice the skipper will probably be asked to come to the office in the dockyard. Incidentally, the call to customs on VHF-16 is the only call yachtsmen may make on that channel, which is reserved for official business and emergency traffic. VHF-68 is where you call your neighbor, your yacht broker or any other marine business, a taxi, or a restaurant.

Having completed the formalities, run quietly down toward the yachts anchored stern-to at the old walls. Space is available on a first-come, first-serve basis. If you think you're up to maneuvering stern-first into a slot that may be just big enough, round up under Point Helena (on which stand the buildings of Antigua Slipway Ltd) and drop back onto the wall. If you'd prefer to anchor out in the stream, carry on around to Ordnance Bay on the northern side of the harbor. This is the traditional anchorage, where cruising yachts drop their mud-stained hooks and pause to regard the dockyard's frantic charter activity with an air of bewildered amusement.

For those who may be attempting the stern-to or Med-moor for the first time, these notes may help avoid a few embarrassing moments.

The first and foremost rule is: Whenever possible, always plan to let out as much chain as you have in the chain locker. You'll see why later. Having dropped the hook in line with the chosen spot, be sure the foredeck hand lets go enough scope to begin with for the anchor to hold, even if the bow begins to swing alarmingly off the wind and the yacht appears to be going at right angles to the dock. With the engine still going gently astern, the chain should then be held so that the vessel is hauled around onto the right approach again. The foredeck man should then work closely with the skipper, easing and holding the chain when necessary and steering the yacht into the berth more with the help of the anchor than anything else.

Try to avoid going ahead on the engine to kick the stern in the right direction; that will only result in slacking the tension on the chain and allowing the bow to fall off even more.

Meanwhile, fenders should be arranged along the topsides at the right height for the vessels on either side, and mooring warps should be led through the fairleads and coiled for heaving. If the wind is more off on one side of the vessel than the other, the windward line should of course be the first ashore.

When the yacht is secured close enough for the crew to step ashore, the chain should be taken up until it can be brought in no farther. In the event of a sudden squall (far from unknown in the islands), the yacht should be unable to fall back more than a few inches toward the stone wall. Obviously, the anchor should hold at all costs, hence the maximum amount of scope. Unfortunately, there are a few isolated patches of rather bad holding ground scattered around the bottom, and to add to the problem, a heavy hurricane chain lies halfway across to Point Helena and parallel to the walls.

Uncle Albert particularly enjoys this whole maneuver. With the aid of several stiff gins, and much to the horror of the already established fleet, he drops his hook halfway to Guadeloupe and steers his hoary old Colin Archer full ahead at a minute gap in the gleaming ranks. With his bowsprit just about to shatter the plate-glass deckhouse of some petrified Panamanian, Uncle Albert is seen to collapse on his windlass brake, and his 30 tons of pitch, oakum, and rust is spun ponderously around in a mad pirouette, sending Auntie Mabel head first across the saloon table into a foc's'le drawer marked "Odds and Ends." Luckily for us all, he doesn't go out very much.

On departure, the master of a foreign-going vessel must fill out an official certificate of clearance, which can be obtained only after all dockyard accounts have been settled and receipts obtained.

Almost all requirements for necessities and amenities can be met at the dockyard. The list of businesses occupying the old buildings and catering to the yachts include a yacht broker and charter agent, marine electronics and electrical specialists, a sailmaker, divers, a travel agency, a provisioning service, a bakery, gift shops, inns with restaurants and bars, and nearby a bank and a post office. Carib Marine at the head of the harbor has a dinghy dock and a pretty good supply of basic and gourmet groceries, as well as marine hardware.

The complex is also a tourist attraction, and the docks are administered by the National Parks Authority.

The Nicholson family is, after Nelson, the name most closely associated with English Harbour. Others may claim to be mainly responsible for the rebirth of Nelson's Dockyard, but without doubt this fascinating Irish family has done more to mold the character of the place than any other group or body combined.

In 1948 Commander V.E.B. Nicholson, his wife, and their two sons sailed from England in their old schooner *Mollihawk,* en route to Australia. Falling in love with a deserted English Harbour, then a place of crumbling buildings, creaking shutters, and magical lonely beauty, the family decided to refit the yacht and stay the winter in the Caribbean. Then an American acquaintance asked if they would sail him south through the islands; *Mollihawk* thus became the first charter yacht in the lower part of the Lesser Antilles.

For many years the Nicholsons lived an idyllic tropical life, cruising in the winters and making homes out of the ruins of the dockyard in the summers. They survived hurricanes, droughts, and the hard times of the early years of charter. The occasional wanderer who sailed into the dockyard was made royally welcome; several whose boats were large enough stayed to join the Nicholson fleet. Nowadays, as 80 or so yachts jostle for mooring space and their hundreds of crewmen turn the place into a facsimile of what it once was, the old commander can be excused if he pauses once in a while and smiles in deep satisfaction.

On the opposite side of the harbor, Antigua Slipway Ltd is well equipped to handle most repairs and can haul vessels up to 160 tons. Unlimited supplies of diesel oil are available alongside a clean but very small fuel dock.

Reliable women from English Harbour Village will do one's laundry, well but not inexpensively, charging by the piece. And there is no shortage of casual labor if it's required; in fact the day workers of the dockyard and the slipway have built up a fine reputation as first-class painters and varnishers. Mail will be held by the Nicholson charter office in English Harbour and should be addressed c/o V.E.B. Nicholson & Sons, Box 103, Saint John's, Antigua, or by the local, very accessible post office, General Delivery, English Harbour Post Office, Antigua, West Indies.

Cables addressed to "Yachts, Antigua" will be read out over English Harbour Radio if so requested. Airline arrangements can also be made through this office. Taxi drivers monitor VHF-68 and can be contacted almost any time of day or night.

A big improvement here is the installation of two telephones, which are direct AT&T lines to the United States. Cellular phones are on the way, too, so you may not be as far out of touch as you expect, or even wish to be. If you prefer to stay in touch by ham radio, it is possible to take a taxi or bus to Saint John's and get your reciprocal license for Antigua on the spot at the Department of Public Works and Communications for a reasonable fee.

If you intend to see more of Antigua (and we thoroughly recommend that you do), your circumnavigation should be clockwise, and you should allow at least five days for the full trip.

Falmouth Harbour (25570, I-A27)

lies less than a mile W of English Harbour. A very large, cool bay, it provides a pleasant alternative to anchoring out in Freeman's Bay, and since the road from Saint John's to English Harbour runs past its eastern shore, Nelson's Dockyard is less than a five-minute walk away. The most pleasant anchorage is just off Saint Ann's Point, at the northern end of Pigeon Point Beach.

Care should be taken entering this harbor, as there are several shoal patches, the most dangerous being Bishop Reef, which lies just inside Black Point, the eastern entrance of the bay.

In the SE corner of the bay, the Antigua Yacht Club, apart from being responsible for the race organization during Antigua Sailing Week, holds regular Thursday evening races open to anything from 100-foot schooners to wind-surfers. Longer races are arranged on the last Sunday of each month and on public holidays. Arbitrary handicaps are allocated if a yacht has no West Indian Yachting Association rating certificate. A certificate can be obtained by contacting the measurer, Bill Fowler, on the yacht *Xicali* anchored adjacent to Antigua Slipway. The club's restaurant, leased to Alberto and Vanessa Ravenello, is considered to be second to none.

Also in the Falmouth area are a floating disco, a first-class pizza parlor, and a newly opened restaurant called the Red Snapper. On the north side of Falmouth Harbour is Hugh Bailey's delightful little Catamaran Hotel. At the head of the harbor is a small grocery, which will take orders by VHF and deliver to your boat with an added charge of 10 percent of the total bill.

This is a growing area, and marine-oriented businesses are locating here as space gets scarce in neighboring English Harbour.

Carlisle Bay (25570, I-A27)

is only 4 miles farther W along the coast, just to windward of Curtain Bluff, on which stands Antigua's premier hotel of the same name.

This bay has a beautiful palm grove at its head and is particularly lovely in the early evening, when the sun paints the mountains and the village of Old Road in pure gold. Sometimes there is an uncomfortable roll, but a shallow-draft vessel can usually escape it by tucking right up into the NE corner.

Curtain Bluff Bay (25570, I-A27)

is also inclined to be rolly, but the hospitality of the hotel makes up for a lot.

Half a mile offshore here is the eastern end of Cades Reef. This large and dangerous obstruction has claimed many vessels, and why its eastern and western ends remain unmarked is a mystery to me. Luckily, however, the seaward side breaks in all but the calmest weather, and an alert crew will have no difficulty spotting it.

If you approach Antigua at night from the NW, be sure to give the SW corner of the island a berth of at least 2 miles. Once you are inside the reef, assuming the light is good—that is, the sun high and the sky clear—a straight course can be held until you are clear of Johnson's Island. The water is calm, and an anchorage can be made anywhere along the edge of the reef and along the shore. The deep-water passage between Cade's Reef and the mainland is never less than one fourth mile wide, and this channel offers a perfect chance for the neophyte reef-hopper to practice eyeball navigation. I would even suggest that the skipper purposely veer back and forth across the channel so that the brilliant blues, greens, and browns begin to mean something to him.

Once past Johnson's Island, stand on 200 yards before turning to the N. Ten feet can safely be carried 200 yards off the shore as far as Ffrye's Point, a distance of 1¾ miles.

Ffrye's Mill Beach (25570, I-A27)

is the most northerly of a succession of palm-fringed beaches that vie with each other in beauty. Ten feet can be carried close inshore here. A rocky patch, accurately positioned on the chart off Ffrye's Mill, covers an area as big as a pair of tennis courts and should be given a wide berth.

Mosquito Cove and Morris Bay (25570, I-A27)

unfortunately are very shallow, and 5 feet should proceed with caution.

An 8-foot draft can proceed in a straight line from Ffrye's Point to the easternmost of the Five Islands, but shoaling may occur in this area after heavy swells.

Five Islands Bay (25570, I-A27),

identified by five rocky islets off its southern arm, offers a whole slew of possibilities. Seven feet can proceed between the easternmost islet and the shore, and the vessel may then turn to the E in deep water close to the beach. This bay boasts some of the most beautiful and secluded beaches on the island—there are at least five to choose from.

Up at the head of the bay, with Maiden Island left to port, a beach that fronts gently rolling meadowland offers perfect solitude (except for the odd local smuggler), but the draft is limited to 6 feet. Head for the rocks at the northern end of the beach, but proceed slowly, since the bottom can change as a result of swells that sometimes plague the whole of the western side of the island.

Deep Bay (25570, I-A271)

is situated immediately W of Saint John's Harbour and is the most secure anchorage under any conditions on this western coast. Eight feet can practically sit on the beach, and the holding is excellent.

The rum punch flows and the music blares, providing a carefree cruise for tourists on the *Jolly Roger*. The tour boat livens up the anchorage at Deep Bay during the day, but leaves the anchorage to yachts for the night.

The wreck of a large three-masted sailing vessel is breaking water right in the middle of the entrance, but there is oodles of water on either side of it. The twisted, cavernous old hull offers some exciting snorkeling.

Saint John's Harbour (25575, I-A271)

is commercial, but it offers good shelter, if necessary, from N through E to S. Warrington Bank is marked by a red spar buoy to the N and a black can flasher to the S. Just NE of the bank is a large mooring complex belonging to the West Indies Oil Refinery. Large vessels frequently refuel at this berth, and the whole thing is surrounded by large mooring buoys. One of Antigua's lights stands on Sandy Island, and in calm weather a landing can sometimes be made on the southern tip. Diving around the island is very good.

Dickinson Bay (25575, I-A271)

should be approached from outside the Sisters Rocks by vessels drawing more than 7 feet. The bay itself, although very popular with local yachts, is quite shallow, but the bottom shelves gently and a controlled approach under Wetherill Point is perfectly safe. Two or three excellent hotels are situated along here, and the area is only 15 minutes away from Saint John's by taxi.

The North Coast (25575, I-A271)

The stretch from Dickinson Bay to Parham Sound is a flat-water windward sail protected by an outlying reef that in good light is clearly visible. Salt Tail and Diamond Banks, at the western end of the reefs, are a real hazard for vessels approaching the island in bad light from the N and NW. A yacht should approach no closer than 4 miles until the black-and-white chimney of the defunct West Indies Oil Refinery bears 100°T.

For coast-hopping yachts, however, the whole chain of coral heads forms an excellent breakwater, and a really delightful two–three hours can be spent working one's way to windward along this coast. A good point of reference along here is Prickly Pear Island, which lies approximately halfway between Dickinson Bay and Parham Harbour. Between the island and the shore 11 feet can just scrape through, provided one favors the island side of the passage.

From Prickly Pear to Maid Island, the preferred course takes one to the NW corner of Maid, which is rather hard to see against the background of Crabb's Peninsula, with its many radio antennas. The channel past Maid is marked by red cans to starboard and black to port, and was dredged during the war by the U.S. government. It is maintained now by the Antigua Cement Company.

A pleasant anchorage can be had anywhere under Maid Island, but don't drop back into the deep channel—a large cement carrier from Puerto Rico is a regular visitor.

Every reef along this N coast offers good snorkeling, and since reefs are littered about like mushrooms in a cow field, the enthusiast can just take his pick.

On the western shore of Crabb's Peninsula is a new and friendly boatyard known as Crabb's Slipway and Marina, run by Mike Piggot and his charming wife. Here you will find full repair facilities, a 50-T travel lift, and a dry storage area. This is a popular place to haul out during the summer season for storage or to have work done or to do it yourself. Rates are reasonable. There is a laundry here. Sun Yacht Charters runs the docks, where transients may moor if there is room.

Long Island (25575, I-A271),

to the N of Maid Island, is being developed as an exclusive resort.

The anchorage in Jumby Bay is cool and beautiful but definitely limited to 6 feet.

In this Parham area are many little sheltered spots, but out to the E we particularly like this next place.

Great Bird Island (25575, I-A271)

lies snuggled up under the windward reef. Uninhabited, windswept, and beautiful, rising to a height of 150 feet and standing in crystal-clear water and white sand, it offers the yachtsman a calm and secure anchorage, with only a colony of long-tailed bosun birds for neighbors.

A yacht should anchor under the two protruding arms of the island, whence you can take your dinghy through the small boat pass at the head of the cove into what must be one of the most beautiful little bays in existence. Lumps of red coral are dotted about like flowers in a carefully planned garden, and the reef fishes gambol about in the shallow, satinlike water off the beach. A path leads up to the weather-blasted cliff, and the view from the top is breathtaking.

Many small islets can be visited by dinghy, and days could be spent exploring. It's actually possible to swim under a little, grottolike islet immediately SE of Bird Island—as long as one isn't panicked by strange, glinting eyes and rather sinister shapes met along the way.

The only problem with Bird Island is that, having found your way in, it's a bit tricky getting your vessel out.

Bird Island Channel (25575, I-A271)

is for the adventurous who have confidence in their motors, for it's a narrow and rather nerve-wracking passage out into open water. I really hesitate to recommend this route: only one mistake is necessary for the yacht to be badly trapped and possibly lost. We have done it in a variety of large vessels drawing up to 11 feet and now think nothing of the channel, but admittedly the first time was decidedly hairy.

The channel actually has over 20 feet of water throughout its length, but is no more than 60 feet wide in places and has a couple of abrupt 90° turns. Nevertheless, viewed from the rigging on a clear West Indian day, the blue-water channel is as well defined as the Connecticut Turnpike.

From the western end of Great Bird, the yacht should pick her way across the shallows heading for the SE end of Long Island. The channel will soon be seen stretching away to the NE, with Little Bird to port and North and South Whelk to starboard. Two right-angle turns, one to port and the other to starboard, follow in quick succession. The yacht will now be feeling the effects of the open sea and should be driven ahead with conviction into clear water. The chart is none too accurate here, and it's definitely up to the watery old eyeballs to keep you in deep water.

The alternative is to return to Prickly Pear, and using this little island in line with Hodges' Point as a range, to proceed out to sea through a 150-yard gap in the coral. A good lookout should nevertheless be maintained until well clear, and neither route should be attempted unless the sky is clear and the sun overhead.

Although the E coast of Antigua between Great Bird and Nonsuch Bay appears to offer an abundance of gunkholes, the prevailing easterlies make any of the approaches decidedly dicey except in the calmest of weather.

Nonsuch Bay and Green Island (25570, I-A27)

are, on the other hand, simple to enter and utterly beautiful. If you are approaching from the N, Green Island should be left to starboard and the yacht should run down into calm water toward Fort Hasman and Submarine Rocks on a heading of 300°T. Take great care to avoid the reef that extends outward from

GREAT BIRD ISLAND
ANTIGUA

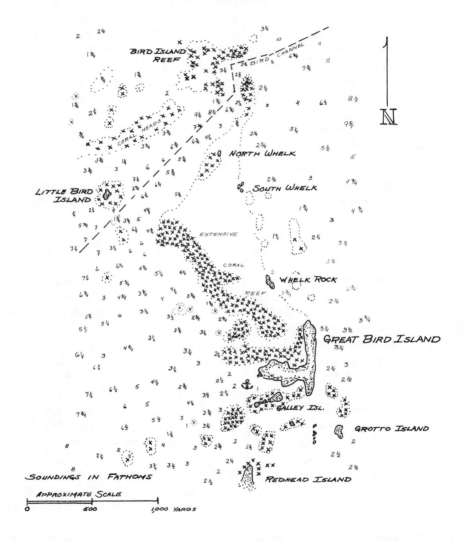

the SW point of Green Island. It is usually clearly visible, white water breaking over brown coral.

Both Green Island and the adjacent mainland are the property of the Mill Reef Club, an extremely elegant retreat frequented only by those whose blood is as blue as the sea at their gilt-edged doorsteps. Nevertheless, despite an insane and idiotic desire to scribble revolutionary rhetoric over their rock gardens, I deeply respect their attempts to keep lovely little Green Island uninhabited.

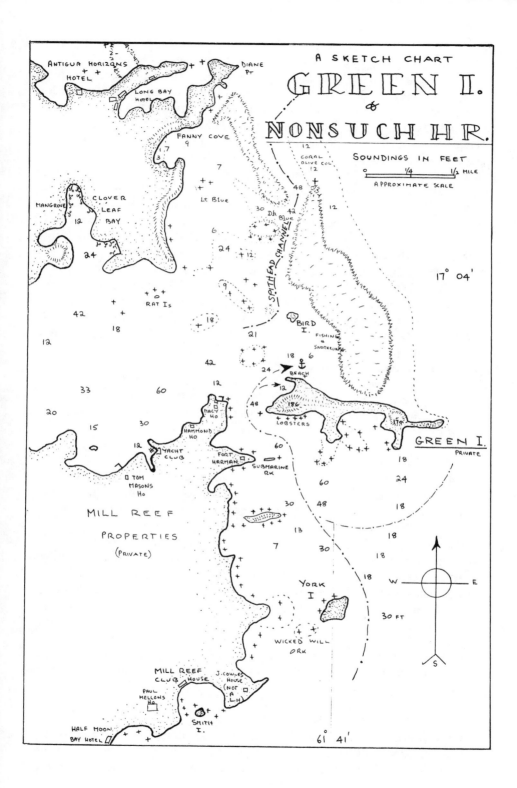

A SKETCH CHART

GREEN I.
&
NONSUCH HR.

SOUNDINGS IN FEET

0   ¼   ½ MILE
APPROXIMATE SCALE

ANTIGUA HORIZONS
HOTEL

DIANE PT

LONG BAY HOTEL

FANNY COVE

CORAL OLIVE COL

MANGROVE

CLOVER LEAF BAY

Lt Blue

Dh Blue

SPITHEAD CHANNEL

17° 04'

RAT Is

BIRD I.

FISHING & SNORKELING

BEACH

GREEN I.
PRIVATE

MACY HO

HAMMOND HO

YACHT CLUB

FORT HARMAN

TOM MASONS HO

SUBMARINE RK

LOBSTERS

MILL REEF

PROPERTIES

(PRIVATE)

N

W   E

S

YORK I.

30 FT

WICKED WILL ORK

MILL REEF CLUB

J. COWLES HOUSE (NOT A L.H.)

PAUL MELLONS HO

SMITH I.

HALF MOON BAY HOTEL

61° 41'

Under a mutual agreement between local yachtsmen and the Mill Reefers, yachts use the N and NW sides of the island, leaving the entire S and SW sides to the club members. It goes without saying that you will not dump garbage in the landlocked Nonsuch Bay, and that the delightful little sandy beach of the NW corner be composed only of clean white sand and not half-eaten hamburgers and buckled beer cans.

Anchorages in Nonsuch can be found almost anywhere. The fabulous windward reef offers complete protection from the seas, and in places 15–20 feet of water can be found right up to the outlying coral heads. A very sheltered little bay just behind the afore-mentioned beach is calm and secure in any conditions. Large patches of coral, clearly seen even on an overcast day, are liberally sprinkled all over the bay, so a good watch should be kept.

The Spithead Channel, a narrow opening through the barrier reef, is fairly easy when used as an exit, but a bit on the teeth-grinding, lip-sucking side if you are going the other way. Going out, the secret is to hug the western or leeward side of the channel until there is no sign whatever of discolored water to windward. Then, and only then, claw out to the deep, me lads! Trying to make an entrance would, in my opinion, be inadvisable until the skipper had come in another way and made a successful exit once or twice.

Anyway, for those who see beauty in the wonders of the Caribbean—the diamond sparkle of early morning over the reef, the soft pastels of the shallowing water, and the constant murmur of the velvet night—Green Island and Nonsuch Bay will never be forgotten.

Willoughby Bay (25570, I-A27)

is a large, reef-sheltered but windswept anchorage seldom used by yachts because of what appears to be a strictly nail-biting entrance. In actual fact, it really presents no problem to the now-expert eyeballer, and once you're inside and tucked up under the reef, the world is indeed a wonderful place.

The best practice is to put a man in the rigging and stand bravely in for the corner of the reef on the eastern side of the very obvious channel, which is at least one-fourth-mile wide. Run close down the side of the reef on a heading of 300°T until all dangers are on the starboard quarter, then turn upwind into the light-blue and turquoise water, and pick a spot behind the reef according to your draft. At certain times of the year, large rollers in the entrance could make entering inadvisable.

At the head of this very large bay, below the village of Bethesda, there are some really excellent clam beds, and you can spend a pleasant morning groveling in the mud up to your nostrils.

Marmora Bay (25570, I-A27)

is distinguished by a large white building that stands on the spit of land to the E. It is not, as you might suspect, an experimental germ-warfare station but the hallowed halls of the Saint James Club, and a very pleasant evening can be spent here in air-conditioned comfort. A draft of 7 or 8 feet can be squeezed into the bay itself. The entrance is marked with buoys. Purchase of a temporary membership is required if you wish to use any of the club's facilities.

Indian Creek (25570, I-A27),

scene of the kidnapping of the governor's lady, is a miniature version of English Harbour, but unfortunately it shallows abruptly halfway in. Nevertheless, it is well worth a visit: it is chock full of fish (tarpon, snook, jack, and the like), and the nesting ground of several kinds of exotic tropical birds.

Watch out for Sunken Rock, a tall pinnacle standing in 6 fathoms less than 100 yards off Indian Point. This dangerous obstacle breaks in nearly all weathers and can be easily seen. There is excellent diving around its craggy sides.

Once inside, stay slap in the middle of the channel. Seven feet can just scrape through the narrows, and once inside the inner basin, the yacht should quickly round up and let go, allowing swinging room for a sometimes flukey wind.

Very still and lonely, and in complete contrast to anything else in Antigua, Indian Creek makes an interesting finish to a round-the-island cruise.

Barbuda (25608, I-A26)

Below the horizon, but just 25 miles N of Antigua, sleeps the flat and sun-drenched island of Barbuda. In the days of sail, it was considered the greatest menace to navigation in the Indies. On moonless nights it lay crouched behind its coral teeth, hungry for the taste of oak, and more than 360 vessels, their lookouts screaming a belated warning, met their fate along its shores. Only the area immediately to windward of Barbuda's 200-foot hill is relatively free of wrecks. The rest of the island, just a few feet above sea level and virtually treeless, is not seen until the navigator finds himself but a few miles offshore.

It's hardly surprising, therefore, that yachtsmen unfamiliar with the area are inclined to give the island a miss. Uncle Albert talks about it in the same hushed tones he uses for the dreaded Skeleton Coast and the Potter Heigham Mothers' Institute. Actually, although not a place to be stumbled upon, Barbuda is not all that difficult to approach, and once you're there, the island offers at least a couple of really secure anchorages.

The ideal time to visit the island is during peaceful conditions in spring, summer, or fall, for sometimes in winter a heavy northwesterly swell turns the shallow but normally calm western side into a very harrowing place indeed, no place to be in a sizable vessel. However, for the greater part of the year a yacht of less than 8-foot draft can be quite secure in the Coco Point area.

If you are approaching Barbuda from the S, the first little problem to be encountered is Codrington Shoal. In normal weather, the sea bottom can be glimpsed all the way from Antigua, the deepest part of the channel being less than 17 fathoms. Wave action, therefore, is pretty short and sharp, and the shoal with

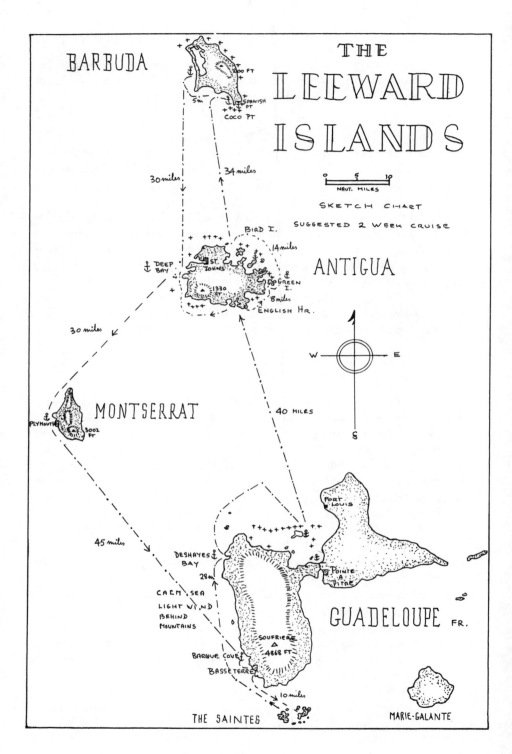

Barbuda to the Saintes

less than 1½ fathoms on it seldom seems to break, as it most certainly would in deeper water. We have usually been able to spot it because of its lighter color or, in brisk conditions, the amount of sand that has been stirred up.

Anyway, once you are outside Antigua's Diamond Bank, you can steer a course of due N, putting the nasty thing safely to windward. On no account should a yacht try to sneak to windward between the shoal and Palaster Reef off Barbuda's S coast. Rather conveniently, however, the old Martello Tower on the SW coast crawls up over the horizon and into view before you reach the shoals, and you should never allow this handy landmark to bear westward of 011°T.

From here on in, it's the old eyeball stuff again, and the intrepid mariner, fresh from his death-defying feats around Antigua, should have no trouble.

Coco Point Hotel,

consisting of one large and several small white buildings, should be approached carefully on a heading of 105°T until a clear path through the reefs becomes obvious. Seven or 8 feet can get very close to the beautiful white beach just N of the hotel. This same beach stretches away out of sight—miles and miles of virgin sand, pastel water, and probably not a soul in sight.

Coco Point Hotel, however, does not welcome yachtsmen; in fact they maintain a decidedly frosty attitude. The management will probably come off in a launch to tell you to move on. To the best of my knowledge, they have no legal right to do this, but since no facilities are available to non-resident guests, there seems to be little point in standing up for any rights.

Close to the Martello Tower a sand-dredging operation is slowly creating a small, protected lagoon behind the breakwater. It could well be that in the near future a yacht of moderate draft will be able to squeeze inside; best to check on this before leaving Antigua. A small guest-house hotel has already been completed in this area. Another small establishment has been constructed in the region of the Martello Tower. Otherwise this island is as close to true isolation as you will probably ever get.

Gravenor Bay (25608, I-A26)

is a reef-fringed anchorage on the eastern side of Coco Point. It affords the best protection on the island, especially if a westerly swell should build up. Eight feet is the absolute maximum draft, but the holding is good and a vessel may safely be left unattended.

The entrance will be clearly seen very close to the hotel boat dock, normally the home of a white sportfisherman and a small motor sailer. Light-tackle fishing is really excellent here, and you can have loads of fun with the dinghy in and around the reefs.

Spanish Point (25608, I-A26),

which lies 1¾ miles E of Coco Point, is yet another long, sandy spit behind which a yacht of no more than 7-foot draft may shelter. The approach should be made only in good light, as there are several isolated coral heads between the two points.

Also, the weather should be settled, because it is impossible to leave in bad light. But what a truly wonderful place it is!

If the crew tires of fishing, snorkeling, or just plain gawking at the view, take a walk across the point and then up the island's wildly windswept eastern coast. If you are a bit of a romantic (and what sailor isn't?), there will be sheer childhood magic in the excitement of exploring a seldom-visited shore, of turning over with sandy feet a battered box inscribed with strange, unreadable letters, and of sharing with the sandpipers the sounds of solitude.

Take a mask and snorkel with you, for the windward reef is only a few feet away from some of the little coves, and here bones of a long-gone fleet, reaching helplessly for the surface, are waiting to be found.

Palaster Reef (25608, I-A26)
has become a national park, administered by the government of Antigua and Barbuda, and fishing with rod or gun is of course strictly *verboten*. A beautiful anchorage can be found right in among the coral in 5–10 fathoms.

The reef, which is only just below the surface, breaks up any sea, and even a large yacht can easily find a spot with room enough to swing. It's quite a sensation to be several miles from land but in calm water and surrounded by some of the most beautiful coral in the world.

West Coast of Barbuda (25608, I-A26)
is shoal infested and inclined to suffer from both the murky water and a north-westerly swell. If neither of these conditions exists, however, give it a try, for it's fun to anchor opposite the town of Codrington and to portage the dinghy over the sand into the lagoon. You can then reach the town and arrange expeditions into the interior of the island, where, according to fancy, one may descend into ancient Darby's Cave, hunt for Arawak and Carib relics, or, rather pointlessly to my mind, hire several antiquated blunderbuses and attempt to blast the few remaining game specimens into Kingdom Come. The latter requires special permission from the warden of Barbuda; having examined some of the guns, I would feel a good deal safer in front of the barrels than behind them.

There are virtually no staple provisions to be had anywhere in Barbuda, but you can buy lobster and fish from almost any fisherman. You can also get fresh local yams, sweet potatoes, pigeon peas, and other vegetables.

Guadeloupe (25563, I-A28)

Guadeloupe is actually two islands in the shape of a flattened butterfly. The wing to the east, Grande Terre, is low, while the western wing, Basse Terre, is high, slightly mysterious, and steep-to along its entire leeward coast. The two halves are joined by a narrow neck of land, and through this neck runs the Salée River.

Thirty years ago I took *Ron of Argyle*, drawing 8½ feet, through the river, and about the same time Carleton Mitchell went through with *Finisterre*. It was a delightful experience, and in addition to giving a better sailing angle to Antigua, the two great bays of Grand and Petit Cul-de-Sac Marin have dozens of excellent reef-fringed anchorages seldom if ever visited by yachts. Then the swing bridge at the river's southern end ceased to swing, the river silted up, and that, *mes amis,* was the end of that for a number of years.

In 1988 the canal reopened, but the new bridge opens only once a day, at 5:30 A.M. This is not very convenient, as it is still dark at that hour during the winter months, but even opening at that early hour causes a huge traffic jam, because the bridge carries the only road between the two islands that make up Guadeloupe. Anchor close by on either the northern or southern side to be ready for the next day's opening. Motoring through the mangrove-lined passage, look for the deepest water in midriver. With care, a boat drawing 7 feet can make the trip. The passage through the reefs on the northern side in Grand Cul-de-Sac Marin is well marked with government aids to navigation. Use French Chart #3287.

Deshaies Bay (25563, I-A28)

is a well-protected and safe anchorage on the NW tip of the island, much used by yachts going to or coming from Antigua. A fairly sizable swell sometimes finds its way into the bay, but owing to the prevailing wind, one normally lies stern-on to it, so that it is seldom uncomfortable.

There are no natural dangers, but when approaching the bay keep a good lookout, as the waters of the W coast of Guadeloupe are absolutely littered with fishpot floats. These used to be large chunks of bamboo up to 6 feet long and very difficult to spot. Now they are apt to be two round floats connected to each other by quite a long line, which can easily wrap around the unwary yachtman's propeller. The floats are connected by rope to chicken-wire traps on the bottom. They are a nuisance up to 5 miles off the coast.

On arrival, dinghy ashore and climb up to the gendarmerie just above and to the right of the little town. Formalities are still fairly informal here. No official was on duty when we checked in. A sign in French and English directed us to fill out a form and put it in the box provided. If we wished official papers saying we had checked out, we should return at 1800, when presumably someone would be there.

On the way down stop in at Madame Racine's famous little bar and restaurant, which totters precariously at the water's edge. Incidentally, the "nosh" at Madame Racine's is *pas mal de tout,* but the garlic can sometimes be detected as far away as Antigua!

A small stream runs into the southern end of the bay, and it's fun to wander up along its course. Follow the little road as far as it goes, then wade across the stream and follow the path.

West Coast of Basse Terre (25563, I-A28)

This stretch is a little barren compared to most parts of the other islands. Perhaps it's the fitful winds that wander gloomily along the shore here, sometimes whispering in from the west, sometimes blasting out from the valleys. Or perhaps it's the deep, still waters and the silent towns. Anyway, to my mind, something is rather sad about this long stretch of coast, especially in contrast to the southwest coast of Guadeloupe's other half, Grande Terre, where all is action, color, and movement.

However, there's a pleasant place to anchor for lunch and snorkeling (Club Med brings its guests here quite often for this purpose) in a small bay on the SW side of Îlot à Goyave, or Pigeon Island, which lies just about halfway down.

The crew with a little time to spare may want to spend the night in Anse-à-la-Barque, a very deep but protected bay 5 miles S of Pigeon Island, marked by a yellow-and-black concrete tower that at night displays a flashing red light. The main coast road runs around this bay, and one may rather get the impression of being in the middle of the Indianapolis 500.

Basse Terre (25567, I-A28),

although a smaller city than Pointe-à-Pitre, is the seat of government for Guadeloupe and its dependencies. It has little to offer the cruising yachtsman except a chance to stock up on some superb French goodies and excellent fresh vegetables in the market.

The Marina de Rivière Sens south of Basse Terre sometimes can find room for a transient boat or two to overnight. It's a good place to take on fresh water and fuel.

South of town you will find the Marina de Rivière Sens, protected by a stone breakwall. Both fuel and water (free) are available. The marina is filled with local boats, and space for transients to tie up, especially large yachts, is not plentiful. If need be, or if you prefer, anchor near the marina off the yacht club and sailing-school docks. You'll be able to identify the general area by the board boats from the sailing school swarming around in the vicinity. From the marina, it is a 20-minute walk to town, where customs may be found at the commercial dock. Buses run about every hour and, of course, taxis are also available.

The coast between Basse Terre and Vieux Fort at the southern end is rugged and hilly, and 90 percent of the time the wind will blow hard here, usually from the S. This means that a yacht under sail, when the point is abeam, will be several miles to leeward. In the channel, of course, the prevailing easterlies will return, and a lengthy beat against wind and current will be required to reach the Saintes.

After many years of being a terribly gung-ho purist, I eventually took to motor sailing along this coast in the permanent calm patch that extends about 200 yards offshore all the way from Basse Terre to the southern point. At the lighthouse, the wind almost immediately frees, and the Saintes can normally be laid in one tack.

Îles des Saintes (25564, I-A281)

have become a showpiece in recent years, and the local residents have suddenly realized the importance of tourism. Already many substantial holiday homes have appeared, most of them built by wealthy Guadeloupeans. The atmosphere ashore is delightful and very French.

As a quick insight into the history of the Saintes, here is a story I once heard from an old priest who had lived there all his life.

It seems that there were some islands that lay a short distance off a much larger island (just like Guadeloupe, in fact), and the inhabitants, being mainly descendants of Breton fishermen, had stuck together rather than intermarry with their darker brothers across the water. Inevitably the stock had weakened, resulting in an illiterate, unhealthy, and slightly barmy population with a future that could only go from bad to worse.

A highly concerned government stepped in, and a team of military doctors was given the unenviable task of cleaning up. Many of the ailing were sent to another small island, where in isolation they ended their days behind the ruined wall of an old leper colony. But what to do with the remaining population? How could new blood be introduced? Then someone came up with a brilliant solution.

The government had a large training fleet that called regularly at other West Indian ports; why not base the fleet (and its sailors of course) in the little archipelago for a couple of weeks each year?

And so it came to pass that healthy children with blond hair and blue eyes once more appeared in the islands, and everyone lived happily ever after, except possibly my friend the priest.

The Îles des Saintes offer pleasant harbors and beautiful vistas.

Other things are changing too. The dozens of graceful fishing boats based in the Saintes were only a few years ago powered by sail alone. Now government-financed outboards are changing the design, and ugly square transoms have appeared.

Both northern entrances are straightforward, and the charts are accurate; however, watch out for Baleine Shoal. On the southern side of the islands, most yachts favor the western passage. The middle passage, between Grand Îlet and La Coche, is perfectly safe in good light. Slightly favor the western side and be aware that rocky outcrops extend farther out than shown on the chart.

My favorite anchorage is under the Pain de Sucre at the western end of Terre d'en Haut. During a northerly spell, Anse Fideling on Terre d'en Basse can be very comfortable, although there is not a great deal of swinging room.

The anchorage off Bourg des Saintes, the main town of the group, is deep, but the holding is excellent. Give the local ferry boats from Guadeloupe enough room to use the pier. They are highly powered and make a large wake. In the Baie de Marigot a small slipway known as Chantier de Bastion has been established; several yachts report the standard of woodwork is excellent but not, alas, cheap.

In settled weather a really pleasant anchorage can be had in the Baie de Pont-pierre, tucked in behind the perforated rocks.

Walking is the great thing in the Saintes. Some of the best strolls are: Across to the beautiful windward beach on Terre d'en Haut for body surfing (sometimes

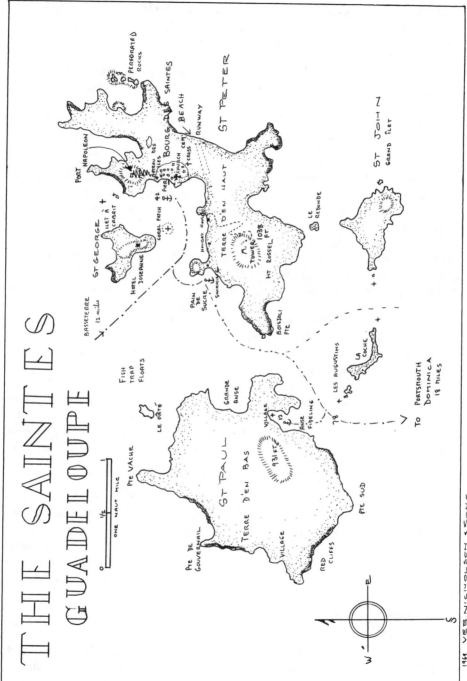

THE SAINTES
GUADELOUPE

ONE NAUT MILE

PTE VACHE
AR DE GOUVERNAIL
FISH TRAP FLOATS
LE PÂTÉ
GRANDE ANSE
ST PAUL
TERRE D'EN BAS
VILLAGE
93 FT
VILLAGE
ANSE FIDELING
RED CLIFFS
PTE SUD

LES AUGUSTINS
LA COCHE

TO PORTSMOUTH
DOMINICA
18 MILES

BASSETERRE
12 miles

ST GEORGE
ILET À CABRIT
HOTEL JOSEPHINE
CORAL PATCH
42

PERFORATED ROCKS
FORT NAPOLEON
BOURG DES SAINTES
ILET DES
CHURCH
RUNWAY
BEACH
ST PETER

HOLIDAY HOUSE
PAIN DE SUCRE
TERRE D'EN HAUT
TOWER 1038
MT ROSSEL FT
SWIMMING
BOISJOLI PTE

LE REDONDE

ST JOHN
GRAND ILET

1964 V.E.B. NICHOLSON & SONS

there is a very strong undertow, so be careful); up to Fort Napoleon (used to imprison Free French supporters by the island's Vichy government during World War II and still in excellent repair); a short stroll to the cross overlooking the harbor, and a long one up to the Napoleonic tower just visible atop the highest point on the island. Then sip a local *ponche* on the balcony of the Coq d'Or and maybe buy one of the coolie hats worn by the local fishermen. But please don't just sit on the yacht; the Saintes are too attractive for that.

From Terre d'en Haut it is sometimes possible to lay Pointe-à-Pitre and the southwestern side of Grande Terre, and if you've got time it's certainly worth it.

Pointe-à-Pitre (25566, I-A28)

is very big, surprisingly modern as well as ramshackle, and full of bustle. Not the best place for a yacht, though, so either nip in behind Gosier Island off the pleasant little town of that name, or find your way into one of the new marinas between Gosier and Pointe-à-Pitre.

The Marina Bas du Fort is comparable to anything found in Europe or the States. After passing Îlet à Cochons (Pig Island) to port, follow the red buoys (leaving them to starboard) until the entrance becomes visible. Still leaving the red buoys to starboard, make a sharp right-hand turn and proceed to the jetty just below the dockmaster's office. There is usually no shortage of berthing space for visitors, and yachts may be left here in perfect safety.

Slightly farther on toward the town of Pointe-à-Pitre is a smaller, not so fancy, family-run marina known as the Carènage. A small floating dry dock capable of prodigious feats of strength is available here, but the whole place is more geared to local business than to visitors.

Fuel, water, ice, and repairs will be found at both places, but vessels of 50 feet or more would do better at Bas du Fort. The town is within easy reach of both marinas by dinghy. Good marine supplies are available from shops in the Marina Bas du Fort and from ElectroNautique, located between town and the marina.

South Coast of Grande Terre (25563, I-A28)

This coast deserves your attention before you leave for Dominica, for there are scads of really beautiful reef-protected anchorages, some a little rolly, some not; some buoyed, some just a narrow hole in the coral. If you can stand the pace, become a temporary member of the Club Méditerranée and spend a day romping with the monokinis in the surf (quite a refreshing change from the blazers of Marblehead and points north). The anchorage off the club is safe but inclined to be rolly. Casual visitors are not allowed, so call up from Pointe-à-Pitre and ask for a temporary membership.

Saint François Harbour (25563, I-A28),

toward the eastern end of Grande Terre, is the site of the new Meridian Hotel and Casino. A first-class small marina operated by the hotel offers full facilities in an atmosphere of peace and quiet. The entrance channel through the reefs is well buoyed.

Marie Galante (25565, 25563, I-A281)

has a convenient lunch stop in good weather off the lovely southwestern beach. Columbus stopped here on his second voyage, but whether or not for lunch we do not know. It is possible to anchor comfortably overnight in calm water behind the breakwater built to protect the ferry dock at Grand Bourg, but the holding in the dredged basin is poor. If you get your anchor in well, you can make an interesting excursion by taxi or on foot to visit the old plantation at Murat.

Petite Terre (25563, I-A28)

is fascinating but seldom visited. Seven feet can just make it across the bar here, and a tolerable anchorage can be found off the little beach on the northern island. If the swell builds up, though, you may get trapped until it goes down again.

The entrance is from the NW and should be attempted only in really good light, since the coral heads are very dangerous although quite obvious to the experienced eyeballer. If there is any sort of swell on the bar, I would forget it.

La Moule (25567, I-A281),

on the windward side of Grand Terre, is for the really adventurous. Maybe one yacht a year visits this place, because the entrance through the reef looks very hairy. Actually it is not too bad, and by the look of the many fine old buildings ashore, it was once a port of some significance.

Stand resolutely on, rather like Lord Cardigan at the head of the Light Brigade. Approach the old battery at the NW end of the town on a SSW heading until the reefs close ashore are nearly under your bowsprit. Turn hard aport and run along the shore into the calm water. Lights and other aids to navigation now mark the way. Consult your chart.

The weathered flukes of old anchors mark the windward reef, and in the old days large vessels would make fast to these and run stern lines to the walls.

Dominica (25561, I-A29)

If there is one island in the West Indies that has hardly changed over the years, it's the great, green jungle wilderness of Dominica. Admittedly, a few freshly hewn roads have appeared, and the odd new hotel waits patiently under the trees for clients, but in truth the sheer ruggedness of the island barely tolerates any attempt to keep pace with the times.

High in the hills, village headmen no doubt still sit in a circle of elders just as they did when their forefathers licked their chops over the occasional exploring European. Red clay paths, made hard and smooth by the tramping of generations of bare feet, wind through the valleys and up to the cool heights. Rivers of pure, rushing water explode from every hillside, their sources in some cases still undiscovered somewhere beneath the island's cloudy cap. Dominica is an island to explore: an island, dare I say, to be almost protected from progress, and to be savored while the taste of purity remains.

For the cruising yachtsman, however, there are some snags, for Dominica is unfortunately rather badly off for anchorages and has a reputation as a place where you must either pay off the boat boys who come out to meet your boat or suffer from thievery, or both.

Prince Rupert Bay (25562, I-A29)

offers the only really good anchorage on the island. Easily recognized by the high, round bulk of Barbers Block to the S and Prince Rupert Bluff to the N, the bay is without doubt one of the most beautiful in the islands.

If the trades are on the move, a real bagful of wind can be encountered at the entrance. Gusts up to 35 knots are ridiculously common, but the water is flat and there is tons of sea room. A really tremendous sail can be enjoyed, and the bay is one of the best places I know to get some good action shots of the boat. Hang on to Grannie, though!

As you proceed to the northeast corner of the bay, where you are most apt to get out of any swell, you will be approached by boys of all ages in craft of all descriptions, who will suggest that they can provide security for your yacht and dinghy, take you up the nearby Indian River by outboard or oar power (either is fine, although if your guide is rowing, you have a better chance to ask any questions about Dominica that may occur to you), or sell you fresh fruit and vegetables. The ride up the Indian River is overrated but enjoyable. The opportunity to get fresh fruit and vegetables, if you have not arrived on a market day (Tuesday and Saturday) is worthwhile. From personal experience and that of others, I can tell you that the boat boys may be a nuisance, but you may patronize them or not, according to your inclination. You are probably better off, however, to pay for a few services and to consider it a modest price of admission to this pleasant anchorage.

At the time of writing, permission had been given to construct a marina in the northwest corner of Prince Rupert Bay, but there was no indication that it would be built anytime soon.

For entry formalities, take the dinghy to the remains of the town dock. The immigration office will be found opposite Barclay's Bank.

A pleasant walk from the anchorage will take you to the ruined fortifications on Prince Rupert Bluff. Just follow the shoreline, and the path will soon appear.

If the swell finds its way to the northern part of the bay, a quiet spot can usually be found somewhere along the beautiful southern shore, across from a small hotel. You may be less bothered by boat boys there.

The Carib Indian Reservation is within easy reach of Portsmouth. Allow the best part of a day and arrange the trip with the many owners of the newest Land Rover you can find.

After clearing at Portsmouth, and if things are not entirely to your liking there, try popping around to Douglas Bay, just N of Prince Rupert Bluff. This is a pleasant anchorage except when a strong northerly swell is running, the people are friendly, and the small boys can be seen but, blissfully, not heard.

West Coast of Dominica (25561, I-A29)

is steep-to and offers little in the way of protection. You can make a lunch stop, however, at the Layou River, and use the dinghy for an expedition to some of the really beautiful pools less than one fourth mile upriver.*

There is also a reasonable anchorage off the Castaways Hotel, halfway down the coast.

Roseau (25562, I-A29)

is the island's dilapidated but strangely attractive capital. Yachts may clear customs and immigration here, but compared to the simple formalities at Portsmouth, it's a bit of a hassle.

Your best bet is to drop an anchor in deep water off the Anchorage Hotel and let Roy, or whoever is there in an outboard, take a line ashore to a bollard for you. Five EC dollars (less than U.S. $2) was the charge for this service when we were there, and you are the guest of the hotel. You are welcome to use their restaurant and bar, and you need pay only a small fee for their showers and freshwater pool. They will arrange tours for you. The most popular is to the falls, where hot sulfur water cascades down the left side and cold water down the right. The hotel is inside the harbor limits, and it is quite legal for the skipper to take a taxi to Roseau to clear with the authorities.

Soufrière Bay (25561, I-A29),

at the S end of the island under Scott's Head, looks excellent on the chart, but on the whole is too deep for secure holding. It is worth trying, however, for the good diving.

This large and beautiful bay produces a distinctly moving phenomenon, known as a white squall: the high mountains to windward play havoc with the trade winds, and once in a while a gust will come tearing down the hillsides and hit the water at about 45°. A curtain of spray rushes off to leeward with the speed and authority of a runaway bus. You can usually see them coming well enough, and the best thing to do is run off for a moment. Uncle Fred steadfastly refused to believe it until one day, while he was suspiciously peering into his leaky lazarette, his whole gaff-topsail disappeared over the leeward horizon, no doubt throwing the radar operators at the Panama Canal into a bit of a dither.

Watch out for the large rocky shoal just to seaward of Scott's Head; it's farther out than indicated.

Martinique (25524, I-A30)

Make no mistake, this is a wonderful island. Apart from its well-known natural beauty, it is brimming over with splendid things such as *boudin créole,* a slightly

---

*Don't forget the snails. See page 32–33.

explosive but delicious pig's-blood-and-spice sausage; *crabes farcis,* made from a large and voracious land crab, which, when alive, is treated with the respect usually shown to a Bengal tiger; and 319,000 characterful and friendly Frenchmen of a rather darker hue than those normally found tottering about the Eiffel Tower.

Many happenings, some tragic, some joyful, have occurred in the history of the island—none was so shattering, though, as the fearsome eruption of the volcano Mont Pelée at the beginning of this century.

It was a morning in May 1902, and the mayor of the city of Saint Pierre had returned from a meeting of the council, feeling relieved. He had just heard a well-known seismologist confirm that Mont Pelée would not erupt. Despite the heavy cloud of volcanic ash that had settled around the town in recent days, he issued instructions that would cancel the evacuation. After all, the volcano had threatened the town many times before, and besides, the next day's elections, which would no doubt assure him of a further term in office, were not to be delayed.

In the anchorage off the town, 30 or so vessels lay stern to the walls. One of them, her loading completed, was slowly getting under way. The time on her wheelhouse clock, the captain noted, was 0750.

Six minutes later Saint Pierre, known as "the Paris of the West Indies," and all its 30,000 proud inhabitants ceased to exist. In a gigantic explosion, the southwestern side of the volcano split open, and a huge quivering mass of flaming gases began to roll down on the town.

In the harbor, as the paint blistered off the hull, the ship's captain watched with horrified fascination as the center of European culture in the Antilles was engulfed in the holocaust. Then, suffering terribly himself, his deck crew already dead from suffocation, the captain managed to maneuver his ship away from the inferno and take the terrible news to the outside world, the only eyewitness to the worst disaster in Caribbean history.

In actual fact there was one more survivor, a condemned man in a stone cell many feet below the city, but he knew nothing of the death and destruction going on around him. Later he was to become a popular exhibit in a world-famous circus.

Saint Pierre (25525, I-A30)

has been rebuilt, but is now only about one fifth the size it was before the volcano erupted, and it has not regained its former importance as a port. Yachts anchor north and south of the two town jetties, where there is a shelf of relatively shallow water. The customs office is south of the jetties. A very good small museum on the north edge of town exhibits many artifacts and describes in both French and English the eruption of the volcano in 1902. Several wrecks dating from the disastrous eruption have been charted. None seem to interfere with anchoring in the areas described.

The West Coast of Martinique (25524, I-A30)

is greatly influenced at its northern end by the massive bulk of Pelée. Heavy rains fall around the mountain when it is completely dry elsewhere, and clouds, which are seldom absent from the summit, shade the surrounding countryside. To leeward, a calm extends up to 12 miles from the coast, and I have sometimes barreled out of a steady Force 5 or 6 into a complete hole in the wind that has left the sea leaping drunkenly about like Uncle Albert at the Christmas office party.

For this reason, yachts approaching from Dominica should hold high and attempt to run up on the island close under the small islet of La Perle. This is one spot where it may really be necessary to exercise the iron topsail. The bay of Saint Pierre is a perfect example of the workings of an island wind pattern: it blows hard down the valley and then fans out to the N and S.

Once you are S of the bay, the wind will again disappear, under the lee of the Pitons du Carbet, a ridge of high, green peaks in the center of the island. From here a yacht under sail alone will have a frustrating time, as the wind will gust fitfully from the SE or S. It might be best to stand offshore and head for Cap Solomon on the southern side of Fort-de-France Bay, where the breeze will be back in the E and strong and steady.

Fort-de-France (25527, I-A30)

lies in the large bay of that name, which has more than its fair share of shallows. The approach to the town anchorage is straightforward, however. Once Pointe à Nègres is rounded, the sheer size and sophistication of the town will be very obvious.

When anchoring under Fort Saint Louis, try to leave the eastern side of the harbor clear, as ferries and cruise ship launches load and unload passengers at the two jetties that extend from the Savane.

On the northern side of the anchorage, a small restaurant building at the head of a wooden jetty is the former headquarters of Daniel Valin's Martinique Charter Service. Yachtsmen owe a lot to Daniel, for not so long ago it was the very devil of a job to find fuel and water in Martinique, and clearance formalities took literally forever. Now, however, thanks to his efforts, things couldn't be easier. Fuel, water, and ice are available on the dock. Customs and immigration men are located in the office next to the restaurant.

At the small bar/restaurant adjacent to the dock, yachtsmen are wont to mingle with visitors, and, with the aid of a few "petit poonchs," all manner of information may be gleaned.

Once upon a time I complained in my then monthly column in *Yachting* that the red tape in Martinique was ridiculous, but owing to the touchiness of the officials, I advised yachtsmen to "grin and bear it." Somewhere along the way the translation from English to French became a little fouled up, and the chief of customs was told by his interpreter that I had warned yachtsmen to "beware the grinning bear." When we see each other now, I grin, but he still looks a little strained.

Then of course there was the matter of Diamond Rock.

In 1804 a party of British sailors garrisoned this almost sheer pinnacle situated just a mile off Martinique's south coast, and by lugging whacking great cannons to the secure heights, completely disrupted French supplies. The gallant party was eventually starved out, and it surrendered with full military honors after 18 months.

One evening when we were young and stupid, John Guthrie, Steph Traptnar, and myself, after partaking of the culinary wonders of the Hotel Europe, decided to honor the Royal Navy on the occasion of the annual visit of the French Training Squadron. We would fly a giant white British ensign from the very top of the Rock. What a splendid idea! Just one more brandy and then to work!

Back on John's lovely old sailing trawler *Pas de Loup*, we fabricated a flag out of a bed sheet and a broken spar and, with piratical cunning, slipped quietly out of the anchorage under cover of night. As John had lightened his ship many years previously by dumping his huge old diesel over the side, it took several hours to work the elderly 100-tonner around the corner, but we pressed on and dropped the hook in the shadow of the Rock about midnight. One hour later we were at the top, which is covered with cactus. We were cut to bits and stone-cold sober, but our makeshift flag fluttered proudly at the summit. What was disturbing, however, was that the moon had fallen behind the Rock, it had started raining, the only way down had completely disappeared from view, and it rather looked as if *Pas de Loup*, 600 feet below, was dragging off the bank and also in danger of disappearing. In desperation we plunged downward, and an hour before dawn were back on the yacht.

With the daylight, the sparks began to fly. A fisherman reported the great flag to the gendarmes. "Mon Dieu," said the gendarmes, "c'est terrible," and they sent a detachment off to the Rock. After much groveling about, they couldn't find the way up. So they sent for a mountain rescue squad, complete with rope ladders, grappling hooks, and anti–snake bite serum. They did manage to find the way but were robbed of the prize by a flight of police helicopters that swooped on the flag at the last minute.

Meanwhile, between Fort-de-France, Paris, and London, cables flew at the highest diplomatic levels. Most unsportingly, the French fleet was diverted around the northern end of the island, while back at the anchorage, gentlemen in soft hats and rimless glasses began stalking around the yachts with nasty black notebooks.

It all blew over eventually.

In Fort-de-France, you should leave dinghies at the immigration dock, not at the town jetty. The shopping in town is superb, but do it early in the morning or late in the afternoon. The huge covered vegetable market is the finest in the West Indies and a sight never to be forgotten.

Fort-de-France has always been proud of its women, and no wonder. Some of them are absolutely gorgeous. They walk well, sit well, drive well, and at weekends, when they flock to the beaches, dress and undress very well. Martinique, and not Arthur Murray, began the beguine, and the motions of a Martiniquan dolly bird make a modern go-go girl look like a spastic giraffe.

Food, however, is the island's pièce de résistance. Allow twice the time you would think necessary anywhere else in the world, and be adventurous in your choice. The restaurant above the Club de Voile is one of the best. Also first class are La Foularde at the village of Schoelcher and Le Gommier in town.

Once, eating in Fort-de-France could be quite an adventure. A wonderful character, Robert Provost, ran a very classy place overlooking the waterfront. Le Foyal, it was called, and usually a large slice of the local elite would refuel there. One night I had a birthday dinner and Robert, knowing I had a passion for his superb baked Alaska, called (for some unearthly reason) an omelette Norwegian in French-speaking countries, cooked the second-largest such dessert in all the world. Then, with great aplomb, he proceeded to throw it at everyone in sight! Chunks of this delicious preparation were still dripping off the ceiling a week later.

Anse Mitan (25527, I-A30)

lies immediately across the bay from Fort-de-France and is marked on some charts as Anse de Cocotiers. From the spit buoy off Fort Saint Louis, head⁻

Anse Mitan, a beach resort across the harbor from Fort-de-France, is a popular anchorage.

straight for Pointe de Bout, on which stands the distinctive red-roofed Bakoua Hotel and the brand new Méridien Hotel. A really beautiful small marina complex lies just to the E of the last-named hotel, but unfortunately there is little or no space for visiting yachts. Most of the buildings have been styled after Port Grimaud in the south of France, and the entire atmosphere is definitely *très européen*. Sad to say, Hurricane David decimated the yachts that stayed alongside here, for Fort-de-France still lacks a good hurricane hole.

To enter Anse Mitan, a black-and-yellow unlit buoy off Pointe de Bout should be left close to port, as should the ferry docks at the Bakoua Hotel. A dangerous unmarked reef lies not more than 130 yards W of the Bakoua dock. An old submerged wreck once lay close to the beach in the middle of the bay, but I have looked for it recently and been able to find nothing.

Anse Mitan is a very popular place with the local residents, has excellent beach restaurants, and is altogether a lot of fun.

Should you wish to visit Fort-de-France, you can leave your boat here and take the ferry across. The trip takes about 20 minutes, and the ferries run about once an hour.

Trois Îlets Bay (25527, I-A30)
(the village is supposedly the birthplace of Empress Josephine) is fun to explore by dinghy. The holding off the little town is not too good, though.

Îlet des Ramiers (25527, I-A30)
makes a good dinghy trip too, although the military sometimes closes up the old fort while they play soldiers.

Halfway along the coast between Îlet des Ramiers and Cap Solomon are two little bays right next to each other. One has a very black beach and the other a very white one. The two tiny villages are primitive and the people delightful.

Grande Anse d'Arlet (25524, I-A30),
just S of Cap Solomon, is one of the most beautiful anchorages on Martinique. Go to either end of the bay, depending on where the swell is coming from. At the S end of the bay, a small beach restaurant has built a dinghy dock for the use of its patrons. The bouillabaisse here is second to none.

Petit Anse d'Arlet (25524, I-A30),
farther to the S, is pretty, with its small village, but more rolly than its larger neighbor.

For the cruiser with a little time to spare, a trip to windward up the island's south coast is very productive.

Diamond Rock (25524, I-A301)
beckons any and all who fancy themselves as mountain-climbing types, and indeed it's fun to clamber around the old fortifications and to wonder at the

HMS *Diamond Rock* rises straight out of the water off the coast of Martinique.

fortitude of the men who manned this towering monolith; it was known in 1804 as HMS *Diamond Rock*.

Anchorage is in 5 fathoms off the NE corner, and the landing place faces N. The only way up is on the eastern side, behind the sole flat piece of land. Many old cannon are in the water at the base of the Rock, and there are some interesting ruins in the caves.

Cul-de-Sac Marin (25524, I-A301)

is a deep bay with shoals projecting irregularly from its perimeter. At the head of the bay there is a yacht club and a marina, well filled with local boats and charter boats from the large ATM fleet. A beautiful anchorage for transients can be found in 2 fathoms one half mile S of Pointe de Marin. A yacht may actually lie alongside beautiful white sand in clear, still water. Farther along still is the Club Mediterranée and the town of Sainte Anne.

The East Coast of Martinique (25524, I-A301)

has several really beautiful anchorages, but on the whole I have found it to be rather too bumpy and harrowing in the blustery winter months to be pleasant.

In the summer it's another story, though, and for the experienced eyeball naviga-tor a whole new Caribbean cruising world is waiting to be discovered.

Don't forget that you must clear with the authorities before leaving Martinique. And you must do it in Fort-de-France.

One more thing. If you are fit and healthy, a great day can be spent in the interior of Martinique. Get a taxi driver and/or a guide to take you to the N end of the island to the entrance of Gorge Falaise, which is halfway up the slopes of Mont Pelée. Climb down through the jungle to the riverbed and follow the stream to the magical waterfall and pool at the head of the gorge. Afterward, drive on to the Plantation Leyritz for a vintage *ponche planter* and a late lunch. I won't attempt to describe it; just go and enjoy it.

Another good excursion is to the Jardins de Balata, a botanical garden exhibit-ing plants from rain forest areas all over the world. You can get there by bus, communal taxi (take the one marked Morne Rouge), or taxi.

Saint Lucia (25521, I-B1)

Once upon a time there was a wonderful laughing lady called Josette Snowball. She was the queen of a beautiful, flower-filled place called Pigeon Island, just a hop, skip, and a jump off the northwestern coast of Saint Lucia. Around her, in a state of joyous confusion, lived her children, grandchildren, and many friends, as well as an assortment of loquacious birds and animals, and for good measure a host of gnomes, pixies, and jumbies. She had a palm-thatched beach bar, its open front just inches from the velvet warm waters of the bay, and for the handful of yachtsmen who in those days led the carefree but hard-working charter life, Pigeon Island days and nights were sheer magic. Maugham, Hemingway, Con-rad, or Gauguin couldn't have created a place of equal enchantment.

Then the government in its farseeing wisdom decided to develop and improve the spot. They pronounced it a national park, and up went signs and picnic tables. A huge causeway was bulldozed out across the bay to connect the island with Saint Lucia. Empty cans and plastic bags soon replaced the children and the birds and animals, and of course no self-respecting jumbie likes transistor radios and rock-and-roll. Then down came Mrs. Snowball's beach bar, and Josette herself fled to a rocky corner of the island, where she lived for several years, a prisoner of progress. She then returned to a quiet corner of England to live out her days with her family and her memories.

Saint Lucia for some reason has always attracted people like Josette, and even now it is probably the last island outpost of the charming, eccentric British colonial who lives in a world of baggy khaki shorts, China tea, and those slow-moving, grimy fans that hang precariously from ceilings like capsized helicopters.

Nevertheless, for the present-day yachtsman, Saint Lucia is still a great place to explore.

Good docks and services keep the slips full at Rodney Bay Marina, Saint Lucia.

Pigeon Island and Rodney Bay (25521, I-B1)

are still very much worth a visit despite the long absence of Mrs. Snowball. After clearing customs and immigration in the artificial lagoon, you may anchor off Pigeon Island so that you will clear its SW end if you should drag during the night, for the holding here is rather dodgy. On the mainland side, the lagoon has been dredged to 8-foot depths to serve as a nucleus for a Florida-style land development project. You can also anchor south of the lagoon entrance, opposite the Saint Lucien Hotel.

The lagoon is the home of Rodney Bay Marina and Stevens' Yachts. Water and fuel may be obtained at Stevens' work facility on the port hand as you enter the lagoon. Laundry can be left at their office in the marina complex, to be returned the following day, and you can get a good variety of supplies at their small commissary. Stevens' can also fill your propane bottle. (This is probably the last place to get propane if you are going south, until you get to Venezuela.) Three other yacht charter companies have offices in the marina, and other businesses located in the complex include a liquor store, drugstore, bread and sandwich shop, car rental, and boutique. A swimming pool is also available to marina patrons. Several restaurants are located within dinghy distance.

Two slips in Rodney Bay Marina, the ones with yellow pilings, are designated for boats wishing to check into customs and can be used without charge. If those are full, drop your anchor and dinghy in. Customs hours are 8:00 A.M.–noon, 4:00–6:00 P.M., but after 4:30 P.M. there is an overtime charge of about U.S. $4. The same charge is also made on Saturday, and is raised to about U.S. $6 on Sunday.

There is usually room at the marina for transients to tie up there and in the lagoon to anchor in its calm water.

This bay was used as a fleet anchorage by Admiral Rodney during his relentless pursuit of de Grasse, which was to end so disastrously for the French in the Saintes Passage. Later, from the fort on top of Pigeon's southern hill, Admiral Hood's men would signal with mirrors to a small sloop on station in the channel between Saint Lucia and Martinique. The sloop would similarly relay the message to the tiny garrison clinging to Diamond Rock. When the French fleet hoisted their yards, spies in Fort-de-France reported to Diamond Rock, and the Royal Navy, a slightly more spirited bunch then than now, was ready to pounce.

The W coast of Saint Lucia has many beautiful and protected anchorages, and I suppose that, of all the islands, Saint Lucia best epitomizes the tropical image of the West Indies.

Castries (25528, B1),

named after a singularly unsuccessful Frenchman, is the capital and main port of entry, although vessels may also enter at Vieux Fort on the island's SE tip, in Rodney Bay, and in Marigot Lagoon.

The harbor is rather deep and has a soft, muddy bottom. Since it usually blows pretty hard from the E, use plenty of scope. For customs and immigration, anchor close to the large black warping buoy opposite the center of the town docks or, if there is space, go alongside—although you may regret this, because the yacht will soon be covered with dust and a multitude of small boys.

Customs and immigration officials share the same office. A cruising permit will be issued, enabling the yacht to depart without having to return to Castries for her final clearance.

On the N side of Castries Harbour is Vigie Cove, home of Saint Lucia Yacht Services, a project started some 25 years ago by Bert and Gracie Ganter. Bert of the booming voice was a master Mr. Fix-it, and in the days when his work shops were the only ones between Trinidad and Saint Thomas, we would all rush in with our sick and stuttering Stuart Turners and bulging and bunged-up Blakes. But "Whiskey Hollow," as it was known among Caribbean yachtsmen, eventually became too much for Bert, and he was forced to move to cooler, calmer climes. Gracie, bless her heart, stuck it out until she sold out to two young American brothers (both positively glowing with enthusiasm) and retired to peace and quietness in England. Castries Yacht Center is also located in Vigie Cove. They can haul your boat and do most kinds of fiberglass and mechanical work. Both Castries Yacht Center and Saint Lucia Yacht Services can supply fuel and water.

Bob Elliot's attractive little restaurant, the Coal Pot, is opposite the marina and is to my mind the best place to eat on the island.

Castries has had a habit of burning down in the past and as a result is horridly modern in appearance. There is good shopping, however. The covered market on Jeremie Street spills out over the surrounding sidewalks and is a good place to restock. Minerval and Chasternets on Bridge Street is, for the islands, a large department store. Leave the dinghy alongside the main dock and, to be on the safe side, engage a small boy to take care of it for you. Don't fall prey to the many helpful types who will insist that they carry your bags, etc.

Grande Cul-de-Sac (25528, I-B1)
is a larger, cool, and usually calm bay 2 miles S of Castries, but unfortunately there is now a hot, large oil depot situated on its shores, which is not exactly the image of the tropics.

Marigot Lagoon (25528, I-B1)
is only a mile S of Grande Cul-de-Sac, and here a yacht would be quite secure even if a hurricane passed overhead. I was in Marigot once when just that happened. The only danger was the threat of flying coconuts, and if you've ever seen an 80-mile-an-hour coconut you'll know it wasn't funny.

Not long ago the lagoon was deserted. At night the beat of drums could be heard coming from the village on the hill, and the only lights to be seen were the fireflies among the palms. It was exciting and somehow all very African.

Then along came our friendly developer and in came suburbia, Saint Lucia style. The tragedy of it all is that, despite the hotels and houses, hardly anyone seems to stick to living there.

On the port hand as you enter is Dolittle's Bar and Restaurant, a very pleasant little spot with a friendly atmosphere. Farther in on the starboard hand is the Hurricane Hole Hotel, which has its own jetty, but don't rely on finding an empty spot there. The Moorings, a bareboat charter company, is based on the eastern side of Marigot's much-photographed sand spit, and has combined the aforementioned establishments into one large entity, known as the Marigot Bay Resort.

The lagoon empties out during the day, then fills up again, chock-a-block, as the charter yachts return from their day's outings. Before you get your anchor down, you'll be visited by boys and young men who would like to sell you fruits, vegetables, and shell and coral jewelry, or do some work on your boat. If you need a shade for your cockpit light, they'll weave you one from coconut palm fronds, to order, while you watch. The vendors may row out in one of the locally made and brightly painted fishing boats, or they may paddle their bananas out on a board boat that is well past its prime.

Our old friend Admiral Rodney, when he in his turn was being hounded around the islands by the unsporting French, hid a small squadron behind the palms by lashing the fronds that are woven today into hats and lamp shades to the mastheads of his ships.

On entering Marigot, favor the southern side of the channel until abeam of Dolittle's. Very shallow water runs out from the northern shore, almost to midchannel. The inner harbor is deep with a muddy bottom. If people anchor close by, don't worry. The lagoon is so well protected that no one dances around on the anchor here.

L'Anse le Raye (25521, I-B1)

is a pleasant enough little spot and a great place to study the local fishing boats, of which about 75 percent are Carib canoes. They still use sails around these parts too.

Beware, inshore mariner, of a devilish rock off Grand Caille Point, the north terminus of Soufrière Bay. The water is very still, and you won't see it break.

Soufrière (25521, I-B1)

is worth a stop if only so that the crew can visit Saint Lucia's drive-in volcano. If you are lucky and the thing is feeling bilious, it's a really worthwhile experience. A bit like a Fellini film: a moonlike landscape wreathed in swirling yellow mists,

The water gets deep quickly right off the beach along the shore of Soufrière Bay.

huge chunks of mud hurtling upward from fiendishly bubbling pools, and a constant rumbling that makes Auntie Mabel's indigestion seem like whispers in a summer's night. At other times, though, these fabled sulfur springs can be about as exciting as a bowl of cold porridge.

A really excellent restaurant, the Hummingbird, is located at the northern end of the town and adjacent to the beach. The water is very deep, so drop a bow anchor and tie a stern line to a tree in front of the restaurant. Or anchor on the narrow shelf on the south side of the harbor where the chart shows about 20 feet.

Anse de Piton (25521, I-B1)

lies around the corner from Soufrière, and if you fail to be thrilled by this gorgeous place, which has become almost a symbol of the West Indies, you really should have stayed at home. Like Soufrière, it is very deep, but the Pitons Bay produces some vicious squalls from time to time, and a yacht must be securely moored. The best method is to approach the beach slowly, having let out 15 fathoms of chain. When the anchor touches bottom, swing around and go stern to the beach. Have a line ready and secure it to a palm tree, then back up to within 30 feet of the beach and take up on the anchor.

The Pitons are magnificent. Nearly 2,700 feet high, they appear to rise almost vertically when you are close under them. Guarded by legions of tall, silent palms and occupied only by the ruins of an old estate house, the area has an atmosphere like nowhere else in the islands. Try to be there on or near the night of the full moon, and watch the shadows inch their way down the mountain.

Laborie (25521, I-B1)

offers a pleasant overnight anchorage for eyeball experts. I have been inside the reef several times and only once found the conditions too rolly to stay.

Don't rely too much on the charts here, and make sure the sky is clear before entering. The village is primitive and the local residents very friendly. Plenty of fish and fresh vegetables can be had ashore.

Vieux Fort Bay (25528, I-B1),

on the extreme southern tip of the island, is seldom visited for two reasons: it is a long, bumpy, upwind sail from almost anywhere, and there is no really good place to anchor. If you put your anchor down on the east side of the commercial dock, you'll be within all too easy earshot of the town's noisy generating plant, but in quiet water. You can tie your dinghy out of harms way on the big dock. If you anchor off town, below the Kimatri Hotel, you will probably roll badly and you'll have to run your dinghy up on the beach with the town's fishing boats. Customs and immigration clearance is available in Vieux Fort at the commercial dock.

Although the old American wartime airfield in Vieux Fort has become Saint Lucia's international airport, and the island's biggest hotel is nearby, this is what

I call a "real" town, not a tourist town. It makes a good contrast to Marigot. And, should you be picking up guests who are flying in, it is easy to do if you are anchored in Vieux Fort. Should you need other reasons to go to Vieux Fort, here are two: it is a good jumping-off place for Barbados, and it also positions you for an easy reach the next day to Saint Vincent.

The Cloud's Nest Hotel, which used to serve very good West Indian food, has been closed, following the death of the owner.

Saint Lucia–Saint Vincent Passage

As spectacular as the Pitons are, I sometimes wish they were not there, for they play absolute havoc with the wind off the southern end of Saint Lucia. Once we tried to work *Lord Jim* up against a blustery northeaster on passage from Saint Vincent to Saint Lucia, and I'll never forget the wracking strain on the gear as the schooner reared and plunged through the confused and tumbling seas with hardly a breath of wind to ease her pain.

Going S, head high after leaving Saint Lucia's Beaumont Point, and keep going high until the true wind fills in. Going N, especially if there is any weight in the wind, do everything in your power to lay the Pitons rather than being swept down to leeward with the 1-knot westerly current.

Saint Vincent (25484, I-B30)

Perhaps the most beautiful island of them all, Saint Vincent is a mass of jagged green peaks and steep-sided, verdant valleys, many of which are partly cultivated. The people of Saint Vincent are industrious both on land and sea, and if it were not for the limitations imposed on air traffic by the very inadequate runway, the island would surely have made great strides. As it is, however, a country-village atmosphere still prevails, and Saint Vincent is utterly delightful.

In Saint Vincent and the Grenadines you'll probably find it worthwhile to troll while you sail. Just be sure to bring your line aboard when in any of the several areas where fishing is prohibited. These include the northeast coast and the Devil's Table in Bequia, Île de Quatre, Grand and Sandy bays in Mustique, the east coast of Canouan, all of Mayero and the Tobago Cays, all of Palm Island, and Petit Saint Vincent and the surrounding reefs.

Apart from being staggeringly beautiful, the northern end of the island beats even Dominica for sheer ruggedness. The lightly slumbering volcano Soufrière (if you have been counting, this is the fifth with that name) dominates the area, and from its 3,600-foot summit one can look down into the dark-green depths of a crater lake that itself is 2,000 feet above sea level. You will remember that Soufrière in 1979, tired of playing second fiddle to Martinique's Mont Pelée, staged a spectacular eruption, which resulted in the rapid evacuation of the entire northern end of the island.

Landmark of the Windwards, the Pitons on Saint Lucia

Although there is no anchorage under even the most perfect conditions, the yachtsman should try to land a party to visit the Falls of Baleine on the northwestern extremity of the island. Get in as close to the little beach as possible and send the dinghy in through the surf. The yacht should then stand well offshore, for there can be some really violent squalls close in under the cliffs.

The tiny village of Wallibu is situated just north of Chateaubelair Bay. When we first went there with *Ron of Argyle*, the inhabitants disappeared from sight,

Villages like this dot the shore of Saint Vincent.

and we were aware only of furtive movements in the surrounding jungle. Later the local people overcame their shyness, and whenever we appeared they would flock out to the yacht in their canoes. The village headman told me that up to the time of our first visit, some of his people had never seen a white woman! The mud and thatch huts are straight from Africa. Take some old clothes ashore, and your kindness will really be appreciated. Here again, the yacht should stand well off rather than attempt to anchor close ashore.

Chateaubelair Bay itself is deep and usually too rolly for anything longer than a lunch stop.

Cumberland Bay (25484, I-B30)

was once a favorite with everyone. Very deep, it is a calm, well protected, and beautiful spot.

For a period, the local residents in this anchorage had a reputation for being a little light-fingered. But the trend in Saint Vincent in recent years has been toward fewer problems of this sort. If you want to leave your boat, you might take the precaution of getting acquainted with your neighbors on other boats in the anchorage and letting them know your plans. The yachtie grapevine should be consulted for the current situation.

Stay in the middle of the bay when you enter; there are rocks off both sides.

Anchor by dropping in 7–8 fathoms and running a line over the stern to a palm tree.

A store, a small restaurant, and a few houses are strung out along the beach. Some of my most pleasant memories are of moon-drenched nights in Cumberland.

Wallilabo Bay (25484, I-B30)

is only 1½ miles S of Cumberland, with just as attractive surroundings. Anchor close to the beach and tie your stern to a tree if you wish. Ashore are a store, a small restaurant, and a few houses.

Layou Bay and Buccament Bay (25484, I-B30)

can, with careful soundings, sometimes be used, but if the anchor ever dragged off the 5-fathom shelf, it would plunge to 30–40 fathoms.

Adventuresome skippers overnight in these bays, generally tie stern lines to a tree ashore.

Kingstown (25483, I-B30)

is the capital and port of entry. A deep-water dock, paid for to a large degree by the Canadian government, has helped the island no end. Yachts, unfortunately, are still not catered to. Considering the amount of business they bring to the island, that is quite surprising.

The only surge-free small-boat anchorage in the harbor is at the extreme ESE end of the bay, in line with the end of the dock. Here it is deep, and the wind can blast in anywhere from the N to the S. The holding is good, though, and as long as there is swinging room, the crew can rest easy. There is no good place to leave a dinghy, and it's best to have someone take the skipper ashore when he goes to clear in, and return the dinghy to the boat.

The Saint Vincent government no longer imposes a tax on yachts cruising in its waters. To check-in is not difficult, but in Kingstown it does entail visits to three separate offices: customs, the port authority, and immigration. Checking in may be done more easily in Bequia or elsewhere.

Once you are away from the dock area, Kingstown is a rather splendid old town, in its way almost as attractive as Saint George's in Grenada. Shopping is reasonable, and most necessities are available, as well as examples of local arts and crafts.

Young Island (25483, I-B30)

is one place to move to after you've cleared at Kingstown. It's a very pretty place, but the current, which runs both ways at anything up to 3 knots, can cause no end of confusion. The least troublesome spot is to the NW of the channel that runs between Young Island and the mainland, but a swell sometimes makes it rolly here. Then there is no choice but to push farther in. A light Danforth or

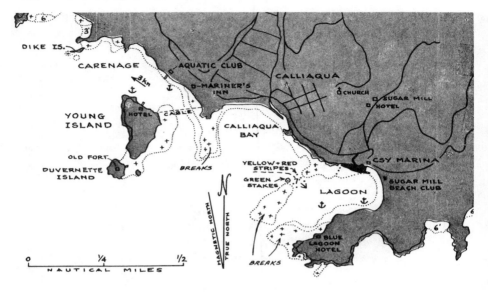

Young Island, Saint Vincent

a CQR will seldom hold in the deepest part of the channel, so if there is room, try to drop in shallower water, opposite the Mariner's Inn. A submerged power cable is clearly marked and should not be used as an aid to anchoring.

When the stream is running to the NW, there is really no problem. The fun begins when it's going the other way against the wind. I remember one night when, at about two in the morning, a whole mass of boats became hopelessly snarled up. *Lord Jim, Redonda, Ticonderoga, Eudroma, Spearhead,* and *Lunaquest* were, I think, the main participants. We eventually gave up the unequal struggle and rafted alongside each other until the tide changed. A yacht lying to a nylon rode will dart about like a tethered stallion, and it doesn't really help to moor fore-and-aft unless everyone else does so too. Despite the problems, though, we have been anchoring there for years and will, I guess, carry on crashing and banging around like jousting juggernauts for a few more years.

Young Island Hotel is the work of John Hauser, a one-time American Express executive. He has created one of the most beautiful tropical retreats in the Caribbean and, quite rightly, has strong feelings about the behavior of visitors to his island. What a pity that some of the concrete-block and tin-roof type of hoteliers could not have shown John Hauser's imagination. The new owners have done their best to preserve the atmosphere and, if anything, the service has improved.

Water can be obtained at the Aquatic Club, opposite Young Island on the mainland. Regarding taxi drivers and their current fares, check with the management there. Adjacent to the Aquatic Club is a native-type slipway for small vessels. Several little restaurants and boutiques now operate in the old houses facing Young Island, and to my mind they only embellish an already delightful spot. Full marks to all concerned!

A fun thing to do is to take the dinghy around to the landing at Fort Duvernette and scramble up the old stone steps to the battery at the top. A craftily placed mortar is still in the position that enabled it to lob a damned great ball over the top of Young Island and into the channel, where even a large vessel would be sheltered from ordinary cannon.

The Blue Lagoon (25483, I-B30)

is one half mile to the SE of Young Island and for smallish craft offers good shelter, although both entrances are narrow and none too easy. It is the home base of Caribbean Sailing Yachts' Grenadine bareboat fleet, and their marina does not really encourage visiting yachts.

The best entrance is through the marked break in the reef on the southwestern side, utilizing a 9-foot channel. Once you are inside, there are no dangers, but the water is deep and I have sometimes seen a roll even here. The northern entrance has little more than 5 feet of water, but it is normally quite calm and the water is clear.

Whales and the Northbound Passage

Cruising the western coast of Saint Vincent, keep a good eye open for the last of a dying breed, the hunters of blackfish. For some reason the blackfish, or pilot whale, is more numerous in the vicinity of Saint Vincent than around the other islands. Their rounded heads and porpoise-like dorsal fins are quite a common sight. Since whaling first began in the island, Vincentian fishermen have hunted the blackfish, and even now the men can be seen in their long, gray whaleboats, quietly waiting for the telltale spouts of spray as the little whales break water to breathe. Although most boats still use a hand-thrown harpoon, some have developed a highly lethal-looking device fashioned out of an old 12-bore shotgun supported on a tripod up in the eyes of the whaleboat. Before the conservationists roar too loudly, let me just say that the Saint Vincent fishermen exist on a pittance and, like the creatures they hunt, are fighting pretty hard to survive.

One last word of advice. If you're headed north from Saint Vincent, there are two paths open. Either press on under sail past Dark Head, in which case you will probably not be able to sail high enough to lay the Pitons without tacking, or motor sail really close under the cliffs until De Volet Point is abeam. The problem with the latter is that in blowy conditions squalls of really ferocious intensity can be encountered as you leave the lee, added to which there is sometimes a healthy tide rip about 4 miles N of the island. Of the two, I prefer motor sailing to De Volet Point unless the wind has a good deal of S in it.

The Grenadines—The Yesterday Islands (25482, I-B3)

In recent years quite a change has taken place in this wonderful 50-mile chain of islands. Hotels and other developments have sprung up, and airstrips have appeared where previously even the seagulls had a hard time taking off. However, to be honest, I don't think anyone could say that the Grenadines have lost much of their charm because of all this. There are still scads of places to hide away from the crowd; quiet beaches where nary a soul will be seen, and water as clear and as pure as it was when the first Arawaks paddled their way north from the vastness of South America.

Some of the following anchorages will not appeal to everyone. They may be too lonely and exposed for the average taste, but to me solitude is a great luxury, becoming rarer as the world gets smaller. I am always amazed at the way most yachtsmen tend to huddle together in a wide-open anchorage. Nothing is more galling, after I have pointedly left the pack for a more isolated spot, than to have some cheerful character, with all the water in the world to choose from, let go within a few yards of me.

Bequia (25483, I-B31)

is the northernmost of the Grenadines, strictly speaking, but somehow the island is a little too grown up to be thought of in the same terms as Union or Mayero. Admiralty Bay on Bequia is a port of entry for Saint Vincent, and the formalities are simple and easy. Just pop into the police station behind the jetty and see what they require.

Should you enter here rather than in Kingstown, and prefer to visit that city without the hassle of anchoring there, it is an easy matter to ride the MV *Admiral* to Kingstown. The vessel departs from Bequia weekdays at 6:30 A.M. and 2:00 P.M., and on Saturdays at 6:30 A.M.; it returns from Kingstown to Bequia at 10:30 A.M. and 4:30 P.M. weekdays, and 12:30 P.M. Saturdays. The trip takes 70 minutes. The sloop *Friendship Rose* makes the same run, leaving Bequia at 6:30 A.M. and returning at 12:30 P.M., Monday through Friday only.

Bequia is only 8 miles S of Saint Vincent and is subject to its large sister's weather; Bequia gets a good deal more rain than the rest of the Grenadines.

Its people, many of whom are descendants of Scots engineers who originally came to Barbados and Saint Vincent to operate the sugar estates, are the most able shipwrights, carpenters, seamen, and general handymen to be found anywhere in the Lesser Antilles. They truly love the sea, and are steeped in the tradition of working sail, thanks to the influence of the New England whaling crews that once were based on the island. There are no keener critics of a sailboat's performance than the old schooner men who sit ashore 'neath the shade of the flamboyant trees watching with knowledgeable eyes all that goes on in the harbor.

Whaling is, in fact, still carried on in Bequia, though not to the extent it once was. (Recent catches are down from six to only one or less per year.) High up on Mount Pleasant, impatient small boys and philosophical old men scan the seas to windward for signs of the migrating humpback whale. Great excitement follows a sighting. The small boys pelt down the hill to the villages of Friendship and Paget Farm, where the 18-foot, 6-oared whaleboats are drawn up on the beach. Once at sea, the whaleboats are guided to the right spot by the old men on the hill, who flash signals by mirror. Should a humpback be sighted to leeward, there is no way that, if killed, its huge bulk can be towed back against the trade winds.

One day we were asked to take *Lord Jim* to sea to stand by three of the more determined whaleboats, which refused to give up the chase even when they were well downwind and in heavy seas. It had been a lean year for the whalers, and so we steamed off, preparing a bridle and a long warp for a possible heavy tow. There were mixed emotions as we watched the tired men row all over the ocean while the whale surfaced and sounded around them. Then there was an unbelievable commotion alongside the lead boat. The harpooner stood poised, and for a split second of time we were with Ahab and the *Pequod*. But it was not to be. The great creature shrugged off the harpoon and sounded, to disappear for good. We towed the exhausted men back to Bequia, feeling strangely sad.

When you have anchored in Admiralty Bay, take time to observe and absorb some small part of the island's atmosphere. On the beach, shipwrights and sailmakers are at work, and fishermen fiddle with their nets and fish traps. Local schooners, most of which were built right on the beach here, come and go. Small boys swim alongside their beautifully made models, some of which are perfect replicas of the charter yachts anchored in the bay. Ashore, the church bell rings, Estelle Fredericks bakes her delicious bread, and across the way in Elizabeth Town a steel band tunes its pans. Have a sundowner at the Frangipani and meet the many happy and relaxed yachtsmen who congregate there. If you like to talk politics, try to engage Frangipani's owner, "Son" Mitchell, an ex-premier of Saint Vincent, in a discussion about the future of the Grenadines. Many small bars, gift shops, and restaurants are dotted about, all within walking distance.

One very soon feels at home in Bequia. Here, more than in any other island, one is inclined to take long, leisurely strolls along winding country lanes. A little over a mile from town, on the S coast just past Friendship Bay, can be found what remains of the whaling fleet drawn up in orderly ranks just above the rumbling surf. Stop along the way for an excellent lunch at the Spring Hotel, part of an active copra plantation.

Or take the dinghy and a jug of rum punch to Princess Margaret Beach, surely one of the most beautiful anywhere.

The yachting boom has not gone unnoticed by the authorities and, in marked contrast to other islands, several useful navigational buoys have appeared between Saint Vincent and Union Island. Of course it's one thing to lay them and another to maintain them. Therefore, there is not much point in noting all their locations, as it appears that several have disappeared already. Hey ho!

If the Bequia slipway is operating, fuel and water can be had from its small dock on the N side of the harbor. The Frangipani Hotel stands by on VHF-16 and SSB 2527 and for a modest sum is delighted to help yachtsmen with travel reservations, cables, etc. Ken Walker operates a Johnson/Evinrude agency, with spare parts and a small machine shop for repairs. Ice may be found in small quantities at many of the bars. Be aware, though, that water is in very short supply in all the Grenadines.

On your way in or out past West Cay, sail close to the coast for a good look at Moon Hole, the weird house in a cave that Tom Johnson built. Several other houses have been built in the same unearthly style on the surrounding rocks. There is a light on West Cay, beyond Moon Hole.

On the other side of the island, Friendship Bay is a pretty anchorage, but it usually rolls badly during the winter months. Petit Nevis has a very pleasant anchorage under its lee, but if a whale has been caught, give it a wide berth, as the smell is horrendous. This is where the unfortunate creatures are cut up, processed, and shared out.

Balliceaux, Battowia, and Île de Quatre (25482, I-B30)

have no really comfortable winter anchorages, which is a pity, because the first two are interesting ashore. In summer, Balliceaux has a lovely hideaway in the bay on the SW side.

Mustique (25482, I-B30)

is a sort of European equivalent of Antigua's Mill Reef Club, having been quite beautifully developed by Colin Tennant, who has hosted Lord Snowden and Princess Margaret among his more notable. As you may well imagine, things are therefore done with a certain style.

Off the N coast of the island is the spectacular wreck of the 20,000-ton French liner *Antilles,* a rather striking example of aberrant piloting.

Close to the small dock in Grand Bay is the best place to anchor, and it is sometimes possible to hang a stern line onto the dock in order to keep your bows into the swell. But the dock may be occupied by interisland boats, so don't count on this manuever.

Half a mile off the dock, on a bearing of 300°T, lies the Montezuma Shoal, where my beloved *Lord Jim,* a year after I sold her, very nearly ended her days. Her Bostonian pride would not allow it, though, and she survived 24 hours of pounding on this treacherous bank with only a damaged rudder to show for it. Old Mr. Lawley apparently knew a thing or two!

There is talk that one day a channel will be dredged into the south pond and a marina constructed.

The Cotton House, a truly delightful club in the center of the island, serves excellent meals, but reservations must be made in advance. Basil's Bar and Restaurant just N of the dock is a great place for a good West Indian jump-up, especially on Wednesday nights. A small provision store, grandiosely named the Great General Store, is across the road from Basil's, and also a boutique known as the Jungle Room. Both the Cotton House and Basil's monitor VHF-16. Off the S end of the island there is excellent trolling from the dinghy.

Savan Island (25482, I-B31)

is a possible overnight anchorage under summer conditions, and a good lunch stop. The snorkeling is good, and apart from a few fishermen camping in some primitive huts ashore, this little island is deserted and seldom visited. Tuck up into the bight and set a stern anchor.

Canouan Island (25482, I-B311)

has a variety of anchorages to suit nearly all wind and sea conditions, but few yachts seem to use the island. In summer only, push right into the SE corner of Maho Bay.

On the west coast, two delightful spots are the minute cove of Corbay or, if the northerly swell is being a pain, behind the point immediately S of Corbay. The latter is nearly always calm, has beautifully clear water, and is seldom used.

Charlestown Bay looks good, but may be rolly. Try anchoring next to the buy boat on station south of the Crystal Sands Hotel beach. The wind blows fairly constantly there and tends to hold your boat bow into the swells. And you'll have a front-row seat to watch the fishermen sail in to sell their catch at the end of the day.

A beautiful anchorage can sometimes be found between Glass Hill and Taffia Hill. An eyeball expert will be required for the anchorage behind Friendship Point, which is good in a northerly breeze, and for the superb hideaway behind the windward reef on the eastern side of the island. Although it will frighten the daylights out of Auntie Mabel, this is one of the best anywhere.

Push on close inshore past Friendship Point until you are behind the barrier reef. Carry on as far as your draft allows and drop back close to one of the beaches. Lay out a second anchor if there is any wind in the offing. Sometimes a strong current runs here, but it slacks off in the shallows close to the reef, and the snorkeling is fabulous. There is great walking ashore, and unless too many people read this, you will have the place to yourself.

Between Canouan and Carriacou

there are so many beautiful and secure anchorages a yachtsman could go bananas worrying about which ones to use. This is the very heart of the Grenadines, and it is safe to say that once you've sailed here, Montauk Point and the Isle of Wight will never seem the same again.

It's a world where wind and sea and land have combined to make a kaleidoscope of color and beauty: a world where even the most hardened Homo sapiens

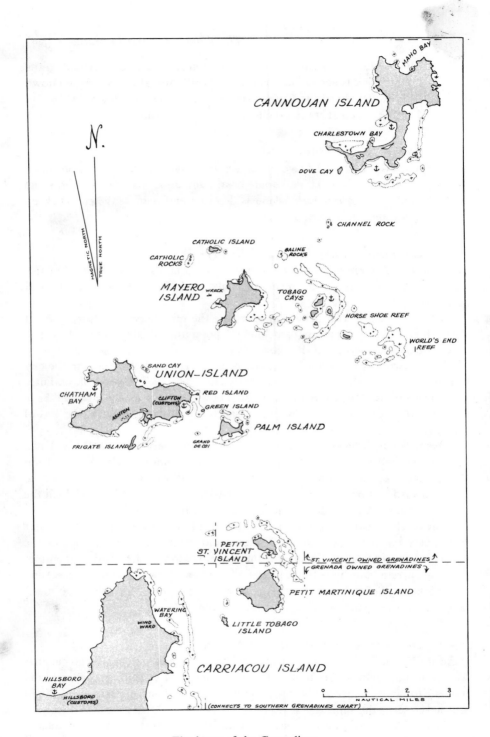

The heart of the Grenadines

may realize that there is more to life than highways and hamburgers and movies and goggle boxes. Even the place names ring with excitement. Roll them around your tongue for a moment: Saltwhistle Bay, World's End Reef, Petit Bateau, and Bloody Bay. You will remember them, all right, as the first snows of the long winter freshen your memory.

The Tobago Cays (25482, I-B31)

lie behind the sheltering barrier of World's End and Horseshoe Reefs. Most famous of all the anchorages in the Grenadines, the cays (provided the weather is its usual benign self) are the epitome of tropical cruising—ringed with beaches, and with deep-water channels winding through the pastel shallows. The yachtsman can spend days living in the midst of their beauty. The cays are inclined to become a little crowded in the height of the winter season, but even then the canny skipper can escape the mob by picking a spot out to windward under the lee of the reef.

The cays are uninhabited, in the sense that there are no villages and no permanent residents. However, a number of men and boys from nearby islands do in fact camp out there during the charter season now, making their living by rowing from boat to boat, selling lobsters, ice, bread, fruits, and vegetables. Fresh water is about the only commodity lacking.

The northern approach to the cays is simple enough. Once past Glass Hill on Canouan, head a little higher than the easternmost of Mayero. Soon the wicked-looking Baline Rocks will be clearly seen. Pass between these rocks and the end of Horseshoe Reef. Two day beacons on the cays will come into line to lead you in. When approaching the cays from the N, the cautious navigator would do well to leave Baline and the unmarked shoal patch to port until the day beacons are in line. Make a cautious approach in good light and be prepared to eyeball your way around.

The southern entrance is more complex, and should be attempted for the first time only in good light. In 18 years I have only once seen one of the two sand cays that are supposed to mark this entrance. From the rigging, though, the dark-blue water of the channel is very obvious.

The most popular anchorage is in the gut between the two islands. A strong current sometimes rushes through the channel, and yachts should lie to a mooring with two anchors off the bow, one to the E and the other to the W. Stern anchors for heavy, deep-drafted vessels seldom hold well, for the strains are enormous.

In summer conditions, my favorite place is just to windward of the little beach on Jamesby, the southernmost of the group, or as far to the SE of Baradal as draft allows. In *Mirage* and *Étoile de Mer,* both trawler types drawing 6 feet, we could roam all over the banks inside the reef.

It was a little different with *Lord Jim*'s 10½ feet, however, as we once found out. For years I had been thoroughly disgusted with the so-called sportsmen (generally from the French islands) who would dash down to the cays in fast motorboats and blast away at every animal and bird in sight. Expended shotgun shells were everywhere, and the iguana and dove population had been decimated.

One day, following our normal practice, which was to give the charter party a bit of a thrill, we executed a quick circumnavigation of the two larger islands under full sail—topsails and the lot aloft. We normally would conclude the tour by strapping everything in tight while running downwind through the narrow gut, then dropping headsails and foresail simultaneously. The 70-ton schooner, under main alone and full helm, would spin around on her heel to drop anchor and fall back alongside the beach. All rather hairy, but a lot of fun.

On this occasion, a fusillade of gunfire from Jamesby attracted our attention to a flotilla of cabin cruisers anchored in the lee of the cay, their crews merrily banging away. Full of righteous fury, I decided to stop this nonsense, and down went *Lord Jim*'s helm. Straight at them we thundered.

Quite what I really intended escapes me now but, with a few feet to go, we ran up the gently sloping sand and stopped dead. Why that long-suffering rig didn't carry on going beats me. Anyway, with gunmen and crew all frozen to the spot in stupefied amazement, I stood up and with imbecilic pomposity shouted, "Vous êtes une vache, alors!" With that brilliant rapier thrust, *Lord Jim* jibed all-standing, heeled over, and trundled off into deep water, and I sat down feeling more stupid than usual. One of the charter party, new to the game, commented seriously, "Hey, how about that? I never thought a sailboat had brakes."

Snorkeling is of course superb out on the Horseshoe Reef, especially due E of the northern tip of Baradal, where there is a break in the reef. A good place for beginners to practice is off the beach on the SE side of Petit Bateau, the southern-most of the two main islands.

Outside the Horseshoe in Petit Tabac, in settled or summer weather, an anchorage can sometimes be found in the Horseshoe's lee. If not, take the dinghy through the small-boat pass up by Baradal and play Robinson Crusoe for a bit. Also in settled weather, eyeball it out to the sprawling World's End Reef, where you will be absolutely alone, seemingly in the middle of the ocean. The holding is good, and there's no reason why you shouldn't overnight there in a calm spell. It's a funny feeling, though—there's not a scrap of land between you and central Africa.

Mayero Island (25482, I-B31)

lies just to the W of the Tobago Cays and has four anchorages, beautiful beaches, wonderful walks, a very interesting wreck, and a population of under a hundred souls. Saltwhistle Bay is tiny, and usually crowded, and more than 9 feet can't really escape the swell. Saline Bay is the better of the other two coves on the W side of the island if there is a northerly swell running. On certain days, you'll share the beach at Saline Bay only with children and fishermen from the village. Other days, you'll find a portion of it covered with tourists who have been lightered ashore from a small cruise ship for swimming, sunning, and a picnic lunch.

The reef that runs out SW from Grand Col Point extends a good deal farther than the chart shows, as the captain of the World War I gunboat *Purina* found out to his cost. She lies about 400 yards NNW of the point, and her shadowy form 35 feet down is an almost irresistible lure for experienced skin divers. Line up the end of the point with the dock in Saline Bay and search with the dinghy. The end of the reef on which *Purina* ran aground is marked with a red buoy. A black buoy now marks the E end of Catholic Island Reef.

A beautiful, seldom-used anchorage is on the eastern side of Mayero behind the reefs. Tuck up to the NE as far as you can go.

The island was once ruled with an iron fist by two West Indian fishermen named the Saint Hilaire brothers. On certain nights of the week, the brothers preferred there to be no yachts around. "Why?" asked one of my charterers. "Because de debil come to talk wid us and you folks might frighten him," replied the Saint Hilaires, leering horribly. "De debil," it seemed, traveled in an unlit sloop.

Union Island (25482, I-B31),

with its spectacular skyline of soaring peaks, always looks bigger than it actually is. Viewed at sundown from the Tobago Cays, it is sensational. Apart from being a port of entry for Saint Vincent, it is the administrative center for the northern Grenadines and enjoys a greater degree of prosperity than its immediate neighbors.

The township of Clifton looks from the harbor to be a badly executed backdrop for Sadie Thompson. On my first trip through, in 1958, I was trying to pretend to the charter party that I had been there before. A rather imposing building displayed a sign which said HOTEL, and with great confidence, I suggested a meal ashore. When we arrived, the "hotel" had chickens in the lobby, goats in the dining room, and a load of saltfish in the bedroom. Now, of course, it's a smart place, with curtains and plants and things in conch shells. The island is still very primitive, but the people are healthy and their laughter is one of the loudest noises to be heard.

A Union Islander, who for purposes of this tale had better remain nameless, once quite literally saved my life. We were in the Martinique drydock, and he was the crew on a friend's boat. One night a young Spanish gent, crew on another boat, went completely off his little rocker and began trying to stick a large rusty chisel into all and sundry. I believe I was relieving myself at the time El Nutcase roared onto the scene waving his trusty chisel. All was very nearly lost, when my Union Island friend leapt out of the rigging and with great dexterity disarmed and disabled the noble Spaniard.

Many years later, my rescuer turned up in Clifton with a huge boatload of lobsters for sale at a most reasonable price. We stacked our deep freeze, and he went off to the other yachts. Later, an acquaintance who had a beach bar in Clifton called me on the ship-to-shore from Grenada to say that his lobster pound had been robbed and would I go ashore and investigate. Being a man of honor, I thoroughly enjoyed the lobster.

Clifton Harbour is simple to enter and very secure, and the outer harbor just behind the reef is beautiful. Don't rely on any of the entrance buoys being in place. A red flasher (6-mile visibility) on Red Island was operating in December 1980. To clear customs, which is necessary only when coming from Grenada, don't forget the Q and courtesy flags, and go ashore to the post office. Immigration is at the airport.

The previously mentioned beach club was taken over and enlarged upon by André and Simone Beaufraund of Martinique. They constructed a slipway for vessels up to 60 feet and allowed crews to do their own work. The place became known as the Anchorage Yacht Club and now again, under new French management, has become one of the "in" places of the Grenadines. Water and ice are available in limited quantities. The restaurant and bar facility is much frequented by yachtsmen, especially the French bareboaters. Of great appeal is the shark cage at the foot of the club's premises.

In 1979 a rather splendid little revolution took place on Union Island. It was felt in some quarters, namely among the Rastifarian sect, that Union was not getting a fair slice of the pie from Mother Saint Vincent. One dark night the Rastas sailed down to neighboring Carriacou and "borrowed" from the authorities there a half dozen elderly Lee Enfield .303 rifles. On the way home, their small whaleboat was swamped and the ammunition lost. Undaunted, the Rastas with their now purely decorative weapons plodded ashore. It so happened that morning that the local constabulary found it necessary to catch the morning schooner for Saint Vincent, so the insurgents found themselves in complete command of Union.

Flushed with victory and ganja, the Rastas then decided to pop over to nearby Palm Island to try their luck there, or at least frighten a few hotel guests into buying some decorated conch shells or suchlike.

Palm Island's John Caldwell had other ideas, though. Digging a hole in the sand, he settled down with a .22 and prepared to repel boarders. The hotel guests, sitting in the cool of the beach bar with their morning rum punches, cheered on their man with polite clapping reminiscent of Wimbledon's center court. The Rastas, after much clicking of empty rifle bolts, found the occasional warning shot much too unfriendly and retired home for tea or whatever, by which time a fresh force of police was on its way from Saint Vincent. So the "boys," after quite a rampage around Union Island, took off for the hills and have not been heard from since.

Leaving Clifton Harbour, beware the Grande de Coi Reef, a very real danger, which, in December 1980, was marked at the western end by a red buoy.

A lovely and secluded anchorage can be had behind Frigate Island. Trolling off the point is very good.

Even more beautiful is Chatham Bay on the W coast of Union. Favor the NE corner and, if there is a fresh trade blowing outside, drop two anchors, for, my goodness, it can squall in there!

Chances are there will be very few boats here, and, if you are looking for a place with a beautiful beach, away from the crowd you encountered at the Tobago Cays, consider this anchorage.

Prune Island (25482, I-B31)

is just across from Clifton. Perhaps I should say it *was,* for it is now called Palm Island and, for that matter, doesn't even look like a prune anymore. The people responsible for the change are John and Mary Caldwell, and whatever your feelings on development in the Grenadines may be, you have to give these two credit for completing a seemingly impossible task. You may remember that John wrote a best-selling book called *Desperate Voyage,* in which he fought against incredible odds, including wrestling with a shark in the cockpit of his tiny boat. More incredible to me is that he has done away with the mosquito on Palm by personally tracking down and killing every land crab on the place, and then filling in thousands of their dank, larvae-infested holes. For that sort of dedication a man has a right to change an island's name, don't you think?

In the days when John chartered *Outward Bound,* the yacht he and Mary built for a world voyage, he amused himself by planting palm trees on every little barren islet and cay he found. In fact, the yacht sometimes looked like a floating coconut grove. But nearly all the palms you now see in the Grenadines were planted by John during his charter years.

The island has one of the most beautiful beaches in the Caribbean, but is plagued with a surging anchorage. The best answer is to stop for lunch and a swim and then pop over to Clifton for the night. Anchor close to the beach, anywhere between the point of sand opposite the beach club and the southwestern corner of the island.

Palm Island's airstrip is now closed, and LIAT and Air Martinique, as well as the various charter companies, now use the strip on neighboring Union Island.

Petit Saint Vincent (25482, I-B31)

is the one of the three "Petit" islands that has made the big time. It has become a justifiably favorite overnight stop for charter yachts. The others, apparently named while someone was in a state of frustration, are Petit Martinique and Petit Tobago.

PSV, as it is affectionately called, was once the property and lonely abode of a splendid West Indian lady named Lily Bethel, who came from neighboring Petit Martinique. Her many sons ran a fleet of schooners engaged in interisland trading. With increasing age, Lily was forced to spend a considerable amount of time in bed. One day a hurricane blew her house off the top of the hill. Lily sat up in bed and peered indignantly out the window while her house took off down the slopes to execute a reasonable landing at the bottom. Apart from breaking her leg when she fell out of bed, Lily enjoyed the flight, or so the story goes, and next day the house was carried back up the hill, where it stands to this day.

In the early 1960s a charter party from the States fell in love with PSV and persuaded Lily to sell. Under the direction of Doug Terman and Haze Richardson, a very tasteful resort has since come into being. Former charter skippers themselves, they realized that yachts would not only bring business but would supply life and interest to the place. Doug and Haze set out from the beginning to encourage yachtsmen in every way possible. Ice and bread are available here. Fuel may be available on the dock. The radio call sign is PSV, and they stand by on VHF-16. All in all, we should be thankful that if the island had to be developed in the first place, such an excellent team was there to do it.

Petit Saint Vincent is sheltered from the seas by a crescent-shaped reef, and except in real blowy conditions an anchorage can be found under its lee on the seldom visited northern side of the island. In general, however, most people use the southern anchorage, but care should be taken to avoid an 8-foot shoal rather inconsiderately placed off the SW corner of the island. It can clearly be seen, since it is a lot lighter in color than the surrounding water.

If there's room, anchor between the shore and the isolated reef almost directly opposite the clubhouse.

Although the holding is poor, it's really great to anchor off the southern side of Mopion, the easternmost of the two tiny sand cays marking the end of the reef to the WNW of PSV. There's wonderful swimming and snorkeling here, and it's a great place to lie in the sun with a pitcher of rum punch.

Petit Martinique (25482, I-B31)
is interesting because you may still be able to buy here a variety of strange liqueurs such as I have never seen, or even heard of, anywhere else in the world. There are no real shops; just ask around. But if you've ever been told that you look even vaguely like a customs man, best forget the whole thing.

They still build the traditional schooner on the beach here, and the shipwrights are a delight to talk with.

Carriacou (25482, I-B32)
is the first port of the Grenadines under Grenada's jurisdiction. Luckily, the political strife that has troubled Grenada seems not to have affected this island. Consequently, of the larger Grenadines, Carriacou has probably changed the least over the past decade. If you plan to stop there, be sure to arrive during daylight, flying the Grenada courtesy flag and the Q flag, and don't delay going ashore to clear with the authorities in Hillsborough. A northbound yacht leaving Carriacou and heading for PSV should very definitely remember to clear in Union Island first.

Carriacou is an island worth more attention than cruising or charter yachtsmen normally give it. Most people, I suppose, are in too much of a hurry to get to the Tobago Cays area, and probably spend only a night in Tyrell Bay before rushing on. However, both the E and S coasts have a variety of good anchorages, and you are almost certain to be alone.

Hillsborough Bay during the winter months can produce a really nasty roll, which reminds me that one of the funniest but most tragic sights I have seen in the islands was watching the Grenada mailboat try to load her cargo alongside the dock there. Cattle and motor cars, cardboard cartons and cooking stoves—all were dropped in the sea or onto the heads of gawking passengers. Anywhere, in fact, except into the hold of the schooner as she plunged and rolled to the swell.

After clearing, provided it is not blowing too hard, you can spend a good night at the south side of Sandy Island. Drop in about 4 fathoms and fall back so that the vessel is in relatively shallow water about 150 yards from shore. The island will break up the northerly swell, and the short easterly chop will hardly be felt. The reef that extends to the E off Sandy Island offers perhaps the most beautiful snorkeling in the Grenadines. Spearfishing is strictly *verboten,* since the island is a Grenadian national park.

Tyrell Bay is almost always snug and naturally popular with yachts. Surprisingly, however, loads of people run happily up onto the shoal opposite the jetty, despite its being accurately marked on the charts and by a series of three white floats on its north side as well. Sometimes, for a change, I drop the hook almost on top of the little island that lies at the entrance to the lagoon, or *carenage.* This is preferable to going all the way inside, unless there is a hurricane around, as the mosquitoes can be bad on windless nights. We used to take the dinghy in and try for tarpon, and there may still be some there. If you want a guide, you can arrange in town to have the self-appointed "manager of the mangroves" take you up. Twelve feet was the least depth we found when we sounded our way in as far as the first little bay, but the water shoaled to 3 feet soon thereafter.

On the S coast, eyeball in anywhere that looks good under the prevailing conditions. Saline Island is excellent, although a quiet night cannot be assured because of the occasional strong current. More interesting is the area behind the windward reef on the E side of Carriacou, where 6 feet can, with care, go all the way from one end to the other.

Provisions can be obtained, and I would suggest that for current information you pop along and chat with the people at the Mermaid Tavern, the pub originally operated by the well-known yachtsman and author Linton Rigg. Linton was a guiding light in organizing the Bahamian Out Island Regatta, and then moved to Carriacou and set up a similar event, which has become extremely popular with the locals.

Île de Ronde (25481, I-B32)

is one of a small group of lonely islands between Carriacou and the north end of Grenada, on which a handful of people exist in very much the same manner as the original settlers. It's most unlikely that things will change much in the near future, and if only to observe a minute part of this globe where the clock has stopped, Île de Ronde is worth a stop.

Although Cornstone Bay on the NW side is supposed to be the best anchorage,

I have always found it more comfortable off the small village on the SW side. Go ashore and, like Alice, step through the looking glass into yesterday.

Kick'em Jenny,

around which flow some of the strongest currents in the West Indies, is uninhabited, has no place to anchor, and is quite literally for the birds.

Grenada (25481, I-B32)

In the days of wine and roses, when crewed chartering was the height of fashion, Grenada was our southern terminal: the end of the line and the place to off-load one "lot" and take on another. With practiced ease we would wash down, clean up, send out laundry, reprovision, refuel, revarnish, change filters, take a shower, grab a beer, meet the new people, and dash off again. A constant stream of charter yachts followed one another out of Saint George's, and there is no doubt that in a modest way we contributed quite a bit to Grenada's prosperity during the 1960s. However, certain elements, both political and commercial, became perhaps a little too greedy, resulting in civil disorders in 1974 and a coup d'état in 1979 that temporarily suspended most tourist-oriented activities in the island, and the yachts mostly took off for new pastures. The coup d'état brought down the government of Eric Gairy, and replaced it with the New Jewel Movement, led by Maurice Bishop. Bishop and several of his close advisers were assassinated by a small group within his own regime on October 19, 1983, and it was at this time that the United States either "invaded" or "intervened," depending on your view of things. Since that time, Grenada has again become a pleasant place to visit.

The sail from Tyrell Bay on Carriacou to Saint George's is one of the most wonderful you can have. On a broad reach, the yacht slips along before the trades while flying fish burst away from the lee bow and frigate and bosun birds come out from the scarred cliffs of Kick'em Jenny to wheel lazily over the masthead. Grenada, cool and green after the sun-bleached Grenadines, calms the seas as you run into her lee. A good breeze, normally from the northeast, will stay with the yacht until the town of Gouyave is abeam, and from then on one flirts with calms and capricious puffs along a coast that is as beautiful as any in the entire island chain.

Halifax Harbour (25481, I-B32),

just S of Black Bay Point, is the only anchorage of note on the W coast N of Saint George's, and here the wind is so flukey that a yacht will swing around and around all night long. If you do stop here, shallow-draft vessels should anchor in the southern bay, but yachts drawing 9 feet or more would do best to find a 5-fathom patch just N of the point that separates the two beaches and run a stern line to a suitable tree.

Driving down toward Saint George's, Grenada

Dragon Bay (25481, I-B32)

is a tiny cove S of Halifax; at a pinch it might accommodate three or four yachts. It is popular with local yachtsmen and day sailers from the hotels.

During the day, between Molinière Point and Grand Anse there is always a splendid breeze to guarantee an exhilarating final sail as the yacht tramps up to Saint George's with the late afternoon sun painting the little town in gold.

Saint George's (25481, I-B32)

has plenty of water inside the channel-marker buoys off the harbor, but don't wander too far to the S of the clearly seen range situated on the hills behind the main docks. The channel into the Lagoon is well marked and should have at least 12 feet of water, although it is very shallow on either side just outside the markers. The water is very calm in the Lagoon and, if you need a respite from rolly anchorages, spend some time here. If you love to hear roosters crowing in the morning, I don't know of a place in the Caribbean where they are louder.

Most yachts clear customs and immigration at Grenada Yacht Services in the Lagoon. It is also possible to clear at the commercial dock in the main harbor, although they are not accustomed to taking care of yachts there. The two facilities were giving different information about cruising permits, so be sure to ask where you can go and how long you can stay there, and where you can check out.

From the Lagoon to the main part of town is just five minutes by dinghy, and it's probably safe to leave the dinghy almost any place along the wall not in use by local craft. If you plan to eat at the Nutmeg or shop at the Food Fair, you

The commercial harbor at Saint George's, Grenada

The Grenada Yacht Services docks are due for repair. The building on the hill was a casualty of the U.S. "intervention" in Grenada in 1983.

can tie up right across the street from these facilities. The Food Fair will be able to supply almost any provisions you need, but if you prefer to browse in the market, there are two places to go. One is the Marketing Board on Young Street, less than two blocks from the waterfront. Local produce, including all the usual fruits and vegetables as well as a variety of nutmeg products and delicious guava candy, can be purchased here at very reasonable prices and without dickering. The open-air market, where the collection of fruits, vegetables, and fresh spices will boggle the mind, is up and over the hill. The fish cooperative store, where you'll find a good variety of fish—frozen only—at very reasonable prices is between the commercial docks and the Grenada Yacht Club, on the point on the north side of the channel into the Lagoon.

Grenadians are, on the whole, a hard-working and intelligent people, and almost any job can be taken care of, provided there's not too much of a rush. To get the most current picture, toddle over to the Grenada Yacht Club and chat with the members. Transient yachtsmen are made welcome.

Saint George's is still the one harbor in the West Indies in which it is possible to get a close look at a large trading schooner. Although most have had their main masts chopped off and garagelike affairs built on their afterdecks, you might be lucky enough to see an original. The schooner men are a proud breed, and some are determined enough to keep on going with only the necessary addition of an engine, making their vessels little different in concept from the Canadian Bluenose fishermen that carried on into the early part of this century.

Grand Anse (25481, I-B32)

is a convenient anchorage off the beach just S of Saint George's, but, unfortunately, a very large swell can ruin this otherwise idyllic spot. The best anchorage is at the NE end of the beach, close to the Silver Sands Hotel. There are two reefs to be avoided, both of them close inshore and clearly visible, so go in when the sun is high.

Long Point Shoal, directly between Saint George's and Point Saline, is dangerous and unmarked.

Port Egmont and Calivigny (25481, I-B32)

are the best of the many excellent harbors along the S coast. Both are in the category of safe hurricane holes. Port Egmont is relatively simple to enter for the confident eyeballer.

These south-coast harbors are seldom visited by yachtsmen, perhaps because

Prickly Bay at the south end of Granada offers a small marina and plenty of room to anchor.

they generally lack the beaches and crystal waters that are so much a part of tropical cruising.

Prickly Bay (L'Anse aux Épines) (25481, I-B32)

is a very pleasant bay in which is situated the boatyard operated by Spice Island Marine. One may receive customs and immigration clearance here and avoid having to pop into Saint George's; this also allows the gung-ho types to sail from Carriacou down the eastern side of Grenada.

You can also have mail sent here. It should be addressed to Spice Island Marine, Box 449, Saint George's, Grenada.

Anchor at least 300 feet off the beach at the head of the bay, where the Calabash Hotel is located, as that buffer zone is reserved for swimming.

Grenville Harbour (25481, I-B32)

is mainly used by fishermen at present. The entrance is through the reef and, although marked, would be difficult for a stranger in windy conditions. For that reason, and because once you are inside the anchorage is rolly, Grenville Harbour is not often visited by yachts. The main attraction in Grenville is the Nutmeg Processing Plant, which offers tours to visitors. If you like to ride the local communal taxi/bus, you can easily catch one at the market square in Saint George's; it will take you up and over the mountain to Grenville. It's a great ride and a good alternative to taking your own boat to Grenville Harbour.

The Northeast Coast (25481, I-B32)

offers three delightful little islands—Levera, Green, and Sandy—definitely worth visiting, but only in pleasant summer weather. The most pleasant anchorage is off the W coast of Sandy Island.

Chapter Ten

BARBADOS

If Carlisle Bay looks like the headquarters of the international yacht set from late November through February, it's only because Barbados (25485, I-B2) is the easternmost and thus the most logical target for the transatlantic sailors who annually scoot across from the Canaries at the end of each hurricane season. Some say that eight out of ten such sailors make for Barbados, and it's not uncommon to find several of them in the bay at one time. And you'll see a mob if you happen to land there just following the finish of the ARC race, an annual transatlantic event with an entry of 150 or more cruising yachts that finishes in Barbados around Christmas.

During the rest of the year, visiting yachts are few and far between, for Barbados really has little to offer in contrast to the cruising attractions of the Windward chain—and Barbados lies a hundred miles dead into the wind. Indeed, the best way to reach this island outpost is downwind from Europe—or south from Martinique, hopefully on one tack.

Perhaps because Barbados is less than 20 miles long and its highest hill only 1,100 feet, Columbus never sighted it on any of his four voyages. While the quest for gold drew sailors farther to the west, this small island to windward lay virtually undiscovered until the British established a colony in 1627. They continued to hold it until 1966, when colonial possessions had become taboo. In the course of those 339 years of uninterrupted British rule, Barbados has, in spite of its climate, absorbed the look and feel of the British countryside, Devon and Cornwall in particular. Ancient stone parish churches, cricket on the green, schoolboys in caps, and girls in starched uniforms and straw boaters are common sights around the island.

Making his landfall after a fast passage from the Canaries with his 47-foot ketch *Xanadu II,* E. Bates McKee, a member of CCA, reports:

> Approaching from the east at night, the light on South Point can be seen 15 miles at sea but the island actually becomes visible far beyond that range because of the loom of the lights of the airport and the metropolis of Bridgetown.

Not only is Barbados so far to windward of her neighbor islands, she lacks any natural harbors for yachts. And so she is even less attractive. Of course, the wind seldom blows from the west, so anchorage may be taken anywhere along the west shore, but there is a persistent surge, and during the summer and fall there is always that worrisome feeling that a tropical storm just might come through to upset the trade wind's steady pattern. If one comes, there's no place to go.

The Careenage, Barbados

Actually, the Careenage, right in the center of Bridgetown, is a natural harbor, but it is too small and too commercially oriented to be suitable for a yacht, and the new commercial harbor N of town is off limits to yachts. The Careenage approach channel carries 12 feet through a restricted entrance that *Xanadu II* found very uncomfortable at 0200 on Christmas morning in 1973.

Frankly admitting that attempting the entrance at night proved to be a mistake in more ways than one, McKee continued:

> In the first place, we were without use of our engine and were almost carried up on the rocks by the surge in the narrow entrance. In the second place, it turned out that one is supposed to anchor off until cleared by customs. However, these gentlemen were most understanding and cleared us next morning at the dock. Once cleared, it soon became apparent that the Careenage was no place to lie alongside for, when the trade wind made up in the morning, the dust of the town completely covered our decks 'til we looked like a sand barge. As soon as it was possible to move we sailed out and joined the other yachts at anchor off the yacht club in Carlisle Bay.

Carlisle Bay (25485)

is the deepest indentation on the lee side of the island and thus the principal anchorage. Although it is protected from the direct blast of the trade winds, a considerable surge makes its way around Needham Point when the wind is easterly, and when the wind is from the NW, rollers come right into the bay. Landing a dinghy on shore is almost always difficult. A commercial yacht facility, the Boatyard, is the best answer. They are located just south of the harbor police pier where the national flag is flying. The Boatyard has a boat landing and runs a shore boat service, and it offers many other services yachtsmen need as well. This landing is within walking distance of shops in town.

Farther south, the Holiday Inn and its pier are flanked by the Barbados Cruising Club to the S and the Barbados Yacht Club to the N.

The Barbados Cruising Club has about 200 members; it's basically a small sailing-boat operation, although it boasts a core of hardy long-distance cruisers. Nothing is fancy here, but the bar on the second story is an ideal place to sit and scan the scene of anchored boats in the background and the bathing types from the inn strewn along the delightful beach below. Visiting yachtsmen are cordially received here. If you wish to anchor off this club, stay N of the tanker mooring buoy that lies off the Hilton Hotel pier.

The Barbados Yacht Club is far more pretentious, and is an important part of the island's social scene, but here too you will find the welcome mat out. The clubhouse is comfortable, and the premises include a nice beach, showers, and tennis courts. Anchor about 200 yards off over a good-holding sand bottom in 20–30 feet. Since there is some coral on the bottom, chain is advised.

Near the innermost of three black can buoys in a line toward the city, snorkeling enthusiasts will find an interesting wreck with about 4 feet of water over it.

Small autos can be rented for sightseeing the island, with its endless miles of sugarcane and dramatic views of the thundering seas on the windward side at Bathsheba, Conger Rocks, and Cherrytree Hill, or for visiting the place whence cometh the yachtsman's favorite rum—the Mount Gay distillery. With right-hand-drive rentals, you'll quickly become accustomed to driving on the left-hand side.

We can't be sure, but Barbados may be the only place in the world where flying fish are harvested commercially, with gill nets or small fishhooks, several to a line. During the January to May peak season they are inexpensive and delicious whether fried, baked, or smoked, and no problem bonewise. Other local food products are limes (December to May), sugar, yams and sweet potatoes, breadfruit, pigeon peas, coconuts, green pawpaws, and onions.

Chapter Eleven

TRINIDAD AND TOBAGO

TRINIDAD (24402, 24405, 24406, I-D11)

Back in 1498, the ubiquitous Columbus came again with his fleet to the New World, this time from the southwest after being becalmed for more than a week in the sweltering doldrums. When finally the southeast trades filled the sails, the fleet made a landfall on three small peaks; the devout admiral named the land for the Holy Trinity. The hills he saw, reportedly from 40 miles out, are still called the Trinity Hills.

Thereafter, Trinidad remained rather removed from the action in the rest of the Caribbean, except for a flurry of activity when a city of gold known as El Dorado was rumored to exist far up the nearby Orinoco River, a rumor that led Sir Walter Raleigh to mount an expedition there. While Raleigh never found a trace of gold, his imagination went wild: he wrote luridly of a country "that hath yet her maidenhead; the graves have not been opened for gold, the miners not broken with sledges nor their images pulled down out of their temples"—in fact a place that was "the very magazine of all rich metals."

Unlike Columbus, most yachtsmen approach Trinidad from the north, often on a close reach from Grenada and usually with some bewilderment as they discover how far the west-going current has set them off course. In fact a landfall during the last hours of darkness makes sense, in order to take advantage of the powerful Chacachare Light. But plan, by all means, to come through the Bocas in daylight!

The usual choice among the Dragon's Mouths is the Boca de Monas, where the current, if you hit it at the wrong time, may be running as much as 5 knots. In this case you will find less current in Boca de Huevos. The current sets north except for about two hours at each change, when, in effect, it is only neutralized. The current almost never sets south. Sea conditions are generally rough as a result of the confluence of winds and currents coming out of the Gulf of Paria and around the north coast of Trinidad.

No Caribbean island is so racially diverse as Trinidad. Most prevalent are the blacks and East Indians, about equal in numbers; then, to add to the mixture, are Chinese, Portuguese, Syrians, Jews, and various Latin Americans. These are the people who stage each year the carnival of all carnivals and who initiated the sly and beguiling calypso, which, in turn, led to the invention of the steel drum. Far from being simply an upside down, sawed-off oil drum, it is in fact a precision

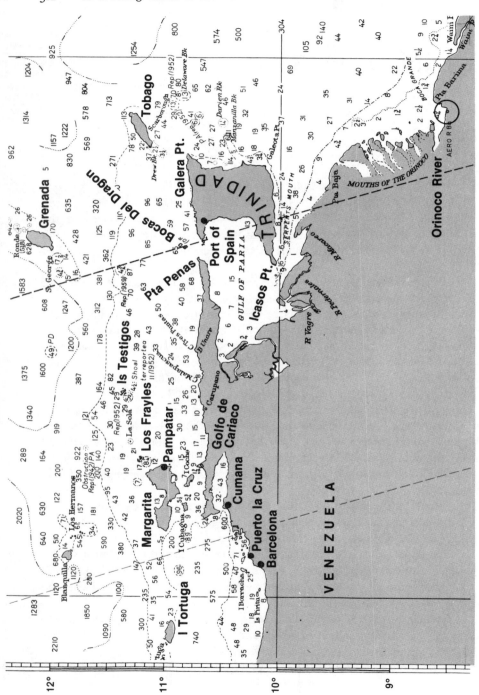

Grenada to Trinidad and the Venezuelan coast

instrument, its top (bottom) hammered to a certain stage of concavity, with the musical notes hammered into oval shapes around the perimeter and tempered by means of glowing charcoal to just the right pitch.

We cannot commend Trinidad as a cruising area, particularly now that the government has clamped down on the mobility of transient yachts and seems bent on discouraging their entry anyway. On top of that the Gulf of Paria is big, and its waters are muddied by the Orinoco River; the southeast wind sweeps across the low plains that border the gulf, and a substantial sea builds up every afternoon to belabor the only popular cruising grounds, which extend from Port-of-Spain out to the islands in the Dragon's Mouths. Most of the southern part of the gulf is taken up with oil rigs. They're not pretty, but at least they're interesting if you want a glimpse of the oil industry at work.

The rainy season comes in June, July, and August; the driest months are March and April. A big plus is that Trinidad lies south of the hurricane paths; in fact on only two or three occasions in the island's recorded history has there been storm damage to crops.

Port-of-Spain (24406),

the only port for entering and clearing, is strictly commercial, dirty, and quite unattractive for a yacht. You will be required to anchor off and to contact the officials every time you may want to shift your anchorage. Furthermore, you will be monitored almost constantly by police boats, and if they don't like you, they may institute a "rummage," which involves unfastening floorboards and a general disassembly of the vessel, all of which you will have to put back when they're finished. Boats with a dog or cat as part of the crew can expect trouble here; there is a regulation against bringing them ashore.

Across Wrightson Road from the quarantine station is the Mariners' Club, a clean, well-run establishment supported by a church auxiliary in England for the benefit of all seamen, and it may still include yachtsmen. Ginnie Higman of *Tormentor III* reports that the amenities include free showers, free movies several times a week, a bar serving beer and soft drinks, a clean swimming pool (for a nominal fee), and a small restaurant producing good, home-cooked meals at very reasonable prices.

Admiralty, U.S. and Imray-Iolaire charts, and a limited stock of chandlery items will be found at R. Landry and Co. Ltd, 12 Borde St., and at Peak and Company, 177 Western Main Rd.

Port-of-Spain to Dragon's Mouths (24405, I-D11)

As we have said, this northern pincer of the island is where the yachts are, but the water is uninviting for swimming and the coast is exposed. We are now progressing west from Port-of-Spain, after getting police permission to move.

Trinidad Yacht Club (24406),

which lies in 61°34.2'W, took a merciless chop every afternoon until a breakwater of sunken wrecks was built and a marina constructed in its lee. Repairs can be made there. Make arrangements with the club manager. Water, fuel, and ice are available.

Trinidad Yachting Association (24406)

is based in the cove on the NE side of Pointe Gourde. Unfortunately, it is also quite open to the prevailing swell, unless a much-discussed breakwater has been built. This club caters to the sailing population hereabouts and has good facilities, but no fuel. The racing season extends from November to May.

Chaguaramas Bay (24405),

formerly the U.S. Navy's lend-lease base, provides one of the snuggest anchorages in the area up in its NE corner, but it's crowded with permanent moorings. The Swan-Hunter Shipyard, which used to repair yachts, is closed. Fuel is available at Island Home.

Staubles Bay (24405)

is the local name of the next bight to the W. Here you will find good shelter, fuel, groceries, and a coast-guard station that is an excellent source of "local knowledge" about this area.

Scotland Bay (24405)

is attractive, very snug, and so popular with local yachtsmen that it is usually crowded on weekends. Contrary to the chart, the deep water runs way up to the end.

Monos Island (24405)

gives you Morris Bay, also the bay on the SE side of the island called Copper Hole by local residents. Though it would not appear so from the chart, this latter bay is quiet at almost all times.

Chacachare Island (24405)

offers good anchorage deep in the western portion of this bay. When you are rounding the SW point of the island, there is safe water for passing inside of Diamond Rock to an excellent anchorage called Tinta Bay. Drop the hook anywhere off this reef-strewn shore.

Lower Gulf of Paria (24404)

Running down the W coast of Trinidad (in case you want to have a look at the forest of drilling platforms and maybe a 200,000-ton tanker or two), stay well off the shallow mud flats all along this shore. On the sail down, the oil rig in about 10°28′ N, 61°33′ W makes a conspicuous mark along an otherwise nondescript shore.

Pointe-à-Pierre (24408)

offers a crowded and uncomfortable anchorage just off the Texaco pier about a cable N of the light near the church. This is the locale of the Pointe-à-Pierre Yacht Club, whose members are employees of Texaco-Trinidad, Inc. The whole area is under Texaco security control.

From here a circular cruise might be made to the fishing port of Guiria, an artificial harbor on the Venezuelan shore, thence back to the island in the Dragon's Mouths. The necessity of clearing in and out of Venezuela keeps most people from doing this. Guiria is a port of entry.

The North Coast of Trinidad (24404)

All the bays along this shore are subject to big swells, but Las Cuevas Bay is said to be tenable when the wind is south of east, generally from March to October.

TOBAGO (24402, I-B4)

Stepchild of Trinidad, to which she has been politically and economically tied ever since the final collapse of her sugar industry in 1888, poor little Tobago languishes in the sun, wearing the wistful smile of an island that once was prosperous and much desired by several of Europe's big powers. In many ways, Tobago (named through some obscure reference to the pipe with which the natives smoked their tobacco) is an example of the West Indian islands-that-were, even though the tourist hotels are there.

Many yachtsmen, lulled by the steady breezes that have let them sail down the island chain in comfortable reaches, think twice before heading out to still another island that actually requires tacking to reach—and against a substantial current, too. Consequently, Tobago remains a neglected island so far as yachts are concerned, and more's the pity, to use a British expression, for in its 26-by-7 mile compass, Tobago offers sandy beaches (albeit dark sand on the windward side) with graceful stands of coconut palms, clear waters, a diving reef to remember, some spectacular rockbound coastal scenery, and a handful of secure anchorages, each picturesque enough to hold a yachtsman for a couple of days or so.

Ginnie Higman and her husband, Bob, spent two months in Tobago aboard their motor sailer, *Tormèntor III,* a 40-foot "Newporter." Ginnie had this to say about getting there:

> This island is easier to reach from Grenada, about 70 miles northwestward, than from Trinidad. However, we left Port-of-Spain, Trinidad, at noon and power-sailed

to Las Cuevas Bay, a rolly but protected roadstead midway along Trinidad's north coast. The next day it took us from 0545 to 1830 to power-sail the 35 miles against wind and current to Milford Bay on the southwest corner of Tobago.

If you are approaching from the southwest, the Drew Shoal is so clear that the bottom can be seen, a welcome relief from the Orinoco mud that taints the waters all around Trinidad. But this area of shoal water is often rough, and depths may be less than shown on charts. It is probably best to avoid it.

Only the north shore of Tobago is a practical cruising area, since the windward side, even when the wind is down, is subject to an incessant ocean swell, except for King's Bay, near the east end of the island, which is sufficiently indented to dissipate most of this swell. The beaches on the windward shore are a dark and unappealing sand, whereas much whiter sand and clearer water will be found on the northern coast.

The northeastern end of Tobago is mountainous and sparsely settled, and most of the activity and the resort operations are at the westerly end, which tapers to a flat plain.

Scarborough (24402)

is the principal town and a rolly anchorage, in addition to being untidy and generally unattractive for a yacht. Unfortunately you must enter here and you can expect the same police surveillance as in Port-of-Spain.

Anchor among the fishing boats or go to the government dock, where you may be allowed to lie alongside or moor in Mediterranean fashion. Ginnie Higman of *Tormentor III* said of the perils of Scarborough:

> Try to tie on the E side of the U-shaped dock because of the havoc created by the Trinidad ferry and freight boats. If you are Med-moored they're liable to set their breast anchor on top of yours and when they weigh it for their 2200 departure, you may be hauled along too! Furthermore, if you are anchored too close, their propeller wash may push your boat right onto the cement quay. Our dinghy, which hangs in stern davits, was crushed this way when we were there.
>
> While in Scarborough, visit the Botanical Gardens and also climb the 430-foot heights to Fort George for a panoramic view of town and countryside, and Trinidad on a clear day. Look for the old water tank shaped like a bell and shout into it: "Bell, tank wants more water," then listen for the results.

In 1801, the old fort was the scene of an interesting subterfuge by a clever officer of the garrison, who, hearing of a planned revolt by the slaves, arrested thirty of the leaders and, to the horror of the townspeople watching from below the walls, summarily hanged them one by one from a conspicuous gallows. Later, to the immense relief of the owners of these valuable slaves, it developed that the same man had been hoisted thirty times to the peak of the gallows.

Milford Bay (24402)

is a far better place to live than Scarborough if you can get permission to go there. Anchor anywhere, according to your draft, off the white sand beach between Sandy and Pigeon Points.

Hotels and shops line the beach.

The vivid colors of the water inside Buccoo Reef add to the beauty of the place. The well-defined reef is constantly breaking, and with some advance soundings from the dinghy, it should be possible to gain the shelter of this pretty body of water through the more northerly of the two obvious reef openings.

Mount Irvine Bay (24402)

provides anchorage anywhere along the reasonably white sand beach. This bay is readily identified by the conspicuous jagged rock off Booby Point and by the hotel of the same name as the bay at the place marked "Chy" on the chart. Expect a low, lazy swell here.

Courland Bay (24402)

affords excellent shelter under the high bluffs toward Plymouth town, and a pleasant anchorage will be found off the Turtle Beach Hotel. The bay gets its name from the Earl of Pembroke, who was also the Duke of Courland and ruled the Baltic principality of that name, now a province of Latvia. Charles I of England gave Tobago to the earl in 1628, as a birthday present.

On the bluff overlooking the bay are the ruins of Fort James, finished in 1666 and the island's oldest fortification. Not far away is a famous gravestone with a baffling epitaph:

> Within these Walls are Deposited the Bodies of Betty Stiven and child. She was the beloved wife of Alex B. Stiven who to the end of his days will deplore her Death which happened upon the 25th day of November, 1783, in the 23rd year of her Age. What was remarkable of her, she was a mother without knowing it and a wife without letting her husband know it, except by her kind indulgences to him.

A household slave and planter's mistress with unborn child? The conjectures go on and on, but no one really knows.

Man of War Bay (24402)

at the NE corner of the island is enclosed by precipitous hills and a curving beach. It is an exceptionally delightful anchorage during the summer months. Ginnie Higman of *Tormentor III* found the people of Charlotteville here not as friendly as elsewhere in Tobago and some of the officials rather rude. She also advises not to put in here without first having cleared immigration and customs at the airport or in Scarborough.

As you are rounding the corner of the island amidst the tide rips, it is best to stay outside the Saint Giles and Marble islands and avoid the awash rocks and

Man of War Bay, northeast end of Tobago

swift current that sluices between Saint Giles and the mainland. Though the anchoring possibilities in the vicinity of Tyrell's Bay look promising on the chart, local sailors warn of difficult winds, seas, and currents here. Anse Bateau is the best choice.

If you want to visit the wildlife refuge on Little Tobago Island, home of the birds of paradise introduced from the Aru Islands of Indonesia in 1909, the Higmans suggest anchoring in King's Bay and coming back 3½ miles by dinghy. Recent reports say the birds of paradise may have disappeared from the island, but the island is worth exploring anyway. It is owned by the Trinidad and Tobago government.

King's Bay (24402)

is surrounded by high hills, and a brook of clear water spills into the cove through a coconut grove. Lieutenant-Governor Alexander Brown, the first British governor of Tobago, landed on the beach here in 1764 and reviewed a guard of honor.

Picture that ceremonial event as you stand into this anchorage in the NE corner of the bay. There will be some motion here, but it is cool and perfectly safe unless the wind is blowing hard from the south.

Prince's Bay (24402)

offers reasonable shelter from the wind up in the NE corner, but the swell makes it uncomfortable, and the rather squalid village of Roxborough doesn't enhance the surroundings. Nearby King's Bay is a much better choice.

Chapter Twelve

THE VENEZUELAN COAST AND ISLANDS

BY KIT S. KAPP

Sailing westward from Grenada or Trinidad, the yachtsman will join and follow the routes sailed by the earliest Spanish explorers, Columbus and Alonso de Ojeda, and later by the Elizabethan opportunists John Hawkins and his nephew Francis Drake. Voyage accounts are sometimes confusing, because many place names have been lost in the fog of history or are seldom used today. "The Spanish Main," for instance, was coined by the English as a contraction of the Spanish-controlled mainland that included the Caribbean coastlines of South and Central America as far as the Miskito Coast of present-day Honduras. Today, the Spanish Main has mostly a romantic meaning, but it applies to the same general area.

The Spaniards had other names for this part of the New World, the most common being Tierra Firma, to denote the first significant body of firm land that Columbus discovered in the course of his third voyage. This time he had sailed westward from Trinidad to touch upon the coast of present-day Venezuela; his previous discoveries had all turned out to be islands.

Shortly afterward an expedition led by Alonso de Ojeda continued along this coast (Ojeda named it "Maracapana") as far as Cabo de la Vela in modern Colombia. Before leaving Tierra Firma, Ojeda discovered the great lake of Maracaibo. The villages there, built out upon the lake itself, so reminded him of Venice that he named the locale Venezuela, or Little Venice, later applied to the whole province and carried down to this day.

By 1525 the limits of the Caribbean had been well defined by the Council of the Indies, the august body in Seville that oversaw for Spain the colonizing and exploiting of this vast, rich New World. First came the large northern islands, the smaller Caribbees in the east, the Antilles, and Tierra Firma, most of them the discoveries of Columbus and his captains. Then, in 1512, Ponce de León, the roving governor of Puerto Rico, discovered Las Floridas. In 1519 Hernán Cortés found a new land mass even farther west than Tierra Firma. He named it Reino de Nueva España: it embraced mainland Mexico and the Yucatán peninsula. Then the council reshuffled its deck: it gave the name Reino de Tierra Firma to present-day Panama and called the eastern part of the mainland, present-day Venezuela, Nueva Andalusia.

Weather Along the Spanish Main

The trade winds blow steadily along the lower Caribbean from the northeast. However, there are seasonal and local variations close in along the shore, which occasionally provides better shelter than you might expect.

Hurricanes are practically unknown. Only one was recorded in the Gulf of Venezuela prior to 1923, and another raged through the Gulf of Cariaco to Bonaire in July 1933. Northers, which are the bane of the upper Caribbean, seem to tucker out by the time they reach the main. However, the ground swells that they generate do not dissipate so easily; they cause tremendous breakers along the coast. Sometimes, for instance, these swells send spume as high as 120 feet into the air at the La Guaira seawall, on the coast near Caracas.

The trades blow strongest from January to May. From July to October they are more variable in direction, and you may expect calms and even mild westerlies. In autumn, look out for *calderetas,* hot, sharp blasts from mountain gorges that are strong enough to take the roofs off houses.

May to November is the season for *chubascos,* local afternoon squalls in the Maracaibo area that blow up to 50 knots from the south to southwest. Fortunately, they are of short duration and are similar to the *chocosanas* in Colombia. Elsewhere along the coast, May to November is a time to expect strong southerly squalls that lose intensity as they blow off the shore.

Close to shore, land breezes, if any, commence toward evening and ease up about dawn. The trades start to pick up in midmorning and tend to drop off after sunset.

West of Aruba, particularly near the Guajira peninsula, and from the Magdalena River to the Rosario Islands, the winter trades reach gale force. Winter winds along the Paria and Araya peninsulas of eastern Venezuela are not quite as strong, and moderate considerably during the summer. Northeasterly winds prevail in the long coastal indentation from Puerto La Cruz west to Carenero. They seldom blow much over 6 knots, and conditions are usually dead calm at sunrise from June to December.

The regular trades produce moderate seas. However, from December to March the seas seem to break more heavily and are often dangerous following strong gales in the Atlantic.

The prevailing westerly current is generally weaker near shore, averaging about one half knot, but sometimes the reinforced trades will increase the rate to 3 knots. Near the coast, countercurrents are sometimes experienced in the summer. Tidal currents are usually weak, since the tidal range is only about a foot. However, spring tides may range to 2¼ feet. When they do, they may speed up surface currents substantially in bottleneck areas such as the lower Gulf of Venezuela. Among the offshore islands, currents set west to west-northwest at one half to 1½ knots, and even more under reinforced trade-wind conditions.

Rainfall on the coasts of Venezuela and Colombia ranges from moderate to extremely light (on the Paraguana and Guajira peninsulas). In general, the wet season is from May to December in eastern Venezuela. In the Puerto Cabello area the rainfall is light from October to May and moderate during the rest of the year. In the Maracaibo area, expect light rain during May and June and downpours from September to December.

Rollers may become heavy when the trades veer northward during November and December.

Entry Procedures and Other Considerations, Venezuela and Colombia

Yachtsmen have long been aware of the reputation of the Venezuelan and Colombian coasts for insurrection, piracy, and smuggling, and for overzealous and trigger-happy patrol-boat crews eager to impound foreign boats on the slightest provocation. We are now happy to report that (except for some smuggling), these are legends of the past insofar as eastern Venezuela and the Dutch A-B-C islands are concerned. A new attitude prevails; it involves just and rigid enforcement of laws and regulations by the Guardia de Costa and port officials, coupled with a sincere desire to encourage the growth of commerce and tourism. This means friendly relations with yachtsmen who are ready to comply with the regulations.

Quite a different situation applies along the coast of the Guajira peninsula, which will be discussed in Chapter Fourteen.

Here are a few rules that will foster mutual respect and make your cruise on the Spanish Main less difficult and more enjoyable:

1. Always fly (correct side up) the national courtesy flag from 0600 to 1800 (never after sunset) from a prominent, high position; also display your vessel's national flag from a lower position.

2. Respect and cooperate with all officials. Don't be in a hurry, and don't expect to be cleared outside of regular hours or on holidays. If you treat those in authority politely, assist them in inspecting your boat, and offer them refreshments and congenial conversation, then, more than likely, they'll go out of their way to assist you.

3. At all ports where there is a port captain's office or customshouse, present your clearance upon request and graciously comply with all paperwork required.

4. Immediately upon entering Venezuelan or Colombian waters, go directly to a port of entry. In Venezuela these are: Güiria, Carúpano, Pampatar, Puerto Sucre (Cumaná), Guanta Puerto La Cruz, La Guaira, Tucacas, Puerto Cabello, La Vela de Coro, Cumarebo, Las Piedras, and Maracaibo. Colombian ports of entry are: Ríohacha, Santa Marta, Barranquilla, Cartagena, Turbo, and Zapzurro.

An official pilot is required to enter Maracaibo, Güiria, and Ciudad Bolivar. In April 1988 a new regulation was issued allowing foreign yachtsmen to obtain a permit/visa for themselves and their vessels to stay in Venezuelan waters for an initial period of 90 days (renewable for a further 90 days upon request). Venezuelan consulates in foreign countries are empowered to issue these permits, after the appropriate application has been made. The Venezuelan consul in Martinique, for instance, has been mentioned as being particularly helpful to yachtsmen in this respect. Passports are essential, especially for crew members expecting to sign off the vessel or desiring to travel to the interior.

It is advisable to list all persons aboard one's vessel as crew members. "Nosotros somos tripulantes" translated means "we are crew members," and "no pasajeros" translates to "no passengers." Your vessel's complement may consist of captain, mate, cook, steward, deckhand, or whatever—but never passengers. If you can communicate at all in Spanish, you should have no need for an agent.

If and when all else fails, try to find a tourist bureau, where English is usually spoken and the staff will probably go out of their way to help.

Customs and immigration offices are seldom open for business on Saturdays and never on Sundays, so time your formal entry accordingly.

When sailing at night along the coast, it is advisable to keep your vessel brightly lit, in addition to the running lights prescribed by international rules. Patrol boats are on the alert for smuggling operations in this area, and a brightly lit boat is unlikely to arouse suspicions.

Although glaringly cheap, (28¢ a gallon in early 1989), Venezuelan diesel fuel is not refined to Stateside standards and burns far less efficiently. Yachtsmen have discovered heavy deposits of chromium in the engine oil, indicating severe piston ring wear due to burning Venezuelan fuel. Mileage per gallon has been reported as dropping from an average of 1.32 to 1.00, while crankcase oil consumption increased from one quart per 22 hours to one quart every 16 hours running.

Isla de Margarita and Isla La Tortuga (24430)

Venezuela's largest island, Margarita, was settled early in the Spanish conquest, as a direct result of the flourishing pearl fisheries found there. It is an island of high, serrated hills and fertile valleys, contrasted with areas of barren, desert scenery dotted with divi-divi trees, their foliage curiously shaped to flow with the sweep of the trade winds. The beaches are magnificent. Margarita's towns are very Spanish, and there are ruins here and there to conjure up a feeling for this island's past.

The Venezuelan government has especially nurtured Porlamar as a resort area, with the result that it is now a bustling community indeed. Downtown streets have been closed off in favor of malls and parks, and the shops carry all sorts of American and European goods, from high fashion to culinary items. Frequent flights and ferries from La Guaira and other mainland points make this a good crew transfer point.

Pampatar (24432),

on the eastern end of Isla Margarita, was founded early in the sixteenth century and is the principal port of entry for the state of Nueva Esparta, which includes

Islas Cubagua, Coche, and Margarita. It may well be your first clearing point in Venezuelan waters, particularly if you are coming from Grenada or Martinique.

The castle of San Carlos Borromeo, built of cut-coral masonry by the engineer Bedin in 1665, is a striking landmark for your approach to the town and is well worth a visit when the hook is down. An older fort, La Caranta, lies in ruins across the bay.

Pampatar appears to be exposed to prevailing winds, and occasionally high seas do indeed make it rough in the harbor. There are no docking facilities for yachts; however, we have anchored off the town in 3 fathoms of clear water and found it to be a fairly quiet place, with some protection even though there was wind enough to sail. The old public pier, reported as functional in earlier editions of this guide, is now in total disrepair and unsuitable for use. A new breakwater, under construction in 1989, south of Punta de la Ballena, will offer additional protection from swells.

The port captain will expect to receive your yacht's papers for entry into Pampatar and endorse your Venezuelan entry permit/visa. We have had good reports of yachtsmen using the services of an agency named Shore Base at Pampatar, whose enterprising owners will clear incoming yachts, organize the paperwork, and visit the port captain's office, for a reasonable sum.

July is the time of a gala fiesta. It includes a water procession of decorated vessels, fireworks, music, and a grandiose parade in honor of Saint Carmen, the patron saint of Margarita.

This town of only 4,000 inhabitants offers little in the way of supplies, but the principal shopping center at Porlamar is only 5 miles away by taxi or motor coach and about the same distance by sea.

We suggest an excursion by public bus to the island's capital, La Asunción. This beautiful town, with its ornate cathedral facing a typical square, was founded in 1565 and has been slumbering ever since. Even today, its population is only 6,000. For a look into the history of the place, see the castle of Santa Rosa and its dungeon, and the Capitular House, now a museum.

Porlamar (24432)

is Margarita's principal resort center and the best place for supplies. The original settlement was called Pueblo de la Mar and was founded in 1536 by Father Francisco de Villacorta. Although there are "free port" shops, you must have been on the island for three days to become eligible to buy the duty-free goods.

Clearance for Porlamar should be made with the port captain at Pampatar. There is a good anchorage in the bay off the high-rise hotel La Margarita Concorde, which is situated at El Morro, the point at the eastern end of the harbor. There is also a marine complex about 250 yards west of the hotel called Puerta Concorde, which has two docks and is protected by a small breakwater, with 6 to 7 feet of water at the head of the docks. Facilities at the marina include ice, essential foods at the small dockside "tienda" (which also handily accepts credit cards), a car rental agency appropriately named Beep Beep, a restaurant and a pleasant beach. No fuel is available at the dock. In the center of town is the public dock, with 15 feet of water at its head, and the Marina el Faro, where gas and diesel may be obtained. Picturesque fishing boats line the leeward side of the dock, where the Guardia Costa keeps its patrol boats. The public market is convenient to the dock and offers a wide selection of vegetables, fruit, and fish at reasonable prices.

Bahía Guamache (24432)

provides refuge anywhere along its shores from the prevailing winds, which may range up to 30 knots by midafternoon. Several small fishing villages dot the shoreline, and there is a deep-water dock for container ships at Puerto Guamache on Punta Mongala.

Punta de Piedras (24432)

is a fishing town of 6,000 inhabitants, the auto-ferry terminal for Cumaná and Puerto La Cruz, and a source of fuel by the drum. Nearby is an oceanographic experimental station.

Boca del Río (24431),

a sizable fishing port accommodating vessels with up to 6 feet draft, lies at the mouth of the Laguna La Arestinga, which almost splits Margarita into two islands. The shallow lagoon, accessible only to dinghies, is thick with mangroves and is a rookery for the rare and beautifully red-plumed scarlet ibis.

Boca de Pozo (24431)

is a small fishing village, and the westernmost anchorage of Isla Margarita, seldom visited by foreign yachts. A dozen fishing vessels anchor there. The bay is exposed to north and west winds—which are infrequent, however. In the northern part of the village boat builders work on large, wooden trawlers. Two miles farther north the village of Robledal has a small dock and a little more protection from north winds.

San Juan Griego (24432)

is a picturesque bay on the N coast of Isla Margarita and a haven for fishing boats. It is considered secure except in a strong northwester—which would be an exceptional occurrence. The town of Juan Griego has a central municipal dock, mainly used by fishermen. There are no facilities, but ice and fuel may be delivered. At the head of the dock there is approximately 10 feet of water. Seafood specialities are served at beachside cafés, and very reasonably priced dinners can be obtained on the beach, under the trees, at the Hotel Fortin's restaurant, where you can curl your toes in the sand under tables set almost at the water's edge. An aesthetic setting for that pleasant evening ashore.

On the east side of the harbor is the old fort Fortín de la Galera, affording a splendid panoramic view of the bay.

Isla Coche (24431, KSK-1)

appears, on first approach, to be a desolate, windswept island with scarcely a tree in sight. However, upon sailing into the anchorage off San Pedro village, a charming view unfolds of adobe houses with old tiled roofs and wide dirt streets, like a bit of old Mexico.

Anchor 300 yards off the small village dock in 9 feet, free from roll. At the head of the dock there is only 4 feet. Show your papers at the office of the Guardia Nacional, east of the dock, in order to avoid arousing any suspicions over your activities in this seldom visited place. You will find a rewarding view from the hill east of the village, where a curiously shaped rock overhangs a shrine.

The bronze-skinned, square-jawed people appear to be of Indian stock. They are, in fact, specialists in farming the famous Margarita pearl beds. These, for the most part, occupy the shallow water of Bahía San Pedro and the coast of Isla Coche. These friendly people engage in sardine fishing as well as pearling. Furthermore, the island has one of the richest salt mines in the country.

Isla Cubagua (24431, KSK-1)

is practically deserted today, yet it was the site of the first settlement in Venezuela. Nueva Cádiz, founded about 1522 on the eastern tip of the island, flourished in the early days when pearls were abundant and valued highly among the other riches of the newly found Indies. But the oyster beds were soon depleted, and in 1541 the place was devastated by a tidal wave. All that remain today are ruined foundations and heaps of pearl shells. Visitors are welcome to look around, but a caretaker quite rightfully discourages souvenir hunters.

Temporary anchorage may be made in 2 fathoms S of a dock situated SE of Punta Las Cabeceras (Nueva Cádiz). However, the best anchorage for overnight is in the northeasterly bay, Ensenada de Charagato, where you should drop the hook deep in the bight, in 2 fathoms, abreast several fishing huts. From here a path crosses a dry salt flat to the Nueva Cadiz archaeological site, a mile away.

Isla La Tortuga (24441)

is low, arid, and practically uninhabited. In colonial times this desolate island was known as Tortuga Salada and was the scene of a salt-panning industry.

On the southeastern shore, a sand spit encloses a shallow lagoon called El Carenero. As its name implies, it was used for careening ships. Altogether contrary to the chart, a coral reef, which breaks in heavy weather, nearly bars the entrance. However, you can edge your way around it via a narrow channel between the reef's end and the sand spit to the E; depths are ample for 6 foot draft. The water is exceptionally clear here.

On the northern side of the island, in the lee of Punta Delgada, is a delightful anchorage along a crescent of white sand beach. Protection is good except in winds from W to NW. The only evidences of civilization are a few fishermen's shacks and a small airstrip.

On the NW side of the island, the islets of Las Tortuguillas may be approached from the SW to a comfortable and secluded anchorage, in 2 fathoms, just S of the islets and in the lee of a reef to the E.

The Northeast Coast, Including Golfo de Cariaco (24420, 24431)

Puerto Santo (24420),

a small settlement with a nice beach and charming anchorage mentioned by the Conquistadores, is located 6 miles E of the much larger port of Carúpano. The beautiful bay, Bahía del Oueste, is formed by a slender sand spit that connects the shore to a lofty rock, El Morro de Puerto Santo. On the sand spit, the village of La Restinga provides a reasonably sheltered anchorage and has a wharf used by commercial fishermen. Islote Puerto Santo, a small island NW of the town, affords additional protection to the anchorage. A paved road runs to Carúpano.

Carúpano (24420)

may well be the entry port to start your cruise of the Spanish Main. In your approach, allow for a substantial current setting W. The high peaks along this coast can be seen for many miles at sea.

Proceed to the dock behind the breakwater, where you will be reasonably free of swells. You may prefer to anchor bow out, and warp your stern into the dock. In any case, avoid the water dock, where the fishing fleet congregates at dawn. The port captain's office is in front of the bus terminal, about half a mile west of the public dock and main plaza. The building, although on the water, is rather insignificant, with no sign to show it contains the Capitanaria. However, the staff members there are pleasant and helpful. Ice, water, fuel, fresh food, and staples are all available in town.

Carúpano was founded in 1647 by Spanish settlers and the bishop of Puerto Rico, Damian Lopez de Haro, although little evidence now remains of the old dwellings. It is a fishing port and a casual town of tiled roofs, many with air plants or cactus growing out of the eaves and decorative spoutings. The walls of adobe and wattle are occasionally interspersed with cement block in bright pastel colors, and, as further signs of modernization, the cobbled streets are now nearly all paved. On the site of a former fort, high up on a hill at Punta Guayacán Este, west of the central plaza, a *mirador* (lookout) and restaurant were under construction in late 1988; they will afford a splendid view of the town and harbor.

At the end of September each year, this small port springs to life with an international carnival, the Feria Exposición Agropecuaria, said to be the most important fair of its kind in Venezuela.

Near town are several splendid beaches for swimming: El Copey, Playa de Oro, Los Uveros, and Playa Caribe.

Esmeralda Bay (24431)

is an open but reasonably protected anchorage in normal weather. We have entered in the dark and found the muddy water extremely phosphorescent. Anchor in 2 fathoms in the lee of Esmeralda Point. This peaceful bay, disturbed only by the putt-putting of fishing smacks, is a handy departure point for Isla Margarita.

Puerto Sucre (24433)

is a port of entry and the seaport for Cumaná, the oldest city in Venezuela. Although the anchorage appears open, it is well protected from both swells and the prevailing winds by the Península de Araya. Just east of the municipal pier is the Marina Cumanágoto, a new large marina slightly west of the Minerva Hotel, where facilities include excellent docking in a secured area, with water and electricity at dockside. There is accommodation for approximately 200 yachts alongside in deep-water docking, and gas and diesel are available. The marina is protected by a breakwater, but care must be taken when entering, as the channel is not well marked and it is not unusual for yachts to ground. A bus stop is within walking distance of the marina for trips into town.

Nearby, a few hundred yards west of the marina, is Varadero Caribe, a shipyard for haul-outs and ship repairs.

Cumaná is a mile away from the port by bus or taxi. Founded by the Spaniards under Gonzalo de Ocampo in 1521 and named Nuevo Toledo, the settlement was rebuilt in 1569 and given its present name after the Cumanágoto Indians, who occupied the land. The old colonial part of the town is centered on the plaza. Nearby, on a small hill, is a dramatic citadel, the Castillo de San Antonio. The view from the ramparts is splendid, and the fortress itself is a seventeenth-century classic, complete with moat, tunnels, and dungeons.

Several restaurants near the plaza feature typical dishes, including such specialties of the state of Sucre as Carúpano mussels *(mejillones carúpaneros),* Cumanese box turtle in garlic and pepper sauce *(olleta cumanesa),* small shark pies *(empanadas de cazón),* Río Manzanares fish eggs *(huevos de lisa),* and saltwater appetizers such as dried octopus with cassava bread or anchovy loaf.

The Museo de Mar is located in the old airport terminal building, west of town on the road to Barcelona. The museum contains one of the rare "coelacanth" fish (famous evolutionary "missing link") from South Africa—supposedly the only specimen on the American continent.

Golfo de Cariaco (24431)

is an inland arm of the sea about 30 miles long and 8 miles wide. Protected from the Caribbean by the Araya peninsula, it offers some remarkable sailing waters, ruffled only by a small chop produced by the afternoon trades, which may pick up to Force 7 before dropping at sundown. One visitor likened it to an oversized Buzzard's Bay (without all the boats and people), and another to Lake Mead in the U.S. Southwest—perhaps a bit of both. In any case, this gulf is seldom visited by commercial craft and is truly a yachtsman's hideaway.

Although much of the surrounding land is semiarid, some of the coves are gracefully fringed with towering coco palms—the anchorage off the sand beach at Punta Guacaparo at the eastern end of the gulf, for instance. There you will find shelter from the afternoon trades, which are strongest from January to July, and good holding in the sand and mud bottom.

The southern shore, which has no anchorages of consequence, is a low, green plain that gradually slopes to a ridge of mountains, the Cerro de Bergantin. The north shore, with its lofty, arid hills, boasts several anchorages. Laguna Chica, where there is a quaint fishing village, is one; but the best is Laguna Grande del Obispo (Bishop's Lagoon), a tranquil bay with a half dozen or more coves to tempt the gunkholer. Take your choice, for there is good holding almost everywhere on a sand and mud bottom. For detail, you will need chart 24421, Plan B.

The rise and fall of the tide is only about 3 inches in the gulf, and the weak current sets generally to the W.

Puerto Mochima (24421, Plan A)
The settlement at Mochima, charmingly nestled at the foot of sharply rising arid hills, has developed into a thriving resort. It is a favorite rendezvous for yachts, particularly at weekends, when two dozen or more tall-masted vessels anchor in the large bight. In the village, which boasts several restaurants, some provisions can be obtained. Ensenada Mochima, with several sandy beaches, offers a deep and secure haven and was considered by early Spanish surveyors to be a tropical storm-proof anchorage for those vessels seeking a respite from the hurricane-prone Caribbean between June and November. A paved road now runs from the village up to the main Cumaná–Puerto La Cruz highway.

Bahía Varadero Oeste (24433)
is on the W side of the Manaure peninsula and about a mile SE of Isla Los Venados. With its sand beach and several attractive shade trees, this is an attractive anchorage.

The nearby Islas Caracas also offer a number of small-craft anchorages, adjacent to a score or more fishing camps.

Puerto Guanta (Bahía de Guanta) (24430, 24434)
is a commercial port for Barcelona and Puerto La Cruz, sheltered by a breakwater. There is a shipping dock on the south shore and various boatyards on adjoining shores. Two small islands in the bay with lighthouses, mark the channel

entrance. Most remarkable is the crumbling old Aduana building, with wrought-iron balconies and a half-collapsed roof—still in use in late 1988! At nearby Punta Chamo is a coast guard and naval maintenance station. The next bay to the SW is Bahía de Bergantin, a deep-water bay with a private marina, Club Chaure, in its innermost harbor. This private club is ostensibly for the use of Corpoven Oil Company employees, but visiting yachtsmen may anchor off the club for a few days and are welcome to use the club facilities, which include a restaurant.

Puerto La Cruz (24434, KSK-1)

faces Bahía de Pozuelos, a large, open bay somewhat protected from wind and swell by the Chimanas Islands to the N. The town has changed tremendously in the last few years, into the Riviera of Venezuela. No longer are you able to tie your dinghy to a tree when visiting the port captain's office, as reported in earlier editions of this cruising guide! Puerto La Cruz is now a lively, mushrooming resort with many hotels and restaurants. Fishing and pleasure boats anchor in 2 fathoms off the shaded beach, where the waterfront drive, Paseo de Colon, fringes Pozuelos Bay. Just west of the landmark Hotel Melia is the Marina Paseo Colon, where water and electricity are available, with approximately 8 feet of water at dockside.

The port captain's office is now west of town, in from the Isla Margarita car-ferry terminal.

Bahía de Pozuelos (24434)

The breakwater entrance to the grandiose marina, Amerigo Vespuccio, part of the El Morro resort development complex, is a long mile west of the Puerto La Cruz ferry terminal. Here are haul-out facilities for yachts at reasonable rates. The marina has restaurants, a few supplies, and motorbikes for hire. A nice convenience is that visitors may rent a nearby waterside apartment at the complex while their boat is being hauled.

Space at the marina docks is run strictly on a first come, first serve basis; however, reservations are accepted for hauling out.

Bahía Barcelona (24434, KSK-1),

also called Old Spanish Port, is where galleons once anchored in the SW cove of the lofty Morro de Barcelona to discharge their cargos to lighters bound for the colonial city of Barcelona 4 miles south. Shoreside from the anchorage is La Lechería, a beach resort along the causeway that links the sugarloaf-shaped El Morro to the mainland. On the SE tip of the promontory is the Club Náutico del Morro, government owned but privately operated. Sailboats may anchor here gratis in about 8 feet of water within the new seawall. Fuel, water, and a few provisions are available at dockside.

All of the yacht clubs along this stretch of coast are private, but presentable yachts can usually expect to be accommodated for a night or two if a slip is available, but that's a big "if."

Islas Pírutu (24442),

about 24 miles W of Barcelona Bay, offers good shelter behind any of the three little islands. Shrimpers anchor here frequently and have been known to trade some fine shrimp for vodka or other spirits.

A long breakwater protects the Boca del Puerto Píritu entrance, a scenic lagoon for shallow-draft vessels. Just to the E is a beach resort, with two hotels and a few restaurants.

Carenero (24442, KSK-1)

is a small, secure port in Bahía Guayacán, a mangrove-lined bay with a maze of small cays and boat passages. Lately the bay has come to be known as Bahía de las Piratas.

Carenero was founded in the 1890s as a narrow-gauge-railroad town. Within the well-protected haven are numerous anchorages and several facilities for docking, repairs, and supplies adjacent to the town. One development is the Varadero Cavafa Marina, where yachts may dock for about $5 a day (1988), including

Carenero Yacht Basin

water and electricity. Near the pilot station, Estación de Pilotos, is the boatyard Talleres Betancourt, offering all types of yacht repairs. Also in the vicinity is a propeller and marine hardware shop. The plush Club Bahía de los Piratas is a private yacht club, with gasoline and diesel fuel available at the dock. Adjoining is the attractive Carenero Yacht Club, with strict security. There is no docking available for visiting yachts, but you may anchor in the east bay and dinghy to shore to use the club facilities. Yachting activities, in general, spring to life during weekends.

Puerto Azul (24440, KSK-1),

at Punta Naiguata, is the artificial harbor of the Club Puerto Azul, one of the most elegant yacht clubs in the Caribbean. The harbor, recreational facilities, and the clubhouse itself were tastefully designed and built, seemingly without regard to cost, by Dr. Daniel Camejo, an ex-commodore of the club.

The whole complex seems to blend comfortably into the natural environment of trees and beach terrain to create a restful, luxurious atmosphere. An informal cafeteria serves snacks and meals, or you may repair to the exotic, formal dining room, with its suspended floor and 90-foot-high ceiling, eminently suitable for the

Puerto Azul

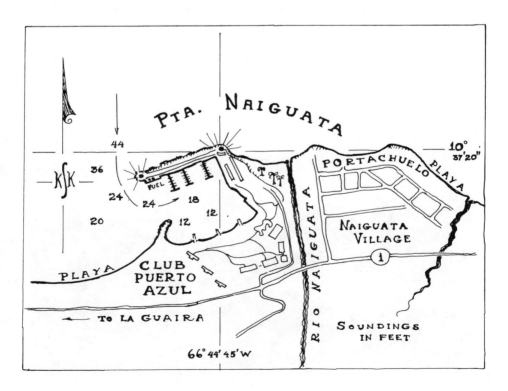

most fashionable of state events. As you would expect in such surroundings, the food is superb.

Visiting yachts are accorded reciprocal yacht club privileges. There is seldom space available at the docks for transients, and even anchoring space (for which there is no charge) is limited; but you should try to visit this place.

Fuel, water, and ice are, of course, available at the modern fuel dock, just inside the entrance.

La Guaira is 20 minutes away by public bus, and downtown Caracas is 35 miles by rapid motorway.

Punta Carabelleda (24440),

5 miles W of Puerto Azul, has a huge breakwater with two marinas in its lee. The Club Náutico de Carabelleda, which is affiliated with Caracas's posh Carabelleda Golf and Country Club, occupies a lagoon dredged to 11 feet, and is accessible by a narrow channel, the Canal Oeste, just to starboard after entry by the breakwater.

Visiting yachts are accorded reciprocal yacht club privileges. If there is room, you will be assigned dock space at the cement guest quay, where you will moor in Mediterranean fashion. All the usual marina facilities are here, including a marine hardware store.

The prominent sign atop the Macuto-Sheraton high-rise is a landmark for your approach to the entrance from seaward. The Marina de Mar, a public facility

Club Náutico de Carabelleda

adjacent to the breakwater, formerly part of the Sheraton Hotel complex, welcomes visiting yachts. The docks there have full facilities, with fuel and ice available. In late 1988 dockage fees were relatively high, although one could anchor off the club gratis and dinghy in to use club facilities.

A large and complete shopping district is within walking distance of both marinas.

La Guaira (24451)

is a port for naval and commercial ships, has no small-boat facilities, and should be avoided unless you must go in for clearance purposes. If you do, turn to starboard after entering the breakwater and try to find a space in the western dock area. All the port regulations and security requirements are administered to the letter here, and every detail of clearance, such as a change in your crew list, will be handled as though you were an ocean liner.

While you are in this vicinity, you should take a day off to see the sights, both colonial and contemporary, of Caracas, Venezuela's majestic capital city. It is only a half-hour ride on the expressway from La Guaira, but the cable car (when in operation) provides a much more thrilling (and cooling) way to go. Departing from Macuto, it rises to the heights of Mount Ávila before descending into downtown Caracas, which is itself at 3,100 feet. The trip by cable car affords spectacular views of the valley and of this ultramodern city during the hour or so in transit.

An interesting side trip well worth taking is to Colonia Tovar, a German settlement in the mountains about 35 miles W of Caracas. The scenery, reminiscent of the Alps, makes a pleasant change from the sea, and the air is refreshingly cool. There are several hotels and restaurants in the Tyrolean-style town, but electricity is turned off every evening promptly at 7:30 P.M. (late 1988).

Punta Calera (24450),

5 miles west of La Guaira port terminal, is the site of the private Playa Grande Club marina, near the old Naval Hotel. This swanky club, with breakwater protection, is situated in front of the high bluff of Catia La Mar, on which are built a half dozen high-rise apartment buildings. The club caters mostly to powerboats, but a few sailboats can be accommodated. Fuel and ice are available, but no shops for provisioning. This otherwise pleasant marina is unfortunately situated within the landing pattern of the nearby Simón Bolívar Airport.

The Offshore Islands: Orchila, Los Roques, and Aves

Isla La Orchila (24443)

is low and arid on its western end, with some 450-foot radio towers that are lighted at night. Although we have anchored in a cove on the SW side near a large dock, there is a military prison here, and the waters for 12 miles around are restricted.

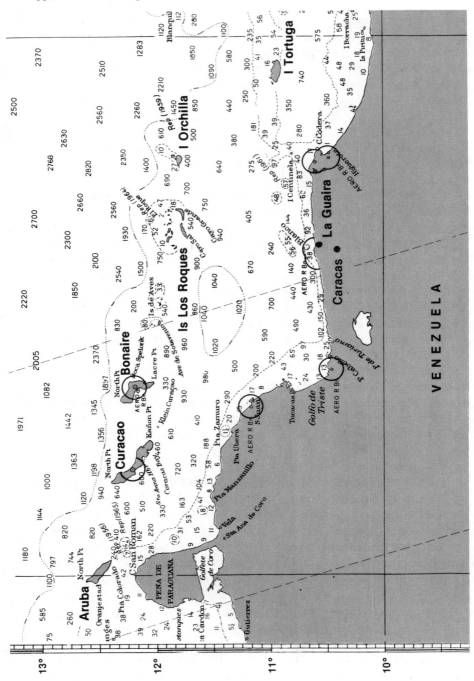

Western Venezuela and the Dutch Islands

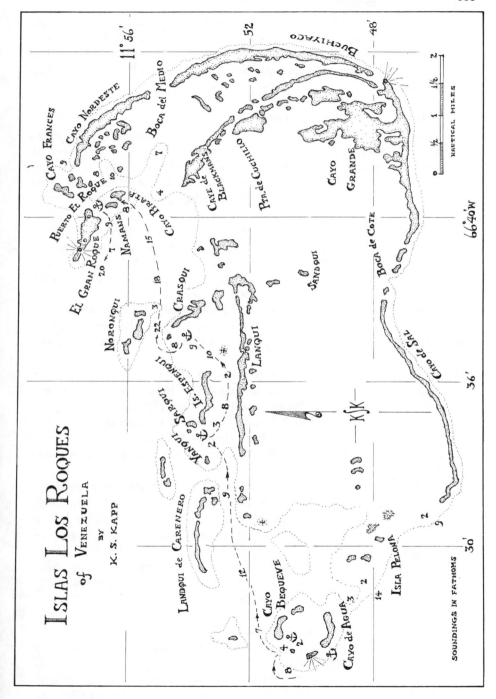

ISLAS LOS ROQUES
of VENEZUELA
BY
K. S. KAPP

SOUNDINGS IN FATHOMS

A special permit must be obtained from officials in La Guaira (or possibly other large Venezuelan cities). Without such a permit, you may have the bad luck to be boarded by the crew of a Venezuelan gunboat and presumed to be smuggling liquor or cigarettes, whereupon you will be relieved of all such stores and thank-you-very-much.

Islas Los Roques (24444)

consist of some 60 attractive, low, sandy cays. They resemble atolls and are spread over about 350 square miles. Only about 25 are named. The majority are less than 30 feet high, with sand dunes, beaches, and a few mangroves. On the principal island, El Gran Roque, the limestone hills rise to 386 feet. A yacht could spend weeks exploring the waterways and protected anchorages, observing the marine and bird life.

Cayo de Agua, the westernmost of the group and a rookery for brown boobies, offers an easily reached anchorage 150 yards off its beautiful sandy beach, not far from a clump of coconut palms. A passage to the NE leads to the sandy, southern shore of Cayo Bequeve. There, fading into the distance, you will see a profusion of sandy islets with scarcely any vegetation.

The channel continues eastward along the S side of Cayo Landquí de Carenero to its eastern end, where you will see a group of 10 huge, thatched buildings; thence eastward of the rockpile of Yanquí to Sarqui Island, where there is a pretty anchorage.

A safe channel passes through the unsurveyed area along the S side of Isla Espenquí to the lee of Crasquí, which has a cluster of drab, wooden houses, then N around Crasquí and across the open water to Cayo Pirata.

From the SW, we suggest you approach Cayo Pirata through the narrow but deep channel between it and Cayo Namans. Here you will come upon an interesting miniature port busily engaged with boat building. True to its name, it somehow seems reminiscent of a pirate hangout.

Within the spacious haven of Puerto El Roque, the most interesting anchorage is off the town of about 60 adobe buildings on El Gran Roque. Fresh fish, bread, canned goods, and diesel fuel are available in limited supply. Anchored here is a fleet of typical Venezuelan fishing smacks, neatly painted white and proudly maintained, each as bright as a new penny. The characteristic features of these powerboats (which carry a steadying sail in rough weather) are a small wheelhouse, a high bow, gunwales that taper to a tumble-home stern, and a symbolic eye, the seaman's protector, carved on the bow.

Aves de Barlovento (24441),

easternmost of the Islas de Aves group, offers a quiet anchorage behind the hook of the southern point. By all means, approach these dangerous coral banks, covered with sand and deposits of phosphate, from the S and in sufficient daylight.

Fishermen occasionally camp out on these forlorn cays; according to Bob and Ginnie Higman of the ketch *Tormentor III,* "The solitude is great, but the fishing is poor." They also reported (1974) that the light was not operating for lack of batteries. It most probably will not be operating when you get there.

The Coast from Puerto Cabello to the Paraguaná Peninsula (24450, 24460)

Isla Larga (24453, KSK-2)

lies 6 miles east of Puerto Cabello and, though only 10 feet high, offers a secluded and well-protected anchorage, free from swell. Approach from E or W to the anchorage in the SE cove, opposite a sandy beach.

On the NE point is a curious blowhole, which usually spouts surf high into the air. Near the SW point of the island lies a mysteriously scuttled German freighter, its hull and 60-foot mast still intact. Good spear fishing is reported in this area, and there is a reef, which may uncover at low water, about 200 yards SW of the wreck.

Puerto Cabello (24454)

has a nearly landlocked inner basin with docking facilities for big ships. If approaching after dark, anchor in 4 fathoms in the roadstead of Bahía San Esteban, about 300 yards SW of the fairway, where it is reasonably quiet. Otherwise pass into the Darsina Canal to the Capitanía de Puerto bulkhead on the town side for clearance when arriving from foreign ports.

Across the canal to the north is the naval dockyard (Base Naval), with heavy-repair facilities, including an 80-ton sheer-leg derrick, a foundry, and a drydock where yachts may be hauled. Naval and civilian craftsmen under government management will take commercial work when time and space are available. In this compound is the impressive Saint Philip Castle, built in 1731. It was a penitentiary for two centuries—until 1949—and was ironically called Liberator's Castle.

In front of the port captain's office is the old plaza and a tall cenotaph, surmounted by an eagle, dedicated to the U.S. citizens Captain Thomas Donohue and others who aided General Francisco Miranda in July 1806 during the Venezuelan struggle for independence.

On the west side of old Puerto Cabello, south of Plaza Flores and facing San Esteban Bay, is the recommended Marina Puerto Cabello. Foreign yachts are welcome to anchor inside the breakwater or at dockside, where there is 15 feet of water. Water, electricity, fuel, and ice are available. Secretaries at the marina office will clear your boat with the port captain for about $8 (September 1988). The shops, markets, and the Buen Hogar hardware store, offering marine items at reasonable prices, are within walking distance. Buses depart outside the marina gate six times a day for Caracas; the one-way fare is about $1. Some foreign yachtsmen have found this a desirable spot to laze about during the Caribbean hurricane season.

The Darsina, a commercial shipping haven on the east side of town, has a number of dredged channels with new docks and warehouses.

In town, there are a few colonial buildings and several old cannon mounted near the western shore at Plaza Flores. You may enjoy a stroll along the promenade or a rest in the pleasant Plaza Bolívar. Or you might take a humorous photo of your companion hugging the stone mermaid. The San José church is an outstanding landmark, built of coral and limestone laid in an unusual pattern. Calle Lanceros is a narrow, cobblestoned alley reminiscent of old Andalusia. Fortín Solana, a small fort on a hill SW of the bay, constructed in 1750–67, offers a splendid view of this historic port.

Tucacas (24455, KSK-2),

formerly a railhead for the Aroa copper mines, is now a fast-growing resort. The old customs dock has been replaced by a large, seven-story apartment building. A bridge across the entrance channel, with a maximum clearance of 15 feet, limits entry to powerboats. This bridge, an obstruction to Tucacas harbor, connects the mainland to Isla Brava for access to the beach-resort part of the Parque Nacional de Morrocoy.

Boca de Suanchez (24455, KSK-2),

located 3 miles ENE of Tucacas, is a narrow inlet to the newly organized Morrocoy National Park, encompassing about 15 square miles of islands, mangroves, and winding waterways. Enter this narrow channel on the NE side of Isla Brava and anchor in 40 feet near the beach on the W side of Cayo Suanchez. A deep-water channel continues around the mangroves on the N side of Cayo Suanchez and out through Boca Ánimas.

A navigable but narrow channel winds north several miles to Lizardo Bay and the hilly mainland of Punta Tucacas. Here, there are several yacht facilities and *embarcaderos,* launching ramps, for small boats. Marina Indunave has about 7 feet of water at dockside, and visitors are welcome. Some repairs, ice, and a restaurant are available. Nearby Cayo del Norte is reputed as being good for diving enthusiasts. Eastward, toward Lizardo village, are several developments, such as Las Luisas Marina, Marina Morrocoy with its adjacent boatyard, and Marina El Ancla, which is managed by a hospitable Cuban, Danilo Cobo. Vessels are charged about $3 a day at the El Ancla, which entitles them to a mooring and use of the club's facilities, including hot showers.

Boca Pailas (24455),

formerly called Boca Ánimas, on the E side of Cayo Suanchez presents a beautiful, remote anchorage just N of Punta Ánimas. Head for the tall tree on the sandy point N of the mangroves. Anchor in 40 feet not far from the tree.

Among the subtle beauties of nature in this lagoon, a bit off the beaten track, are the rookeries of the scarlet ibis and several varieties of herons.

Chichiriviche (24455, KSK-2)

is a commercial port, with more attractive anchorages in the vicinity. The town has mostly unpaved streets, although there are plans for a seaside resort, as several hotels have been recently built amazingly near the cement company's silos! Nearby lagoons are seasonably filled with flocks of flamingos, providing a colorful, spectacular sight.

You will find a more picturesque anchorage one half mile NE, in the lee of Cayo Los Muertos, a miniature resort with beach cottages. Anchor off the beach in 12 feet. A half mile farther N is a less frequented anchorage in 3 fathoms, off the beautiful beach on the W side of Cayo Sal.

An exceptionally secure refuge will be found in Chichiriviche's grand lagoon, Golfete de Guare, near the wreck of the *Gaviota,* an old sailing vessel whose clipper bow and helm are still intact. Proceed 1 mile S of Puerto Chichiriviche, past the commercial complex, and make a semicircular turn W around the mangrove point. This channel runs from 2 to 4 fathoms in depth. Continue another mile W, then turn NW past two small islets and drop the hook in the vicinity of the wreck, in 2 fathoms, sand and mud.

From here, by outboard, you may explore the lagoon that extends for several miles beyond Cayo Villalba. In this area we found an abundance of tasty mangrove oysters, ranging up to 4 inches long. But because they are so thin, it took a 10-quart bucketful to make a proper treat.

Preparing mangrove oysters isn't all that different from preparing steamed clams or mussels in northern waters. First brush off the mud film with several saltwater rinses; then steam (do not boil) the bivalves for 10 minutes, or until the shells open easily. Try dipping the pea-sized morsels into a seasoned, warm butter-lemon sauce. Delicious!

Punta San Juan (24450, 24460)

This area is flat and presents no visible characteristic landmarks from seaward, except for the detached Cayo San Juan. There is a narrow channel between the cay and the anvil-shaped point, but there is little gain in trying to locate this channel when you can simply round the north end of Cayo San Juan, which has trees rising to 30 feet, a nice beach, and a secluded anchorage in 3 fathoms just S of the island. The town of San Juan de los Cayos, 1 mile S of the cay, has limited supplies available. Cayo Noroeste, 2 miles NW, is as flat as the proverbial pancake, although it displays a 33-foot-high black beacon, which flashes a white light every six seconds. This light establishes an identifiable point along this rather nondescript, low-lying coast, fringed with palms.

Punta Aguide (24460)

is a heavily eroded beige-red escarpment, approximately 90 feet high, prominent from sea from either north or east. The town of Aguide is situated high on the bluff, with an oil derrick type of light tower. The anchorage at Punta Aguide offers only limited shelter in 2 fathoms, and is best avoided when easterly trades are in force because of the offshore shoaling areas at Bajo Aguide and Bajo Uveros. This whole coastal area is dangerous for after-dark navigation; in times of rain, the water around the area becomes murky because of numerous streams that empty into the sea.

Puerto Cumarebo (24443)

is an open roadstead, sheltered somewhat from the prevailing wind and current. Anchor in 2 fathoms off the small floating dock. There is no fuel available, except for a gasoline station two blocks from the dock. A new breakwater was being constructed in September 1988 just east of the new dock. This is a favorite mooring for small fishing vessels, which can be seen gently bobbing in this semiprotected anchorage. On Calle Guzmán, near the waterfront is a marvelous old building, Balcón de Jurado, a testimony to the former grandeur of Cumarebo. Very Spanish in design, it was once the courthouse and Aduana (customshouse). It now has weeds and cacti growing, quite artistically, out of the empty window-frames and between the roof tiles.

This sleepy little town has an attractive plaza and two nearby beach resorts Santa Rosa and Bella Vista—also a small hotel for that meal ashore.

For a specialty of the region, try *talkary,* a tasty curry dish made of goat meat and coconut. Incidentally, the goat is the prized animal of this state of Falcón, and is the source of leathercraft and numerous other local items, including unique preserves made from the goat's milk.

We first visited Cumarebo on a Sunday morning when church services were being held. At the same time four *cantinas* surrounding the square were doing a land-office business. People were enjoying billiards and dominoes, *cerveze,* and *música*—and the genial port captain waived all formalities.

The former lighthouse provides a fine panorama of the port. We found weeds growing inside the light lens, which probably had not functioned for years.

This again brings to mind the unreliability of lighthouses and buoys in the Caribbean. For instance, in one cruising season alone, we found the following lights not operating, although they were supposed to be in service according to the charts and light lists: Punta Hermano (Colombia), Isla Tesoro (Colombia), Half Moon Bay (Belize), Little Corn Island (Nicaragua), and Isla Providencia (Colombia).

La Vela de Coro (24460, KSK-2)

offers only limited shelter. We recommend anchoring NW of the town in 2 fathoms. Since the bottom is hard clay, it is advisable to set two anchors.

The old Aduana building opposite the newly constructed floating dock is now an interesting marine museum. A small breakwater, in the process of construction in September 1988, extends from the sandy shore directly in front of the General

Miranda monument. Miranda landed at Vela de Coro on August 3, 1806, and raised the Venezuelan national flag for the first time. The city of Coro, 10 miles from the port of La Vela, was founded in 1527, becoming the capital of Venezuela and the first diocese of South America in 1531. Truly rich in Hispanic heritage, it is well worth a visit, since it has some of the best examples of colonial architecture in the republic.

Not to be missed are the cathedral, built in 1583; the José Garces House with its iron windows; and the Diocese Museum, where you may learn more of the history of Nueva Andalusia. Elsewhere, the cobbled streets and the houses of whitewashed adobe with tiled, terra-cotta roofs help to frame the city within its colonial past.

At nearby Port Muaco, 1 mile E of the La Vela breakwater, car and passenger ferries leave on a scheduled basis to Aruba and Curaçao.

We also recommend a visit farther afield, to Los Médanos, a miniature desert of remarkable sand dunes facing the shallow Golfete de Coro. Prey to the vagaries of the winds, the dunes constantly change their delightful, capricious forms.

La Paraguaná (24470)

Most of the Paraguaná peninsula is a low, arid, windswept region surrounded by beaches, and relieved only by a ridge of hills in the central area, culminating in the 2,800-foot peak of Pan de Santa Ana. An outstanding landmark resembling a miniature Matterhorn, it often rises into the clouds, and may be seen up to 40 miles at sea. At night the sky glows from the huge refineries at Amuay and Punta Cardón on the west coast of the peninsula. Similar glows illuminate the sky over Curaçao and Aruba, and all of them make useful after-dark navigational aids.

The northeast shore, from Punta Braya to Punta Tumatey, is a veritable graveyard of ships that have unsuspectingly grounded because of the strong current that sets directly onto this very low coast. Beware!

Punta Adicora (24460)

is a small peninsula and fishing village with limited supplies. Boats anchor behind the reef in Morrocoy Bay, south of the town. Entrance through the reef is SE of the point, although anchorage here is not readily endorsed, as depth is uncertain. However, power smacks to 40 feet frequent the anchorage. Those adventurous seamen with shallow-draft boats may be encouraged to try, especially for a base anchorage, if intending to explore the shipping graveyard on the Paraguaná NE coast. Just north of Adicora is a wide crescent-shaped beach, which has the potential for an attractive anchorage. On a small sand cay off the point is a 39-foot black iron-frame light tower, flashing a white light every 15 seconds.

The older houses in town have a quaint architectural style, with a Dutch influence from the nearby Netherlands Antilles. The scroll-scalloped gables are flush, and the distinctive windows have protruding barred casements with decorative pedestals.

Pueblo Nuevo, 9 miles west and accessible by public bus, is the capital of the Paraguaná canton. The name is misleading, as the town is actually one of the oldest on the peninsula, with a church that dates back to 1758. The old houses there are of wattle and daub construction, with barrel-tile roofs.

Moruy, another accessible town and at the foot of the majestic Santa Ana peak, was founded by the Caquetio Indians prior to 1621.

The Gulf of Venezuela and Lake Maracaibo (24470, 24481)

The west coast of La Paraguaná, south of Punta Salina, has numerous anchorages protected from prevailing weather and, for the most part, free of roll.

The daily weather here is phenomenal. Almost without fail, the wind starts to blow off the land at midmorning and picks up to about 35 knots before dying down after dark. Out in the Gulf of Venezuela, from December until March, the winds blow almost constantly at Force 5 to 7. Only occasionally, during the summer, will the wind blow from west of north.

This area of the southwestern Paraguaná, from Los Taques to Punta Cardón, is the fastest-growing development on the Spanish Main. The mammoth oil refineries at Amuay and Cardón provide the principal employment, but there is also shrimp fishing, ship building, and light industries.

Bahía Salina (24471)

is a spacious, deep-enough bay away from industrial development, except for the Astilleros Navales Venezuelanos shipyard. Anchor about 500 yards NE of Punta Salina, near the beach, in 15 feet of water. There is a small fishing village, and El Pico restaurant is at the water's edge serving tasty meals of freshly caught *carita, chivo, jurel, rey,* and other seafood.

Bahía Estanques (24471),

located 3 miles S of El Pico, affords a similar anchorage, in 20 feet of water NE of Punta Estanques formerly called Los Taques. Be sure to round this point with caution because of the shoal that extends 500 yards to the south. The town of Los Taques rambles along the sandy beach. On the NW shore there is a deep-water cement dock next to Diques y Astilleros Villa Marina, a shipyard for all types of repairs and haul-outs, with a restaurant adjacent.

Carirubana (24471)

The S side of Punta Carirubana provides a less congested anchorage, away from commercial traffic, except for small fishing boats. Anchor in 12 feet of water in the center of the bay. The shipyards, half a mile S of the bay, were building a number of large fishing trawlers in September 1988. Most of the town of Carirubana is built on the bluff above, while the landmark church is situated near the bay. There are facilities for outfitting vessels. Hardware supplies, food, and ice are available.

Puerto de Guaranao (24471, KSK-2)

is the port of entry for the west coast of the Paraguaná peninsula. The authorities prefer that a yacht entering from a foreign port dock at the customshouse pier in Ensenada Caleta Guaranao, where all formalities may be completed before moving to other anchorages. Water is piped to the dock, and fuel by truck or drum may be ordered for delivery here.

Just south of the Guaranao docks and warehouse complex (sometimes called Punta Fijo, for the adjoining urban area) is the Cardón Yacht Club (formerly Club Náutico Shell). Fuel, water, and restaurant facilities are available to visiting yachts. Dockage is scarce although we have anchored off and dinghied in to enjoy the club's hospitality. On rare occasions, sea swells will accompany a northwester to make the anchorage rather uncomfortable.

Canal-Barra de Maracaibo (24481)

is the dredged entrance channel to the city and lake of Maracaibo. We suggest you plan to arrive at Isla San Carlos at about low water, so that the flood current will carry you through the well-marked and well-lighted channel with less swell and current eddies. Conversely, plan your exit to pick up an ebbing current. The current here may run up to 5 knots, and when opposed by the wind, will produce some frightening, steep waves.

The ship traffic in the channel and its approaches is considerable, so remember the ditty about Michael O'Day and his fight for the right-of-way, and be warned! Stay clear of the large ships; they certainly will not alter their course or speed.

Windwise the best time to pass through the outer bar, N of Isla San Carlos, is between 0700 and 1000, when the wind is usually moderate.

Your first sight of land will probably be the 400-foot hills of Isla de Toas; all of the rest of the surrounding shore is very low. A pilot from the station at San Carlos Point may board your vessel for the passage down the channel and will possibly remain aboard all the way to port captain's dock at Maracaibo. You must present your papers at Maracaibo, and chances are you may be able to stay at the dock for a day or two, gratis. Water is available, but fuel and ice must be ordered.

Maracaibo (24481)

is, understandably, rather congested at the dock. After clearing, you may wish to anchor SW of the wharf, or perhaps berth at one of the two pleasant yacht clubs, which have breakwaters protecting their docks. You must telephone these clubs—better still, visit them by taxi—to obtain permission and instructions on where to tie up. Both clubs extend reciprocal yacht club privileges, but their docking basins are limited to vessels of about 5–6 feet draft.

Club Náutico de Maracaibo is a handsome, fashionable private club with all sorts of sports facilities, situated next to the 15-story lakeside Hotel del Lago on the N side of the city (Calle 70). Dock space is limited, but diesel, gasoline, electricity, and water are all available dockside. There are haul-out facilities for boats up to 45 feet. The club also has tennis courts, a swimming pool, helpful staff, and a well-recommended restaurant. If your boat's draft is too deep to dock, anchor off the S side of the dock and dinghy in to use the club's facilities.

The Los Andes Yacht Club at Calle 75 (formerly the Caribbean Yacht Club), founded by Shell Oil employees, makes use of an old two-deck ferryboat as its clubhouse—once floating, but now set into cement at dockside. The vessel forms part of the shelter for a mooring basin, along with a circular breakwater. Water is available at dockside, but there is no electricity or fuel. Less formal than the Club Náutico, the club places more emphasis on small, class-sailing designs. However, foreign yachts are welcome. Two blocks to the N is the 12-story Hotel el Paseo, with a penthouse revolving restaurant affording excellent dining and a fine panoramic view of the city and waterways. Jackets are not required.

The old part of Maracaibo city, founded in 1570, is within walking distance of the steamer docks and centers on the tiled walks of the Plaza Bolívar. Here you may hear a lively concert played by La Banda Bolívar, watch the vendors with their fold-away stands offering all sorts of tidbits, sip a demitasse of coffee served from a large thermos (sometimes mounted on the vendor's head), or puff on one of the hand-rolled mild, savory cigars offered for sale. Then visit the Mercado Central, just off the Paseo Las Ciencias, for a wide variety of fresh foods and assorted handcrafts made and sold by Indians, some dressed in colorful traditional costume.

For a full-day's excursion, take a bus to Sinamaica Lagoon, 45 miles NNE of the city, where the Goaro Indians live in primitive dwellings built on pilings in the lake. The bird life and natural surroundings are most interesting.

In general, yachting on Lake Maracaibo is confined to the western shore, south of Cabimas city, because oil rigs, dangerous high-voltage wires, submerged pilings, and pipe lines congest the eastern side. We also noticed a number of fast-moving hydrofoil vessels, used for servicing the oil rigs.

Incidentally, a phenomenon in the Lake Maracaibo area worth mentioning is the *relampagos,* heat flashes that occur nightly during the May-to-December rainy season with utmost regularity. They appear as lightning flashes but without thunder, originating in the SW Río Catatumbo area.

The Lake Maracaibo region is not the oil-polluted sump you might think it is. In fact, if you are not pressed for time, it may prove to be a rewarding detour to cruise the remote western and southern shores. There the land animal, bird, and aquatic life is in abundance, far from urban developers. Truly a gunkholer's delight!

Chapter Thirteen

THE DUTCH
A-B-C ISLANDS

Sailing into the Dutch Leeward Islands from the generally somnolent and happy-go-lucky mainland is like sailing into another world: a vibrant one, in which efficiency is a habit, cleanliness a trait, and courtesy a custom. Here live the people who built the dikes of Holland to hold back the sea and make land where there had been only water. These are descendants of the same people, intermixed with other European stocks, transplanted to a balmy climate. They have thrived on adversity, and to them, almost any project is a challenging possibility.

Nobody really wanted these low, rocky, barren islands at first, although they had been discovered for Spain in 1499 by one of Columbus's roving captains, Alonzo de Ojeda. Since the Dutch were at war with Spain anyway, and needed a base in the fast-developing Caribbean for their traditionally mercantile aspirations, it was only natural that the Dutch should take over This they did in proper fashion, in 1634, by establishing the Dutch West India Company, whose purpose was to trade along the Spanish Main, pan salt, and market slaves from Africa. Except for two brief periods of British sovereignty, the islands have been Dutch ever since. In 1954 they became self-governing.

Of those original industries, the slave trade especially boomed—and then went bust in 1863, when the trade was outlawed. After a period of economic doldrums came the discovery of oil in Lake Maracaibo in 1915. Quick to capitalize on their location, only 180 miles from the source of this "black gold," the Dutch set about to build a huge refinery on Curaçao to process the crude into usable products.

Refining oil was the mainstay of the islands' economy. In fact, your landmarks approaching Curaçao, and Aruba were the smoking refinery stacks by day and their flickering reflected torchlight by night. Another smelly industrial jungle, no place for a yacht, you might have thought—but not so. Even within the commercial harbors there were attractive yacht anchorages, upwind or otherwise separated from the refinery ports. As a matter of fact, the first of these islands, if you're coming from the east, is Bonaire, which has no refineries at all, and Aruba's closed in 1985.

Language problems seldom arise in the Dutch islands. In contrast to the average American, who tends only to talk louder and louder in English when his English is not understood, the Dutch are usually fluent in several languages, most commonly in English, Spanish, and French. And so it is in these islands.

They even have a working language of their own, Papiamento, a fascinating mixture of Portuguese, Spanish, some Dutch, and a little English, an appropriate reflection of these islands' history. It is more than a dialect or patois; newspapers and books are published in this unique language. Some say that if there is ever to be an international language, it should be Papiamento. In any case, it is a living, growing language, which Esperanto is not.

We have never heard anything but praise for the attitude of officialdom in the Duch Leewards. U.S. and Canadian citizens need produce only proof of identity. (A passport is good for this, and is always a good document to have aboard.) And the population enjoys a well-earned reputation for friendliness, honesty, and helpfulness.

To tune in on the cruising party line, try Channel 77 on your VHF.

Bonaire (24661 I-D23)

Approaching from the southeast around Lacre Punt, you can expect a smooth, soul-satisfying reach up to the island's only port, Kralendijk (meaning "coral dike" and pronounced "crawlen-dike"). Though you will have no sea in the lee of the island, this low land of salt flats hardly disturbs the trade wind. In the *salinas* you will see flight after flight of pink flamingos enjoying their sanctuary (their droppings actually contribute to the salt-making process).

Kralendijk (24461, Plan)

is an almost open roadstead, protected only by a low and reef-fringed island, Kleine Bonaire, but you're likely to be in dangerous trouble here only if you get caught in southwesterly winds. According to the *Sailing Directions*, these may occur from August through the first part of November.

Fortunately for the cruising fraternity, a marina has been created by dredging through to the salt pond about 0.75 miles N of the town. A group of red-tile-roof condos is a landmark, and the entrance to the marina will be found through the rock breakwater. Customs will come to your boat here. Facilities include water, electricity (115V, 50 cycles), and a laundry.

Alternatively take your boat to the main pier and tie up while you visit customs and immigration. Then anchor on the narrow shelf north of the main pier. A secondary anchorage can be found south of the pier, in 15 to 20 feet of water, with a sand and coral bottom.

After clearing customs, to regain your land legs briefly, take an excursion out to the 13,500-acre Washington/Slagbaii National Park, a wildlife sanctuary in the "mountainous" (Mount Brandaris, 781 feet, the highest point on Bonaire, is found here) NW end of the island. This is desert country, with forests of cactus; iguanas scurry across the road, and you'll see, perhaps for the first time in your life, uncaged parrots roosting in the trees. One hundred and fifty different species of migratory birds have been sighted in this park.

Bonaire is a mecca for diving and snorkeling enthusiasts. The waters extending from the coast of the island out 3 miles and down 200 feet are protected as the Bonaire Marine Park, so the spectacular coral formations and colorful fish population are preserved for looking and are not for collecting.

It is possible to get visas to visit Venezuela at the Venezuelan consulate here.

Kralendijk's biggest market is Cultimara. There are quite a few smaller markets as well. In addition to replenishing the larder, it is also possible to get fuel, propane, and computer supplies here.

Curaçao (22462, I-D23)

Curaçao is the largest of the six islands that make up the Netherlands Antilles. The population of 165,000 is cosmopolitan. Beaches suffer by comparison with the neighboring islands of Bonaire and Aruba, but are still excellent by most standards. And to supplement their God-given portion, the people of Curaçao have constructed what is probably the longest man-made beach in the world (6,000 feet), in Willemstad. There are many interesting and historic forts and museums to visit here. The distinctly Dutch colonial look to the architecture may make you forget you are only 40 miles N of South America!

Fuik Bay, Caracas Bay, and Bullen Bay are not suitable havens for yachts on this foremost island of the Netherlands Antilles. Fuik Bay is a phosphate-loading port; Caracas Bay is full of cruise ships; Bullen Bay is full of VLCCs (very large crude carriers). That leaves three good places for yachtsmen—Willemstad Harbor (just inside the entrance in Saint Anna Bay); Spanish Water, a large and almost landlocked lagoon a few miles east of Willemstad; and snug Piscadera Bay, on the west side of the big city.

You are requested to enter first at Willemstad, although yachtsmen will be accommodated by the officials' coming out, on call, to vessels at the Concorde Hotel at Piscadera Bay and at Spanish Water.

In all these Dutch islands guns and ammunition are impounded until half an hour before your departure, a minor inconvenience but nothing to be alarmed about, as you will probably not need to defend yourself in these friendly islands.

Willemstad, Saint Anna Bay (24465)

dockage is just inside the Queen Emma Pontoon bridge, which, since 1888, has been handling street traffic from Punda, the main part of town, to Otrabanda (meaning, of course, "the other side"). Now the bridge carries only pedestrian traffic—vehicular traffic has been diverted over the modern, high Queen Juliana Bridge farther in. The pontoon bridge hinges on the western side of the bay and swings inward; it opens an average of 30 times daily.

A good deal of ship traffic is usually waiting to get through, so just stand by patiently and await developments. If you seem to be unnoticed after a long wait, call Curaçao Radio on 2181 kHz for advice; their operators speak English.

Once past the pontoon bridge, proceed to the commercial docks on your

Entrance to Saint Anna Bay, Willemstad

starboard hand, where you will receive berthing instructions from the port authorities. Under the bridge abutments on the other side of the channel is a dock where fuel and delicious distilled water may be taken on.

Whether or not you stay here after clearing customs and immigration depends on whether you prefer activity or peace. You and your yacht will be perfectly safe here, and the procession of big ships in and out of the huge Schottegat Bay is a sight to see; among Dutch ports, Willemstad is second in importance only to Rotterdam. The city itself is a shopper's paradise, even if you only look through the store windows. Then, too, you will be only a few steps from the bustling Waaigat, where, awnings rigged, sailing coasters have come from Aruba, Bonaire, and Venezuela to sell their produce right off their decks. Come in the morning and barter for fresh fruits and vegetables and fish.

Of course, you can make excursions from Spanish Water or Piscadera Bay to see all this, and you'll keep your topsides clean if you don't stay in Saint Anna Bay. It is, after all, a refinery port.

The American Express office here is run by the Maduro Travel Agency; it is prepared to do an efficient job for you in receiving and forwarding your mail.

Complete repairs to large and small yachts can be handled by Small Craft Yard

Antilles, Inc., on the west side of the Schottegat, at Batipanja, close to the Otrabanda ramp of the Queen Juliana Bridge. Of the two slipways, the smaller one will handle craft up to 50 tons. This yard has been in operation since 1968 and is engaged mostly in the construction and repair of tugs, pilot launches, and similar commercial vessels.

Spanish Water (24462)

is about halfway between Curaçao's easternmost point and Willemstad. Coming from the SE, you will see the phosphate port of Newport, distinguished by a white mountain of phosphate and a high stack, just N of the entrance to Newport. Continuing W another mile, you will come to the rather obscure entrance to Spanish Water. A cluster of oil storage tanks jut up on the top and sides of the hill that forms the left bank of the entrance into this lagoon. The entrance channel is narrow and buoyed, although the water is clear enough to eyeball your way in anyway. This is not a place to enter at night.

The Curaçao Yacht Club has limited space for transients, but diesel fuel and gas are available at the club. Club Asiento (also called the Shell Club) is located in the NE corner of the NW arm of the bay, and is primarily a small-boat club. Sairfundy's Marina (Brakkeput, Ariba 5, Curaçao, Netherlands Antilles) is a

Spanish Water, Curaçao

relatively new facility, which offers many services to transients. These include receiving mail (address above), the availability of ice and water and a rental car, and care of your boat should you need to be away for a time. Their Sunday barbecue is popular and inexpensive.

Spanish Water is a delightful and secure spot to stay for a while, and many cruising people do just that. To visit Willemstad from here, it is easy to take a bus for a very nominal charge.

Piscadera Bay (24462)

is about 2 miles W of Willemstad. The government has dredged the entrance to 20 feet and deepened a basin for anchoring just inside.

At the entrance to this bay, the Concorde Hotel operates a marina that makes use of a former government dock; here they tie up the boats that provide various types of water sports for their guests. There has been space for transients in the past and there may still be.

West Punt Bay (24462)

is an open roadstead about 1½ miles S of the NW tip of Curaçao. An attractive beach and a well-known native fish restaurant called Janchie's are there. You will have to move close in to the beach before letting go; the bottom shelves steeply.

This might be a useful temporary stop to break the usually tempestuous passage between Curaçao and Aruba.

Aruba (24463, I-D23)

Aruba, the easternmost of this group of Dutch islands, lies about 15 miles N of Venezuela, at roughly 12 degrees N latitude. Like Bonaire and Curaçao, Aruba is very dry. The island receives only about 20 inches of rainfall annually. The island is noted for beautiful beaches, and its economy has relied primarily on tourism since the Lago Oil refinery closed in 1985. Gold mining was a mainstay during the nineteenth century, and an old smelting works may be visited near Frenchman's Pass.

Aruba gained its independence from the Netherlands Antilles on January 1, 1986. It will maintain its ties directly with the Netherlands until it achieves full independence in 1996. In the meantime fly a Dutch courtesy flag here, not a Netherlands Antilles courtesy flag.

Of the three commercial harbors on Aruba, only Oranjestad is suitable for yachts. San Nicolas Harbor at the eastern end of the island is the huge refinery port of Lago Oil and Transport, an Exxon affiliate; the barren, windswept quay and dredged basin inside the reef at Barcadera is strictly an industrial development project of the government.

Approaching from the east, lay a course that you feel is a safe distance south of Point Basora, to avoid being unexpectedly set toward the dangerous windward coast of Aruba. The currents in this strait are capricious, although they set generally to the west. The land is very low, so you may not have much time on an adjusted course after you sight the island.

Oranjestad (24463, Plan A)

lies completely sheltered behind an outlying reef, with a straightforward, buoyed channel at each end of this reef. We would not hesitate to enter at night. Big ships enter through the western channel and exit through the eastern, but small craft are free to enter and leave from either direction. If you are coming from Curaçao, your clue to the eastern entrance will be the airport control tower 1½ miles SE.

The yacht anchorage is in the lagoon near the floating Bali Restaurant, which is an extension of a pier making out from the city's waterfront. The Bali dock is within a block of the customs and immigration office and very convenient to a well-stocked supermarket.

One of Aruba's exports is coffee, notwithstanding the fact that there is not a coffee tree on the island. It is smuggled in from Colombia to avoid levies by the coffee growers' federation there, processed in Aruba, and shipped out as "Aruban" coffee. This activity has brought a lot of sleazy Colombians to Aruba; thievery is their way of life, so be wary of leaving your boat at anchor and unmonitored.

A full-service marina within a breakwatered harbor has been created between the wooded peninsula that juts out from the waterfront boulevard and the commercial docks. When it opened in 1989, rates were $1 a foot. That price was also levied on dinghies left at their docks for more than one hour. As few long-distance cruisers would be prepared to pay those rates, at least for any prolonged stay, it would be worthwhile inquiring to find out if any adjustments have been made.

Southeast down the coast, and entered via Haven Barcadera, is Aruba Nautical Club, primarily a local yacht club but available to cruising yachtsmen with yacht club credentials. Rather than going in unannounced, it would be appropriate to make prior arrangements by calling the club manager. Proceed southeasterly beyond the bulkheaded wharfs, following the line of mangroves close to starboard, until you come approximately abeam of what was once the island's distillation plant. This indentation in the mainland is just before the point that juts out from Spanish Lagoon, where the label "stack" appears on Chart 24463. Line up a front range on the yacht club building with a back range on a high TV antenna situated on the E side of Spanish Lagoon, and cross over to the club on this range. This is a comfortable and protected spot for yachts that plan to tarry more than a few days in Aruba.

Chapter Fourteen

THE COAST OF COLOMBIA

BY KIT S. KAPP

The north Colombian coast, formerly the province Castilla del Oro, offers the greatest contrasts in natural scenery to be found in the Caribbean. From the sand dunes and flat, arid cactus country of the Guajira peninsula, almost devoid of vegetation, the landscape gradually changes. As you sail west, pine-clad slopes and lofty peaks begin to appear, including the magnificent, snow-capped Mount Cristóbal Colón of the Sierra Nevada de Santa Marta, often visible 100 miles at sea. The land breeze becomes refreshingly cool, for the descending air is chilled by the perpetual snow that caps this 18,900-foot peak only 22 miles from your Caribbean anchorage.

The coast continues southwestward past Cartagena, clothed in semitropical forests and rolling green savannas with cattle ranches, fringed by mile after mile of sand beaches. Farther west, the lush, primeval forests of Darien reach down to the water's edge. From an anchorage here, one can hear the roar of a cougar and the chatter of howler monkeys.

Part of the delight of cruising this western half of the Spanish Main is the pervading atmosphere of yesteryear. Everywhere is the awareness of the Spanish Conquest, of the wars seeking to unseat the Spaniards, and of daring adventures in piracy. Defenses all along the coast of Nueva Andalusia, old cannon on the beach at Ríohacha, forts in ruins since the War of Jenkins's Ear, and the skeletons of galleons on Salmedina Reef are all there today for the skin diver and beach-comber to explore.

Colombia produces 95 percent of the world's emeralds. These precious stones, a worthy souvenir of your cruise, were being mined here more than 300 years before the Spanish Conquest. The Conquistadores were quick to take possession of the fabulously wealthy mines and to enslave the Indians to work them. Mostly for humanitarian reasons, the mines were closed by order of King Charles II in 1675. Dense jungle vegetation gradually obliterated all traces of them, especially of the famous Chivor excavation of Boyaca, the location of which was lost for over two centuries. Then, in 1899, in a stirring tale of adventure, Dr. Francisco Restrepo rediscovered the lost mine after a three-year search.

Today the emerald mines are again in operation, and splendid stones may be purchased in Bogotá, Barranquilla, and Cartagena. When buying an emerald, keep in mind that stones of deep green are more esteemed than the paler ones;

that all emeralds are flawed to some extent; and that the clearer the stone and the greater the sparkle, the more valuable it is. Resist buying emeralds from street vendors, who tempt the novice with low prices and questionable quality. Always buy from a reputable dealer in an established shop.

La Guajira Peninsula to Cartagena

Centuries ago, lustful freebooters, headed by the likes of Morgan, Ringrose, and Montbars the Exterminator, struck fear into the hearts of those who sailed the Spanish Main. Their depredations so hampered international trade that the Spanish Guardia de Costa even joined with British Men-of-War in an effort to make the sea lanes safe to sail. Later, with the advent of the Monroe Doctrine, the fledgling United States Navy took over the task of maintaining order in the West Indies. Then came the Castro takeover, the political injustices in Jamaica, "Papa Doc" in Haiti, the Sandinista upheaval in Nicaragua, and guerrilla strife in El Salvador. More recently, the drug traffickers, with their related piracy on the high seas, have brought another era of instability to the Caribbean. As a result we now have, so to speak, zones of "no-man's seas"—areas to be avoided by gunkholing, fun-loving yachtsmen.

One of these zones is the Guajira peninsula, which has become a haunt for traffickers in contraband and leads us to issue some words of caution to the casual yachtsman who may still harbor the naive belief that atrocities at sea, hijacking, and piracy are things of the past.

In waters of questionable safety, be alert on all quarters, and stay well offshore at night, 20 miles or so. Be prepared with engine, radio, and all sails in good condition. Be suspicious of distress signals and approaching vessels and aircraft. While at anchor, maintain an around-the-clock watch and by all means be adequately armed. Construct a mental plan concerning how you will go about repelling boarders. This author, for one, would not be here to write this advice were it not for his armed capability to defend himself, his crew, and his vessel. By all means keep your cool and try to avoid anxieties by planning ahead for the possibility of dangerous or at least unpleasant situations.

Islas Las Monjes (24470)

are sugarloaf-like rocks, which, although possessions of Venezuela, serve as distinguishing landmarks for the approach to the low, barren Guajira peninsula. In this area, the current may be set as much as 3 knots to the W, so keep close track of your position by identifying such unmistakable landmarks as the 2,800-foot peaks of the Sierra de Chimare. Point Cañón, a 120-foot-high rock, half a mile off the point, is also easy to distinguish.

Vessels carrying contraband navigate these waters at night without lights. Colombian gunboats also patrol without lights and may take aggressive action towards unidentifiable vessels. While the patrol boats usually base at Puerto de

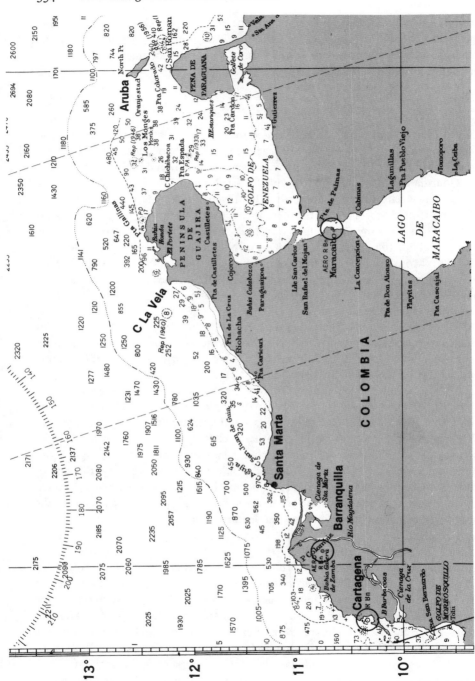

Aruba to Cartagena

Chimare and do not bother yachts, it is best to keep your vessel well lit in addition to using your usual running lights, and to display your flag prominently, even during darkness.

Bahía Honda (24473)
offers the first comfortable anchorage along the arid, desertlike Guajira peninsula.

It is difficult to understand why, in 1502, the Conquistadores under Alonso de Ojeda chose this low, windswept spot for the first settlement on the Spanish Main. The colony, unable to eke out an existence in this sterile land, proved to be short-lived, but beachcombers today will be intrigued with the assortment of ruins that abound in the vicinity.

Anchor in 2 fathoms S of Punta Soldado, where the water is usually calm. The point has been abandoned for the past 15 years. The white customshouse has been destroyed, perhaps bombed, and a few other ruins are to be seen, among them a curious concrete block inscribed "U.S.S. *Niagara,* June 18, 1927." Along the shore are numerous mounds of seashells that resemble white roofs on a moonlit night. These old shell heaps are probably pre-Columbian. Many bricks lie about on the ridge; several cisterns and two water holes, usually dry, are nearby.

Incidentally, the large Bahía de Portete appears at first glance to provide small-craft protection. However, the entrance is too tricky to be recommended.

Cabo de la Vela (24470)
was an anchorage recommended by Ojeda and other early sea rovers because of its wide-open approach and splendid protection. With a fresh N wind, seas can be steep off the cape, so round the small island, Isla Farallon, into the lee of the cape, and anchor in 2 fathoms of quiet water. Here the wind will sing in your rigging while tumbleweeds roll along the barren shore, which seems to resemble a moonscape.

When eastbound, one may choose to pass between Isla Farallon and the cape. Favor the island side, where a 3-fathom channel will be found; a shoal patch extends 400 yards N of Cabo de la Vela.

Ríohacha (KSK-2)
was founded by the German conquistador Nicholas Feldman, for whom the town's main plaza is named. Sir Francis Drake raided this village on several occasions (first in 1565) to revictual his vessels with corn and fresh meat. Since then this old port has mercifully suffered no growth pains. The avenues are still only partly paved; the adobe buildings are mostly one story, with tiled roofs. Several ancient cannon still lie in the streets, too heavy and too much trouble to mount in the plaza near the statue of Feldman.

When you are sailing westward, Ríohacha is the first Colombian port of entry. From seaward, only the high water tower and white church are landmarks on this low coast. Anchor anywhere off the pier in 12 feet of water, where there is good holding ground. If the port authorities do not come out within a reasonable time, take your papers to the customs office at the far end of the dock.

The open roadstead is subject to swells in fresh winds, but if the sea is calm enough, you may prefer to use the dock, providing lighters are not loading an anchored ship at the time.

This dusty little town has an air of intrigue, resembling in some aspects a frontier settlement west of the Pecos. Adobe houses are built of knitted sticks and wattle plastered with red clay; some are topped with thatched roofs. Guajira Indians come into town to sell their handicrafts and produce. Outstanding is the *chinchorro,* a beautifully woven and extremely large hammock.

Guajira men have a stately bearing and a disconcerting, icy stare; their cheek-bones are high beneath a drum-tight, dark-brown skin. They wear mustaches and their jet-black hair long. Their costume includes a felt sombrero and, for city wear, a towel wrapped around their middle to cover the traditional loin cloth. In modest contrast, the tall women dress in a commodious, toe-length, Arab-like smock, a drab bandana around the head, and sandals with large, brilliantly colored pompons.

To the E of town, the Rancheria River empties swiftly into the sea, and there a number of flat-bottomed *piraguas,* dugout canoes, will probably be engaged in river fishing. Nearby is a thatched-roof turtle store, where often a score of gigantic, whimpering sea turtles will be seen, turned helplessly on their backs and awaiting coastal transport to Barranquilla.

Bahía Cinto (KSK-3)

is the first of numerous snug anchorages to be found along the northern coast of Colombia. Although open to the NW, the anchorage is well protected from the prevailing weather, and the same can be said of the neighboring bays of Ancon Nenguange and Bahía Guayraca farther to the W.

A sand-and-silt bottom at 5 fathoms provides a good holding with few swells. Opposite the hacienda at the head of the bay is an attractive mountain stream, which may be explored in the dinghy and is a source of good drinking water. This bay, with its sandy Caribbean beach, seems, however, more like a Scandinavian fjord—with steep slopes and the fleeting scent of pine in the air. To counter the "willywaws" that swirl down unexpectedly from the surrounding heights, we suggest mooring with two anchors on a bridle to avoid doubling over the hook, as the boat may swing in all directions.

Ancon Concha (KSK-3)

has an anchorage bold to the beach, in 8 fathoms and good holding in sand, where there are several small docks and cabanas. A primitive road connects with Santa Marta, and on weekends this is a favorite rendezvous for local yachtsmen.

With snowcapped Mount Cristóbal Colón scarcely 25 miles away, you can expect land breezes and downright cool evenings. The northers that are seasonally common to this coast of South America are seldom experienced here. The SE section of this bay is generally free from swells.

Isla de la Aguja (24491, KSK-3)

is a barren, windswept island 3 miles W of Ancon Concha, inhabited only by wild goats. It resembles a mesa on the Arizona desert. A landing may be made on the small beach on the NW (lee) side, a spot that is also frequented by the *contrabandistos.*

This island is mentioned not for its anchorage, however, but for the Pasaje La Mesa (Table Passage) on its S side. Many a small eastbound vessel has pounded its caulking loose trying to fight the strong current and rips in order to round the N end of this island, only because they did not have a chart of the convenient passage. Even if the passage looks rough, don't change your mind at the last moment. There is sufficient depth—18 feet on the S side of Mesa Rock, which lies in the center of this channel, and deeper water on the N side of that rock. The current may be running in either direction, so approach under power at 5 knots or more on a due E or due W heading through the center of either channel. Although the surf on the cliffy W side of Isla Aguja may be disconcerting, have faith in those who have sailed through here before you; this passage is safe even in rough weather.

Santa Marta (24492),

a large banana port and tourist resort, still retains its colonial charm despite the recent high-rise and cement-jungle invasion. In any conditions, this port is easily accessible, even at night, and is well protected from the weather at all times.

Upon entry, proceed to a berth along the southeast dock; if no space is available, anchor 100 yards S of this bulkhead in 2 fathoms. Even though you may have cleared the yacht at Ríohacha, you must show all your papers and obtain a fresh clearance if you come in here. There is usually no charge during normal office hours, but the officials prefer to board at the dock.

Water is available, but fuel must be ordered for delivery to the dock in drums or by tank truck. The ice-delivery truck will be found only after diligent inquiry. Ten blocks E of the beach on Calle #11 is a large city market that offers a variety of tropical fruits, vegetables, and meats. The old cathedral, downtown plaza, and balconied colonial homes are all within strolling distance of the scenic beach boulevard.

Caution: This place has an almost universal reputation for burglary, especially the "swim-aboard" type. Be extremely vigilant after dark and secure all deck gear, particularly outboard motors. Sleep below with hatches secured so a sneak entry can be detected. Have a horn and flare gun handy, with a switch for the spreader lights nearby.

Crossing the Mouth of the Río Magdalena (24491)

presents an obstacle to all who pass along this coast. Having traversed this bumpy and sometimes treacherous piece of water at least a score of times, in all seasons and in good and bad weather, we advise staying offshore at least 4 miles in

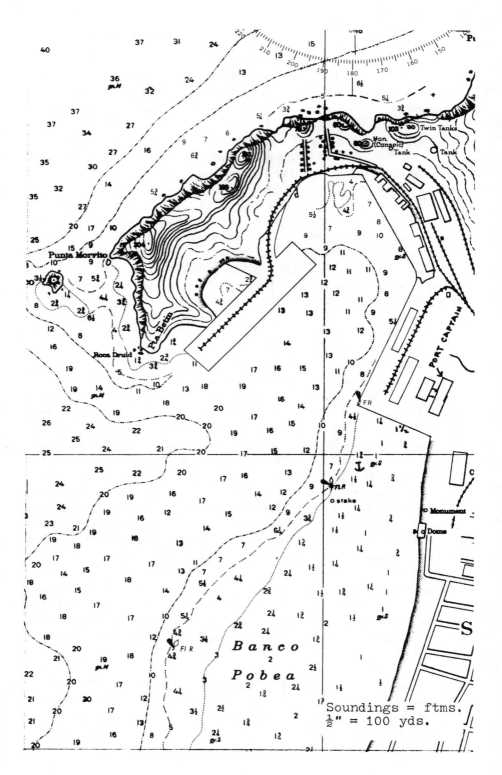

Santa Marta, Colombia

daylight and 8 miles at night. Why be uncomfortably wet, or needlessly slat about in the usually steep rollers closer in? The possibility of haze, which rises off the marshes; the lowness of the terrain; the unreliability of the navigational lights— all combine to make your piloting more difficult than might appear from the charts. Waterlogged debris, including huge trees barely awash, represents the greatest hazard during the rainy season, or during the night at any time. If you have a choice, we recommend crossing just after daylight, when it tends to be calm and you can see and avoid these floating menaces.

Barranquilla (24502)

is visited by yachts not for its charm but for the convenience of its facilities as a port along a difficult coast. We would normally avoid this haven; it is a detour, and there are complications in entering the mouth of the Magdalena (it is very fast-flowing). But on the other hand, there are the advantages of cranes for lifting smaller vessels onto the pier for hull repairs, drive-on pier service for speedy removal of an engine directly to a repair shop, international agencies with stocks of repair parts, and generally good facilities for hull and machinery repairs.

The city is large, dusty, relatively new, and devoid of character. The two yacht clubs, Club Náutico Barranquilla and Club de Pesca, are cordial to visitors, but docking facilities are limited, and then only for 5-foot draft or less. Yachts usually have no alternative but to use the high-walled and dirty commercial docks. Anchorage in the river is dangerous and strictly not recommended. The river traffic is heavy and hectic, since the "bongo" boat helmsmen do not always observe the rules of the road. Beware of bumboats and pilferage, and never leave your yacht unguarded.

Do not be tempted to take overnight shelter outside the entrance to leeward of the western breakwater, which appears, by the chart, to offer protection. The soundings are very unreliable.

Entering the mouth of the Magdalena should be attempted only when you know you have sufficient daylight to see you all the way to the city. This mightiest of rivers on the Spanish Main is compressed at the entrance to less than half a mile from seawall to breakwater, so the convulsions of the water at this point are understandable. Close all ports and hatches and secure loose gear. You can expect waves to break completely over the deck when you enter the breakwater, depending on river height, current, sea temperature, and the phase of the tide. Small craft should favor the east seawall on a straight, speedy approach—and never, never try to turn in the steep troughs. Do not depend on the range lights.

Once inside the breakwaters, be prepared for a current of 3 to 5 knots. The flow of water is tremendous, although the wave action is reduced. In any case, the 10-mile run upriver to Barranquilla will be a memorable experience of dodging driftwood, trees, floating hyacinth "islands," and other assorted debris.

Enter Barranquilla flying the Q flag, dock where you can, and then ask for a berthing assignment. Expect to show your papers in the port captain's office.

Taxi service from the docks to downtown should be reasonably priced, especially if you speak Spanish. There are several nice restaurants: the Yacht Club and the fashionable Del Prado Hotel are among them.

Puerto Colombia (24503)

formerly bustled with steamer traffic, before the mouth of the Río Magdalena was dredged to enable big ships to reach Barranquilla. The majestic four-track railway pier still dominates the port, although it's now ravaged by time. Puerto Colombia has become a resort town; vacationers stroll along this pier, which strangely seems to move farther and farther inland each year. In fact the entire shoreline has silted in considerably. Even the large, charted island of Isla Verde has completely vanished since we first anchored here 29 years ago. Punta Velilla and its light tower have also disappeared, and only the curling, white breakers in rough weather indicate where they once were.

At best, this is a rolly anchorage, but in moderate weather temporary anchorage may be taken in 3 fathoms, 50 yards S of former Punta Velilla. A steamer wreck, barely awash, lies 1,700 yards WSW of the pier head.

Punta Las Canoas (24504)

is mentioned only as a refuge from the ferocious afternoon winds and steep chop or, at most, as an emergency overnight stop. The open roadstead is subject to swells but does offer some shelter from the prevailing weather. We have anchored here many a time for a few hours' pause when beating up the coast from Cartagena to Santa Marta. Take great care in approaching Punta Canoas in poor visibility, because the water N of the point has shoaled considerably since the last hydrographic survey. The light here, as well as Punta Hermano light, is occasionally not operating.

Boca Chica (24505)

is the only entrance to Cartagena Bay safe for strangers. Guarding the narrows are the formidable strongholds of Castilla San José and Fortaleza San Fernando, which are visited daily by excursion boats from Cartagena, 9 miles away. Adjacent to Fortaleza San Fernando, on Isla Tierra Bomba, is a beach and refreshment area. Still another fort, Castel Angelo, in poor repair, is located on the hill 500 yards to the north.

Anchor in 4 fathoms 100 yards SW of the pilot-boat dock at Boca Chica village. Since the sand and mud bottom provides only fair holding, you had best put out a second hook if the wind is strong. There is no objection to anchoring for a short time closer to Fort San Fernando, but the greater depth involves a lot more scope. Incidentally, much of the Marlon Brando movie *La Quemada* was filmed at this fort.

Boca Chica village is perhaps best known for the *canoas* built here with adze and cross saw; they are widely used in river and coastwise trade. This double-ended, distinctly Colombian vessel is beamy and of shallow draft. Some are large enough to carry 150,000 coconuts and a crew of 10. Many schooner-rigged *canoas* line the picturesque inner harbor of Cartagena and engage in coastwise trade with the people of the San Blas Islands.

Cartagena (24505)

"of the Indies" was for several centuries the most important Spanish port in the New World, and certainly the most heavily fortified city. The spacious, thoroughly protected anchorages within the bay could comfortably accommodate the largest sailing vessels. Moreover, its strategic location made it the ideal western base for the Plate Fleet sent from Spain every other year to gather the riches of the Indies. Here the galleons could be careened for repairs in perfect safety, and the fleet regrouped after taking delivery of its precious cargo at Porto Bello. Here, too, the fleet was able to establish a suitable windward position for the close-hauled passage to the Yucatán Straits.

Cartagena must be entered through the Boca Chica Channel. The wider Boca Grande entrance is shallow and studded with submerged rocks, the remnants of a seawall built for defense purposes two centuries ago. Actually, there is an obscure, 9-foot-deep channel through here about midway between the two points of land, but with murky water. However, it is narrow and too risky to warrant describing.

Proceed to Cartagena's inner harbor, favoring a route close to the naval base on Boca Grande peninsula, then turn right when the yacht club bears due E. This L turn will avoid a 6-foot shoal SW of old Fort Pastilello (now the attractive dining terrace of the Club de Pesca).

Most yachts prefer to dock at the club. However, if no berth is available, anchor W of the club, where the bottom is mud and debris, with only fair holding. Use two anchors for the heavy blows that may be expected January through March, or the occasional *chocosana* in the summer months. Fly your Q flag and request the *jefe de muelle,* dockmaster at the Club de Pesca, to telephone for the clearance officials.

The Club de Pesca and its Grandee Board of Governors are particularly hospitable to yachtsmen. Diesel, gasoline, water, ice, and shallow-draft haul-out facilities are all here. Other supplies, including bottled gas, can be ordered for delivery to the dock. For major repairs, the Colombian naval base has machine and electric shops (for balancing propellers and regrinding armatures, for instance) and also a huge marine railway that we have used for years. However, they are now less inclined to haul yachts. A new establishment, Compañía Vikingos de Colombia, at Mamonal on the southeast side of Cartagena Harbor, is operated by the veteran yachtsman José (Pepino) Moggolon, who has always been most cordial to visitors. This yard, which caters to fishing vessels and yachts, has a modern machine shop, shipwrights, sandblaster, and facilities for hauling six vessels to 140 tons. Contact may be made by phone from Club de Pesca.

The walled city of Cartagena, 15 minutes' walk from the Club de Pesca, has

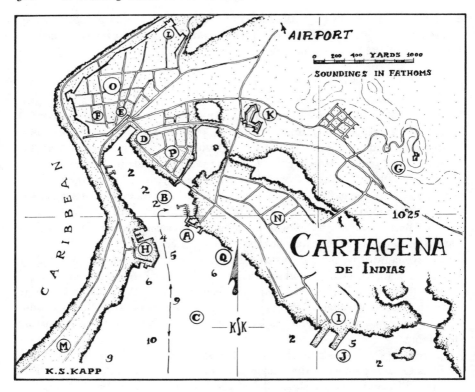

Key to city of Cartagena: (A) Club de Pesca; (B) Yacht anchorage; (C) Ship anchorage (restricted); (D) Public market; (E) Old Clock Gate; (F) San Pedro Claver church; (G) La Popa convent; (H) Naval base; (I) Customs; (J) Commercial docks; (K) Fort San Felipe; (L) Fort Tenaza and old dungeons; (M) Boca Grande, a residential suburb; (N) Manga, another residential suburb; (O) Old city; (P) Gethsemane; (Q) Restaurant

preserved much of its colonial charm. In particular, don't miss the cathedral, the Clock Gate, the church of San Pedro Claver, the Plaza de la Aduana, and the Palace of the Inquisition, now a museum, which faces Plaza Bolívar.

This heroic city endured many a battle for its survival. In 1543 it was sacked by the Frenchman Robert Baal's corsairs while the treasure fleet was assembling to sail for Spain. Then came Martin Cote, followed in 1586 by the much feared Sir Francis Drake, who started to burn the city block by block until the ransom he demanded was paid. Eleven years later, the French Baron de Pointis looted the city with 9,000 buccaneers. Thus many a good ship has gone to the bottom of this harbor, especially during the War of Jenkins's Ear.

The dungeons and high ramparts of the majestic fortress of San Felipe, which so courageously withstood Admiral Vernon's three-month siege in 1741, are within walking distance of the Club de Pesca. La Popa monastery, a fascinating place to visit, dominates the skyline 1½ miles to the E and is a conspicuous landmark for many miles at sea, as are the new high-rises on Boca Grande.

Cartagena has a number of fashionable restaurants, featuring *de la costa* cuisine. Most notable of the time-tested establishments specializing in fresh seafood are: Capilla del Mar and Club de Pesca, the latter renowned for its *pargo a la cosquera,* a red snapper broiled in wine sauce. Among the newer restaurants serving fine foods in a pleasant atmosphere are: La Fragata, Arabe, La Escollera, El Galeón, and La Quemada; all are within 10 minutes by taxi from the yacht club. This small but cosmopolitan city stages numerous colorful events, such as the annual film festival and religious fiestas.

Cartagena to Zapzurro

El Dique Canal (24511, KSK-4)

connects Cartagena with Colombia's mighty Río Magdalena at Calamar. This waterway, 62 nautical miles long, begins at the bottom of the bay, at Punta Pascaballo, and was first opened to navigation in 1650 by Don Pedro Zapata. By 1726 it had silted so badly that traffic was restricted to canoes. After a long history of widening and dredging, El Dique was opened to 500-ton vessels in 1903, although the channel, lined with mangroves and interlocking lagoons, has shallowed to 8½ feet in some sections.

Today, with ever-increasing commercial traffic, project dimensions call for a width of 260 feet and a depth of 8—but from time to time, when the water is low in the Magdalena, the "guaranteed" depth is only 6 feet. In 1970 we found only 6 feet on the sand bar at Pasa Cabellos, where one enters the canal at the Cartagena end. There are two bridges, one near Pasa Cabellos and the other about midway, each having a vertical clearance of 49 feet.

If you're passaging against the trades, this bypass from Cartagena can save a yacht a nasty dusting while working some 70 miles to windward to the mouth of Río Magdalena.

Islas del Rosario (24511, KSK-4)

are an attractive group of islands only a few hours by boat from the metropolis of Cartagena, where a yachtsman could spend an enjoyable week or more fishing, skin diving, and exploring the lovely coves of these enchanting, palm-fringed islands. From time to time for over a decade, we've enjoyed gunkholing and hydrographic surveying in these sparkling, clear waters. Another cruising man, Dick Johnson of the schooner *Migrant,* sums it up neatly: "The Rosarios offer the visiting yachtsman a mini–South Sea experience without having to leave the Caribbean."

The Rosarios are a popular weekend retreat for businessmen from Bogotá and

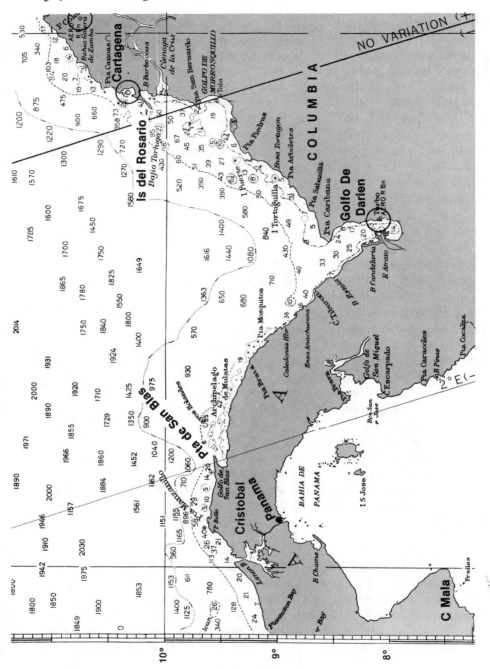

Cartagena to Panama Canal

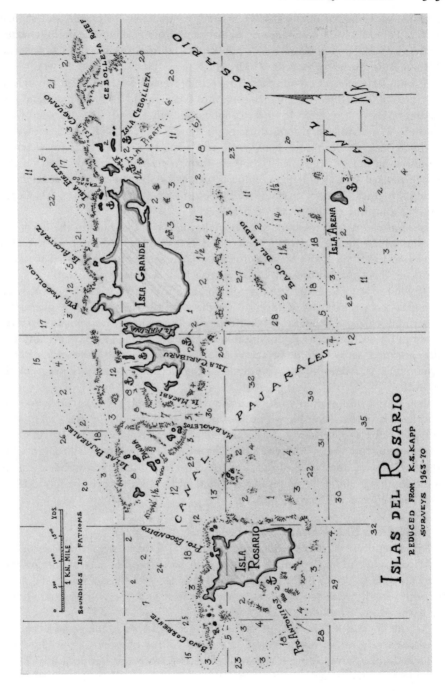

ISLAS DEL ROSARIO

REDUCED FROM K.S.KAPP

SURVEYS 1963-70

are also renowned as a sportfishing ground, particularly for marlin and sailfish. J. V. ("Pepino") Mogollon has written an account of his technique in these waters entitled *Sailfishing in Cartagena,* published (in English) by the Corporación Nacional de Turismo, Bogotá, 1972.

From Cartagena, approach these low-profile islands with sufficient daylight to navigate the Canal Rosario, which separates Isla Grande from the mainland area of Punta Baru. The reef, Arrecife Cebolleta, which extends 1½ miles E of Isla Grande, is not so easily defined as might appear from Chart 24511. However, proceed on a SW course for Isla Arena, and when Isla Tesora light tower comes in line with the W tip of Isla Cebolleta, turn to starboard and proceed on that range toward Isla Cebolleta, keeping a watch for the few isolated coral heads along this track. Anchor over the sandy bottom about 100 yards S of Isla Cebolleta, or continue to the S side of Isla Pirata.

Several secure and reasonably deep anchorages will be found in the lee of Isla Fiesta, which lies between the N shore of Isla Grande and the barrier reef to seaward. Enter from the S through Pirata Channel, which is limited to 6-foot draft, or from the N through Canal Seco, which will carry 7½ feet.

If you are approaching the Rosarios from the SW, the W coast of Isla Rosario presents a convenient anchorage, although there may be a little roll during the December-to-April dry season. Isla Rosario has some lovely beaches, but to move close in for secure anchorages, you'll need Chart KSK-4. This is especially true for entering Puerto Antonio on the W side of Isla Rosario, or for reaching Puerto Escondido, a delightful and thoroughly protected port on the N shore of the island.

Isla Caribaru is dotted with picturesque cottages and provides attractive anchorages in Bahía Macabi, where the quiet is broken only by the putt-putt of generators on the weekends. In good light this area is easily reached via Canal Marmoleto from the S. Approach on course 010°T, then turn to starboard when Punta Obregon, the N tip of Isla Caribaru, bears E. Bahía Macabi is spacious, with depths of 90 feet. Anchorages of the gunkhole variety will be found SE of Isla Macabi and in Puerto Caribaru.

Islas San Bernadinos (24512)

offers several comfortable, roll-free anchorages. A bay on the lee side of Isla Tintipan is the most popular and could even be entered by moonlight. Anchor here about 200 yards S of the eastern beach in 15 feet, where there is good holding in white sand. Moor too close to shore, however, and you will become victims of carnivorous sandflies!

To the W, and within view of this anchorage, is Islote, a village island of 250 souls, scarcely an acre in size and crammed full of chickens, dogs, pigs, and thatched huts. How strange it is that these natives from a primitive culture prefer to crowd together when there is so much unoccupied land all around. Their chief occupations are fishing, mostly for conch, and hollowing out log canoes by adze.

The San Bernadino Islands, now so pleasantly quiet and insignificant, were featured on a 1681 Dutch chart by Johan van Keulen as a haven for the corsairs who lay in wait for the treasure fleets sailing between Cartagena and Porto Bello.

Isla Fuerte (24512, 24514)

is frequently used as a rest stop, until the wind abates, by the large *canoas,* schooner rigged and double ended, making their passage from the San Blas coast laden with coconuts. Unlike the rather dry San Bernadino cays with their mangroves, this island evidently enjoys heavier rainfall and is correspondingly lush, green, and typically tropical. In a short stroll ashore, you will see trees of guava, sugar apple, Spanish plum *(Spondias purpurea),* coco sea plum, papaya, almond, and sea grape.

If you are approaching by night, head NW toward the light tower and anchor in 15 feet about 300 yards from shore. There is a light swell and a current that sets NE, but you can expect considerable protection from the winter winds.

Puerto Limón is a settlement of some 300 persons living in thatch-roofed houses, many with wattle walls and portways with swinging half doors. The village supports a small boat-repair industry, and occasionally a large vessel is built on the beach. A limited variety of fruit may be purchased.

Tortuguilla (24514)

is a tiny island like Robinson Crusoe's, but is a distinctive landmark along an otherwise nondescript coast; that is undoubtedly why it was noted on the early charts. Only a stone's throw wide, the island is flat and studded with towering coco palms, but there are no sandy beaches. We have anchored here several times, 100 yards off the E shore, and found current eddies that make the water confused at times. Otherwise the current sets steadily NW.

Laguna Aguila (24515, KSK-5)

offers a landlocked, uninhabited anchorage in a maze of mangroves. This place is a paradise for bird lovers. Strangely enough, the "bug menace," which usually applies to mangrove swamps, does not seem to be too troublesome here.

Access is limited, since the channel into the lagoon shallows to 6 feet just off Punta Negro, a sand spit.

Note that Punta Aguila and the dangerous shoals that extend 5 miles off this point have sent many a vessel to a watery grave. We recommend circumventing this reef. Even in light weather, a misty haze may obscure the hills of Cerro de Aguila, which are your best landmarks for determining distance offshore.

There is a rather shallow passage inside the reef close to Punta Aguila, but we do not recommend it, due to the vagaries of wind, current, and tide—and especially the murky water all about this coast. If you must try this channel, which we found shallows to 12 feet, the easiest entrance is from the SW.

Bahía de Turbo (24515, KSK-5)

is shallow, although a narrow channel has been dredged partway to the town. The recommended anchorage is in a small cove 600 yards NE of Punta Las Vacas, where diesel, gasoline, and water are dispensed at a dock. The water is so murky that a submerged wreck bordering the E side of the channel is difficult to detect. If your vessel draws over 5 feet, proceed to the basin very slowly, sounding as you go. This is a port of entry; the port captain's launch usually comes alongside to check your papers.

To visit the town of Turbo, take the dinghy N about 1½ miles to the town canal's honkytonk, water-rat setting, the like of which you have never seen before. Dock at the foot of Main Street, where there is a large public market selling fresh meat, vegetables, and ice. Turbo is a rugged frontier town, with unpaved streets shared by transport trucks and horsemen alike. In the commercial bustle, you will see Indians, barefoot *campesinos,* Choco bushmen, wranglers, and ranchers. Meantime, keep an eye on your dinghy!

A 9- to 12-foot-deep channel has lately been dredged from the south end of Punta Las Vacas, extending E to the mangroved mainland, where there is a government docking facility for the tugs and lighters that assist freighters loading bananas in the roadstead.

Bahía Pinololo (24515, KSK-5)

is a picturesque, secluded anchorage, flanked all around by a sandy beach and towering coco palms. On the western side, at the base of a steeply sloping, dense jungle, is an unobtrusive hamlet called Pino Roja.

Isla Los Deseos has a small cottage, the retreat of a Colombian; it is seldom occupied. Around the island reef there is good spear fishing and lobstering. This is a lovely anchorage except from January through March, when a swell usually creeps in. It is untenable, however, in the event of a winter norther.

In this pretty anchorage, we once experienced a *chocosana* that sent our Alden ketch onto the beach. *Chocosana* (also known as *chubasco*) is the local term for a mini-hurricane. We have personally experienced them as far E as Punta Las Canoas and as far W as the Gulf of San Blas. These miniature tropical disturbances, which occur from June through November, give distinct warning of their approach. The *chocosana* usually originates in Choco Province in the early hours of the morning. The telltales are a deathly quiet atmosphere and noiseless lightning flashes in the S. When you observe these signs, set out two or more anchors, expecting to be blown in any direction, and ready a larger hook on deck as a standby. Keep a watch for a sound like Niagara Falls approaching. When it hits, with winds of hurricane force, use the engine to ease the strain on any one of the anchors. The rain will be blinding. The duration is about 15 minutes, usually not long enough to build up a large sea—but it seems like an age.

Incidentally, if a *chocosana* catches you at sea, take down *every* sail, or they'll be blown to shreds. The vessel will heel right over, even under bare sticks.

Maintaining steerageway is not really important, as the front will pass through very quickly. These violent but short-lived storms occasionally range as far as Cartagena and along the San Blas coast, appearing before or shortly after daybreak.

Zapzurro (24515, KSK-5)

is an obscure little keyhole-shaped harbor and, like the Z in its name, is the last anchorage in Colombia when going westward. Quite naturally, it is a port of entry, and the customs office here handles a considerable amount of paper in clearing the coastwise coconut carriers.

The harbor entrance is deep, but frequently subjected to huge swells. Keep to the center when entering and turn N to anchor in 3 fathoms, sandy bottom, E of the dock. If you already have a Republic of Colombia *zarpe,* don't fly the Q flag. Present your papers ashore to the port captain, explaining you just stopped in Zapzurro to enjoy a rest, and they will probably not bother to issue new papers.

A pleasant walk N of the customs office will bring you to a saddle on the ridge with a good view of the Caribbean. A plinth there marks the frontier with Panama, agreed to in 1921.

Back in town is a charming *cantina* serving cold beer to barefoot *campesinos,* and a general store with a genuine Butch Cassidy atmosphere of the Old West. This is truly the Republic of Colombia's *frontera.*

Chapter Fifteen

PANAMA AND THE SAN BLAS COAST

BY KIT S. KAPP

Rodrigo de Bastidas, in 1501, was the first of the busy Conquistadores to discover the San Blas coast, during the feverish search for a water route to the East Indies. Christopher Columbus, who arrived the following year, noted in his log that the islands, which he named Las Cativas, were more numerous than the days of the year, which proved to be a nearly accurate appraisal.

Panama, a mystical-sounding name derived from an Indian word meaning "abundance of fish," with which the waters on the Pacific side still abound, is a land of lofty, verdant mountains, rolling savannas, and luxuriant rain forests. Much of that can be seen while you are cruising along the shores of the isthmus. Nowhere else along the coasts of the Americas, in the Atlantic or Pacific, can a yachtsman see at such close range the high summits of the Continental Divide. In fact, two characteristic peaks in the Darien Cordillera—Obo Yala, rising to 5,000 feet, and Ella Popa, slightly lower—are imposing landmarks for the coast-wise navigator.

Panama has maintained a strategic position ever since Vasco Nuñez de Balboa crossed the isthmus from San Blas in 1513 to discover what was then called the great South Sea. Verbally he took formal possession of "all the lands and islands bordering upon the sea . . . for our Sovereign of Castile and Léon till the day of judgment." Rather an ambitious claim even in those days of speculative imperialism! However, Spanish sovereignty over Darien proved to be a futile claim, for nowhere else in North or Central America have the indigenous people held more continuous control of their land. The fact is that the Kuna Indians, who have inhabited this country ever since history began here, have never been conquered and are today unique in having maintained tribal customs by openly opposing the inroads of civilization.

All who have seen the San Blas Islands have been captivated by the profusion of coconut palms, white-sand beaches, unexplored coral reefs, and luxuriant jungle spreading to the water's edge. The cruising yachtsman will appreciate the lack of commercialism, the clarity of the water, and the many opportunities for deep-water gunkholing. (Note that anything over 15 feet is deep in our book!)

The Kuna Indians are thought to be the last of the full-blooded Carib strain that inhabited the Caribbean before the Spanish conquest. The women are spec-

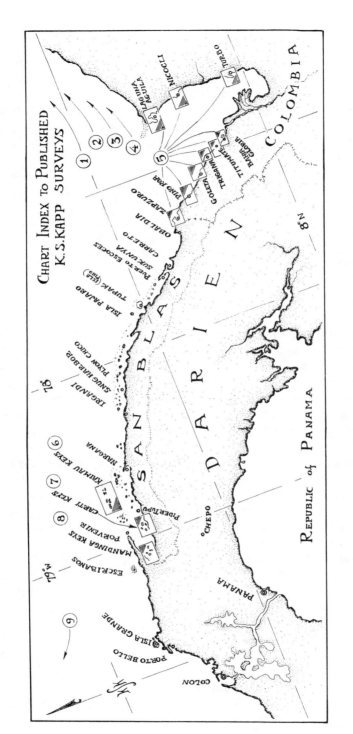

The San Blas coast (see Appendix B for Kapp charts indicated here)

tacularly attired in gold jewelry, red-and-yellow cotton headdresses, sarong-type skirts, and the multicolored *mola* blouses. The front and back panels of the *molas* have become a popular souvenir of primitive art, used for home decor in the United States and Europe, and most visitors to the San Blas Islands are tempted to purchase a *mola* or two. The Kunas consider a bright, new *mola* to be more valuable than a worn and faded one, although from an aesthetic point of view an older *mola* may be superior in both design and workmanship. Today the more modern, acculturated designs are growing in popularity with the Kuna women, although traditional motifs featuring flora, fauna, and geometric designs are still prevalent. In making your choice, a rule of thumb for judging the quality of a *mola* is to compare these basic points: (1) design, (2) color with balance and harmony, and (3) workmanship. A detailed treatise of this subject will be found in the publication *Mola Art,* by this writer, available at bookstores in Panama and the U.S.

San Blas Etiquette

The San Blas people have been accustomed to sailing and trading vessels visiting their islands for many years and are quite friendly toward strangers, providing the strangers follow the unwritten rules of the territory. However, don't feel slighted if some Kunas seem to show a studied indifference to you; it is part of their impassive nature. Others may appear to you to be too "pushy," especially the women, who often approach visiting vessels in dugout canoes and will clamber aboard, without invitation, to try to sell their *molas* and trinkets. Be patient, be firm, and laugh in face of argument, for you will find they respond well to a sense of humor.

Upon entering a village, strangers should go first to the Congress House and introduce themselves to the *saila,* the chief, or to one of the secondary chiefs, for the traditional approval to visit the village. Just speak up—there is bound to be someone about who knows some English or Spanish, even though the local language is, of course, Kuna. Additional permission should be obtained if you intend to remain ashore after dark.

The San Blas islanders lead an idyllic life. They divide work equally between men and women, which affords ample time for handicrafts, for relaxation at the end of the day, and for talking over village affairs. The crime rate is unbelievably low, due to religious and traditional beliefs, so there are no jails. Furthermore, the islanders live so close to one another that they take a keen interest in watching everyone else and their movements about the village, especially those of the *wakas,* or strangers. The *suaribeti* are plainclothes policemen who will not hesitate to snatch an offender off to the Congress Hall for swift but democratic justice. For minor offenses, this usually involves only a stiff fine, but for more serious cases, such as smuggling marijuana, the culprit is turned over to the Guardia Nacionál for a second trial in Panamanian courts.

Life in the islands for the most part is easygoing and relaxing, as we have said, but there are a few rules of the territory to bear in mind. For instance: never, but *never,* help yourself to coconuts, even though you may see some lying on the ground on an uninhabited island. Coconuts are the mainstay of economic life in the San Blas, and *all* of them should be purchased. Coconut thievery in these islands is considered nearly as bad as horse thievery was in the Old West. Another point: if a village has red flags flying or posted at the dock, it strictly means do not enter, or you will be subject to a heavy fine. In such cases the village is undergoing a *nia*-exorcising ritual (*nia* means devil), which may last up to 10 days.

Photographing an Indian or his village may require special permission, which usually involves a fee. The Kuna have a traditionally negative superstition about the photographing of their persons, so be discreet with your camera. Usually an offer of 10¢ or so per person for a series of shots will remove the shy hesitation of photogenic subjects! On the other hand, snapshots of scenery that may catch an Indian or two in the foreground are not chargeable.

One can hardly fail to enjoy cruising in tropical waters of such exceptional beauty. In addition, there is an unusual opportunity to observe at close hand a life-style entirely different from your own, one that contains much to be admired and respected.

Entry Procedures

Procedures for entering the Republic of Panama are rather cumbersome, and the distinction must be recognized between the republic itself and the Comarca de San Blas, which is the semiautonomous Kuna Indian territory. As explained later (see Porvenir, page 379), separate permission is required to cruise the San Blas Islands.

When entering Panama, you are expected to produce the following papers:

1. *Zarpe,* or clearance document, from your last foreign port, designating your port of entry in Panama, which should be Obaldía or Colón.

2. *Lista de trabajandos,* or crew list.

3. *Lista de ranchos,* or inventory of food stores.

4. *Lista de pasajeros,* a passenger list—but all persons aboard a yacht are normally listed in some crew capacity, so simply state "No pasajeros."

5. *Aviso de yates y lista de carga* provides for listing the vessel's particulars. This should include: name, official number, flag, radio call sign, captain's name, tonnage, where from, and where bound, plus the statement "No lleve carga" to signify "Carrying no cargo."

These documents should be typed in Spanish and in triplicate, and signed and dated by the master. If this all seems too complicated, then hire an agent upon the port captain's advice.

There is a small charge made for cruising permits, depending on the size of your vessel. Charges are usually higher when permits are issued outside normal working hours (evenings, weekends, and holidays)—if the officials are willing to open the office at all. Special clearance to cruise the San Blas Islands, obtainable from the *intendencia* at Porvenir, should be issued without charge during office hours. However, a charge may be made when entering at Obaldía, the eastern end of San Blas.

Charts

The San Blas coast E of 78°W is inadequately charted both as to scale and coverage. The coastline E of 78°09′W is taken from a small-scale Spanish chart of 1817, and BA1278 is needed to fill most of the gap in the small-scale coverage of this area by U.S. charts. This British chart, albeit on a scale of 1:200,000, substantially covers the coastal section between Charts 24514 and 26061.

Obaldía to Tup-Pak (Isla Pino) (BA1278)

Obaldía (24514)

is a miserable anchorage at best, but an unavoidable one because it is an obligatory port of entry for those who intend to cruise the San Blas en route to Cristóbal.

After spotting the few roofs camouflaged among the palms, approach the anchorage in range SE toward the beach S of the town in order to avoid the reef that juts out westerly from the offices of the port captain and the Guardia. Feel your way in among the several schooner-rigged *goletas* that are usually anchored in the best spots. The sand-mud bottom at 4 fathoms provides reasonable holding, but it is advisable to use two anchors to reduce the risk of dragging on a short scope in the heavy swells.

The ideal mooring position is closer to the beach in 3 fathoms, just S of the town-creek mouth, where the roll is less. The cove appears wide open, but is used throughout the winter by local coasters, which must come here for clearance. The winter rollers are tremendous and would make anchoring impossible, except for the fact that the wind is generally light in the roadstead.

Put up your Q and Panamanian courtesy flags, and wait to be boarded by the port officials—but don't expect any action on Sundays or holidays. Obtain if you can a stamped endorsement of your *zarpe,* signifying approval of entry into the Republic of Panama and thereby postponing the formality of a cruising permit until you reach Cristóbal/Colon.

The territory of San Blas begins 1 mile W of Obaldía and extends through to Porvenir, about 110 miles away.

Carreto (BA1278)

is a commodious bay where, in 1510, Nuñez de Balboa befriended the Indian chief Carreta, and took his daughter for a wife. Today, descendants of the same Kuna live in Carreto village, which is nestled among giant palm trees.

Do not enter the village or the river unless you are invited. The Indians in this part of the San Blas shun strangers and have been known to shoot at anyone "toting" coconuts. Be sure to read our previous section on Kuna etiquette before attempting to trespass onto San Blas cultivations, rivers, or villages. Best to befriend a Kuna man and ask him to show you around ashore. A pack or two of cigarettes should do the trick.

The bay has a wide mouth and is easy to enter despite the caution in the U.S. chart about the Carreto Shoals. The writer has extensively surveyed this coast and found a least depth of 3 fathoms on the shoals, which break in rough weather. Upon entry, select an anchorage well up into the lee of the NW point, where there is good holding in sand and silt in 3 fathoms 100 yards from shore. A slight swell may enter the anchorage even during the quiet summer and fall.

Looking SW from the anchorage you will observe a low section of the Darien mountain range. This is Carreto Pass, which Balboa traversed on his memorable expedition to discover the Pacific Ocean in 1513.

Puerto Escocés (26041)

is entered by bearing SE around Patterson Hill and Point, which stand out distinctly against the distant hills of the inner bay. A reasonably quiet anchorage will be found immediately ESE of Fort Saint Andrew Point in 4 fathoms.

You will see the Kuna village of Sukunya bearing ENE, where remnants have been found of the moat built by Scottish colonials in 1699 under the direction of William Patterson, financial wizard and cofounder of the Bank of England. A score of books have been written about this fantastic two-year venture; one title, *The Disaster of Darien,* by Russel Hart, best sums up the only attempt the Scots ever made to colonize in America.

A quiet, down-to-nature anchorage can be found deep in the bay in the lee of Cullen's Islands, but unless there is a breeze, the sand fleas may disturb your sleep. Also, the wild-animal calls that come out of the darkness add to the drama of the jungle surroundings. Beware—don't swim here; the writer has been chased on two different occasions by an 18-foot "macho" crocodile, named Charlie by an IAGS survey crew. Special behavior in the Comarca de San Blas dictates that you respect nature and don't try to molest Charlie. The people of Sukunya, a nearby village, believe his untimely death would release malevolent spirits, and besides, their *tiolele* (god) would be greatly displeased. Where else in the Caribbean does a yachtsman have the chance to see a granddaddy crocodile in the wild?

Tup-Pak, or Isla Pino (BA1278),

is an anchorage that was used by none other than Sir Francis Drake, in 1572, when he lay here to stage his surprise attack on the Spanish gold port of Nombre de Dios. He called the anchorage "Port Plentie" and noted that it was a fine watering place with an abundance of pines for making ship repairs. Later, privateers Basil Ringrose and John Esquemeling (see Esquemeling's *Buccaneers of America,* written in 1684 and republished by Dover Publications, Inc., New York) wrote in their journals that the best landfall when sailing for the coast of Darien was to sight the Isle of Pines and lie in peaceful haven there. The Kuna call the island Tup-Pak, meaning "whale island;" it resembles a whale in profile.

Approach the island from the SE and come in on Point Mami Mulu, the low

SW point of Tup-Pak. Beware of a submerged rock, difficult to detect, one half mile S of the SE point.

A delightful, protected anchorage will be found in 3 fathoms off Mami Mulu, an attractive beach with a small village. Fresh drinking water may be obtained from a spring a short walk into the coconut grove. The channel between Tup-Pak and the low-lying mangroves on the mainland is navigable for vessels drawing up to 6 feet. Freshly baked Kuna bread can usually be obtained at Tup-Pak village, 1 mile to the N.

Tup-Pak to Plyón Chico (BA1278)

This route skirts approximately 60 miles of coastline dotted with tiny islands and hundreds of uncharted reefs. The writer has conducted 10 years of hydrographic surveying in this area and expects to publish the charts in 1989. Meantime, it is hardly possible to explain safe passage among the reefs without those charts.

In general, the treacherous barrier reefs, not always visible, extend up to 6 miles offshore. We suggest departing at daybreak, circling to the S of Tup-Pak, and giving Pajaro Tupu (Isla Pajaro) a berth of at least 1 mile to port. Take the blue-water route to the NW, maintaining a comfortable distance outside the reefs and arriving at Snug Harbor, the beginning of the upper San Blas, before sundown.

Upper San Blas Islands (26061)

Snug Harbor (26042),

a spacious landlocked anchorage, was a favorite of the Yankee square-rigged merchant ships that came to the San Blas Islands to trade for coconuts and tortoise shells a century ago. Today it is just as delightfully uninhabited. The bay is protected by an assemblage of Ratones Cays, the largest and westernmost being Tia Tupu, so called because fresh water may be obtained by digging a hole several feet into the sand.

Frankie Kilu, who cultivated the coconut grove here and comes from the village of Plyón Chico, 3 miles to the E, told us stories of the windjammers that formerly visited the harbor and of the old vessels wrecked on the coast. His testimony led us to bronze pieces from an ancient wreck on a reef near the village of Irgandi.

Enter Snug Harbor from the W, steering 075°T on the SW point of Tia Tupu. Beware of a submerged and uncharted reef that juts out about 75 yards from the midside of Tia Tupu. Pass Aquadin, the charted reef, close on your starboard side (it breaks in all but a calm sea), then round the SW point into the lee, and anchor most anywhere you please. The holding ground is good and the water deep. Mooring closer than 100 yards to shore here—or, for that matter, any other parts of the coast of Panama—you may attract a few sand fleas in the late afternoon.

Nargana, or Río Diablo Village (26063),

and the island of Corazón de Jesus are connected by a long wicker-and-plank bridge. These two villages, with their contrary names, are an interesting example of the impact of Christianity and its brand of civilization upon the Kuna way of life. In 1920 Anna Coope, using fiery evangelistic tactics, was the first missionary to force the Bible upon this community. So great was her zeal that she brought about insurrections among the villagers, who objected to her teaching such new, non-Indian philosophy to their impressionable children. But today an imposing church, a covered gymnasium, and a cement hot-dog stand are evidence of the accultural evolvement and the Kunas' acceptance of this non-Indian culture.

On an adjacent island, E of Nargana, there is an airport office and a landing strip. Light-commercial air service is maintained daily with Panama City.

Limited supplies of diesel, gasoline, cold beer, and canned goods may be purchased in several shops near the bridge.

The white cement belfry of the church at Corazón de Jesus is easy to spot from seaward. On this mark, enter from the N, passing three picturesque cays on your port hand, which you may care to return to later for a picnic and swim. Favor the channel close to the E side of the villages, and anchor in 4 fathoms due E of the bridge. The mud-sand bottom provides excellent holding ground, and the anchorage is free from swells.

Pider Tupu (26063)

has become a favorite anchorage for visiting yachts. There was formerly a small beach resort on this island, run by a cordial American, Tom Moodie, and his wife. However, the American's claim to this acre-sized isle and years of constant bickering with the elders of the Urgandi Congreso caused a mini-insurrection, and Tom was almost burnt at the stake (a coconut tree on Pider Tupu) by the neighboring Kunas. A lesson can be learned from this event. While the Kunas will tolerate strangers visiting their islands for a short while, they are not prepared for *wakas* (foreigners) to put down roots in the San Blas or engage in business there.

The anchorage, with good sandy holding ground, is on the west side of the island and appears to be open to the N, but the swells are broken somewhat by an outlying reef just to the N.

Visitors arrive from Panama City by daily air service. The gravel airstrip lies 3 miles S of Pider Tupu and may be handy for flying into the "big city" for a desperately needed replacement part, help for a sick crew member, or for a change of crew. The fare is about $65 round trip, and the single-engine flight over the cloudy Continental Divide is a thrill to remember.

The village of Urgandi (Río Siedra) is 1½ miles S of Pider Tupu, where fresh bread, canned food, and the usual Kuna supplies may be found, including (depending on the season) plantains, coconuts, breadfruit, limes, bananas, pineapples, and, without doubt, the finest avocados to be found anywhere.

Carti Keys (26063, KSK-7)

are a group of seven inhabited islands representing the largest concentration of Kuna life in Panama. There's a constant stream of sailing *cayucos* and coastal chuggers engaged in agrarian commerce, and it might be said that this is the metropolis of the San Blas. Although a number of cement structures have been built here, the traditional Indian culture generally prevails. The making and selling of *molas,* and the wearing of gold nose rings and *wini* leg bands are typical of the women's way of life in this unique matriarchal society. Strangers to this group of islands are tolerated, if not welcomed.

Approach the Carti Keys from any direction, since the reefs can be distiguished in good light. The waters of the anchorage are surprisingly clear, considering the close proximity of numerous muddy rivers along this coast. The most accessible anchorage is 80 yards due S of the island of Yan Tupu, where the sand and coral bottom at 3 fathoms or more provides very good holding, free from swells.

A visit to the San Blas Islands wouldn't be complete without ascending at least one of the larger rivers to experience the awesome nature of the jungle and to see the wildlife and the Indian cultivations. Permission or, better still, a young Kuna guide is required before you enter the Carti Tummadi River with your dinghy. The water hole, where the villagers obtain their drinking water in calabashes and plastic jugs, is at the end of the navigable section of the river. Just before the water hole is the spectacular "washing" beach, where visitors may do their laundry alongside jovial women bathing and washing their *molas.*

Mandinga Keys, or Robeson Islands (26064, KSK-8),

are a group of nine islands and numerous detached reefs offering a multitude of picturesque and roll-free anchorages. Here are good spearfishing, lobstering, or just plain snorkeling in the relatively clear, protected waters of the Gulf of San Blas.

Anchor on the lee (southern) side of most any of the larger reefs, where the holding is good on a sand-coral bottom. The prevailing wind is N, but during the rainy season, from June to December, you may expect the *mandi-purwar,* a local west wind, to grace the anchorage on showery afternoons and evenings. However, this breeze is generally not enough to cause discomfort in the anchorages.

Each year in February, Mandinga is host to a small but colorful regatta. Kuna dugout *cayucos* compete under sail in and around the Mandinga Keys. An adventurous American, John Mann, took kindly to the laid-back life-style of the Kuna people and instigated these San Blas regattas in the 1960s. For a number of years the writer also enjoyed owning and sailing one of the classic race contenders, a 28-foot white cedar log canoe—which afforded much enjoyment.

Tia Tupu in the Holandes, or Kaimau, Cays (26063, KSK-6)

is a favorite yacht anchorage. Drop your hook about 100 yards W of this island, where a few Kuna coconut retrievers live. Here, and on the nearby islands of

Tigre Tupu and Moro Tupu, are some beautiful, small sand beaches. The SW end of Tigre Tupu is especially pleasant for swimming, free of weed and coral. Towering coconut trees gracefully shade the beach. In general, the Holandes Cays have clearer water than anchorages closer to the mainland, because the nearest river mouth is 16 miles away. Closer to the San Blas rivers, especially in the rainy season, the water is more murky.

Porvenir (26064)

is the port of entry for the Comarca de San Blas, or Kuna Indian territory, and is the residence of the *intendente,* who acts as governor and liaison between Panama and the triumvirate Kuna government.

Cruising vessels, even the Kuna coastal carriers, must stop here in any event to show their previous clearance and a crew list, which is all that is required when proceeding eastbound from Cristóbal/Colón to the San Blas. However, on a westbound passage from Obaldía most yachts bypass Porvenir en route to the canal.

On this tiny island, which lies 2 miles E of San Blas Point, is a much-used landing strip providing daily commercial air service to Panama City.

The anchorage just S of the *intendente*'s residence, about 75 yards offshore in 8 fathoms, is well protected in all weather and provides very good holding in sand, free from swells. There are several entry possibilities, somewhat encumbered with dangers, so (for clarity's sake) enter the E channel heading WSW on the S tip of Porvenir, and anchor just clear of the airstrip approach. Marking the S side of the channel is a conspicuous wrecked barge.

Farther W, and easy enough to visit by dinghy, are the island villages of Wichupwala and, beyond that, Nalunega. Both are reasonably cordial. In fact Nalunega once received a government tourist citation for friendliness to visitors.

Porvenir to Colón (26065, 26066)

The Coast from Porvenir to Isla Grande (26065)

is exposed and subject to seas that roll in from the N. We recommend an inside passage westbound—that is, inside the chain of Escribanos Shoals, keeping a comfortable 2 miles or so offshore to take advantage of the westbound current. Closer inshore there is less current and so the best track for eastbound small craft. This coast is navigable in all weather for sturdy vessels, but beware the 2–4 fathom string of shoals, which break with the heavy winter swells. Escribanos Reef itself is now marked with a lighted buoy.

Isla Grande (26066)

has a powerful lighthouse and may be approached at night. The preferred passage is to enter close to the S side of Los Magotes, a remarkable haystack-shaped rock. Turn SW and keep to the center of the Isla Grande Channel, which is deep enough, although the swells in rough weather can be frightening, especially if you are unfortunate enough to be towing a dinghy. The swells diminish as you pass the settlement of Isla Grande. We suggest anchoring 200 yards E of the beach on the SW point, where the sand-mud bottom gives fine holding. The current here usually runs 1 knot to the SW. Bananas, plaintains, limes, and occasionally tomatoes are available in the nearby village of Magote.

This anchorage was frequently used by early navigators taking shelter from adverse weather. Columbus spent 10 days here tending his ships, and named the island Isla Bastimentos. On the SE side of the neighboring Isla San Joaquin is an extremely tranquil, landlocked anchorage.

Cruising to the W, depart through the wide channel W of Isla Grande, favoring a course rather close to shore, where the current is less. There is usually a strong N-to-NE-setting current off Isla Grande. For this reason, we recommend the inside passage.

Porto Bello (26067)

is a spacious yet uniquely snug harbor, flanked on three sides by land and wide open to the W. The unknowing navigator would expect the anchorage to be untenable in case of a wester—but relax, this has simply never happened! In fact, the last turmoil recorded here was the storming of Iron Castle Fort at the harbor mouth in 1741, when Admiral Vernon took Porto Bello, as he had promised, "with six men-of-war only."

Porto Bello has a fantastic past. For nearly two centuries it was the western terminus of the Spanish Plate Fleet. The gold and other treasures of South America were transported here by mule train over the Camino Real from Panama City. Every other year, a large and roisterous fair was held. Cacao, vicuña wool, and quinine were traded for cloth, rice, and furniture that the fleet had brought from Europe. In turn, the armada of galleons stacked their holds with precious metal and set sail back to Spain. In *Buccaneers of America,* John Esquemeling described Porto Bello just prior to Henry Morgan's sacking of the city in 1668:

> The city which bears this name in America is seated in the Province of Costa Rica, under the latitude of ten degrees North, at the distance of fourteen leagues from the Gulf of Darien, and eight westwards from the port called Nombre de Dios. It is judged to be the strongest place that the King of Spain possesses in all the West Indies, excepting two, that is to say Havana and Cartagena. Here are two castles, almost inexpugnable, that defend the city, being situated at the entry of the port; so that no ship or boat can pass without permission. The garrison consists of three hundred soldiers, and the town constantly inhabited by four hundred families, more or less. The merchants dwell not here, but only reside for awhile, when the galleons come or go from Spain; by reason of the unhealthiness of the air, occasioned by certain vapours that exhale from the mountains. Notwithstanding, their chief warehouses are at Porto Bello, howbeit their habitations be all the year long at Panama, whence they bring the plate upon mules at such times as the fair begins, and when the ships, belonging to the Company of Negroes, arrive here to sell slaves.

Today Porto Bello is a sleepy little town, invaded only on weekends by tourists who come to photograph the moss-covered ruins, especially San Geronimo and the treasury building. A public bus runs to Colón in less than an hour, convenient for replenishing your supplies of fresh meat and vegetables.

An "Ice for Sale" truck calls every morning, but you need a sharp eye to catch him. Local shops carry a limited supply of canned goods, bananas, limes, and bread. There is also a local *abbatoir,* where fresh meat is sold twice a week, early in the morning. In fact, the earlier you arrive the better, as there would be fewer flies buzzing around the meat!

Two anchorages are suggested. The first is 100 yards N of Fort Gloria and the dilapidated town dock, where there is good holding in green mud in 3 fathoms. The second is a more secluded anchorage, away from town to the N, in about the same depth, 100 yards off Fort San Fernando.

Yachts frequently rendezvous here, some to spend a week or more. In addition to its historical significance, this harbor holds the dubious distinction of having the greatest average yearly rainfall, 240 inches, of any place on the North American continent. Even in the dry season it may rain twice a day, so don't plan to catch up on any varnishing here!

Colón (26068),

until recently, was seldom considered by yachtsmen, since the erstwhile American port of Cristóbal and the Panama Canal Yacht Club (also called Cristóbal Yacht Club) were so close at hand. However, better political relations and improved facilities have changed this attitude, especially in the case of yachts not intending to transit the canal. Colón may indeed be a better choice, where a cordial welcome is extended to visiting yachts by the Club Náutico, a welcome personally endorsed for years by a fellow member and yachtsman, the former President Lakas of the Republic of Panama.

Commercial shipping and large yachts should anchor or dock on the W side of Colón, but the preferred anchorage is 75 yards E of the Club Náutico dock on the E shore of Colón.

The sand-mud bottom provides good holding in 2 fathoms, and shallows to 6 feet on the bar and 6½ feet at the dock. During a winter norther, the anchorage is rough but not untenable. Clearance from foreign ports may be arranged through the yacht club. Gasoline and fresh water are available there, while ice and diesel fuel must be ordered. Just prior to departure from Panama, certain items of food and liquor may be purchased in bond, with substantial savings, through the Colón Free Zone.

In Folk's River, 1 mile S of the yacht club, is a marine railway capable of hauling vessels up to 100 tons with drafts to 10 feet.

Chapter Sixteen

THE PANAMA CANAL TO SWAN ISLAND

As you are running up or down the western Caribbean, the wind and current patterns should be your primary consideration in deciding whether to stay offshore via San Andrés Island or to hug all or part of the relatively dull coastline of Costa Rica and Nicaragua. Although this stretch seems to present an uncomfortable lee shore, it does afford some reasonably quiet anchorages in the lee of capes and off-lying cays. For reasons that will become evident later, we recommend pivoting on San Andrés northbound and following the coast southbound. The distances are nearly equal either way.

A compromise route north (especially from May to September, when the winds are down) is to run from San Andrés to Puerto Cabezas (Bragman's Bluff), with its good light and the dock serving as landmarks . . . and thence through the Miskito Channel to the Vivario Cays. This track is of course especially desirable when making for Roatán.

On the offshore route, the wind is generally NE to E between the canal and Swan Island; a southerly component works into the pattern from there northward. On the other hand, particularly from November through March, the wind along the coastal route is likely to be N as often as it is NE or E, and Force 5 is not uncommon.

From November to early April, this whole area is unfortunately subject to the long reach of northers that sweep across the Gulf of Mexico at a rate of one a week and sometimes even more frequently. Although the *Sailing Directions* note at one point that their strength tends to diminish with the latitude, a statistical table in another section shows a higher frequency of northers of Force 7 or more between Cabo Gracias a Dios and Cristóbal than in the sea area from the Cabo to Cozumel. Then, there is a distinction drawn between "true northers" and "intensified trades," the latter being, as the name implies, the cumulative result of a norther combined with strong NE trades.

In *Yellow Bird*'s passage from Cristóbal to San Andrés, we ran into seas of 20 feet or more just off the bow, and while winds of Force 8–9 howled around our wheelhouse, we could hear distress messages from big ships farther north, where it was blowing Force 11; in fact we were later to see salvage operations under way on one of those vessels, which had blown high on the Quita Sueño Reef. Undoubtedly we were caught in a "true norther," but the distinction becomes rather academic when you are actually at sea in such a gale.

On the offshore route, you will benefit from the full sweep of the Equatorial Current when making for the Yucatán Channel. Along the Miskito Coast, a somewhat inconsistent countercurrent makes south but becomes regular and stronger in its counterclockwise movement along the coast southeast of San Juan del Norte.

Inshore Route, Cristóbal to Swan Island or Roatán (26000, 21500, 28041, 28000)

Running direct to the Corn Islands, this passage is about 560 miles all the way to Swan Island and only about 10 miles shorter than the route via San Andrés and Gorda Cay. From the standpoint of wind direction, it should be comfortable during spring and summer, although you will be bucking a current much of the way. Then, too, it offers overnight anchorages instead of the day-and-night running involved with the offshore route.

On the other hand, this is a hot and steamy coast all year, but worst during the wet season, from June through December. For example, the rainfall at Bluefields is 250 inches a year, and the littoral of Nicaragua is not named the Miskito Coast without good reason!

We will now list the most useful layover places northward from the canal, although you would do well to make directly for the Corn Islands or Bluefields rather than buck the worst of the perpetual counterclockwise current along the Costa Rican coast.

Laguna de Chiriqui (28042)

is easy to enter and offers numerous anchoring possibilities, the most sheltered being in the NW section of the lagoon. The shoreline is mostly mangrove and a clear sand beach is hard to find. The human inhabitants are scarce, but the area abounds in herons, terns, pelicans, crabs, oysters, iguanas, and some 'gators; and where there are mangroves, there are usually insects.

The chart is unusually well detailed for so wild an area, but the soundings in the Split Hill Channel are not reliable. Kit Kapp, with the ketch *Fairwinds,* drawing 6½ feet, grounded here in several places, but not seriously, for the bottom is merely sand or mud.

Bahía de Almirante (28044, 28045, 28046, 28047)

was named after Columbus, the Admiral of the Ocean Seas, who discovered this spacious, landlocked haven and used it on several occasions, particularly Careening Cay, where his vessels were repaired.

The main settlements are Almirante and Bocas del Toro, the latter being a port of entry and a quiet little town of Victorian frame houses with leaky, wooden water tanks, and a general appearance of "has-been" prosperity. Fruit is available, and fresh meat if you get there early enough on slaughtering days. Supplies in

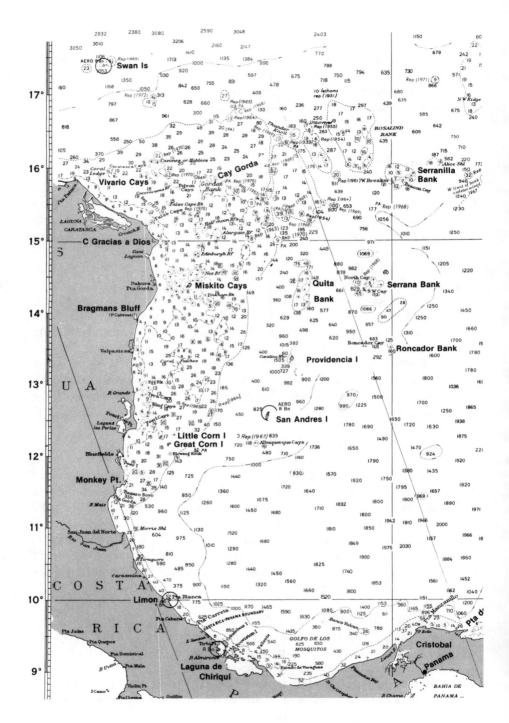

Cristóbal to Swan Island, with offshore islands and banks

general are scarce, especially drinking water. You may be able to tie to the public quay, but commercial coasters are given preference.

Almirante is a fruit company town with a population of about 3,000. The commissary and hospital are open only to company employees, but you may be able to make an "arrangement" with a local resident who has commissary privileges. Fresh water and usually ice are available at the large banana-loading wharf.

Puerto Limón (28049)

offers little shelter and constant swell but good holding in mud. The town lacks charm but is a place to replenish your supply of meats, vegetables, and ice.

Apparently the economy of the area has not recovered from a blight that necessitated destroying the banana trees some years back. However, it is Costa Rica's only port on the Atlantic side and is the railhead for the Northern Railroad to the capital of San José.

Incidentally, this Toonerville-type transportation is your golden opportunity to see Central America at close hand, as well as a chance to gain some welcome relief from the heat and humidity of sea-level living. For five hours and 103 miles, this little train winds its clacking, narrow-gauge way through tropical forest, across spidery trestles, and along verdant mountainsides until it crosses the Continental Divide and ends its tortuous journey in the blessed coolness of San José, 4,000 feet up on the plateau that gives Costa Rica its second climate.

If, after a night's rest in what we think must be the cleanest city in the world, you're still game for more railroading, you can take a similar ride down to the Pacific Ocean at Puntarenas, as described in Chapter Three.

Along the beach some 50 miles N of Limón, at isolated Tortuguero, green turtles come from all over the western Caribbean to breed and lay as many as a hundred eggs at a time in pits in the dark sand, then to wriggle their 200–300 pounds back to their natural habitat, the sea. Although the turtles habitually use this particular 22-mile stretch of beach, the whole shoreline of Costa Rica is protected by law against poachers. Nevertheless, they still come by night, goaded by the high prices that turtle meat commands, to tip as many of these female turtles as they can onto their backs, where they lie helplessly until picked up by boats for transport back to Limón.

San Juan del Norte, or Greytown (28062),

was the terminus of a canal project that would have linked the Atlantic and Pacific oceans via the San Juan River and Lake Nicaragua. In fact construction carried on from 1889 to 1893, when the private company, having run through $4 million, was unable to persuade the U.S. government to invest $100 million more to keep the project alive.

Kit Kapp advises that the entrance to the river mouth is, for all practical purposes, closed. In calm conditions local coasters occasionally pick up light cargo and passengers, which are brought across the bar in canoes or small lighters. To take even a shallow-draft yacht across the shifting bar into the river would be tricky and hazardous.

Monkey Point (28063)

is well protected from W through N to E, and the high bluff makes it a particularly good refuge in a norther.

Approach the anchorage cautiously, especially when within a half mile of the shore. Although the chart gives no such indication, the Niemeiers of the powerboat *Shield* report reefs and shoals in the bay, and Kit Kapp of *Fairwinds* tells us he hit bottom where the chart showed 17 feet. Under the circumstances, the large-scale chart noted above is not really needed; 28061 should suffice.

Bluefields (28082)

will carry 4½ feet all the way into the town dock, but you should engage a local pilot, at least the first time.

There is no need, however, to proceed beyond the deep-water anchorage just inside Casaya Cay, whence you can easily dinghy into the town, which is neither quaint nor modern. Report to the port captain's office on El Bluff. Some English is spoken here and at other places from here northward.

There is a slipway capable of hauling the shrimpers that base here.

Río Escondido is navigable by scheduled passenger boats for 55 miles to the town of Rama. This might make an interesting side cruise for a yacht.

Great Corn Island (28083)

is ringed with white sandy beaches, literally rustles with coconut palms, and is lightly sprinkled with friendly and cooperative people who make their living primarily from fishing—and they all speak English. In addition to having banana and coconut plantations, the island is base for a huge shrimper and lobster fleet, with an attendant cold-storage plant. If in need of repairs, you will find a good machine shop and expert mechanics and electronics technicians ready and willing to help you.

Brig Bay is the preferred anchorage, but if the swell is uncomfortable you might be better situated in Southwest Bay, near the end of the airstrip. If caught in the early stages of a norther, go around into Long Bay. Beware Scylla Rock—it has less than 6 feet over it and lies about a mile 250°T from West Point.

Little Corn Island (28083)

affords good shelter in Pelican Bay due S of the light. Only about 50 people live here, and if you are only stopping overnight and want to forego the Nicaraguan entry formalities, this might be a better choice than Great Corn.

Tungwarra Cays (28083)

are favored by the fishermen as an anchorage, which of course is a pretty good recommendation. From the SW, approach the anchorage between Buttonwood and Little Tungwarra Cays and anchor in the vicinity of the mooring buoy.

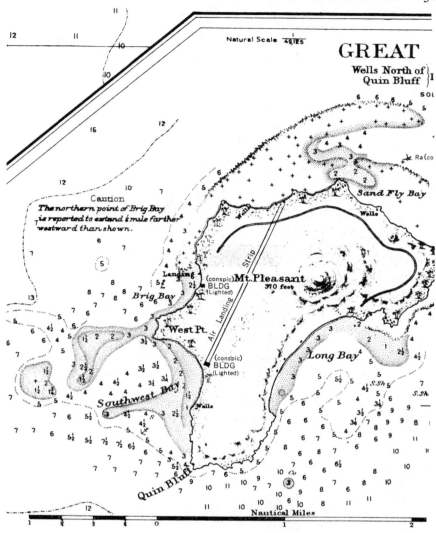

Great Corn Island, Nicaragua (soundings in fathoms)

Obviously, there are other suitable anchorages in this area, known as the Pearl Cays, but very cautious piloting is required because the water is too murky for eyeballing.

Man of War Cays (28081)

once served as a loading port for fruit, which was lightered out from the mainland. The ships lay along pilings in a cove on the W side of the westernmost islet,

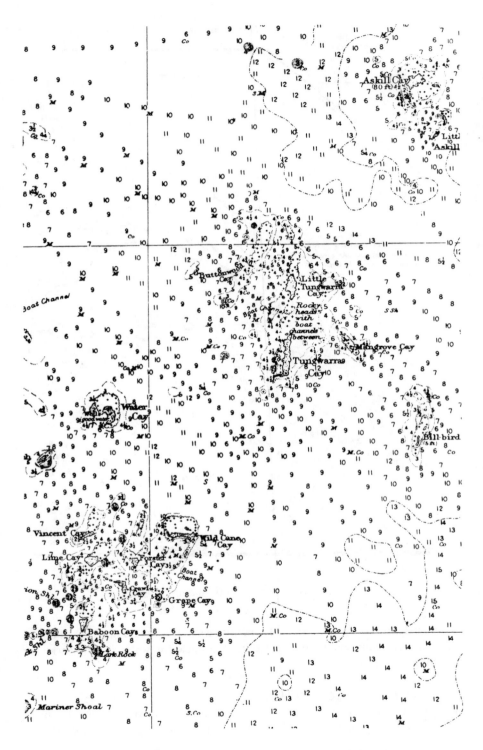

Tungwarra Cays, or Pearl Islands (soundings in fathoms)

where shelter is adequate from NW through N to E. Some shelter may also be found just S of the cluster of easternmost cays.

Puerto Cabezas (Bragman's Bluff) (28102),

with its dilapidated long wooden pier, is an impoverished port town devoted to the shipping of bananas and timber and has nothing to attract yachts except in emergencies. The roadstead is open, the pier pilings don't break the sea, and mainland Nicaragua is not noted for its hospitality toward yachtsmen. Entry and clearing formalities have been reported to cost $25, although there is no consistency in such charges in any Central American ports.

Miskito Channel to Cabo Gracias a Dios (28101)

presents a low swampy shoreline with no identifiable objects to check your progress; judging distance off is very deceptive. When rounding the cape itself, stay at least 2 miles off but never in less than 5 fathoms, and even farther off in bad weather, since the seas are then actually breaking in 4–5 fathoms.

If you're caught by a norther, you can take shelter in Sunbeam Bay, S of Cabo Gracias a Dios, with good holding in the mud bottom, but expect to roll in the swell.

If you are held up waiting for the weather to clear, dinghy into the lagoon at the mouth of the river, which is surrounded by a pristine, brackish marsh.

Cabo Falso (28101)

is imperfectly charted, low-lying, and as dangerous as its name implies. Give it a wide berth.

Vivario Cays (28103),

which lie about 50 miles N of Cabo Gracias a Dios and 100 miles S of Swan Island, have become a popular stopping place for the few yachts that come this way. The approach is easy, the protection rather remarkable, and the setting idyllic, for here you lie in the lee of a 2-mile-long natural breakwater of exposed or awash reefs interspersed with a chain of tiny islets.

Anchor in the lee of Grand Vivario itself, where the palms give shelter from the wind. You may find better holding about 6 cables S of the northernmost cay, where the shrimpers usually anchor to rest after their all-night trawling operations.

When the husky powercruiser *Eventide* passed through here in 1968, Esther Newmark, in an article in *Yachting,* wrote eloquently of this lonely haven in the middle of the sea, and it probably has not changed much:

> Gratefully we sighted Grand Vivario Cay at 0600 one morning. A semicircle of reefs forms a lee from the easterly trades and seas, and it's always a source of wonderment to me to find a patch of calm water in the open sea created by those walls of coral.
>
> One of the cays was a natural bird sanctuary, the prominent species being the black man-of-war frigate. Even though it was December, it must have been "spring" to

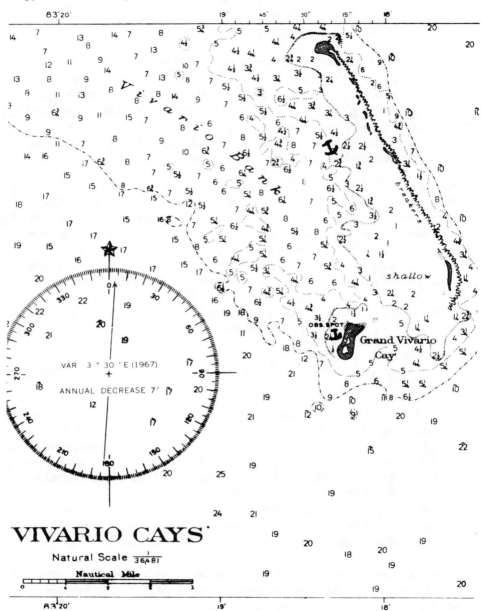

VIVARIO CAYS

Natural Scale $\frac{1}{36,481}$

Nautical Mile

Vivario Cays (soundings in fathoms)

them, for the males were blowing up their beautiful red pouches and flying back and forth among the females, not at all disturbed by us in the Whaler.

Shrimp boats from Guanaja, the mainland of Honduras, and elsewhere, anchored here during the day. Usually the first one in after the night's shrimping drops a hook, then the succeeding arrivals merely toss a line to be secured to the stern of the preceding boat. As many as seven would tie up in this fashion. We traded some canned goods and paperbacks for buckets of shrimp and lobsters. For those who like the serenity of a lonely seascape, with only the call of the birds and the sound of seas breaking on reefs, and the breathtaking beauty of an unmarred sunset, Vivario Cays is such a place.

Swan Island (28121),

which lies about 100 miles off the NE shoulder of Honduras and about halfway between San Andrés and Cozumel, could hardly have been set down in a more convenient spot for yachtsmen. Actually, there are two of these little coral lime-stone islands, each about 1½ miles long and only 60 feet high, and separated by a narrow channel that may or may not be foul.

In 1972 they were ceded by the U.S. to Honduras under the interesting claim that, since they had once been a part of the Spanish Empire, they should belong to the nearest formerly Spanish country. Until 1980 the U.S. National Weather Service continued to operate their facilities on Swan, but now these, too, have been donated to the Honduras government "with sufficient resources to continue synoptic observations from the island and to broadcast these via voice of Teguci-galpa." A new operating aircraft beacon system was also left on the station.

In the prevailing NE to SE winds, the bight at the western end of Great Swan gives adequate protection, provided you go all the way into the concrete quay. For some reason, the swell seems to dissipate down in this corner, but if you are anchored off, the motion is very uncomfortable. When we were there, the wind came in from the SSE, setting up a dangerous surge at the quay, and we had to move around to an anchorage on the NW side of uninhabited Little Swan, about 150 yards off, where it was smooth and well sheltered from the wind. In a strong norther, shelter may be taken along the S shore.

Since Swan is such a small speck in the ocean, an early morning approach is helpful, in order to take advantage of the aircraft beacon visible for some 30 miles in clear weather. Presumably the Hondurans will continue to operate this aid.

A walk around the island will show only traces of the old plantation days when United Fruit harvested coconuts from some 15,000 trees. Hurricane *Janet,* in 1955, wiped this all out. Some 15–20 people from the Caymans and the Bay Islands of Honduras live here, raising cattle and a few crops.

Offshore Route, Cristóbal to Swan Island or Jamaica (26000, 28000, 26010)

This 570-mile route to Swan, with San Andrés the first stop, takes the current on the beam for the first 215-mile leg. From Providencia on, you begin to feel the powerful effect of the steady current that sweeps through the Caribbean and up through the Yucatán Channel. It is perfectly safe for night passaging, whereas the inshore route is encumbered by the Miskito Cays.

The deserted Quita Sueño, Serrana, and Serranilla banks project themselves ever so slightly above the surface to offer a small measure of protection for overnight stops, particularly if you're bound for Jamaica.

San Andrés Island (26081)

is only a flyspeck in the middle of the western Caribbean Sea, yet this little Colombian possession has more to offer in facilities and amusement than any place for hundreds of miles in any direction. Any ordinary mechanical or electrical repairs can be effected here, and should it be parts you need, there is almost daily air service nonstop from Miami and New Orleans. As for amusement, the resort atmosphere is pleasantly low key.

Lying within the protecting arm of the long barrier reef that creates the harbor, the water is so transparent and the colors are so exquisite that the rather numerous brown bars stand out sharply against the sandy bottom, and just to make it easier in poor light conditions, the channel is well buoyed as far as the commercial dock (where there is too much activity and dirt for a yacht). Coming in after dark, you would have to anchor near the entrance buoy, where you are somewhat protected from the surge. While the channel is straightforward, the buoys may not be as charted and the lights are unreliable. Pilots are available only from 0600 to 1800.

Two yacht anchorages are available, both inshore of Cayo Santander but reached by different routes.

One is approached if you head initially toward the commercial docks, then turn to the NNE toward a wreck between the shore and Cayo Santander. Leave the wreck close to port and the cay of course to starboard. Ahead is a 2- to 3-fathom anchorage with good holding ground, but beware the shallow bank at the N end of this anchorage, which connects Cayo Santander with the shore and effectively blocks this anchorage from the one we next describe.

The perferred anchorage, off the Club Náutico, is reached by turning wide to the NNE after passing the last channel buoy, heading toward the 3-story round buildings on Punta Hansa until you are past the cay and able to turn NNW toward the steep, green roof of the Club Náutico. The anchorage here is in 10 to 15 feet over a sandy bottom. Just to the right of the club is the Hansa Restaurant, which serves some of the island's best seafood in a pleasant atmosphere and allows dinghies to be tied up.

Two blocks inland brings you to the commercial district, with its almost endless succession of shops devoted to the sale of radios, china, watches, cameras, and all the other geegaws that entice tourists to a free port—which San Andrés is. After a session of what we thought was very sharp bargaining in one of these stores (the clerk even telephoned the boss for his approval to sell at such a low price), we bought a portable Japanese radio for keeping in touch with the weather

San Andrés Island: one ship that didn't quite make it over the bar

and news, only to find when we got back to the States that we'd saved only $2 on the list price!

Turning to the right on the shore road brings you to the beach front and the hotels, bars, and bistros that line such places the world over. No Hiltons, Sheratons, or Holiday Inns yet, for this is basically an unsophisticated resort frequented mostly by Colombians. With the new air service from Miami, this modest state of affairs probably won't last long, especially considering that this is a truly beautiful island with wide, white beaches, palm-covered sandy islets just offshore, and a smooth bay of clear aquamarine enclosed by a fringing reef. All add up to a convincing South Sea–island impression.

If you rent a car, drive up on the hill behind the town where two-storied clapboard houses with brightly painted balconies line the road. The views of the bay through the waving trees are rewarding. Then continue on around the island, where still-working plantations provide vistas of slanting coconut palms and orderly rows of banana trees. Here today is a remnant of the West Indian scene as it was on most of the Caribbean islands a quarter century ago, before the concerted tourist assault.

That almost respectable buccaneer Henry Morgan was here, too, and no wonder, because San Andrés sits exactly astride the route of the gold- and silver-laden galleons that plied from the ports of the isthmus through the Yucatán Channel

San Andrés feels the trades

on their way to Spain. A cave, purported to be one of his lairs, is just off the road on the W side of the island.

We were held up on San Andrés for several days waiting for the wind to drop, and liked every minute of our stay. A couple of good restaurants will be found along the playa: the Oasis for one, and off on one of the side streets is the relatively elegant Romano's, serving the finest food in town.

Entry formalities will probably change as yacht traffic increases. According to our last information, the port captain at the naval base requires yachts to engage an agent for entry and exit procedures for a fee totaling $35 or more. Some agents speak English.

On the opposite side of the island from town, Southwest Cove is a snug and quiet anchorage with a bottom of sand and mud. Yachts making for the Miskito Channel will find this a convenient departure point.

Providencia (26083, 26082),

within an easy day's sail of San Andrés, is obviously of volcanic origin. Its jagged peaks rising to 1,200 feet make this almost forgotten island, also a Colombian possession, an easy target from almost 20 miles at sea. Yachtsmen have long recognized Providencia as a convenient and secure stepping-stone in the vastness of the western Caribbean. The cistern water is good, and international phone service is available. An ancient amphibian plane makes regular flights to and from San Andrés.

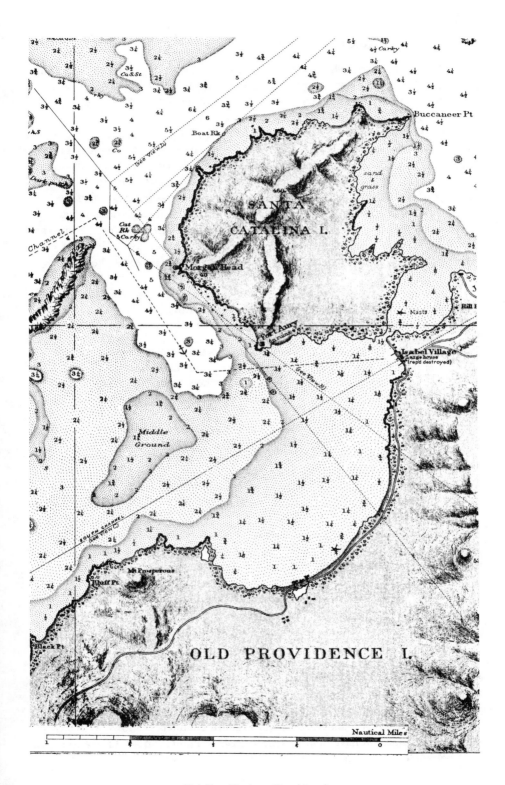

Catalina Harbor, Providencia

The 4,000 islanders, who eke out a living through fishing and cattle raising, proudly trace their ancestry through Negro, Spanish, and English blood to that great ruffian, Henry Morgan, who was so widely respected by the British and just as widely hated and feared by the Spaniards.

In those mid-seventeenth-century days, pirates took this strategic island from the Spaniards to use as a base for savage forays upon Spanish colonies on the mainland and upon shipping that had to pass their way. They also took advantage of the richness of the land to grow vegetables and to raise cattle to provision their fleets. It was called Santa Catalina then, referring more specifically to the small island at the NW corner of Old Providence, where the fortifications stood.

Two avid cruising people, Bob and Rosie Cullen of *El Sonador*, became so entranced with this primitive island that they stayed for almost two years. Our visit was only overnight, so we prefer to let the Cullens describe the place:

> Port Isabel has a very secure anchorage with sand bottom and is sheltered from the NE trades that continually bathe the island. The village consists of four small general stores and a new 3-story hotel building housing the government offices, the post office, and a bakery.
>
> A road circles the island and transportation is by horse and 8 pick-up trucks. Cattle graze on the green slopes and cows and pigs join the traffic on main street. In case of a news event, a town crier circles the island on horseback, stopping at intervals to shout the news.
>
> The settling of Providencia has resulted in a multi-colored society, ranging from almost white to almost black. There are no color barriers, and the children can only be described as absolutely beautiful. Six names of English origin dominate: Archibald, Newball, Howard, Rankin, Robinson, and Taylor, but inbreeding has not produced the serious effects that it has elsewhere. The people speak English, but with a dialect that is sometimes difficult to understand. Spanish is also spoken. They are without doubt the most friendly people Rosie and I have ever met.

Another who liked Providencia, enough to stay for several months, was Ginnie Higman of *Tormentor III*. Commenting on how small the island is, she observed that it takes only five-six hours to sail around it in a dinghy. She also tells us:

> At Fresh Water Bay, a lovely, coconut-bordered white-sand beach on the SW side of Providencia, there's a public building with two adequate freshwater showers which yachtsmen may like to know about. Via dinghy from Isabel Village it's about 2 miles.

The Cullens also report that for years ships have sailed hundreds of miles out of their way just to obtain a pair of Providencia crickets, which are said not only to help greatly with a cockroach problem but bring good luck to the ship as well.

Indeed, the enticements of Providencia seem truly overwhelming!

The entrance to Catalina Harbor via the south channel, as shown in 26082, is quite simple after you have finally identified Black Point, and with the afternoon light behind you, you should have no difficulty.

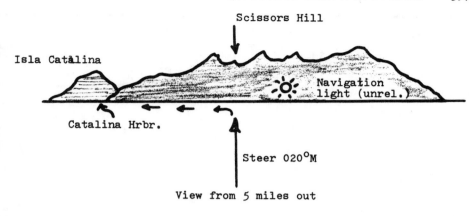

Approach to Isla Providencia from the south (inshore route)

Bob Cullen, however, has given us a sketch of the south approach (which first appeared in the SSCA *Bulletin*), which he says is the best when coming from San Andrés and the one that the islanders use all the time. Since the navigation light is out most of the time, and the structure difficult to see against the greenery anyway, he advises entering on Scissors Hill on a heading of 020°M, this being the small hill in a saddle between two sharp and prominent peaks. Continuing Bob's instructions:

> The last mile before reaching the island you will be over 2–3 fathoms but you can read the water as it is crystal clear. Go right up to within 200–300 feet of the island and turn to port. Go up the western shore, staying in close. Enter the harbor and anchor anywhere E of the cement wharf.

The extensive breaking reef and Low Cay, some 7 miles N of Catalina Island, will be your reference mark when approaching Providencia from the N. The harbor approach on a southeasterly course, as shown in 26082, is not as difficult as it may appear, because Morgan Head is prominent, and Lawrence Reef is barely covered and thus easily seen.

Quinta Sueño Bank (28000)

may hardly seem appropriate as an anchorage, lying as it does 120 miles off the mainland and some 60 miles N of Providencia; yet the low reef, barely awash in places, breaks up most of the sea, and you can at least expect a reasonably comfortable sleep literally miles from nowhere.

The "landmarks" here are the wrecks along the weather side of the reef, but it is nearly impossible to know which wreck is which on the chart, if indeed they are all shown. We anchored in approximately 14°15'N, 81°11'W, in 6 fathoms, sand. A new stranding, still with steam up, lay about 1½ miles from us across

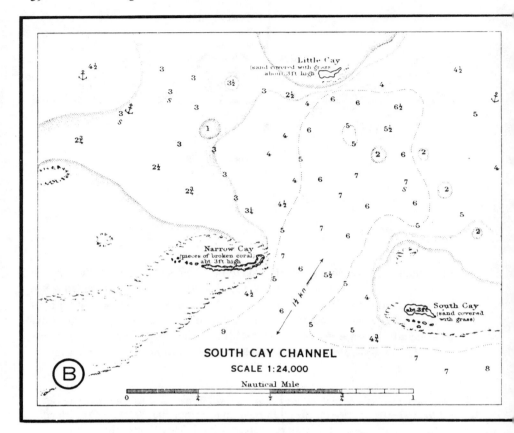

Preferred anchorage on Serrana Bank (soundings in fathoms)

the reef, and there were two other wrecks in sight, to the NE and SE of us. There may be more now, for the reef is very steep-to on its eastern side, the currents are strong, and the whole area is a trap for the unwary.

Serrana Bank (26101)

lies about 50 miles E of Quinta Sueño and actually offers some solid land in the form of a half dozen tiny cays widely scattered over its 17-by-8-mile area. The largest is Southwest Cay, standing all of 32 feet high with a light structure and a couple of palms, but the best anchorage is in South Cay Channel, within the triangle of three tiny cays that are hardly more than sand piles. The one-half-mile-wide, unobstructed entrance is 10 miles NE of Southwest Cay. Be prepared for a 2–3 knot current.

On passage to or from Jamaica and the canal, this is a useful and surprisingly good shelter. Some of these cays are occasionally inhabited by lobster and turtle fishermen.

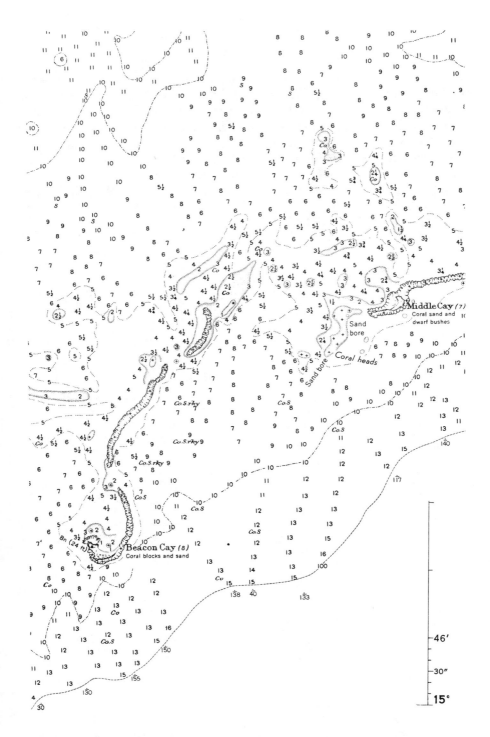

Serranilla Bank, best anchorage in lee of Beacon Cay (soundings in fathoms)

Serranilla Bank (26102)

is another useful overnight stop when you are bound to or from Jamaica or the Caymans. Beacon Cay can be recognized by the steep sand beach on its north side and several coconut palms clustered in the center. It is the most southerly of the three cays that just barely protrude from the vast underwater plateau extending from Cabo Gracias a Dios irregularly to Jamaica. Anchor in the lee of the curving reef. Water from a brackish well near the palm trees can be used for washing. Beacon Cay is home for vast flocks of frigate and booby birds.

Still another stepping-stone is Southwest Cay on the Pedro Bank, mentioned in Chapter Twenty-two.

Chapter Seventeen

THE GULF OF HONDURAS AND THE BAY ISLANDS

Only yesterday, or so it seems, this corner of the western Caribbean was aptly called the Unknown Caribbean. Most cruising yachts making the direct passage between Florida and the Panama Canal studiously bypassed the Gulf of Honduras and the Bay Islands. When we first explored this area between 1974 and 1976 for the first edition of this guide, we encountered scarcely more than a half dozen cruising yachts. These historic islands and coastal waters of the Spanish Main are just beginning to be discovered by cruising sailors from the U.S. and other countries.

The Gulf of Honduras occupies the western part of the huge bight that cuts deeply into the coast of Central America north of Cape Gracias a Dios (latitude 15°) and south of Mexico's Yucatán peninsula. It covers a triangular-shaped water area of approximately 10,000 square miles, bordered on the south by the mountainous coast of Honduras; on the west by the low, sandy coastline of Belize and its outlying barrier reef; and in the SW corner by Guatemala's short coastal region, with its spectacular Río Dulce tucked in between them at the apex of the triangle.

Inside the triangle, there are three quite different subregions, each of which has its own distinctive characteristics and cruising attractions. In this chapter we discuss two of the subregions—the Bay Islands of Honduras and the Río Dulce basin of Guatemala—and the navigational problems likely to be encountered in approaching them from sea. The third area, Belize and its barrier reef, is covered in Chapter Eighteen.

APPROACHES TO THE GULF OF HONDURAS (28001)

No one planning to cruise the Gulf of Honduras in his own boat should take lightly the navigational problems of getting there or the skills required to pilot safely in this extensive area of outlying reefs and shoals. It's not that the gulf is geographically remote. Actually, Belize and the Bay Islands are closer to Florida than Puerto Rico and the Virgins are. It is only about 615 miles from Key West to Belize by way of Cozumel and the Yucatán Channel, plus another 100 miles or so to the Bay Islands, compared with about 900 miles from Miami to Puerto Rico or about 1,000 miles direct to the Virgin Islands. But the westward passage around Cuba and southward through the chain of reefs off Yucatán and Belize can be more taxing than the straightforward ocean passage to the Virgins, particularly when winter northers sweep across the Gulf of Mexico, affecting both the direction and intensity of ocean currents that are erratic and difficult to judge even under the best of conditions.

The Yucatán route can be done in relatively easy stages by making the first leg from Key West to Isla Mujeres or Cozumel, and then proceeding down the coast of Yucatán inside the Chinchorro Bank and Turneffe Islands to English Cay and the Eastern Channel across the bank to Belize Harbor, a track distance of about 220 miles. The chief problems are likely to arise in northers and periods of unsettled weather, when you have to be concerned about poor visibility and erratic currents. You must also constantly keep track of your position in the vicinity of three particularly dangerous reefs that are inadequately charted and not visible until you are close upon them. These areas are described in Chapter Eighteen.

Yachts making a direct passage offshore from Cozumel to the Bay Islands should note that the current generally sets strongly to the NW and W. A few vessels (including more than one yacht) have failed to take this into account and have made unexpected landfalls on Chinchorro or Lighthouse Reefs and even at Puerto Cortes on the coast of Honduras instead of at Roatán.

Eastern and Southern Approaches (28001)

In periods of unsettled weather, it might almost be easier for yachts heading south from Florida to make their approach from the eastward to Swan Island, keeping clear of the banks and reefs, or to cruise through the Bahamas, around the eastern end of Cuba through the Windward Passage, and then run back west with the trade winds to Swan Island and the Bay Islands of Honduras. We followed this route under sail in *Brer Fox* on a winter passage via Jamaica and Swan Island, logging over 1,400 miles, downwind all the way with successive northers on our heels. In 1980 Bates McKee sailed *Xanadu* from the Virgin Islands to Roatán with the trade winds at his back all the way. This is almost always a comfortable, "fun" route if you can spare the time.

Approaches from eastward and southward are generally free of dangers until you are close to the outlying reefs. Swan Island lies approximately 240 miles east of Belize and about 200 miles east of Lighthouse Reef, outermost of the offshore reefs, but it is only about 150 miles northeast of Roatán, largest of the Bay Islands, with nothing but deep water between. We'll have more to say about the inadequacies of existing charts, but here it is sufficient to note that even the most recent U.S. and British editions are of limited use in identifying island landmarks or determining the course of channels through the reefs.

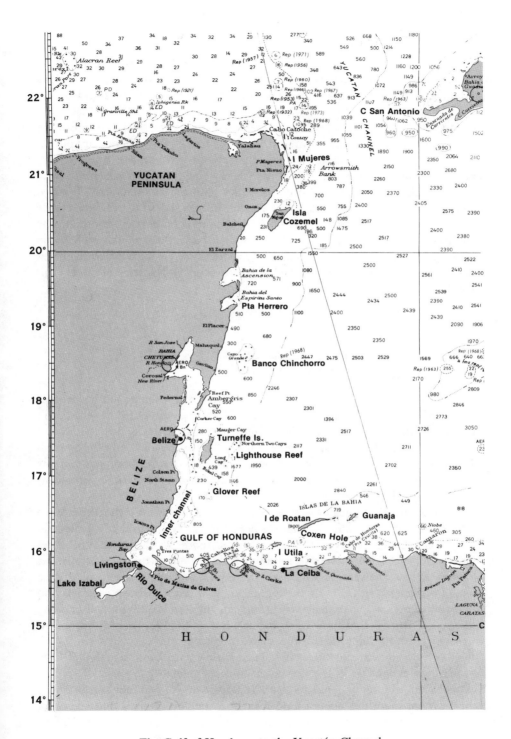

The Gulf of Honduras to the Yucatán Channel

For yachts approaching the Bay Islands from the south and eastward, however, there are no serious problems in making a landfall under good weather conditions with average visibility—the islands are relatively high and can be seen from 15 or 20 miles at sea. If you are coming north from Panama, you have a choice: you can stand well off the coast of Central America until clear of the shoals northeast of Cape Gracias a Dios before turning westward for the Bay Islands, or you can follow the coastline of Honduras from the cape as it trends northwesterly for about 125 miles to Cape Cameron. From there you continue on much the same course; it takes you offshore another 60 miles until the mountains of Guanaja, most easterly of the Bay Islands, become visible over the horizon. Columbus made the first recorded approach to the Gulf of Honduras on his last voyage to the Caribbean, in 1502, when he felt his way cautiously through the reefs to an anchorage off those same mountains of Guanaja. A customs office has been opened in the main settlement of Guanaja, making it possible for yachts approaching from the east to enter here.

THE BAY ISLANDS—ROATÁN, UTILA, GUANAJA (28001)

Although Columbus claimed the Bay Islands for Spain when he put his brother Bartolomé ashore at Guanaja on July 30, 1502, the Spanish failed to settle there and showed little interest in the islands until after buccaneers of five nations had made them a base for raiding treasure ships homeward bound from the Spanish Main. The Brethren of the Coast found the reef-locked harbors and lagoons perfect hideouts for their fast ships, and established some of the first permanent settlements in the islands.

The first British settlement on Roatán was established by the Providence Company in 1638, but the site has not been found. By the mid-1650s, British, French, and Dutch buccaneers had established footholds they successfully defended against Spanish attacks from the mainland. Henry Morgan was only one of many British buccaneers who used the Bay Islands as a base prior to the sacking of Panama in 1671. By the middle and late 1700s, British colonists had a number of permanent settlements throughout the Bay Islands as well as along the coast of British Honduras (now Belize). But in 1859 the British negotiated a treaty, returning the islands to Spanish Honduras.

Today the islands are no longer as isolated as they once were, though they have not yet been caught up in the Caribbean tourist current.

On Roatán, the most populous, with 18,000 of the 21,500 inhabitants of the island group, there are no fast-food franchises or golf courses, but there are telephones, electricity in the towns, and a modern airport with a 6,000-foot runway.

The islands can be reached by air in a few hours from Miami and New Orleans, but the outlying reefs and shoals still make them somewhat difficult of access by sea. Still, how long can it be before more yachtsmen discover this 1,700-square-mile cruising ground—an area larger than the Virgin Islands—with deep, sheltered, and largely empty harbors.

There are three main islands, three smaller inhabited islands, and scores of islets and cays in this enticing group that rises steeply from the blue-green sea close behind the fringing reefs. Roatán, the largest of the group, occupies the central position, between Guanaja to the east and Utila to the west. The entire chain extends for 75 miles on its east-west axis, 20–30 miles off the mountainous northern coast of Honduras.

Each of the main islands is easy to identify on approaching from sea. Roatán and Guanaja are heavily wooded and hilly or mountainous, with numerous distinguishing peaks and rocky outcroppings, some of which are shown in sketch views in the British *Pilot*. Utila is the lowest of the group, but has a rim of hills near its only harbor at the eastern end. All of the main islands are surrounded by reefs and banks, which rise steeply from the seabed. The principal openings are shown on the charts, but the scale is not adequate for close-in piloting around the reefs, and yachts must depend largely on their own careful soundings and eyeball navigation.

Aids to navigation are virtually nonexistent in the Bay Islands. Currents are erratic outside the reefs. But inside the reefs there are many fine harbors comparable to the best in the eastern Caribbean. Here you will find a small segment of the Caribbean that still looks much as it did half a century ago. You won't find many marinas or plush shoreside hotels, or TV or telephones, and you may have to anchor out in most of the harbors and lagoons. Provisions and ship supplies are hard to come by in the small villages that cluster around the harbors, but if you carry your own basic supplies you won't have too much trouble supplementing them with an assortment of imported canned goods and native staples usually available at the local stores. Rice, beans, potatoes, and cabbage are the main staples.

There are other drawbacks, too, ones you are likely to find in most of the tropic isles. Pests, for example: mosquitos in the mangrove swamps, sand flies on sandy beaches, and "no-see-ums," which appear mysteriously at dusk with a hunter's instinct for exposed flesh and yachtsmen among their preferred targets. Roatán seems to have a particularly aggressive breed, although the native population is virtually immune. When we asked for an effective preventive lotion at a store in French Harbour, the proprietor looked surprised and said, "Oh, they don't bother us none." Fortunately, the faithful trade winds keep most of the insect pests a safe distance from your boat, and if you select an anchorage where the breeze blows at night, you are unlikely to be bothered. Some cruising boats don't bother to carry screens, and we've been more pestered by mosquitos on the Chesapeake than in the Caribbean.

The people in all the Bay islands are friendly and eager to help visiting mariners. The population of about 21,500 is a mixture of British, Spanish, Black Carib, and Creole, speaking both English and Spanish. The Honduras government requires Spanish in the public schools, but a substantial part of the population trace their ancestry to the British buccaneers and colonists and are proud of their English-speaking heritage. They resist interference from the mainland and support English-speaking church schools in many of the villages.

In the following sections we take a closer look at each of the three main islands and cruising conditions in the area.

PLANNING A CRUISE IN THE BAY ISLANDS

Whether you are cruising your own boat or a charter yacht, certain basic considerations must be kept in mind in planning a Bay Islands cruise. First, there's the dearth of navigational aids, as mentioned above—when we were last there, none of the lights was operating. Then, one must accept that the U. S. charts are useless for navigating around the reefs, with the exception of a harbor chart of Coxen Hole on Roatán, Utila (28143), and Guanaja (28123). British Admiralty charts are somewhat better but still not adequate for piloting through the reefs. Essential for the visiting yachtsman is the *Cruising Guide to the Bay Islands* by Julius Wilensky, published by Wescott Cove Publishing Co., Stamford, Conn. This guide includes excellent sketch charts by Jo Haight, based on soundings and local information compiled during Wilensky's data-gathering cruise for CSY in 1978.

For those who have cruised the protected waters of the Virgins or the Bahama Banks, the deep-water passages between the Bay Islands are sure to seem rough and turbulent, even with the trade wind at its normal 20–25 knots. The 100-fathom line runs close to the reefs around all of these islands, with the result that you may encounter 10-foot seas immediately on leaving the entrance channels of any of Roatán's fine harbors. It's smart to plan your windward sailing in the morning before the trade wind has reached its afternoon peak. It's also wise to get as far upwind as possible early in your cruise so that you will have an easy downwind return to your starting point or another destination. Power-driven vessels will do well to follow the same rule, so steep are the seas in the open passages.

In a week's charter cruise, one cannot expect to visit more than three or four of Roatán's fine harbors, plus an overnight run to the Cayos Cochinos (Hog Cays), a delightful little archipelago reminiscent of the South Pacific. Starting from Coxen Hole or Brick Bay, your itinerary might include Port Royal Harbour as your most easterly anchorage for the first two days on Roatán. Then a 25-mile passage takes you south to the Cochinos, usually on a broad reach, where there's a choice of exotic anchorages. The return passage northbound takes you to the W end of Roatán, where there are several good harbors on both the N and S shores of the island. More about these later.

Two weeks is barely long enough to visit two of the three main islands—either

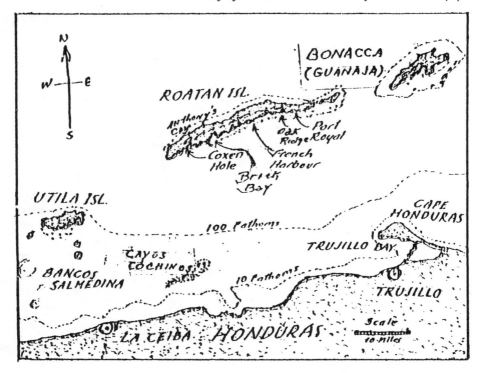

The Bay Islands of Honduras

Roatán and Guanaja, or Roatán and Utila—plus the Cochinos. In settled weather you might be able to include all the main islands in two weeks, but three weeks would allow time to sample the attractions of each of the larger island groups.

The weather is not very different from the Windwards and Leewards. The trades blow more or less constantly but with significant variations in the mountainous islands and coastal regions. Winter northers sweep down from the Yucatán peninsula, often accompanied by squalls and heavy rains that may keep boats in port for a day or two. Cruising the Bay Islands is best in late winter and early spring when the northers have ended and the trades are most dependable.

Roatán Island (28154)

Isla de Roatán is not only the largest of the Bay Islands, but its many fine harbors make it the most attractive of the group to cruising yachtsmen. Its eastern tip lies about 15 miles W of Guanaja, across a deep channel with soundings of 700 fathoms close to its fringing reefs. The island is about 28 miles long and 2–4½ miles wide, with densely wooded hills and ridges rising to heights of 700 feet or more toward the E end and a peak of 900 feet toward the W end. Three small inhabited islands lie off the easternmost tip of Roatán, so close together within the same encircling reef that they seem to be a part of the main island. They are called Santa Elena, Morat, and Barbareta.

For vessels entering Honduran waters, Coxen Hole on the S coast of Roatán is the main port of entry in the islands. Roatán is the official name of the town, which is the capital of the Bay Islands. Known locally as Coxen Hole, this little bight is named after Captain John Coxen, a British buccaneer who made the port his private hideaway. It lies about 4½ miles E of West Point. Entry procedures are not difficult, but there have been numerous complaints in the past about delays and often exorbitant charges imposed on visiting yachts.

Customs charges and port fees vary from time to time, so it is difficult to predict what kind of treatment a visiting yacht will encounter. You may be approached by a customs agent offering his services in processing your papers. If you think he may be helpful, discuss with him in advance what government fees are involved and the cost of his services. Recently charges have varied from $15 to $30.

The usual customs and immigration forms have to be filled out. It's necessary to have passports and health certificates for all persons aboard, and a crew list prepared in advance saves time. Regular hours for customs at Coxen Hole are 9:00 A.M. to 5:00 P.M. weekdays, and 9:00 to 12:00 Saturdays, with overtime charges for entering at other hours and on Sundays and holidays. There is a small departure tax similar to that imposed on passengers at the airport. Conditions seemed to be improving in 1976, when we cleared in with *Brer Fox* without delay and minimal port charges, and in 1980, when the Cruising Club of America held its winter cruise in the Bay Islands.

The customshouse is located near the head of the government dock. Anchorage may be found a hundred yards offshore, and your flag should bring a boarding party in due course. The officials are Spanish-speaking Hondurans from the mainland, but some of them usually have enough English to conduct the necessary entry business without trouble. We found them friendly and courteous, and the procedures here are undoubtedly simpler and less time-consuming than in the larger ports of entry on the coast.

Harbors and Anchorages

Coxen Hole is by no means the best harbor on Roatán; in fact, it is hardly more than an open bight protected from the prevailing trade winds by Coxen Cay and Reef. The town is picturesque when seen from a distance in the harbor but dusty and bedraggled when inspected at close hand. Most of the houses facing the harbor are built on stilts over the water, with outbuildings at the end of rickety piers extending into deeper water. Not long ago most of the island's travel was by boat, and Bay Island dories, fishing smacks, and small interisland freight boats are still much in evidence. TAN/SAHSA has daily flights into Coxen Hole's airstrip at the eastern end of the harbor. The new airport, with a 6,000-foot runway, a small terminal, and a control tower, may have direct jet traffic from Miami.

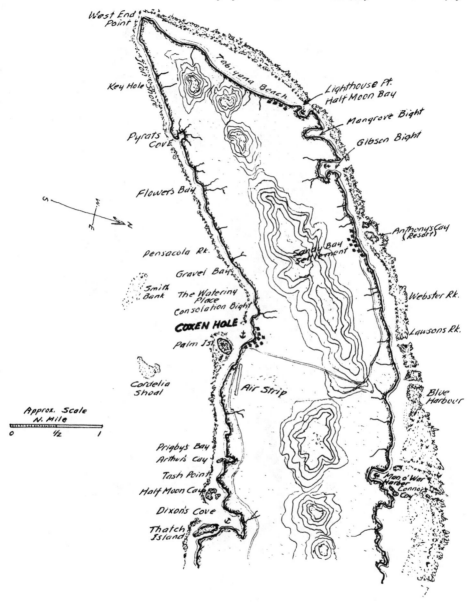

West End
Point

Key Hole

Tabi yena Beach

Lighthouse Pt.
Half Moon Bay

Pyrats
Cove

Mangrove Bight

Gibson Bight

Flowers Bay

Pensacola Rk.

Sandy Bay
Settlement

Anthonys Cay
(Resort)

Gravel Bay

Smith
Bank

The Watering
Place
Consolation Bight

Webster Rk.

COXEN HOLE

Lausons Rk.

Palm Isl.

Cordelia
Shoal

Air Strip

Blue
Harbour

Approx. Scale
N. Mile

0   ½   1

Prigbys Bay
Arthurs Cay

Tash Point

Half Moon Cay

Man o'War
Harbour
Connett
Cay

Dixons Cove

Thatch
Island

Roatán, west end to Thatch Island

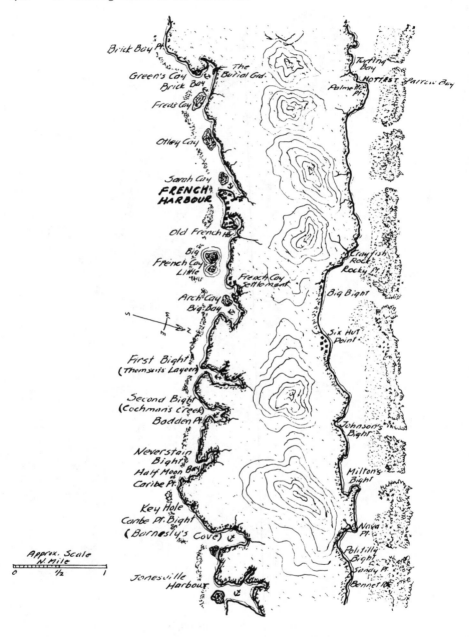

Roatán, Brick Bay to Jonesville Harbour

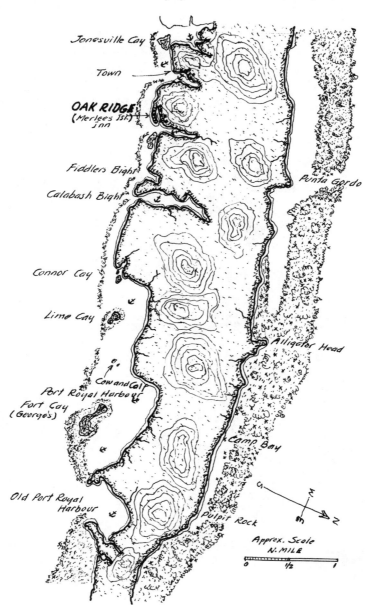

Roatán, Oak Ridge to Old Port Royal Harbour

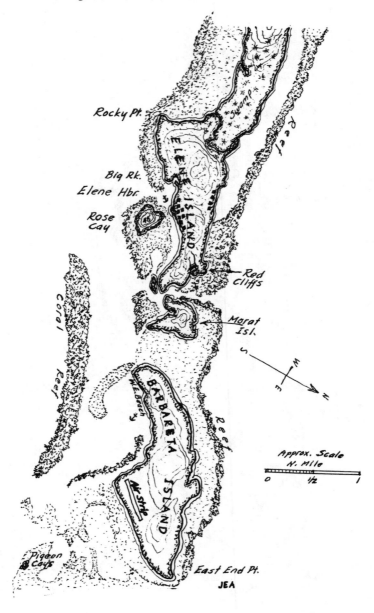

East end of Roatán, Santa Elena, and Barbareta islands

You will find supplies and provisions in a large supermarket and in the small shops along the half-mile "downtown" shopping street. Most supplies can be obtained at the general market at the head of the dock, but at many of the smaller shops groceries seem to consist chiefly of canned goods and such staples as cabbage, rice, and beans. Diesel and gasoline are available on the waterfront, but ice and fresh drinking water are harder to find. Since most of these basic necessities are also available at other harbors a few miles away, you may wish to start your further exploration without delay.

Few islands in the Caribbean have more harbors, coves, and protected anchorages than Roatán. With one or two exceptions, all the best harbors are to be found along the south coast, in the 24-mile stretch between Coxen Hole and the eastern end of the island. Here you'll find more than a dozen all-weather harbors, protected from northers by the high ridges and wooded hills that extend the full length of the island, and sheltered from other directions by small cays and connecting reefs close in along the south shore. None of the U.S. or British charts provides enough detail for small-boat piloting, and the *Sailing Directions* and British *Pilot* describe only major anchorages for larger commercial vessels. The sketch maps shown on pages 492–95 should not be used for navigation, but they indicate topographical features of the island and locations of the principal harbors. Wilensky's Guide shows additional anchorages in coves and bights that are easy to enter with careful eyeball navigation, but beware uncharted shoals in the murkier waters of landlocked harbors.

Here is the overall picture, based on our own observations by plane and small boat and advice by local boatmen and others who know the area well.

Reefs and Entrances

With the exception of the western end of the island, which is steep-to, Roatán is completely surrounded by a reef that rises abruptly from the deep seabed. The entire island lies outside the 100-fathom curve of the Honduran continental shelf, with recorded soundings of 1,000 to 2,000 fathoms a few miles north of Roatán. The barrier reef lies about 1 mile or less off the north coast of the island and continues (with only a narrow opening at the eastern end) around Isla Barbareta. As early as 1704, a map by Thomas Jeffreys warned unwary mariners that "The N side is bounded, in its whole extent, by a Reef of Rocks that have not few passages through, and these of small note." While it is possible to take shoal-draft boats through several small openings in the north reef, we do not recommend attempting to enter for the first time anywhere along that coast without a local pilot. In poor visibility and high seas, this reef is quite impassable.

This advice is still valid, although Wilensky's sketch charts and text suggest several channels that may be entered safely in fair weather.

Most of the south coast of Roatán is, by contrast, relatively free of dangers, with many entrances into the principal harbors. From the eastern point of Barbareta, the edge of the reef extends at least 3 miles offshore, curving around to the southeast and south, then trending west to Isla Elena, close off the southeast end of Roatán. While there are several delightful small-boat anchorages inside the reef between Barbareta and Roatán, they should be reserved for exploration by dinghy, at least until after the visiting boat has become familiar with reading depths in these waters. In any case, the remainder of the south coast is bold and clear, with well-defined channels between the small cays and through connecting reefs that lie close inshore.

After several months of cruising we learned to run close along the fringing reef line in deep water generally free of outlying dangers. This made it easier to keep track of the narrow openings in the reef, which are difficult to identify from only a mile or so offshore.

Protected Coves and Lagoons

Without writing an entire book about the harbors of Roatán it's impossible to describe all of the sheltered coves and lagoons that invite inspection by cruising boats with time to explore. Here's a brief inventory of what you might expect to find in the course of a week's leisurely cruising around the island.

Port Royal Harbour (28154, KSK-9)

is one of the finest anywhere in the Caribbean. It is said to have been used by Henry Morgan and other British buccaneers as a major base for freebooting raids on the Spanish Main; British fortifications, or what remains of them, may still be found on George Cay, locally known as Fort Cay, guarding the main entrance to the harbor. The channel is about 200 yards wide, with depths of 18–27 feet between a short reef, just W of Fort Cay, and Long Reef, extending about three fourths of a mile W. Both reefs are visible, and parts of Long Reef are exposed and almost dry at low tide. There are two other charted entrances W of Long Reef, but both are narrower and more intricate than the main channel. A good landmark for vessels approaching from the S is the conspicuous 735-foot peak about three quarters of a mile W of the harbor entrance.

Good anchorages may be found almost anywhere inside the protecting reefs, in depths that range from 12 to 60 feet or more, over a bottom that provides good holding. Six feet can be carried close up to the beaches on the northern and western shore. In buccaneer days, large fleets of privateers based in the harbor and careened their ships on the gently sloping sand beach inside the eastern rim of George Reef. Careening Cay is the name of the small islet with coconut palms at the E end of the reef, and it's still used for that purpose by native boats. The wreck of *Rambler,* an oceanographic research vessel lost in a December storm in 1972, lies hard in the sand nearby, and many earlier wrecks are hidden beneath the sand.

Speaking of wrecks and ocean research, Port Royal Harbour was the site of extensive archaeological exploration for many years, resulting in the discovery of several historic wrecks.

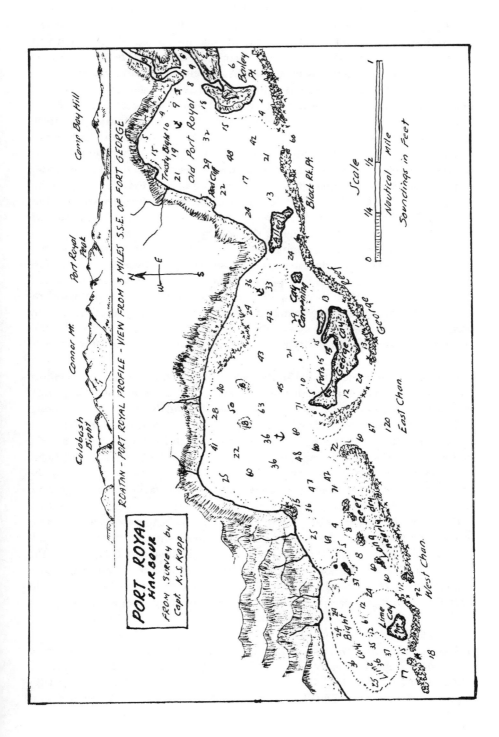

PORT ROYAL
HARBOUR

FROM SURVEY by
Capt. K.S. Kopp

ROATAN - PORT ROYAL PROFILE - VIEW FROM 3 MILES S.S.E. OF FORT GEORGE

Scale

Nautical mile

Soundings in Feet

The first discoveries were made in 1968 by a cruising yachtsman from the Pacific Northwest named Nicholas Johnston, who attracted a number of adventurous divers and marine scientists to the site and negotiated an agreement with the Honduras government sanctioning further exploration. The group, known officially as Oceanographicos de Honduras, developed its own techniques for identification of subsurface sites and found evidence of 11 wrecks in the harbor, one of which turned out to be the remains of a 120-foot hull deep under the sand bottom of the harbor, close by Careening Cay. For many months, the divers dredged sand from the hulk, laboriously moving ballast stones and finding perfectly preserved sherds that proved—believe it or not—to be about 40 large unbroken amphorae, or Mediterranean jars, with insignia that could not readily be identified. Samples were sent to the government of Honduras and to scientific institutions in the U.S., including the University of Pennsylvania's Museum and Applied Science Center for Archaeology. Results of tests based on a modern thermoluminescence technique dated the pottery samples from as early as A.D. 570 to as late as 1470, plus or minus 150 years! Later tests and "corrections" by the Pennsylvania Center suggested other possible dates, between 1510 and 1716, but noted that "dating is not very precise at the 'modern' endpoint of the scale."

When we visited Port Royal in 1980, most of the formal archaeological research had terminated, but some members of the original group were still seeking verification of the age of pottery jars discovered on the first ancient wreck. Informal archaeological activity and scuba diving are continuing from time to time.

In the early 1980s, Port Royal Harbor was able to offer its fair share of facilities for cruising yachtsmen and scuba divers. But by the late 1980s, Roatán Lodge, which stood on a bluff at the west end of the harbor, had discontinued operations.

Today there are few visible reminders of the old Port Royal, where the Spaniards once destroyed 500 houses in the town in retribution for buccaneer attacks on their ships. The Port Royal Farms Company, owned by Eric Anderson, holds extensive acreage around the shores of the bay and has plans for developing the property as a resort, with marina and other waterfront facilities; we're glad we saw it in its pristine beauty.

Port Royal offers good protection in a norther and is frequented by local shrimp boats, fishing vessels, and visiting yachts. One interesting anchorage for small boats is just north of the two rocky cays known as Cow and Calf, toward the western end of the harbor, where you'll find the remains of buccaneer gun emplacements. Other good anchorages may be found N of Lime Cay and in Old Port Royal Harbour, about 1½ miles E of the Fort Cay channel entrance.

Oak Ridge Harbour,

or Pitt's Lagoon, as it was once called, is located about 4 miles W of Port Royal, providing a deep-water harbor entered through a narrow channel with depths of 12 feet over the bar. The channel opens into two forks of the inner harbor, with depths of 12 to 30 feet. The channel over the bar is marked by a damaged and

Josefine lies at anchor in the deserted harbor of Port Royal, once a hidden base for the pirates of five nations.

unlighted light structure on the E side, and by the bow section of a wreck stranded on the reef W of the entrance.

Oak Ridge settlement, with a population of about 1,200 in 1990, is an active shipping port built close around the shores of both forks. The E harbor directly N of the entrance channel is lined with small clapboard houses built to (or over) the water's edge. There is a shipyard and marine railway, with facilities for hauling large shrimp boats. This yard, which has hauled yachts up to 80 feet in length, has a well-equipped machine shop, and may by now have some slips for visiting yachts. Another machine shop and outboard repair facility is located at the E entrance.

The W fork of the harbor has depths of 8 to 20 feet, with numerous private piers and the docks of a shrimp-packing plant. When we first visited Oak Ridge in 1974, the 72-foot Baltic ketch *Josefine* was lying alongside the bulkhead dock near the entrance to the W fork. Owned by Nelson and Jane McClary of Middleburg, Virginia, *Josefine* was built in Denmark in 1895; it sailed for more than half a century as a Baltic cargo boat before her conversion to a yacht. We'll have more to report about her cruise in the Gulf of Honduras later in this chapter.

Fuel, ice, water, and groceries may be obtained nearby.

French Harbour

is the second commercial harbor on the S shore, 7 miles WSW of Oak Ridge. The entrance is marked by a light (unreliable), which you leave to starboard in rounding the town point. The channel is deep enough for ocean steamers as far as the Hyber Shrimp Company docks and packing plant at the W side of the harbor, where a fleet of shrimp boats will usually be seen. This is a locally owned firm that packs and ships frozen shrimp (and crayfish, in season) from Honduras to Miami twice a month in its own refrigerated vessel, the *Hyber Transport.* Two shipyards with marine railways are just W of the Hyber docks, with facilities for handling vessels up to 100 feet. Gasoline and diesel fuel are available at a Texaco dock at the head of the harbor, just N of the Hyber plant; groceries and other supplies may be had at the docks and stores alongside the E shore of the harbor.

The town of French Harbour, with a population of approximately 1,100 in 1982, is almost completely surrounded by water, as a deep lagoon known as Old French Harbour lies back of the settlement, with its entrance to the E. While the entrance channel to this lagoon is deep enough for the large, deep-draft schooner we found moored inside at the time of our visit, the unmarked approach should be explored by dinghy before attempting to enter the first time. Despite its name, French Harbour is populated by McNabs, Dixons, Elwins, and Arches, who trace their ancestry to the first English colonists. The Elwins are descendents of Thomas Elwin, the first English governor, and the McNabs, who operate the public bus service (Jeeps and Land Rovers) between Coxen Hole and French Harbour, look back to even earlier buccaneer days. The French Harbour Yacht Club occupies an attractive site on a hill overlooking both the harbor and lagoon, with guest facilities in the hilltop lodge and boat slips in the lagoon.

The French Harbour Yacht Club facilities and services were upgraded in the late 1980s and reported slips with 9-foot draft, water, power, and laundry facilities, as well as food and drink.

Coves and Anchorages on the South Shore

In cruising the south coast, you will be able to identify at least a dozen more coves and lagoons that invite closer inspection. All of these inlets may be entered through narrow openings in the reef, which lie close to shore in the 20-mile stretch between Old Port Royal Harbour and Coxen Hole. The prevailing trade winds make this a downhill run for yachts heading westward, and a close beat to windward eastbound. But the orientation and distance between ports are comparable to Sir Francis Drake Channel in the British Virgins; the coves are even more protected, though there are not as many good beaches. Here are some of the best.

Calabash Lagoon
lies between Port Royal and Oak Ridge. Vessels running outside the reef must keep a sharp lookout for the narrow, unmarked entrance to this mile-long lagoon that indents the coast. Inside the entrance channel, you can find protected anchorages almost anywhere in the deep bight (also known as Manatee Lagoon), completely surrounded by green hillsides rising steeply from the water. This deep harbor extends almost halfway to the island's northern coast.

Fiddler's Bight

is an intriguing little cove between Calabash Lagoon and Oak Ridge. A connecting shoal-draft channel leads inside the reef and back of the mangrove keys to Oak Ridge Harbour, and is used by local dories and outboards. However, don't try to enter with more than 3-feet draft.

Jonesville Harbour,

once known as Falmouth Harbour, is a two-pronged basin providing several safe anchorages off the town of Jonesville. Island trading boats call regularly at the town docks. Limited supplies are available ashore, but fuel and water are more conveniently obtained at Oak Ridge or French Harbour.

Caribe Point Bight,

also known as Barnsley's Cove, is a large bay that must be approached cautiously, since the reef extends S and W beyond Moley Key before revealing its narrow, unmarked opening. The next bay to the W is more protected and is becoming a popular anchorage for cruising charter boats.

Neverstain Bight

lies half a mile W of Caribe Point. Here the reef opens into a tight little anchorage close to shore, known also as Dalrymple's Bay. Halfmoon Bay at the E end of the bight provides an attractive daytime anchorage off a tiny palm-fringed beach.

First and Second Bight

are two deep indentations W of Neverstain Bight. Yachts proceeding in deep water outside the reef should be able to identify two narrow openings leading into these protected bays, otherwise known respectively as Thompson's Lagoon and Cochman's Creek. Both should be approached with caution, as the entrances are narrow, unmarked, and difficult to read in poor light. First Bight is in fact quite impassable for cruising yachts. A channel is being opened into Second Bight, leading to Parrott Tree Plantation, a resort hotel in the planning stage in 1982, which fronts a completely landlocked lagoon that looks like a mountain lake.

Arch Key and Big Bay

are too intricate for strangers to enter safely, although there are inside channels behind Arch Key and Big and Little French Key leading to Old French Harbour and the lagoon mentioned above. Several sandy beaches are visible from beyond the reef, with a small settlement inside the French Keys having good anchorage just offshore.

Brick Bay,

formerly Roatán headquarters for the bareboat charter operation of Caribbean Sailing Yachts (CSY), this tight little lagoon still provides an anchorage for a limited number of cruising yachts. If it is too crowded at Brick Bay, you should find plenty of anchoring room in 10 to 12 feet behind Big or Little French cays, about 1 mile to the east.

The CSY facilities were taken over by a local operator who had dive boats, a gift store, and a liquor store. These had been closed by 1988–89.

Dixon's Cove

was once a favorite anchorage of British buccaneers, rivaling Coxen Hole, 3 miles to the W. The entrance channel lies between the two easternmost keys. It is marked by the edges of the reefs, which are clearly visible on both sides. Depths up to 15 fathoms are found in the ship anchorage near the center of the cove. Yachts can anchor in 12–18 feet close to the shores, which are fairly steep-to. When we were there in 1980, we joined a fleet of 30 yachts, including CSY bareboats and visiting members of the Cruising Club of America.

In the late 1980s, a family of scientists and naturalists was operating a small resort in this cove.

West of Coxen Hole,

the coastline is steep and provides no all-weather anchorage for almost 4 miles to West End Point. Pyrates Cove, a small bight 1½ miles E of the point, does not provide an anchorage, but may be entered by dinghy in settled weather.

The North Shore of Roatán

As already noted, there are very few harbors on the N coast of Roatán that can be entered safely through the continuous line of reefs, and almost none we recommend attempting for the first time without a local guide or pilot. However, there are several interesting bays and bights used by boatmen, scuba divers, and sportfishermen who know their way around the reefs and can guide visiting yachts to safe anchorages. Here are the principal bays, from west to east.

West Bay

is not really a bay at all but a 3-mile-long bight (Tabiyana Beach), rising steep-to at West End Point, with deep water off the sandy beach and bluffs that trend NE to Lighthouse Point. The bight provides protection in the easterly trades but is wide open to northers and occasional westerly winds. It's not a good overnight anchorage, although boats can lie safely off the beach in settled weather. Halfmoon Bay is entered through a narrow opening in the reef just N of lovely little Lighthouse Point. It's a cove just as attractive as its name.

Mangrove Bight,

also known as Cahoon Hole, is larger than Halfmoon, but it's not recommended as an anchorage for cruising yachts. Tom Fool Bight, as the name suggests, is a place to keep clear of.

Gibson's Bight

affords protected anchorage in the middle of the bight, which may be entered in settled weather a mile NE of Halfmoon Bay. The holding is poor in mud.

Anthony's Cay

is the center of scuba-diving activity on Roatán, with several sportfishing and reef-fishing boats operated in conjunction with the resort. This is becoming the most popular anchorage for cruising yachts on the north shore. The entrance channel through the reef is extremely narrow but is clearly marked and presents no problem in good weather. A small anchorage basin lies just inside Anthony's Cay, with 13–18 feet of water. It is protected in almost any weather, but a 2½-knot current sets across the basin, making two anchors advisable. Anthony's Resort runs a small ferry between the palm-fringed area (where its cay guest cottages are located) and the beach on the main island, where the central lodge and dining room are perched on a steep hillside overlooking the cay and reef. Yachtsmen are welcome, and the meals are generally excellent. A small native settlement and resort-type lodge, the Pirate's Den, are situated close by at Sandy Bay, where the controlling depth for anchoring is only 4 feet.

Man-o-War Harbour

lies about 4 miles E of Anthony's Cay and provides temporary and fair protection behind Man-o-War and Conner's cays. Our repeated caution about entering

Anthony's Cay resort, on the north coast of Roatán

through the narrow openings in the outer reef holds especially good from here to the eastern end of the island, despite the tempting names along the 20-mile stretch of coast—names like Turtling Bay, Hottest Sparrow Bay, Polittily Bight, and Barbarossa Bay.

Islas Barbareta, Morat, and Santa Elena

These three small islands lying within the reef off the east tip of Roatán should be approached only from the south, as the break in the northern reef leads one into strong tidal currents and uncharted shoals and coral heads. About 1½ miles S of Barbareta, on the edge of the reef, there are two small cays between which an opening leads northward (toward the high land at the center of island) into a clear basin in the protected bight between West End Beach and Pelican, or Pelham, Rock. The island is privately owned. Another opening in the reef lies about half a mile S of Elena and E of Rose Cay, leading NE toward a narrow channel into the S end of Morat. Elena harbor is entered through a channel W of Rose Cay, which leads to a small settlement. While these channels are visible to the eye in good weather, they should always be approached with caution, using a depth finder or lead line. The canal at the E end of Roatán is navigable only by canoe, dory, or small outboard.

Isla Guanaja (28123)

Guanaja, the most easterly of the Bay Islands, lies about 15 miles ENE of Roatán and 24 miles off the mainland of Honduras. Columbus is believed to have anchored here in 1502, and Guanaja's green hills, rising to heights of 1,200 feet, are easily identified, and provide the first landfall for vessels approaching the Gulf of Honduras from the east. There is now a customs office at Guanaja Settlement, making it possible to enter here before proceeding to Roatán. For eastbound vessels with time to visit all the Bay Islands, Guanaja is worth returning to, even though it usually means a windward beat across the channel from Roatán. Like all the main islands, Guanaja rises from a very steep coral bank and is completely surrounded by a barrier reef that extends several miles offshore on the northern and northeasterly sides.

The island is about 8 miles long and 2½ miles wide at its widest point, but it has few harbors comparable to Roatán. Its charm lies in the rugged, heavily wooded hills that rise steeply from the water's edge and the lines of palm-fringed cays that lie just inside the reef along the southwestern shore.

The principal town and anchorage are at the southwestern end of the island, where a large fleet of shrimp boats may often be seen at anchor in the roadstead or tied up alongside the docks of the settlement. There are depths of 20–60 feet in the anchorage, but the surge is uncomfortable in northers, and there are numerous shallow banks and sand bores. Two deep channels lead through the reefs, which are clearly visible in good weather but may be confusing when entered for the first time. Pilots are not required, but can be obtained if needed.

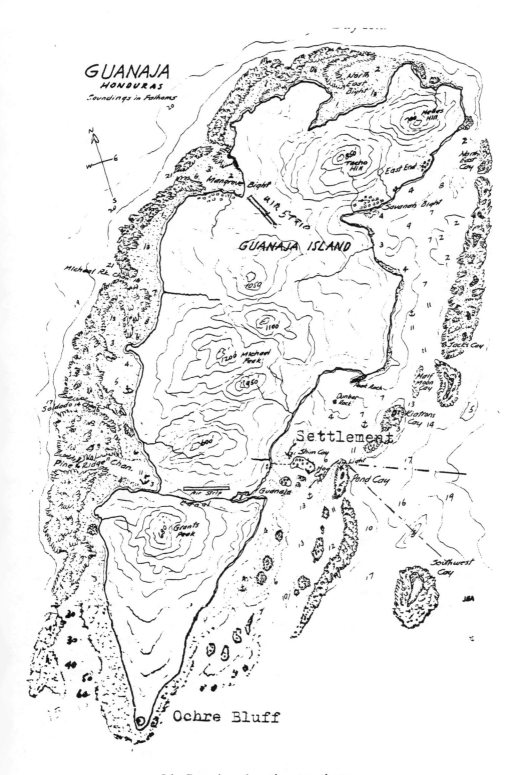

Isla Guanaja and southwest anchorages

BA 1718 and the British *Pilot* provide adequate directions for entering. A light standing 30 feet high on a metal column just E of Pond Cay marks the inner entrance leading to the town, which is situated on two small sandy islets named the Sheen Cays.

Most of the population of Guanaja, estimated to be about 3,600 in the mid-1980s, lives on these tiny cays in one of the most unique coastal settlements of the Americas. The highest "land" on the cays is scarcely 18 inches above high water, and most of the frame houses are built on poles extending over water. Bridges and narrow causeways connect the two islands. Storms and hurricanes have submerged the town more than once, but it has been quickly rebuilt on the same low site—"to avoid flies and insects," as they say on the higher shores of the main island. Good water is piped in from the main island. There are two "downtown" hotels and numerous small shops, churches, bars, and restaurants along the crowded main street and alleys. Spanish and English are both spoken, although Spanish seems to be more prevalent here than on Roatán. Fishing, chiefly for shrimp and crayfish, is the principal occupation, and you'll often see 50 or more shrimp boats in the harbor. Daily airline service is maintained between the island and La Ceiba on the mainland. The airstrip is on the main island, at the end of a lagoon that provides the only fully protected small craft harbor, half a mile from the town. Small ferries ply between the lagoon and the settlement. You will find plenty of deep water with good anchorages in the channel leading northward to Savannah Bight, with good snorkeling on the reefs behind nine small cays. You can also continue counterclockwise around the N end of Guanaja, with anchorages behind the reefs at Mangrove Bight and Michael Rock Channel, where there is an attractive small resort. Still another good anchorage is found in El Soldado Channel in 23 feet at the end of La Laguna Airport. Wilensky's excellent sketch charts are essential in piloting through the reefs on this side of the island.

Isla de Utila (28143)

Smallest of the Bay Islands, Utila lies at the southwestern end of the group, about 19 miles offshore and 16 miles WSW of Roatán. It is lower than the other islands; its ridge of wooded hills reaches a maximum height of about 290 feet at the northeastern end, where a red framework tower (no longer lighted) provides a distinctive landmark. The principal harbor, Puerto Este, is located at the southeastern end of the island, in a natural bight that provides good protection in northers and the prevailing trades. While the harbor is exposed to the S and SW, a fringing reef affords sufficient shelter except in severe weather. The entrance should be approached from the SW, and vessels entering from N or E must be careful to keep well outside the fringing reef that extends for at least a mile and a half southwesterly from the dark, reddish cliffs that mark the southeastern end of the island. A light is usually visible from a small wooden building about 400 yards from the eastern side of the entrance, but the channel must be navigated carefully by eye to avoid the two shallow ledges, on either side of the 300-yard-

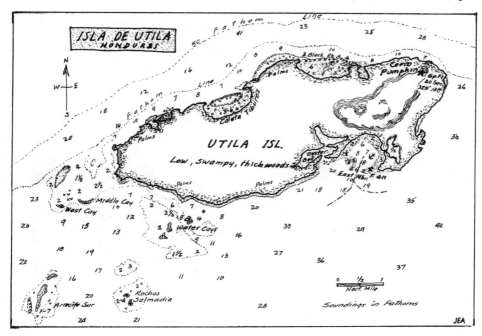

wide entrance, and two small submerged coral heads with 6 feet or less over them inside the harbor. A controlling depth of 20 feet can be carried all the way into the harbor. Local pilots use a range of 020°, formed by a church steeple and a conspicuous tree. Yachts can find good anchorage in the northwestern side of the harbor, in 10 to 20 feet; most of the eastern side is shallower, with foul ground and coral heads.

The Utila settlement, built around the shores of the harbor, is smaller than Coxen Hole on Roatán, and is also a port of entry. It boasts several general stores where limited provisions may be found; gas and diesel fuel are available at the Texaco dock, also water and ice plus groceries at a store. A small resort hotel rents scuba, snorkeling, and fishing gear, and has outboards for exploring the reefs and cays. There are two restaurants and several local boardinghouses; they serve home-cooked meals at reasonable prices. Daily air flights from La Ceiba were discontinued for a time in the early 1980s, following storm damage to the airstrip, but were resumed shortly afterward, bringing a few more tourists to the island. But the island and its settlement remain much as they were 50 years ago. Both English and Spanish are spoken.

There are many other fine anchorages for cruising yachts in the small cays that extend off the southwestern end of the island, and there is plenty of water in the deep, winding channels that lead between the sandy shoals. Here you can find some of the best snorkeling and diving anywhere in the Bay Islands, with protected anchorages in pools and basins behind the cays. Two of the cays, Pigeon and Sucsuc, are populated by an interesting fishing community, which supports

View of Utila, westernmost of the Bay Islands, a boat-building and deeply religious community

several churches, grocery stores, and shrimp boats; these cays are well worth a visit. Although the principal cays, shoals, rocks, and ledges are clearly shown in the large-scale charts and Wilensky's sketch charts, we recommend exploring the area first, by dinghy or with a local guide.

The northern side of Utila is fringed by reefs that extend up to 400 yards offshore, with only a few narrow entrance channels, which are hard to identify from seaward. Inside the reef, however, there are two shallow basins, or lagoons, used by local fishermen. They are worth exploring by dinghy but are not as rewarding as the cays to the SW. Black Rock Basin, the eastern one, is entered through a channel that lies about midway between Black Rock and the east end of the reef, where it converges with the shore. Depths of 6 feet can be carried over the channel bar, and anchorage inside may be found in 6–18 feet S of the entrance. The basin shoals rapidly at the western end.

Utila is a pleasant place to linger for a few days. It was a favorite port of call for *Brer Fox,* and we found it a convenient point of departure for a daylight passage to Puerto Cortés on the mainland.

Cayos Cochinos, or Hog Cays (28143)

No cruise in the Bay Islands is complete without a visit to these exotic little islands, which look as if they had been transplanted from the South Pacific.

The Cochinas lie on a coral bank between Roatán and the mainland, about 20 miles S of Coxen Hole and the same distance NE of the mainland port of La Ceiba. When the trades are blowing, they can be reached in a few hours from almost any point on Roatán or Guanaja.

Two large hilly islands, Cayos Grande at the NE end of the bank and Cayos Pequeño less than a mile to the SW, are separated by a deep open channel that divides both islands from a dozen tiny, sandy cays that fringe the entire eastern side of the coral bank. In settled weather the best anchorage is off a sandy beach on the SW side of Cochino Grande in depths of 10 to 30 feet. The palm-covered hillside behind the beach rises to a height of 469 feet, and the Griffith family, original owners of the Cochinos, live at the N end of this beach. Several other homes and beach cottages have been built along the shore in recent years but have not disturbed the tranquillity of this island group.

In a winter norther the anchorage at Cochino Grande becomes rough, in fact untenable if the storm lasts more than 24 hours. Under such circumstances, better anchorage will be found on the E side of the large island, near a pier built by Ed Kaunitz, an American boat builder and engineer.

Another good anchorage is on the SE shore of Cochinos Pequeño, in 12 to 15 feet off a sandy beach, part of which serves as a small aircraft runway built by a retired airline pilot.

About half of the small fringing cays are inhabited, at least part of the year, by their local or North American owners, most of whom discovered these islands while cruising the area by boat. There's an Indian village on the E side of Cochino Grande, just S of Ed Kaunitz's place inside the close-in reef. You could well spend several days exploring this lovely island paradise.

THE NORTH COAST OF HONDURAS

Some of the most exciting scenery in the Caribbean is found along the mountainous north coast of Honduras, but the steep-to shorefront provides almost no protection along the 130-mile section between Cabo Honduras and the border of Guatemala to the west. The prevailing trade winds make this an uncomfortable lee shore for most of the year; winter northers can be dangerous for small vessels, and during the hurricane season it would be one of the worst places imaginable for any vessel to be caught. Although most of the hurricanes recorded during this century have turned north before reaching the Gulf of Honduras, there have been notable exceptions, like Hurricane Fifi in 1974, which caused great damage along this coast and in the interior of Honduras. Coastal areas fared better in this instance than mountain districts, where torrential rains created flash floods that took a heavy toll of life, while the Bay Islands suffered relatively little damage.

The principal ports on this section of the coast are open roadsteads, with only one partially protected harbor, Puerto Castilla, really worth considering for an overnight anchorage.

Islas de Cochinas
HONDURAS

Scale 1 N.M.

Soundings in Feet

COCHINA GRANDE

Breaks

N.E. Cay

Upper Long Cay

Lower Long Cay

Lamb Cay

Round Cay

Upper Monitor

Lower Monitor

COCHINA PEQUENO

Chicken Cay

Baby Cay

N.W. Cay

SEA

Puerto Castilla (28142)

is a small port on the south side of Cabo Honduras on the peninsula that forms Bahía Trujillo. It provides shelter from northers and easterly winds. Anchorage may be found off the town about 2 miles SE of Punta Castilla. This was once a major shipping port, but the old pier is in ruins and the town largely abandoned. The lagoon at the eastern end of the bay makes an excellent all-weather boat harbor for vessels that can clear the shallow bar off the entrance channel, where depths vary after each major storm.

Puerto Trujillo (28142)

is a port of entry on the south side of Trujillo Bay. It has little to offer visiting yachts, and the anchorage is exposed to all but southerly winds. This town played an important role in the early years of Spanish colonial rule. Several expeditions were launched against Roatán when that island was occupied by British pirates in the 1700s.

La Ceiba (28144)

is one of the principal ports of Honduras and a growing commercial city of about 40,000. It has a 1,400-foot pier for loading bananas and lumber, but no facilities for yachts. The anchorage is an open roadstead, and during northers vessels must put to sea. There is daily air service to Roatán and the Bay Islands. Water and fuel are available at all of the major mainland ports, but the process of fueling yachts may be time-consuming.

Puerto Tela (28161)

lies about 32 miles westward of La Ceiba, in a section where the low coastal plain rises a few miles inland to jagged mountain peaks that are often lost in the clouds. Rivers flow down from the mountains, spilling over their banks in the rainy season and disgorging tons of yellow silt into the blue Caribbean Sea. The anchorage at Tela is another open roadstead off the commercial pier. It has little to recommend it to yachts and is unsafe in a norther.

Punta Sal (28162)

is a bold rocky promontory on the coast between Tela and Puerto Cortés, which affords protection from the prevailing trades in a small cove and lagoon on the western side of the point. The eastern side of the point provides shelter from northers and is sometimes used as a harbor of refuge by native coasters who have been forced to leave the exposed roadstead at Tela. We bypassed the lagoon entrance on a westbound passage several years ago, but returned later to discover a completely landlocked basin with good anchorages reached through a narrow entrance on the western side of the point. It's worth exploring and makes a good overnight stopping place on a passage between Puerto Cortes and Utila.

Puerto Cortés (28163)

is a major banana port about 15 miles E of the Guatemalan border and 30 miles
W of Tela. Cortés is a principal port of entry for Honduras. Our friends the
McClarys entered here on a passage from Guatemala to the Bay Islands in their
Baltic trader *Josefine,* but reported later, "This was a mistake. Anyone bound for

Approaches to Puerto Cortés

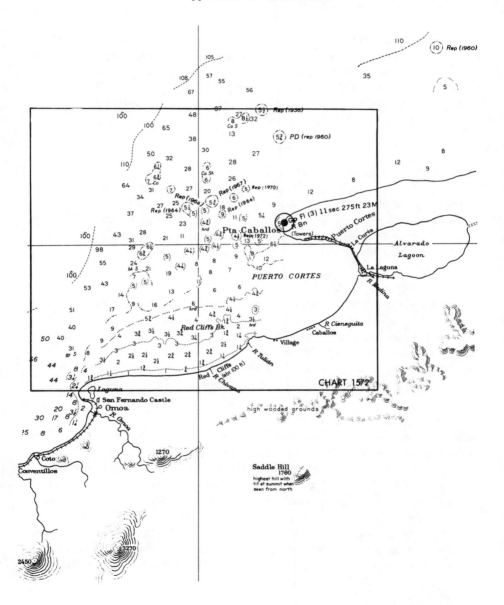

the Bay Islands should bypass the mainland and clear at English-speaking Coxen Hole on Roatán." Finding no one among the officialdom who could speak English, and having no one aboard with much more than high-school Spanish, the McClarys were delayed 48 frustrating hours, ended up paying $130 in assorted fees and gratuities, and narrowly avoided a fine for not having five stars in the center of their home-sewn blue-and-white Honduran courtesy flag. Their warning to other visitors by sea: "Be sure you have the proper flags for all of the countries you intend to visit."

The town of Cortés, with a population of about 25,000, straggles along the shoreline of a deep bay that extends SE of Punta Cabellos for about 2½ miles. There are two commercial wharfs, one of which is a 960-foot banana-loading facility with a movable crane and conveyor belt, and a T-headed oil pier. Fuel and water are available at both piers, but don't expect pumping facilities for yachts. The anchorage off the town is protected from northers and the easterly trades, but is exposed to the westward. Yachts bound for Guatemala should be sure to get their clearance papers before leaving Puerto Cortés; it is the last port on the Honduran side of the border.

EAST COAST OF GUATEMALA TO THE RÍO DULCE (28162)

The ultimate destination of every cruising yacht entering the Gulf of Honduras is bound to be the Río Dulce, that fabulous Guatemalan river that empties into the Bahía de Amatique at the head of the gulf. But before reaching that destination, navigators should familiarize themselves with coastal features of this area and keep their charts and *Sailing Directions* handy for eyeball piloting in the shoaler bank waters, which are a distinct change from the steep-to coast of Honduras.

The coastline of Guatemala is scarcely 45 miles long, as the crow flies, from the eastern border on the Río Motagua to the boundary with Belize on the Sarstoon River in the northwest—but it's more than double that distance if you follow the winding shoreline that meanders inland around Bahía de Amatique and the three smaller bays that form this estuary. From the mouth of Río Motagua, the coast is low, swampy, and bordered by dark-sand beaches that have few distinguishing features for about 27 miles, until you sight the lighthouse and water tower on Cabo Tres Puntas at the eastern entrance to Amatique. Vessels approaching the bay are cautioned against deceptive tidal currents that vary in direction and strength.

You may see one of the American-Canadian Caribbean Line's small cruise ships—6-foot draft and 80 passengers—along this coast, heading up the Río Dulce.

In the late 1980s cruisers were regularly reporting that cruising in Guatemala was "great," citing low prices, stable government, pleasant climate, dramatic scenery, historic sites to visit, and friendly people.

Bahía de Amatique (28162, BA1573)

The entrance to this large bay (also called Honduras Bay) is over 13 miles wide between Cabo Tres Puntas and Punta Gorda, with depths of 6–18 fathoms, shoaling to less than 2 fathoms near the shores and on several sand banks within the bay. Ox Tongue Shoal, the largest of these banks, extends about 7½ miles off the eastern shore and is at its western end marked by a light buoy with radar reflector. All three of Guatemala's east-coast seaports are situated on estuaries of Amatique Bay. Anchorage may be found in Ox Tongue Bight, north of the shoal in the lee of Punta Manabique and clear of the steamer lanes that lead to Puerto Barrios and Santo Tomás.

Livingston, Puerto Barrios, and Puerto Santo Tomás, all on Bahía de Amatique, are ports of entry for yachts. The general consensus is that clearance is easiest in Livingston, with Puerto Santo Tomás the second choice. Clearing out is probably equally easy at any one of the three towns. In the late 1980s earlier restrictions on cruising had been eased, and permits for as long as one month, with possible extensions, were available.

Puerto Barrios (28165)

lies on the eastern shore of Bahía de Santo Tomás de Castilla, about 14 miles SSE of Cabo Tres Puntas. Although Puerto Barrios is somewhat exposed to the prevailing winds, it is convenient to anchor near the Tecno Marine boat and dinghy dock, S of the main pier. Provided they have already checked in, cruisers may use the dinghy dock, which is lighted and guarded 24 hours a day. Water is available here. Tecno Marine is equipped to make extensive repairs, should you require them. In town you'll find good provisioning, good ice cream, and good bus service to the capital, Guatemala City. The open market at Puerto Barrios is said to be one of the largest in the country.

For a more protected anchorage not too far from the town, go over to Esperanza Bay, 1 ½ miles W of the main pier, where you'll find a mud bottom and about 8 feet of water. This is a good place from which to launch a dinghy trip up the nearby San Carlos River. Another anchorage can be found N of Esperanza Bay in 9 to 12 feet of water.

A ferry runs between Puerto Barrios and Livingston, a trip of about 9 miles, which takes about 1½ hours and costs about 30¢.

Puerto Santo Tomás (28165)

is almost an extension of Puerto Barrios and is reached through the same dredged channel that leads into the Bay of Santo Tomás and continues about 2½ miles southward to the end of that bay. There are berthing facilities for commercial vessels at both ports, and a naval installation at Santo Tomás with facilities for lifting 60–80-foot patrol boats. We found good anchorage W of the naval station and in the large bight at the foot of the mountains farther westward. Deep water carries close in to the shoreline, where the wooded slopes rise steeply to mountain ridges 1,500 feet above the bay.

Livingston (28164)

is a small river port at the mouth of the Río Dulce on the western shore of the Bay of Amatique. As noted earlier, it is a port of entry and the most convenient place for yachts to enter and clear. During most of the 1970s, Livingston enjoyed a good reputation with visiting yachtsmen. In the early 1980s, however, the Guatemalan government began restricting cruising permits to a week or less, thus making it almost impossible to cruise the Río Dulce and Lake Izabal. And, after Belize announced its full independence from Honduras in September 1981, with the blessing of Great Britain, Guatemala closed the borders between the two countries and stopped entry by boat at Livingston and Puerto Barrios. In the later 1980s restrictions on cruising on private yachts had eased considerably, and Livingston regained its popularity with yachtsmen.

Once known as the Gateway to Guatemala, Livingston was a bustling center of shipping and commerce at the turn of the century, when coffee, bananas, and timber came down the river by boat from the plantations and hardwood forests of the interior. Planters and the wealthy German owners of the coffee and banana *fincas* traveled by the sternwheeler that carried mail and passengers across Lago

Livingston Bar

de Izabal and down the winding gorge of the Río Dulce. Today the town has lost all traces of its earlier glamour, and the population has dwindled to an estimated 1,500—predominantly Mayan, Ladino, and Black Carib. The Caribs are descendants of early settlers who had been forcibly transported to the Gulf of Honduras from Saint Vincent in the eastern Caribbean during the 1790s and then had migrated here to establish the first community, which they named Labuga, "Mouth of the River." Half a century later, Guatemala's president Francisco Morazán renamed it Livingston after a then-famous Louisiana lawyer who wrote a new penal code, which Morazan adopted, introducing trial by jury to Guatemala in 1823.

Now the little town has surrendered its trade and commerce to Puerto Barrios and Santo Tomás across the bay, but it retains the advantages of its geographic position at the mouth of the Río Dulce and continues its intimate association with the unique waterway that still carries native small craft between the interior and the seacoast of Guatemala. It can be reached only by boat—no roads connect it with the interior.

The Río Dulce to Lago Izabal (BA1219)

When we were in the Bay Islands, the marine archaeologists at Port Royal said of the Río Dulce: "The Mississippi is longer, the Amazon wider, the Yukon colder, but the Río Dulce is the ultimate!"

There are several practical problems for yachts planning to cruise the Río Dulce. One is the 6-foot controlling depth over the extensive bar at the mouth of the river, where the mean rise and fall of the tide is less than a foot. However, the afternoon sea breeze may produce greater depths by backing up the river stream about one half foot or more on a rising tide. *Josefine* needed the assistance of the tug *Río Dulce,* aided by a second tug, *Guatemala,* to clear her 7½-foot draft over the bar, but yachts drawing 6 feet or less should not have serious trouble.

Another problem is the lack of nautical charts. The inland waters of Guatemala are completely uncharted, and the U.S. charts don't go beyond the river delta and a few miles upstream. BA1219 includes the lake but is almost too small in scale to be useful. However, Río Dulce and Lago Izabal have been navigated for more than three centuries by all manner of deep-draft vessels, and, after cruising the river and lake several times over a two-year period, we never encountered any difficulty in piloting by eye and sounding our way to the headwaters of this fascinating river-and-lake system almost 50 miles inland from the Caribbean Sea. We did find it useful to carry a set of aeronautical charts produced by the U. S. Air Force (series ONC J-24, Belize, Guatemala, Mexico) and distributed by the Defense Mapping Agency's Aeronautical Chart and Information Center, Saint Louis, Missouri 63118. While these show no water depths, they do indicate the course of the river and the topographical features around the lake.

Once you are safely across the two sandbars at Livingston, the river flows for

Hotel Catamaran on the Río Dulce

about 8 miles through a winding gorge between steep limestone cliffs backed by heavily wooded hills, with midchannel depths of 16–60 feet. Jane McClary wrote:

> Suddenly the sea lay behind us, we were enclosed in shadow, by walls of living green. Waterfalls cascaded from the sheer cliffs, hundreds of feet high, wreathed in mist. Graceful clusters of mauve candelaria and other rare varieties of *Bromeliad* grew to the water's edge. Here and there branches were hung with the curious nests of the *Oropendula,* the orioles that build their hanging compartments, sometimes as many as a hundred to a single tree. The river twisted and turned, changing direction so sharply that we virtually boxed the compass. Occasionally, in an angle of turns, the rising sun lit the leafy walls with scorching force, only to vanish again leaving us in dense shade. We saw caves in the limestone cliffs. The graffiti of generations decorated the rock where it was exposed. Our boys wondered if the pirates who besieged the fortress guarding the Spanish ships anchored in Lake Izabal had left their mark. These, the buccaneers of the Honduran coast, followed in the wake of the Spaniards soon after Pedro de Alvarado, a 34-year-old captain in Cortés' army, subjugated the Indians of Guatemala in 1526.

El Golfete

suddenly comes into view around a bend in the river as the mountains recede into the distance. It is a "sweet-salt" basin about 9 miles in length with an average width of 2 miles and depths of 12–24 feet. There are several small islands that afford protection in their lee and are well worth exploring. At the western end, the basin narrows and the river continues its winding course through wooded hills, with depths of 12–36 feet in the channel, for about 6 miles where it connects with Lake Izabal. A substantial current flows through the narrow sections of the river at most times of the year, becoming stronger in the rainy season, when you must keep a sharp watch for floating logs.

El Golfete, "the little gulf," is bordered by the jagged splendor of the Mico Mountains to the southeast, the jungle and foothills of the Sierra de Santa Cruz to the northwest. The crocodiles and turtles that old-timers say consorted in the shallows are no longer in evidence. But the McClarys found it possible, literally, to run into manatees, the sea cows that the Caribs feature in their dance, Pio Manati. These beasts may be seen feeding on water plants. Along the shores you pass the thatch-roofed huts of the Indians, half hidden amidst coconut palms, with their small plots of corn and beans nearby. For the Indians, writes Jane McClary, "life flows on, like the river, its course unchanged for centuries." According to tradition, the Indians believe that the river is a vein in God's body, providing the fish they eat and the water they drink, clean, and sweet—*dulce!*

The last mile of the river before you reach Lake Izabal and the new high bridge is full of surprises. It discloses, of all things, a modern marina-hotel on a lush little island, owned and operated by an American couple, Louisa and Kevin Lucas. It's called Catamaran, and has a good anchorage, a dockside bar topped with palm thatch, a swimming pool, and a group of hotel units that can accommodate 36 guests. Kevin Lucas was a navy pilot in 1962 when he met and married Louisa, daughter of a United Fruit Company official; in 1969, after Kevin had left the service, the couple bought the island and became the first Americans to own and operate a hotel in that area.

Catamaran is a fine base for exploring the lake and surrounding country. Fresh water and fuel are available at the Lucases' marina, and at the Marimonte Marina and Hotel dock across the river. Food may be bought at the little marketplace of Relleno, at the bridge crossing 10 minutes away by dugout canoe. Catamaran is now accessible from Guatemala City, 165 miles by the road that opened in 1971, linking the capital with Tikal in the Petén rain forest, where the great city of the Mayan civilization is being restored. One may travel by bus, an experience no intrepid traveler should miss, or charter Kevin Lucas's plane for trips to the historic capital of Antigua, the market at Chichicastenango, and Lake Atitlán.

Lago de Izabal

Offering another kind of cruising, Lake Izabal is almost 30 miles long from E to W and 10 to 12 miles wide, with depths of 36 to 48 feet in most of the center area and shoaling to 6 feet around its sparsely settled shores. There are only two towns of any size around the lake—Mariscos on the S shore at the foot of the heavily wooded Mico Mountains, and El Estor on the N shore only a few miles from the western end of the lake. The large International Nickel mine at El Estor is inoperative due to the depressed world price for nickel.

The new highway bridge at the confluence of the Río Dulce and Lago de Izabal

There are few protected anchorages and, while it is usually safe enough to anchor almost anywhere along the lake's shores, you are likely to have high winds during thunder squalls in the mountains. Perhaps the best and most interesting anchorage we found was in the large bight at the SW end of the lake, shown as Puerto Refugio in the sketch chart and described later.

Castillo San Felipe de Lara,

which stands at the entrance to Lake Izabal, has been rebuilt on its original foundations from plans found in the Spanish archives. The restoration of this structure, built in 1652, offers a tourist version of the colonial outpost that once played an important strategic role in defending the treasure ships that loaded here awaiting shipment to Spain. In fact it was captured three times by pirates, sacked and burned once, and finally destroyed by an earthquake.

A circumnavigation of the lake is very interesting. Starting from Catamaran, our three-day cruise took us along the mountainous south shore past Mariscos, where port facilities were then being built to handle nickel shipments from El Estor across the lake. Since the dock was crowded with small boats and the anchorage looked exposed, we continued to the SW corner of the lake, where we came upon a delightful, protected harbor in a lagoonlike bight called Ensenada

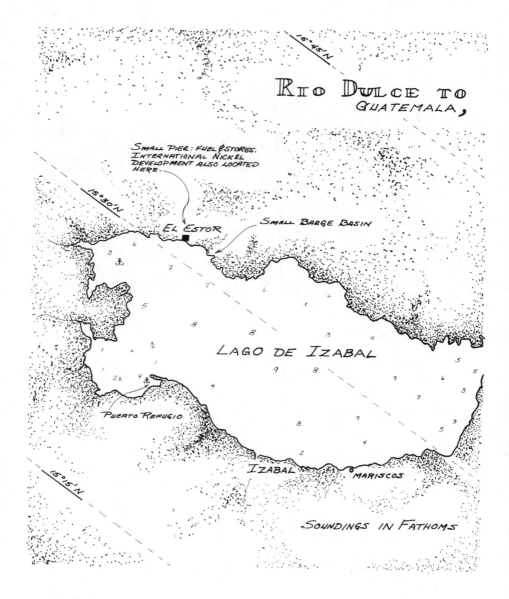

RIO DULCE TO GUATEMALA,

SMALL PIER: FUEL & STORES.
INTERNATIONAL NICKEL
DEVELOPMENT ALSO LOCATED
HERE.

EL ESTOR

SMALL BARGE BASIN

LAGO DE IZABAL

PUERTO REFUGIO

IZABAL   MARISCOS

SOUNDINGS IN FATHOMS

15°45'N

15°30'N

15°15'N

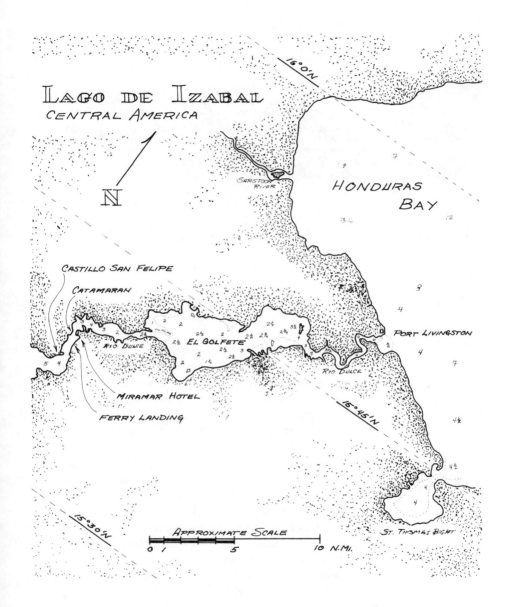

LAGO DE IZABAL
CENTRAL AMERICA

N

16° 0' N

SARSTOON RIVER

HONDURAS
BAY

CASTILLO SAN FELIPE

CATAMARAN

RIO DULCE

EL GOLFETE

PORT LIVINGSTON

RIO DULCE

MIRAMAR HOTEL

FERRY LANDING

15° 45' N

15° 30' N

APPROXIMATE SCALE

0   1   5   10 N.MI.

ST. THOMAS BIGHT

Castillo San Felipe on the shores of Lake Izabal

de Balandroa, or Puerto Refugio on older Spanish charts. Here we spent a peaceful night at anchor in 8 to 10 feet near the head of the bight, with the deep tropical jungle close around us.

From the lagoon you can explore by dinghy a number of small streams that penetrate several miles into the deep jungle. Here we saw a half dozen varieties of brightly colored parrots, along with cranes, egrets, and wading birds. Along the banks were turtles sunning themselves, huge orange-colored iguanas, and, believe it or not, real live howling monkeys! Now, to be completely truthful, we *heard* the monkeys howling over our heads in the trees, for they quite successfully hid themselves from our view.

The next morning we were under way shortly after sunrise, crossing the end of the lake to explore the headwaters of the Polochick River basin, which lies between two mountain ranges and forms a delta fed by numerous tributaries. These jungle rivers are still completely unspoiled, and the wildlife is unbelievable. It was in this area, on the Zarquita River, that we stalked a noisy band of howling monkeys while following a winding channel into a tropical forest where the tall trees touched overhead. The monkeys swung through the trees, only rarely giving us a glimpse of their gymnastic abilities. Giant iguanas sunned themselves lazily in the lower branches. Here, too, we saw scores of tiny hummingbirds feeding on clusters of wild orchids, and we marveled at hundreds of hanging bird nests in the branches of a tall ceiba tree, which looked like huge oriole nests. The birds resembled jackdaws more than orioles, but we were later told that they were the *orependula,* a Central American variety of oriole that often builds as many as a hundred nests in a single tall tree.

Signs of encroaching civilization begin to appear as you sail across the western end of the lake toward El Estor at the foot of the mountain spur on the N shore. A tall smokestack provides a landmark where once there was only an Indian village on the waterfront. It stands about 4 miles W of the village and is part of the large industrial complex of International Nickel Company. In 1977 large piers were built and channel markers set in place for the barges that carry fuel from Puerto Barrios and ore shipments to Mariscos on the other side of the lake. Company executives built a small, enclosed basin with slips about 2 miles E of the main plant. Visiting yachts drawing less than 4 feet are welcome if slips are available at the time. If not, you can anchor off El Estor town docks another few miles to the E. There are several good native restaurants in El Estor, and the old town is definitely worth a visit.

Despite the industrial presence of the mine and refinery, the remainder of the lake is quite isolated and remote, looking much as it did more than a century ago

Western end of Lake Izabal, El Estor, and International Nickel Mine

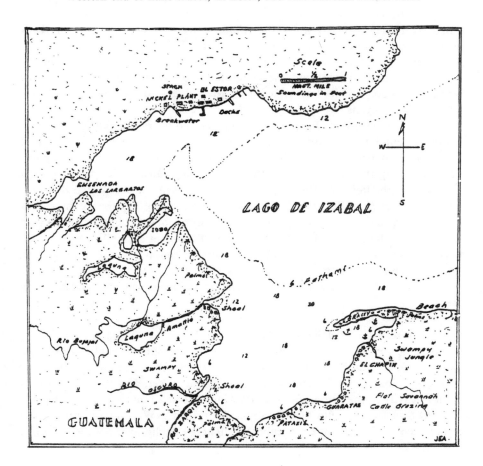

when John L. Stevens, the first discoverer of the Mayan ruins of Central America, described it as "a fairy scene of Titan land."

The prevailing NE winds are generally moderate during the winter months, when cruising conditions are best. From May to September, the winds are frequently strong, with heavy thunder squalls at night during the rainy season. Hurricanes are rare, but Fifi did considerable damage in Guatemala after it passed through Honduras in September 1974.

Coastal Waters Between Livingston and Sarstoon River

There are no protected anchorages in the coastal waters between Livingston and the Sarstoon River, which forms the boundary between Guatemala and Belize (formerly British Honduras). Most of this 10-mile coastal section is low, with little to attract cruising yachts; about 2 miles inland the Santa Cruz mountains rise to a height of 1,395 feet.

The Seven Altars.

There is one major attraction that should not be overlooked by any cruising yacht, especially one with children or teenagers aboard. This is the fascinating series of waterfalls about 5 miles N of Livingston called The Seven Altars, so named because the stream flows down the mountain across seven limestone ledges into seven crystal pools on its way to the sea. These ledges and pools were ceremonial sites for the Mayans.

The first time we visited the falls, the skipper and his rather elderly crew were content to climb to the third altar, but when we returned a few months later with a crew of teenagers, our youthful explorers climbed of course to the very top. Clambering up the slippery bed of the stream, they paused at each rocky ledge to dive over the falls into the deep sparkling pool below and reported that each altar was more beautiful than the one below. At the top they found an artesian spring that gushed from an opening in the limestone rock. On both visits we were lucky to find the spring full and the pools overflowing at each altar. Because the falls may be reduced to a trickle during the dry season, it's best to inquire about the water level before starting from Livingston.

There is good anchorage a hundred yards off the beach where the stream enters the sea.

The Sarstoon River (28162)

is navigable for about 10 miles above the entrance, but the banks are so low, swampy, and covered with mangroves that it's difficult to land anywhere along its shores. The bar at the entrance carries about 6 feet, and the sea generally breaks heavily in the prevailing onshore winds. Vessels bound for Belize usually proceed directly to Punta Gorda, about 16 miles NNW of Livingston, or the Snake Cays, which provide a number of sheltered anchorages another 15 miles to the NE.

Chapter Eighteen

Belize and Its Great Barrier Reef

Cruising the Great Barrier Reef of Belize is full of surprises, even for experienced sailors familiar with the waters of the Bahamas and the eastern Caribbean. Furthermore, these reef waters are different from other parts of the western Caribbean, and even different parts of the same reef have individual characteristics, which makes sailing in each area an experience in itself.

Extending 120 miles north and south between Guatemala and Yucatán, the Belize Reef in terms of length is second only to the barrier reef off Australia. Standing 10 to 22 miles off the sandy Belize coast, it provides a broad belt of protected bank water with a wide choice of anchorages. For its entire length the reef is skirted by hundreds of small islands, sandy cays, atolls, and Pacific-like lagoons.

Whether you sail your own or a charter yacht, you will quickly observe the many subtle differences that make each segment of this fabulous reef a unique cruising experience. You'll discover, for instance, that the cays fall into two basic categories with, of course, nature's customary variations: there are the mangrove cays, locally called the "wet cays"; then there are the sandy, or "dry," cays, which usually have tall palm trees fringing a sandy beach. Most, but not all, of the dry cays are found on or near the outer edge of the barrier reef; in fact some are actually a part of the reef wall, which drops precipitously to the 100-fathom line. Most, but again not all, of the wet cays lie along the Inner Channel, 10 or more miles inside the outer reef. These are often difficult to approach, since many of them lie in shallow, muddy water, and they tend to be covered with impenetrable growth anyway.

Outside the barrier reef, there are two large isolated reefs atop submerged plateaus that rise from the deep seabed to form atolls much like those found in the South Pacific. These are Lighthouse Reef and Glover Reef, which lie 10–30 miles seaward of the barrier reef in the eastern approaches to Belize. Another group of submerged islands, Turneffe, lies beyond the 100-fathom curve between Lighthouse Reef and the entrance channel to Belize City.

Each of these areas is described in the following sections, starting with the Inner Channel, which is the preferred route for small coastal vessels and yachts making the southern approach to Belize. The northern and eastern approaches are discussed in connection with the barrier reef and the outlying reefs and islands.

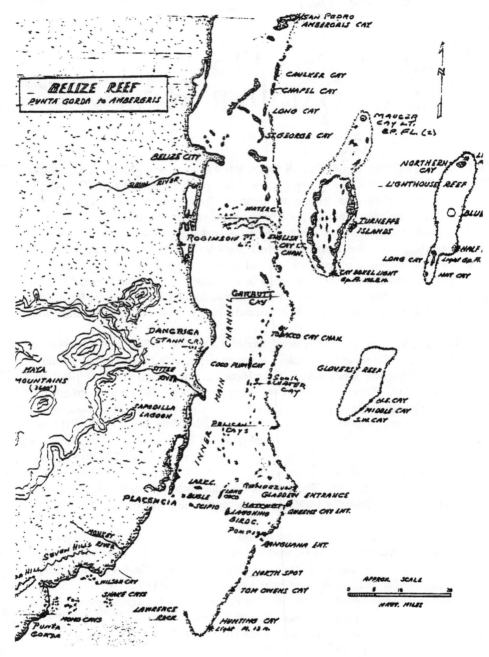

Planning a Cruise on the Belize Reef

Despite our background of cruising in the Bahamas and other parts of the Caribbean, very few of the lessons learned there apply on the Belize Reef. It took us the better part of two years to reach this conclusion, but, from then on, it stood us in good stead in planning any cruise, from an overnight jaunt to one of the barrier cays to a two-week cruise along the full length of the Belize section of the reef.

The first requirement in planning is to study the available charts, such as they are. The U.S. charts for Belize waters are considerably better than those for Honduras and Guatemala. These are the issues you are likely to need:

28167—covers northern area, also approaches to Belize Harbour, scale 1:125,000

28162—covers southern coast and reef, including approaches from Guatemala and the Gulf of Honduras, scale 1:125,640

28168—is a harbor chart for Belize City, the Belize River, and surrounding cays in detail, also the cays to the north of Belize

28000—is a planning chart essential only for those who will cruise their own boats to Belize. It covers the western Caribbean from Yucatán to Honduras, including the approaches from Swan Island and the Caymans, scale 1:936,430

Although the above government charts are remarkably accurate (considering that they are based on British surveys dating to the 1830s), they are not sufficiently detailed to identify many of the smaller cays. In addition to the sketch charts herein, we recommend *Belize Cruising Guide,* by Bill Sorem and used by the Belize charter fleets, which includes sketch charts and air photos and indicates anchorages recommended for their charter clients. These anchorages are generally between Placencia Cay to the south and Ambergris Cay to the north. The islands and cays at the southern end of the reef are not included.

A glance at the charts will tell you that you cannot expect to cruise the entire area inside the barrier reef in less than two or three weeks. In fact, three weeks would be about the minimum time one should allow to visit all of the three main areas, with time to explore the most interesting islands and cays in each.

Each area has its own distinctive characteristics:

1. *The Northern Cays,* starting with Ambergris Cay at the tip of Mexico's Yucatán peninsula, extend southward to Belize City and the main ship channel. Most of this area is shallow, with soft mud bottom, and numerous "wet" mangrove cays along the coast. Close to the reef, however, is a string of small "dry" cays with sandy beaches and coconut palms. The entire area covers some 600 square miles.

2. *The Central Cays* extend southward from the ship channel to Ranguana Entrance, approximately 65 NM along the barrier reef, which is 10 to 22 miles from the coastline, consisting of an area of approximately 1,000 square miles. The most interesting cays lie in a belt between the barrier reef and the wide Inner Channel that extends all the way from Belize City to the border of Guatemala. Most of the "dry" cays face the barrier reef, while most (but not all) of the "wet" cays lie along the Inner Channel.

3. *The Southern Cays* extend southward from Ranguana Entrance for about 18 miles to the Zapotilla Cays at the southern tip of the reef, and along the Belize coastline from Monkey River to Punta Gorda and the Guatemalan border. The reef in this sector lies from 22 to 35 miles offshore. As in the other areas, most of the "dry" cays are found close to the edge of the reef, while the "wet" cays are more likely to be found along shore on the western side of the channel.

The following list is a partial inventory of "wet" and "dry" cays frequently visited by cruising yachts:

A PARTIAL INVENTORY OF BELIZE CAYS

"Wet," or Mangrove Cays (Mostly along coast or the Inner Channel)	*"Dry," or Sandy Cays* (Mostly near edge of the barrier reef)
I. The Northern Cays	
Hicks Cays	Ambergris Cay
Drowned Cays	Cay Caulker
Water Cay	Cay Chapel
	Saint George's Cay
	Goffs Cay
	English Cay (Lt.Ho.)
	Robinson Cay (Lt. Ho.)
II. The Central Cays	
Garbutt Cay	Tobacco Cay
Coco Plum Cay	South Water Cay
Bluegrass Range	Rendezvous Cay
Pelican Cays	Cary Cay
Elbow Cays	Moho Cays
Lark Cays	Long Coco Cay
	Bugle Cays

THE INNER CHANNEL—PUNTA GORDA TO BELIZE CITY

With a few zigs and zags, the 100-mile Inner Channel runs almost due north and south across the easterly trade winds, in generally protected waters with controlling depths of 24–30 feet in the fairways. For the most part, the coastline is low, with long stretches of palm-fringed beaches indented by small streams, jungle rivers, lagoons, and coastal salt ponds, some of which provide sheltered anchorages. There are several small coastal towns and villages, with a friendly English-speaking population of mixed Indian-African-European stock. Most make their living from the sea or as plantation workers. Here the dugout canoes are called dories; they range in size from 12 feet to 30 feet or more and are used for fishing and all forms of water transportation. Some have outboards, some have sails, some are only paddled.

Most of the villages have one or more small piers, but don't expect to find fuel pumps or other yacht facilities along this waterway. Fresh water and limited provisions are usually available, but water from village wells should be boiled for drinking purposes. There are a few small, first-class hotels with good restaurants and some more informal hotels and diving and fishing camps along the coast and in the cays, but, as Dorwin Teague wrote some years ago after cruising the area, "If you aren't happy unless you can get a room in a plush hotel on your vacation, don't go. Epicures will be wasting their time, as the food is rough and ready, service is haphazard and supplies of most kinds are hard to obtain."

On the other hand, if you are not too finicky, you will find much of interest on this primitive coast and among the unspoiled islands and cays along the waterway. If you like to go in style, try a cruise on the American Canadian Caribbean Line, which now cruises in Belize.

From Punta Gorda to Placencia

This section of the coast trends northeast for 38 miles, indented by several bays, rivers, and lagoons. They provide some good anchorages in 2–6 fathoms, but better anchorages may be found in the lee of numerous small cays that lie only a few miles off the shore on the eastern side of the channel. The shorefront is generally low except in the southwest, where it is backed by hills that rise to heights of 400 to 728 feet at Gorda Hill north of Punta Gorda.

Punta Gorda (28162)

is the largest town on the southern coast of Belize, with a population of about 2,500 in 1980. It is a major port of entry used by vessels making the coastal passage between Honduras, Guatemala, and Belize, and is only 16 miles from Livingston across the Bay of Amatique. When we were last there, the beacon shown on the chart was missing (and had not been operative for more than a decade, according to local authorities), but the saddleback mountain behind the town provides a good landmark when you are approaching from eastward. Shoals to the N and S can be avoided on a course of 305° to the government dock off the customshouse and immigration office. This is a good place to check in or out. The anchorage is exposed, but you can lie at the dock in 6 feet in settled weather. The town is connected with the interior by road.

The Seven Hills

shown on the chart a few miles NE of Punta Gorda provide a landmark for vessels entering the large bay of Port Honduras, which is sheltered from the easterly sea breeze by two groups of low islands and sandy cays. The Mangrove Cays at the SW entrance to the bay offer a number of anchorages in depths from 1–6 fathoms. We visited here several times in 1976–77, finding good shelter in a large bight just a quarter mile SW of Frenchman's Cay. In settled weather you can anchor in depths of 30 feet off the wooden pier on the W side of Frenchman's. This exotic little palm island was then owned by Dick More, an ex-navy American whose house was surrounded by lush tropical plants, coconut palms, and livestock, including a 1,000-pound hog who was Dick's special pet. Since then Dick More has passed on, but the island is well worth a visit.

The Bedford Cays

lie about 3 miles N of Mangrove and Frenchman's cays, with anchorage in 2–4 fathoms. In the northern group, Wild Cane Cay, with a caretaker's house on it,

The Seven Hills near Punta Gorda, Belize

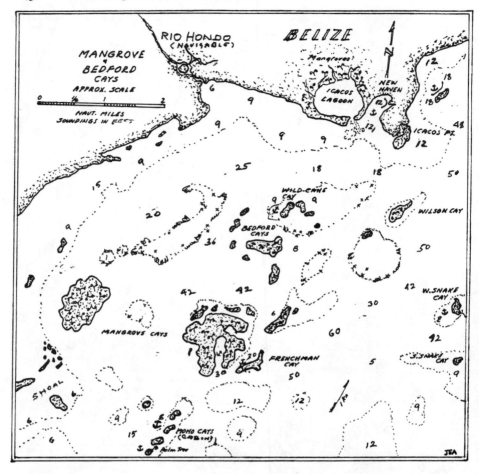

There are a good many anchorages in the Mangrove Cays, the Bedford Cays, and the Rio Hondo.

has some Indian mounds as evidence that the cays were once the site of a Mayan settlement.

Icacos Point

is the southern tip of a long tongue of land that extends S of Punta Negra to form a cove on its western side with depths of 9–15 feet inside and pine trees along the shore. It gives good protection in a norther. Just westward of the cove is a narrow channel with 6 feet in the entrance, leading into Icacos Lagoon, a completely landlocked basin, with numerous mangrove cays and islands. It's best to explore the entrance by dinghy before trying to enter with a keel boat.

The Snake Cays

are four little wooded islets about 3 to 5 miles SE of Icacos Point, surrounded by a number of detached shoals providing temporary anchorage in settled weather. East Snake Cay is marked by a 65-foot concrete lighthouse, but West Snake has the best anchorage. Good diving around coral heads; small sandy beach.

Monkey River

lies about 7 miles NE of Punta Negra, with a conspicuous light on a 54-foot white mast at the river mouth. The stream is blocked by a 2-foot bar across the entrance, and the anchorage off the small town of Monkey River is exposed and uncomfortable in strong on-shore winds. Great Monkey Cay, NNE of the town, is too small to offer much protection, but the bight to the N provides good shelter. This is a "wet" cay with heavy mangrove cover.

Placencia Cay

provides a well-protected anchorage with a fascinating little village on the Placencia peninsula.

You may be able to work your way into the lagoon behind the town with a shallow-draft boat, but most will prefer the anchorage between Placencia Cay and the peninsula, south of the town dock.

The southern approach is straightforward, with the main channel leading through the Narrows between Bugle Cay (marked by a 52-foot light) and Placencia Cay, off the southern end of the peninsula. If you are making an approach from the N, you can enter through the narrow but deep channel between the crescent beach on the peninsula and the tall palm trees on Placencia Cay. Once inside, you can anchor anywhere south of the town pier and westward of the cay in 12–18 feet of clear blue water over a good-looking sand bottom.

The town pier is usually crowded with local fishing boats, dories, and dugout canoes, and there may not be room to tie alongside, although you'll be welcome for a few hours when the fishing fleet is out working on the banks. There is a refrigerated-fish storage plant at the inner end of the pier, where a narrow path leads to the village between tall, waving palm trees. If you are interested in a shore meal, there are a couple of very informal places to eat, and bars with music in town. Rum Point Resort and Placencia Cove Resort north of town serve good dinners, but require 24-hours notice. You may be able to raise them on VHF Channel 16 to make a reservation. To be closer to the resorts, anchor south of the resort dock on the north side of the cove, north of town, over sand bottom.

The village of Placencia occupies the sandy spit behind the crescent-shaped beach; most of its white framed houses are perched high above the ground on piles to keep them from flooding when tropical storms sweep across the peninsula. The houses are laid out in neat rows on either side of the "main street"—actually a mile-long narrow cement sidewalk built to carry wheelbarrows—with separate

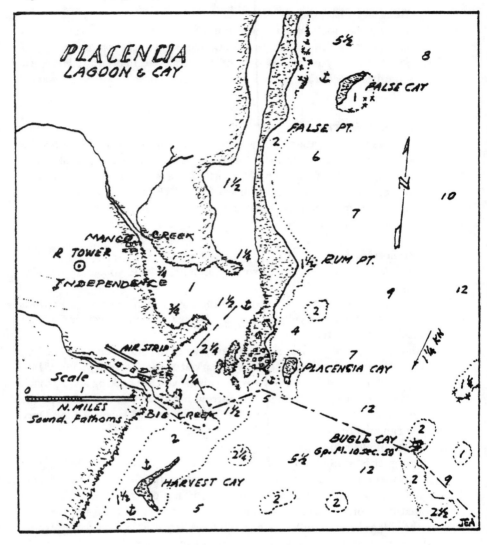

Placencia provides the best all-weather harbor on the coast of Belize.

cookhouses, outbuildings, and sheds scattered round about. The population, about 350, is typical of the coastal villages—a mixture of English, Scotch, Irish, Spanish, Black Carib, Mayan, and African stock. Fishing and processing frozen fish for market are the principal occupations.

At the north end of the white crescent beach there are the two small tourist resorts. The first along the beach consists of half a dozen white framed cottages with a pier and sportfishing boat. The place once belonged to Jim Gavagan, who sailed a Chapelle-designed charter schooner, *Leprechaun,* which you may still see cruising this coast. Bill and Joy Billings replaced him as proprietors. At Rum Point you'll find George and Carol Bevier, who operate the Rum Point Inn, an interesting establishment with interesting people usually around, and an unusual group of housekeeping cottages just back of the sandy beach. The cottages are built of ferroconcrete, like a boat, and look like Eskimo igloos from offshore.

The lagoon at Placencia is a long, shallow estuary extending about 10 miles N and S behind the sandy peninsula. The shoreline near the entrance and well into the lagoon is low, swampy and covered with mangroves, but affords good all-weather protection for shallow-draft boats that is particularly welcome in a norther or strong easterly trades; old Chart 28166 showed depths ranging from one half to 2 fathoms in the southern part of the lagoon, but we found too many discrepancies to use the chart with any assurance. (Big Creek just to the S, which is used by commercial vessels, is not shown at all.) However, with careful sounding it is possible to take vessels drawing 6 feet to protected anchorages far into the lagoon. Starting from the deep water westward of Placencia Cay, we kept about 100 yards S of Little Harvest Cay (identified only as "Cay" on the chart) before turning northwesterly for one half mile toward a conspicuous clump of tall palm trees on the western shore, then heading NNE for about 2 miles into the lagoon. But we'd recommend exploring by dinghy or using a local guide for your first trip into the lagoon.

The anchorage in Placencia off the town dock

The channel into Big Creek is marked with day beacons and carries 7 feet over the bar, with depths of 9–12 feet in the creek. There's a wooden wharf near the airstrip about a mile upstream. Good running water is usually available at the dock. Maya Airways has daily flights to Belize.

Other interesting anchorages in the Placencia area may be found S and W of Harvest Cay, which is easily identified by the tall stand of palm trees SW of the Big Creek entrance channel, with sandy beaches and unspoiled tropical foliage. The Bugle Cays, 3½ miles SE of Placencia Cay, are four little wooded islets providing temporary anchorage on the eastern side of the Inner Channel.

Placencia to Belize City (28167)

The 60-mile coastline between Placencia and Belize City is generally low and marshy in spots, with long stretches of yellow sandy beachfront intersected by small rivers, creeks, and lagoons backed by wooded hills a few miles inland. From Placencia northward, the Inner Channel widens gradually into a broad sound, free of hidden dangers and sheltered by the barrier reef and its fringing islands, cays, and rocks. For coasting schooners and cruising yachts, it's an exhilarating daylight sail up or down the channel, with the trade winds abeam, a blue sky overhead, and sparkling clear water on the bank. In settled weather, the channel is relatively simple to navigate, despite the paucity of navigational aids, and one has a choice of safe temporary anchorages along the coast or under the lee of islands and cays on the reef. In a winter norther or hard easterly blow, however, there's no good protection on the reef and very few all-weather anchorages on the coast. Cruising skippers should be particularly careful to keep track of their position at all times in this area, and to know what anchorages may be within reach during an unexpected blow.

Sapodilla Lagoon

is the only fully protected harbor on this section of the coast. It's about 16 miles N of Placencia and 3 miles SW of Sittee Point. Its narrow entrance is difficult to see from midchannel, but the general location can be identified by houses in the small village of All Pines about a mile N of the entrance and by the extensive pine ridges, 50 to 100 feet high, behind the lagoon. There are depths of 6–12 feet inside the entrance, with good anchorage just west of the southern sandy spit or near the tiny cay N of the entrance. The lagoon is fed by a freshwater stream known as Cabbage Haul Creek.

Sittee Point

stands at the shallow mouth of the Sittee River, about 3 miles NE of the entrance to Sapotilla Lagoon. It provides some protection in a norther. It is marked by a 30-foot light. Coastal vessels anchor SW of the island and S of the river bar in depths of 18–30 feet. Yachts drawing up to 6 feet are much better off in Sapodilla Lagoon.

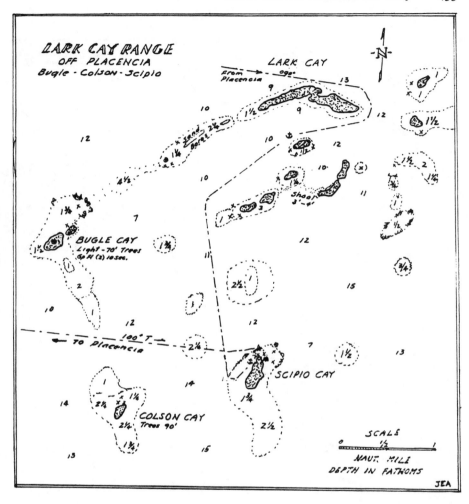

Lark Cay Range, Scipio Cay, and Colson Cay

Dangriga,

formerly known by its Carib name Stann Creek, is the largest town on this section of the coast, fronting the Inner Channel about 10 miles NNE of Sittee Island. Two towers, one for telephone and one for water, mark the town.

There is a 400-foot jetty at the N end of the town that is used by local boats. The anchorage off the town is exposed to winds from N to E to S, but is not uncomfortable in settled weather. Limited provisions are available in the town, which extends along the waterfront for about a mile. The district commissioner has his office here, and there are several small tourist facilities that serve meals. North of Stann Creek the coast trends NNW past Colson Point and the Manatee

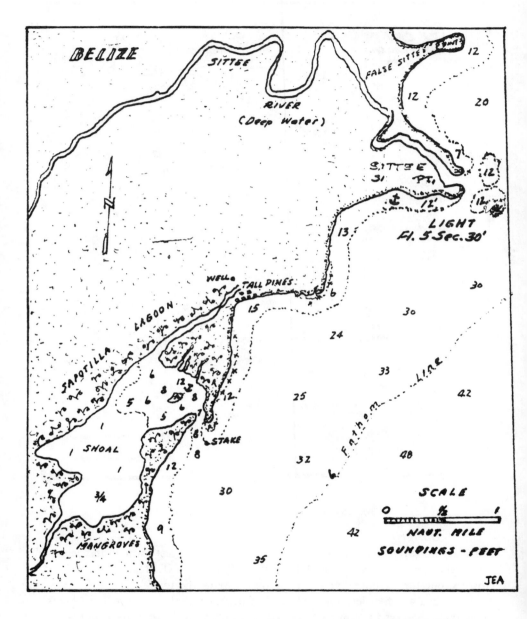

Sapodilla Lagoon, a fine hurricane hole 3 miles southwest of Sittee Point

River, which leads into a large lagoon, but the entrance bar is very shallow and prevents access to boats drawing over 3 feet. There are no good anchorages in the 30-mile coastal section between Stann Creek and Belize City.

Islands and cays

on the eastern side of the main channel provide shelter for vessels making the passage between Placencia and Belize City, and those closest to the channel may be approached safely in fair weather with good visibility. They carry intriguing names like Coco Plum Cay, Crawl Cay, Sandfly Cay, and believe it or not, Wee Wee Cay! Not all of them are as attractive as they sound, for a goodly number of them are low mangrove islets often surrounded by flats and coral heads, typical of the wet cays we have already described.

There are several good dry cays on the channel side of the reef bank. We won't attempt to name them individually, because they are difficult to identify from the chart and even more difficult to distinguish one from another when seen from a distance. The British *Pilot* gives a good description of some of the best cays in its sections covering the reef and Inner Channel, and the charts often indicate those that have conspicuous palms or other trees, showing that they are more than wet mangrove cays. But as we've pointed out before, the charts cannot be depended upon and are unreliable guides once you are off the fairways of the Inner Channel. The configuration of many of the islands has changed radically in the century or more since the original British surveys were made in the 1830s and 1840s. Several large islands north of Belize have actually been cut into two or more small islands, so that you may now follow a deep channel directly across what the chart still shows as dry land. In some cases, hurricanes have completely washed away charted cays.

We don't want these necessary words of caution to discourage you from keeping a sharp lookout for tall palms and sandy patches of beach if you sail along the eastern side of the fairway. Some of your most likely sightings may turn out to be the tall trees on Crawl Cay, about 4 miles E of the main channel line opposite Rocky Point on the Placencia peninsula, where our friend Dave Kimball once found boa constrictors, or the 50-foot trees on the largest of the Pelican Cays, about 4 miles northward. Kimball, who explored the cays for two months from an inflatable outboard boat, found hundreds of boobies, pelicans, and other water birds nesting on tiny Man-of-War Cay, a mile E of Coco Plum Cay.

APPROACHES TO BELIZE CITY (28167)

The approaches from both N and S on the Inner Channel are clearly marked and present no problems. North of Stann Creek the main fairway is wide and clear, with depths ranging from 6 to 10 fathoms until you sight the 42-foot light off Robinson's Point, where soundings drop off to 2 to 5 fathoms for the remaining 8 miles through Belize Harbor and the roadstead off the city.

If you know the worst about Belize Harbor and its open roadstead before you arrive, perhaps the anchorage and shoreside facilities may not seem as disappointing as they do to most visiting yachtsmen. But after cruising in clear bank waters or arriving from a hard ocean passage outside the reefs, you're bound to feel somewhat depressed when you drop your anchor in the dirty, murky-brown waters off the mouth of Haulover Creek and scan the dilapidated waterfront in search of the customshouse. Even with forewarning, it's hard to believe that this is the principal port of what was formerly British Honduras. Deeper-draft vessels are required to anchor from 1½ to 2 miles off the entrance SW of Fort George on the north shore of the river, but yachts drawing 6–7 feet can approach to within 200 yards of the white light tower on the point or about the same distance off the Fort George Hotel. The customshouse is just inside the mouth of the river, readily identified by its flagstaff and orange-red rooftop. A patrol boat or pilot vessel is usually moored in the entrance, with small boats lying alongside the customshouse wharf and bulkhead.

Clearance procedures are handled rather better here than in some other Central American ports. In the 1980s, officials sometimes gathered and came out to your boat, and at other times the skipper had to take the papers ashore to visit customs, immigration, and the port captain's office. The best thing to do is to call the port authority on VHF Channel 16 for instructions, or, for help with the authorities, call Personalized Services, also on Channel 16.

The Eastern Channel to Belize Harbor (28168)

is used by vessels entering from seaward through a wide opening in the barrier reef NE of English Cay, a small island with a 62-foot light structure visible for 13 miles. The winding channel is marked by lighted beacons for about 9 miles to One Man Channel, leading NW into the harbor. Yachts drawing 7 feet or less can steer a course of 325°T from the second beacon W of English Cay across "the Flat" directly to Fort George, a distance of about 8½ miles, as shown in the accompanying sketch. Licensed Belize pilots have a station at English Cay.

Fort George Anchorage

is protected from the easterly trade winds by the Drowned Cays, a group of low mangrove islands 5 miles to the E behind the reef, but it is exposed to northers and uncomfortable in a blow. The current generally sets southward through the harbor at about 1½ knots, but during northers the rate may increase to 2½ or 3 knots. Under such conditions, yachts may find it more comfortable in Siburn Bight, SW of the city or at Robinson Point, at the western end of the ship channel 8 miles S of Belize City. Northers are most apt to occur during November and December, according to the *Sailing Directions,* but they may come with a cold front at any time during the winter months and last two or three days. We encountered one with Force 8 winds in late February, preceded by several days of almost flat calms.

Belize City,

formerly the capital of British Honduras, has a population of about 50,000, nearly a third of the total population of the country. The city is built on low, swampy land, in some places no more than 2 feet above sea level, and has suffered severely from hurricanes. Hurricane Hattie swept a 10-foot tidal wave over the city on October 31, 1961, causing such great damage and loss of life that the capitol and many government offices were moved 50 miles inland, where a new capitol was constructed at Belmopan. Most of the people remained in the old city, however, rebuilding their clapboard houses on piles and mahogany posts on the same

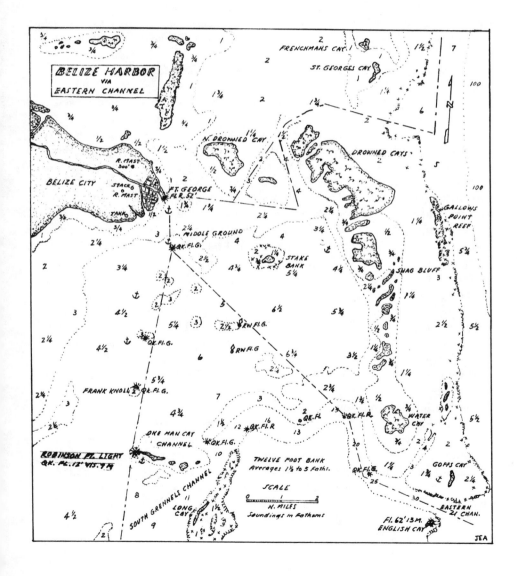

narrow streets on both sides of Haulover Creek. Two bridges connect the two parts of the city, with the town center and market on the south side and larger residences and several foreign consulates on the north side. There are three first-class hotels, the Fort George and the Villa on the north point, and the Bellevue facing the river on the south shore. The Fort George has a long dock that may be reached by dinghy from boats anchored off the point. Fuel, water, and electricity are available, and there is said to be about 8 feet of water at the dock's outer end. A dinghy could be left here fairly safely during daylight hours.

English is the official language, although Spanish is widely spoken throughout the city and countryside. The people are of mixed racial origins, with African and Afro-Europeans accounting for about 60 percent of the total population; Mayan and Mestizo (Spanish-Maya), 26 percent; Afro-Carib, about 7 percent; British and other Europeans, 4 percent, and East Indians and Asiatics, the remaining 3 percent.

Berthing facilities for boats are limited in town, despite the large number of local fishing craft, canoes, dories, tugs, barges, and lighters seen in the river mouth. Fishing sloops up to 40 feet in length are moored bow-and-stern to stakes below the first bridge in the river, and lighters unload cargo at wharfs along the north shore. Sugar is loaded onto barges at a large dock and warehouse between the customshouse and the bridge. Fuel and water may be obtained at two filling stations, both on the north side of the river, one below the bridge, the other just above it. We don't recommend bringing yachts into the river, which is shallow, crowded, and very dirty. There is seldom room to tie alongside the bulkhead at either of the filling stations, or at the market dock on the south side by the bridge, except with a dinghy. So if you require fuel, it's best to carry your own portable tanks, have them filled at the gas station, and take them back to your boat by dinghy. Fairly well-stocked supermarkets and hardware stores can be found in town.

There are several shipyards with repair facilities above the first bridge on the river. Belize has had a reputation for boat building, and most of the yards have had some experience in building or repairing yachts. The fine Honduras mahogany of former years is becoming scarce but is still available in limited quantities, and skilled carpenters and shipwrights have not yet disappeared entirely. When we were first there in 1974, the U.S. consul Robert Driscoll was having a classic Atkin-designed sloop built at one of the yards; he hoped to sail it back to the States at the end of his tour of duty. The hull we saw would compare favorably in workmanship with anything we've seen done by the few remaining wooden-boat builders in the U.S. All parts, machinery, and fittings have to be imported, however, and if your own spare-parts kit doesn't have what you need, you'll have a difficult time indeed in getting replacements of any kind in Belize. We had *Brer Fox* hauled at Jones Shipyard, where they used greased ways and a 12-man wooden windlass. The work was excellent.

Airlines schedule daily flights to Belize City from Miami, Houston, and New Orleans.

The bridge over Haulover Creek, Belize City

Native fishing boats moored off the market, Belize

The Cays North of Belize (28167)

are worth exploring if your boat draws no more than 6½ feet or if you have access to a shoal-draft outboard. The Inner Channel ends just S of Belize, and the entire bank shoals rapidly to depths of 1 and 2 fathoms over sand and mud bottom for about 25 miles on a northeasterly track a few miles inside the reef. There are no recent charts of this area, and the positions and configuration of islands shown on 28167 bear little resemblance to what you will see today. Yet these cays are interesting historically and for their close proximity to the edge of the barrier reef, where some of the finest reef fishing is found. Archaeological research has disclosed evidence of early aboriginal fishing sites on several cays that were later occupied by buccaneers in the early 1600s and permanently settled by the British in the 1760s. We'd recommend using a local pilot on your first venture into these shallow waters. We found the following cays of interest.

Moho Cay,

approximately one fourth mile N of Belize City, is the site of a developing resort. The entrance to the Maya Landing Marina there is marked, and the basin is well protected. Sail Belize, the only bareboat charter business presently operating in Belize, is located here. They offer nine boats, power and sail, from 31 to 52 feet in length. Transients may find a slip here on a space-available basis, fuel, and possibly water.

Saint George's Cay,

about 7½ miles NE of Belize and 2 miles N of the Drowned Cays, was used as a buccaneer stronghold before 1650, when turtling was a favorite occupation. The earliest map of the island, in 1764, when it had been settled by British colonists, shows five large turtle pens and more than 70 houses and other structures on the tiny island, which is used today as an offshore beach colony by well-to-do residents of Belize. There is one good hotel on the small island. A famous battle was fought on Saint George's Cay in 1798 between the Baymen (Belizeans) and some Spanish invaders, and the Baymen's victory is celebrated each year on September 10.

Hicks Cays

are an uninhabited group of mangrove cays on the flats about 9 miles NE of Belize, with little to distinguish them from dozens of other "wet" cays, except for an Indian mound that has provided rich archaeological evidence of a very early pre-Columbian settlement that must have existed a long time. This is one of the best examples of how hurricanes can change the configuration of low islands and cays: the southeastern island of the Hicks Cays group was cut apart by Hurricane Hattie in 1961, and the main channel now leads directly through the middle of what is still shown as a single 4-mile-long mangrove cay on Chart 28167. The new channel has a controlling depth of 10–12 feet. Tugs tow sugar barges through this cut, which is on the main water route to Chetumal Bay and the ports of Corozal and Chetumal. The cut is also used by fishing boats and pleasure craft.

Someone must have had trouble squeezing through, however, as the cut is shown as "Port Stuck" on local sketch charts!

A second passage, Short Cut, W of Montego Cay, has calmer but shallower water—only about 4 feet.

Cay Chapel,

about 5 miles NE of the cut through Hicks Cays, is the first of two inhabited "dry" cays, complete with sandy beaches and waving palm groves and close to the edge of the barrier reef. Cay Chapel is the site of an aboriginal Indian village and a large resort. On the W side, a marina with a well-marked entrance and good protection offers fuel, water, and electricity. It is also possible to anchor on the west side of the island, and on the east side as well, where the reef provides good protection even when the trades are blowing, and especially when a norther is blowing.

Cay Corker,

or "Caulker" as it was called in earlier times, is the northern of the two reef-edge cays, and the site of a native fishing village that has managed to survive successive hurricanes, keeping alive a way of life that can't be too different from that of the Indians and early European settlers. Prior to Hurricane Hattie, most of the 100 or more houses in the village were built along a sandy path close to the exposed eastern shoreline and a few feet back of the sandy beach. Many of these older houses were swept away in the space of 15 minutes during the 1961 blow by a series of huge surge waves that came roaring in from the reef not much more than a mile off the beach. The "main street" has been relocated nearer the middle of the narrow neck of the island, with new houses, outbuildings, and community structures clustered along both sides. A map of the village, made during a 1965 study (*The Geography of Fishing in British Honduras,* conducted by Alan E. Craig), shows 101 structures at that time, including a "hurricane-proof" school, a "cricket pitch," a fisherman's cooperative warehouse, and several wooden piers and docks.

The village looked much the same on another visit, 15 years later, a few months before another hurricane bypassed Belize but swept all the reef cays with gale-force winds and high seas. We enjoyed meeting several of the natives, including the local master boat builders, Simeon Young and his brother, then in their late seventies, and the eighty-year-old sailmaker. The Youngs took us out to the edge of the reef in their small outboard on a clear, calm day; you could see the beautiful coral heads rising from the sandy bottom in 2 fathoms of crystal-clear water only a stone's throw from the precipitous drop-off ledge, with depths of 100 fathoms a few hundred yards beyond. There are depths of 1½ to 2 fathoms between the reef and the eastern shore of Cay Corker, where it's safe to anchor, in settled weather, and take your dinghy ashore to one of the small piers. In a northerly or easterly blow, fishing vessels move around to the western side of the island, where there's good holding ground (look for sandy patches) in an anchorage within the bight west of the village. Sometimes you'll see a sizable fleet of Creole smacks and small trading vessels lying at anchor or tied to the pier in the bight. The 600 inhabitants make their living lobster fishing. Lobster is plentiful during the season, July 15 to March 14.

Unfortunately, things sometimes change rather abruptly, for on our last visit we found several hundred young North American hippies overrunning the island and occupying every available house thereon. Now the Villa Adventure resort here provides tents for its guests on a budget. A ferry from Belize City gives easy access.

Bahía Chetumal (BA 1204),

which extends northwestward from Cay Corker to Corozal and the Río Hondo and forms part of the border between Belize and Mexico, is a large, very shallow bay. It is poorly charted and not covered at all by any published U.S. Navy chart. Although local boats and shoal-draft barges carry cargo between Belize and Chetumal, it is not an area to attract yachts, and we have made no attempt to include sailing directions to the few ports that might be reached by cruising boats. However, you can take 5 feet up to Chetumal; some of our friends who've made the passage enjoyed the experience and recommend it to others.

APPROACHES TO THE BARRIER REEF (28167)

However it is approached, whether from the N or E or S, the great barrier reef of Belize is impressive. Furthermore, this coral-fringed shelf at the edge of the Belize coastal bank offers a more formidable challenge to mariners than any comparable shorefront we know about in the Caribbean or Bahamas. For amateur skippers cruising this coast, here are three major navigational cautions: (1) be sure of your precise position at all times in the vicinity of the reef, (2) positively identify small islands and cays on the edge of the bank, and (3) carefully pinpoint those in the vicinity of the few openings that provide safe channels onto the bank. We suggest you keep a copy of the *Pilot* aboard as a constant necessity!

Openings are shown on the charts, but as we've mentioned before, the features of the cays are so similar that it's often difficult or impossible to determine the location of critical entrance channels. The British *Pilot* for the east coasts of Central America gives a detailed description of the principal openings, but cautions its readers that the information is "only given with a view to assisting a vessel in case of necessity." Below is a partial inventory of cays with protected anchorages, from S to N.

Zapotilla Cays to Gladden Spit (BA 1573)

The Zapotilla Cays are a group of small islets at the southern end of the long barrier reef, about 30 miles eastward of Punta Gorda. Vessels proceeding north-westward from Puerto Cortés, on the coast of Honduras, may enter the Inner Channel through Zapotilla Cut, an opening about half a mile wide NE of Zapo-tilla Cay, which can be identified by a clump of coconut palms. The cut has a controlling depth of 24 feet in the channel, bounded on the NE by Low Cay and a 57-foot light structure on Hunting Cay half a mile northward. One can anchor W of Hunting Cay in 9 to 12 feet. Fishing and diving boats from Guatemala are often found here. Both cays are inhabited, and there are likely to be fishing nets and fish traps in the area.

Many interesting anchorages are found in the Zapotilla Cays, with excellent snorkeling and fishing close by. Although the cays may seem too small to provide much protection, you can usually find a lee, even in a norther. The following are good overnight anchorages.

Nicolas Cay,

a wooded, sandy cay less than a mile N of Hunting Cay, where the best anchorage is on the N side close to the reef.

Tom Owen's Cay,

about 6 miles N of Nicolas, with protection in a tiny basin formed by the reef just E of the cay.

Ranguana Entrance

is the next navigable opening, about 14 miles NNE of Hunting and Nicolas Cays, in a section of the reef presenting few distinguishing features along the edge of the bank. We would not care to be caught here in a norther or a hard squall with poor visibility, since the 50-foot trees on Ranguana Cay provide the only identifi-cation nearly a mile W of the breaking edge of the reef. However, this entrance and two others to the NE are used by local vessels approaching the Inner Channel at Placencia, 15 miles NW of Ranguana entrance.

Queen Cay and Gladden Entrance

are the two most easterly openings on the entire barrier reef, about 22 miles E of Placencia. They are not easy to identify from seaward, as the edge of the reef rises steeply from depths of 400 to 600 fathoms, and the only distinguishing landmarks lie almost a mile westward of the Queen's entrance. These are the three low sandy islets covered with bushes, known as the Queen Cays. There are depths of 18 to 24 feet in the mile-wide Queen Cay channel and similar depths in Gladden

Entrance, about 3 miles NE, but the bank within both entrances is so studded with shoals, cays, and isolated coral heads as to make navigation hazardous. "Neither channel," says the British *Pilot,* "should be attempted without local knowledge or a local pilot." Yet given a competent pilot, you'll find some of the most interesting cays anywhere around in this wide section of the bank on both sides of Victoria Channel and the Inner or Main Channel.

Victoria Channel and the Central Cays

combine to form a fascinating cruising ground. Here are some of the cays we found most interesting, starting S of Ship Channel and continuing S to Gladden Entrance and Victoria Channel.

Tobacco Cay,

at the very edge of the Barrier Reef just N of the entrance of that name, is a tiny sand cay easily identified by an exceptionally tall stand of palms. There are fishermen's huts among the trees and good diving along the reef. Tobacco Entrance is one of the two best departure points for Glover Reef.

South Water Cay,

about 6 miles S of Tobacco Entrance, is an inhabited island directly fronting the edge of the reef, with a good anchorage on the W side and a deep channel on the S end, almost as wide as Tobacco Entrance.

Pelican Cays,

on the Inner Channel side and SW of Water Cay, offer perhaps the best all-weather anchorages in the Central Cays. These six or so small mangrove cays form a protected lagoon with depths of 40 to 60 feet in the center. Unlike other mangrove cays these little islets sit atop coral banks and are surrounded by deep water. We moored to a mangrove stump while our stern swung free in 60 feet. The staghorn coral beneath us was teeming with tropical fish.

Crawl Cay

lies at the N end of a long narrow coral reef at the juncture of Victoria Channel and the Inner Channel, with 60- to 80-foot depths right up to the beach. It was here that our crew member Dave Kimball found a boa constrictor, and many varieties of water birds.

Lagoon Cays,

3 miles N of Crawl Cay, are not as attractive as they may appear on the chart. The anchorage is S of the entrance to the lagoon, which can only be entered by dinghy.

Moho Cay,

a small, isolated dry cay near the S end of Victoria Channel and due E of Placencia, is inhabited by native fishermen. The chart indicates good water.

Long Coco Cay,

3 miles W of Moho, has a good anchorage on its W side in 20 feet.

Laughing Bird Cay,

with its tall palm trees visible SW of Moho Cay, is one of our favorites in the Central Cays group. When we were there in June, the laughing gulls were hatching their eggs on the beach—literally hundreds of male birds circling the nesting area with shrill cries while the females hovered over their chicks on the beach. If you encounter them at hatching time, be careful not to disturb their nests.

This anchorage is exposed in a norther.

Hatchett Cay and Little Water Cay

lie close to each other at the southern end of Victoria Channel, only a few miles from Queen's Cay entrance. They are worth a visit in settled weather.

Ambergris Cay to English Cay Channel (28167)

From Ambergris Cay at the southern tip of Mexico's Yucatán peninsula, the long, breaking fringe of the barrier reef trends southward for about 35 miles to English Cay and the ship channel to Belize City. The reef in this section is steep-to, with only a few openings for small boats. None are safe to enter from seaward without local knowledge. All the small cays—Saint George's, Cay Chapel, and Cay Corker—should be approached only from the bank side, as previously described, although it's possible to take vessels drawing 6 feet or less through several small openings in the reef between those cays.

Ambergris Cay,

25 miles long and one half mile wide, is the largest, most developed cay. It is low and swampy, but has a long sandy beach facing the reef, which is only about half a mile offshore along parts of the eastern side of the island and even closer at the northern end. The island is separated from the mainland of Yucatán peninsula by a shallow boat channel called Boca Bacalar Chico, used by local fishing smacks and dories but not recommended for yachts without local knowledge. From offshore, it is difficult to see the opening, and the island appears to be part of the coast.

San Pedro, the largest village on Ambergris, is fast becoming a popular beach resort town, with daily air service linking it with Belize City and Corozal. It has an attractive beach fringed with tall palms, several small resort hotels, and close access to reef fishing and snorkeling.

Just S of the town is an opening in the reef, but the channel is difficult to spot from seaward. When we last entered there, a yachtsman, responding to our call on VHF-16, came out in a dinghy to direct us in. Ken Saylor took his 40-foot Allied-Wright through the opening on a 300° heading on a green-roofed house at the S end of town. However you come in, keep a sharp eye for a rock to port, which breaks gently in the usual swell.

To check in here, you'll have to pay to fly customs officers over from Belize City, which will cost U.S. $35 or more.

Yachts with 6 ½ feet of draft will have more than enough depth to proceed S inside the reef.

OUTLYING ISLANDS, REEFS, AND ATOLLS

Lying outside the great barrier reef and athwart the principal deep-sea approaches to Belize are two large isolated reefs and the uncharted Turneffe Islands we spoke of in the introduction to this chapter. Columbus never sighted the reefs when he first approached the Gulf of Honduras in 1502, but for centuries afterward mariners from many nations found them a major navigational hazard, as numerous stranded wrecks still attest. Today they continue to present a challenge to yachtsmen who venture into these waters.

Obviously, these outlying dangers must be approached with great caution. The reefs rise suddenly, without warning, from depths of 500 to more than 1,000 fathoms, and are steep-to on all sides, so that soundings give no advance notice of shoaling. Currents often set strongly around them, and they are so low that they are seldom visible for any distance.

Glover Reef

Named after the English buccaneer John Glover, who operated off the coast of Belize in the early 1700s, Glover lies approximately 12 miles eastward of the barrier reef and about 40 miles southeast of Belize City. The reef is some 15 miles long from north to south and 4½ to 6 miles wide, enclosing a shallow lagoon of about 80 square miles. Seen from a high-flying aircraft, it looks more like a South Pacific atoll than anything you are likely to see anywhere else in the Caribbean. Geologically, it was formed by coral growing around the edges of a steep limestone plateau that was flooded by the sea after the last glacial period; as the sea level continued to rise, the coral growth kept pace with it, until today it is several hundred feet thick, forming a wall 44 miles long that drops off steeply to the seabed all around the rim of the reef. Some 24 different species of coral have been identified, and the reef is still growing and changing its shape. The northeast side was reported to be extending eastward in 1969, and must be given a wide berth. In fact this edge of the reef is now reported to lie 1.5 miles eastward of its charted position!

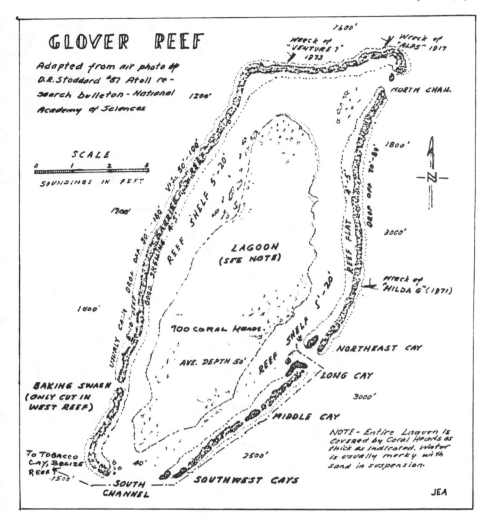

Glover Reef: South Channel and Northeast Channel are the safest entrances for yachts.

Inside the elliptical rim of the reef, the pale-green waters of the lagoon show depths of 1 to 3 or more fathoms over a sandy bottom. The largest opening permitting entrance into the lagoon is at the extreme southern end of the reef, southwest of five small sandy cays with palm trees and other tropical growth.

Once inside, you will have to eyeball your way around hundreds of coral heads and shallow patches to find a safe place to drop the hook. By far the best anchorage is off the western side of Glover Reef Village on Long Cay, where Gil Lomont's Glover Reef Lodge is located. Another is on the W side of Long Cay

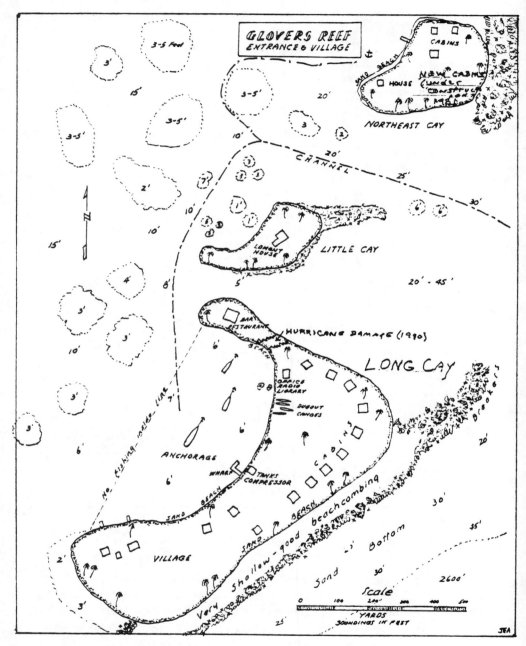

Entrance channel to Glover Reef anchorages at Long Cay and Northeast Cay

off a dive camp, with some marks to help you in. Call the dive camp on VHF Channel 16 if you need help coming in.

Boats bringing supplies and guests to the Village use the deep, natural entrance channel between Long and Northeast cays. When we first visited Glover in 1976, we departed from South Water Cay at the edge of the Belize barrier reef and had no trouble identifying the five small cays that fringe the SE corner of Glover and the Northeast Cay entrance. We spent almost a week weathering a winter norther during which several local vessels were lost.

Lighthouse Reef (28167)

Situated about 13 miles NNE of the northern tip of Glover, Lighthouse Reef is the outermost of the offshore islands and shoals. Like Glover, it is completely surrounded by its own barrier reef, which forms a lagoon with several islands and small cays. The reef is about 22 miles long and 2 to 5 miles wide; the only navigable openings are at the southern end, west of Half Moon Cay, where there is a lighthouse. The British *Pilot* reminds mariners to approach with caution, as the only chart of this reef is an enlargement of a survey made in 1830.

The Lomonts of Glover Reef and charter groups from Belize occasionally bring diving groups here.

Half Moon Cay

is about 10 feet high and covered with trees and bushes. The light structure is a 70-foot white metal tower, and there is a lighthouse keeper on the island. The anchorage NW of the island is exposed, with an uncomfortable surge in almost any weather, but there is said to be good holding ground in depths of 2 to 5 fathoms off the sandy beach on the S side of Half Moon Cay, giving better protection from the normal trade winds. The entrance into the lagoon is about half a mile westward of the cay, with depths of 2 fathoms, but keep a sharp watch for numerous coral heads around the cay.

Hat Cay

is a tiny sandy islet on the SW side of the reef, where temporary anchorage may be found under the lee of the cay in prevailing easterly winds.

The Blue Hole

near the center of the lagoon is a remarkable natural phenomenon, now part of an Underwater National Park. Jacques Cousteau spent a month on *Calypso* here in 1971, filming a sequence for his TV program. The "hole" is a deep circular pit surrounded by a rim of coral that rises to the surface of the lagoon. The hole was originally said to be "bottomless," but lead-line soundings have shown depths of 464 feet, and divers have found a huge underwater cavern with stalactites, some of them 40 feet long, hanging from the ceiling. The rim of the Blue Hole is 1,000

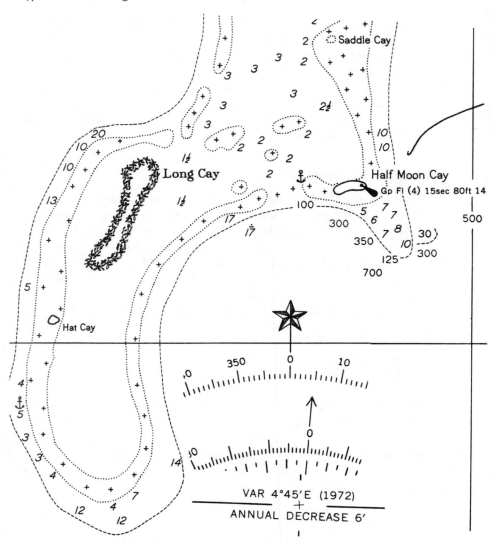

Entrance to Lighthouse Reef at its southern end

feet in diameter and is clearly visible from aircraft flying over the reef. Several divers were lost when their equipment was damaged by contact with submerged portions of the reef.

Sandbore Cay

is a small wooded island at the northern end of Lighthouse Reef, with a red-and-white metal light structure at the end of a jetty off the N shore of the cay. The chart shows what appears to be an opening in the reef one half mile N of the light, but there is a wreck in the entrance, and a warning note: "Many rocks, shoals, and coral formations exist in the north end of the reef." We don't recommend entering here or exploring nearby Northern Cay without a local pilot, although the chart shows depths of 1 to 2 fathoms in the lagoon.

Turneffe Island and Cays (28167)

This large group of low mangrove islands and cays lies between Lighthouse Reef and the main barrier reef off Belize. It covers an area almost 30 miles long from north to south and from 3 to 10 miles wide, completely surrounded by its own barrier reef. The mangrove islands are so close together that from seaward they look like a single island. Although there are several openings leading into interior channels and lagoons, they are uncharted and should only be entered with a competent local guide. The only aids to navigation are a 64-foot light on Mauger Cay, at the northern end of the Turneffe barrier reef, and a 33-foot light structure on Cay Bokel, at the southern end of the archipelago. The 100-fathom curve is close to the fringing reef, which is awash at many places.

Cay Bokel (28167, Plan)

is a tiny islet with sandy beach and palm trees, lying just off the SW corner of the reef, with an anchorage charted from a British survey in 1921. There's a fishing lodge there with an anchorage that appears feasible according to the chart but is actually too shallow for boats drawing over 3 feet. Ron Barr took his seagoing charter ketch through a supposedly 6-foot channel on the S side of the reef at its westernmost end. Entering on a 160° heading, he grounded several times on a muddy bottom before finding swinging room near the fishing camp.

The lodge is used by fishermen who come out from Belize in fast, shoal-draft powerboats. Deep-draft sailboats will find better anchorages at Lighthouse and Glover reefs.

Chapter Nineteen

MEXICO'S QUINTANA ROO

This wild and almost roadless eastern part of Mexico's Yucatán peninsula, its miles on miles of straight coastline made up of powdery sand hills and turquoise lagoons, would hardly be known today were it not for Cozumel, the sportfishing mecca and resort island a few miles off its northeastern shore. But in this day and age, such enticing areas cannot long retain their natural state, and sleepy Cozumel, which has now sprouted its own high-rises and a real marina, is already mightily overshadowed by another island just up the coast, Cancún by name, where big government has masterminded and put up the ante for a huge resort and residential complex: a sort of eastern Acapulco, but without the cliffs and mountainous backdrop.

Mysterious Yucatán, which saw the rise and fall of the mighty Mayan Empire, now lives to see the rise of a tourist empire, with all the civilized trappings this entails, and cruising there will never again be quite the adventure it once was, although there is still the formidable Yucatán Channel to cross to reach it.

Here you will probably contract "Mayan fever," which is the natural and healthy desire to see, and let your imagination be titillated by, the baffling ruins left by a cultured and progressive people who, having been a nation for perhaps three thousand years, simply disappeared from the face of the earth even before the Spaniards arrived to "Christianize" and decimate the Indians. Apparently the Mayans were a hyper-religious people in their own way, for it is said that, quite apart from the cities that have been unearthed, the whole Yucatán countryside remains literally unscratched and that temples can be found in the underbrush all over this flat land if only you have the tenacity to hack your way through it. Temples and other remnants of their civilization along the shore have already been vandalized; you have to go farther back into the hinterland now. Incidentally, earth moving for the Cancún development turned up Mayan ruins.

If you've got a day to spare, a guide can take you on horseback to temple ruins on the weather side of Cozumel, or you can cruise or fly to Tulum, on the mainland coast, said to have been a Mayan seaport, although this seems a rather grandiose claim, since there isn't even an indentation in the coast here. The ruins themselves have been dutifully excavated; you can get a glimpse of what this walled town might have been like in its heyday. The main temple, with its carvings to the upside-down god, stands high on the cliff and is an inspiring sight.

Farther afield, Mérida is the center for sightseeing other Mayan city sites, notably Chichén Itzá, Uxmal, and Dzibilchaltún.

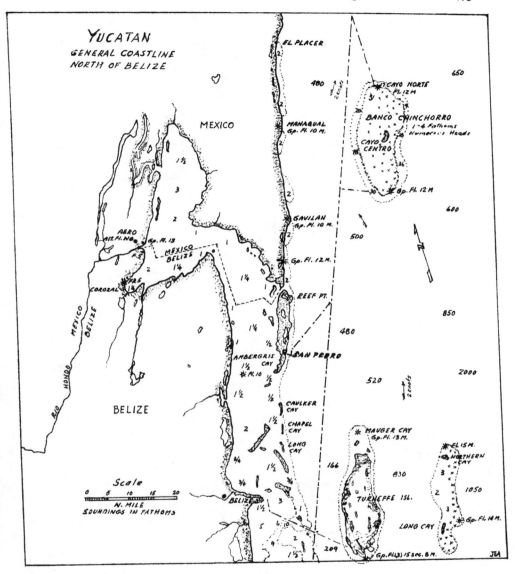

Although most yachts tend to run the 185 miles direct from Cay Corker to Cozumel, there are several reasonably sheltered stopovers along this route.

Banco Chinchorro (28001)

is not covered in sufficient detail on any chart, and the U.S. *Sailing Directions* give no directions whatsoever. The British *Pilot,* while it gives a complete description of the bank, avoids detailing the anchoring possibilities for small vessels,

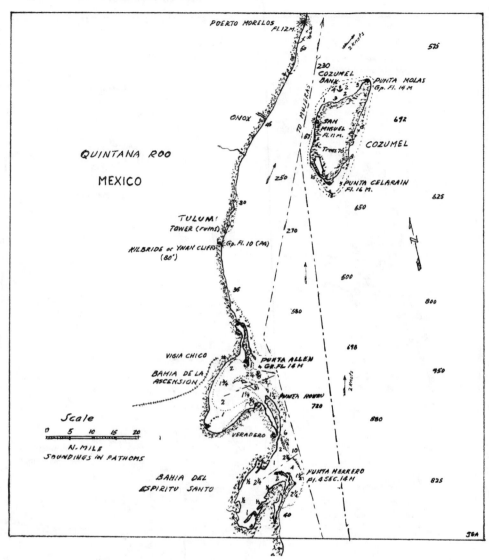

except to mention that several small openings exist for eyeballing through the reef into a lagoon in a 3½-mile stretch NW of Cayo Lobos, a very low islet of sand and coral with an unreliable light on it.

Ron Barr of the ketch *Cibola* approached the light on the S end of Chinchorro on about 085°M until about 1 mile off, then altered to 065°M, following a sandy streak with a light-blue cast and dodging heads, to come to anchor in 25 feet about one fourth mile NW of the light on Cayo Lobos. Assuredly this is not the only way to come in nor the only place to anchor, but good light is necessary in any approach; the whole area abounds with coral heads, and lobsters! In this vicinity,

Skylark Ledges, which dry, lie about one half mile W of Cayo Lobos, while Blackford Ledge, always awash, is about 2 miles WNW of Lobos.

At the N end of Chinchorro, we have anchored comfortably overnight, approaching the light on Cayo Norte on a 135°M heading and dropping the hook near the light per our sketch chart.

Firefly Bight is on the eastern side of the banks. The current set is in excess of 6 knots, extremely dangerous, and to be avoided, as the sighted wrecks give testimony.

Bahía del Espíritu Santo (28001)

provides a straightforward entrance, steering 260°T on the NW tip of Owen Island, with suggested anchorages as shown in our sketch chart.

There is a strong in-setting current around Punta Herrero. When heading south, be aware of it and the off-lying shoal area, which can be uncomfortable.

Bahía de la Ascensión (28001)

may be entered through a wide opening in the barrier reef. Take up a position with tangent bearings of 286°T on Allen Point (Punta Nicchehabin) and 244°T on the northernmost shoulder of the Culebra Cays and come in on a generally westerly heading, but beware a dangerous rock about 1.5 cables SW of the drying reef to starboard of the entrance.

Tulum (28001),

with its well-preserved ruins of what was once a Mayan "seaport," lies 25 miles N of Ascension Bay. How it came to be termed a "seaport" along this unindented

Approaches, north end of Chinchorro Reef

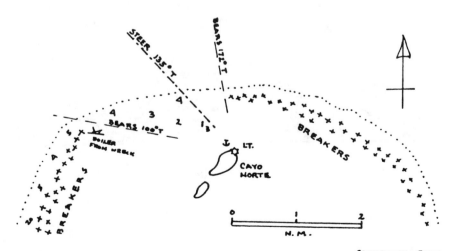

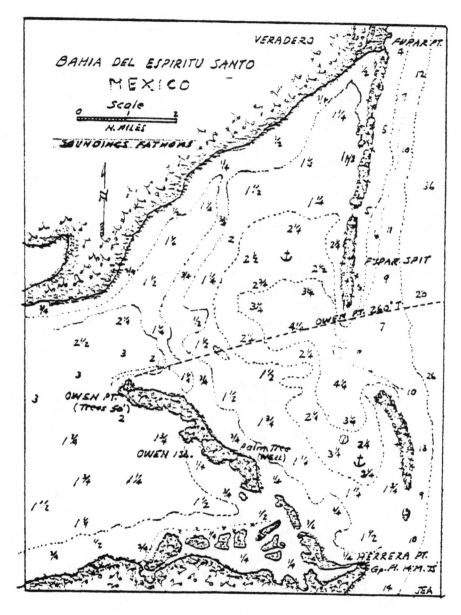

Approach to Bahía del Espiritu Santo, Quintana Roo, Mexico

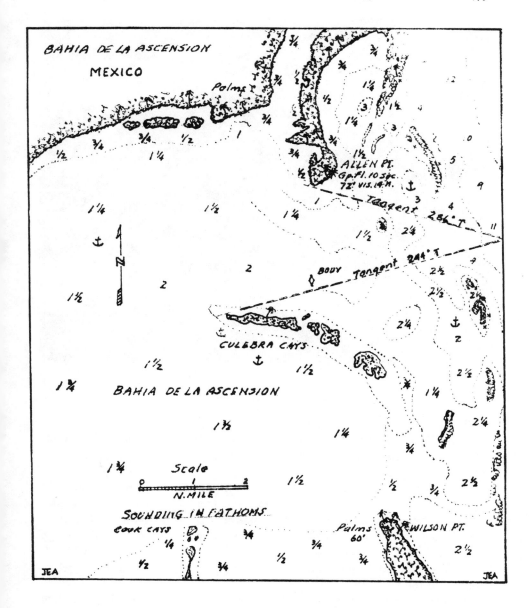

Approaches to Bahía de la Ascensión, Quintana Roo, Mexico

Tulum—Mayan "seaport"

stretch of coast is rather a mystery, but the short strand N of the higher temple was probably considered an appropriate place for beaching the hardy canoes of those days.

South of the lighthouse is a wide break in the barrier reef that may safely be used in good light and moderate sea conditions. Ron Barr of *Cibola* recommends that you orient yourself by identifying some resort houses and a beach, farther S some low cliffs, and still farther S a stand of palms with one particularly high one on its N end. Coming in on this conspicuous palm tree on a course of 310°M, you will pass to port a prominent flat-topped and nearly awash rock just before you get to the reef opening itself.

Hold over to starboard after clearing the reef and anchor along the beach S of the light in 10 or 12 feet, but be sure your anchor is well set, for the bottom is hard.

Isla de Cozumel (28196, 28197)

is low and flat, and the terrain is surprisingly dull, considering its prominence as a resort. There is, however, incredible snorkeling and scuba diving.

The anchorage behind San Miguel is well protected from the trade winds, but the bottom is extremely hard, and anchoring can be difficult. During the winter it is best to be aware of the approaching northers and scoot across to Playa del Carmen (mentioned later), which offers good protection from the northwest, north, and northeast. The marina north of town is well maintained, but during a norther it can get sloppy.

Hang up your Q flag, telephone the port captain's office, and wait patiently for the officials to find *you;* do not go ashore to seek *them* unless requested to do so. We have had varying reports of entry fees charged at Cozumel, usually quite reasonable, but one in particular a real rip-off. The Glindmeiers of the motor yacht *Summer Wind,* who used the yacht harbor in 1980, were obliged to pay about $150 for port charges, customs, health clearance, immigration, and "pilotage," a service that of course was neither needed nor rendered. Incidentally, the Glindmeiers report that in the course of a round-trip cruise from Florida to Alaska they were never required to pay any charges, other than agent's fees, at any other port on either side of Mexico.

Cozumel's self-appointed yacht agent is Wilson the "Legend," who is likely to call soon after your arrival. To save some money it might be well to engage him to negotiate with the officials for you. Despite the possibility of formidable port charges, there is some consolation: Cozumel is unusually clean and a pleasant place for a bit of R and R; also, the marina charges are very modest by U. S. standards.

If you are adventurous and draw less than 5½ feet, you might try Caleta Bay, which is about 8 miles S of town and a few hundred yards N of the towering El Presidente Hotel. The entrance is narrow and obstructed by some massive boulders; they are, however, easily seen in the clear water. The cove itself is some 200 yards in diameter, with a rocky perimeter to which you will moor Med-fashion. You can use the amenities of the swank El Presidente, rent a car in the lobby there, or use buses and taxis to get to town.

Playa del Carmen (28001)
is a quaint town with beautiful beaches. The holding ground is good. The best anchoring is just south of the ferry dock, but be sure to give the water jet and the ferryboats enough room to maneuver. South of Playa is Puerto Aventuras, a new and sophisticated resort with a marina dredged right out of the rock. There is plenty of dock space, restaurants, bars, and condos, and it is well protected. During strong southeasters I suspect there may be slop.

Puerto Morelos (28001)
is adequately protected by a low-lying reef about a mile off, where there is great diving. The easiest access to the town is via the ship's channel from the south, which is well marked. There is a small American community, and the town is home to UNAM—the University of Mexico's Marine Research Branch. The

largest boat-building and repair facility on the Mexican Caribbean can be found here, with a large travel lift and work force—and high prices.

When traveling north, keep off a bit from Punta Nizuc (Club Med). The outlying reef can be messy and has caught a few people unaware. Although it is very wise to travel the reef in close during daylight hours to avoid the strong north-setting current, you must be aware of those few, possibly fatal, points.

Cancún (28202),

a skinny, L-shaped island about 9 miles long and separated from the mainland by a lagoon, has, during several years of intensive development by the Mexican government, become a major tourist and residential attraction, with numerous hotels, condos, fancy restaurants, a Bobby Jones golf course, and shopping plazas. However, nobody thought about cruising yachts when a marina was built with a 4-foot-deep channel on the far side of a fixed bridge with 12-foot vertical clearance. But this is probably no great loss; having cruised this far from Florida, yachtsmen are not likely to be looking for another Miami Beach or Fort Lauderdale. Those who really want to see the fleshpots of Cancún can—by taking advantage of the frequent ferry service from nearby Mujeres. Bring money.

Miles and miles of sandy coast stretch S to Tulum and beyond, interspersed with lagoons that appear to be navigable from the sea but have never been charted on a useful scale. With Cancún as the catalyst, we expect that not many years will pass before this now inhospitable coast will be dotted with resort establishments and associated marinas dredged into the lagoons.

Isla Mujeres (28202)

may be entered by passing about one half mile N of the square black rock called the Anvil, then rounding gradually down toward the settlement, where anchorage may be taken anywhere along the shore S of the village.

The more customary entrance, however, is to come in from the S, passing about halfway between the southern end of Mujeres and Becket Rock and steering toward the northern end of the sand hills on the mainland shore, where you will see a bouy when the village bears due N, then turning toward it and eventually picking up the charted range. Give the front range a good berth before turning in to the anchorage. There is good protected anchoring in the harbor.

At present there are two marinas. The one in town is relatively unprotected from a southeaster. The sportfishing boats from the U.S. use this marina during the late winter/early spring fishing season. The other is farther up the anchorage, near the shrimp docks (Mairina Paraiso).

A very ambitious project in the lagoon was under way as this book was being updated. A 150+ slip marina was being completed, which will be a bonded marina. The bonded marina will enable foreign vessels to remain in Mexico for five years and work in the charter trade. This is a relatively new concept, which several other charter services and individuals are taking advantage of on the west coast of Mexico.

The lagoon at Isla Mujeres is a good hurricane hole. The holding ground is not the best, but the lagoon is surrounded by mangroves that can be tied to.

The Spanish explorers heard of temples on Isla Mujeres decorated with female idols; hence they called the place "Island of Women." The town is typically Spanish and appealingly primitive, with two nice hotels and a charming French restaurant right on the beach, where the meals are truly worthy of the French tradition.

You are expected to go ashore and present yourself with your papers to the port captain, which will involve a trip to the hospital for health clearance and to the airport for immigration, then back to the port captain for the remaining details. You repeat all that when you are ready to depart.

Isla Contoy (27120)

is a Mexican national park and a bird sanctuary. It is worth a stopover because of its fantastic diving and snorkeling. The famous Sleeping Shark Caves are nearby. There are two entrances: one to the north, which is easy, and one to the south, which is more difficult. C. H. Murphy provided us with these directions and the accompanying sketch chart, which details the southern entrance, based on his observations in 1987:

> Steer 340 degrees from the Nautibeach Pier until the reef can be seen to the E. Hold just W of the reef, threading the needle between it and the sand bars off the SE shore of Isla Blanca. All reefs and rocks are visible in good light. Then take up 350 degrees until the rocks of the S point of Isla Contoy are sighted. Eyeball it more westerly to avoid shoal and rocks, which are clear.
>
> The lagoon one-half mile north of the observation tower has a controlling depth of 5½ feet at the entrance. The bottom is mud and grass, enabling a 6-foot-draft vessel to tiptoe in at half-tide. Once inside, there is 7 feet, ample swinging room with two anchors, and 360-degree protection.

The anchorage close under the lighthouse at the north end is reasonably protected from N and E.

Just beware of the mosquitoes if you are planning to spend the night.

Isla Contoy can be used as a jumping-off point for the usually boisterous passage to the Dry Tortugas or Key West.

Yucatán Channel and the Loop Current

The Equatorial Current, which has been flowing so freely through the Caribbean Sea, becomes markedly compressed when it reaches the straits between Yucatán and Cuba. As it enters the Gulf of Mexico, with its axis about 35 miles off the Yucatán coast, it becomes known as the Loop Current and spreads out erratically to the N, W, and E. The northerly branch circles into the Gulf clockwise toward New Orleans while the easterly branch becomes the Florida Current (more commonly known as the Gulf Stream) and is later augmented by the Loop Current coming out of the Gulf of Mexico.

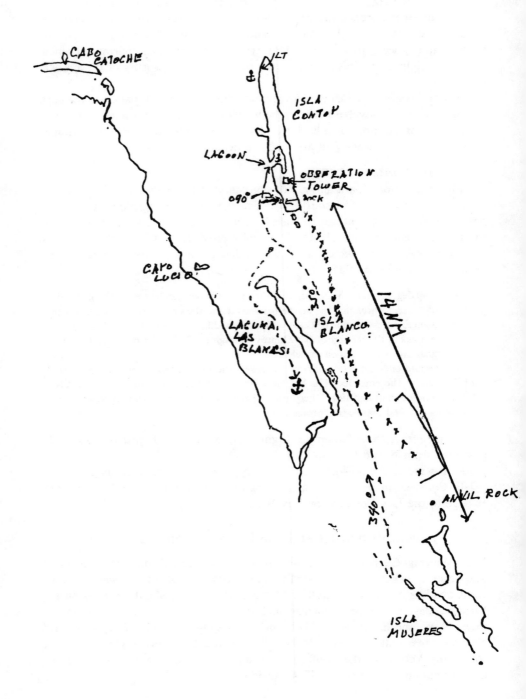

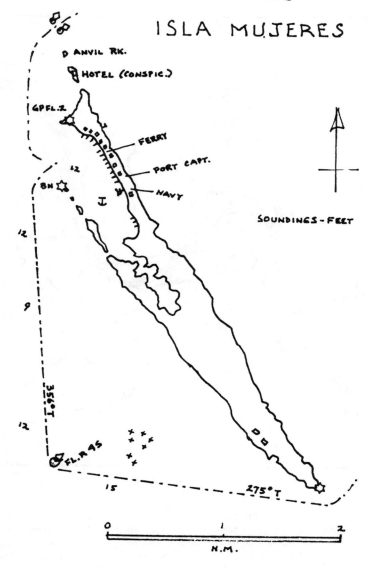

ISLA MUJERES

D ANVIL RK.

HOTEL (CONSPIC.)

GP FL.2

FERRY

PORT CAPT.

NAVY

BN

SOUNDINGS - FEET

12

9

356°T

12

FL.R 4S

15

275°T

0   1   2

N.M.

Where these currents diverge and rejoin, how strong they run, and what's happening within the loop are of course questions of immense interest to those who race from Biloxi to Cozumel and from Saint Pete to Mujeres; but race results and careful post-race study of the relative positions of the boats at different times during the race show that even these astute sailors are easily foiled by the inconsistencies of the stream. Some racers sailing along smoothly at 5 knots couldn't believe their instruments when they discovered that they were actually

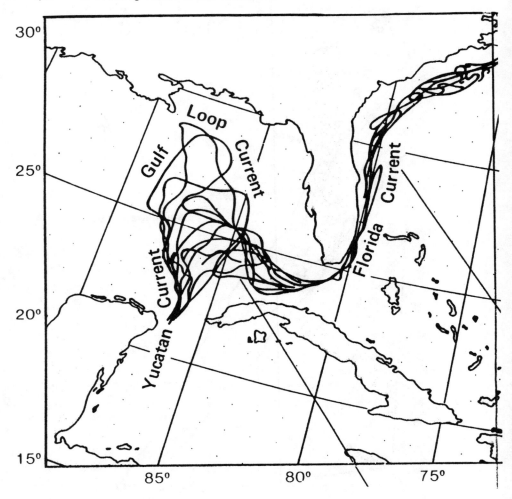

The Gulf Loop Current: This diagram, developed from satellite and surface sensing of water temperatures, gives some idea of the vagaries of the currents between Yucatán and Florida, before they consolidate into the relatively narrow Gulf Stream (officially called the Florida Current at this point). The government bulletin in which this diagram appears tells us that it "is meant as a guide to the spatial nonuniformity one can expect to find" and goes on, rather discouragingly, to say that "the mean picture of the oceans—the atlas image—may be largely a figment of our mathematics; one should not expect to encounter mean conditions at any given time."

making no progress over the bottom; they were roundly beaten by others who sailed a long course toward Cuba and back across the channel.

If there is any strategy for the cruising sailor to follow when making from, say, Mujeres to Key West, we would advise a straight track across, while allowing for 4k of north-setting current until about abeam of Cabo San Antonio, then for 2k of southeasterly set for the next 125 miles, and thereafter little or no current.

Since the 290-mile run in the opposite direction is navigationally much more difficult, perhaps it will be helpful to describe our findings on a recent passage from Dry Tortugas to Isla Mujeres aboard a 40-foot sailboat making a pretty steady 6k in moderate trade-wind conditions and equipped with Loran-C.

Departing at noon from the Tortugas we encountered no perceptible current for the first 6 hours on a 235° course. Our midnight log reading showed we had covered 72.5 miles, and our Loran reading was within 1 mile of our DR position.

Then we entered the southerly flowing Loop Current, which carried us 14 miles SSE of our DR position at 0600 and another 14 miles in the same direction by the noon reading, at which time we were one day out and about halfway across. During this 12-hour period in the Loop Current we logged 79 miles through the water, with Loran-C readings confirming the drift and enabling us to adjust our course every 6 hours. Had we failed to correct course we would have been very close to the fringing reefs off the western tip of unfriendly Cuba.

The north-setting current became fairly evident during the afternoon watch of the second day when we were some 40 miles NW of Cuba's Cabo San Antonio. In adjusting course for Mujeres, we allowed for an average 2k set in the midchannel portion of the Yucatán Straits, trusting successive Loran-C readings, which turned out to be very accurate. As we neared the Mexican coast, the northerly current increased to 4k, which would of course have carried us well N of our intended landfall had we not made course corrections every few hours.

Several hours of squalls with heavy rain and limited visibility gave us an uncomfortable second night in the shipping lanes; but any uncertainty about our position vanished when our last Loran fix brought us in less than a half mile from the lighthouse on the S end of Mujeres. Our taffrail log showed 320 miles, which we'd made in just under 51 hours from the Dry Tortugas.

Chapter Twenty

CUBA

Depending upon your nationality, it is possible to enter Cuba with as little documentation for yourself and your crew as tourist cards, available through Cuban consulates or even travel agents. Yachtsmen of certain other nationalities must produce passports and visas. U.S. citizens, like ourselves, are in a separate, third category. As of this writing, U.S. citizens were being "discouraged" by the U.S. government from visiting Cuba, and few were making the trip.

Although Cuban authorities are said to be encouraging tourism, the system of clearing private vessels into the country is somewhat intimidating. Reports from non-U.S. cruisers who have been to Cuba make the following points.

Barlovento (10 miles E of Havana) and Key Largo (E of Isle of Youth on the S coast) have marinas and tourist facilities and are easier to enter than commercial harbors such as Santiago and Mariel.

When 12 NM out, call on VHF Channel 16 to request permission to proceed, and do not proceed until you make contact with either a pilot station or the Guarda Frontera. A boat will probably come out to escort you in, which is actually helpful when approaching an unfamiliar harbor.

Be sure to have the required papers for ship and crew. Checking in is apt to be a lengthy but friendly process. Get permission from the authorities before moving to other ports.

As an introduction to the country and to whet your appetite for a cruise when once again we are all free to travel there, we include an itinerary of ports and places that would seem to be worth seeing around Cuba, based on earlier information and on information received from non-U.S. citizens who have cruised in Cuba recently.

We have made assumptions right and left. Nevertheless, the land configurations that produce Cuba's maze of sheltered passages and idyllic anchorages have surely not changed, and we give you these now, not only for dreaming purposes but also to serve as an outline for a properly documented chapter on Cuba in a later edition of this guide.

Cuba is a shark-shaped island of about the same size as England, and is situated in a SE–NW direction. The prevailing winds are a little north of east; it follows that a circumnavigation should be counterclockwise. Although Havana Harbor is now an oil-polluted commercial port and no place for a yacht, in addition to being currently off limits, it is nevertheless the capital, and we shall start our imaginary cruise from there.

Cuba, so near and yet so far

Havana to Cabo San Antonio

Havana to La Mulata (27084, 27101)

is an exposed passage with three nicely spaced and completely landlocked bays along the way: Mariel (Barlovento), Cabanas, and Bahía Honda, all of them free of any dangers in entering.

Laberinto de los Colorados (27101, 27121),

which you will enter at La Mulata, is a barricade of reefs affording protection in any weather all the way to Cabo San Antonio. This should present no difficulty to skippers with a trained eye for piloting through reef areas, but if you don't feel confident, a pilot may be picked up at Morrillo, La Mulata, or Cayo Paraiso. Esperanza and Santa Lucia are easy to enter, but the best port along this stretch is La Fé.

La Fé (27121)

affords excellent protection and is the last possibility for food, fuel, and water until you get all the way around to La Columa in the Gulf of Batabano.

Ensenada Cajon (27121)

or, more specifically, the arm of the Cayos de Lena, is the last anchorage before rounding Cabo San Antonio. Depths are ample and the protection is complete, even in a strong NW blow.

Golfo de Batabano

La Coloma (27141)

is the first real shelter following an exposed passage of over 80 miles. This tuna and lobster fishing port has a marked channel, fuel, and some supplies.

Batabano (27142)

lies some 85 miles farther E across the comparatively shallow gulf via the Hacha Channel. Exposed to southeasterly winds, this small port has supplies and a commercial pier used by coasters.

Ensenada de la Broa (27142)

is the mouth of the Hatiguanico River, which is entered via a staked channel. The Stevensons, on *Sea Eagle,* anchored for a week up in one of the tributaries of this large river that flows out of the Zapata Swamp, concentrating on the superb tarpon fishing. During the rainy season the mosquitoes are said to be "a torment."

Isle of Youth (Isla de Juventad), Formerly Isle of Pines (Isla de Pinos)

A succession of names—Isle of Santiago, Isle of Pines, Island of Parrots—has identified this island, which lies just 53 NM from the S coast of the mainland. The most recent name was earned when 50,000 teenagers were brought here to learn to farm. Citrus plantations, fishing, and tourism are the chief industries. Tourists come for hunting, diving, and fishing and to enjoy the beaches. There are two yacht harbors.

Nueva Gerona (27142)
is the principal port and capital city of the island. During the 1950s Fidel Castro and some of his followers were held in a prison here. The prison is now the Museo del Presidio. There are other museums, hotels and restaurants, beaches, and lakes.

Río Jucaro (27142)
on the E side of the island may be entered for several miles until the river narrows abruptly. Depths are ample, the banks are high, and there are mangroves and palm trees to moor to in case of a hurricane.

Ensenada de los Barcos (27141)
offers splendid protection in normal weather.

Bahía Siguanea (27141)
is said to have one of the finest beaches on Cuba's south coast, with a protected anchorage at the southern end in the deep coves, if you can get in over the bars between the caylets.

Puerto Francés (27141),
just around the point of that name, gives perfect protection from the NW; Caleta Grande, just beyond, is said to be safe in all winds except from W and N.

Southwest Coast

Isle of Youth to Cienfuegos (27142, 27161)
requires some delicate navigation via the Canal del Ingles to a point just S of Cay Palanca, thence 102°T to the Diego Perez Channel and on past the famous, or infamous, Bay of Pigs to Cienfuegos.

Cienfuegos (27161)
is a thriving modern city and one of the best and largest ports in Cuba. Here there is a naval base, a large sugar terminal, Cuba's largest oil refinery and her largest cement plant, silos and flour mills, and more in the big industrial complex. There

are also many elegant nineteenth-century mansions on Punta Gorda. A small yacht and dinghy club is located near the Hotel Jagua, E of Punta Gorda.

Casilda (27181)

is a must stop. The oldest and most picturesque town in all Cuba, Trinidad, lies 3 miles inland, while the port itself was the scene of Hernán Cortés's departure for the conquest of Mexico.

Trinidad, with its narrow and twisting cobblestoned streets, was settled in 1514 and was once the wealthiest town in Cuba. During the previous regime, it was declared a national monument. Some say the Spanish architecture is in a class with Toledo in Spain and Taxco in Mexico.

Twelve League Labyrinth (27181, 27184, 27201, 27206)

is a vast, relatively shoal area stretching 180 miles from Casilda to Cabo Cruz. Though infested with cays, rocky islets, and banks, it is regularly navigated by large ships loading sugar and other agricultural products from Cuba's central-plains region. The muddy bottom discolors the water, but the charts are detailed, and we presume the buoyage is being maintained in the numerous channels leading through the tight spots.

Twenty-five years ago, Ernesto Aguilera told of bringing *Indra,* a 47-foot Chris Craft, through here, and has left us the following specific directions.

> Depart Casilda by the La Mulata Channel and return to the bank S of the Machos de Afuera Cays, thence to Punta Ladrillo and the large sugar port of Tunas de Zaza. Then run close along the shore past what our guide claims is the most beautiful cay in Cuba, Obispito, on the way to another important sugar port, Jucaro.

From Jucaro, Aguilera's route leaves Flamenco, Flamenquito, and Guasimas cays to port, passes through the Ana Maria group of cays, then on to the Pinque Channel after leaving Algodon Grande and Malabrigo cays to starboard on the way.

From the SE end of the Pinque Channel he tells us to run 093°T to Santa Cruz del Sur, an important shrimp port.

Cruising in the Gulf of Guacanayabo beyond Santa Cruz is somewhat less obstructed, with stops suggested at the small sugar-and-molasses port of Guayabal, where ice used to be available, as well as safe water, which has always been a problem in these parts. Also recommended is the large commercial port of Manzanillo, and lastly Campechuela and Niquero, before turning the corner into the trade winds again at Cabo Cruz.

Southeast Coast

With the five- and six-thousand-foot peaks of the Sierra Maestra dropping sheer to the sea, much like Spain's own south coast, the 220-mile passage from Cabo

Cruz to Cabo Maisi is surely the most magnificent along Cuba's coastline. Since the powerful trades draw in upon this exposed coast, it would be a most uncomfortable stretch were it not for several very secure harbors along the way.

Pilon (27221)

is strewn with reefs and shoals across the entrance, but their very presence provides excellent protection, and the channel is buoyed.

Santiago (26222)

was once the capital of Cuba. In fact, its Morro Castle is even older than Havana's. Through the years, Cortés was the city's first mayor; the slave revolts in Haiti in 1776 sent many Frenchmen here to leave an indelible French influence; Teddy's Rough Riders made history here in 1898, winning the decisive battle for Cuban independence; and Fidel Castro used this mountainous countryside to build his revolutionary movement and gather his faithful adherents about him.

Once you are inside the 60-yard-wide entrance, the protection is complete and the anchoring possibilities many and varied. Punta Gorda used to be the site of one of Cuba's most active yacht clubs, the Club Amateur de Pesca.

Guantanamo Bay (26222)

is a U.S. naval base situated in the midst of an avowedly hostile country. It's one of the great anomalies of the world today, but it stands in fact upon land that has been leased for this purpose since 1903, shortly after Cuba won her independence from Spain with immense assistance from the United States, military and otherwise.

Even after a healing of U.S. and Cuban relationships, it's doubtful that the port would be open to small craft except in emergencies. Needless to say, the shelter is more than adequate.

Puerto Baitiquero (26235)

is a landlocked inlet completely surrounded by high hills, with a 10-foot-deep channel only 50 feet wide between the awash reefs on each side.

Cabo Maisi to Nuevitas (26241, 26244, 27041)

This portion of the northeast coast is a sailor's delight when traveling counterclockwise, with the wind on the beam and a snug harbor every 25–30 miles; and many of these ports are commodious coves entered via narrow, winding channels that completely filter out the swells. Ernesto Aguilera of *Indra* has recommended Baracoa, Moa Bay, and Tanamo, this last having such a twisting entrance that it cannot be seen until you are almost on it. Landlocked Nipe Bay is so huge that the problem is to find a shelter for the particular conditions at the time. If you must have your daily swim, better go elsewhere, because Nipe Bay is famous for its shark population.

Puerto Banes, Vita, and Puerto Padres are all sugar and molasses ports with circuitous, high-walled entrances. The one at Banes, in fact, is called "the Canyon." Currents run strong in these entrance canyons, and there is of course the danger of meeting a big ship where you least want to find it. Food and fuel should be available in any of these ports and some repairs as well, since all the sugar mills have machine shops and mechanics.

Nuevitas Bay to Havana

Nuevitas to Caibarien (27041, 27045, 27047)
poses a 45-mile run along the Bahama Channel to Cayo Verde, where you can duck inside the reef to anchor on a sandy bottom, with reasonable protection even in a norther. The next anchorage in northeasterly winds is under the light at Paredon Grande.

The mainland port of Caibarien lies some 15 miles in from the line of the outer reefs and is hardly worth the detour unless you are desperate for provisions. Better to go on to Isabella.

Isabella (27061)
is only 6 miles in from the open sea. Before Castro, it had a special pier maintained by Amigos del Mar, an association devoted to the "development of seamanship and love of the sea among Cubans," with several chapters around the island.

Cardenas (27081)
marks the end of the long chain of off-lying cays that has stretched 215 miles from Cayo Verde. Few yachts would, however, be likely to use this huge sugar port, considering the nearness of Kawama.

Varadero, or Kawama Lagoon (27081),
has been reactivated under Castro as a spic-and-span marina with all modern facilities. Once again it has become Cuba's preeminent yachting center. Entry may be made by well-marked channel from the sea or from Cardenas Bay.

Havana (27084)
was like this to the Stevensons when they came up to the coast in their 46-foot power cruiser, *Sea Eagle,* one day in 1952 after a bumpy passage from Key West:

> We were able to see the wide stretch of Havana suburbs and the lovely homes along the shore, including the Havana Yacht Club, the Biltmore Yacht and Country Club—an amazing community.
>
> We eased into the channel to Havana Harbor on the lookout for the Club Náutico

Internacional, of which we had heard a great deal. We could see the traffic on Avenida del Puerto and hear the constant blare of horns from the buses and autos. Suddenly the club came in view, a modern building completely clean in character, an incongruous sight in this ancient harbor.

This description should give you something to compare with your own impressions when you make your cruise in the 1990s or perhaps even in the year 2000.

Chapter Twenty-one

THE CAYMAN ISLANDS

Almost in dead center of the western Caribbean, yet off the usual sailing routes to anywhere, the Caymans seemed to have been hardly worth fighting for, and were very late in being settled. Even Columbus missed them until he was returning from the isthmus on his fourth and final voyage, and he sighted only the Lesser Caymans, which lie some 80 miles east of Grand Cayman. Sugarcane had no part in the development of this island group; in fact the islands are so low and thus so subject to hurricane destruction that agricultural enterprises have hardly had a chance.

Although the Caymans take their name from the Spanish word for crocodile, and these reptiles have been seen on Little Cayman (the island most visited in the early days), it was the turtle that for many years provided these islands with their livelihood. In fact, had it not been for the availability of turtle steaks, and water from wells deep in the limestone, few of the early sailors would have bothered to set foot in these remote islands. In 1592 the log of a Captain William King, sailing from Jamaica to Grand Cayman, tells us:

> . . . we found no people, but a river of fresh water, and there we turned up three score great tortoises or turtles. Two of these, with their eggs, fed ten men for a day.

Since the Caymans were so isolated and provided such good sustenance, the pirates of the early eighteenth century quite naturally made good use of them. This in turn made the islands quite unsuitable for God-fearing settlers. It was not until 1734 that the first grant of crown land was made in Grand Cayman—to the first of the Boddens, who, with two pages in the telephone book, have been a prominent family in the islands ever since, exceeded only by the slightly more prolific Ebanks, who fill three pages.

The lack of big plantations led to a more limited need for slaves than on the other West Indian Islands, with the result that the races were about evenly divided when slavery ended in 1834. There has since been enough intermarrying in the population of 20,000 to make racial tensions almost nonexistent. And so the Caymans have slumbered their way into modern times, sending their men to seek the turtle as far as the Nicaraguan coast and to serve, in great demand, among the merchant fleets of the world.

Rediscovery of Grand Cayman has come about relatively recently, and a "Gold Coast" has built up along its beautiful western beach. It is rated now as one of

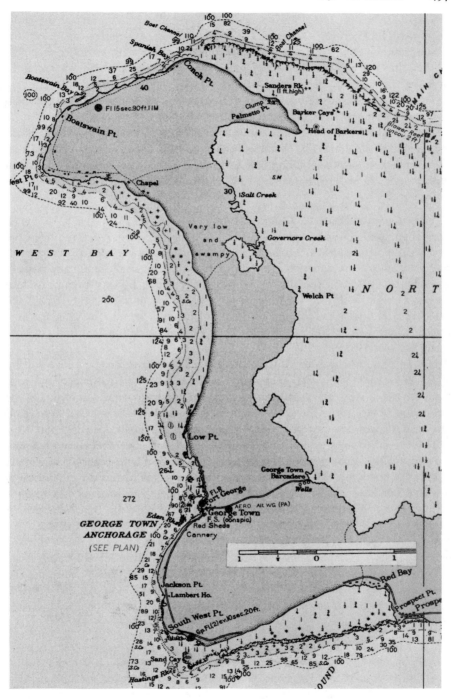

West Bay, Grand Cayman

the top four scuba-diving destinations and is also a popular port for big-game fishermen. Furthermore, George Town has become a popular tax haven for offshore money. Stark white and cream-colored bank buildings (more than 450 of them in George Town) have created a skyline where once the town's tallest building was a red-roofed, two-story customshouse.

The Cayman Islands remain a British Crown Colony, and are among the most politically stable of the Caribbean countries.

Though Grand Cayman can hardly be classed as a cruising ground in itself, it has enough amenities and facilities to attract yachts for a safe and restful stay of several days or weeks along the gorgeous beach on its generally sheltered western end, or within the expansive North Sound, protected by a formidable barrier reef.

George Town (27141, 27243),

port of entry for pleasure craft, is an open roadstead, yet is protected from the prevailing northeasterlies. Anchorage may be taken anywhere clear of the commercial traffic. The Cayport is in almost constant use by small freight and passenger vessels and would be uncomfortable for a yacht anyway because of the constant surge. A tiny cove with a pile of rocks in the middle is directly off the town's center and has a convenient beach for landing the dinghy. The customshouse, where you will have to report upon arrival, is only a hundred yards N along the waterfront.

If there is a northwester blowing, Port Security will probably advise you by VHF-16 that you should go around to Spott Bay (an open roadstead, but protected to the northwest) or little Southwest Sound (shallow and large enough for only a few boats). Even the cruise ships and cargo vessels take shelter here. And during northwesters, customs will clear yachts at the small dock in Spott Bay.

These northwesters, which are most prevalent from November through April, are a part of the storm systems that sweep across the States throughout the winter. Unlike the northers in the Bahamas, which are presaged by a wind shift through S with a fair blow from the SW on the way around, these storms come in with little warning to strangers, sometimes right out of a blue sky. The local people seem to have a sixth sense about these blows; perhaps they feel the shift in direction of the swell, or notice the sea fans beginning to bend toward the SE, or maybe they've simply heard the 1205 forecast from Swan Island. In any case, if there is a general exodus of vessels from George Town or West Bay around the corner to Spott Bay and Southwest Bay, by all means follow the crowd! And remember, the colder the forecast for Miami, the more violent the northwester will be.

West Bay (27241)

is made beautiful as an anchorage by Seven Mile Beach, which is really only 4 miles long. Already this gorgeous strip of white sand is pocked with hotels, and more are abuilding. Anchor anywhere along here, according to the chart and your

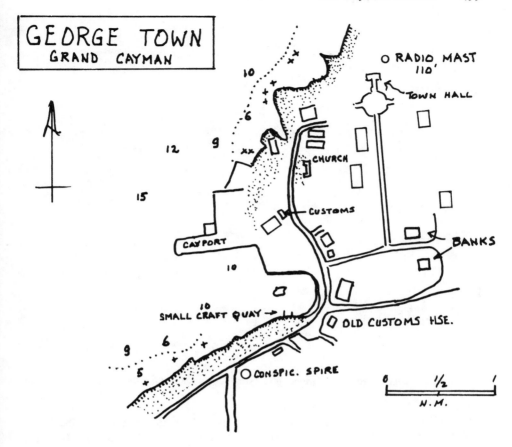

GEORGE TOWN
GRAND CAYMAN

draft. Mosquitoes may bother you, especially from May to October, so it may be best not to anchor too close in. Mosquitoes are a very real problem here. Although they are being vigorously attacked, they're far from being under control.

The light near Boatswain Point now has 15-mile visibility.

A short distance N of the village of West Bay is one of the prime attractions of the island, the only sea-turtle farm in the world, operated by Mariculture Ltd. Having been fished practically out of existence, the turtles are (quite appropriately) back in the Caymans now, 120,000 strong, being bred in tanks, where the survival rate of hatchlings is about 85 percent, compared with 1 percent under natural conditions. Conducted tours and a gift shop are part of the act here.

Reef Entrances to North Sound (27241)

are not difficult to negotiate by anyone familiar with piloting in such waters, for the bottom is clearly visible and the barrier reef itself is very distinct.

The Big Channel shown in our sketch is actually the one entitled "Main

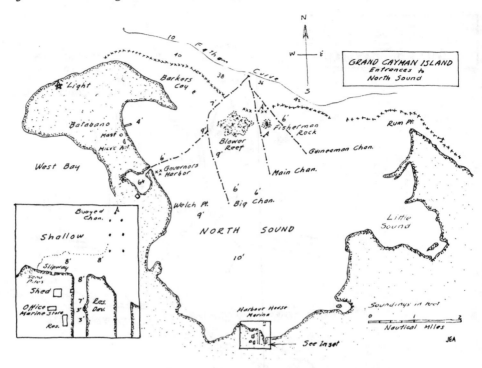

The three reef channels into North Sound, Grand Cayman

Channel" in 27241; we have simply used the name by which it is known locally. On your first approach you will be coming from George Town, having cleared customs there. After passing Conch Point, stand along the barrier reef to its conspicuous termination about 2 cables NW of Blower Reef. You should further orient yourself by noting Barker Cay, which is a single, low rock easily identified off the Head of Barkers. Other prominent objects against a rather featureless shore are a dish-shaped microwave antenna (not shown on the chart), at 19°22.2′ N, and Welch Point.

Leave the end of the barrier reef fairly close to starboard while heading into the sound on a southwesterly course, until Barker Cay bears about NW, then take up about 172°T toward some sand piles to be seen on the far southern shore. After clearing Blower Reef, there are essentially no other dangers within North Sound except for the shallowness near the shores and the 1-fathom patches near the center.

The Main Channel, as it is called locally, enters just W of a short breaking reef, which itself is about 60 yards W of the continuation of the barrier reef. The key to this channel is Fisherman Rock, which is a jagged nubbin of coral not more than 2 feet high. Pass the above-mentioned short reef patch close on the port hand, on a course about S by E, calculated to pass Fisherman Rock about 50 yards to port. In 1982 this channel was reported to have 3 red and 1 black day markers with reflectors.

Guineaman Channel starts where the barrier reef recommences, on a SE heading toward the center of Little Sound. Leave the end of the main breaking reef close to port, a small reef patch close to starboard, and carry on in with a sharp eye to starboard for the brown bar that surrounds Fisherman Rock. This channel is narrow at the start and carries barely 6 feet just inside in places.

While we have described and sketched three channels, we urge that only the first (Big Channel) be used for the first time. This is the first prominent break in the long reef that you will come to and is by far the widest. Note, however, that Blower Reef is very dangerous; it covers a wide area, it does not always break conspicuously, nor does it have the continuity of the outer reef line, which is very obvious.

Do not try to come into North Sound even in the early stages of a northwester. Take shelter instead along the island's S coast as described earlier.

Batabano (27241)
is situated at the termination of a road crossing the peninsula from West Bay, just N of a microwave antenna and red-and-white radio mast; neither is shown on the chart. Anchorage may be taken in 4 feet about 50 yards off the dock and the weirs, but we would be inclined to anchor in deeper water farther out to avoid the bugs. The shoreside surroundings are not attractive.

Governor's Harbour
is a blossoming real-estate development with some "waterfront" homes already built on its conventional, Florida-inspired canal system. There are few if any facilities for yachts, but if not, there is plenty of room to anchor and lie snug while a northwester blows around your ears. On a still evening in the mosquito season, this anchorage would be a horror, since the creek is almost surrounded by mangroves.

Stand in for the entrance at a right angle to the shoreline, to avoid shoal water that will appear on your port hand and to miss a sunken wreck to starboard about 100 yards off the shore. Hold to the center of the entrance creek, which has been dredged to 6 feet but may have shoaled since we were last there. Once you are inside, there is plenty of water except on the eastern side.

Two miles S of Governor's Harbour a canal has been dredged to a club and marina that is expected to be available for the use of visiting yachts.

On the E side of North Sound, yachts may use the facilities at North Sound Estates at Duck Pond.

Harbour House Marina,
in 81°20.0′W, can be identified at the bottom of North Sound by the dredging and land-development operations on each side of it.

The marina monitors VHF-16.

The Lesser Caymans (27241)

Lying almost 80 miles dead to windward from Grand Cayman, and considerably off the direct route from Jamaica to the Yucatán Channel, these two slim islands hold little attraction for a yachtsman, except perhaps to his more adventurous spirit. Separated by a 4-mile strait, lacking any significant indentations along either coasts, and pointed almost directly into the prevailing wind, these island slivers offer minimal protection, and the selection of an anchorage (in any case at the western end of either island) depends on whether the wind happens to be blowing a little N or a little E of NE.

Fewer than 50 souls live on Little Cayman, which boasts only one village, Blossom, one partially paved road, and a grass airstrip. Cayman Brac ("bluff" in Gaelic), where some 1,700 people live, mostly along the northern shore, has been invaded by some tourist hotels, so there is an airport that can accommodate jets, several settlements connected by paved roads, a hospital, and a worldwide, direct-dial telephone system. At the west end of this island, close in on the south side, yachts up to 5-foot draft will find a small sheltered area for anchoring. At the opposite end of the Brac, commercial vessels use the open roadstead at the Creek, where a 200-foot finger pier has been constructed.

A few miles south of the Cayman Islands the ocean floor plunges to 24,576 feet, the deepest point in the Caribbean.

Chapter Twenty-two

JAMAICA

A huge and impressive island, with almost 300 miles of coastline, her 7,000-foot mountain peaks usually wreathed in clouds, Jamaica boasts no less than 14 truly authentic and neatly spaced harbors giving shelter to yachts. Furthermore, she is, via the Windward Passage, one of the easiest islands to sail to from Florida, and back again.

The Arawaks called her Xaymaca, or "Isle of Rivers"; indeed, a number of the harbors we will describe stand at the mouths of small rivers or streams. Jamaica is much too big to miss; Columbus was here, of course, probably bitterly disappointed that he had found yet another island instead of the mainland of Asia. The Spaniards did little with Jamaica during their long occupation but probably wished later that they had realized the island's strategic position, for in 1655, after an abortive attempt on well-defended Santo Domingo, the British took over the island for the specific purpose of establishing a West Indian base from which to try to topple the Spanish supremacy in these parts, a plan which succeeded admirably with major help from the cutthroat Brethren of the Coast, who knew no laws at all. After more than 300 years of British rule, Jamaica followed the popular trend to independence in 1962 and has been falling apart ever since. Government ineptitude during the long-term domination of Prime Minister Michael Manley fostered anarchy and brought the island's economy to the brink of bankruptcy. In a pronounced surge to the right, Manley's pro-Castro regime was thrown out in favor of Edward Seaga, the Harvard-educated leader of the Jamaica Labour Party.

In 1989 Manley returned to the post of prime minister, with promises to foster good relations with Jamaica's Caribbean neighbors and with the United States, in hope of bringing better times to the island. So perhaps Jamaica will become again a pleasant destination, overcoming its present reputation as a dangerous place to cruise because of drug trafficking, a high crime rate, unpleasant incidents on the streets, and onerous customs and immigration regulations. In the 1980s, most cruisers passed Jamaica by.

If you do go, pay strict attention to customs and immigration requirements and procedures. These are, of course, subject to change, but the following points should give you some idea of how it may go. Enter only at large, commercial ports. Report immediately. Officials will probably come to the dock to clear you, at least in Port Antonio. You will have to report to officials again whenever you move the boat. You will be issued a transire and allowed to visit only those places listed on the transire. Unauthorized stops may result in large fines. Firearms will be impounded. If these requirements have eased by the time you visit, so much the better.

If these regulations seem overly stringent, remember that *ganja* (marijuana) has been an illegal but rather abundant crop for years, and the government is finally taking stern measures to halt this trade, which is also linked with gunrunning. When we were last there, a 35-foot sloop sailed by a young couple was inspected by customs officers every day for 10 days and finally told to leave the port.

Like so many Caribbean islands, Jamaica prospered mightily from the sugar industry until 1805, when, mostly through absentee ownership and attendant mismanagement, the bottom fell out of their market. But sugarcane is again a very major crop, along with bananas, cocoa, some coffee, and, unfortunately, the ubiquitous *ganja* (marijuana). As you coast along her eastern and northern shores, you will see a verdant island with a patchwork of plantations made luxuriant by the rains brewed in the mountains. In other places, however, you will see land laid open in brick-red scars where bauxite is being mined. And some parts of the south coast, especially in the vicinity of Kingston, are parched and dusty, the lower hillsides drab and eroded.

The prevailing wind is north of east, with a southerly component thrown in during the summer. Unfortunately, Jamaica's proximity to the North American mainland brings dreaded northers in the winter season to the western and northern coasts, where many of the harbors offer little protection from this quarter.

Taking advantage of the way the island presents itself to the prevailing winds, you will find it far more comfortable to circle Jamaica counterclockwise. This puts the wind and sea on your stern along the exposed north coast, and after rounding the west end, you will have some lee at least as far as Great Pedro Bay.

Most yachts coming from the Bahamas or the east will make for Port Antonio, which is the most convenient and probably the safest place to enter. We will,

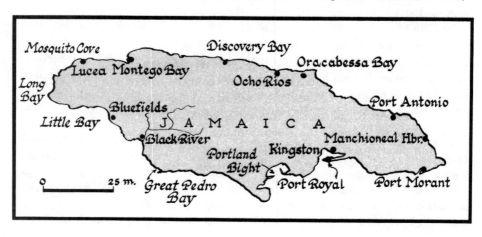

however, start our circular cruise from Kingston, since it is the capital and chief port.

Kingston Harbour (26128)

is so expansive and so ruffled by the afternoon breeze that a yacht can only consider berthing at Morgan's Harbour Club, next to old Port Royal, or at the Royal Jamaica Yacht Club, about a half mile E of Manley Airport.

Morgan's Harbour, at the end of the Palisades, the long, low spit of land that creates Kingston Harbour, is a 12-mile taxi ride from the city center (although there is an inexpensive ferry service across); the RJYC is only 8 miles from town. Both places are relatively safe and quiet and afford a magnificent view of the towering Blue Mountains. But you might be taking your life into your hands to go into shabby, dirty, gutted Kingston anyway. The city was in fact a combat zone during the last years of the first Manley regime, and the same perils that years ago caused the Maroon country of central Jamaica to be dubbed the "Land of Look Behind" might now be applied to Kingston, and to a lesser extent to the rest of this tortured island.

You will be welcome at the Royal Jamaica Yacht Club if you are a member of another recognized yacht club. The out-of-town premises (17°56.5′ N, 76°46.5′ W) were built in 1971 and include an attractive clubhouse, bar, and clean swimming pool, overlooking a dredged basin set about with mangroves. Most of the 70 or more slips are occupied by local boats. The entrance channel is good for at least 9-foot draft, and the basin is perfectly protected. Fuel and electricity are laid on, and a marine railway will take modest-size boats. You may also anchor just outside the basin in reasonable comfort.

Morgan's Harbour Club, at Port Royal, is a small hotel-and-restaurant establishment. Adjacent is a fuel dock and small-boat marina with what appears to be a rather improvised marine railway. Mooring at the club is stern-to at the wooden dock fronting the bar and restaurant; it's best to use your anchor rather than tie to the rotted pilings off the dock. There is at least 6 feet alongside, but even if there is plenty of room, we recommend mooring off because of the slight swell and the wakes of passing boats.

For convenient sightseeing, Morgan's Harbour Club stands literally in the outskirts of what was old Port Royal, a prominent port for supplies and repairs. It was also the scene of such debauchery among the hard-living, devil-may-care buccaneers who frequented the place between their seagoing forays, that it was called the wickedest city in the whole world. An earthquake in 1692 unceremoniously dumped most of the town into the bay, with the loss of 2,000 lives and a lot of booze. This was followed up by a fire in 1703, a severe storm in 1722, another fire in 1816, and a second earthquake in 1907, which seems like divine justice with a vengeance.

Of the original three forts that guarded Port Royal in the days of Henry Morgan, only Fort Charles, which controlled the outer channel, has survived. Its

The Royal Jamaica Yacht Club's modern marina near the airport at Kingston

brick walls and interior buildings are slowly being restored to make it an imagin-able point of historic interest, but much more needs doing. A plaque on one of the parapets draws attention to the memory of Admiral Lord Nelson, who, at the ripe age of 21, commanded this fort for a time. In grave tones is inscribed: "You who tread his footsteps, remember his glory."

Port Morant (26129),

near the E end of the island, has a well-buoyed entrance into a quiet harbor in a lush tropical setting with clear, clean water. There are no facilities, no small-craft docks, in fact few signs of any habitation or activity except the Bowden Dock of United Fruit Ja. Ltd, where small freighters load sugar and bananas from plantations served by a narrow-gauge railroad that runs 7 miles back into the hinterland.

We suggest anchoring slightly beyond the Bowden Dock, where protection is complete and free of surge.

Manchioneal Harbour (Plan from cancelled BA 459)

is only partly protected by a breaking bar that makes out from the northern arm of this small bay; thus it is uncomfortable in the usual northeasterlies and untena-ble in a real norther. The entrance through the reefs is difficult to identify. Run

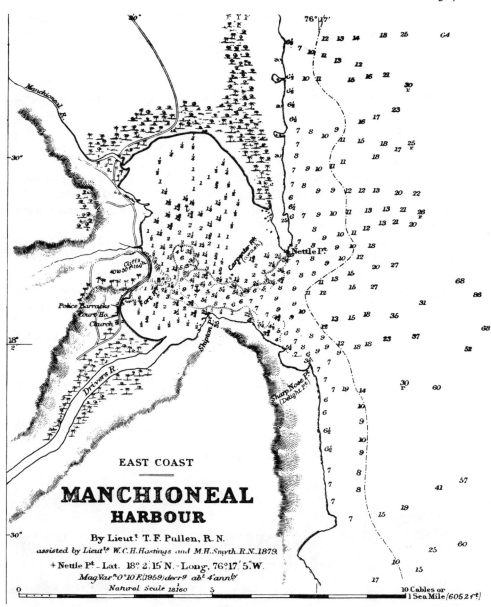

EAST COAST

MANCHIONEAL
HARBOUR

By Lieut.ᵗ T. F. Pullen, R. N.

assisted by Lieut.ᵗˢ W. C. H. Hastings and M. H. Smyth. R. N. 1879.

+ Nettle Pᵗ – Lat. 18°. 2. 15ʺ N. – Long. 76°17. 5ʺ W.

MagVar.ⁿ0°10.E.(1959) decr⁹ abᵗ 4'ann⁹ʸ

Natural Scale 18160

10 Cables or
1 Sea Mile (6052 ft)

This plan no longer appears in current charts and is reproduced from cancelled chart BA 459 with the sanction of the Controller, H. M. Stationery Office, and of the Hydrographer of the Navy.

well up into the N end, where a line may be run ashore to hold your bow against the river current and into the swell. Small freighters used to load bananas here, so there is ample depth and room to maneuver.

Blue Hole

is a gorgeous and justly famous spot, well protected by high, steep hills all around, but the entrance is limited to 4 feet over the bar, and a local pilot is essential. You can engage one in Port Antonio.

Port Antonio (26129)

is two harbors divided by the Tichfield peninsula, but the eastern one is sufficiently exposed to the prevailing wind and swell to be completely ignored. Take the channel into the W harbor between the peninsula and Navy Island toward the Boundbrook commercial wharf.

Huntress Marina and the Admiralty Club are the facilities most frequented and recommended by cruisers for docking and repairs. Grocery stores and markets are available for provisioning, with good fresh vegetables in season.

For a remarkable view and a breath of cool air, take a taxi to Bonnie View Hotel, a half-mile ride "straight up" from town. It's a toss-up whether the panorama or the ride will thrill you more.

Port Antonio is a deservedly popular yacht stop, well protected in all weather

Port Antonio

and picturesque when seen from the water. Although Columbus didn't come here, Captain Bligh, R.N., did—with the first shipment of breadfruit from the South Seas.

Welshwoman's Point
makes a welcome lee when you are making for Port Antonio in heavy weather.

Oracabessa Bay (26130)
is undergoing intermittent harbor development to make it safe for banana ships against the northers that are the bane of this coast, but none of this shows on the charts as yet. As our sketch indicates, breakwaters have been built atop the reefs,

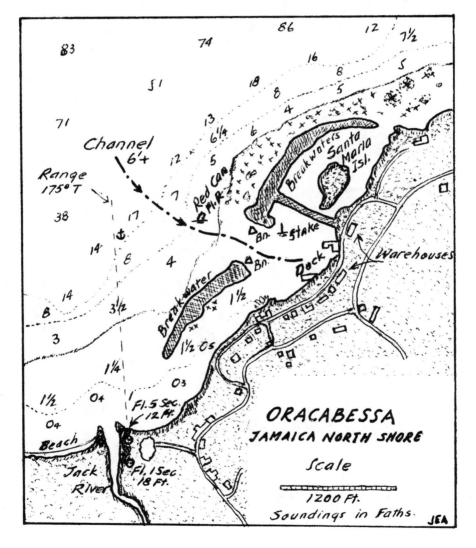

ORACABESSA
JAMAICA NORTH SHORE
Scale
1200 Ft.
Soundings in Faths.

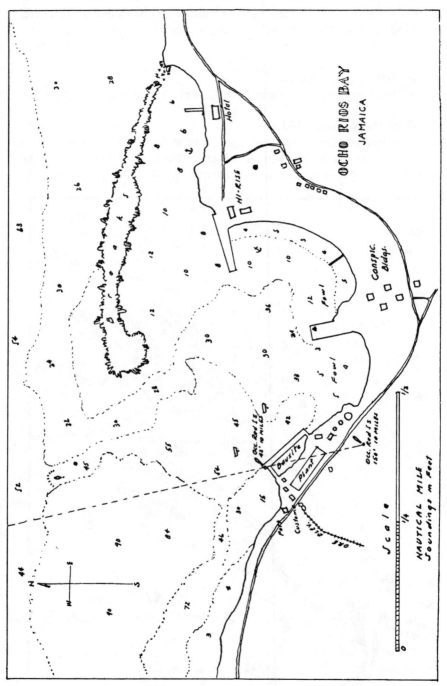

Ocho Ríos, Jamaica, north shore (soundings in feet)

and the channel and basin have been dredged deeper than now charted. There really is nothing here to attract yachts.

The late Ian Fleming wrote the James Bond 007 thrillers at his estate here.

Río Nuevo Bay (26220)

provides a good lee, but it may be necessary to set a stern anchor to hold your bow into the swell against the river current.

Ocho Ríos (26130)

has been breakwatered against the northernly blows. We have anchored at the extreme NE corner of the harbor beyond the high-rise hotels where the reef is only a few hundred feet off the beach and the protection is good in normal tradewind conditions.

Saint Ann's Bay (26130)

presents an easy entrance through the reef, as the chart shows, but, with its rather messy waterfront and muddy water, it can hardly qualify as a yacht stop.

Discovery Bay (26122)

is named after who else but Columbus, who landed here during his second voyage, in 1494, when the accompanying royal historian recorded for Queen Isabela that Jamaica "is the fairest island that eyes have beheld; mountainous and the land seems to touch the sky . . . and all full of valleys and fields and plains."

Ten years later, on his fourth and final voyage, whereby the "Admiral of the Ocean Sea" hoped to regain favor with the king and queen, Columbus was forced to beach his last two worm-riddled ships at Saint Ann's Bay. Having lost almost all his influence, he and what was left of his company spent a year in this area before he was able to arrange passage in another ship back to Spain.

Discovery Bay is surely one of the most attractive anchorages on the whole northern coast, especially close under the shore in the SE corner adjacent to the park. The best anchorage is off the beach park maintained by Kaiser Aluminum Company on the E side of the harbor, opposite the bauxite shipping pier on the western shore.

An interesting phenomenon is the freshwater spring that bubbles up in the W side of this bay near the 46-meter sounding NE of the white flasher.

Río Bueno (26122)

is excellent shelter in normal weather. The smoothest anchorage is under the hill on the E side, near the range beacons. Here again a stern anchor will be helpful to counter the river current, which tends to lay you broadside to the swell. For those interested in native art, there are two galleries in the village exhibiting the work of local artists.

Falmouth (26130)

lies in a low, swampy area surrounded by mangroves and infested with insects, but the town is attractive. This harbor is much too exposed for comfort in moderate N to NE winds.

Montego Bay (26122)

boasts a fine headquarters for yachts in the Montego Bay Yacht Club, located in the port area. Although 3½ miles from town, the club and grounds are pleasant and tidy, with all the customary facilities. Shelter is complete, and a cooling breeze comes into the basin.

If there are no northers in the offing and you want to be near town, come in on the hotel immediately S of Sandy Reef and the famous Doctor's Cave Beach. This beach is named after one Dr. McCatty, who, near the turn of the century, when swimming meant bathing in full costume and shoes, felt so strongly about the therapeutic value of this daring sport that he donated the beautiful white beach that he owned for the establishment of Doctor's Cave Bathing Club.

When a hurricane threatens Mo' Bay, yachtsmen take their boats into the Bogue Island area to moor among the mangroves in the extreme SE portion of this bay. The charted beacons clearly show the way in.

Mosquito Cove (26122),

with its 500-foot-wide opening, is surely Jamaica's finest gunkhole. Keep to midchannel and proceed straight in for excellent protection. To avoid Buckner Reef when entering or leaving, be very sure of your distance off before turning along the coast.

Lucea Harbour (26122)

is an agreeable place to drop anchor for a night, though the town is uninspiring. Pronounce it "Lucy."

Negril Harbour (Bloody Bay) (26150)

affords good anchorage in the middle and southern parts of the bay. The bottom is flat, and 2 fathoms extend for quite a long distance off the beach. For a more snug anchorage, tuck in behind the rock in the northern corner of the bay.

Negril (or Long) Bay (26150)

is unquestionably one of the most beautiful stretches of beach on the whole island, a fact that has been appreciated by resort developers and is evident in the new hotels near the original Sundowner Hotel and in the shopping center and villa complex down at the village of Negril itself.

The most attractive anchorage for yachts is at the N end of the strand. Keep 150 yards off Booby Cay and come in by eye toward the Sundowner Hotel

(18°19.5′ N). Though you will be crossing solid reef, according to the chart, actually there is a 17-foot channel all the way in. However, if you prefer to be conservative, enter this NE corner of the bay by passing S of Sandy Reef, which is clearly visible. In normal weather you will also find good anchorages in the middle and southern parts of the bay, in 2 fathoms over a level bottom.

Little Bay (26150)

requires caution entering. Hug the shoreline as you enter from the SE, and go into the anchorage behind the rocks at the extremity of the bay. Stay only 50 feet off the shore and do not be deterred by the fact that the passage is only 30 feet wide. The bottom is mud and grass.

Savannah la Mar (26124)

is an important commercial center, but is drab and dingy and definitely no place for a yacht.

Bluefields (26150)

is a pretty spot with high hills all around and attractive beaches. The approach is straightforward with no hidden dangers, the snuggest anchorage being close under the point with the fort ruins.

White House Point (26123)

offers similarly good shelter with no approach problems. You may drop the hook within 20 yards of the point. This section of coast is extremely beautiful, with its sloping pasture land and high hills beyond.

Black River (26150)

should be entered via the northern half of the bay, toward the church spire, then angling slightly S to the river mouth, which you may actually enter and tie to the wall on either side, being prepared of course to maneuver in a current. Or simply anchor off the village, as convenient.

Parotte Point (26150)

anchorage must be entered from due W through the break in the reef about three fourths of a mile N of the point itself.

Great Pedro Bay (26150)

is the last real shelter before you turn the corner into the full sweep of the trade wind, and even here you will feel the constant and sometimes heavy swell.

From here, if not from farther W, the proper strategy is to start in the small hours of the morning to take advantage of the night breezes, which will be flowing off the land and at least neutralizing the regular trade wind.

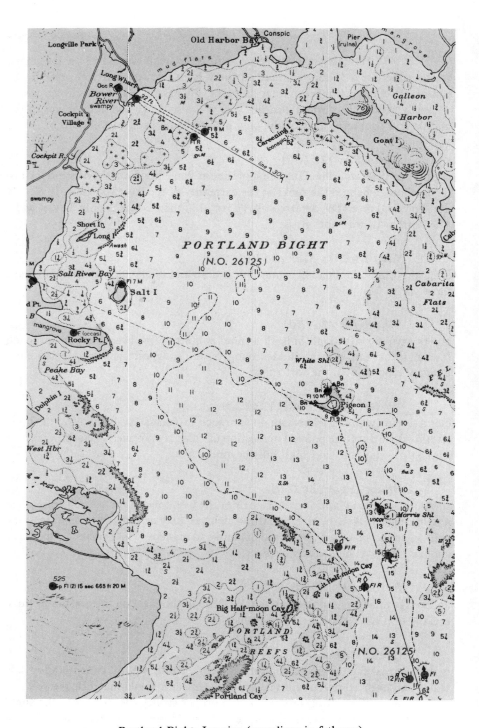

Portland Bight, Jamaica (soundings in fathoms)

Alligator Reef (26150)

affords a better lee than one might suspect.

Portland Bight (26125)

is a delightful area and quite unmarred by the bauxite-loading operations of Alcoa at Peake Bay and Alcan at Port Esquivel. About a half mile W of Old Harbour Bay are the conspicuous stacks of a power station. Entrance to the bight from the W may be safely taken close around the shore of Portland Point, but with due regard for the rocky patch along the shore just before you come abeam of Portland Cay. Those who are familiar with these waters enter even in darkness, by following the shoreline of the point until on a line between the forward range light on Pigeon Island and the 20-mile light on Portland Ridge, thence to a pretty anchorage off a sandy beach with waving palms on the N side of Pigeon Island. In judging your swinging room, allow for the usual night breeze from the N. The bottom is grass, so care must be given to setting your anchor.

Alternative anchorages are NW of Little Half Moon Cay and W of Wreck Reef, although the latter is considerably more exposed.

Pedro Cays (26150),

some 50 miles S of Jamaica, provide fair shelter, but expect a swell. The best anchorage is in the lee of South West Cay, where you will see the huts of fishermen from Kingston. These cays could make a useful rest stop when you are bound north, via the banks, from Providencia, but don't stop without permission.

Morant Cays (26129),

lying 35 miles SE of Port Morant, offer good shelter from the E, and better fishing. The run from Jamaica is best made at night, when the wind is down and advantage may be taken of the lights on Morant Point and the cays themselves, since the arcs of visibility come within 5–6 miles of overlapping.

APPENDIX A

The Leeward and Windward Islands and Vice Versa

When the West Indies were first a "Spanish Sea," the islands were grouped as Barlovento and Sotavento, or Windward and Leeward. The Leewards, quite logically, were the large islands from Puerto Rico toward the west; the Windwards were considered to be all the island chain east of Puerto Rico.

Later, when the British secured most of the previously termed Windwards, they divided their islands into Windwards and Leewards for administrative purposes. Dominica and the other British islands to the south were in the Windward group; the cluster from Montserrat and Antigua north were administratively the Leewards. However, the modern division, geographically, puts Dominica and the islands north of it among the Leewards, and all the islands southward, beginning with Martinique, in the Windwards. How this classification came into being is not at all clear, for it depends where you are sailing from. Since most landfalls from Europe were (and still are) made on Barbados, it follows that the Leewards were just that, but this doesn't explain the designation of Windwards except as you beat back from the Virgins.

The term "Antilles" is also bandied about, deriving from the name of a legendary "Island of the Seven Cities," which appeared in very early charts of the waters west of the Azores and which Columbus believed he would sight on his voyage to the Indies. Today, the Greater Antilles are known as the Leeward Islands of the Spaniards, and the Lesser Antilles are the Spaniards' Windwards—that is, from Puerto Rico to the east.

If this explanation clears up all the confusion so far, we are happy; but now bear in mind that the Dutch islands of Saba, Sint Maarten, and Statia are called the Dutch Windwards, although they lie among the formerly British Leewards. This appellation, however, makes some sense, because the Dutch Leewards— Aruba, Bonaire, and Curaçao—definitely lie to leeward of their cousins to the north.

APPENDIX B

Nautical Charts from K. S. Kapp Surveys, 1962–1989

KSK-1 Republic of Venezuela North Coast Anchorages
11 small port plans: Carenero, Pto. Azul, Ocumare, Cato, Chiao, Pto. Colombia, Maya, La Cruz, Barcelona, Isla Coche, and Cubagua.
Average scale: 1:15,200   Size: 28″ × 18″

KSK-2 Colombia and Venezuela Anchorages
10 remote ports: Isla Larga, Chichiriviche, Ríohacha, Manaure, Tucacas, Isla Suanchez, La Vela, Pto. Estrella, Santa Ana, and Guaranao.
Average scale: 1:15,200   Size: 28″ × 18″

KSK-3 Republica Colombia, Costa Norte
5 anchorages: Bahía Cinto, Nenguange, Gayraca, Chengue, Ancon Concha.
Scale: 1:21,150   Size: 30″ × 16″

KSK-4 Islas del Rosario Anchorages, with inset: Isla Tesoro
Scale: 1:15,200   Size: 26″ × 20″

KSK-5 Republica Colombia, Costa Norte, Fondeaderos, Golfo de Uraba
Features anchorages of the Conquistadores: Zapzurro, Turbo, Bahía Gloria, Necocli, Titumate, Pinololo, Trigana, and Goleta.
Scale: 1:14,500   Size: 22″ × 15″

KSK-6 Kaimau Keys (Holandes Cays), San Blas Coast, Panama
Scale: 1:34,500   Size: 26″ × 20″

KSK-7 Carti Keys, San Blas Gulf, Panama North Coast
Locale of the Republic of Tule Indian war in 1925.
Scale: 1:8,500   Size: 24″ × 20″

KSK-8 Mandinga Keys (Islas Robeson), San Blas Gulf, Panama North Coast
Inhabited isles of the Kuna Indians.
Scale: 1:8,500   Size: 24″ × 20″

KSK-9   Port Royal Harbour, Isla Roatán, Honduras
Includes profile from seaward and historical notes of this pirate haven.
Scale: 1:10,400   Size: 28″ × 18″

BIBLIOGRAPHY

UNITED STATES AND UNITED KINGDOM GOVERNMENT PUBLICATIONS

Defense Mapping Agency. *Altas of Pilot Charts, Central American Waters and South America.* D.M.A. Hydrographic/Topographic Center, Washington, D.C. 20315-0030, 1955 (with later revisions).
———. *Catalog of Maps, Charts, and Related Products, Part 2, Vol. II.* D.M.A. Hydrographic/Topographic Center, Washington, D.C. 20315-0030, May 1, 1988.
———. *Sailing Directions, Vol. 20.* D.M.A. Hydrographic/Topographic Center, Washington, D.C. 20315-0030, 1952 (with supplements). Comprising Colombia and the east coast of Central America.
———. *Sailing Directions, Vol. 21.* D.M.A. Hydrographic/Topographic Center, Washington, D.C. 20315-0030, 1958 (with supplements). Comprising the Bahamas, Turks and Caicos Islands, Hispaniola, Puerto Rico, Cuba, Jamaica, and the Caymans.
———. *Sailing Directions, Vol. 22.* D.M.A. Hydrographic/Topographic Center, Washington, D.C. 20315-0030, 1963 (with supplements). Comprising the Lesser Antilles and Venezuela.
Hydrographer of the Navy. *East Coasts of Central America and Gulf of Mexico Pilot.* Taunton, Somerset, England: Hydrographic Dept., 1975 (with supplements). Comprising Costa Rica, the Miskito Coast, the Bay of Honduras, and the Yucatán peninsula.
———. *South America Pilot, Vol. IV.* Taunton, Somerset, England: Hydrographic Dept., 1969 (with supplements to 1980). Comprising Trinidad and Tobago, the A-B-C Islands, and the Spanish Main as far west as Almirante Bay.
———. *West Indies Pilot, Vol. I.* Taunton, Somerset, England: Hydrographic Dept., 1971 (with supplements to 1979). Comprising the Bahamas, Florida Straits, Hispaniola, Cuba, Jamaica, and the Caymans.
———. *West Indies Pilot, Vol. II.* Taunton, Somerset, England: Hydrographic Dept., 1969 (with supplements to 1978). Comprising the Mona Passage, Puerto Rico, and the island chain to Grenada.
National Ocean Survey. *Coast Pilot, Vol. 5.* Riverdale, MD, 20737-1199. Published annually. Comprising Puerto Rico, Culebra, and the U.S. Virgin Islands.
National Oceanic and Atmospheric Administration Service. *Charts and Publications #1.* U.S. Atlantic and Gulf Coasts, including Puerto Rico and the Virgin Islands. Distribution Branch, NOS, Riverdale, MD 20737-1199.
———. *Worldwide Marine Weather Broadcasts.* Revised annually. The principal source of information on marine weather broadcasts for ships. Distribution Branch, NOS, Riverdale, MD 20737-1199.

CRUISING GUIDES

Allen, Philip, ed. *The Atlantic Crossing Guide.* New York and London: W. W. Norton, 1983.

Auger, Raymond N. *Westward from the Virgins.* Aspen, Colo.: Columbine Books, 1971. Paperback. Covers eastern Puerto Rico, Vieques, and Culebra.

Cary, C. G., and E. A. Rainold III. *Virgin Anchorages.* Road Town, Tortola, B.V.I.: The Moorings Ltd., 1980, and later revisions. Paperback.

Cornell, Jimmy. *World Cruising Routes.* Camden, Maine: International Marine Press, 1987.

Doyle, Chris. *Sailor's Guide to the Windward Islands.* Clearwater, Fla.: Chris Doyle Publishing and Cruising Guide Publications. 1988. Paperback. Advertisers mentioned preferentially.

————. *Stevens Cruising Guide to the Windward Islands.* Stevensville, Md.: Stevens Yachts of Annapolis, 1979. Paperback. Large format, beautifully illustrated in color, good advice.

Eiman, William J. *St. Maarten/St. Martin Area Cruising Guide.* Philadelphia, Pa.: Virgin Islands Plus Yacht Charters, Inc., 1980. Paperback.

Kline, Harry. *Yachtsman's Guide to the Bahamas.* Coral Gables, Fla.: Tropic Isle Publishers, published annually. Paperback.

————. *Yachtsman's Guide to the Virgin Islands, Puerto Rico, Republic of Haiti, Dominican Republic.* Coral Gables, Fla.: Tropic Isle Publishers, published annually. Paperback.

Kline, Harry, and J. Linton Rigg. *Bahama Islands.* New York: Charles Scribner's Sons, 1973.

Robinson, Bill. *The Caribbean Cruising Handbook.* New York: Dodd, Mead & Co., 1986.

Roscoe, Robert S., and Fessenden S. Blanchard. *A Cruising Guide to the Southern Coast.* New York: Dodd, Mead & Co., 1974. Covers the East Coast "jumping-off" points to the Caribbean.

Sorem, Bill. *Belize Cruising Guide.* Treasure Island, Fla., 1984. Paperback.

————. *Virgin Cruising.* Treasure Island, Fla.: Fleet Indigo Ltd., 1980. Paperback.

Street, Donald M. *Street's Cruising Guide to the Eastern Caribbean, Vol. I—Getting There; Vol. II—Puerto Rico to Dominica; Vol. III—Martinique to Trinidad; Vol. IV—Venezuela.* New York: W. W. Norton & Co., 1980, and later revisions (all volumes). Paperback.

Van Sant, Bruce. *The Gentleman's Guide to Passages South.* Self-published. Distributed by Cruising Guide Publications, Inc., Clearwater, Fla. Second edition, 1989.

Voegeli, Michael. *Yachtsmen's Guide to the Bermuda Islands.* Bermuda, 1981. Paperback.

Wilensky, Julius M. *Cruising Guide to the Abacos and the Northern Bahamas.* Stamford, Conn.: Wescott Cove Publishing Co., 1980. Paperback.

————. *Cruising Guide to the Bay Islands of Honduras.* Stamford, Conn.: Wescott Cove Publishing Co., 1979. Paperback.

————. *Cruising Guide to the Windward Islands.* Stamford, Conn.: Wescott Cove Publishing Co., 1979. Paperback.

CRUISE ACCOUNTS

Cottman, Evans W. *Out-Island Doctor.* London: Hodder and Stoughton, 1963. The adventures of a doctor sailing his Bahamian ketch among the islands to minister to his isolated patients.

Eggleston, George T. *Virgin Islands.* Princeton, N.J.: D. Van Nostrand, 1959.

Fenger, Frederic A. *The Cruise of the Diablesse.* New York: Yachting, Inc., 1926. A classic pre–World War I account of a cruise by schooner from Boston to Tobago and back.

Hiscock, Eric C. *Atlantic Cruise in Wanderer III.* London: Oxford University Press, 1968. Chapters on the trade-wind passage from the Canaries to Antigua, thence through the Turks and Caicos Islands and the Bahamas.

———. *Cruising Under Sail.* London: Oxford University Press, rev. ed., 1981, incorporating *Voyaging Under Sail.* Useful chapters on planning a transatlantic passage to the West Indies.

———. *Sou'west in Wanderer IV.* London: Oxford University Press, 1973. Chapters on crossing to Barbados, thence to Antigua, Grenada, the Panama Canal, and coastwise to California.

Mitchell, Carleton. *Islands to Windward.* Princeton, N.J.: D. Van Nostrand, 1955. From Trinidad, *Carib* sails the island chain north to Annapolis. Includes useful appendices on pilotage and routes.

———. *Isles of the Caribbees.* Washington, D.C.: National Geographic Society, 1966. From Grenada to the Virgins, with the usual top-flight color photography.

Niemeier, Jean. *Wild Blue Water.* Portland, Ore.: Metropolitan Press, 1962. The powerboat *Shield* cruises from the West Coast to the Great Lakes via the western Caribbean.

Puleston, Dennis. *Blue Water Vagabond.* New York: Doubleday, Doran, 1939. Chapters on a passage from England to Antigua in a 31-foot yawl and of cruising in the West Indies in the early 1930s.

Robinson, William W. *South to the Caribbean.* New York: W. W. Norton, 1982.

———. *Where the Trade Winds Blow.* New York: Charles Scribner's Sons, 1963.

HISTORY AND BACKGROUND

Albury, Paul. *The Story of the Bahamas.* London: MacMillan Publishers, 1984.

Craig, Alan K. *Geography of Fishing in British Honduras and Adjacent Coastal Waters.* Baton Rouge, La.: Louisiana State University Press, 1966. Paperback. A study of fishing in the area of the barrier reef, with chapters on the development of fishing techniques and boat building from the colonial period to the present, with maps.

Craton, Michael. *A History of the Bahamas.* London: Collins, 1962. From the Ice Age to the twentieth century.

Davidson, William J. *Historical Geography of the Bay Islands.* Birmingham, Ala.: Southern University Press, 1974.

Dodge, Steve. *Abaco—The History of an Out Island and Its Cays.* Decatur, Ill: White Sound Press, 1984.

Dupuch, S. P., editorial director. *Bahamas Handbook and Businessman's Annual.* Nassau: Etienne DuPuch, Jr., Publications, 1989.

Esquemeling, John. *The Buccaneers of America.* New York: Dover Publications, 1967. Paperback. Written in the late seventeenth century by an eyewitness to events at the time of Henry Morgan, this fascinating book purports to be "A true account of the most remarkable assaults committed of late years upon the coasts of the West Indies by Buccaneers of Jamaica and Tortuga (both English and French)."

Gravette, A. Gerald. *Cuba—Official Guide.* London and Basingstoke: MacMillan Caribbean, 1988. Paperback.

Harman, Carter, and the editors of *Life. The West Indies.* New York: Time, Inc., 1963. An overview of the history of the region, the impact of slavery and European culture, and the economic and political aspirations of the people.

Johnston, Michael C., and James L. Radawski. "Marine Archaeological Investigations of the Bay Islands and North Coast of Honduras, 1968 to 1975." Roatán: Oceanographicos de Honduras, 1975. A report presented at the Sixth International Conference on Underwater Archaeology, Charleston, S.C., Jan. 7–11, 1975.

Lewisohn, Florence. *The Romantic History of St. Croix.* Christiansted, St. Croix: St. Croix Landmarks Society, 1964. Paperback.

———. *Tales of Tortola and the British Virgin Islands.* 1966. Paperback.

Macpherson, John. *Caribbean Lands—A Geography of the West Indies.* London: Longmans Group Ltd., 1973. Paperback. An easy-to-use reference book on the formation and development of the West Indies.

Masefield, John. *On the Spanish Main.* Annapolis, Md.: Naval Institute Press, 1972. A somewhat disjointed but extensively researched word picture of the prowess of English adventurers, from Drake through Morgan, as well as the life-style of the buccaneers. Engrossing background reading for those who will cruise the western Caribbean.

Michener, James A. *Caribbean.* New York: Random House, 1989.

Morison, Samuel Eliot. *Admiral of the Ocean Sea.* Boston: Little, Brown, 1942. The Pulitzer Prize–winning biography of Columbus.

———. *The European Discovery of America—The Southern Voyages, 1492–1616.* Boston: Oxford University Press, 1974. The concluding volume of Morison's monumental study, with much new material on the voyages of Columbus, Magellan, Drake, and other early explorers.

Parry, J. H., Philip Sherlock, and Anthony Maingot. *A Short History of the West Indies.* London: MacMillan Publishers, 1987.

Waugh, Alec. *A Family of Islands.* A History of the West Indies from 1492 to 1898. New York: Doubleday, 1964.

INDEX

Page references for charts are in italics.

Other SHERIDAN HOUSE Titles of Interest

The Boating Bible—
An Essential Handbook
for Every Sailor **Jim Murrant**

This handbook contains all the essential information sailors need in one easy-to-use volume. Thorough descriptions are given for all the topics covered.

Effective Skippering—
A Comprehensive Guide to
Yacht Mastery **John Myatt**

Packed with practical tips and sensible ideas, this book covers a variety of topics. The manual all yacht owners should possess.

The Sailing Dictionary
Second Edition **Joachim Schult**

A completely revised and updated edition of a highly respected and authoritative sailing dictionary. This comprehensive reference work has over 3500 entries and 1500 line drawings.

By Way of the Wind
Jim Moore

A fascinating tale of a memorable circumnavigation by Jim and Molly Moore who, without any experience, decided to build their own boat and sail it around the world. "The best sailboat cruising book to come out in a long time."
—Washington Post

Around the World Rally
Jimmy Cornell

A detailed analysis of how 36 different cruising boats, their equipment and crew performed during 16 months and 24,000 miles of tough ocean sailing. EUROPA 92 took the yachts to places that dreams, and tourist brochures, are made of—the Caribbean, the Marquesas, Tahiti, Phuket, and a lot more...

Innocents Afloat—
Close Encounters with Sailors,
Boats and Places from Maine
to Florida **Ken Textor**

An entertaining insight of what Textor calls 'the chief reason' for going to sea: people's dreams, schemes and their 'expect the unexpected' sense of adventure.

Castaway in Paradise—
The Incredible Adventures of
True-Life Robinson Crusoes
James C. Simmons

A fascinating array of castaways and their adventures from Alexander Selkirk, Defoe's model for Robinson Crusoe, to Herman Melville on Typee, coming to the present time with Tom Neale, a New Zealand drifter who became the 'hermit of Suwarrow.' Gripping stories of adventure and survival in the South Pacific.

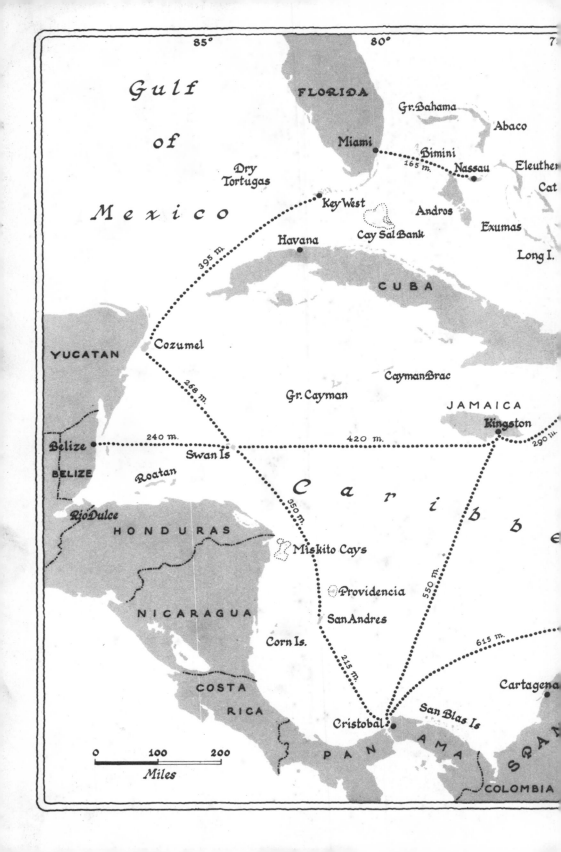